Data Analysis with Open Source Tools

Data Analysis with Open Source Tools

Philipp K. Janert

O'REILLY®

Beijing • Cambridge • Farnham • Köln • Sebastopol • Tokyo

Data Analysis with Open Source Tools

by Philipp K. Janert

Published by O'Reilly Media, Inc. 1005 Gravenstein Highway North, Sebastopol, CA 95472.

O'Reilly books may be purchased for educational, business, or sales promotional use. Online editions are also available for most titles (*http://my.safaribooksonline.com*). For more information, contact our corporate/institutional sales department: (800) 998-9938 or *corporate@oreilly.com*.

Editor: Mike Loukides	**Indexer:** Fred Brown
Production Editor: Sumita Mukherji	**Cover Designer:** Karen Montgomery
Copyeditor: Matt Darnell	**Interior Designer:** Edie Freedman and Ron Bilodeau
Production Services: MPS Limited, a Macmillan Company, and Newgen North America, Inc.	**Illustrator:** Philipp K. Janert

Printing History:

   November 2010: First Edition.

ISBN: 978-0-596-80235-6

[M]

Furious activity is no substitute for understanding.

—H. H. Williams

CONTENTS

PART III   Computation: Mining Data

Preface

THIS BOOK GREW OUT OF MY EXPERIENCE OF WORKING WITH DATA FOR VARIOUS COMPANIES IN THE TECH industry. It is a collection of those concepts and techniques that I have found to be the most useful, including many topics that I wish I had known earlier—but didn't.

My degree is in physics, but I also worked as a software engineer for several years. The book reflects this dual heritage. On the one hand, it is written for programmers and others in the software field: I assume that you, like me, have the ability to write your own programs to manipulate data in any way you want.

On the other hand, the way I think about data has been shaped by my background and education. As a physicist, I am not content merely to describe data or to make black-box predictions: the purpose of an analysis is always to develop an understanding for the processes or mechanisms that give rise to the data that we observe.

The instrument to express such understanding is the *model*: a description of the system under study (in other words, not just a description of the data!), simplified as necessary but nevertheless capturing the relevant information. A model may be crude ("Assume a spherical cow . . . "), but if it helps us develop better insight on how the system works, it is a successful model nevertheless. (Additional precision can often be obtained at a later time, if it is really necessary.)

This emphasis on models and simplified descriptions is not universal: other authors and practitioners will make different choices. But it is essential to my approach and point of view.

This is a rather personal book. Although I have tried to be reasonably comprehensive, I have selected the topics that I consider relevant and useful in practice—whether they are part of the "canon" or not. Also included are several topics that you won't find in any other book on data analysis. Although neither new nor original, they are usually not used or discussed in this particular context—but I find them indispensable.

Throughout the book, I freely offer specific, explicit advice, opinions, and assessments. These remarks are reflections of my personal interest, experience, and understanding. I do not claim that my point of view is necessarily correct: evaluate what I say for yourself and feel free to adapt it to your needs. In my view, a specific, well-argued position is of greater use than a sterile laundry list of possible algorithms—even if you later decide to disagree with me. The value is not in the opinion but rather in the arguments leading up to it. If your arguments are better than mine, or even just more agreeable to you, then I will have achieved my purpose!

Data analysis, as I understand it, is not a fixed set of techniques. It is a way of life, and it has a name: curiosity. There is always something else to find out and something more to learn. This book is not the last word on the matter; it is merely a snapshot in time: things I knew about and found useful today.

"Works are of value only if they give rise to better ones."

(Alexander von Humboldt, writing to Charles Darwin, 18 September 1839)

Before We Begin

More data analysis efforts seem to go bad because of an excess of sophistication rather than a lack of it.

This may come as a surprise, but it has been my experience again and again. As a consultant, I am often called in when the initial project team has already gotten stuck. Rarely (if ever) does the problem turn out to be that the team did not have the required skills. On the contrary, I usually find that they tried to do something unnecessarily complicated and are now struggling with the consequences of their own invention!

Based on what I have seen, two particular risk areas stand out:

- The use of "statistical" concepts that are only partially understood (and given the relative obscurity of most of statistics, this includes virtually *all* statistical concepts)

- Complicated (and expensive) black-box solutions when a simple and transparent approach would have worked at least as well or better

I strongly recommend that you make it a habit to avoid all statistical language. Keep it simple and stick to what you know for sure. There is absolutely nothing wrong with speaking of the "range over which points spread," because this phrase means exactly what it says: the range over which points spread, and only that! Once we start talking about "standard deviations," this clarity is gone. Are we still talking about the *observed* width of the distribution? Or are we talking about one specific *measure* for this width? (The standard deviation is only one of several that are available.) Are we already making an implicit *assumption* about the nature of the distribution? (The standard deviation is only suitable under certain conditions, which are often not fulfilled in practice.) Or are we even confusing the *predictions* we could make if these assumptions were true with the actual data? (The moment someone talks about "95 percent anything" we know it's the latter!)

I'd also like to remind you not to discard simple methods until they have been *proven* insufficient. Simple solutions are frequently rather effective: the marginal benefit that more complicated methods can deliver is often quite small (and may be in no reasonable relation to the increased cost). More importantly, simple methods have fewer opportunities to go wrong or to obscure the obvious.

True story: a company was tracking the occurrence of defects over time. Of course, the actual number of defects varied quite a bit from one day to the next, and they were looking for a way to obtain an estimate for the typical number of expected defects. The solution proposed by their IT department involved a compute cluster running a neural network! (I am not making this up.) In fact, a one-line calculation (involving a moving average or single exponential smoothing) is all that was needed.

I think the primary reason for this tendency to make data analysis projects more complicated than they are is *discomfort*: discomfort with an unfamiliar problem space and uncertainty about how to proceed. This discomfort and uncertainty creates a desire to bring in the "big guns": fancy terminology, heavy machinery, large projects. In reality, of course, the opposite is true: the complexities of the "solution" overwhelm the original problem, and nothing gets accomplished.

Data analysis does not have to be all that hard. Although there are situations when elementary methods will no longer be sufficient, they are much less prevalent than you might expect. In the vast majority of cases, curiosity and a healthy dose of common sense will serve you well.

The attitude that I am trying to convey can be summarized in a few points:

> Simple is better than complex.
> Cheap is better than expensive.
> Explicit is better than opaque.
> Purpose is more important than process.
> Insight is more important than precision.
> Understanding is more important than technique.
> Think more, work less.

Although I do acknowledge that the items on the right are necessary at times, I will give preference to those on the left whenever possible.

It is in this spirit that I am offering the concepts and techniques that make up the rest of this book.

Conventions Used in This Book

The following typographical conventions are used in this book:

Italic
    Indicates new terms, URLs, and email addresses

`Constant width`
    Used to refer to language and script elements

Using Code Examples

This book is here to help you get your job done. In general, you may use the code in this book in your programs and documentation. You do not need to contact us for permission unless youre reproducing a significant portion of the code. For example, writing a program that uses several chunks of code from this book does not require permission. Selling or distributing a CD-ROM of examples from OReilly books does require permission. Answering a question by citing this book and quoting example code does not require permission. Incorporating a significant amount of example code from this book into your products documentation does require permission.

We appreciate, but do not require, attribution. An attribution usually includes the title, author, publisher, and ISBN. For example: *"Data Analysis with Open Source Tools*, by Philipp K. Janert. Copyright 2011 Philipp K. Janert, 978-0-596-80235-6."

If you feel your use of code examples falls outside fair use or the permission given above, feel free to contact us at *permissions@oreilly.com*.

Safari® Books Online

Safari ·> Safari Books Online is an on-demand digital library that lets you easily search
Books online   over 7,500 technology and creative reference books and videos to find the answers you need quickly.

With a subscription, you can read any page and watch any video from our library online. Read books on your cell phone and mobile devices. Access new titles before they are available for print, and get exclusive access to manuscripts in development and post feedback for the authors. Copy and paste code samples, organize your favorites, download chapters, bookmark key sections, create notes, print out pages, and benefit from tons of other time-saving features.

O'Reilly Media has uploaded this book to the Safari Books Online service. To have full digital access to this book and others on similar topics from OReilly and other publishers, sign up for free at *http://my.safaribooksonline.com*.

How to Contact Us

Please address comments and questions concerning this book to the publisher:

O'Reilly Media, Inc.
1005 Gravenstein Highway North
Sebastopol, CA 95472
800-998-9938 (in the United States or Canada)
707-829-0515 (international or local)
707-829-0104 (fax)

We have a web page for this book, where we list errata, examples, and any additional information. You can access this page at:

http://oreilly.com/catalog/9780596802356

To comment or ask technical questions about this book, send email to:

bookquestions@oreilly.com

For more information about our books, conferences, Resource Centers, and the O'Reilly Network, see our website at:

http://oreilly.com

Acknowledgments

It was a pleasure to work with O'Reilly on this project. In particular, O'Reilly has been most accommodating with regard to the technical challenges raised by my need to include (for an O'Reilly book) an uncommonly large amount of mathematical material in the manuscript.

Mike Loukides has accompanied this project as the editor since its beginning. I have enjoyed our conversations about life, the universe, and everything, and I appreciate his comments about the manuscript—either way.

I'd like to thank several of my friends for their help in bringing this book about:

- Elizabeth Robson, for making the connection
- Austin King, for pointing out the obvious
- Scott White, for suffering my questions gladly
- Richard Kreckel, for much-needed advice

As always, special thanks go to PAUL Schrader (Bremen).

The manuscript benefited from the feedback I received from various reviewers. Michael E. Driscoll, Zachary Kessin, and Austin King read all or parts of the manuscript and provided valuable comments.

I enjoyed personal correspondence with Joseph Adler, Joe Darcy, Hilary Mason, Stephen Weston, Scott White, and Brian Zimmer. All very generously provided expert advice on specific topics.

Particular thanks go to Richard Kreckel, who provided uncommonly detailed and insightful feedback on most of the manuscript.

During the preparation of this book, the excellent collection at the University of Washington libraries was an especially valuable resource to me.

Authors usually thank their spouses for their "patience and support" or words to that effect. Unless one has lived through the actual experience, one cannot fully comprehend how true this is. Over the last three years, Angela has endured what must have seemed like a nearly continuous stream of whining, frustration, and desperation—punctuated by occasional outbursts of exhilaration and grandiosity—all of which before the background of the self-centered and self-absorbed attitude of a typical author. Her patience and support were unfailing. It's her turn now.

## CHAPTER ONE

Introduction

IMAGINE YOUR BOSS COMES TO YOU AND SAYS: "HERE ARE 50 GB OF LOGFILES—FIND A WAY TO IMPROVE OUR business!"

What would you do? Where would you start? And what would you do next?

It's this kind of situation that the present book wants to help you with!

Data Analysis

Businesses sit on data, and every second that passes, they generate some more. Surely, there *must* be a way to make use of all this stuff. But how, exactly—that's far from clear.

The task is difficult because it is so vague: there is no specific problem that needs to be solved. There is no specific question that needs to be answered. All you know is the overall *purpose*: improve the business. And all you have is "the data." Where do you start?

You start with the only thing you have: "the data." What is it? We don't know! Although 50 GB sure sounds like a lot, we have no idea what it actually contains. The first thing, therefore, is to *take a look*.

And I mean this literally: the first thing to do is to *look* at the data by plotting it in different ways and looking at graphs. Looking at data, you will notice things—the way data points are distributed, or the manner in which one quantity varies with another, or the large number of outliers, or the total absence of them. . . . I don't know what you will find, but there is no doubt: if you look at data, you will observe things!

These observations should lead to some reflection. "Ten percent of our customers drive ninety percent of our revenue." "Whenever our sales volume doubles, the number of returns goes up by a factor of four." "Every seven days we have a production run that has twice the usual defect rate, and it's always on a Thursday." How very interesting!

Now you've got something to work with: the amorphous mass of "data" has turned into ideas! To make these ideas concrete and suitable for further work, it is often useful to capture them in a mathematical form: a *model*. A model (the way I use the term) is a mathematical description of the system under study. A model is more than just a description of the data—it also incorporates your understanding of the process or the system that produced the data. A model therefore has *predictive power*: you can predict (with some certainty) that next Thursday the defect rate will be high *again*.

It's at this point that you may want to go back and alert the boss of your findings: "Next Thursday, watch out for defects!"

Sometimes, you may already be finished at this point: you found out enough to help improve the business. At other times, however, you may need to work a little harder. Some data sets do not yield easily to visual inspection—especially if you are dealing with data sets consisting of many different quantities, all of which seem equally important. In such cases, you may need to employ more-sophisticated methods to develop enough intuition before being able to formulate a relevant model. Or you may have been able to set up a model, but it is too complicated to understand its implications, so that you want to implement the model as a computer program and simulate its results. Such computationally intensive methods are occasionally useful, but they always come later in the game. You should only move on to them after having tried all the simple things first. And you will need the insights gained from those earlier investigations as input to the more elaborate approaches.

And finally, we need to come back to the initial agenda. To "improve the business" it is necessary to feed our understanding back into the organization—for instance, in the form of a business plan, or through a "metrics dashboard" or similar program.

What's in This Book

The program just described reflects the outline of this book.

We begin in Part I with a series of chapters on graphical techniques, starting in Chapter 2 with simple data sets consisting of only a single variable (or considering only a single variable at a time), then moving on in Chapter 3 to data sets of two variables. In Chapter 4 we treat the particularly important special case of a quantity changing over time, a so-called time series. Finally, in Chapter 5, we discuss data sets comprising more than two variables and some special techniques suitable for such data sets.

In Part II, we discuss models as a way to not only describe data but also to capture the understanding that we gained from graphical explorations. We begin in Chapter 7 with a discussion of order-of-magnitude estimation and uncertainty considerations. This may seem odd but is, in fact, crucial: all models are approximate, so we need to develop a sense for the accuracy of the approximations that we use. In Chapters 8 and 9 we introduce basic building blocks that are useful when developing models.

Chapter 10 is a detour. For too many people, "data analysis" is synonymous with "statistics," and "statistics" is usually equated with a class in college that made *no sense* at all. In this chapter, I want to explain what statistics really is, what all the mysterious concepts mean and how they hang together, and what statistics can (and cannot) do for us. It is intended as a travel guide should you ever want to read a statistics book in the future.

Part III discusses several computationally intensive methods, such as simulation and clustering in Chapters 12 and 13. Chapter 14 is, mathematically, the most challenging chapter in the book: it deals with methods that can help select the most relevant variables from a multivariate data set.

In Part IV we consider some ways that data may be used in a business environment. In Chapter 16 we talk about metrics, reporting, and dashboards—what is sometimes referred to as "business intelligence." In Chapter 17 we introduce some of the concepts required to make financial calculations and to prepare business plans. Finally, in chapter 18, we conclude with a survey of some methods from classification and predictive analytics.

At the end of each part of the book you will find an "Intermezzo." These intermezzos are not really part of the course; I use them to go off on some tangents, or to explain topics that often remain a bit hazy. You should see them as an opportunity to relax!

The appendices contain some helpful material that you may want to consult at various times as you go through the text. Appendix A surveys some of the available tools and programming environments for data manipulation and analysis. In Appendix B I have collected some basic mathematical results that I expect you to have at least passing familiarity with. I assume that you have seen this material at least once before, but in this appendix, I put it together in an application-oriented context, which is more suitable for our present purposes. Appendix C discusses some of the mundane tasks that—like it or not—make up a large part of actual data analysis and also introduces some data-related terminology.

What's with the Workshops?

Every full chapter (after this one) includes a section titled "Workshop" that contains some programming examples related to the chapter's material. I use these Workshops for two purposes. On the one hand, I'd like to introduce a number of open source tools and libraries that may be useful for the kind of work discussed in this book. On the other hand, some concepts (such as computational complexity and power-law distributions) must be seen to be believed: the Workshops are a way to demonstrate these issues and allow you to experiment with them yourself.

Among the tools and libraries is quite a bit of Python and R. Python has become somewhat the scripting language of choice for scientific applications, and R is the most popular open source package for statistical applications. *This choice is neither an endorsement nor a recommendation* but primarily a reflection of the current state of available software. (See Appendix A for a more detailed discussion of software for data analysis and related purposes.)

My goal with the tool-oriented Workshops is rather specific: I want to enable you to decide whether a given tool or library is worth spending time on. (I have found that evaluating open source offerings is a necessary but time-consuming task.) I try to demonstrate clearly what purpose each particular tool serves. Toward this end, I usually give one or two short, but not entirely trivial, examples and try to outline enough of the architecture of the tool or library to allow you to take it from there. (The documentation for many open source projects has a hard time making the bridge from the trivial, cut-and-paste "Hello, World" example to the reference documentation.)

What's with the Math?

This book contains a certain amount of mathematics. Depending on your personal predilection you may find this trivial, intimidating, or exciting.

The reality is that if you want to work *analytically*, you will need to develop some familiarity with a few mathematical concepts. There is simply no way around it. (You can work with *data* without any math skills—look at what any data modeler or database administrator does. But if you want to do any sort of *analysis*, then a little math becomes a necessity.)

I have tried to make the text accessible to readers with a minimum of previous knowledge. Some college math classes on calculus and similar topics are helpful, of course, but are by no means required. Some sections of the book treat material that is either more abstract or will likely be unreasonably hard to understand without some previous exposure. These sections are optional (they are not needed in the sequel) and are clearly marked as such.

A somewhat different issue concerns the notation. I use mathematical notation wherever it is appropriate and it helps the presentation. I have made sure to use only a very small set of symbols; check Appendix B if something looks unfamiliar.

Couldn't I have written all the mathematical expressions as computer code, using Python or some sort of pseudo-code? The answer is no, because quite a few *essential* mathematical concepts cannot be expressed in a finite, floating-point oriented machine (anything having to do with a limit process—or real numbers, in fact). But even if I could write all math as code, I don't think I should. Although I wholeheartedly agree that mathematical notation can get out of hand, simple formulas actually provide the easiest, most succinct way to express mathematical concepts.

Just compare. I'd argue that:

$$\sum_{k=0}^{n} \frac{c(k)}{(1+p)^k}$$

is clearer and easier to read than:

```
s = 0
for k in range( len(c) ):
    s += c[k]/(1+p)**k
```

and certainly easier than:

```
s = ( c / (1+p)**numpy.arange(1, len(c)+1) ).sum(axis=0)
```

But that's only part of the story. More importantly, the first version expresses a *concept*, whereas the second and third are merely specific prescriptions for how to perform a certain calculation. They are *recipes*, not ideas.

Consider this: the formula in the first line is a description of a sum—not a specific sum, but any sum of this form: it's the *idea* of this kind of sum. We can now ask how this abstract sum will behave under certain conditions—for instance, if we let the upper limit n go to infinity. What value does the sum have in this case? Is it finite? Can we determine it? You would not even be *able* to ask this question given the code versions. (Remember that I am not talking about an approximation, such as letting n get "very large." I really do mean: what happens if n goes all the way to infinity? What can we say about the sum?)

Some programming environments (like Haskell, for instance) are more at ease dealing with infinite data structures—but if you look closely, you will find that they do so by being (coarse) approximations to mathematical concepts and notations. And, of course, they still won't be able to evaluate such expressions! (All evaluations will only involve a finite number of steps.) But once you train your mind to think in those terms, you can evaluate them *in your mind* at will.

It may come as a surprise, but mathematics is *not* a method for calculating things. Mathematics is a theory of *ideas*, and ideas—not calculational prescriptions—are what I would like to convey in this text. (See the discussion at the end of Appendix B for more on this topic and for some suggested reading.)

If you feel uncomfortable or even repelled by the math in this book, I'd like to ask for just one thing: try! Give it a shot. Don't immediately give up. Any frustration you may experience at first is more likely due to lack of familiarity rather than to the difficulty of the material. I promise that none of the content is out of your reach.

But you have to let go of the conditioned knee-jerk reflex that "math is, like, *yuck*!"

What You'll Need

This book is written with programmers in mind. Although previous programming experience is by no means required, I assume that you are able to take an idea and implement it in the programming language of your choice—in fact, I assume that this is your prime motivation for reading this book.

I don't expect you to have any particular mathematical background, although some previous familiarity with calculus is certainly helpful. You will need to be able to count, though!

But the most important prerequisite is not programming experience, not math skills, and certainly not knowledge of anything having to do with "statistics." The most important prerequisite is *curiosity*. If you aren't curious, then this book is not for you. If you get a new data set and you are not *itching* to see what's in it, I won't be able to help you.

What's Missing

This is a book about data analysis and modeling with an emphasis on applications in a business settings. It was written at a beginning-to-intermediate level and for a general technical audience.

Although I have tried to be reasonably comprehensive, I had to choose which subjects to include and which to leave out. I have tried to select topics that are useful and relevant in practice and that can safely be applied by a nonspecialist. A few topics were omitted because they did not fit within the book's overall structure, or because I did not feel sufficiently competent to present them.

Scientific data.   This is not a book about scientific data analysis. When you are doing scientific research (however you wish to define "scientific"), you really need to have a solid background (and that probably means formal training) in the field that you are working in. A book such as this one on general data analysis cannot replace this.

Formal statistical analysis.   A different form of data analysis exists in some particularly well-established fields. In these situations, the environment from which the data arises is fully understood (or at least believed to be understood), and the methods and models to be used are likewise accepted and well known. Typical examples include clinical trials as well as credit scoring. The purpose of an "analysis" in these cases is not to find out anything new, but rather to determine the model parameters with the highest degree of accuracy and precision for each newly generated set of data points. Since this is the kind of work where details matter, it should be left to specialists.

Network analysis.   This is a topic of current interest about which I know nothing. (Sorry!) However, it does seem to me that its nature is quite different from most problems that are usually considered "data analysis": less statistical, more algorithmic in nature. But I don't know for sure.

Natural language processing and text mining.   Natural language processing is a big topic all by itself, which has little overlap (neither in terms of techniques nor applications) with the rest of the material presented here. It deserves its own treatment—and several books on this subject are available.

Big data.   Arguably the most painful omission concerns everything having to do with *Big Data*. Big Data is a pretty new concept—I tend to think of it as relating to data sets that not merely don't fit into main memory, but that no longer fit comfortably on a single *disk*, requiring compute clusters and the respective software and algorithms (in practice, map/reduce running on Hadoop).

The rise of Big Data is a remarkable phenomenon. When this book was conceived (early 2009), Big Data was certainly on the horizon but was not necessarily considered mainstream yet. As this book goes to print (late 2010), it seems that for many people in the tech field, "data" has become nearly synonymous with "Big Data." That kind of development usually indicates a fad. The reality is that, in practice, many data sets are "small," and in particular many *relevant* data sets are small. (Some of the most important data sets in a commercial setting are those maintained by the finance department—and since they are kept in Excel, they *must* be small.)

Big Data is not necessarily "better." Applied carelessly, it can be a huge step backward. The amazing insight of classical statistics is that you don't need to examine every single member of a population to make a definitive statement about the whole: instead you can sample! It is also true that a carefully selected sample may lead to better results than a large, messy data set. Big Data makes it easy to forget the basics.

It is a little early to say anything definitive about Big Data, but the current trend strikes me as being something quite *different*: it is not just classical data analysis on a larger scale. The approach of classical data analysis and statistics is *inductive*. Given a part, make statements about the whole: from a sample, estimate parameters of the population; given an observation, develop a theory for the underlying system. In contrast, Big Data (at least as it is currently being used) seems primarily concerned with individual data points. Given that *this specific* user liked *this specific* movie, what other *specific* movie might he like? This is a very different question than asking which movies are most liked by what people in general!

Big Data will not replace general, inductive data analysis. It is not yet clear just where Big Data will deliver the greatest bang for the buck—but once the dust settles, somebody should definitely write a book about it!

## PART I

Graphics: Looking at Data

## CHAPTER TWO

A Single Variable: Shape and Distribution

WHEN DEALING WITH UNIVARIATE DATA, WE ARE USUALLY MOSTLY CONCERNED WITH THE OVERALL *SHAPE* OF the distribution. Some of the initial questions we may ask include:

- Where are the data points located, and how far do they spread? What are typical, as well as minimal and maximal, values?

- How are the points distributed? Are they spread out evenly or do they cluster in certain areas?

- How many points are there? Is this a large data set or a relatively small one?

- Is the distribution symmetric or asymmetric? In other words, is the tail of the distribution much larger on one side than on the other?

- Are the tails of the distribution relatively heavy (*i.e.*, do many data points lie far away from the central group of points), or are most of the points—with the possible exception of individual outliers—confined to a restricted region?

- If there are clusters, how many are there? Is there only one, or are there several? Approximately where are the clusters located, and how large are they—both in terms of spread and in terms of the number of data points belonging to each cluster?

- Are the clusters possibly superimposed on some form of unstructured background, or does the entire data set consist only of the clustered data points?

- Does the data set contain any significant outliers—that is, data points that seem to be different from all the others?

- And lastly, are there any other unusual or significant features in the data set—gaps, sharp cutoffs, unusual values, anything at all that we can observe?

As you can see, even a simple, single-column data set can contain a lot of different features!

To make this concrete, let's look at two examples. The first concerns a relatively small data set: the number of months that the various American presidents have spent in office. The second data set is much larger and stems from an application domain that may be more familiar; we will be looking at the response times from a web server.

Dot and Jitter Plots

Suppose you are given the following data set, which shows all past American presidents and the number of months each spent in office.[*] Although this data set has three columns, we can treat it as univariate because we are interested only in the times spent in office—the names don't matter to us (at this point). What can we say about the typical tenure?

1	Washington	94
2	Adams	48
3	Jefferson	96
4	Madison	96
5	Monroe	96
6	Adams	48
7	Jackson	96
8	Van Buren	48
9	Harrison	1
10	Tyler	47
11	Polk	48
12	Taylor	16
13	Filmore	32
14	Pierce	48
15	Buchanan	48
16	Lincoln	49
17	Johnson	47
18	Grant	96
19	Hayes	48
20	Garfield	7
21	Arthur	41
22	Cleveland	48
23	Harrison	48
24	Cleveland	48
25	McKinley	54
26	Roosevelt	90
27	Taft	48
28	Wilson	96
29	Harding	29

---

[*]The inspiration for this example comes from a paper by Robert W. Hayden in the *Journal of Statistics Education*. The full text is available at *http://www.amstat.org/publications/jse/v13n1/datasets.hayden.html*.

30	Coolidge	67
31	Hoover	48
32	Roosevelt	146
33	Truman	92
34	Eisenhower	96
35	Kennedy	34
36	Johnson	62
37	Nixon	67
38	Ford	29
39	Carter	48
40	Reagan	96
41	Bush	48
42	Clinton	96
43	Bush	96

This is not a large data set (just over 40 records), but it is a little too big to take in as a whole. A very simple way to gain an initial sense of the data set is to create a *dot plot*. In a dot plot, we plot all points on a single (typically horizontal) line, letting the value of each data point determine the position along the horizontal axis. (See the top part of Figure 2-1.)

A dot plot can be perfectly sufficient for a small data set such as this one. However, in our case it is slightly misleading because, whenever a certain tenure occurs more than once in the data set, the corresponding data points fall right on top of each other, which makes it impossible to distinguish them. This is a frequent problem, especially if the data assumes only integer values or is otherwise "coarse-grained." A common remedy is to shift each point by a small random amount from its original position; this technique is called *jittering* and the resulting plot is a *jitter plot*. A jitter plot of this data set is shown in the bottom part of Figure 2-1.

What does the jitter plot tell us about the data set? We see two values where data points seem to cluster, indicating that these values occur more frequently than others. Not surprisingly, they are located at 48 and 96 months, which correspond to one and two full four-year terms in office. What may be a little surprising, however, is the relatively large number of points that occur *outside* these clusters. Apparently, quite a few presidents left office at irregular intervals! Even in this simple example, a plot reveals both something expected (the clusters at 48 and 96 months) and the unexpected (the larger number of points outside those clusters).

Before moving on to our second example, let me point out a few additional technical details regarding jitter plots.

- It is important that the amount of "jitter" be small compared to the distance between points. The only purpose of the random displacements is to ensure that no two points fall exactly on top of one another. We must make sure that points are not shifted significantly from their true location.

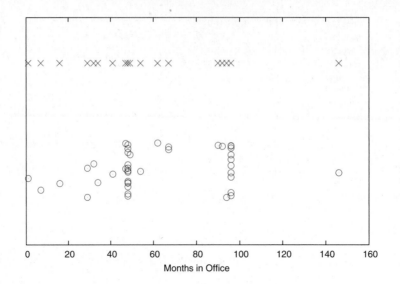

FIGURE 2-1. Dot and jitter plots showing the number of months U.S. presidents spent in office.

- We can jitter points in either the horizontal or the vertical direction (or both), depending on the data set and the purpose of the graph. In Figure 2-1, points were jittered only in the vertical direction, so that their horizontal position (which in this case corresponds to the actual data—namely, the number of months in office) is not altered and therefore remains exact.

- I used open, transparent rings as symbols for the data points. This is no accident: among different symbols of equal size, open rings are most easily recognized as separate even when partially occluded by each other. In contrast, filled symbols tend to hide any substructure when they overlap, and symbols made from straight lines (*e.g.*, boxes and crosses) can be confusing because of the large number of parallel lines; see the top part of Figure 2-1.

Jittering is a good trick that can be used in many different contexts. We will see further examples later in the book.

Histograms and Kernel Density Estimates

Dot and jitter plots are nice because they are so simple. However, they are neither pretty nor very intuitive, and most importantly, they make it hard to read off *quantitative* information from the graph. In particular, if we are dealing with larger data sets, then we need a better type of graph, such as a histogram.

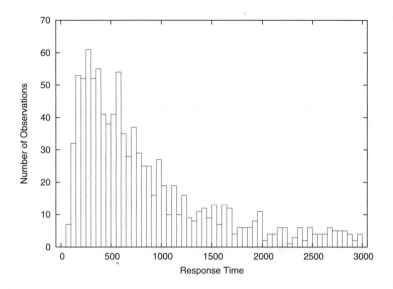

FIGURE 2-2. A histogram of a server's response times.

Histograms

To form a *histogram*, we divide the range of values into a set of "bins" and then count the number of points (sometimes called "events") that fall into each bin. We then plot the count of events for each bin as a function of the position of the bin.

Once again, let's look at an example. Here is the beginning of a file containing response times (in milliseconds) for queries against a web server or database. In contrast to the previous example, this data set is fairly large, containing 1,000 data points.

```
 452.42
 318.58
 144.82
 129.13
1216.45
 991.56
1476.69
 662.73
1302.85
1278.55
 627.65
1030.78
 215.23
  44.50
...
```

Figure 2-2 shows a histogram of this data set. I divided the horizontal axis into 60 bins of 50 milliseconds width and then counted the number of events in each bin.

What does the histogram tell us? We observe a rather sharp cutoff at a nonzero value on the left, which means that there is a minimum completion time below which no request can be completed. Then there is a sharp rise to a maximum at the "typical" response time, and finally there is a relatively large tail on the right, corresponding to the smaller number of requests that take a long time to process. This kind of shape is rather typical for a histogram of task completion times. If the data set had contained completion times for students to finish their homework or for manufacturing workers to finish a work product, then it would look qualitatively similar except, of course, that the time scale would be different. Basically, there is some minimum time that nobody can beat, a small group of very fast champions, a large majority, and finally a longer or shorter tail of "stragglers."

It is important to realize that a data set does not determine a histogram uniquely. Instead, we have to fix *two* parameters to form a histogram: the bin width and the alignment of the bins.

The quality of any histogram hinges on the proper choice of bin width. If you make the width too large, then you lose too much detailed information about the data set. Make it too small and you will have few or no events in most of the bins, and the shape of the distribution does not become apparent. Unfortunately, there is no simple rule of thumb that can predict a good bin width for a given data set; typically you have to try out several different values for the bin width until you obtain a satisfactory result. (As a first guess, you can start with *Scott's rule* for the bin width $w = 3.5\sigma/\sqrt[3]{n}$, where σ is the standard deviation for the entire data set and n is the number of points. This rule assumes that the data follows a Gaussian distribution; otherwise, it is likely to give a bin width that is too wide. See the end of this chapter for more information on the standard deviation.)

The other parameter that we need to fix (whether we realize it or not) is the alignment of the bins on the x axis. Let's say we fixed the width of the bins at 1. Where do we now place the first bin? We could put it flush left, so that its left edge is at 0, or we could center it at 0. In fact, we can move all bins by half a bin width in either direction.

Unfortunately, this seemingly insignificant (and often overlooked) parameter can have a large influence on the appearance of the histogram. Consider this small data set:

```
1.4
1.7
1.8
1.9
2.1
2.2
2.3
2.6
```

Figure 2-3 shows two histograms of this data set. Both use the same bin width (namely, 1) but have different alignment of the bins. In the top panel, where the bin *edges* have been aligned to coincide with the whole numbers (1, 2, 3, . . .), the data set appears to be flat. Yet in the bottom panel, where the bins have been *centered* on the whole numbers, the

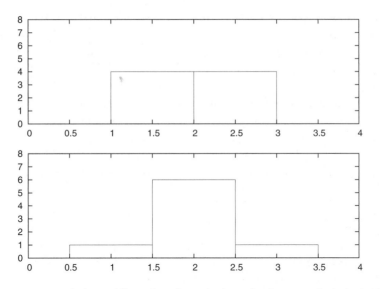

FIGURE 2-3. Histograms can look quite different, depending on the choice of anchoring point for the first bin. The figure shows two histograms of the same data set, using the same bin width. In the top panel, the bin edges are aligned on whole numbers; in the bottom panel, bins are centered on whole numbers.

data set appears to have a rather strong central peak and symmetric wings on both sides. It should be clear that we can construct even more pathological examples than this. In the next section we shall introduce an alternative to histograms that avoids this particular problem.

Before moving on, I'd like to point out some additional technical details and variants of histograms.

- Histograms can be either normalized or unnormalized. In an *unnormalized* histogram, the value plotted for each bin is the absolute count of events in that bin. In a *normalized* histogram, we divide each count by the total number of points in the data set, so that the value for each bin becomes the fraction of points in that bin. If we want the percentage of points per bin instead, we simply multiply the fraction by 100.

- So far I have assumed that all bins have the same width. We can relax this constraint and allow bins of differing widths—narrower where points are tightly clustered but wider in areas where there are only few points. This method can seem very appealing when the data set has outliers or areas with widely differing point density. Be warned, though, that now there is an additional source of ambiguity for your histogram: should you display the absolute number of points per bin regardless of the width of each bin; or should you display the density of points per bin by normalizing the point count per bin by the bin width? Either method is valid, and you cannot assume that your audience will know which convention you are following.

- It is customary to show histograms with rectangular boxes that extend from the horizontal axis, the way I have drawn Figures 2-2 and 2-3. That is perfectly all right and has the advantage of explicitly displaying the bin width as well. (Of course, the boxes should be drawn in such a way that they align in the same way that the actual bins align; see Figure 2-3.) This works well if you are only displaying a histogram for a single data set. But if you want to compare two or more data sets, then the boxes start to get in the way, and you are better off drawing "frequency polygons": eliminate the boxes, and instead draw a symbol where the top of the box would have been. (The horizontal position of the symbol should be at the center of the bin.) Then connect consecutive symbols with straight lines. Now you can draw multiple data sets in the same plot without cluttering the graph or unnecessarily occluding points.

- Don't assume that the defaults of your graphics program will generate the best representation of a histogram! I have already discussed why I consider frequency polygons to be almost always a better choice than to construct a histogram from boxes. If you nevertheless choose to use boxes, it is best to avoid filling them (with a color or hatch pattern)—your histogram will probably look cleaner and be easier to read if you stick with just the box outlines. Finally, if you want to compare several data sets in the same graph, always use a frequency polygon, and stay away from stacked or clustered bar graphs, since these are particularly hard to read. (We will return to the problem of displaying composition problems in Chapter 5.)

Histograms are very common and have a nice, intuitive interpretation. They are also easy to generate: for a moderately sized data set, it can even be done by hand, if necessary. That being said, histograms have some serious problems. The most important ones are as follows.

- The binning process required by all histograms loses information (by replacing the location of individual data points with a bin of finite width). If we only have a few data points, we can ill afford to lose any information.

- Histograms are not unique. As we saw in Figure 2-3, the appearance of a histogram can be quite different. (This nonuniqueness is a direct consequence of the information loss described in the previous item.)

- On a more superficial level, histograms are ragged and not smooth. This matters little if we just want to draw a picture of them, but if we want to feed them back into a computer as input for further calculations, then a smooth curve would be easier to handle.

- Histograms do not handle outliers gracefully. A single outlier, far removed from the majority of the points, requires many empty cells in between or forces us to use bins that are too wide for the majority of points. It is the possibility of outliers that makes it difficult to find an acceptable bin width in an automated fashion.

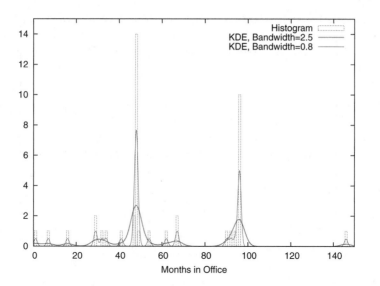

FIGURE 2-4. Histogram and kernel density estimate of the distribution of the time U.S. presidents have spent in office.

Fortunately, there is an alternative to classical histograms that has none of these problems. It is called a *kernel density estimate*.

Kernel Density Estimates

Kernel density estimates (KDEs) are a relatively new technique. In contrast to histograms, and to many other classical methods of data analysis, they pretty much *require* the calculational power of a reasonably modern computer to be effective. They cannot be done "by hand" with paper and pencil, even for rather moderately sized data sets. (It is interesting to see how the accessibility of computational and graphing power enables new ways to think about data!)

To form a KDE, we place a *kernel*—that is, a smooth, strongly peaked function—at the position of each data point. We then add up the contributions from all kernels to obtain a smooth curve, which we can evaluate at any point along the *x* axis.

Figure 2-4 shows an example. This is yet another representation of the data set we have seen before in Figure 2-1. The dotted boxes are a histogram of the data set (with bin width equal to 1), and the solid curves are two KDEs of the same data set with different bandwidths (I'll explain this concept in a moment). The shape of the individual kernel functions can be seen clearly—for example, by considering the three data points below 20. You can also see how the final curve is composed out of the individual kernels, in particular when you look at the points between 30 and 40.

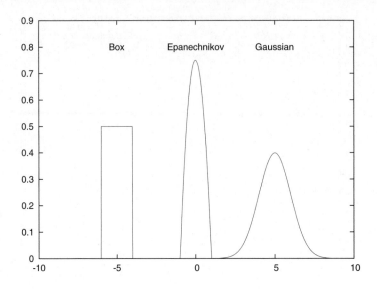

FIGURE 2-5. Graphs of some frequently used kernel functions.

We can use any smooth, strongly peaked function as a kernel provided that it integrates to 1; in other words, the area under the curve formed by a single kernel must be 1. (This is necessary to make sure that the resulting KDE is properly normalized.) Some examples of frequently used kernel functions include (see Figure 2-5):

$$K(x) = \begin{cases} \frac{1}{2} & \text{if } |x| \leq 1 \\ 0 & \text{otherwise} \end{cases} \qquad \text{box or boxcar kernel}$$

$$K(x) = \begin{cases} \frac{3}{4}\left(1 - x^2\right) & \text{if } |x| \leq 1 \\ 0 & \text{otherwise} \end{cases} \qquad \text{Epanechnikov kernel}$$

$$K(x) = \frac{1}{\sqrt{2\pi}} \exp\left(-\frac{1}{2}x^2\right) \qquad \text{Gaussian kernel}$$

The box kernel and the Epanechnikov kernel are zero outside a finite range, whereas the Gaussian kernel is nonzero everywhere but negligibly small outside a limited domain. It turns out that the curve resulting from the KDE does not depend strongly on the particular choice of kernel function, so we are free to use the kernel that is most convenient. Because it is so easy to work with, the Gaussian kernel is the most widely used. (See Appendix B for more information on the Gaussian function.)

Constructing a KDE requires to things: first, we must move the kernel to the position of each point by shifting it appropriately. For example, the function $K(x - x_i)$ will have its peak at x_i, not at 0. Second, we have to choose the kernel *bandwidth*, which controls the spread of the kernel function. To make sure that the area under the curve stays the same as we shrink the width, we have to make the curve higher (and lower if we increase the

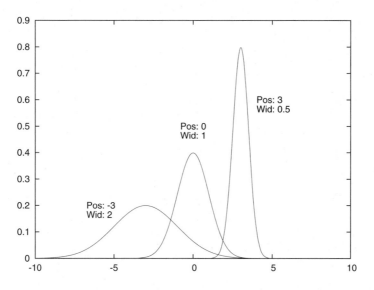

FIGURE 2-6. The Gaussian kernel for three different bandwidths. The height of the kernel increases as the width decreases, so the total area under the curve remains constant.

width). The final expression for the shifted, rescaled kernel function of bandwidth h is:

$$\frac{1}{h} K \left(\frac{x - x_i}{h} \right)$$

This function has a peak at x_i, its width is approximately h, and its height is such that the area under the curve is still 1. Figure 2-6 shows some examples, using the Gaussian kernel. Keep in mind that the area under all three curves is the same.

Using this expression, we can now write down a formula for the KDE with bandwidth h for any data set $\{x_1, x_2, \ldots, x_n\}$. This formula can be evaluated for any point x along the x axis:

$$D_h \left(x; \{x_i\} \right) = \sum_{i=1}^{n} \frac{1}{h} K \left(\frac{x - x_i}{h} \right)$$

All of this is straightforward and easy to implement in any computer language. Be aware that for large data sets (those with many thousands of points), the required number of kernel evaluations can lead to performance issues, especially if the function $D(x)$ needs to be evaluated for many different positions (*i.e.*, many different values of x). If this becomes a problem for you, you may want to choose a simpler kernel function or not evaluate a kernel if the distance $x - x_i$ is significantly greater than the bandwidth h.[*]

[*]Yet another strategy starts with the realization that forming a KDE amounts to a convolution of the kernel function with the data set. You can now take the Fourier transform of both kernel and data set and make use of the Fourier convolution theorem. This approach is suitable for very large data sets but is outside the scope of our discussion.

Now we can explain the wide gray line in Figure 2-4: it is a KDE with a larger bandwidth. Using such a large bandwidth makes it impossible to resolve the individual data points, but it does highlight entire *periods* of greater or smaller frequency. Which choice of bandwidth is right for you depends on your purpose.

A KDE constructed as just described is similar to a classical histogram, but it avoids two of the aforementioned problems. Given data set and bandwidth, a KDE is unique; a KDE is also smooth, provided we have chosen a smooth kernel function, such as the Gaussian.

Optional: Optimal Bandwidth Selection

We still have to fix the bandwidth. This is a different *kind* of problem than the other two: it's not just a technical problem, which could be resolved through a better method; instead, it's a fundamental problem that relates to the data set itself. If the data follows a smooth distribution, then a wider bandwidth is appropriate, but if the data follows a very wiggly distribution, then we need a smaller bandwidth to retain all relevant detail. In other words, the optimal bandwidth is a property of the data set and tells us something about the nature of the data.

So how do we choose an optimal value for the bandwidth? Intuitively, the problem is clear: we want the bandwidth to be narrow enough to retain all relevant detail but wide enough so that the resulting curve is not too "wiggly." This is a problem that arises in every approximation problem: balancing the faithfulness of representation against the simplicity of behavior. Statisticians speak of the "bias–variance trade-off."

To make matters concrete, we have to define a specific expression for the error of our approximation, one that takes into account both bias and variance. We can then choose a value for the bandwidth that minimizes this error. For KDEs, the generally accepted measure is the "expected mean-square error" between the approximation and the true density. The problem is that we don't know the true density function that we are trying to approximate, so it seems impossible to calculate (and minimize) the error in this way. But clever methods have been developed to make progress. These methods fall broadly into two categories. First, we could try to find explicit expressions for both bias and variance. Balancing them leads to an equation that has to be solved numerically or—if we make additional assumptions (*e.g.*, that the distribution is Gaussian)—can even yield explicit expressions similar to Scott's rule (introduced earlier when talking about histograms). Alternatively, we could realize that the KDE is an approximation for the probability density from which the original set of points was chosen. We can therefore choose points from this approximation (*i.e.*, from the probability density represented by the KDE) and see how well they replicate the KDE that we started with. Now we change the bandwidth until we find that value for which the KDE is best replicated: the result is the estimate of the "true" bandwidth of the data. (This latter method is known as *cross-validation*.)

Although not particularly hard, the details of both methods would lead us too far afield, and so I will skip them here. If you are interested, you will have no problem picking up the details from one of the references at the end of this chapter. Keep in mind, however, that these methods find the optimal bandwidth *with respect to the mean-square error*, which tends to overemphasize bias over variance and therefore these methods lead to rather narrow bandwidths and KDEs that appear too wiggly. If you are using KDEs to generate graphs for the purpose of obtaining intuitive visualizations of point distributions, then you might be better off with a bit of manual trial and error combined with visual inspection. In the end, there is no "right" answer, only the most suitable one for a given purpose. Also, the most suitable to develop intuitive understanding might not be the one that minimizes a particular mathematical quantity.

The Cumulative Distribution Function

The main advantage of histograms and kernel density estimates is that they have an immediate intuitive appeal: they tell us how probable it is to find a data point with a certain value. For example, from Figure 2-2 it is immediately clear that values around 250 milliseconds are very likely to occur, whereas values greater than 2,000 milliseconds are quite rare.

But how rare, exactly? That is a question that is much harder to answer by looking at the histogram in Figure 2-2. Besides wanting to know how much weight is in the tail, we might also be interested to know what fraction of requests completes in the typical band between 150 and 350 milliseconds. It's certainly the majority of events, but if we want to know exactly how many, then we need to sum up the contributions from all bins in that region.

The *cumulative distribution function* (CDF) does just that. The CDF at point x tells us what fraction of events has occurred "to the left" of x. In other words, the CDF is the fraction of all points x_i with $x_i \leq x$.

Figure 2-7 shows the same data set that we have already encountered in Figure 2-2, but here the data is represented by a KDE (with bandwidth $h = 30$) instead of a histogram. In addition, the figure also includes the corresponding CDF. (Both KDE and CDF are normalized to 1.)

We can read off several interesting observations directly from the plot of the CDF. For instance, we can see that at $t = 1,500$ (which certainly puts us into the tail of the distribution) the CDF is still smaller than 0.85; this means that fully 15 percent of all requests take longer than 1,500 milliseconds. In contrast, less than a third of all requests are completed in the "typical" range of 150–500 milliseconds. (How do we know this? The CDF for $t = 150$ is about 0.05 and is close to 0.40 for $t = 500$. In other words, about 40 percent of all requests are completed in less than 500 milliseconds; of these, 5 percent are completed in less than 150 milliseconds. Hence about 35 percent of all requests have response times of between 150 and 500 milliseconds.)

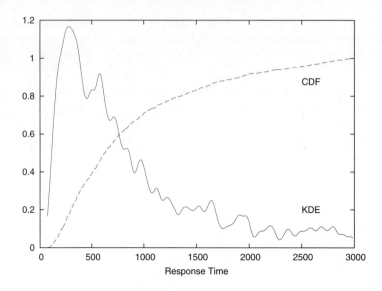

FIGURE 2-7. Kernel density estimate and cumulative distribution function of the server response times shown in Figure 2-2.

It is worth pausing to contemplate these findings, because they demonstrate how misleading a histogram (or KDE) can be despite (or because of) their intuitive appeal! Judging from the histogram or KDE alone, it seems quite reasonable to assume that "most" of the events occur within the major peak near $t = 300$ and that the tail for $t > 1,500$ contributes relatively little. Yet the CDF tells us clearly that this is not so. (The problem is that the eye is much better at judging distances than areas, and we are therefore misled by the large values of the histogram near its peak and fail to see that nevertheless the area beneath the peak is not that large compared to the total area under the curve.)

CDFs are probably the least well-known and most underappreciated tool in basic graphical analysis. They have less immediate intuitive appeal than histograms or KDEs, but they allow us to make the kind of quantitative statement that is very often required but is difficult (if not impossible) to obtain from a histogram.

Cumulative distribution functions have a number of important properties that follow directly from how they are calculated.

- Because the value of the CDF at position x is the fraction of points to the left of x, a CDF is always monotonically increasing with x.

- CDFs are less wiggly than a histogram (or KDE) but contain the same information in a representation that is inherently less noisy.

- Because CDFs do not involve any binning, they do not lose information and are therefore a more faithful representation of the data than a histogram.

- All CDFs approach 0 as x goes to negative infinity. CDFs are usually normalized so that they approach 1 (or 100 percent) as x goes to positive infinity.
- A CDF is unique for a given data set.

If you are mathematically inclined, you have probably already realized that the CDF is (an approximation to) the antiderivative of the histogram and that the histogram is the derivative of the CDF:

$$\text{cdf}(x) \approx \int_{-\infty}^{x} dt \, \text{histo}(t)$$

$$\text{histo}(x) \approx \frac{d}{dx} \text{cdf}(x)$$

Cumulative distribution functions have several uses. First, and most importantly, they enable us to answer questions such as those posed earlier in this section: what fraction of points falls between any two values? The answer can simply be read off from the graph. Second, CDFs also help us understand how imbalanced a distribution is—in other words, what fraction of the overall weight is carried by the tails.

Cumulative distribution functions also prove useful when we want to compare two distributions. It is notoriously difficult to compare two bell-shaped curves in a histogram against each other. Comparing the corresponding CDFs is usually much more conclusive.

One last remark, before leaving this section: in the literature, you may find the term *quantile plot*. A quantile plot is just the plot of a CDF in which the x and y axes have been switched. Figure 2-8 shows an example using once again the server response time data set. Plotted this way, we can easily answer questions such as, "What response time corresponds to the 10th percentile of response times?" But the information contained in this graph is of course exactly the same as in a graph of the CDF.

Optional: Comparing Distributions with Probability Plots and QQ Plots

Occasionally you might want to confirm that a given set of points is distributed according to some specific, known distribution. For example, you have a data set and would like to determine whether it can be described well by a Gaussian (or some other) distribution.

You could compare a histogram or KDE of the data set directly against the theoretical density function, but it is notoriously difficult to compare distributions that way—especially out in the tails. A better idea would be to compare the cumulative distribution functions, which are easier to handle because they are less wiggly and are always monotonically increasing. But this is still not easy. Also keep in mind that most probability distributions depend on location and scale parameters (such as mean and variance), which you would have to estimate *before* being able to make a meaningful comparison. Isn't there a way to compare a set of points directly against a theoretical distribution and, in the process, read off the estimates for all the parameters required?

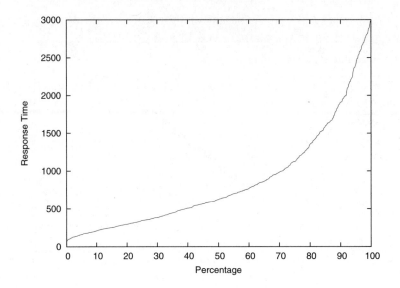

FIGURE 2-8. *Quantile plot of the server data. A quantile plot is a graph of the CDF with the x and y axes interchanged. Compare to Figure 2-7.*

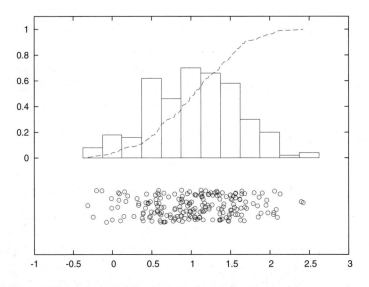

FIGURE 2-9. *Jitter plot, histogram, and cumulative distribution function for a Gaussian data set.*

As it turns out, there is. The method is technically easy to do, but the underlying logic is a bit convoluted and tends to trip up even experienced practitioners.

Here is how it works. Consider a set of points $\{x_i\}$ that we suspect are distributed according to the Gaussian distribution. In other words, we expect the cumulative distribution function of the set of points, $y_i = \text{cdf}(x_i)$, to be the Gaussian cumulative

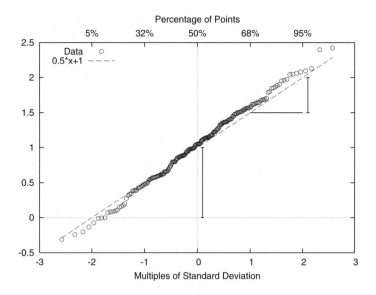

FIGURE 2-10. Probability plot for the data set shown in Figure 2-9.

distribution function $\Phi\left((x - \mu)/\sigma\right)$ with mean μ and standard deviation σ:

$$y_i = \Phi\left(\frac{x_i - \mu}{\sigma}\right) \quad \text{only if data is Gaussian}$$

Here, y_i is the value of the cumulative distribution function corresponding to the data point x_i; in other words, y_i is the *quantile* of the point x_i.

Now comes the trick. We apply the *inverse* of the Gaussian distribution function to both sides of the equation:

$$\Phi^{-1}(y_i) = \frac{x_i - \mu}{\sigma}$$

With a little bit of algebra, this becomes

$$x_i = \mu + \sigma\,\Phi^{-1}(y_i)$$

In other words, if we plot the values in the data set as a function of $\Phi^{-1}(y_i)$, then they should fall onto a straight line with slope σ and zero intercept μ. If, on the other hand, the points do not fall onto a straight line after applying the inverse transform, then we can conclude that the data is not distributed according to a Gaussian distribution.

The resulting plot is known as a *probability plot*. Because it is easy to spot deviation from a straight line, a probability plot provides a relatively sensitive test to determine whether a set of points behaves according to the Gaussian distribution. As an added benefit, we can read off estimates for the mean and the standard deviation directly from the graph: μ is the intercept of the curve with the y axis, and σ is given by the slope of the curve. (Figure 2-10 shows the probability plot for the Gaussian data set displayed in Figure 2-9.)

One important question concerns the *units* that we plot along the axes. For the vertical axis the case is clear: we use whatever units the original data was measured in. But what about the horizontal axis? We plot the data as a function of $\Phi^{-1}(y_i)$, which is the inverse Gaussian distribution function, applied to the percentile y_i for each point x_i. We can therefore choose between two different ways to dissect the horizontal axis: either using the percentiles y_i directly (in which case the tick marks will not be distributed uniformly), or dividing the horizontal axis uniformly. In the latter case we are using *the width of the standard Gaussian distribution* as a unit. You can convince yourself that this is really true by realizing that $\Phi^{-1}(y)$ is the inverse of the Gaussian distribution function $\Phi(x)$. Now ask yourself: what units is x measured in? We use the same units for the horizontal axis of a Gaussian probability plot. These units are sometimes called *probits*. (Figure 2-10 shows both sets of units.) Beware of confused and confusing explanations of this point elsewhere in the literature.

There is one more technical detail that we need to discuss: to produce a probability plot, we need not only the data itself, but for each point x_i we also need its quantile y_i (we will discuss quantiles and percentiles in more detail later in this chapter). The simplest way to obtain the quantiles, given the data, is as follows:

1. Sort the data points in ascending order.
2. Assign to each data point its rank (basically, its line number in the sorted file), starting at 1 (not at 0).
3. The quantile y_i now is the rank divided by $n + 1$, where n is the number of data points.

This prescription guarantees that each data point is assigned a quantile that is strictly greater than 0 and strictly less than 1. This is important because $\Phi^{-1}(x)$ is defined only for $0 < x < 1$. This prescription is easy to understand and easy to remember, but you may find other, slightly more complicated prescriptions elsewhere. For all practical purposes, the differences are going to be small.

Finally, let's look at an example where the data is clearly *not* Gaussian. Figure 2-11 shows the server data from Figure 2-2 plotted in a probability plot. The points don't fall on a straight line at all—which is no surprise since we already knew from Figure 2-2 that the data is not Gaussian. But for cases that are less clear-cut, the probability plot can be a helpful tool for detecting deviations from Gaussian behavior.

A few additional comments are in order here.

- Nothing in the previous discussion requires that the distribution be Gaussian! You can use almost any other commonly used distribution function (and its inverse) to generate the respective probability plots. In particular, many of the commonly used probability

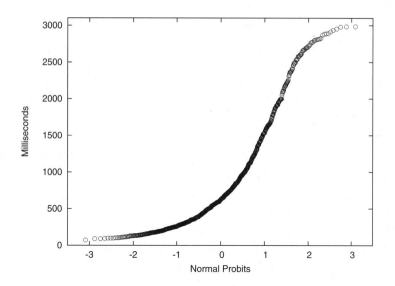

FIGURE 2-11. A probability plot of the server response times from Figure 2-2. The data does not follow a Gaussian distribution and thus the points do not fall on a straight line.

distributions depend on location and scale parameters in exactly the same way as the Gaussian distribution, so all the arguments discussed earlier go through as before.

- So far, I have always assumed that we want to compare an *empirical* data set against a *theoretical* distribution. But there may also be situations where we want to compare two empirical data sets against each other—for example, to find out whether they were drawn from the same family of distributions (without having to specify the family explicitly). The process is easiest to understand when both data sets we want to compare contain the same number of points. You sort both sets and then align the points from both data sets that have the same rank (once sorted). Now plot the resulting pairs of points in a regular scatter plot (see Chapter 3); the resulting graph is known as a *QQ plot*. (If the two data sets do not contain the same number of points, you will have to interpolate or truncate them so that they do.)

Probability plots are a relatively advanced, specialized technique, and you should evaluate whether you really need them. Their purpose is to determine whether a given data set stems from a specific, known distribution. Occasionally, this is of interest in itself; in other situations subsequent analysis depends on proper identification of the underlying model. For example, many statistical techniques assume that the errors or residuals are Gaussian and are not applicable if this condition is violated. Probability plots are a convenient technique for testing this assumption.

Rank-Order Plots and Lift Charts

There is a technique related to histograms and CDFs that is worth knowing about. Consider the following scenario. A company that is selling textbooks and other curriculum materials is planning an email marketing campaign to reach out to its existing customers. For this campaign, the company wants to use personalized email messages that are tailored to the job title of each recipient (so that teachers will receive a different email than their principals). The problem is the customer database contains about 250,000 individual customer records with over 16,000 different job titles among them! Now what?

The trick is to sort the job titles by the number of individual customer records corresponding to each job title. The first few records are shown in Table 2-1. The four columns give the job title, the number of customers for that job title, the fraction of all customers having that job title, and finally the cumulative fraction of customers. For the last column, we sum up the number of customers for the current and all previously seen job titles, then divide by the total number of customer records. This is the equivalent of the CDF we discussed earlier.

We can see immediately that fully two thirds of all customers account for only 10 different job titles. Using just the top 30 job titles gives us 75 percent coverage of customer records. That's much more manageable than the 16,000 job titles we started with!

Let's step back for a moment to understand how this example is different from those we have seen previously. What is important to notice here is that *the independent variable has no intrinsic ordering*. What does this mean?

For the web-server example, we counted the number of events for each response time; hence the count of events per bin was the dependent variable, and it was determined by the independent variable—namely, the response time. In that case, the independent variable had an inherent ordering: 100 milliseconds are always less than 400 milliseconds (and so on). But in the case of counting customer records that match a certain job title, the independent variable (the job title) has no corresponding ordering relation. It may appear otherwise since we can sort the job titles alphabetically, but realize that this ordering is entirely arbitrary! There is nothing "fundamental" about it. If we choose a different font encoding or locale, the order will change. Contrast this with the ordering relationship on numbers—there are no two ways about it: 1 is always less than 2.

In cases like this, where the independent variable does not have an intrinsic ordering, it is often a good idea to sort entries by the *dependent* variable. That's what we did in the example: rather than defining some (arbitrary) sort order on the job titles, we sorted by the number of records (*i.e.*, by the dependent variable). Once the records have been sorted in this way, we can form a histogram and a CDF as before.

TABLE 2-1. The first 30 job titles and their relative frequencies.

Title	Number of customers	Fraction of customers	Cumulative fraction
Teacher	66,470	0.34047	0.340
Principal	22,958	0.11759	0.458
Superintendent	12,521	0.06413	0.522
Director	12,202	0.06250	0.584
Secretary	4,427	0.02267	0.607
Coordinator	3,201	0.01639	0.623
Vice Principal	2,771	0.01419	0.637
Program Director	1,926	0.00986	0.647
Program Coordinator	1,718	0.00880	0.656
Student	1,596	0.00817	0.664
Consultant	1,440	0.00737	0.672
Administrator	1,169	0.00598	0.678
President	1,114	0.00570	0.683
Program Manager	1,063	0.00544	0.689
Supervisor	1,009	0.00516	0.694
Professor	961	0.00492	0.699
Librarian	940	0.00481	0.704
Project Coordinator	880	0.00450	0.708
Project Director	866	0.00443	0.713
Office Manager	839	0.00429	0.717
Assistant Director	773	0.00395	0.721
Administrative Assistant	724	0.00370	0.725
Bookkeeper	697	0.00357	0.728
Intern	693	0.00354	0.732
Program Supervisor	602	0.00308	0.735
Lead Teacher	587	0.00300	0.738
Instructor	580	0.00297	0.741
Head Teacher	572	0.00292	0.744
Program Assistant	572	0.00292	0.747
Assistant Teacher	546	0.00279	0.749

This trick of sorting by the dependent variable is useful whenever the independent variable does not have a meaningful ordering relation; it is not limited to situations where we count events per bin. Figures 2-12 and 2-13 show two typical examples.

Figure 2-12 shows the sales by a certain company to different countries. Not only the sales to each country but also the cumulative sales are shown, which allows us to assess the importance of the remaining "tail" of the distribution of sales.

In this example, I chose to plot the independent variable along the vertical axis. This is often a good idea when the values are strings, since they are easier to read this way. (If you plot them along the horizontal axis, it is often necessary to rotate the strings by 90 degrees to make them fit, which makes hard to read.)

Figure 2-13 displays what in quality engineering is known as a *Pareto chart*. In quality engineering and process improvement, the goal is to reduce the number of defects in a

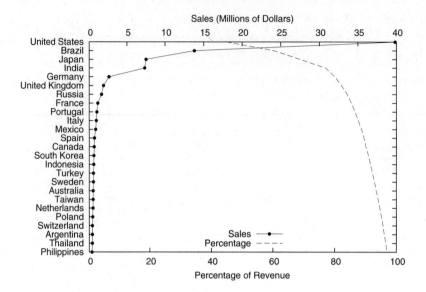

FIGURE 2-12. A rank-order plot of sales per country. The independent variable has been plotted along the vertical axis to make the text labels easier to read.

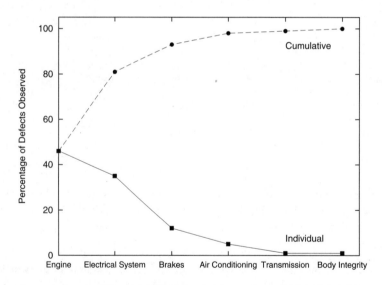

FIGURE 2-13. The Pareto chart is another example of a rank-order plot.

certain product or process. You collect all known causes of defects and observe how often each one occurs. The results can be summarized conveniently in a chart like the one in Figure 2-13. Note that the causes of defects are sorted by their frequency of occurrence. From this chart we can see immediately that problems with the engine and the electrical system are much more common than problems with the air conditioning, the brakes, or the transmission. In fact, by looking at the cumulative error curve, we can tell that fixing just the first two problem areas would reduce the overall defect rate by 80 percent.

Two more bits of terminology: the term "Pareto chart" is not used widely outside the specific engineering disciplines mentioned in the previous paragraph. I personally prefer the expression *rank-order chart* for any plot generated by first sorting all entries by the dependent variable (*i.e.*, by the *rank* of the entry). The cumulative distribution curve is occasionally referred to as a *lift curve*, because it tells us how much "lift" we get from each entry or range of entries.

Only When Appropriate: Summary Statistics and Box Plots

You may have noticed that so far I have not spoken at all about such simple topics as mean and median, standard deviation, and percentiles. That is quite intentional. These *summary statistics* apply only under certain assumptions and are misleading, if not downright wrong, if those assumptions are not fulfilled. I know that these quantities are easy to understand and easy to calculate, but if there is one message I would like you to take away from this book it is this: the fact that something is convenient and popular is no reason to follow suit. For any method that you want to use, make sure you understand the underlying assumptions and *always* check that they are fulfilled for the specific application you have in mind!

Mean, median, and related summary statistics apply only to distributions that have a single, central peak—that is, to *unimodal* distributions. If this basic assumption is not fulfilled, then conclusions based on simple summary statistics will be wrong. Even worse, nothing will tip you off that they are wrong: the numbers will look quite reasonable. (We will see an example of this problem shortly.)

Summary Statistics

If a distribution has only a single peak, then it makes sense to ask about the properties of that peak: where is it located, and what is its width? We may also want to know whether the distribution is symmetric and whether any outliers are present.

Mean and standard deviation are two popular measures for location and spread. The *mean* or average is both familiar and intuitive:

$$m = \frac{1}{n} \sum_i x_i$$

The standard deviation measures how far points spread "on average" from the mean: we take all the differences between each individual point and the mean, and then calculate the average of all these differences. Because data points can either overshoot or undershoot the mean and we don't want the positive and negative deviations to cancel each other, we sum the *square* of the individual deviations and then take the mean of the square deviations. (The second equation is very useful in practice and can be found from the first after plugging in the definition of the mean.)

$$s^2 = \frac{1}{n} \sum_i (x_i - m)^2$$
$$= \frac{1}{n} \sum_i x_i^2 - m^2$$

The quantity s^2 calculated in this way is known as the *variance* and is the more important quantity from a theoretical point of view. But as a measure of the spread of a distribution, we are better off using its square root, which is known as the *standard deviation*. Why take the square root? Because then both measure for the location, and the measure for the spread will have the same units, which are also the units of the actual data. (If our data set consists of the prices for a basket of goods, then the variance would be given in "square dollars," whereas the standard deviation would be given in dollars.)

For many (but certainly not all!) data sets arising in practice, one can expect about two thirds of all data points to fall within the interval $[m - s, m + s]$ and 99 percent of all points to fall within the wider interval $[m - 3s, m + 3s]$.

Mean and standard deviation are easy to calculate, and have certain nice mathematical properties—provided the data is symmetric and does not contain crazy outliers. Unfortunately, many data sets violate at least one of these assumptions. Here is an example for the kind of trouble that one may encounter. Assume we have 10 items costing $1 each, and one item costing $20. The mean item price comes out to be $2.73, even though no item has a price anywhere near this value. The standard deviation is even worse: it comes out to $5.46, implying that most items have a price between $2.73 − $5.46 and $2.73 + $5.46. The "expected range" now includes negative prices—an obviously absurd result. Note that the data set itself is not particularly pathological: going to the grocery store and picking up a handful of candy bars and a bottle of wine will do it (pretty good wine, to be sure, but nothing outrageous).

A different set of summary statistics that is both more flexible and more robust is based on the concepts of *median* and *quantiles* or *percentiles*. The median is conventionally defined as the value from a data set such that half of all points in the data set are smaller and the other half greater that that value. Percentiles are the generalization of this concept to other fractions (the 10th percentile is the value such that 10 percent of all points in the data set are smaller than it, and so on). Quantiles are similar to percentiles, only that they are taken with respect to the fraction of points, not the percentage of points (in other words, the 10th percentile equals the 0.1 quantile).

Simple as it is, the percentile concept is nevertheless ambiguous, and so we need to work a little harder to make it really concrete. As an example of the problems that occur, consider the data set {1, 2, 3}. What is the median? It is not possible to break this data set into two equal parts each containing exactly half the points. The problem becomes even more uncomfortable when we are dealing with arbitrary percentile values (rather than the median only).

The Internet standard laid down in RFC 2330 ("Framework for IP Performance Metrics") gives a definition of percentiles in terms of the CDF, which is unambiguous and practical, as follows. The pth percentile is the smallest value x, such that the cumulative distribution function of x is greater or equal $p/100$.

$$p\text{th percentile: smallest } x \text{ for which } \text{cdf}(x) \geq p/100$$

This definition assumes that the CDF is normalized to 1, not to 100. If it were normalized to 100, the condition would be $\text{cdf}(x) \geq p$.

With this definition, the median (*i.e.*, the 50th percentile) of the data set $\{1, 2, 3\}$ is 2 because the $\text{cdf}(1) = 0.33\ldots$, $\text{cdf}(2) = 0.66\ldots$, and $\text{cdf}(3) = 1.0$. The median of the data set $\{1, 2\}$ would be 1 because now $\text{cdf}(1) = 0.5$, and $\text{cdf}(2) = 1.0$.

The median is a measure for the location of the distribution, and we can use percentiles to construct a measure for the width of the distribution. Probably the most frequently used quantity for this purpose is the *inter-quartile range* (IQR), which is the distance between the 75th percentile and 25th percentile.

When should you favor median and percentile over mean and standard deviation? Whenever you suspect that your distribution is not symmetric or has important outliers.

If a distribution is symmetric and well behaved, then mean and median will be quite close together, and there is little difference in using either. Once the distribution becomes skewed, however, the basic assumption that underlies the mean as a measure for the location of the distribution is no longer fulfilled, and so you are better off using the median. (This is why the average wage is usually given in official publications as the median family income, not the mean; the latter would be significantly distorted by the few households with extremely high incomes.) Furthermore, the moment you have outliers, the assumptions behind the standard deviation as a measure of the width of the distribution are violated; in this case you should favor the IQR (recall our shopping basket example earlier).

If median and percentiles are so great, then why don't we always use them? A large part of the preference for mean and variance is historical. In the days before readily available computing power, percentiles were simply not practical to calculate. Keep in mind that finding percentiles requires to *sort* the data set whereas to find the mean requires only to add up all elements in any order. The latter is an $\mathcal{O}(n)$ process, but the former is an $\mathcal{O}(n^2)$ process, since humans—being nonrecursive—cannot be taught Quicksort and therefore need to resort to much less efficient sorting algorithms. A second reason is that it is much harder to prove rigorous theorems for percentiles, whereas mean and variance are mathematically very well behaved and easy to work with.

Box-and-Whisker Plots

There is an interesting graphical way to represent these quantities, together with information about potential outliers, known as a *box-and-whisker plot*, or *box plot* for short. Figure 2-15 illustrates all components of a box plot. A box plot consists of:

- A *marker* or symbol for the median as an indicator of the *location* of the distribution

- A *box*, spanning the inter-quartile range, as a measure of the *width* of the distribution

- A set of *whiskers*, extending from the central box to the upper and lower adjacent values, as an indicator of the *tails* of the distribution (where "adjacent value" is defined in the next paragraph)

- Individual *symbols* for all values outside the range of adjacent values, as a representation for *outliers*

You can see that a box plot combines a lot of information in a single graph. We have encountered almost all of these concepts before, with the exception of upper and lower *adjacent values*. While the inter-quartile range is a measure for the width of the central "bulk" of the distribution, the adjacent values are one possible way to express how far its tails reach. The upper adjacent value is the largest value in the data set that is less than twice the inter-quartile range greater than the median. In other words: extend the whisker upward from the median to twice the length of the central box. Now trim the whisker down to the largest value that actually occurs in the data set; this value is the upper adjacent value. (A similar construction holds for the lower adjacent value.)

You may wonder about the reason for this peculiar construction. Why not simply extend the whiskers to, say, the 5th and 95th percentile and be done with it? The problem with this approach is that it does not allow us to recognize true outliers! Outliers are data points that are, *when compared to the width of the distribution*, unusually far from the center. Such values may or may not be present. The top and bottom 5 percent, on the other hand, are always present even for very compact distributions. To recognize outliers, we therefore cannot simply look at the most extreme values, instead we must *compare their distance from the center to the overall width of the distribution*. That is what box-and-whisker plots, as described in the previous paragraph, do.

The logic behind the preceding argument is extremely important (not only in this application but more generally), so I shall reiterate the steps: *first* we calculated a measure for the width of the distribution, *then* we used this width to identify outliers as those points that are far from the center, where (and this is the crucial step) "far" is measured in units of the width of the distribution. We neither impose an arbitrary distance from the outside, nor do we simply label the most extreme x percent of the distribution as outliers—instead, we determine the width of the distribution (as the range into which points "typically" fall) and then use it to identify outliers as those points that deviate from this range. The important insight here is that the distribution itself determines a typical *scale*, which provides a natural unit in which to measure other properties of the distribution. This idea of using some typical property of the system to describe other parts of the system will come up again later (see Chapter 8).

Box plots combine many different measures of a distribution into a single, compact graph. A box plot allows us to see whether the distribution is symmetric or not and how the weight is distributed between the central peak and the tails. Finally, outliers (if present) are not dropped but shown explicitly.

Box plots are best when used to compare several distributions against one another—for a single distribution, the overhead of preparing and managing a graph (compared to just quoting the numbers) may often not appear justified. Here is an example that compares different data sets against each other.

Let's say we have a data set containing the index of refraction of 121 samples of glass.[*] The data set is broken down by the type of glass: 70 samples of window glass, 29 from headlamps, 13 from containers of various kinds, and 9 from tableware. Figures 2-14 and 2-15 are two representations of the same data, the former as a kernel density estimate and the latter as a box plot.

The box plot emphasizes the overall structure of the data sets and makes it easy to compare the data sets based on their location and width. At the same time, it also loses much information. The KDE gives a more detailed view of the data—in particular showing the occurrence of multiple peaks in the distribution functions—but makes it more difficult to quickly sort and classify the data sets. Depending on your needs, one or the other technique may be preferable at any given time.

Here are some additional notes on box plots.

- The specific way of drawing a box plot that I described here is especially useful but is far from universal. In particular, the specific definition of the adjacent values is often not properly understood. Whenever you find yourself looking at a box plot, always ask what exactly is shown, and whenever you prepare one, make sure to include an explanation.

- The box plot described here can be modified and enhanced. For example, the width of the central box (*i.e.*, the direction orthogonal to the whiskers) can be used to indicate the size of the underlying data set: the more points are included, the wider the box. Another possibility is to abandon the rectangular shape of the box altogether and to use the local width of the box to display the density of points at each location— which brings us almost full circle to KDEs.

[*] The raw data can be found in the "Glass Identification Data Set" on the UCI Machine Learning Repository at *http://archive.ics.uci.edu/ml/*.

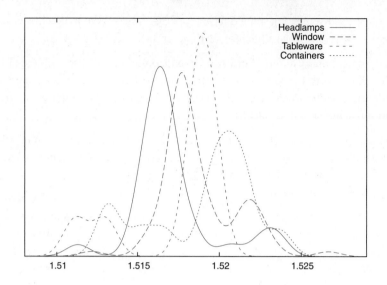

FIGURE 2-14. Comparing data sets using KDEs: refractive index of different types of glass. (Compare Figure 2-15.)

Workshop: NumPy

The NumPy module provides efficient and convenient handling of large numerical arrays in Python. It is the successor to both the earlier Numeric and the alternative numarray modules. (See the Appendix A for more on the history of scientific computing with Python.) The NumPy module is used by many other libraries and projects and in this sense is a "base" technology.

Let's look at some quick examples before delving a bit deeper into technical details.

NumPy in Action

NumPy objects are of type `ndarray`. There are different ways of creating them. We can create an `ndarray` by:

- Converting a Python list
- Using a factory function that returns a populated vector
- Reading data from a file directly into a NumPy object

The listing that follows shows five different ways to create NumPy objects. First we create one by converting a Python list. Then we show two different factory routines that generate equally spaced grid points. These routines differ in how they interpret the provided boundary values: one routine includes both boundary values, and the other includes one and excludes the other. Next we create a vector filled with zeros and set each element in a loop. Finally, we read data from a text file. (I am showing only the simplest

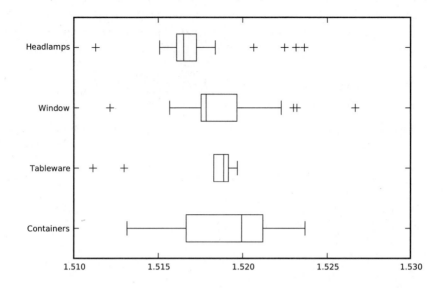

FIGURE 2-15. Comparing data sets using box plots: refractive index of different types of glass. (Compare Figure 2-14.)

or default cases here—all these routines have many more options that can be used to influence their behavior.)

```
# Five different ways to create a vector...

import numpy as np

# From a Python list
vec1 = np.array( [ 0., 1., 2., 3., 4. ] )

# arange( start inclusive, stop exclusive, step size )
vec2 = np.arange( 0, 5, 1, dtype=float )

# linspace( start inclusive, stop inclusive, number of elements )
vec3 = np.linspace( 0, 4, 5 )

# zeros( n ) returns a vector filled with n zeros
vec4 = np.zeros( 5 )
for i in range( 5 ):
    vec4[i] = i

# read from a text file, one number per row
vec5 = np.loadtxt( "data" )
```

In the end, all five vectors contain identical data. You should observe that the values in the Python list used to initialize vec1 are floating-point values and that we specified the *type* desired for the vector elements explicitly when using the arange() function to create vec2. (We will come back to types in a moment.)

Now that we have created these objects, we can operate with them (see the next listing). One of the major conveniences provided by NumPy is that we can operate with NumPy objects as if they were atomic data types: we can add, subtract, and multiply them (and so forth) *without the need for explicit loops*. Avoiding explicit loops makes our code clearer. It also makes it faster (because the entire operation is performed in C without overhead— see the discussion that follows).

```
# ... continuation from previous listing

# Add a vector to another
v1 = vec1 + vec2

# Unnecessary: adding two vectors using an explicit loop
v2 = np.zeros( 5 )
for i in range( 5 ):
    v2[i] = vec1[i] + vec2[i]

# Adding a vector to another in place
vec1 += vec2

# Broadcasting: combining scalars and vectors
v3 = 2*vec3
v4 = vec4 + 3

# Ufuncs: applying a function to a vector, element by element
v5 = np.sin(vec5)

# Converting to Python list object again
lst = v5.tolist()
```

All operations are performed element by element: if we add two vectors, then the corresponding elements from each vector are combined to give the element in the resulting vector. In other words, the compact expression `vec1 + vec2` for `v1` in the listing is equivalent to the explicit loop construction used to calculate `v2`. This is true even for multiplication: `vec1 * vec2` will result in a vector in which the corresponding elements of both operands have been multiplied element by element. (If you want a true vector or "dot" product, you must use the `dot()` function instead.) Obviously, this requires that *all operands have the same number of elements*!

Now we shall demonstrate two further convenience features that in the NumPy documentation are referred to as *broadcasting* and *ufuncs* (short for "universal functions"). The term "broadcasting" in this context has nothing to do with messaging. Instead, it means that if you try to combine two arguments of different shapes, then the smaller one will be extended ("cast broader") to match the larger one. This is especially useful when combining scalars with vectors: the scalar is expanded to a vector of appropriate size and whose elements all have the value given by the scalar; then the operation proceeds, element by element, as before. The term "ufunc" refers to a scalar function that can be applied to a NumPy object. The function is applied, element by element, to all entries in the NumPy object, and the result is a new NumPy object with the same shape as the original one.

Using these features skillfully, a function to calculate a kernel density estimate can be written as a *single* line of code:

```
# Calculating kernel density estimates

from numpy import *

# z: position, w: bandwidth, xv: vector of points
def kde( z, w, xv ):
    return sum( exp(-0.5*((z-xv)/w)**2)/sqrt(2*pi*w**2) )

d = loadtxt( "presidents", usecols=(2,) )

w = 2.5

for x in linspace( min(d)-w, max(d)+w, 1000 ):
    print x, kde( x, w, d )
```

This program will calculate and print the data needed to generate Figure 2-4 (but it does not actually draw the graph—that will have to wait until we introduce matplotlib in the Workshop of Chapter 3).

Most of the listing is boilerplate code, such as reading and writing files. All the actual work is done in the one-line function kde(z, w, xv). This function makes use of both "broadcasting" and "ufuncs" and is a good example for the style of programming typical of NumPy. Let's dissect it—inside out.

First recall what we need to do when evaluating a KDE: for each location *z* at which we want to evaluate the KDE, we must find its distance to all the points in the data set. For each point, we evaluate the kernel for this distance and sum up the contributions from all the individual kernels to obtain the value of the KDE at *z*.

The expression z-xv generates a vector that contains the distance between z and all the points in xv (that's broadcasting). We then divide by the required bandwidth, multiply by 1/2, and square each element. Finally, we apply the exponential function exp() to this vector (that's a ufunc). The result is a vector that contains the exponential function evaluated at the distances between the points in the data set and the location z. Now we only need to sum all the elements in the vector (that's what sum() does) and we are done, having calculated the KDE at position z. If we want to plot the KDE as a curve, we have to repeat this process for each location we wish to plot—that's what the final loop in the listing is for.

NumPy in Detail

You may have noticed that none of the warm-up examples in the listings in the previous section contained any matrices or other data structures of higher dimensionality—just one-dimensional vectors. To understand how NumPy treats objects with dimensions greater than one, we need to develop at least a superficial understanding for the way NumPy is implemented.

It is misleading to think of NumPy as a "matrix package for Python" (although it's commonly used as such). I find it more helpful to think of NumPy as a wrapper and access layer for underlying C buffers. These buffers are contiguous blocks of C memory, which—by their nature—are one-dimensional data structures. All elements in those data structures must be of the same size, and we can specify almost any native C type (including C structs) as the type of the individual elements. The default type corresponds to a C `double` and that is what we use in the examples that follow, but keep in mind that other choices are possible. All operations that apply to the data overall are performed in C and are therefore very fast.

To interpret the data as a matrix or other multi-dimensional data structure, the shape or layout is imposed during element access. The same 12-element data structure can therefore be interpreted as a 12-element vector or a 3×4 matrix or a $2 \times 2 \times 3$ tensor—the shape comes into play only through the way we access the individual elements. (Keep in mind that although reshaping a data structure is very easy, resizing is not.)

The encapsulation of the underlying C data structures is not perfect: when choosing the types of the atomic elements, we specify C data types not Python types. Similarly, some features provided by NumPy allow us to manage memory manually, rather than have the memory be managed transparently by the Python runtime. This is an intentional design decision, because NumPy has been designed to accommodate *large* data structures—large enough that you might want (or need) to exercise a greater degree of control over the way memory is managed. For this reason, you have the ability to choose types that take up less space as elements in a collection (*e.g.*, C `float` elements rather than the default `double`). For the same reason, all ufuncs accept an optional argument pointing to an (already allocated) location where the results will be placed, thereby avoiding the need to claim additional memory themselves. Finally, several access and structuring routines return a *view* (not a copy!) of the same underlying data. This does pose an aliasing problem that you need to watch out for.

The next listing quickly demonstrates the concepts of shape and views. Here, I assume that the commands are entered at an interactive Python prompt (shown as >>> in the listing). Output generated by Python is shown without a prompt:

```
>>> import numpy as np

>>> # Generate two vectors with 12 elements each
>>> d1 = np.linspace( 0, 11, 12 )
>>> d2 = np.linspace( 0, 11, 12 )

>>> # Reshape the first vector to a 3x4 (row x col) matrix
>>> d1.shape = ( 3, 4 )
>>> print d1
```

```
[[  0.   1.   2.   3.]
 [  4.   5.   6.   7.]
 [  8.   9.  10.  11.]]

>>> # Generate a matrix VIEW to the second vector
>>> view = d2.reshape( (3,4) )

>>> # Now: possible to combine the matrix and the view
>>> total = d1 + view


>>> # Element access: [row,col] for matrix
>>> print d1[0,1]
1.0
>>> print view[0,1]
1.0
>>> # ... and [pos] for vector
>>> print d2[1]
1.0


>>> # Shape or layout information
>>> print d1.shape
(3,4)
>>> print d2.shape
(12,)
>>> print view.shape
(3,4)

>>> # Number of elements (both commands equivalent)
>>> print d1.size
12
>>> print len(d2)
12

>>> # Number of dimensions (both commands equivalent)
>>> print d1.ndim
2
>>> print np.rank(d2)
1
```

Let's step through this. We create two vectors of 12 elements each. Then we *reshape* the first one into a 3 × 4 matrix. Note that the shape property is a data member—not an accessor function! For the second vector, we create a *view* in the form of a 3 × 4 matrix. Now d1 and the newly created view of d2 have the same shape, so we can combine them (by forming their sum, in this case). Note that even though reshape() is a member function, it does *not* change the shape of the instance itself but instead returns a new view object: d2 is still a one-dimensional vector. (There is also a standalone version of this function, so we could also have written view = np.reshape(d2, (3,4)). The presence of such redundant functionality is due to the desire to maintain backward compatibility with both of NumPy's ancestors.)

We can now access individual elements of the data structures, depending on their shape. Since both d1 and view are matrices, they are indexed by a pair of indices (in the order [row,col]). However, d2 is still a one-dimensional vector and thus takes only a single index. (We will have more to say about indexing in a moment.)

Finally, we examine some diagnostics regarding the shape of the data structures, emphasizing their precise semantics. The shape is a tuple, giving the number of elements in each dimension. The size is the total number of elements and corresponds to the value returned by len() for the entire data structure. Finally, ndim gives the number of dimensions (*i.e.*, d.ndim == len(d.shape)) and is equivalent to the "rank" of the entire data structure. (Again, the redundant functionality exists to maintain backward compatibility.)

Finally, let's take a closer look at the ways in which we can access elements or larger subsets of an ndarray. In the previous listing we saw how to access an individual element by fully specifying an index for each dimension. We can also specify larger subarrays of a data structure using two additional techniques, known as *slicing* and *advanced indexing*. The following listing shows some representative examples. (Again, consider this an interactive Python session.)

```
>>> import numpy as np

>>> # Create a 12-element vector and reshape into 3x4 matrix
>>> d = np.linspace( 0, 11, 12 )
>>> d.shape = ( 3,4 )
>>> print d
[[  0.   1.   2.   3.]
 [  4.   5.   6.   7.]
 [  8.   9.  10.  11.]]

>>> # Slicing...
>>> # First row
>>> print d[0,:]
[ 0.  1.  2.  3.]

>>> # Second col
>>> print d[:,1]
[ 1.  5.  9.]

>>> # Individual element: scalar
>>> print d[0,1]
1.0

>>> # Subvector of shape 1
>>> print d[0:1,1]
[ 1.]

>>> # Subarray of shape 1x1
>>> print d[0:1,1:2]
[[ 1.]]
```

```
>>> # Indexing...
>>> # Integer indexing: third and first column
>>> print d[ :, [2,0] ]
[[  2.   0.]
 [  6.   4.]
 [ 10.   8.]]

>>> # Boolean indexing: second and third column
>>> k = np.array( [False, True, True] )
>>> print d[ k, : ]
[[  4.   5.   6.   7.]
 [  8.   9.  10.  11.]]
```

We first create a 12-element vector and reshape it into a 3 × 4 matrix as before. Slicing uses the standard Python slicing syntax `start:stop:step`, where the start position is inclusive but the stopping position is exclusive. (In the listing, I use only the simplest form of slicing, selecting all available elements.)

There are two potential "gotchas" with slicing. First of all, specifying an explicit subscripting index (not a slice!) reduces the corresponding dimension to a scalar. Slicing, though, does not reduce the dimensionality of the data structure. Consider the two extreme cases: in the expression `d[0,1]`, indices for both dimensions are fully specified, and so we are left with a scalar. In contrast, `d[0:1,1:2]` is sliced in both dimensions. Neither dimension is removed, and the resulting object is still a (two-dimensional) matrix but of smaller size: it has shape 1 × 1.

The second issue to watch out for is that *slices return views*, not copies.

Besides slicing, we can also index an `ndarray` with a vector of indices, by an operation called "advanced indexing." The previous listing showed two simple examples. In the first we use a Python list object, which contains the integer indices (*i.e.*, the positions) of the desired columns and in the desired order, to select a subset of columns. In the second example, we form an `ndarray` of Boolean entries to select only those rows for which the Boolean evaluates to True.

In contrast to slicing, *advanced indexing returns copies*, not views.

This completes our overview of the basic capabilities of the NumPy module. NumPy is easy and convenient to use for simple use cases but can get very confusing otherwise. (For example, check out the rules for general broadcasting when both operators are multi-dimensional, or for advanced indexing).

We will present some more straightforward applications in Chapters 3 and 4.

Further Reading

- *The Elements of Graphing Data*. William S. Cleveland. 2nd ed., Hobart Press. 1994.
  A book-length discussion of graphical methods for data analysis such as those described in this chapter. In particular, you will find more information here on topics such as

box plots and QQ plots. Cleveland's methods are particularly careful and well thought-out.

- *All of Statistics: A Concise Course in Statistical Inference.* Larry Wasserman. Springer. 2004.
  A thoroughly modern treatment of mathematical statistics, very advanced and condensed. You will find some additional material here on the theory of "density estimation"—that is, on histograms and KDEs.

- *Multivariate Density Estimation.* David W. Scott. 2nd ed., Wiley. 2006.
  A research monograph on density estimation written by the creator of Scott's rule.

- *Kernel Smoothing.* M. P. Wand and M. C. Jones. Chapman & Hall. 1995.
  An accessible treatment of kernel density estimation.

## CHAPTER THREE

Two Variables: Establishing Relationships

WHEN WE ARE DEALING WITH A DATA SET THAT CONSISTS OF *TWO* VARIABLES (THAT IS, A *BIVARIATE* DATA SET), we are mostly interested in seeing whether some kind of relationship exists between the two variables and, if so, what kind of relationship this is.

Plotting one variable against another is pretty straightforward, therefore most of our effort will be spent on various tools and transformations that can be applied to characterize the nature of the relationship between the two inputs.

Scatter Plots

Plotting one variable against another is simple—you just *do* it! In fact, this is precisely what most people mean when they speak about "plotting" something. Yet there are differences, as we shall see.

Figures 3-1 and 3-2 show two examples. The data in Figure 3-1 might come from an experiment that measures the force between two surfaces separated by a short distance. The force is clearly a complicated function of the distance—on the other hand, the data points fall on a relatively smooth curve, and we can have confidence that it represents the data accurately. (To be sure, we should ask for the accuracy of the measurements shown in this graph: are there significant error bars attached to the data points? But it doesn't matter; the data itself shows clearly that the amount of *random* noise in the data is small. This does not mean that there aren't problems with the data but only that any problems will be *systematic* ones—for instance, with the apparatus—and statistical methods will not be helpful.)

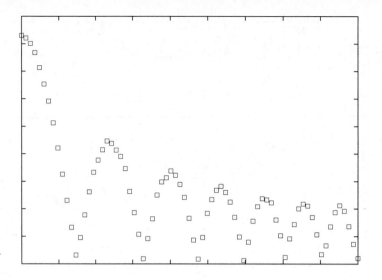

FIGURE 3-1. Data that clearly shows that there is a relationship, albeit a complicated one, between x and y.

In contrast, Figure 3-2 shows the kind of data typical of much of statistical analysis. Here we might be showing the prevalence of skin cancer as a function of the mean income for a group of individuals or the unemployment rate as a function of the frequency of high-school drop-outs for a number of counties, and the primary question is whether there is any relationship at all between the two quantities involved. The situation here is quite different from that shown in Figure 3-1, where it was obvious that a strong relationship existed between x and y, and therefore our main concern was to determine the precise nature of that relationship.

A figure such as Figure 3-2 is referred to as a *scatter plot* or *xy plot*. I prefer the latter term because scatter plot sounds to me too much like "splatter plot," suggesting that the data necessarily will be noisy—but we don't know that! Once we plot the data, it may turn out to be very clean and regular, as in Figure 3-1; hence I am more comfortable with the neutral term.

When we create a graph such as Figure 3-1 or Figure 3-2, we usually want to understand whether there is a relationship between x and y as well as what the nature of that relationship is. Figure 3-3 shows four different possibilities that we may find: no relationship; a strong, simple relationship; a strong, not-simple relationship; and finally a multivariate relationship (one that is not unique).

Conquering Noise: Smoothing

When data is noisy, we are more concerned with establishing *whether* the data exhibits a meaningful relationship, rather than establishing its precise character. To see this, it is

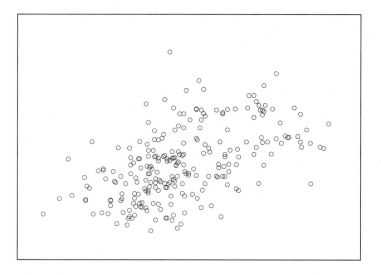

FIGURE 3-2. A noisy data set. Is there any relationship between x and y?

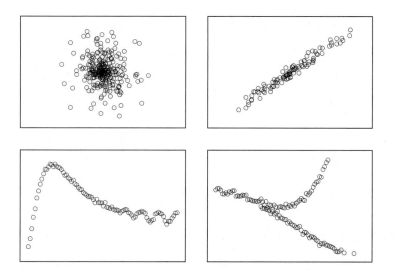

FIGURE 3-3. Four types of functional relationships (left to right, top to bottom): no relationship; strong, simple relationship; strong, not-simple relationship; multivariate relationship.

often helpful to find a smooth curve that represents the noisy data set. Trends and structure of the data may be more easily visible from such a curve than from the cloud of points.

Two different methods are frequently used to provide smooth representation of noisy data sets: *weighted splines* and a method known as *LOESS* (or LOWESS), which is short for locally weighted regression.

Both methods work by approximating the data in a small neighborhood (*i.e.*, locally) by a polynomial of low order (at most cubic). The trick is to string the various local approximations together to form a single smooth curve. Both methods contain an adjustable parameter that controls the "stiffness" of the resulting curve: the stiffer the curve, the smoother it appears but the less accurately it can follow the individual data points. Striking the right balance between smoothness and accuracy is the main challenge when it comes to smoothing methods.

Splines

Splines are constructed from piecewise polynomial functions (typically cubic) that are joined together in a smooth fashion. In addition to the local smoothness requirements at each joint, splines must also satisfy a global smoothness condition by optimizing the functional:

$$J[s] = \alpha \int \left(\frac{d^2 s}{dt^2}\right)^2 dt + (1 - \alpha) \sum_i w_i \, (y_i - s(x_i))^2$$

Here $s(t)$ is the spline curve, (x_i, y_i) are the coordinates of the data points, the w_i are weight factors (one for each data point), and α is a mixing factor. The first term controls how "wiggly" the spline is overall, because the second derivative measures the curvature of $s(t)$ and becomes large if the curve has many wiggles. The second term captures how accurately the spline represents the data points by measuring the squared deviation of the spline from each data point—it becomes large if the spline does not pass close to the data points. Each term in the sum is multiplied by a weight factor w_i, which can be used to give greater weight to data points that are known with greater accuracy than others. (Put differently: we can write w_i as $w_i = 1/d_i^2$, where d_i measures how close the spline should pass by y_i at x_i.) The mixing parameter α controls how much weight we give to the first term (emphasizing overall smoothness) relative to the second term (emphasizing accuracy of representation). In a plotting program, α is usually the dial we use to tune the spline for a given data set.

To construct the spline explicitly, we form cubic interpolation polynomials for each consecutive pair of points and require that these individual polynomials have the same values, as well as the same first and second derivatives, at the points where they meet. These smoothness conditions lead to a set of linear equations for the coefficients in the polynomials, which can be solved. Once these coefficients have been found, the spline curve can be evaluated at any desired location.

LOESS

Splines have an *overall* smoothness goal, which means that they are less responsive to *local* details in the data set. The LOESS smoothing method addresses this concern. It consists of approximating the data locally through a low-order (typically linear) polynomial (regression), while weighting all the data points in such a way that points close to the location of interest contribute more strongly than do data points farther away (local weighting).

Let's consider the case of first-order (linear) LOESS, so that the local approximation takes the particularly simple form $a + bx$. To find the "best fit" in a least-squares sense, we must minimize:

$$\chi^2 = \sum_i w(x - x_i; h)\,(a + bx_i - y_i)^2$$

with respect to the two parameters a and b. Here, $w(x)$ is the weight function. It should be smooth and strongly peaked—in fact, it is basically a kernel, similar to those we encountered in Figure 2-5 when we discussed kernel density estimates. The kernel most often used with LOESS is the "tri-cube" kernel $K(x) = \left(1 - |x|^3\right)^3$ for $|x| < 1$, $K(x) = 0$ otherwise; but any of the other kernels will also work. The weight depends on the distance between the point x where we want to evaluate the LOESS approximation and the location of the data points. In addition, the weight function also depends on the parameter h, which controls the bandwidth of the kernel: this is the primary control parameter for LOESS approximations. Finally, the value of the LOESS approximation at position x is given by $y(x) = a + bx$, where a and b minimize the expression for χ^2 stated earlier.

This is the basic idea behind LOESS. You can see that it is easy to generalize—for example, to two or more dimensions or two higher-order approximation polynomials. (One problem, though: explicit, closed expressions for the parameters a and b can be found only if you use first-order polynomials; whereas for quadratic or higher polynomials you will have to resort to numerical minimization techniques. Unless you have truly compelling reasons, you want to stick to the linear case!)

LOESS is a computationally intensive method. Keep in mind that the entire calculation must be performed for *every* point at which we want to obtain a smoothed value. (In other words, the parameters a and b that we calculated are themselves functions of x.) This is in contrast to splines: once the spline coefficients have been calculated, the spline can be evaluated easily at any point that we wish. In this way, splines provide a summary or approximation to the data. LOESS, however, does not lend itself easily to semi-analytical work: what you see is pretty much all you get.

One final observation: if we replace the linear function $a + bx$ in the fitting process with the constant function a, then LOESS becomes simply a weighted moving average.

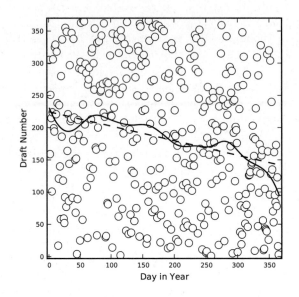

F I G U R E 3-4. *The 1970 draft lottery: draft number versus birth date (the latter as given in days since the beginning of the year). Two LOESS curves with different values for the smoothing parameter h indicate that men born later in the year tended to have lower draft numbers. This would not be easily recognizable from a plot of the data points alone.*

Examples

Let's look at two examples where smoothing reveals behavior that would otherwise not be visible.

The first is a famous data set that has been analyzed in many places: the 1970 draft lottery. During the Vietnam War, men in the U.S. were drafted based on their date of birth. Each possible birth date was assigned a draft number between 1 and 366 using a lottery process, and men were drafted in the order of their draft numbers. However, complaints were soon raised that the lottery was biased—that men born later in the year had a greater chance of receiving a low draft number and, consequentially, a greater chance of being drafted early.[*]

Figure 3-4 shows all possible birth dates (as days since the beginning of the year) and their assigned draft numbers. If the lottery had been fair, these points should form a completely

[*] More details and a description of the lottery process can be found in *The Statistical Exorcist.* M. Hollander and F. Proschan. CRC Press. 1984.

random pattern. Looking at the data alone, it is virtually impossible to tell whether there is any structure in the data. However, the smoothed LOESS lines reveal a strong falling tendency of the draft number over the course of the year: later birth dates are indeed more likely to have a lower draft number!

The LOESS lines have been calculated using a Gaussian kernel. For the solid line, I used a kernel bandwidth equal to 5, but for the dashed line, I used a much larger bandwidth of 100. For such a large bandwidth, practically all points in the data set contribute equally to the smoothed curve, so that the LOESS operation reverts to a linear regression of the entire data set. (In other words: if we make the bandwidth very large, then LOESS amounts to a least-squares fit of a straight line to the data.)

In this draft number example, we mostly cared about a *global* property of the data: the presence or absence of an overall trend. Because we were looking for a global property, a stiff curve (such as a straight line) was sufficient to reveal what we were looking for. However, if we want to extract more detail—in particular if we want to extract *local* features—then we need a "softer" curve, which can follow the data on smaller scales.

Figure 3-5 shows an amusing example.[*] Displayed are the finishing times (separately for men and women) for the winners in a marathon. Also shown are the "best fit" straight-line approximations for all events up to 1990. According to this (straight-line) model, women should start finishing faster than men before the year 2000 and then continue to become faster at a dramatic rate! This expectation is not borne out by actual observations: finishing times for women (and men) have largely leveled off.

This example demonstrates the danger of attempting to describe data by using a model of fixed form (a "formula")—and a straight line is one of the most rigid models out there! A model that is not appropriate for the data will lead to incorrect conclusions. Moreover, it may not be obvious that the model is inappropriate. Look again at Figure 3-5: don't the straight lines seem reasonable as a description of the data prior to 1990?

Also shown in Figure 3-5 are smoothed curves calculated using a LOESS process. Because these curves are "softer" they have a greater ability to capture features contained in the data. Indeed, the LOESS curve for the women's results does give an indication that the trend of dramatic improvements, seen since they first started competing in the mid-1960s, had already begun to level off before the year 1990. (All curves are based strictly on data prior to 1990.) This is a good example of how an adaptive smoothing curve can highlight local behavior that is present in the data but may not be obvious from merely looking at the individual data points.

---

[*]This example was inspired by *Graphic Discovery: A Trout in the Milk and Other Visual Adventures.* Howard Wainer. 2nd ed., Princeton University Press. 2007.

.

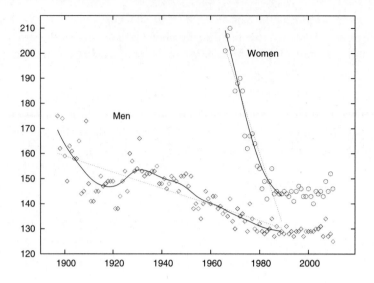

F I G U R E 3-5. Winning times (in minutes) for an annual marathon event, separately for men and women. Also shown are the straight-line and smooth-curve approximations. All approximations are based entirely on data points prior to 1990.

Residuals

Once you have obtained a smoothed approximation to the data, you will usually also want to check out the *residuals*—that is, the remainder when you subtract the smooth "trend" from the actual data.

There are several details to look for when studying residuals.

- Residuals should be balanced: symmetrically distributed around zero.

- Residuals should be free of a trend. The presence of a trend or of any other large-scale systematic behavior in the residuals suggests that the model is inappropriate! (By construction, this is never a problem if the smooth curve was obtained from an adaptive smoothing model; however, it is an important indicator if the smooth curve comes from an analytic model.)

- Residuals will necessarily straddle the zero value; they will take on both positive and negative values. Hence you may also want to plot their absolute values to evaluate whether the overall magnitude of the residuals is the same for the entire data set or not. The assumption that the magnitude of the variance around a model is constant throughout ("homoscedasticity") is often an important condition in statistical methods. If it is not satisfied, then such methods may not apply.

- Finally, you may want to use a QQ plot (see Chapter 2) to check whether the residuals are distributed according to a Gaussian distribution. This, too, is an assumption that is often important for more advanced statistical methods.

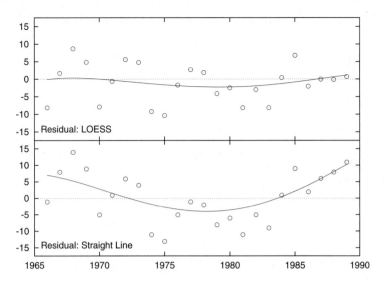

FIGURE 3-6. Residuals for the women's marathon results, both for the LOESS smoothing curve and the straight-line linear regression model. The residuals for the latter show an overall systematic trend, which suggests that the model does not appropriately describe the data.

It may also be useful to apply a smoothing routine to the *residuals* in order to recognize their features more clearly. Figure 3-6 shows the residuals for the women's marathon results (before 1990) both for the straight-line model and the LOESS smoothing curve. For the LOESS curve, the residuals are small overall and hardly exhibit any trend. For the straight-line model, however, there is a strong systematic trend in the residuals that is increasing in magnitude for years past 1985. This kind of systematic trend in the residuals is a clear indicator that the model is not appropriate for the data!

Additional Ideas and Warnings

Here are some additional ideas that you might want to play with.

As we have discussed before, you can calculate the residuals between the real data and the smoothed approximation. Here an isolated large residual is certainly odd: it suggests that the corresponding data point is somehow "different" than the other points in the neighborhood—in other words, an outlier. Now we argue as follows. If the data point is an outlier, then it should contribute less to the smoothed curve than other points. Taking this consideration into account, we now introduce an additional weight factor for each data point into the expression for $J[s]$ or χ^2 given previously. The magnitude of this weight factor is chosen in such a way that data points with large residuals contribute less to the smooth curve. With this new weight factor reducing the influence of points with large residuals, we calculate a *new* version of the smoothed approximation. This process is iterated until the smooth curve no longer changes.

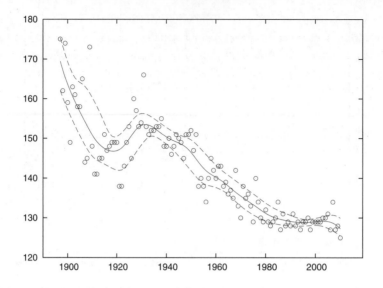

FIGURE 3-7. A "smooth tube" for the men's marathon results. The solid line is a smooth representation of the entire data set; the dashed lines are smooth representations of only those points that lie above (or below) the solid line.

Another idea is to split the original data points into two classes: those that give rise to a positive residual and those with a negative residual. Now calculate a smooth curve for each class separately. The resulting curves can be interpreted as "confidence bands" for the data set (meaning that the majority of points will lie between the upper and the lower smooth curve). We are particularly interested to see whether the width of this band varies along the curve. Figure 3-7 shows an example that uses the men's results from Figure 3-5.

Personally, I am a bit uncomfortable with either of these suggestions. They certainly have an unpleasant air of circular reasoning about them.

There is also a deeper reason. In my opinion, smoothing methods are a quick and useful but entirely nonrigorous way to explore the structure of a data set. With some of the more sophisticated extensions (*e.g.*, the two suggestions just discussed), we abandon the simplicity of the approach without gaining anything in rigor! If we need or want better (or deeper) results than simple graphical methods can give us, isn't it time to consider a more rigorous toolset?

This is a concern that I have with many of the more sophisticated graphical methods you will find discussed in the literature. Yes, we certainly *can* squeeze ever more information into a graph using lines, colors, symbols, textures, and what have you. But this does not necessarily mean that we *should*. The primary benefit of a graph is that it speaks to us directly—without the need for formal training or long explanations. Graphs that require training or complicated explanations to be properly understood are missing their mark no matter how "clever" they may be otherwise.

Similar considerations apply to some of the more involved ways of graph preparation. After all, a smooth curve such as a spline or LOESS approximation is only a rough approximation to the data set—and, by the way, contains a huge degree of arbitrariness in the form of the smoothing parameter (α or h, respectively). Given this situation, it is not clear to me that we need to worry about such details as the effect of individual outliers on the curve.

Focusing too much on graphical methods may also lead us to miss the essential point. For example, once we start worrying about confidence bands, we should really start *thinking more deeply* about the nature of the local distribution of residuals (Are the residuals normally distributed? Are they independent? Do we have a reason to prefer one statistical model over another?)—and possibly consider a more reliable estimation method (*e.g.*, bootstrapping; see Chapter 12)—rather than continue with hand-waving (semi-)graphical methods.

Remember: The purpose of computing is insight, not pictures! (L. N. Trefethen)

Logarithmic Plots

Logarithmic plots are a standard tool of scientists, engineers, and stock analysts everywhere. They are so popular because they have three valuable benefits:

- They rein in large variations in the data.
- They turn multiplicative variations into additive ones.
- They reveal exponential and power law behavior.

In a logarithmic plot, we graph the *logarithm* of the data instead of the raw data. Most plotting programs can do this for us (so that we don't have to transform the data explicitly) and also take care of labeling the axes appropriately.

There are two forms of logarithmic plots: *single* or *semi-logarithmic* plots and *double logarithmic* or *log-log* plots, depending whether only one (usually the vertical or y axis) or both axes have been scaled logarithmically.

All logarithmic plots are based on the fundamental property of the logarithm to turn products into sums and powers into products:

$$\log(xy) = \log(x) + \log(y)$$
$$\log(x^k) = k\log(x)$$

Let's first consider semi-log plots. Imagine you have data generated by evaluating the function:

$$y = C\exp(\alpha x) \quad \text{where } C \text{ and } \alpha \text{ are constants}$$

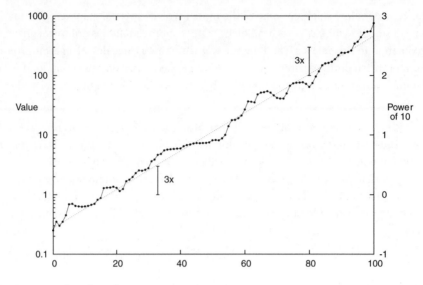

FIGURE 3-8. A semi-logarithmic plot.

on a set of *x* values. If you plot *y* as a function of *x*, you will see an upward- or downward-sloping curve, depending on the sign of α (see Appendix B). But if you instead plot the *logarithm* of *y* as a function of *x*, the points will fall on a straight line. This can be easily understood by applying the logarithm to the preceding equation:

$$\log y = \alpha x + \log C$$

In other words, the logarithm of *y* is a linear function of *x* with slope α and with offset $\log C$. In particular, by measuring the slope of the line, we can determine the scale factor α, which is often of great interest in applications.

Figure 3-8 shows an example of a semi-logarithmic plot that contains some experimental data points as well as an exponential function for comparison. I'd like to point out a few details. First, in a logarithmic plot, we plot the logarithm of the values, but the axes are usually labeled with the actual values (not their logarithms). Figure 3-8 shows both: the actual values on the left and the logarithms on the right (the logarithm of 100 to base 10 is 2, the logarithm of 1,000 is 3, and so on). We can see how, in a logarithmic plot, the logarithms are equidistant, but the actual values are not. (Observe that the distance between consecutive tick marks is constant on the right, but not on the left.)

Another aspect I want to point out is that on a semi-log plot, all *relative* changes have the same size no matter how large the corresponding absolute change. It is this property that makes semi-log plots popular for long-running stock charts and the like: if you lost $100, your reaction may be quite different if originally you had invested $1,000 versus $200: in the first case you lost 10 percent but 50 percent in the second. In other words, relative change is what matters.

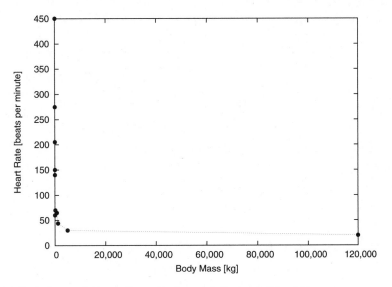

FIGURE 3-9. Heart rate versus body mass for a range of mammals. Compare to Figure 3-10.

The two scale arrows in Figure 3-8 have the same length and correspond to the same relative change, but the underlying absolute change is quite different (from 1 to 3 in one case, from 100 to 300 in the other). This is another application of the fundamental property of the logarithm: if the value before the change is y_1 and if $y_2 = \gamma y_1$ after the change (where $\gamma = 3$), then the change in absolute terms is:

$$y_2 - y_1 = \gamma y_1 - y_1 = (\gamma - 1)y_1$$

which clearly depends on y_1. But if we consider the change in the logarithms, we find:

$$\log y_2 - \log y_1 = \log(\gamma y_1) - \log y_1 = \log \gamma + \log y_1 - \log y_1 = \log \gamma$$

which is independent of the underlying value and depends only on γ, the size of the relative change.

Double logarithmic plots are now easy to understand—the only difference is that we plot logarithms of both x *and* y. This will render all power-law relations as straight lines—that is, as functions of the form $y = Cx^k$ or $y = C/x^k$, where C and k are constants. (Taking logarithms on both sides of the first equation yields $\log y = k \log x + \log C$, so that now $\log y$ is a linear function of $\log x$ with a slope that depends on the exponent k.)

Figures 3-9 and 3-10 provide stunning example for both uses of double logarithmic plots: their ability to render data spanning many order of magnitude accessible and their ability to reveal power-law relationships by turning them into straight lines. Figure 3-9 shows the typical resting heart rate (in beats per minute) as a function of the body mass (in kilograms) for a selection of mammals from the hamster to large whales. Whales weigh in at 120 tons—nothing else even comes close! The consequence is that almost all of the data points are squished against the lefthand side of the graph, literally crushed by the whale.

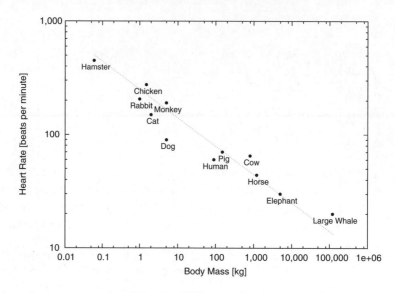

FIGURE 3-10. The same data as in Figure 3-9 but now plotted on a double logarithmic plot. The data points seem to fall on a straight line, which indicates a power-law relationship between resting heart rate and body mass.

On the double logarithmic plot, the distribution of data points becomes much clearer. Moreover, we find that the data points are not randomly distributed but instead seem to fall roughly on a straight line with slope −1/4: the signature of power-law behavior. In other words, a mammal's typical heart rate is related to its mass: larger animals have slower heart beats. If we let f denote the heart rate and m the mass, we can summarize this observation as:

$$f \sim m^{-1/4}$$

This surprising result is known as *allometric scaling*. It seems to hold more generally and not just for the specific animals and quantities shown in these figures. (For example, it turns out that the lifetime of an individual organism also obeys a 1/4 power-law relationship with the body mass: larger animals live longer. The surprising consequence is that the total number of heartbeats per life of an individual is approximately constant for all species!) Allometric scaling has been explained in terms of the geometric constraints of the vascular network (veins and arteries), which brings nutrients to the cells making up a biological system. It is sufficient to assume that the network must be a space-filling fractal, that the capillaries where the actual exchange of nutrients takes place are the same size in all animals, and that the overall energy required for transport through the network is minimized, to derive the power-law relationships observed experimentally![*] We'll have more to say about scaling laws and their uses in Part II.

---

[*]The original reference is "A General Model for the Origin of Allometric Scaling Laws in Biology." G. B. West, J. H. Brown, and B. J. Enquist. *Science* 276 (1997), p. 122. Additional references can be found on the Web.

Banking

Smoothing methods and logarithmic plots are both tools that help us recognize structure in a data set. Smoothing methods reduce noise, and logarithmic plots help with data sets spanning many orders of magnitude.

Banking (or "banking to 45 degrees") is another graphical method. It is different than the preceding ones because it does not work on the *data* but on the plot as a whole by changing its aspect ratio.

We can recognize *change* (*i.e.*, the slopes of curves) most easily if they make approximately a 45 degree angle on the graph. It is much harder to see change if the curves are nearly horizontal or (even worse) nearly vertical. The idea behind *banking* is therefore to adjust the aspect ratio of the entire plot in such a way that most slopes are at an approximate 45 degree angle.

Chances are, you have been doing this already by changing the plot *ranges*. Often when we "zoom" in on a graph it's not so much to see more detail as to adjust the slopes of curves to make them more easily recognizable. The purpose is even more obvious when we zoom *out*. Banking is a more suitable technique to achieve the same effect and opens up a way to control the appearance of a plot by actively adjusting the aspect ratio.

Figures 3-11 and 3-12 show the classical example for this technique: the annual number of sunspots measured over the last 300 years.[*] In Figure 3-11, the oscillation is very compressed, and so it is difficult to make out much detail about the shape of the curve. In Figure 3-12, the aspect ratio of the plot has been adjusted so that most line segments are now at roughly a 45 degree angle, and we can make an interesting observation: the rising edge of each sunspot cycle is steeper than the falling edge. We would probably not have recognized this by looking at Figure 3-11.

Personally, I would probably not use a graph such as Figure 3-12: shrinking the vertical axis down to almost nothing loses too much detail. It also becomes difficult to compare the behavior on the far left and far right of the graph. Instead, I would break up the time series and plot it as a *cut-and-stack plot*, such as the one in Figure 3-13. Note that in this plot the aspect ratio of each subplot is such that the lines are, in fact, banked to 45 degrees.

As this example demonstrates, banking is a good technique but can be taken too literally. When the aspect ratio required to achieve proper banking is too skewed, it is usually better to rethink the entire graph. No amount of banking will make the data set in Figure 3-9 look right—you need a double logarithmic transform.

There is also another issue to consider. The purpose of banking is to improve human perception of the graph (it is, after all, exactly the same data that is displayed). But graphs

---

[*]The discussion here is adapted from my book *Gnuplot in Action*. Manning Publications. 2010.

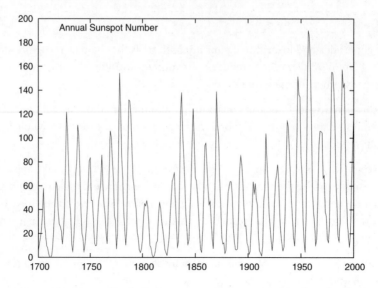

F I G U R E 3-11. The annual sunspot numbers for the last 300 years. The aspect ratio of the plot makes it hard to recognize the details of each cycle.

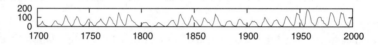
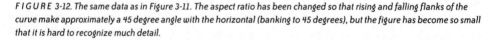

F I G U R E 3-12. The same data as in Figure 3-11. The aspect ratio has been changed so that rising and falling flanks of the curve make approximately a 45 degree angle with the horizontal (banking to 45 degrees), but the figure has become so small that it is hard to recognize much detail.

with highly skewed aspect ratios violate the great affinity humans seem to have for proportions of roughly 4 by 3 (or 11 by 8.5 or $\sqrt{2}$ by 1). Witness the abundance of display formats (paper, books, screens) that adhere approximately to these proportions the world over. Whether we favor this display format because we are so used to it or (more likely, I think) it is so predominant because it works well for humans is rather irrelevant in this context. (And keep in mind that squares seem to work particularly badly—notice how squares, when used for furniture or appliances, are considered a "bold" design. Unless there is a good reason for them, such as graphing a square matrix, I recommend you avoid square displays.)

Linear Regression and All That

Linear regression is a method for finding a straight line through a two-dimensional scatter plot. It is simple to calculate and has considerable intuitive appeal—both of which together make it easily the single most-often misapplied technique in all of statistics!

There is a fundamental misconception regarding linear regression—namely that it is a good and particularly rigorous way to *summarize* the data in a two-dimensional scatter

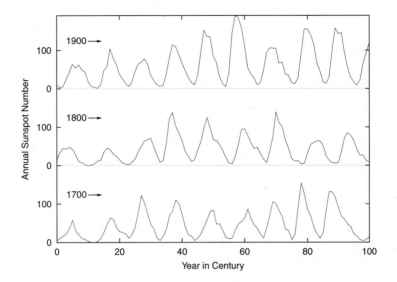

FIGURE 3-13. A cut-and-stack plot of the data from Figure 3-11. By breaking the time axis into three chunks, we can bank each century to 45 degrees and still fit all the data into a standard-size plot. Note how we can now easily recognize an important feature of the data: the rising flank tends to be steeper than the falling one.

plot. This misconception is often associated with the notion that linear regression provides the "best fit" to the data.

This is not so. Linear regression is not a particularly good way to summarize data, and it provides a "best fit" in a much more limited sense than is generally realized.

Linear regression applies to situations where we have a set of input values (the controlled variable) and, for each of them, we measure an output value (the response variable). Now we are looking for a linear function $f(x) = a + bx$ as a function of the controlled variable x that reproduces the response with the least amount of error. The result of a linear regression is therefore a function that minimizes the error in the responses for a given set of inputs.

This is an important understanding: the purpose of a regression procedure is not to *summarize* the data—the purpose is to obtain a function that allows us to *predict* the value of the response variable (which is affected by noise) that we expect for a certain value of the input variable (which is assumed to be known exactly).

As you can see, there is a fundamental asymmetry between the two variables: the two are not interchangeable. In fact, you will obtain a *different* solution when you regress x on y than when you regress y on x. Figure 3-14 demonstrates this effect: the same data set is fitted both ways: $y = a + bx$ and $x = c + dy$. The resulting straight lines are quite different.

This simple observation should dispel the notion that linear regression provides *the* best fit—after all, how could there be two different "best fits" for a single data set? Instead,

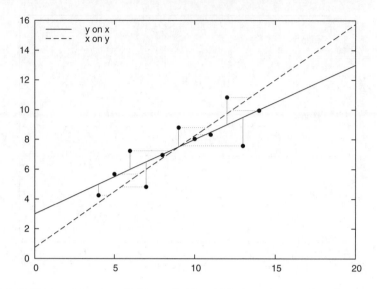

FIGURE 3-14. *The first data set from Anscombe's quartet (Table 3-1), fit both ways:* $y = a + bx$ *and* $x = c + dy$. *The thin lines indicate the errors, the squares of which are summed to give* χ^2. *Depending on what you consider the input and the response variable, the "best fit" turns out to be different!*

linear regression provides the most faithful representation of an output in response to an input. In other words, *linear regression is not so much a best fit as a best predictor*.

How do we find this "best predictor"? We require it to minimize the error in the responses, so that we will be able to make the most accurate predictions. But the error in the responses is simply the sum over the errors for all the individual data points. Because errors can be positive or negative (as the function over- or undershoots the real value), they may cancel each other out. To avoid this, we do not sum the errors themselves but their squares:

$$\chi^2 = \sum_i (f(x_i) - y_i)^2$$
$$= \sum_i (a + bx_i - y_i)^2$$

where (x_i, y_i) with $i = 1 \ldots n$ are the data points. Using the values for the parameters a and b that minimize this quantity will yield a function that best explains y in terms of x.

Because the dependence of χ^2 on a and b is particularly simple, we can work out expressions for the optimal choice of both parameters explicitly. The results are:

$$b = \frac{n \sum x_i y_i - \left(\sum x_i \right) \left(\sum y_i \right)}{n \left(\sum x_i^2 \right) - \left(\sum x_i \right)^2}$$
$$a = \frac{1}{n} \left(\sum y_i - b \sum x_i \right)$$

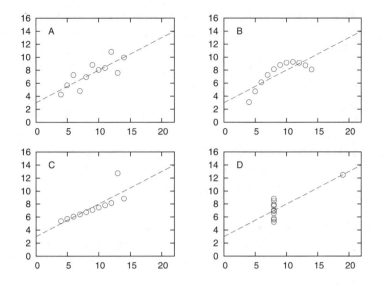

FIGURE 3-15. Anscombe's quartet: all summary statistics (in particular the regression coefficients) for all four data sets are numerically equal, yet only data set A is well represented by the linear regression function.

TABLE 3-1. Anscombe's quartet.

A		B		C		D	
x	y	x	y	x	y	x	y
10.0	8.04	10.0	9.14	10.0	7.46	8.0	6.58
8.0	6.95	8.0	8.14	8.0	6.77	8.0	5.76
13.0	7.58	13.0	8.74	13.0	12.74	8.0	7.71
9.0	8.81	9.0	8.77	9.0	7.11	8.0	8.84
11.0	8.33	11.0	9.26	11.0	7.81	8.0	8.47
14.0	9.96	14.0	8.10	14.0	8.84	8.0	7.04
6.0	7.24	6.0	6.13	6.0	6.08	8.0	5.25
4.0	4.26	4.0	3.10	4.0	5.39	19.0	12.50
12.0	10.84	12.0	9.13	12.0	8.15	8.0	5.56
7.0	4.82	7.0	7.26	7.0	6.42	8.0	7.91
5.0	5.68	5.0	4.74	5.0	5.73	8.0	6.89

These results are simple and beautiful—and, in their simplicity, very suggestive. But they can also be highly misleading. Table 3-1 and Figure 3-15 show a famous example, *Anscombe's quartet*. If you calculate the regression coefficients *a* and *b* for each of the four data sets shown in Table 3-1, you will find that they are exactly the same for all four data sets! Yet when you look at the corresponding scatter plots, it is clear that only the first data set is properly described by the linear model. The second data set is not linear, the third is corrupted by an outlier, and the fourth does not contain enough independent *x* values to form a regression at all! Looking only at the results of the linear regression, you would never know this.

I think this example should demonstrate once and for all how dangerous it can be to rely on linear regression (or on any form of aggregate statistics) to summarize a data set. (In fact, the situation is even worse than what I have presented: with a little bit more work, you can calculate confidence intervals on the linear regression results, and even *they* turn out to be equal for all four members of Anscombe's quartet!)

Having seen this, here are some questions to ask *before* computing linear regressions.

Do you need regression?
    Remember that regression coefficients are not a particularly good way to *summarize* data. Regression only makes sense when you want to use it for *prediction*. If this is not the case, then calculating regression coefficients is not useful.

Is the linear assumption appropriate?
    Linear regression is appropriate only if the data can be described by a straight line. If this is obviously not the case (as with the second data set in Anscombe's quartet), then linear regression does not apply.

Is something else entirely going on?
    Linear regression, like all summary statistics, can be led astray by outliers or other "weird" data sets, as is demonstrated by the last two examples in Anscombe's quartet.

Historically, one of the attractions of linear regression has been that it is easy to calculate: all you need to do is to calculate the four sums $\sum x_i$, $\sum x_i^2$, $\sum y_i$, and $\sum x_i y_i$, which can be done in a single pass through the data set. Even with moderately sized data sets (dozens of points), this is arguably easier than plotting them using paper and pencil! However, that argument simply does not hold anymore: graphs are easy to produce on a computer and contain so much more information than a set of regression coefficients that they should be the preferred way to analyze, understand, and summarize data.

Remember: The purpose of computing is insight, not numbers! (R. W. Hamming)

Showing What's Important

Perhaps this is a good time to express what I believe to be the most important principle in graphical analysis:

Plot the pertinent quantities!

As obvious as it may appear, this principle is often overlooked in practice.

For example, if you look through one of those books that show and discuss examples of poor graphics, you will find that most examples fall into one of two classes. First, there are those graphs that failed *visually*, with garish fonts, unhelpful symbols, and useless embellishments. (These are mostly presentation graphics gone wrong, not examples of bad graphical analysis.)

The second large class of graphical failures consists of those plots that failed *conceptually* or, one might better say, *analytically*. The problem with these is not in the technical aspects of drawing the graph but in the conceptual understanding of what the graph is trying to show. These plots displayed something, but they failed to present what was most important or relevant to the question at hand.

The problem, of course, is that usually it is not at all obvious *what* we want to see, and it is certainly not obvious at the beginning. It usually takes several iterations, while a mental model of the data is forming in your head, to articulate the proper question that a data set is suggesting and to come up with the best way of answering it. This typically involves some form of transformation or manipulation of the data: instead of the raw data, maybe we should show the difference between two data sets. Or the residual after subtracting a trend or after subtracting the results from a model. Or perhaps we need to normalize data sets from different sources by subtracting their means and dividing by their spreads. Or maybe we should not use the original variables to display the data but instead apply some form of transformation on them (logarithmic scales are only the simplest example of such transformations). Whatever we choose to do, it will typically involve some form of transformation of the data—it's rarely the raw data that is most interesting; but any deviation from the expected is almost always an interesting discovery.

Very roughly, I think we can identify a three-step (maybe four-step) process. It should be taken not in the sense of a prescriptive checklist but rather in the sense of a gradual process of learning and discovery.

First: The basics.   Initially, we are mostly concerned with displaying what is there.

- Select proper ranges.
- Subtract a constant offset.
- Decide whether to use symbols (for scattered data), lines (for continuous data), or perhaps both (connecting individual symbols can help emphasize trends in sparse data sets).

Second: The appearance.   Next, we work with aspects of the plot that influence its overall appearance.

- Log plots.
- Add a smoothed curve.
- Consider banking.

Third: Build a model.   At this point, we start building a mathematical model and compare it against the raw data. The comparison often involves finding the differences between the model and the data (typically subtracting the model or forming a ratio).

- Subtract a trend.
- Form the ratio to a base value or baseline.
- Rescale a set of curves to collapse them onto each other.

Fourth (for presentation graphics only): Add embellishments. Embellishments and decorations (labels, arrows, special symbols, explanations, and so on) can make a graph much more informative and self-explanatory. However, they are intended for an audience beyond the actual creator of the graph. You will rarely need them during the *analysis* phase, when you are trying to find out something new about the data set, but they are an essential part when *presenting* your results. This step should only occur if you want to communicate your results to a wider and more general audience.

Graphical Analysis and Presentation Graphics

I have used the terms *graphical analysis* and *presentation graphics* without explaining them properly. In short:

Graphical analysis

Graphical analysis is an investigation of data using graphical methods. The purpose is the discovery of *new* information about the underlying data set. In graphical analysis, the proper question to ask is often not known at the outset but is discovered as part of the analysis.

Presentation graphics

Presentation graphics are concerned with the communication of information and results that are *already understood*. The discovery has been made, and now it needs to be communicated clearly.

The distinction between these two activities is important, because they do require different techniques and yield different work products.

During the analysis process, convenience and ease of use are the predominant concerns—any amount of polishing is too much! Nothing should keep you from redrawing a graph, changing some aspect of it, zooming in or out, applying transformations, and changing styles. (When working with a data set I haven't seen before, I probably create dozens of graphs within a few minutes—basically, "looking at the data from all angles.") At this stage, any form of embellishment (labels, arrows, special symbols) is inappropriate—you know what you are showing, and creating any form of decoration on the graph will only make you more reluctant to throw the graph away and start over.

For presentation graphics, the opposite applies. Now you already know the results, but you would like to communicate them to others. Textual information therefore becomes very important: how else will people know what they are looking at?

You can find plenty of advice elsewhere on how to prepare "good" presentation graphics—often strongly worded and with an unfortunate tendency to use emotional responses (ridicule or derision) in place of factual arguments. In the absence of good empirical evidence one way or the other, I will not add to the discussion. But I present a *checklist* below, mentioning some points that are often overlooked when preparing graphs for presentation:

- Try to make the text self-explanatory. Don't rely on a (separate) caption for basic information—it might be removed during reproduction. Place basic information on the graph itself.

- Explain what is plotted on the axes. This can be done with explicit labels on the axes or through explanatory text elsewhere. Don't forget the units!

- Make labels self-explanatory. Be careful with nonstandard abbreviations. Ask yourself: If this is all the context provided, are you *certain* that the reader will be able to figure out what you mean? (In a recent book on data graphing, I found a histogram labeled *Married*, *Nvd*, *Dvd*, *Spd*, and *Wdd*. I could figure out most of them, because at least *Married* was given in long form, but I struggled with *Nvd* for quite a while!)

- Given how important *text* is on a graph, make sure to pick a suitable font. Don't automatically rely on the default provided by your plotting software. Generally, sans-serif fonts (such as Helvetica) are preferred for short labels, such as those on a graph, whereas serif fonts (such as Times) are more suitable for body text. Also pick an appropriate size—text fonts on graphics are often too large, making them look garish. (Most text fonts are used at 10-point to 12-point size; there is no need for type on graphics to be much larger.)

- If there are error bars, be sure to explain their meaning. What are they: standard deviations, inter-quartile ranges, or the limits of experimental apparatus? Also, choose an appropriate measure of uncertainty. Don't use standard deviations for highly skewed data.

- Don't forget the basics. Choose appropriate plot ranges. Make sure that data is not unnecessarily obscured by labels.

- Proofread graphs! Common errors include: typos in textual labels, interchanged data sets or switched labels, missing units, and incorrect order-of-magnitude qualifiers (*e.g.*, milli- versus micro-).

- Finally, choose an appropriate output format for your graph! Don't use bitmap formats (GIF, JPG, PNG) for print publication—use a scalable format such as PostScript or PDF.

One last piece of advice: creating good presentation graphics is also a matter of *taste*, and taste can be acquired. If you want to work with data, then you should develop an interest in graphs—not just the ones you create yourself, but all that you see. If you notice one that seems to work (or not), take a moment to figure out what makes it so. Are the lines too thick? The labels too small? The choice of colors just right? The combination of curves helpful? Details matter.

Workshop: matplotlib

The matplotlib module is a Python module for creating two-dimensional xy plots, scatter plots, and other plots typical of scientific applications. It can be used in an interactive session (with the plots being shown immediately in a GUI window) or from within a script to create graphics files using common graphics file formats.

Let's first look at some examples to demonstrate how matplotlib can be used from within an interactive session. Afterward, we will take a closer look at the structure of the library and give some pointers for more detailed investigations.

Using matplotlib Interactively

To begin an interactive matplotlib session, start IPython (the enhanced interactive Python shell) with the -pylab option, entering the following command line like at the shell prompt:

```
ipython -pylab
```

This will start IPython, load matplotlib *and* NumPy, and import both into the global namespace. The idea is to give a Matlab-like experience of interactive graphics together with numerical and matrix operations. (It is important to use IPython here—the flow of control between the Python command interpreter and the GUI eventloop for the graphics windows requires it. Other interactive shells can be used, but they may require some tinkering.)

We can now create plots right away:

```
In [1]: x = linspace( 0, 10, 100 )

In [2]: plot( x, sin(x) )
Out[2]: [<matplotlib.lines.Line2D object at 0x1cfefd0>]
```

This will pop up a new window, showing a graph like the one in Figure 3-16 but decorated with some GUI buttons. (Note that the sin() function is a ufunc from the NumPy package: it takes a vector and returns a vector of the same size, having applied the sine function to each element in the input vector. See the Workshop in Chapter 2.)

We can now add additional curves and decorations to the plot. Continuing in the same session as before, we add another curve and some labels:

```
In [3]: plot( x, 0.5*cos(2*x) )
Out[3]: [<matplotlib.lines.Line2D object at 0x1cee8d0>]

In [4]: title( "A matplotlib plot" )
Out[4]: <matplotlib.text.Text object at 0x1cf6950>

In [5]: text( 1, -0.8, "A text label" )
Out[5]: <matplotlib.text.Text object at 0x1f59250>

In [6]: ylim( -1.1, 1.1 )
Out[6]: (-1.1000000000000001, 1.1000000000000001)
```

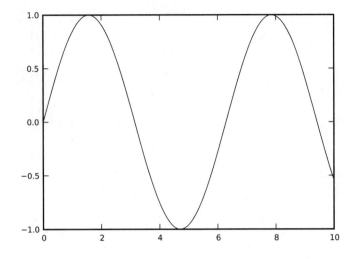

F I G U R E 3-16. A simple matplotlib figure (see text).

In the last step, we increased the range of values plotted on the vertical axis. (There is also an `axis()` command, which allows you to specify limits for both axes at the same time. Don't confuse it with the `axes()` command, which creates a new coordinate system.) The plot should now look like the one in Figure 3-17, except that in an interactive terminal the different lines are distinguished by their color, not their dash pattern.

Let's pause for a moment and point out a few details. First of all, you should have noticed that the graph in the plot window was updated after every operation. That is typical for the interactive mode, but it is not how matplotlib works in a script: in general, matplotlib tries to delay the (possibly expensive) creation of an actual plot until the last possible moment. (In a script, you would use the `show()` command to force generation of an actual plot window.)

Furthermore, matplotlib is "stateful": a new plot command does not erase the previous figure and, instead, adds to it. This behavior can be toggled with the `hold()` command, and the current state can be queried using `ishold()`. (Decorations like the text labels are not affected by this.) You can clear a figure explicitly using `clf()`.

This implicit state may come as a surprise: haven't we learned to make things explicit, when possible? In fact, this stateful behavior is a holdover from the way Matlab works. Here is another example. Start a new session and execute the following commands:

```
In [1]: x1 = linspace( 0, 10, 40 )

In [2]: plot( x1, sqrt(x1), 'k-' )
Out[2]: [<matplotlib.lines.Line2D object at 0x1cfef50>]
```

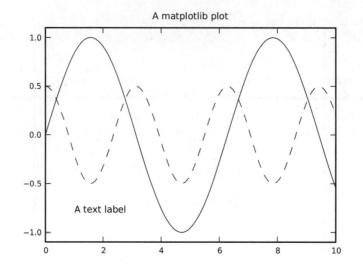

FIGURE 3-17. The plot from Figure 3-16 with an additional curve and some decorations added.

```
In [3]: figure(2)
Out[3]: <matplotlib.figure.Figure object at 0x1cee850>

In [4]: x2 = linspace( 0, 10, 100 )

In [5]: plot( x1, sin(x1), 'k--', x2, 0.2*cos(3*x2), 'k:' )
Out[5]:
[<matplotlib.lines.Line2D object at 0x1fb1150>,
 <matplotlib.lines.Line2D object at 0x1fba250>]

In [6]: figure(1)
Out[6]: <matplotlib.figure.Figure object at 0x1cee210>

In [7]: plot( x1, 3*exp(-x1/2), linestyle='None', color='white', marker='o',
   ...: markersize=7 )
Out[7]: [<matplotlib.lines.Line2D object at 0x1d0c150>]

In [8]: savefig( 'graph1.png' )
```

This snippet of code demonstrates several things. We begin as before, by creating a plot. This time, however, we pass a third argument to the plot() command that controls the appearance of the graph elements. That matplotlib library supports Matlab-style mnemonics for plot styles; the letter k stands for the color "black" and the single dash - for a solid line. (The letter b stands for "blue.")

Next we create a second figure in a new window and switch to it by using the figure(2) command. All graphics commands will now be directed to this second figure—until we switch back to the first figure using figure(1). This is another example of "silent state." Observe also that figures are counted starting from 1, not from 0.

In line 5, we see another way to use the plot command—namely, by specifying two sets of curves to be plotted together. (The formatting commands request a dashed and a dotted line, respectively.) Line 7 shows yet a different way to specify plot styles: by using named (keyword) arguments.

Finally, we save the currently active plot (*i.e.*, figure 1) to a PNG file. The `savefig()` function determines the desired output format from the extension of the filename given. Other formats that are supported out of the box are PostScript, PDF, and SVG. Additional formats may be available, depending on the libraries installed on your system.

Case Study: LOESS with matplotlib

As a quick example of how to put the different aspects of matplotlib together, let's discuss the script used to generate Figure 3-4. This also gives us an opportunity to look at the LOESS method in a bit more detail.

To recap: LOESS stands for *locally weighted* linear regression. The difference between LOESS and regular linear regression is the introduction of a weight factor, which emphasizes those data points that are close to the location x at which we want to evaluate the smoothed curve. As explained earlier, the expression for squared error (which we want to minimize) now becomes:

$$\chi^2(x) = \sum_i w(x - x_i; h)\,(a + bx_i - y_i)^2$$

Keep in mind that this expression now depends on x, the location at which we want to evaluate the smoothed curve!

If we minimize this expression with respect to the parameters a and b, we obtain the following expressions for a and b (remember that we will have to evaluate them from scratch for every point x):

$$b = \frac{\sum w_i \sum w_i x_i y_i - \left(\sum w_i x_i\right)\left(\sum w_i y_i\right)}{\sum w_i \left(\sum w_i x_i^2\right) - \left(\sum w_i x_i\right)^2}$$

$$a = \frac{\left(\sum w_i y_i - b \sum w_i x_i\right)}{\sum w_i}$$

This can be quite easily translated into NumPy and plotted with matplotlib. The actual LOESS calculation is contained entirely in the function `loess()`. (See the Workshop in Chapter 2 for a discussion of this type of programming.)

```
from pylab import *

# x: location; h: bandwidth; xp, yp: data points (vectors)
def loess( x, h, xp, yp ):
    w = exp( -0.5*( ((x-xp)/h)**2 )/sqrt(2*pi*h**2) )

    b = sum(w*xp)*sum(w*yp) - sum(w)*sum(w*xp*yp)
```

```
        b /= sum(w*xp)**2 - sum(w)*sum(w*xp**2)
        a = ( sum(w*yp) - b*sum(w*xp) )/sum(w)

        return a + b*x

    d = loadtxt( "draftlottery" )

    s1, s2 = [], []
    for k in d[:,0]:
        s1.append( loess( k,    5, d[:,0], d[:,1] ) )
        s2.append( loess( k, 100, d[:,0], d[:,1] ) )

    xlabel( "Day in Year" )
    ylabel( "Draft Number" )

    gca().set_aspect( 'equal' )

    plot( d[:,0], d[:,1], 'o', color="white", markersize=7, linewidth=3 )
    plot( d[:,0], array(s1), 'k-', d[:,0], array(s2), 'k--' )

    q = 4
    axis( [1-q, 366+q, 1-q, 366+q] )

    savefig( "draftlottery.eps" )
```

We evaluate the smoothed curve at the locations of all data points, using two different
values for the bandwidth, and then proceed to plot the data together with the smoothed
curves. Two details require an additional word of explanation. The function gca() returns
the current "set of axes" (*i.e.*, the current coordinate system on the plot—see below for
more information on this function), and we require the aspect ratio of both x and y axes
to be equal (so that the plot is a square). In the last command before we save the figure to
file, we adjust the plot range by using the axis() command. This function must *follow* the
plot() commands, because the plot() command automatically adjusts the plot range
depending on the data.

Managing Properties

Until now, we have ignored the values returned by the various plotting commands. If you
look at the output generated by IPython, you can see that all the commands that add
graph elements to the plot return a reference to the object just created. The one exception
is the plot() command itself, which always returns a *list* of objects (because, as we have
seen, it can add more than one "line" to the plot).

These references are important because it is through them that we can control the
appearance of graph elements once they have been created. In a final example, let's study
how we can use them:

    In [1]: x = linspace(0, 10, 100)

    In [2]: ps = plot(x, sin(x), x, cos(x))

```
In [3]: t1 = text( 1, -0.5, "Hello" )

In [4]: t2 = text( 3, 0.5, "Hello again" )

In [5]: t1.set_position( [7, -0.5] )

In [6]: t2.set( position=[5, 0], text="Goodbye" )
Out[6]: [None, None]

In [7]: draw()

In [8]: setp( [t1, t2], fontsize=10 )
Out[8]: [None, None]

In [9]: t2.remove()

In [10]: Artist.remove( ps[1] )

In [11]: draw()
```

In the first four lines, we create a graph with two curves and two text labels, as before, but now we are holding on to the object references. This allows us to make changes to these graph elements. Lines 5, 6, and 8 demonstrate different ways to do this: for each property of a graph element, there is an explicit, named accessor function (line 5). Alternatively, we can use a generic setter with keyword arguments—this allows us to set several properties (on a single object) in a single call (line 6). Finally, we can use the standalone setp() function, which takes a list of graph elements and applies the requested property update to all of them. (It can also take a single graph element instead of a one-member list.) Notice that setp() generates a redraw event whereas individual property accessors do not; this is why we must generate an explicit redraw event in line 7. (If you are confused by the apparent duplication of functionality, read on: we will come back to this point in the next section.)

Finally, we remove one of the text labels and one of the curves by using the remove() function. The remove() function is defined for objects that are derived from the Artist class, so we can invoke it using either member syntax (as a "bound" function, line 9) or the class syntax (as an "unbound" function, line 10). Keep in mind that plot() returns a *list* of objects, so we need to index into the list to access the graph objects themselves.

There are some useful functions that can help us handle object properties. If you issue setp(r) with only a single argument in an interactive session, then it will print all properties that are available for object r together with information about the values that each property is allowed to take on. The getp(r) function on the other hand prints all properties of r together with their current values.

Suppose we did not save the references to the objects we created, or suppose we want to change the properties of an object that we did not create explicitly. In such cases we can use the functions gcf() and gca(), which return a reference to the current figure or axes object, respectively. To make use of them, we need to develop at least a passing familiarity with matplotlib's object model.

The matplotlib Object Model and Architecture

The object model for matplotlib is constructed similarly to the object model for a GUI widget set: a plot is represented by a tree of widgets, and each widget is able to render itself. Perhaps surprisingly, the object model is not flat. In other words, the plot elements (such as axes, labels, arrows, and so on) are not properties of a high-level "plot" or "figure" object. Instead, you must descend down the object tree to find the element that you want to modify and then, once you have an explicit reference to it, change the appropriate property on the element.

The top-level element (the root node of the tree) is an object of class `Figure`. A figure contains one or more `Axes` objects: this class represents a "coordinate system" on which actual graph elements can be placed. (By contrast, the actual axes that are drawn on the graph are objects of the `Axis` class!) The `gcf()` and `gca()` functions therefore return a reference to the root node of the entire figure or to the root node of a single plot in a multiplot figure.

Both `Figure` and `Axes` are subclasses of `Artist`. This is the base class of all "widgets" that can be drawn onto a graph. Other important subclasses of `Artist` are `Line2D` (a polygonal line connecting multiple points, optionally with a symbol at each point), `Text`, and `Patch` (a geometric shape that can be placed onto the figure). The top-level `Figure` instance is owned by an object of type `FigureCanvas` (in the `matplotlib.backend_bases` module). Most likely you won't have to interact with this class yourself directly, but it provides the bridge between the (logical) object tree that makes up the graph and a backend, which does the actual rendering. Depending on the backend, matplotlib creates either a file or a graph window that can be used in an interactive GUI session.

Although it is easy to get started with matplotlib from within an interactive session, it can be quite challenging to really get one's arms around the whole library. This can become painfully clear when you want to change some tiny aspect of a plot—and can't figure out how to do that.

As is so often the case, it helps to investigate how things came to be. Originally, matplotlib was conceived as a plotting library to emulate the behavior found in Matlab. Matlab traditionally uses a programming model based on functions and, being 30 years old, employs some conventions that are no longer popular (*i.e.*, implicit state). In contrast, matplotlib was implemented using object-oriented design principles in Python, with the result that these two different paradigms clash.

One consequence of having these two different paradigms side by side is redundancy. Many operations can be performed in several different ways (using standalone functions, Python-style keyword arguments, object attributes, or a Matlab-compatible alternative syntax). We saw examples of this redundancy in the third listing when we changed object properties. This duplication of functionality matters because it drastically increases the size of the library's interface (its application programming interface or API), which makes it that much harder to develop a comprehensive understanding. What is worse, it tends to spread information around. (Where should I be looking for plot attributes—among functions, among members, among keyword attributes? Answer: everywhere!)

Another consequence is inconsistency. At least in its favored function-based interface, matplotlib uses some conventions that are rather unusual for Python programming—for instance, the way a figure is created *implicitly* at the beginning of every example, and how the pointer to the current figure is maintained through an invisible "state variable" that is opaquely manipulated using the `figure()` function. (The `figure()` function actually returns the figure object just created, so the invisible state variable is not even necessary.) Similar surprises can be found throughout the library.

A last problem is namespace pollution (this is another Matlab heritage—they didn't have namespaces back then). Several operations included in matplotlib's function-based interface are not actually graphics related but do generate plots as *side effects*. For example, `hist()` calculates (and plots) a histogram, `acorr()` calculates (and plots) an autocorrelation function, and so on. From a user's perspective, it makes more sense to adhere to a separation of tasks: perform all calculations in NumPy/SciPy, and then pass the results explicitly to matplotlib for plotting.

Odds and Ends

There are three different ways to import and use matplotlib. The original method was to enter:

```
from pylab import *
```

This would load all of NumPy as well as matplotlib and import both APIs into the global namespace! This is no longer the preferred way to use matplotlib. Only for interactive use with IPython is it still required (using the `-pylab` command-line option to IPython).

The recommended way to import matplotlib's function-based interface together with NumPy is by using:

```
import matplotlib.pyplot as plt
import numpy as np
```

The pyplot interface is a function-based interface that uses the same Matlab-like stateful conventions that we have seen in the examples of this section; however, it does *not* include the NumPy functions. Instead, NumPy must be imported separately (and into its own namespace).

Finally, if all you want is the object-oriented API to matplotlib, then you can import just the explicit modules from within matplotlib that contain the class definitions you need (although it is customary to import `pyplot` instead and thereby obtain access to the whole collection).

Of course, there are many details that we have not discussed. Let me mention just a few:

- Many more options (to configure the axes and tick marks, to add legend or arrows).
- Additional plot types (density or "false-color" plots, vector plots, polar plots).
- Digital image processing—matplotlib can read and manipulate PNG images and can also call into the Python Image Library (PIL) if it is installed.
- Matplotlib can be embedded in a GUI and can handle GUI events.

The Workshop of Chapter 4 contains another example that involves matplotlib being called from a script to generate image files.

Further Reading

In addition to the books listed below, you may check the references in Chapter 10 for additional material on linear regression.

- *The Elements of Graphing Data.* William S. Cleveland. 2nd ed., Hobart Press. 1994. This is probably the definitive reference on graphical analysis (as opposed to presentation graphics). Cleveland is the inventor of both the LOESS and the banking techniques discussed in this chapter. My own thinking has been influenced strongly by Cleveland's careful approach. A companion volume by the same author, entitled *Visualizing Data*, is also available.

- *Exploratory Data Analysis with MATLAB.* Wendy L. Martinez and Angel R. Martinez. Chapman & Hall/CRC. 2004. This is an interesting book—it covers almost the same topics as the book you are reading but in *opposite* order, starting with dimensionality reduction and clustering techniques and ending with univariate distributions! Because it demonstrates all techniques by way of Matlab, it does not develop the conceptual background in great depth. However, I found the chapter on smoothing to be quite useful.

## CHAPTER FOUR

Time As a Variable: Time-Series Analysis

IF WE FOLLOW THE VARIATION OF SOME QUANTITY OVER TIME, WE ARE DEALING WITH A *TIME SERIES*. TIME series are incredibly common: examples range from stock market movements to the tiny icon that constantly displays the CPU utilization of your desktop computer for the previous 10 seconds. What makes time series so common and so important is that they allow us to see not only a single quantity by itself but at the same time give us the typical "context" for this quantity. Because we have not only a single value but a bit of history as well, we can recognize any changes from the typical behavior particularly easily.

On the face of it, time-series analysis is a bivariate problem (see Chapter 3). Nevertheless, we are dedicating a separate chapter to this topic. Time series raise a different set of issues than many other bivariate problems, and a rather specialized set of methods has been developed to deal with them.

Examples

To get started, let's look at a few different time series to develop a sense for the scope of the task.

Figure 4-1 shows the concentration of carbon dioxide (CO_2) in the atmosphere, as measured by the observatory on Mauna Loa on Hawaii, recorded at monthly intervals since 1959.

This data set shows two features we often find in a time-series plot: trend and seasonality. There is clearly a steady, long-term growth in the overall concentration of CO_2; this is the *trend*. In addition, there is also a regular periodic pattern; this is the *seasonality*. If we look closely, we see that the period in this case is exactly 12 months, but we will use the term

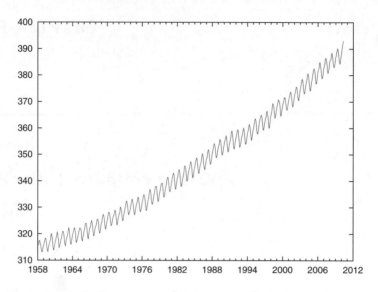

F I G U R E 4-1. Trend and seasonality: the concentration of CO_2 (in parts per million) in the atmosphere as measured by the observatory on Mauna Loa, Hawaii, at monthly intervals.

"seasonality" for any regularly recurring feature, regardless of the length of the period. We should also note that the trend, although smooth, does appear to be nonlinear, and in itself may be changing over time.

Figure 4-2 displays the concentration of a certain gas in the exhaust of a gas furnace over time. In many ways, this example is the exact opposite of the previous example. Whereas the data in Figure 4-1 showed a lot of regularity and a strong trend, the data in Figure 4-2 shows no trend but a lot of noise.

Figure 4-3 shows the dramatic drop in the cost of a typical long-distance phone call in the U.S. over the last century. The strongly nonlinear trend is obviously the most outstanding feature of this data set. As with many growth or decay processes, we may suspect an exponential time development; in fact, in a semi-logarithmic plot (Figure 4-3, inset) the data follows almost a straight line, confirming our expectation. Any analysis that fails to account explicitly for this behavior of the original data is likely to lead us astray. We should therefore work with the logarithms of the cost, rather than with the absolute cost.

There are some additional questions that we should ask when dealing with a long-running data set like this. What exactly is a "typical" long-distance call, and has that definition changed over the observation period? Are the costs adjusted for inflation or not? The data itself also begs closer scrutiny. For instance, the uncharacteristically low prices for a couple of years in the late 1970s make me suspicious: are they the result of a clerical error (a typo), or are they real? Did the breakup of the AT&T system have

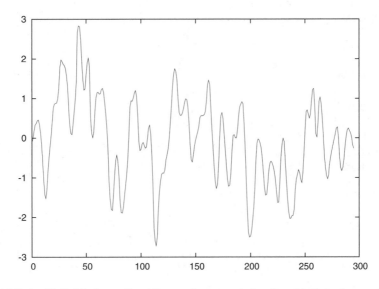

FIGURE 4-2. No trend but relatively smooth variation over time: concentration of a certain gas in a furnace exhaust (in arbitrary units).

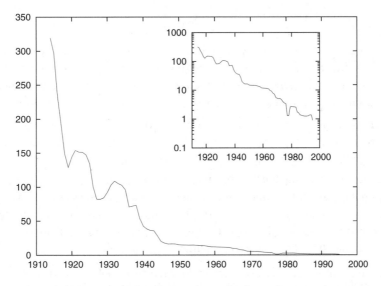

FIGURE 4-3. Nonlinear trend: cost of a typical long-distance phone call in the U.S.

anything to do with these low prices? We will not follow up on these questions here because I am presenting this example only as an illustration of an exponential trend, but any serious analysis of this data set would have to follow up on these questions.

Figure 4-4 shows the development of the Japanese stock market as represented by the Nikkei Stock Index over the last 40 years, an example of a time series that exhibits a

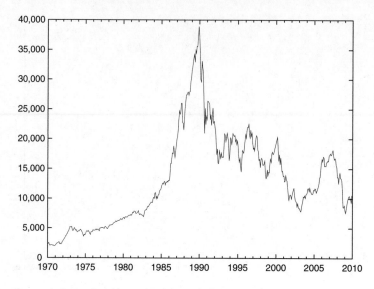

FIGURE 4-4. Change in behavior: the Nikkei Stock Index over the last 40 years.

marked change in behavior. Clearly, whatever was true before the New Year's Day 1990 was no longer true afterward. (In fact, by looking closely, you can make out a second change in behavior that was more subtle than the bursting of the big Japanese bubble: its beginning, sometime around 1985–1986.)

This data set should serve as a cautionary example. All time-series analysis is based on the assumption that the processes generating the data are stationary in time. If the rules of the game change, then time-series analysis is the wrong tool for the task; instead we need to investigate what caused the break in behavior. More benign examples than the bursting of the Japanese bubble can be found: a change in sales or advertising strategy may significantly alter a company's sales patterns. In such cases, it is more important to inquire about any further plans that the sales department might have, rather than to continue working with data that is no longer representative!

After these examples that have been chosen for their "textbook" properties, let's look at a "real-world" data set. Figure 4-5 shows the number of daily calls placed to a call center for a time period slightly longer than two years. In comparison to the previous examples, this data set has a lot more structure, which makes it hard to determine even basic properties. We can see some high-frequency variation, but it is not clear whether this is noise or has some form of regularity to it. It is also not clear whether there is any sort of regularity on a longer time scale. The amount of variation makes it hard to recognize any further structure. For instance, we cannot tell if there is a longer-term trend in the data. We will come back to this example later in the chapter.

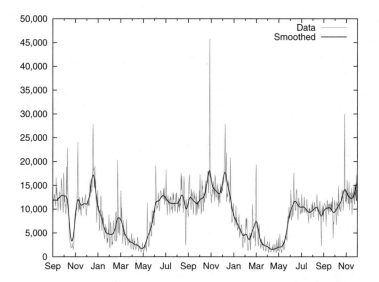

FIGURE 4-5. A real-world data set: number of daily calls placed to a call center. The data exhibits short- and long-term seasonality, noise, and possibly changes in behavior. Also shown is the result of applying a 31-point Gaussian smoothing filter.

The Task

After this tour of possible time-series scenarios, we can identify the main components of every time series:

- Trend

- Seasonality

- Noise

- Other(!)

The trend may be linear or nonlinear, and we may want to investigate its magnitude. The seasonality pattern may be either additive or multiplicative. In the first case, the seasonal change has the same *absolute* size no matter what the magnitude of the current baseline of the series is; in the latter case, the seasonal change has the same *relative* size compared with the current magnitude of the series. Noise (*i.e.*, some form of random variation) is almost always part of a time series. Finding ways to reduce the noise in the data is usually a significant part of the analysis process. Finally, "other" includes anything else that we may observe in a time series, such as particular significant changes in overall behavior, special outliers, missing data—anything remarkable at all.

Given this list of components, we can summarize what it means to "analyze" a time series. We can distinguish three basic tasks:

- Description

- Prediction
- Control

Description attempts to identify components of a time series (such as trend and seasonality or abrupt changes in behavior). Prediction seeks to forecast future values. Control in this context means the monitoring of a process over time with the purpose of keeping it within a predefined band of values—a typical task in many manufacturing or engineering environments. We can distinguish the three tasks in terms of the time frame they address: description looks into the past, prediction looks to the future, and control concentrates on the present.

Requirements and the Real World

Most standard methods of time-series analysis make a number of assumptions about the underlying data.

- Data points have been taken at equally spaced time steps, with no missing data points.
- The time series is sufficiently long (50 points are often considered as an absolute minimum).
- The series is *stationary*: it has no trend, no seasonality, and the character (amplitude and frequency) of any noise does not change with time.

Unfortunately, most of these assumptions will be more or less violated by any real-world data set that you are likely to encounter. Hence you may have to perform a certain amount of data cleaning before you can apply the methods described in this chapter.

If the data has been sampled at irregular time steps or if some of the data points are missing, then you can try to interpolate the data and resample it at equally spaced intervals. Time series obtained from electrical systems or scientific experiments can be almost arbitrarily long, but most series arising in a business context will be quite short and contain possibly no more than two dozen data points. The exponential smoothing methods introduced in the next section are relatively robust even for relatively short series, but somewhere there is a limit. Three or four data points don't constitute a series! Finally, most interesting series will not be stationary in the sense of the definition just given, so we may have to identify and remove trend and seasonal components explicitly (we'll discuss how to do that later). Drastic changes in the nature of the series also violate the stationarity condition. In such cases we must not continue blindly but instead deal with the break in the data—for example, by treating the data set as two different series (one before and one after the event).

Smoothing

An important aspect of most time series is, the presence of *noise*—that is, random (or apparently random) changes in the quantity of interest. Noise occurs in many real-world

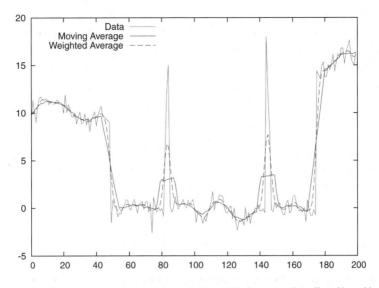

FIGURE 4-6. Simple and a Gaussian weighted moving average: the weighted average is less affected by sudden jumps in the data.

data sets, but we can often reduce the noise by improving the apparatus used to measure the data or by collecting a larger sample and averaging over it. But the particular structure of time series makes this impossible: the sales figures for the last 30 days are fixed, and they constitute all the data we have. This means that removing noise, or at least reducing its influence, is of particular importance in time-series analysis. In other words, we are looking for ways to *smooth* the signal.

Running Averages

The simplest smoothing algorithm that we can devise is the *running*, *moving*, or *floating average*. The idea is straightforward: for any odd number of consecutive points, replace the centermost value with the average of the other points (here, the $\{x_i\}$ are the data points and the smoothed value at position i is s_i):

$$s_i = \frac{1}{2k + 1} \sum_{j=-k}^{k} x_{i+j}$$

This naive approach has a serious problem, as you can see in Figure 4-6. The figure shows the original signal together with the 11-point moving average. Unfortunately, the signal has some sudden jumps and occasional large "spikes," and we can see how the smoothed curve is affected by these events: whenever a spike enters the smoothing window, the moving average is abruptly distorted by the single, uncommonly large value until the outlier leaves the smoothing window again—at which point the floating average equally abruptly drops again.

We can avoid this problem by using a *weighted moving average*, which places less weight on the points at the edge of the smoothing window. Using such a weighted average, any new point that enters the smoothing window is only gradually added to the average and then gradually removed again:

$$s_i = \sum_{j=-k}^{k} w_j x_{i+j} \quad \text{where} \quad \sum_{j=-k}^{k} w_j = 1$$

Here the w_j are the weighting factors. For example, for a 3-point moving average, we might use $(1/4, 1/2, 1/4)$. The particular choice of weight factors is not very important provided they are peaked at the center, drop toward the edges, and add up to 1. I like to use the Gaussian function:

$$f(x, \sigma) = \frac{1}{\sqrt{2\pi\sigma^2}} \exp\left(-\frac{1}{2}\left(\frac{x}{\sigma}\right)^2\right)$$

to build smoothing weight factors. The parameter σ in the Gaussian controls the width of the curve, and the function is essentially zero for values of x larger than about 3.5σ. Hence $f(x, 1)$ can be used to build a 9-point kernel by evaluating $f(x, 1)$ at the positions $[-4, -3, -2, -1, 0, 1, 2, 3, 4]$. Setting $\sigma = 2$, we can form a 15-point kernel by evaluating the Gaussian for all integer arguments between -7 and $+7$. And so on.

Exponential Smoothing

All moving-average schemes have a number of problems.

- They are painful to evaluate. For each point, the calculation has to be performed from scratch. It is not possible to evaluate weighted moving averages by updating a previous result.

- Moving averages can never be extended to the true edge of the available data set, because of the finite width of the averaging window. This is especially problematic because often it is precisely the behavior at the leading edge of a data set that we are most interested in.

- Similarly, moving averages are not defined *outside* the range of the existing data set. As a consequence, they are of no use in forecasting.

Fortunately, there exists a very simple calculational scheme that avoids all of these problems. It is called *exponential smoothing* or *Holt–Winters method*. There are various forms of exponential smoothing: single exponential smoothing for series that have neither trend nor seasonality, double exponential smoothing for series exhibiting a trend but no seasonality, and triple exponential smoothing for series with both trend and seasonality. The term "Holt–Winters method" is sometimes reserved for triple exponential smoothing alone.

All exponential smoothing methods work by updating the result from the previous time step using the new information contained in the data of the current time step. They do so by "mixing" the new information with the old one, and the relative weight of old and new information is controlled by an adjustable mixing parameter. The various methods differ in terms of the number of quantities they track and the corresponding number of mixing parameters.

The recurrence relation for single exponential smoothing is particularly simple:

$$s_i = \alpha x_i + (1 - \alpha)s_{i-1} \quad \text{with } 0 \leq \alpha \leq 1$$

Here s_i is the smoothed value at time step i, and x_i is the actual (unsmoothed) data at that time step. You can see how s_i is a mixture of the raw data and the previous smoothed value s_{i-1}. The mixing parameter α can be chosen anywhere between 0 and 1, and it controls the balance between new and old information: as α approaches 1, we retain only the current data point (*i.e.*, the series is not smoothed at all); as α approaches 0, we retain only the smoothed past (*i.e.*, the curve is totally flat).

Why is this method called "exponential" smoothing? To see this, simply expand the recurrence relation:

$$
\begin{aligned}
s_i &= \alpha x_i + (1 - \alpha)s_{i-1} \\
&= \alpha x_i + (1 - \alpha) \left[\alpha x_{i-1} + (1 - \alpha)s_{i-2} \right] \\
&= \alpha x_i + (1 - \alpha) \left[\alpha x_{i-1} + (1 - \alpha) \left[\alpha x_{i-2} + (1 - \alpha)s_{i-3} \right] \right] \\
&= \alpha \left[x_i + (1 - \alpha)x_{i-1} + (1 - \alpha)^2 x_{i-2} \right] + (1 - \alpha)^3 s_{i-3} \\
&= \dots \\
&= \alpha \sum_{j=0}^{i} (1 - \alpha)^j x_{i-j}
\end{aligned}
$$

What this shows is that in exponential smoothing, *all* previous observations contribute to the smoothed value, but their contribution is suppressed by increasing powers of the parameter α. That observations further in the past are suppressed multiplicatively is characteristic of exponential behavior. In a way, exponential smoothing is like a floating average with infinite memory but with exponentially falling weights. (Also observe that the sum of the weights, $\sum_j \alpha(1 - \alpha)^j$, equals 1 as required by virtue of the geometric series $\sum_i q^i = 1/(1 - q)$ for $q < 1$. See Appendix B for information on the geometric series.)

The results of the simple exponential smoothing procedure can be extended beyond the end of the data set and thereby used to make a forecast. The forecast is extremely simple:

$$x_{i+h} = s_i$$

where s_i is the last calculated value. In other words, single exponential smoothing yields a forecast that is absolutely flat for all times.

Single exponential smoothing as just described works well for time series without an overall trend. However, in the presence of an overall trend, the smoothed values tend to lag behind the raw data unless α is chosen to be close to 1; however, in this case the resulting curve is not sufficiently smoothed.

Double exponential smoothing corrects for this shortcoming by retaining explicit information about the trend. In other words, we maintain and update the state of two quantities: the smoothed signal *and* the smoothed trend. There are two equations and two mixing parameters:

$$s_i = \alpha x_i + (1 - \alpha)(s_{i-1} + t_{i-1})$$
$$t_i = \beta(s_i - s_{i-1}) + (1 - \beta)t_{i-1}$$

Let's look at the second equation first. This equation describes the smoothed trend. The current unsmoothed "value" of the trend is calculated as the difference between the current and the previous smoothed signal; in other words, the current trend tells us how much the smoothed signal changed in the last step. To form the smoothed trend, we perform a simple exponential smoothing process on the trend, using the mixing parameter β. To obtain the smoothed signal, we perform a similar mixing as before but consider not only the previous smoothed signal but take the trend into account as well. The last term in the first equation is the best guess for the current smoothed signal—assuming we followed the previous trend for a single time step.

To turn this result into a forecast, we take the last smoothed value and, for each additional time step, keep adding the last smoothed trend to it:

$$x_{i+h} = s_i + h\,t_i$$

Finally, for triple exponential smoothing we add yet a third quantity, which describes the seasonality. We have to distinguish between additive and multiplicative seasonality. For the additive case, the equations are:

$$s_i = \alpha(x_i - p_{i-k}) + (1 - \alpha)(s_{i-1} + t_{i-1})$$
$$t_i = \beta(s_i - s_{i-1}) + (1 - \beta)t_{i-1}$$
$$p_i = \gamma(x_i - s_i) + (1 - \gamma)p_{i-k}$$
$$x_{i+h} = s_i + h\,t_i + p_{i-k+h}$$

For the multiplicative case, they are:

$$s_i = \alpha\frac{x_i}{p_{i-k}} + (1 - \alpha)(s_{i-1} + t_{i-1})$$
$$t_i = \beta(s_i - s_{i-1}) + (1 - \beta)t_{i-1}$$
$$p_i = \gamma\frac{x_i}{s_i} + (1 - \gamma)p_{i-k}$$
$$x_{i+h} = (s_i + h\,t_i)p_{i-k+h}$$

Here, p_i is the "periodic" component, and k is the length of the period. I have also included the expressions for forecasts.

All exponential smoothing methods are based on recurrence relations. This means that we need to fix the start-up values in order to use them. Luckily, the specific choice for these values is not very critical: the exponential damping implies that all exponential smoothing methods have a short "memory," so that after only a few steps, any influence of the initial values is greatly diminished. Some reasonable choices for start-up values are:

$$s_0 = x_0 \quad \text{or} \quad s_0 = \frac{1}{n} \sum_i^n x_i \quad \text{with } 1 < n < 5, \ldots, 10$$

and:

$$t_0 = 0 \quad \text{or} \quad t_0 = x_1 - x_0$$

For triple exponential smoothing we must provide one full season of values for start-up, but we can simply fill them with 1s (for the multiplicative model) or 0s (for the additive model). Only if the series is short do we need to worry seriously about finding good starting values.

The last question concerns how to choose the mixing parameters α, β, and γ. My advice is trial and error. Try a few values between 0.2 and 0.4 (very roughly), and see what results you get. Alternatively, you can define a measure for the error (between the actual data and the output of the smoothing algorithm), and then use a numerical optimization routine to minimize this error with respect to the parameters. In my experience, this is usually more trouble than it's worth for at least the following two reasons. The numerical optimization is an iterative process that is not guaranteed to converge, and you may end up spending way too much time coaxing the algorithm to convergence. Furthermore, any such numerical optimization is slave to the expression you have chosen for the "error" to be minimized. The problem is that the parameter values minimizing that error may not have some other property you want to see in your solution (*e.g.*, regarding the balance between the accuracy of the approximation and the smoothness of the resulting curve) so that, in the end, the manual approach often comes out ahead. However, if you have many series to forecast, then it may make sense to expend the effort and build a system that can determine the optimal parameter values automatically, but it probably won't be easy to really make this work.

Finally, I want to present an example of the kind of results we can expect from exponential smoothing. Figure 4-7 is a classical data set that shows the monthly number of international airline passengers (in thousands of passengers).[*] The graph shows the actual data together with a triple exponential approximation. The years 1949 through 1957 were used to "train" the algorithm, and the years 1958 through 1960 are forecasted. Note how well the forecast agrees with the actual data—especially in light of the strong seasonal pattern—for a rather long forecasting time frame (three full years!). Not bad for a method as simple as this.

[*] This data is available in the "airpass.dat" data set from R. J. Hyndman's Time Series Data Library at *http://www.robjhyndman.com/TSDL*.

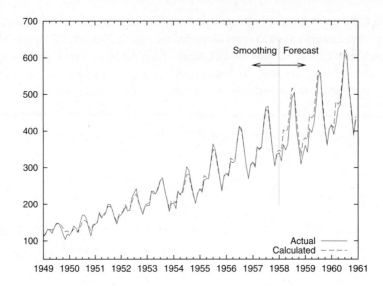

FIGURE 4-7. *Triple exponential smoothing in action: comparison between the raw data (solid line) and the smoothed curve (dashed). For the years after 1957, the dashed curve shows the forecast calculated with only the data available in 1957.*

Don't Overlook the Obvious!

On a recent consulting assignment, I was discussing monthly sales numbers with the client when he made the following comment: "Oh, yes, sales for February are always somewhat lower—that's an after effect of the Christmas peak." Sales are always lower in *February*? How interesting.

Sure enough, if you plotted the monthly sales numbers for the last few years, there was a rather visible dip from the overall trend every February. But in contrast, there wasn't much of a Christmas spike! (The client's business was not particularly seasonal.) So why should there be a corresponding dip two months later?

By now I am sure you know the answer already: February is *shorter* than any of the other months. And it's not a small effect, either: with 28 days, February is about three days shorter than the other months (which have 30–31 days). That's about 10 percent—close to the size of the dip in the client's sales numbers.

When monthly sales numbers were normalized by the number of days in the month, the February dip all but disappeared, and the *adjusted* February numbers were perfectly in line with the rest of the months. (The average number of days per month is 365/12 = 30.4.)

Whenever you are tracking aggregated numbers in a time series (such as weekly, monthly, or quarterly results), make sure that you have adjusted for possible variation in the aggregation time frame. Besides the numbers of days in the month, another likely candidate for hiccups is the number of *business days* in a month (for months with five weekends, you can expect a 20 percent drop for most business metrics). But the problem is, of course, much more general and can occur whenever you are reporting aggregate *numbers* rather than *rates*. (If the client had been reporting average sales per day for each month, then there would never have been an anomaly.)

This specific problem (*i.e.*, nonadjusted variations in aggregation periods) is a particular concern for all business reports and dashboards. Keep an eye out for it!

The Correlation Function

The *autocorrelation function* is the primary diagnostic tool for time-series analysis. Whereas the smoothing methods that we have discussed so far deal with the raw data in a very direct way, the correlation function provides us with a rather different view of the same data. I will first explain how the autocorrelation function is calculated and will then discuss what it means and how it can be used.

The basic algorithm works as follows: start with two copies of the data set and subtract the overall average from all values. Align the two sets, and multiply the values at corresponding time steps with each other. Sum up the results for all time steps. The result is the (unnormalized) correlation coefficient at *lag* 0. Now shift the two copies against each other by a single time step. Again multiply and sum: the result is the correlation coefficient at lag 1. Proceed in this way for the entire length of the time series. The set of all correlation coefficients for all lags is the autocorrelation function. Finally, divide all coefficients by the coefficient for lag 0 to normalize the correlation function, so that the coefficient for lag 0 is now equal to 1.

All this can be written compactly in a single formula for $c(k)$—that is the correlation function at lag k:

$$c(k) = \frac{\sum_{i=1}^{N-k}(x_i - \mu)(x_{i+k} - \mu)}{\sum_{i=1}^{N}(x_i - \mu)^2} \quad \text{with } \mu = \frac{1}{N}\sum_{i=1}^{N}x_i$$

Here, N is the number of points in the data set. The formula follows the mathematical convention to start indexing sequences at 1, rather than the programming convention to start indexing at 0. Notice that we have subtracted the overall average μ from all values and that the denominator is simply the expression of the numerator for lag $k = 0$. Figure 4-8 illustrates the process.

The meaning of the correlation function should be clear. Initially, the two signals are perfectly aligned and the correlation is 1. Then, as we shift the signals against each other, they slowly move out of phase with each other, and the correlation drops. How quickly it

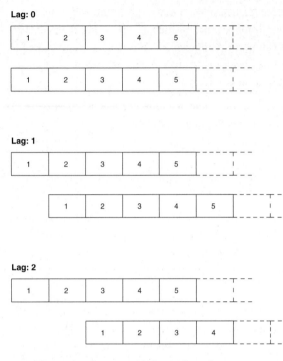

Lag: 0

Lag: 1

Lag: 2

FIGURE 4-8. Algorithm to compute the correlation function.

drops tells us how much "memory" there is in the data. If the correlation drops quickly, we know that, after a few steps, the signal has lost all memory of its recent past. However, if the correlation drops slowly, then we know that we are dealing with a process that is relatively steady over longer periods of time. It is also possible that the correlation function first drops and then rises again to form a second (and possibly a third, or fourth, . . .) peak. This tells us that the two signals align again if we shift them far enough—in other words, that there is periodicity (*i.e.,* seasonality) in the data set. The position of the secondary peak gives us the number of time steps per season.

Examples

Let's look at a couple of examples. Figure 4-9 shows the correlation function of the gas furnace data in Figure 4-2. This is a fairly typical correlation function for a time series that has only short time correlations: the correlation falls quickly, but not immediately, to zero. There is no periodicity; after the initial drop, the correlation function does not exhibit any further significant peaks.

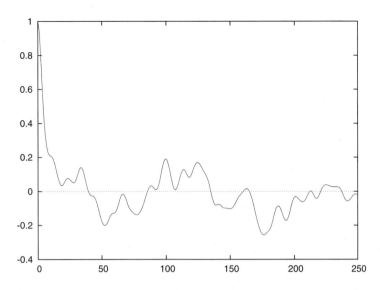

F I G U R E 4-9. The correlation function for the exhaust gas data shown in Figure 4-2. The data has only short time correlations and no seasonality; the correlation function falls quickly (but not immediately) to zero, and there are no secondary peaks.

Figure 4-10 is the correlation function for the call center data from Figure 4-5. This data set shows a very different behavior. First of all, the time series has a much longer "memory": it takes the correlation function almost 100 days to fall to zero, indicating that the frequency of calls to the call center changes more or less once per quarter but not more frequently. The second notable feature is the pronounced secondary peak at a lag of 365 days. In other words, the call center data is highly seasonal and repeats itself on a yearly basis. The third feature is the small but regular sawtooth structure. If we look closely, we will find that the first peak of the sawtooth is at a lag of 7 days and that all repeating ones occur at multiples of 7. This is the signature of the high-frequency component that we could see in Figure 4-5: the traffic to the call center exhibits a secondary seasonal component with 7-day periodicity. In other words, traffic is weekday dependent (which is not too surprising).

Implementation Issues

So far I have talked about the correlation function mostly from a conceptual point of view. If we want to proceed to an actual implementation, there are some fine points we need to worry about.

The autocorrelation function is intended for time series that do not exhibit a trend and have zero mean. Therefore, if the series we want to analyze does contain a trend, then we must remove it first. There are two ways to do this: we can either subtract the trend or we can difference the series.

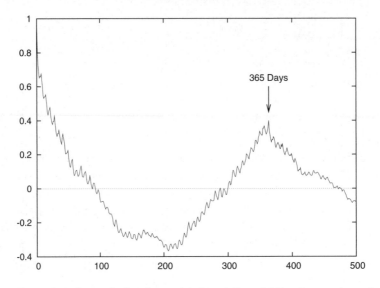

F I G U R E 4-10. The correlation function for the call center data shown in Figure 4-5. There is a secondary peak after exactly 365 days, as well as a smaller weekly structure to the data.

Subtracting the trend is straightforward—the only problem is that we need to determine the trend first! Sometimes we may have a "model" for the expected behavior and can use it to construct an explicit expression for the trend. For instance, the airline passenger data from the previous section, describes a growth process, and so we should suspect an exponential trend ($a \exp(x/b)$). We can now try guessing values for the two parameters and then subtract the exponential term from the data. For other data sets, we might try a linear or power-law trend, depending on the data set and our understanding of the process generating the data. Alternatively, we might first apply a smoothing algorithm to the data and then subtract the result of the smoothing process from the raw data. The result will be the trend-free "noise" component of the time series.

A different approach consists of *differencing* the series: instead of dealing with the raw data, we instead work with the *changes* in the data from one time step to the next. Technically, this means replacing the original series x_i with one consisting of the differences of consecutive elements: $x_{i+1} - x_i$. This process can be repeated if necessary, but in most cases, single differencing is sufficient to remove the trend entirely.

Making sure that the time series has zero mean is easier: simply calculate the mean of the (de-trended!) series and subtract it before calculating the correlation function. This is done explicitly in the formula for the correlation function given earlier.

Another technical wrinkle concerns how we implement the sum in the formula for the numerator. As written, this sum is slightly messy, because its upper limit depends on the lag. We can simplify the formula by *padding* one of the data sets with N zeros on the right and letting the sum run from $i = 1$ to $i = N$ for all lags. In fact, many computational

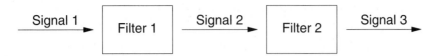

FIGURE 4-11. A filter chain: each filter applied to a signal yields another signal, which itself can be filtered.

software packages assume that the data has been prepared in this way (see the Workshop section in this chapter).

The last issue you should be aware of is that there are two different normalization conventions for the autocorrelation function, which are both widely used. In the first variant, numerator and denominator are not normalized separately—this is the scheme used in the previous formula. In the second variant, the numerator and denominator are each normalized by the number of nonzero terms in their respective sum. With this convention, the formula becomes:

$$c(k) = \frac{\dfrac{1}{N-k}\sum_{i=1}^{N-k}(x_i - \mu)(x_{i+k} - \mu)}{\dfrac{1}{N}\sum_{i=1}^{N}(x_i - \mu)^2} \qquad \text{with } \mu = \frac{1}{N}\sum_{i=1}^{N} x_i$$

Both conventions are fine, but if you want to compare results from different sources or different software packages, then you will have to make sure you know which convention each of them is following!

Optional: Filters and Convolutions

Until now we have always spoken of time series in a direct fashion, but there is also a way to describe them (and the operations performed on them) on a much higher level of abstraction. For this, we borrow some concepts and terminology from electrical engineering, specifically from the field of digital signal processing (DSP).

In the lingo of DSP, we deal with *signals* (time series) and *filters* (operations). Applying a filter to a signal produces a new (filtered) signal. Since filters can be applied to any signal, we can apply another filter to the output of the first and in this way chain filters together (see Figure 4-11). Signals can also be combined and subtracted from each other.

As it turns out, many of the operations we have seen so far (smoothing, differencing) can be expressed as filters. We can therefore use the convenient high-level language of DSP when referring to the processes of time-series analysis. To make this concrete, we need to understand how a filter is represented and what it means to "apply" a filter to a signal.

Each digital filter is represented by a set of coefficients or weights. To apply the filter, we multiply the coefficients with a subset of the signal. The sum of the products is the value of the resulting (filtered) signal:

$$y_t = \sum_{i=-k}^{k} w_i x_{t+i}$$

This should look familiar! We used a similar expression when talking about moving averages earlier in the chapter. A moving average is simply a time series run through an n-point filter, where every coefficient is equal to $1/n$. A weighted moving average filter similarly consists of the weights used in the expression for the average.

The filter concept is not limited to smoothing operations. The differencing step discussed in the previous section can be viewed as the application of the filter $[1, -1]$. We can even shift an entire time series forward in time by using the filter $[0, 1]$.

The last piece of terminology that we will need concerns the peculiar sum of a product that we have encountered several times by now. It's called a *convolution*. A convolution is a way to combine two sequences to yield a third sequence, which you can think of as the "overlap" between the original sequences. The convolution operation is usually defined as follows:

$$y_t = \sum_{i=-\infty}^{\infty} w_i x_{t-i}$$

Symbolically, the convolution operation is often expressed through an asterisk: $y = w \star x$, where y, w, and x are sequences.

Of course, if one or both of the sequences have only a finite number of elements, then the sum also contains only a finite number of terms and therefore poses no difficulties. You should be able to convince yourself that every application of a filter to a time series that we have done was in fact a convolution of the signal with the filter. This is true in general: applying a filter to a signal means forming the convolution of the two. You will find that many numerical software packages provide a convolution operation as a built-in function, making filter operations particularly convenient to use.

I must warn you, however, that the entire machinery of digital signal processing is geared toward signals of infinite (or almost infinite) length, which makes good sense for typical electrical signals (such as the output from a microphone or a radio receiver). But for the rather short time series that we are likely to deal with, we need to pay close attention to a variety of *edge effects*. For example, if we apply a smoothing or differencing filter, then the resulting series will be shorter, by half the filter length, than the original series. If we now want to subtract the smoothed from the original signal, the operation will fail because the two signals are not of equal length. We therefore must either pad the smoothed signal or truncate the original one. The constant need to worry about padding and proper alignment detracts significantly from the conceptual beauty of the signal-theoretic approach when used with time series of relatively short duration.

Workshop: scipy.signal

The `scipy.signal` package provides functions and operations for digital signal processing that we can use to good effect to perform calculations for time-series analysis. The `scipy.signal` package makes use of the signal processing terminology introduced in the previous section.

The listing that follows shows all the commands used to create graphs like Figures 4-5 and 4-10, including the commands required to write the results to file. The code is heavily commented and should be easy to understand.

```python
from scipy import *
from scipy.signal import *
from matplotlib.pyplot import *

filename = 'callcenter'


# Read data from a text file, retaining only the third column.
# (Column indexes start at 0.)
# The default delimiter is any whitespace.
data = loadtxt( filename, comments='#', delimiter=None, usecols=(2,) )

# The number of points in the time series. We will need it later.
n = data.shape[0]

# Finding a smoothed version of the time series:
# 1) Construct a 31-point Gaussian filter with standard deviation = 4
filt = gaussian( 31, 4 )
# 2) Normalize the filter through dividing by the sum of its elements
filt /= sum( filt )
# 3) Pad data on both sides with half the filter length of the last value
#    (The function ones(k) returns a vector of length k, with all elements 1.)
padded = concatenate( (data[0]*ones(31//2), data, data[n-1]*ones(31//2)) )
# 4) Convolve the data with the filter. See text for the meaning of "mode".
smooth = convolve( padded, filt, mode='valid' )

# Plot the raw data together with the smoothed data:
# 1) Create a figure, sized to 7x5 inches
figure( 1, figsize=( 7, 5 ) )
# 2) Plot the raw data in red
plot( data, 'r' )
# 3) Plot the smoothed data in blue
plot( smooth, 'b' )
# 4) Save the figure to file
savefig( filename + "_smooth.png" )
# 5) Clear the figure
clf()

# Calculate the autocorrelation function:
# 1) Subtract the mean
tmp = data - mean(data)
# 2) Pad one copy of data on the right with zeros, then form correlation fct
#    The function zeros_like(v) creates a vector with the same dimensions
#    as the input vector v but with all elements zero.
corr = correlate( tmp, concatenate( (tmp, zeros_like(tmp)) ), mode='valid' )
# 3) Retain only some of the elements
corr = corr[:500]
```

```
# 4) Normalize by dividing by the first element
corr /= corr[0]


# Plot the correlation function:
figure( 2, figsize=( 7, 5 ) )
plot( corr )
savefig( filename + "_corr.png" )
clf()
```

The package provides the Gaussian filter as well as many others. The filters are not normalized, but this is easy enough to accomplish.

More attention needs to be paid to the appropriate padding and truncating. For example, when forming the smoothed version of the data, I pad the data on both sides by half the filter length to ensure that the smoothed data has the same length as the original set. The mode argument to the convolve() and correlate functions determines which pieces of the resulting vector to retain. Several modes are possible. With mode="same", the returned vector has as many elements as the largest input vector (in our case, as the padded data vector), but the elements closest to the ends would be corrupted by the padded values. In the listing, I therefore use mode="valid", which retains only those elements that have full overlap between the data and the filter—in effect, removing the elements added in the padding step.

Notice how the signal processing machinery leads in this application to very compact code. Once you strip out the comments and plotting commands, there are only about 10 lines of code that perform actual operations and calculations. However, we had to pad all data carefully and ensure that we kept only those pieces of the result that were least contaminated by the padding.

Further Reading

- *The Analysis of Time Series*. Chris Chatfield. 6th ed., Chapman & Hall. 2003.
  This is my preferred text on time-series analysis. It combines a thoroughly practical approach with mathematical depth and a healthy preference for the simple over the obscure. Highly recommended.

## CHAPTER FIVE

More Than Two Variables: Graphical Multivariate Analysis

AS SOON AS WE ARE DEALING WITH MORE THAN TWO VARIABLES SIMULTANEOUSLY, THINGS BECOME MUCH MORE complicated—in particular, graphical methods quickly become impractical. In this chapter, I'll introduce a number of graphical methods that can be applied to multivariate problems. All of them work best if the number of variables is not *too* large (less than 15–25).

The borderline case of *three* variables can be handled through *false-color plots*, which we will discuss first.

If the number of variables is greater (but not much greater) than three, then we can construct multiplots from a collection of individual bivariate plots by scanning through the various parameters in a systematic way. This gives rise to scatter-plot matrices and co-plots.

Depicting how an overall entity is composed out of its constituent parts can be a rather nasty problem, especially if the composition changes over time. Because this task is so common, I'll treat it separately in its own section.

Multi-dimensional visualization continues to be a research topic, and in the last sections of the chapter, we look at some of the more recent ideas in this field.

One recurring theme in this chapter is the need for adequate tools: most multi-dimensional visualization techniques are either not practical with paper and pencil, or are outright impossible without a computer (in particular when it comes to animated techniques). Moreover, as the number of variables increases, so does the need to look at a data set from different angles; this leads to the idea of using interactive graphics for exploration. In the last section, we look at some ideas in this area.

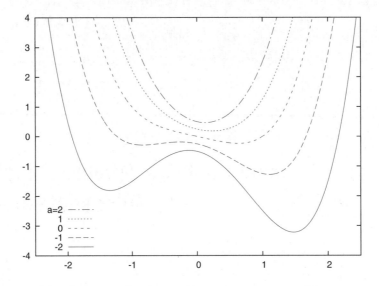

FIGURE 5-1. A simple but effective way to show three variables: treat one as parameter and draw a separate curve for several parameter values.

False-Color Plots

There are different ways to display information in three variables (typically, two independent variables and one dependent variable). Keep in mind that simple is sometimes best! Figure 5-1 shows the function $f(x, a) = x^4/2 + ax^2 - x/2 + a/4$ for various values of the parameter a in a simple, two-dimensional xy plot. The shape of the function and the way it changes with a are perfectly clear in this graph. It is very difficult to display this function in any other way with comparable clarity.

Another way to represent such trivariate data is in the form of a *surface plot*, such as the one shown in Figure 5-2. As a rule, surface plots are visually stunning but are of very limited practical utility. Unless the data set is very smooth and allows for a viewpoint such that we can look *down* onto the surface, they simply don't work! For example, it is pretty much impossible to develop a good sense for the behavior of the function plotted in Figure 5-1 from a surface plot. (Try it!) Surface plots can help build intuition for the overall structure of the data, but it is notoriously difficult to read off quantitative information from them.

In my opinion, surface plots have only two uses:

1. To get an intuitive impression of the "lay of the land" for a complicated data set

2. To dazzle the boss (not that this isn't important at times)

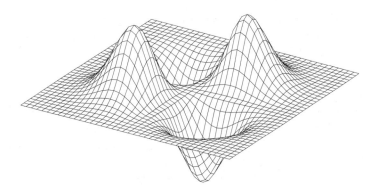

FIGURE 5-2. Surface plots are often visually impressive but generally don't represent quantitative information very well.

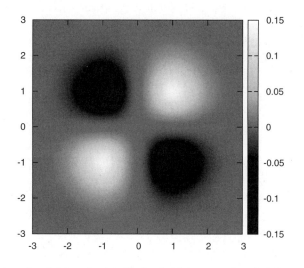

FIGURE 5-3. Grayscale version of a false-color plot of the function shown as a surface plot in Figure 5-2. Here white corresponds to positive values of the function, and black corresponds to negative values.

Another approach is to project the function into the base plane below the surface in Figure 5-2. There are two ways in which we can represent values: either by showing contours of constant alleviation in a *contour plot* or by mapping the numerical values to a palette of colors in a *false-color plot*. Contour plots are familiar from topographic maps—they can work quite well, in particular if the data is relatively smooth and if one is primarily interested in local properties.

The false-color plot is an alternative and quite versatile technique that can be used for different tasks and on a wide variety of data sets. To create a false-color plot, all values of the dependent variable z are mapped to a palette of colors. Each data point is then plotted as a region of the appropriate color. Figure 5-3 gives an example (where the color has been replaced by grayscale shading).

I like false-color plots because one can represent a lot of information in a them in a way that retains quantitative information. However, false-color plots depend crucially on the quality of the palette—that is, the mapping that has been used to associate colors with numeric values.

Let's quickly recap some information on color and computer graphics. Colors for computer graphics are usually specified by a triple of numbers that specify the intensity of their red, green, and blue (RGB) components. Although RGB triples make good sense technically, they are not particularly intuitive. Instead, we tend to think of color in terms of its hue, saturation, and value (*i.e.*, luminance or lightness). Conventionally, hue runs through all the colors of the rainbow (from red to yellow, green, blue, and magenta). Curiously, the spectrum of hues seems to circle back onto itself, since magenta smoothly transforms back to red. (The reason for this behavior is that the hues in the rainbow spectrum are arranged in order of their dominant electromagnetic frequency. For violet/magenta, no frequency dominates; instead, violet is a mixture of low-frequency reds and high-frequency blues.) Most computer graphics programs will be able to generate color graphics using a hue–saturation–value (HSV) triple.

It is surprisingly hard to find reliable recommendations on good palette design, which is even more unfortunate given that convenience and what seems like common sense often lead to particularly *bad* palettes. Here are some ideas and suggestions that you may wish to consider:

Keep it simple
> Very simple palettes using red, white, and blue often work surprisingly well. For continuous color changes you could use a blue-white-red palette, for segmentation tasks you could use a white-blue-red-white palette with a sharp blue–red transition at the segmentation threshold.

Distinguish between segmentation tasks and the display of smooth changes
> Segmentation tasks (*e.g.*, finding all points that exceed a certain threshold, finding the locations where the data crosses zero) call for palettes with sharp color transitions at the respective thresholds, whereas representing smooth changes in a data set calls for continuous color gradients. Of course, both aspects can be combined in a single palette: gradients for part of the palette and sharp transitions elsewhere.

Try to maintain an intuitive sense of ordering
> Map low values to "cold" colors and higher values to "hot" colors to provide an intuitive sense of ordering in your palette. Examples include the simple blue-red palette and the "heat scale" (black-red-yellow-white—I'll discuss in a moment why I don't recommend the heat scale for use). Other palettes that convey a sense of ordering (if only by convention) are the "improved rainbow" (blue-cyan-green-yellow-orange-red-magenta) and the "geo-scale" familiar from topographic maps (blue-cyan-green-brown-tan-white).

Place strong visual gradients in regions with important changes

Suppose that you have a data set with values that span the range from −100 to +100 but that all the really interesting or important change occurs in the range −10 to +10. If you use a standard palette (such as the improved rainbow) for such a data set, then the actual region of interest will appear to be all of the same color, and the rest of the spectrum will be "wasted" on parts of the data range that are not that interesting. To avoid this outcome, you have to compress the rainbow so that it maps only to the region of interest. You might want to consider mapping the extreme values (from −100 to −10 and from 10 to 100) to some unobtrusive colors (possibly even to a grayscale) and reserving the majority of hue changes for the most relevant part of the data range.

Favor subtle changes

This is possibly the most surprising recommendation. When creating palettes, there is a natural tendency to "crank it up full" by using fully saturated colors at maximal brightness throughout. That's not necessarily a good idea, because the resulting effect can be so harsh that details are easily lost. Instead, you might want to consider using soft, pastel colors or even to experiment with mixed hues in favor of the pure primaries of the standard rainbow. (Recent versions of Microsoft Excel provide an interesting and easily accessible demonstration for this idea: all default colors offered for shading the background of cells are soft, mixed pastels—to good effect.) Furthermore, the eye is quite good at detecting even subtle variations. In particular, when working with luminance-based palettes, small changes are often all that is required.

Avoid changes that are hard to detect

Some visual changes are especially hard to perceive visually. For example, it is practically impossible to distinguish between different shades of yellow, and the transition from yellow to white is even worse! (This is why I don't recommend the heat scale, despite its nice ordering property: the bottom third consists of hard-to-distinguish dark reds, and the entire upper third consists of very hard-to-distinguish shades of light yellow.)

Use hue- and luminance-based palettes for different purposes

In particular, consider using a luminance-based palette to emphasize fine detail and using hue- or saturation-based palettes for smooth, large-scale changes. There is some empirical evidence that luminance-based palettes are better suited for images that contain a lot of fine detail and that hue-based palettes are better suited for bringing out smooth, global changes. A pretty striking demonstration of this observation can be found when looking at medical images (surely an application where details matter!): a simple grayscale representation, which is pure luminance, often seems much clearer than a multicolored representation using a hue-based rainbow palette. This rule is more relevant to image processing of photographs or similar images (such as that in our medical example) than to visualization of the sort of abstract information that we consider here, but it is worth keeping in mind.

Don't forget to provide a color box

No matter how intuitive you think your palette is, nobody will know for sure what you are showing unless you provide a color box (or color key) that shows the values and the colors they are mapped to. Always, always, provide one.

One big problem not properly addressed by these recommendations concerns *visual uniformity*. For example, consider palettes based on the "improved rainbow," which is created by distributing the six primaries in the order blue-cyan-green-yellow-red-magenta across the palette. If you place these primaries at equal distances across from each other and interpolate linearly between them in color space, then the fraction of the palette occupied by green appears to be much larger than the fraction occupied by either yellow or cyan. Another example is that when placing a fully saturated yellow next to a fully saturated blue, then the blue region will appear to be more intense (*i.e.*, saturated) than the yellow. Similarly, the browns that occur in a geo-scale easily appear darker than the other colors in the palette. This is a problem with our *perception* of color: simple interpolations in color space do not necessarily result in visually uniform gradients!

There is a variation of the HSV color space, called the *HCL* (hue–chroma–luminance) space that takes visual perception into account to generate visually uniform color maps and gradients. The HCL color model is more complicated to use than the HSV model, because not all combinations of hue, chroma, and luminance values exist. For instance, a fully saturated yellow appears lighter than a fully saturated blue, so a palette at full chroma and with high luminance will include the fully saturated yellow but not the blue. As a result, HCL-based palettes that span the entire rainbow of hues tend naturally toward soft, pastel colors. A disadvantage of palettes in the HCL space is that they often degrade particularly poorly when reproduced in black and white.[*]

A special case of false-color plots are geographic *maps*, and cartographers have significant experience developing color schemes for various purposes. Their needs are a little different and not all of their recommendations may work for general data analysis purposes, but it is worthwhile to become familiar with what they have learned.[†]

Finally, I'd like to point out two additional problems with all plots that depend on color to convey critical information.

- Color does not reproduce well. Once photocopied or printed on a black-and-white laser printer, a false-color plot will become useless!

---

[*] An implementation of the transformations between HCL and RGB is available in R and C in the "colorspace" module available from CRAN.

[†] An interesting starting point is Cynthia Brewer's online ColorBrewer at *http://colorbrewer2.org/*.

- Also keep in mind that about 10 percent of all men are at least partially color blind; these individuals won't be able to make much sense of most images that rely heavily or exclusively on color.

Either one of these problems is potentially serious enough that you might want to reconsider before relying entirely on color for the display of information.

In my experience, preparing good false-color plots is often a tedious and time-consuming task. This is one area where better tools would be highly desirable—an interactive tool that could be used to manipulate palettes directly and in real time would be very nice to have. The same is true for a publicly available set of well-tested palettes.

A Lot at a Glance: Multiplots

The primary concern in all multivariate visualizations is finding better ways to put more "stuff" on a graph. In addition to color (see the previous section), there are basically two ways we can go about this. We can make the graph elements themselves richer, so that they can convey additional information beyond their position on the graph; or we can put several similar graphs next to each other and vary the variables that are not explicitly displayed in a systematic fashion from one subgraph to the next. The first idea leads to *glyphs*, which we will introduce later in this chapter, whereas the latter idea leads to scatter-plot matrices and co-plots.

The Scatter-Plot Matrix

For a *scatter-plot matrix* (occasionally abbreviated SPLOM), we construct all possible two-dimensional scatter plots from a multivariate data set and then plot them together in a matrix format (Figure 5-4). We can now scan all of the graphs for interesting behavior, such as a marked correlation between any two variables.

The data set shown in Figure 5-4 consists of seven different properties of a sample of 250 wines.[*] It is not at all clear how these properties should relate to each other, but by studying the scatter-plot matrix, we can make a few interesting observations. For example, we can see that sugar content and density are positively correlated: if the sugar content goes up, so does the density. The opposite is true for alcohol content and density: as the alcohol content goes up, density goes down. Neither of these observations should come as a surprise (sugar syrup has a higher density than water and alcohol a lower one). What may be more interesting is that the wine quality seems to increase with increasing alcohol content: apparently, more potent wines are considered to be better!

---

[*] The data can be found in the "Wine Quality" data set, available at the UCI Machine Learning repository at *http://archive.ics.uci.edu/ml/*.

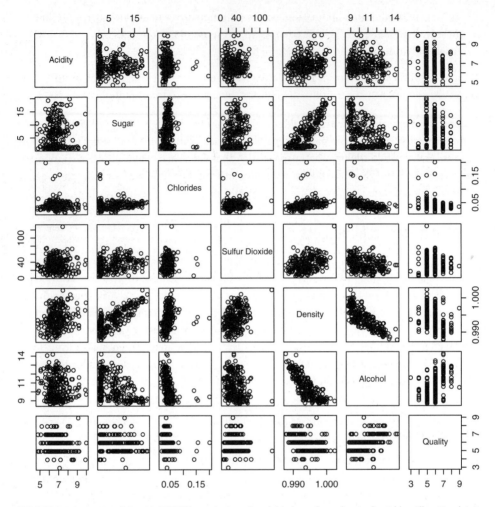

FIGURE 5-4. In a scatter-plot matrix (SPLOM), a separate scatter plot is shown for each pair of variables. All scatter plots in a given row or column have the same plot range, so that we can compare them easily.

One important detail that is easy to overlook is that all graphs in each row or column show the same plot range; in other words, they use *shared scales*. This makes it possible to compare graphs across the entire matrix.

The scatter-plot matrix is symmetric across the diagonal: the subplots in the lower left are equal to the ones in the upper right but rotated by 90 degrees. It is nevertheless customary to plot both versions because this makes it possible to scan a single row or column in its entirety to investigate how one quantity relates to each of the other quantities.

Scatter-plot matrices are easy to prepare and easy to understand. This makes them very popular, but I think they can be overused. Once we have more than about half a dozen variables, the individual subplots become too small as that we could still recognize anything useful, in particular if the number of points is large (a few hundred points or more). Nevertheless, scatter-plot matrices are a convenient way to obtain a quick overview and to find viewpoints (variable pairings) that deserve a closer look.

The Co-Plot

In contrast to scatter-plot matrices, which always show all data points but *project* them onto different surfaces of the parameter space, *co-plots* (short for "conditional plots") show various *slices* through the parameter space such that each slice contains only a subset of the data points. The slices are taken in a systematic manner, and we can form an image of the entire parameter space by mentally gluing the slices back together again (the salami principle). Because of the regular layout of the subplots, this technique is also known as a *trellis plot*.

Figure 5-5 shows a trivariate data set projected onto the two-dimensional xy plane. Although there is clearly structure in the data, no definite pattern emerges. In particular, the dependence on the third parameter is entirely obscured!

Figure 5-6 shows a co-plot of the same data set that is sliced or *conditioned* on the third parameter a. The bottom part of the graph shows six slices through the data corresponding to different ranges of a. (The slice for the *smallest* values of a is in the lower left, and the one for the largest values of a is in the upper righthand corner.) As we look at the slices, the structure in the data stands out clearly, and we can easily follow the dependence on the third parameter a.

The top part of Figure 5-6 shows the range of values that a takes on for each of the slices. If you look closely, you will find that there are some subtle issues hidden in (or rather revealed by) this panel, because it provides information on the details of the slicing operation.

Two decisions need to be made with regard to the slicing:

1. By what method should the overall parameter range be cut into slices?

2. Should slices overlap or not?

In many ways, the most "natural" answer to these questions would be to cut the entire parameter range into a set of adjacent intervals of equal width. It is interesting to observe (by looking at the top panel in Figure 5-6) that in the example graph, a different decision was made in regard to both questions! The slices are not of equal width in the range of parameter values that they span; instead, they have been made in such a way that each slice contains *the same number of points*. Furthermore, the slices are not adjacent but partially overlap each other.

The first decision (to have each slice contain the same number of points, instead of spanning the same range of values) is particularly interesting because it provides additional information on how the values of the parameter a are distributed. For instance,

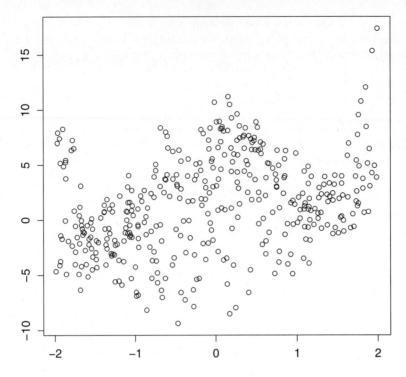

FIGURE 5-5. Projection of a trivariate data set onto the xy plane. How does the data vary with the third variable?

we can see that large values of a (larger than about $a = -1$) are relatively rare, whereas values of a between -4 and -2 are much more frequent. This kind of behavior would be much harder to recognize precisely if we had chopped the interval for a into six slices of equal width. The other decision (to make the slices overlap partially) is more important for small data sets, where otherwise each slice contains so few points that the structure becomes hard to see. Having the slices overlap makes the data "go farther" than if the slices were entirely disjunct.

Co-plots are especially useful if some of the variables in a data set are clearly "control" variables, because co-plots provide a systematic way to study the dependence of the remaining ("response") variables on the controls.

Variations

The ideas behind scatter-plot matrices and co-plots are pretty generally applicable, and you can develop different variants depending on your needs and tastes. Here are some ideas:

- In the standard scatter-plot matrix, half of the individual graphs are redundant. You can remove the individual graphs from half of the overall matrix and replace them with something different—for example, the numerical value of the appropriate correlation

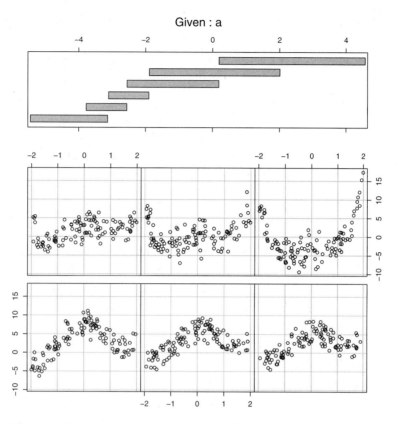

FIGURE 5-6. A co-plot of the same data as in Figure 5-5. Each scatter plot includes the data points for only a certain range of a values; the corresponding values of a are shown in the top panel. (The scatter plot for the smallest value of a is in the lower left corner, and that for the largest value of a is in the upper right.)

coefficient. However, you will then lose the ability to visually scan a full row or column to see how the corresponding quantity correlates with all other variables.

- Similarly, you can place a histogram showing the distribution of values for the quantity in question on the diagonal of the scatter-plot matrix.

- The slicing technique used in co-plots can be used with other graphs besides scatter plots. For instance, you might want to use slicing with rank-order plots (see Chapter 2), where the conditioning "parameter" is some quantity not explicitly shown in the rank-order plot itself. Another option is to use it with histograms, making each subplot a histogram of a subset of the data where the subset is determined by the values of the control "parameter" variable.

- Finally, co-plots can be extended to *two* conditioning variables, leading to a matrix of individual slices.

By their very nature, all multiplots consist of many individual plot elements, sometimes with nontrivial interactions (such as the overlapped slicing in certain co-plots). Without a good tool that handles most of these issues automatically, these plot types lose most of their appeal. For the plots in this section, I used R (the statistical package), which provides support for both scatter-plot matrices and co-plots as built-in functionality.

Composition Problems

Many data sets describe a *composition problem*; in other words, they describe how some overall quantity is composed out of its parts. Composition problems pose some special challenges because often we want to visualize two *different* aspects of the data simultaneously: on the one hand, we are interested in the relative magnitude of the different components, and on the other, we also care about their absolute size.

For one-dimensional problems, this is not too difficult (see Chapter 2). We can use a histogram or a similar graph to display the absolute size for all components; and we can use a cumulative distribution plot (or even the much-maligned pie chart) to visualize the relative contribution that each component makes to the total.

But once we add additional variables into the mix, things can get ugly. Two problems stand out: how to visualize *changes* to the composition over time and how to depict the breakdown of an overall quantity along *multiple axes* at the same time.

Changes in Composition

To understand the difficulties in tracking compositional problems over time, imagine a company that makes five products labeled A, B, C, D, and E. As we track the daily production numbers over time, there are two different questions that we are likely to be interested in: on the one hand, we'd like to know how many items are produced overall; on the other hand, we would like to understand how the item mix is changing over time.

Figures 5-7, 5-8, and 5-9 show three attempts to plot this kind of data. Figure 5-7 simply shows the absolute numbers produced per day for each of the five product lines. That's not ideal—the graph looks messy because some of the lines obscure each other. Moreover, it is not possible to understand from this graph how the total number of items changes over time. Test yourself: does the total number of items go up over time, does it go down, or does it stay about even?

Figure 5-8 is a *stacked plot* of the same data. The daily numbers for each product are added to the numbers for the products that appear lower down in the diagram—in other words, the line labeled B gives the number of items produced in product lines A *and* B. The topmost line in this diagram shows the total number of items produced per day (and answers the question posed in the previous paragraph: the total number of items does *not* change appreciably over the long run—a possibly surprising observation, given the appearance of Figure 5-7).

Stacked plots can be compelling because they have intuitive appeal and appear to be clear and uncluttered. In reality, however, they tend to hide the details in the development of

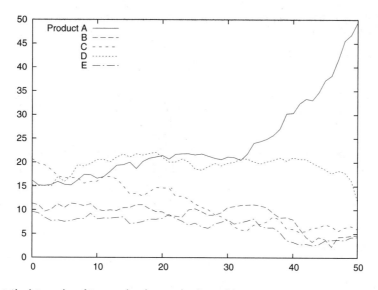

FIGURE 5-7. Absolute number of items produced per product line and day.

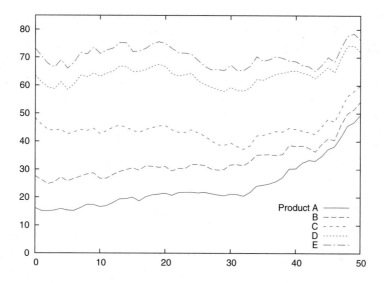

FIGURE 5-8. Stacked graph of the number of items produced per product line and day.

the individual components because the changing baseline makes comparison difficult if not impossible. For example, from Figure 5-7 it is pretty clear that production of item D increased for a while but then dropped rapidly over the last 5 to 10 days. We would never guess this fact from Figure 5-8, where the strong growth of product line A masks the smaller changes in the other product lines. (This is why you should order the components in a stacked graph in ascending order of variation—which was intentionally *not* done in Figure 5-8.)

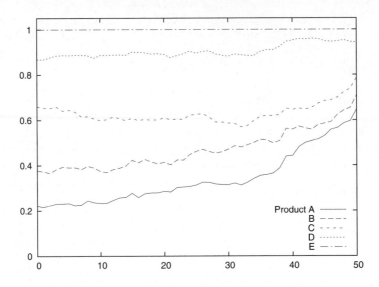

FIGURE 5-9. *Stacked graph of the relative contribution that each product line makes to the total.*

Figure 5-9 shows still another attempt to visualize this data. This figure is also a stacked graph, but now we are looking not at the absolute numbers of items produced but instead at the relative fraction that each product line contributes to the daily total. Because the change in the total number of items produced has been eliminated, this graph can help us understand how the item mix varies over time (although we still have the changing baseline problem common to all stacked graphs). However, information about the total number of items produced has been lost.

All things considered, I don't think any one of these graphs succeeds very well. No single graph can satisfy both of our conflicting goals—to monitor both absolute numbers as well as relative contributions—and be clear and visually attractive at the same time.

I think an acceptable solution for this sort of problem will always involve a combination of graphs—for example, one for the total number of items produced and another for the relative item mix. Furthermore, despite their aesthetic appeal, stacked graphs should be avoided because they make it too difficult to recognize relevant information in the graph. A plot such as Figure 5-7 may seem messy, but at least it can be read accurately and reliably.

Multidimensional Composition: Tree and Mosaic Plots

Composition problems are generally difficult even when we do not worry about changes over time. Look at the following data:

```
Male    BS    NYC    Engineering
Male    MS    SFO    Engineering
Male    PhD   NYC    Engineering
```

```
Male    BS    LAX   Engineering
Male    MS    NYC   Finance
Male    PhD   SFO   Finance
Female  PhD   NYC   Engineering
Female  MS    LAX   Finance
Female  BS    NYC   Finance
Female  PhD   SFO   Finance
```

The data set shows information about ten employees of some company, and for each employee, we have four pieces of information: gender, highest degree obtained, office where they are located (given by airport code—NYC: New York, SFO: San Francisco, LAX: Los Angeles), and their department. Keep in mind that each line corresponds to a single person.

The usual way to summarize such data is in the form of a *contingency table*. Table 5-1 summarizes what we know about the relationship between an employee's gender and his or her department. Contingency tables are used to determine whether there is a correlation between categorical variables: in this case, we notice that men tend to work in engineering and women in finance. (We may want to divide by the total number of records to get the *fraction* of employees in each cell of the table.)

The problem is that contingency tables only work for two dimensions at a time. If we also want to include the breakdown by degree or location, we have no other choice than to repeat the basic structure from Table 5-1 several times: once for each office or once for each degree.

A *mosaic plot* is an attempt to find a graphical representation for this kind of data. The construction of a mosaic plot is essentially recursive and proceeds as follows (see Figure 5-10):

1. Start with a square.

2. Select a dimension, and then divide the square proportionally according to the counts for this dimension.

3. Pick a second dimension, and then divide each subarea according to the counts along the second dimension, separately for each subarea.

4. Repeat for all dimensions, interchanging horizontal and vertical subdivisions for each new dimension.

TABLE 5-1. A contingency table: breakdown of male and female employees across two departments

	Male	Female	Total
Engineering	4	1	5
Finance	2	3	5
Total	6	4	10

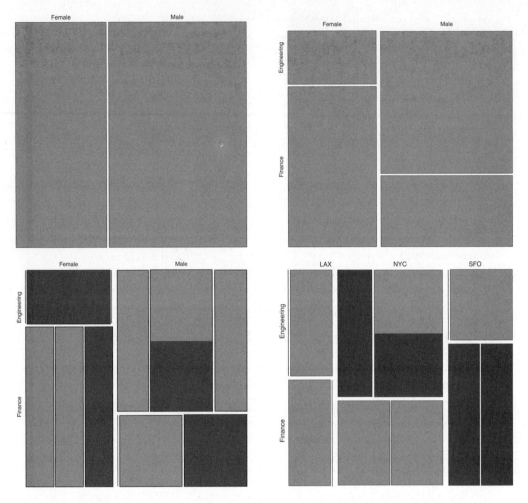

FIGURE 5-10. Mosaic plots. In the top row, we start by dividing by gender, then also by department. In the bottom row, we have divided by gender, department, and location, with doctorate degrees shaded. The graph on the left uses the same sort order of dimensions as the graphs in the top row, whereas the graph on the bottom right uses a different sort order. Notice how the sort order changes the appearance of the graph!

In the lower left panel of Figure 5-10, location is shown as a secondary vertical subdivision in addition to the gender (from left to right: LAX, NYC, SFO). In addition, the degree is shown through shading (shaded sections correspond to employees with a Ph.D.).

Having seen this, we should ask how much mosaic plots actually help us understand this data set. Obviously, Figure 5-10 is difficult to read and has to be studied carefully. Keep in mind that the information about the number of data points within each category is represented by the area—recursively at all levels. Also note that some categories are empty and therefore invisible (for instance, there are no female employees in either the Los Angeles or San Francisco engineering departments).

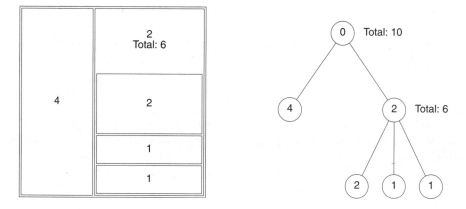

FIGURE 5-11. A tree map (left) and the corresponding tree (right). The numbers give the weight of each node and, if applicable, also the weight of the entire subtree.

I appreciate mosaic plots because they represent a new idea for how data can be displayed graphically, but I have not found them to be useful. In my own experience, it is easier to understand a data set by poring over a set of contingency tables than by drawing mosaic plots. Several problems stand out.

- The order in which the dimensions are applied matters greatly for the appearance of the plot. The lower right panel in Figure 5-10 shows the same data set yet again, but this time the data was split along the location dimension first and along the gender dimension last. Shading again indicates employees with a Ph.D. Is it obvious that this is the same data set? Is one representation more helpful than the other?

- Changing the sort order changes more than just the appearance, it also influences what we are likely to recognize in the graph. Yet even with an interactive tool, I find it thoroughly confusing to view a large number of mosaic plots with changing layouts.

- It seems that once we have more than about four or five dimensions, mosaic plots become too cluttered to be useful. This is not a huge advance over the two dimensions presented in basic contingency tables!

- Finally, there is a problem common to all visualization methods that rely on *area* to indicate magnitude: human perception is not that good at comparing areas, especially areas of different shape. In the lower right panel in Figure 5-10, for example, it is not obvious that the sizes of the two shaded areas for engineering in NYC are the same. (Human perception works by comparing visual objects to each other, and the easiest to compare are lengths, not areas or angles. This is also why you should favor histograms over pie charts!)

In passing, let's quickly consider a different but related concept: *tree maps*. Tree maps are area-based representations of hierarchical tree structures. As shown in Figure 5-11, the area of each parent node in the tree is divided according to the weight of its children.

Tree maps are something of a media phenomenon. Originally developed for the purpose of finding large files in a directory hierarchy, they seem to be more talked about then used. They share the problems of all area-based visualizations already discussed, and even their inventors report that people find them hard to read—especially if the number of levels in the hierarchy increases. Tree maps lend themselves well to interactive explorations (where you can "zoom in" to deeper levels of the hierarchy).

My greatest concern is that tree maps have abandoned the primary advantage of graphical methods without gaining sufficiently in power, namely *intuition*: looking at a tree map does not conjure up the image of, well, a *tree*! (I also think that the focus on treelike hierarchies is driven more by the interests of computer science, rather than by the needs of data analysis—no wonder if the archetypical application consisted of browsing a file system!)

Novel Plot Types

Most of the graph types I have described so far (with the exception of mosaic plots) can be described as "classical": they have been around for years. In this section, we will discuss a few techniques that are much more recent—or, at least, that have only recently received greater attention.

Glyphs

We can include additional information in any simple plot (such as a scatter plot) if we replace the simple symbols used for individual data points with *glyphs*: more complicated symbols that can express additional bits of information by themselves.

An almost trivial application of this idea occurs if we put two data sets on a single scatter plot and use different symbols (such as squares and crosses) to mark the data points from each data set. Here the symbols themselves carry meaning but only a simple, categorical one—namely, whether the point belongs to the first or second data set.

But if we make the symbols more complicated, then they can express more information. Textual labels (letters and digits) are often surprisingly effective when it comes to conveying more information—although distinctly low-tech, this is a technique to keep in mind!

The next step up in sophistication are arrows, which can represent both a direction and a magnitude (see Figure 5-12), but we need not stop there. Each symbol can be a fully formed graph (such as a pie chart or a histogram) all by itself. And even that is not the end—probably the craziest idea in this realm are "Chernoff faces," where different quantities are encoded as *facial features* (*e.g.*, size of the mouth, distance between the eyes), and the faces are used as symbols on a plot!

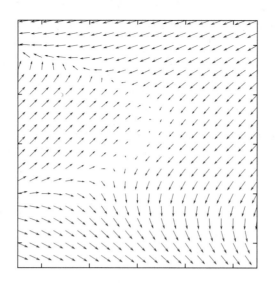

FIGURE 5-12. *Simple glyphs: using arrows to indicate both direction and magnitude of a field. Notice that the variation in the data is smooth and that the data itself has been recorded on a regular grid.*

As you can see, the problem lies not so much in putting more information on a graph as in being able to interpret the result in a useful manner. And that seems to depend mostly on the *data*, in particular on the presence of large-scale, regular structure in it. If such structure is missing, then plots using glyphs can be very hard to decode and quite possibly useless.

Figures 5-12 and 5-13 show two extreme examples. In Figure 5-12, we visualize a four-dimensional data set using arrows (each point of the two-dimensional plot area has both a direction and a magnitude, so the total number of dimensions is four). You can think of the system as flow in a liquid, as electrical or magnetic field lines, or as deformations in an elastic medium—it does not matter, the overall nature of the data becomes quite clear. But Figure 5-13 is an entirely different matter! Here we are dealing with a data set in seven dimensions: the first two are given by the position of the symbol on the plot, and the remaining five are represented via distortions of a five-edged polygon. Although we can make out some regularities (*e.g.*, the shapes of the symbols in the lower lefthand corner are all quite similar and different from the shapes elsewhere), this graph is hard to read and does not reveal the overall structure of the data very well. Also keep in mind that the appearance of the graph will change if we map a different pair of variables to the main axes of the plot, or even if we change the order of variables in the polygons.

Parallel Coordinate Plots

As we have seen, a scatter plot can show two variables. If we use glyphs, we can show more, but not all variables are treated equally (some are encoded in the glyphs, some are

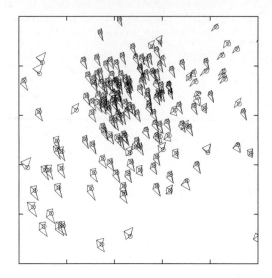

FIGURE 5-13. *Complex glyphs: each polygon encodes five different variables, and its position on the plot adds another two.*

encoded by the position of the symbol on the plot). By using *parallel coordinate plots*, we can show all the variables of a multivariate data set on equal footing. The price we pay is that we end up with a graph that is neither pretty nor particularly intuitive, but that can be useful for exploratory work nonetheless.

In a regular scatter plot in two (or even three) dimensions, the coordinate axes are at right angles to each other. In a parallel coordinate plot, the coordinate axes instead are *parallel* to each other. For every data point, its value for each of the variables is marked on the corresponding axis, and then all these points are connected with lines. Because the axes are parallel to each other, we don't run out of spatial dimensions and therefore can have as many of them as we need. Figure 5-14 shows what a single record looks like in such a plot, and Figure 5-15 shows the entire data set. Each record consists of nine different quantities (labeled A through J).

The main use of parallel coordinate plots is to find clusters in high-dimensional data sets. For example, in Figure 5-15, we can see that the data forms two clusters for the quantity labeled B: one around 0.8 and one around 0. Furthermore, we can see that most records for which B is 0, tend to have higher values of C than those that have a B near 0.8. And so on.

A few technical points should be noted about parallel coordinate plots:

- You will usually want to rescale the values in each coordinate to the unit interval via the linear transformation (also see Appendix B):

$$x_{\text{scaled}} = \frac{x - x_{\min}}{x_{\max} - x_{\min}}$$

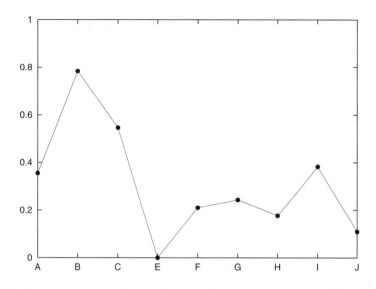

FIGURE 5-14. A single record (i.e., a single data point) from a multivariate data set shown in a parallel coordinate plot.

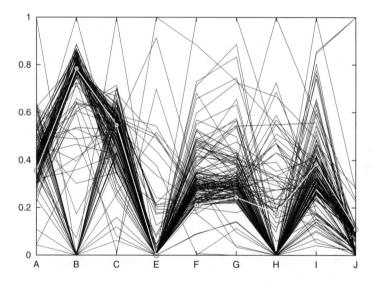

FIGURE 5-15. All records from the data set shown in a parallel coordinate plot. The record shown in Figure 5-14 is highlighted.

This is not mandatory, however. There may be situations where you care about the absolute positions of the points along the coordinate axis or about scaling to a different interval.

- The appearance of parallel coordinate plots depends strongly on the order in which the coordinate lines are drawn: rearranging them can hide or reveal structure. Ideally, you have access to a tool that lets you reshuffle the coordinate axis interactively.

- Especially for larger data sets (several hundreds of points or more), overplotting of lines becomes a problem. One way to deal with this is through "alpha blending": lines are shown as semi-transparent, and their visual effects are combined where they overlap each other.

- Similarly, it is often highly desirable to be able to select a set of lines and highlight them throughout the entire graph—for example, to see how data points that are clustered in one dimension are distributed in the other dimensions.

- Instead of combining points on adjacent coordinate axes with straight lines that have sharp kinks at the coordinate axes, one can use smooth lines that pass the coordinate axes without kinks.

All of these issues really are *tool* issues, and in fact parallel coordinates don't make sense without a tool that supports them natively and includes good implementations of the features just described. This implies that parallel coordinate plots serve less as finished, static graphs than as an interactive tool for exploring a data set.

Parallel coordinate plots still seem pretty novel. The idea itself has been around for about 25 years, but even today, tools that support parallel coordinates plots *well* are far from common place.

What is not yet clear is how useful parallel coordinate plots really are. On the one hand, the concept seems straightforward and easy enough to use. On the other hand, I have found the experience of actually trying to apply them frustrating and not very fruitful. It is easy to get bogged down in technicalities of the plot (ordering and scaling of coordinate axes) with little real, concrete insight resulting in the end. The erratic tool situation of course does not help. I wonder whether more computationally intensive methods (*e.g.*, principal component analysis—see Chapter 14) do not give a better return on investment overall. But the jury is still out.

Interactive Explorations

All the graphs that we have discussed so far (in this and the preceding chapters) were by nature *static*. We prepared graphs, so that we then could study them, but this was the extent of our interaction. If we wanted to see something different, we had to prepare a new graph.

In this section, I shall describe some ideas for *interactive* graphics: graphs that we can change directly in some way without having to re-create them anew.

Interactive graphics cannot be produced with paper and pencil, not even in principle: they *require* a computer. Conversely, what we can do in this area is even more strongly limited by the tools or programs that are available to us than for other types of graphs. In this sense, then, this section is more about *possibilities* than about *realities* because the tool support for interactive graphical exploration seems (at the time of this writing) rather poor.

Querying and Zooming

Interaction with a graph does not have to be complicated. A very simple form of interaction consists of the ability to select a point (or possibly a group of points) and have the tool display additional information about it. In the simplest case, we hover the mouse pointer over a data point and see the coordinates (and possibly additional details) in a tool tip or a separate window. We can refer to this activity as *querying*.

Another simple form of interaction would allow us to change aspects of the graph directly using the mouse. Changing the plot range (*i.e.*, *zooming*) is probably the most common application, but I could also imagine to adjust the aspect ratio, the color palette, or smoothing parameters in this way. (Selecting and highlighting a subset of points in a parallel coordinate plot, as described earlier, would be another application.)

Observe that neither of these activities is inherently "interactive": they all would also be possible if we used paper and pencil. The interactive aspect consists of our ability to invoke them in real time and by using a graphical input device (the mouse).

Linking and Brushing

The ability to interact directly with graphs becomes much more interesting once we are dealing with multiple graphs at the same time! For example, consider a scatter-plot matrix like the one in Figure 5-4. Now imagine we use the mouse to select and highlight a group of points in one of the subplots. If the graphs are *linked*, then the symbols corresponding to the data points selected in one of the subplots will also be highlighted in all other subplots as well.

Usually selecting some points and then highlighting their corresponding symbols in the linked subgraphs requires two separate steps (or mouseclicks). A real-time version of the same idea is called *brushing*: any points currently under the mouse pointer are selected and highlighted in all of the linked subplots.

Of course, linking and brushing are not limited to scatter-plot matrices, but they are applicable to any group of graphs that show different aspects of the same data set. Suppose we are working with a set of histograms of a multivariate data set, each histogram showing only one of the quantities. Now I could imagine a tool that allows us to select a bin in *one* of the histograms and then highlights the contribution from the points in that bin in all the other histograms.

Grand Tours and Projection Pursuits

Although linking and brushing allow us to interact with the data, they leave the graph itself static. This changes when we come to *Grand Tours* and *Projection Pursuits*. Now we are talking about truly animated graphics!

Grand Tours and Projection Pursuits are attempts to enhance our understanding of a data set by presenting many closely related projections in the form of an animated "movie."

The concept is straightforward: we begin with some projection and then continuously move the viewpoint around the data set. (For a three-dimensional data set, you can imagine the viewpoint moving on a sphere that encloses the data.)

In Grand Tours, the viewpoint is allowed to perform essentially a random walk around the data set. In Projection Pursuits, the viewpoint is moved so that it will improve the value of an index that measures how "interesting" a specific projection will appear. Most indices currently suggested measure properties such as deviation from Gaussian behavior. At each step of a Pursuit, the program evaluates several possible projections and then selects the one that most improves the chosen index. Eventually, a Pursuit will reach a local maximum for the index, at which time it needs to be restarted from a different starting point.

Obviously, Tours and Pursuits require specialized tools that can perform the required projections—and do so in real time. They are also exclusively exploratory techniques and not suitable for preserving results or presenting them to a general audience.

Although the approach is interesting, I have not found Tours to be especially useful in practice. It can be confusing to watch a movie of essentially random patterns and frustrating to interact with projections when attempting to explore the neighborhood of an interesting viewpoint.

Tools

All interactive visualization techniques require suitable tools and computer programs; they cannot be done using paper-and-pencil methods. This places considerable weight on the quality of the available tools. Two issues stand out.

- It seems difficult to develop tools that support interactive features and are sufficiently general at the same time. For example, if we expect the plotting program to show additional detail on any data point that we select with the mouse, then the input (data) file will have to contain this information—possibly as metadata. But now we are talking about relatively complicated data sets, which require more complicated, structured file formats that will be specific to each tool. So before we can do anything with the data, we will have to transform it into the required format. This is a significant burden, and it may make these methods infeasible in practice. (Several of the more experimental programs mentioned in the Workshop section in this chapter are nearly unusable on actual data sets for exactly this reason.)

- A second problem concerns performance. Brushing, for instance, makes sense only if it truly occurs in real time—without any discernible delay as the mouse pointer moves. For a large data set and a scatter-plot matrix of a dozen attributes, this means updating a few thousand points in real time. Although by no means infeasible, such responsiveness does require that the tool is written with an eye toward performance and using appropriate technologies. (Several of the tools mentioned in the Workshop exhibit serious performance issues on real-world data sets.)

A final concern involves the overall design of the user interface. It should be easy to learn and easy to use, and it should support the activities that are actually required. Of course, this concern is not specific to data visualization tools but common to all programs with a graphical user interface.

Workshop: Tools for Multivariate Graphics

Multivariate graphs tend to be complicated and therefore require good tool support even more strongly than do other forms of graphs. In addition, some multivariate graphics are highly specialized (*e.g.*, mosaic plots) and cannot be easily prepared with a general-purpose plotting tool.

That being said, the tool situation is questionable at best. Here are three different starting points for exploration—each with its own set of difficulties.

R

R is not a plotting tool per se; it is a statistical analysis package and a full development environment as well. However, R has always included pretty extensive graphing capabilities. R is particularly strong at "scientific" graphs: straightforward but highly accurate line diagrams.

Because R is not simply a plotting tool, but instead a full data manipulation and programming environment, its learning curve is rather steep; you need to know a lot of different things before you can do anything. But once you are up and running, the large number of advanced functions that are already built in can make working with R very productive. For example, the scatter-plot matrix in Figure 5-4 was generated using just these three commands:

```
d <- read.delim( "wines", header=T )

pairs(d)

dev.copy2eps( file="splom.eps" )
```

(the R command `pairs()` generates a plot of all pairs—*i.e.*, a scatter-plot matrix). The scatter plot in Figure 5-5 and the co-plot in Figure 5-6 were generated using:

```
d <- read.delim( "data", header=F )
names( d ) <- c( "x", "a", "y" )

plot( y ~ x, data=d )
dev.copy2eps( file='coplot1.eps' )

coplot( y ~ x | a, data=d )
dev.copy2eps( file='coplot2.eps' )
```

Note that these are the *entire* command sequences, which include reading the data from file and writing the graph back to disk! We'll have more to say about R in the Workshop sections of Chapters 10 and 14.

R has a strong culture of user-contributed add-on packages. For multiplots consisting of subplots arranged on a regular grid (in particular, for generalized co-plots), you should consider the `lattice` package, which extends or even replaces the functionality of the basic R graphic systems. This package is part of the standard R distribution.

Experimental Tools

If you want to explore some of the more novel graphing ideas, such as parallel coordinate plots and mosaic plots, or if you want to try out interactive ideas such as brushing and Grand Tours, then there are several options open to you. All of them are academic research projects, and all are highly experimental. (In a way, this is a reflection of the state of the field: I don't think any of these novel plot types have been refined to a point where they are clearly useful.)

- The ggobi project (*http://www.ggobi.org*) allows brushing in scatter-plot matrices and parallel coordinate plots and includes support for animated tours and pursuits.

- Mondrian (*http://www.rosuda.org/mondrian*) is a Java application that can produce mosaic plots (as well as some other multivariate graphs).

Again, both tools are academic research projects—and it shows. They are technology demonstrators intended to try out and experiment with new graph ideas, but neither is anywhere near production strength. Both are rather fussy about the required data input format, their graphical user interfaces are clumsy, and neither includes a proper way to export graphs to file (if you want to save a plot, you have to take a screenshot). The interactive brushing features in ggobi are slow, which makes them nearly unusable for realistically sized data sets. There are some lessons here (besides the intended ones) to be learned about the design of tools for statistical graphics. (For instance, GUI widget sets do not seem suitable for interactive visualizations: they are too slow. You have to use a lower-level graphics library instead.)

Other open source tools you may want to check out are Tulip (*http://tulip.labri.fr*) and ManyEyes (*http://manyeyes.alphaworks.ibm.com/manyeyes*). The latter project is a web-based tool and community that allows you to upload your data set and generate plots of it online.

A throwback to a different era is OpenDX (*http://www.research.ibm.com/dx*). Originally designed by IBM in 1991, it was donated to the open source community in 1999. It certainly feels overly complicated and dated, but it does include a selection of features not found elsewhere.

Python Chaco Library

The Chaco library (*http://code.enthought.com/projects/chaco/*) is a Python library for two-dimensional plotting. In addition to the usual line and symbol drawing capabilities, it includes easy support for color and color manipulation as well as—more importantly—for real-time user interaction.

Chaco is an exciting toolbox if you plan to experiment with writing your own programs to visualize data and interact with it. However, be prepared to do some research: the best available documentation seems to be the set of demos that ship with it.

Chaco is part of the Enthought Tool Suite, which is developed by Enthought, Inc., and is available under a BSD-style license.

Further Reading

- *Graphics of Large Datasets: Visualizing a Million.* Antony Unwin, Martin Theus, and Heike Hofmann. Springer. 2006.
  This is a modern book that in many ways describes the state of the art in statistical data visualization. Mosaic plots, glyph plots, parallel coordinate plots, Grand Tours—all are discussed here. Unfortunately, the basics are neglected: standard tools like logarithmic plots are never even mentioned, and simple things like labels are frequently messed up. This book is nevertheless interesting as a survey of some of the state of the art.

- *The Elements of Graphing Data.* William S. Cleveland. 2nd ed., Hobart Press. 1994.
  This book provides an interesting counterpoint to the book by Unwin and colleagues. Cleveland's graphs often look pedestrian, but he thinks more deeply than almost anyone else about ways to incorporate more (and more quantitative) information in a graph. What stands out in his works is that he explicitly takes human perception into account as a guiding principle when developing new graphs. My discussion of scatter-plot matrices and co-plots is heavily influenced by his careful treatment.

- *Gnuplot in Action: Understanding Data with Graphs.* Philipp K. Janert. Manning Publications. 2010.
  Chapter 9 of this book contains additional details on and examples for the use of color to prepare false-color plots, including explicit recipes to create them using gnuplot. But the principles are valid more generally, even if you use different tools.

- *Why Should Engineers and Scientists Be Worried About Color?* B. E. Rogowitz and L. A. Treinish. *http://www.research.ibm.com/people/l/lloydt/color/color.HTM*. 1995. This paper contains important lessons for false-color plots, including the distinction between segmentation and smooth variation as well as the difference between hue- and luminance-based palettes. The examples were prepared using IBM's (now open source) OpenDX graphical Data Explorer.

- *Escaping RGBland: Selecting Colors for Statistical Graphics.* A. Zeileis, K. Hornik, and P. Murrell. *http://statmath.wu.ac.at/~zeileis/papers/Zeileis+Hornik+Murrell-2009.pdf*. 2009. This is a more recent paper on the use of color in graphics. It emphasizes the importance of perception-based color spaces, such as the HCL model.

## CHAPTER SIX

Intermezzo: A Data Analysis Session

OCCASIONALLY I GET THE QUESTION: "HOW DO YOU ACTUALLY WORK?" OR "HOW DO YOU COME UP WITH THIS stuff?" As an answer, I want to take you on a tour through a new data set. I will use gnuplot, which is my preferred tool for this kind of interactive data analysis—you will see why. And I will share my observations and thoughts as we go along.

A Data Analysis Session

The data set is a classic: the CO_2 measurements above Mauna Loa on Hawaii. The inspiration for this section comes from Cleveland's *Elements of Graphical Analysis*,[*] but the approach is entirely mine.

First question: what's in the data set? I see that the first column represents the date (month and year) while the second contains the measured CO_2 concentration in parts per million. Here are the first few lines:

```
Jan-1959      315.42
Feb-1959      316.32
Mar-1959      316.49
Apr-1959      317.56
...
```

The measurements are regularly spaced (in fact, monthly), so I don't need to parse the date in the first column; I simply plot the second column by itself. (In the figure, I have

---

[*] *The Elements of Graphing Data.* William S. Cleveland. Hobart Press. 1994. The data itself (in a slightly different format) is available from StatLib: *http://lib.stat.cmu.edu/datasets/visualizing.data.zip* and from many other places around the Web.

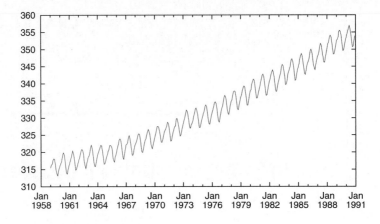

FIGURE 6-1. The first look at the data: plot "data" u 1 w l

added tick labels on the horizontal axis for clarity, but I am omitting the commands required here—they are not essential.)

```
plot "data" u 1 w l
```

The plot shows a rather regular short-term variation overlaid on a nonlinear upward trend. (See Figure 6-1.)

The coordinate system is not convenient for mathematical modeling: the x axis is not numeric, and for modeling purposes it is usually helpful if the graph goes through the origin. So, let's make it do so by subtracting the vertical offset from the data and expressing the horizontal position as the number of months since the first measurement. (This corresponds to the line number in the data file, which is accessible in a gnuplot session through the pseudo-column with column number 0.)

```
plot "data" u 0:($2-315) w l
```

A brief note on the command: the specification after the u (short for using) gives the columns to be used for the x and y coordinates, separated by a colon. Here we use the line number (which is in the pseudo-column 0) for the x coordinate. Also, we subtract the constant offset 315 from the values in the second column and use the result as the y value. Finally, we plot the result with lines (abbreviated w l) instead of using points or other symbols. See Figure 6-2.

The most predominant feature is the trend. What can we say about it? First of all, the trend is nonlinear: if we ignore the short-term variation, the curve is convex downward. This suggests a power law with an as-yet-unknown exponent: x^k. All power-law functions go through the origin $(0, 0)$ and also through the point $(1, 1)$. We already made sure that the data passes through the origin, but to fix the upper-right corner, we need to rescale both axes: if x^k goes through $(1, 1)$, then $b\left(\frac{x}{a}\right)^k$ goes through (a, b).

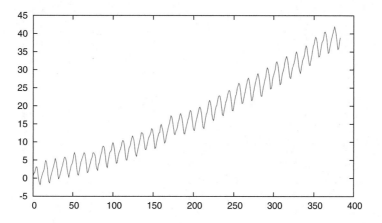

FIGURE 6-2. Making the x values numeric and subtracting the constant vertical offset: plot "data" u 0:($2-315) w l

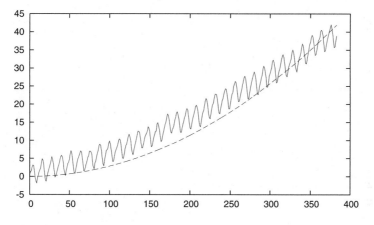

FIGURE 6-3. Adding a function: plot "data" u 0:($2-315) w l, 35*(x/350)**2

What's the value for the exponent *k*? All I know about it right now is that it must be greater than 1 (because the function is convex). Let's try *k* = 2. (See Figure 6-3.)

```
plot "data" u 0:($2-315) w l, 35*(x/350)**2
```

Not bad at all! The exponent is a bit too large—some fiddling suggests that *k* = 1.35 would be a good value (see Figure 6-4).

```
plot "data" u 0:($2-315) w l, 35*(x/350)**1.35
```

To verify this, let's plot the residual; that is, we subtract the trend from the data and plot what's left. If our guess for the trend is correct, then the residual should not exhibit any trend itself—it should just straddle *y* = 0 in a balanced fashion (see Figure 6-5).

```
plot "data" u 0:($2-315 - 35*($0/350)**1.35) w l
```

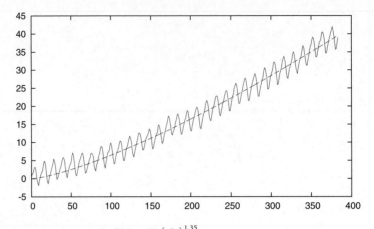

FIGURE 6-4. Getting the exponent right: $f(x) = 35 \left(\frac{x}{350}\right)^{1.35}$

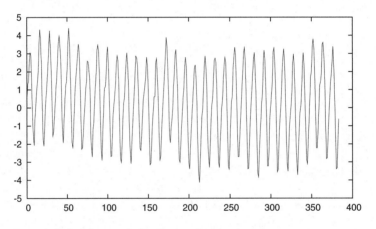

FIGURE 6-5. The residual, after subtracting the function from the data.

It might be hard to see the longer-term trend in this data, so we may want to approximate it by a smoother curve. We can use the weighted-spline approximation built into gnuplot for that purpose. It takes a third parameter, which is a measure for the smoothness: the smaller the third parameter, the smoother the resulting curve; the larger the third parameter, the more closely the spline follows the original data (see Figure 6-6).

```
plot "data" u 0:(2 − 315 − 35 ∗ (0/350)**1.35) w l, \
     "" u 0:($2-315 - 35*($0/350)**1.35):(0.001) s acs w l
```

At this point, the expression for the function that we use to approximate the data has become unwieldy. Thus it now makes sense to define it as a separate function:

```
f(x) = 315 + 35*(x/350)**1.35
plot "data" u 0:($2-f($0)) w l, "" u 0:($2-f($0)):(0.001) s acs w l
```

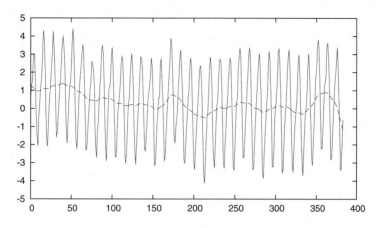

FIGURE 6-6. Plotting a smoothed version of the residual together with the unsmoothed residual to test whether there is any systematic trend remaining in the residual.

From the smoothed line we can see that the overall residual is pretty much flat and straddles zero. Apparently, we have captured the overall trend quite well: there is little evidence of a systematic drift remaining in the residuals.

With the trend taken care of, the next feature to tackle is the seasonality. The seasonality seems to consist of rather regular oscillations, so we should try some combination of sines and cosines. The data pretty much starts out at $y = 0$ for $x = 0$, so we can try a sine by itself. To make a guess for its wavelength, we recall that the data is meteorological and has been taken on a monthly basis—perhaps there is a year-over-year periodicity. This would imply that the data is the same every 12 data points. If so, then a full period of the sine, which corresponds to 2π, should equal a horizontal distance of 12 points. For the amplitude, the graph suggests a value close to 3 (see Figure 6-7).

```
plot "data" u 0:($2-f($0)) w l, 3*sin(2*pi*x/12) w l
```

Right on! In particular, our guess for the wavelength worked out really well. This makes sense, given the origin of the data.

Let's take residuals again, employing splines to see the bigger picture as well (see Figure 6-8):

```
f(x) = 315 + 35*(x/350)**1.35 + 3*sin(2*pi*x/12)
plot "data" u 0:($2-f($0)) w l, "" u 0:($2-f($0)):(0.001) s acs w l
```

The result is pretty good but not good enough. There is clearly some regularity remaining in the data, although at a higher frequency than the main seasonality. Let's zoom in on a smaller interval of the data to take a closer look. The data in the interval [60:120] appears particularly regular, so let's look there (see Figure 6-9):

```
plot [60:120] "data" u 0:($2-f($0)) w lp, "" u 0:($2-f($0)):(0.001) s acs w l
```

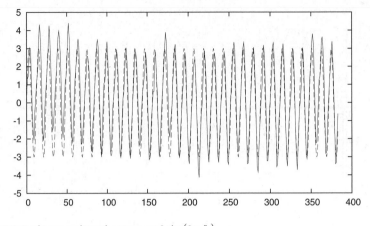

FIGURE 6-7. Fitting the seasonality with a sine wave: $3 \sin\left(2\pi \frac{x}{12}\right)$

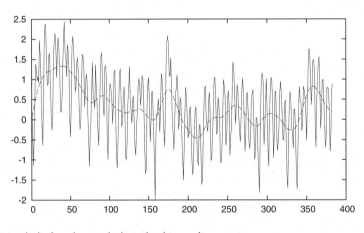

FIGURE 6-8. Residuals after subtracting both trend and seasonality.

I have indicated the individual data points using gnuplot's `linespoints` (`lp`) style. We can now count the number of data points between the main valleys in the data: 12 points. This is the main seasonality. But it seems that between any two primary valleys there is exactly one secondary valley. Of course: higher harmonics! The original seasonality had a period of exactly 12 months, but its shape was not entirely symmetric: its rising flank comprised 7 months but the falling flank only 5 (as you can see by zooming in on the original data with only the trend removed). This kind of asymmetry implies that the seasonality cannot be represented by a simple sine wave alone but that we have to take into account higher harmonics—that is, sine functions with frequencies that are integer multiples of the primary seasonality. So let's try the first higher harmonic, again punting a little on the amplitude (see Figure 6-10):

```
f(x) = 315 + 35*(x/350)**1.35 + 3*sin(2*pi*x/12) - 0.75*sin(2*pi*$0/6)
plot "data" u 0:($2-f($0)) w l, "" u 0:($2-f($0)):(0.001) s acs w l
```

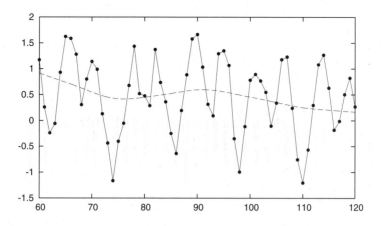

FIGURE 6-9. *Zooming in for a closer look. Individual data points are marked by symbols.*

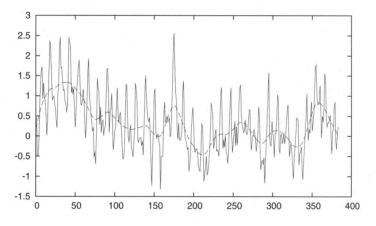

FIGURE 6-10. *Residual after removing trend and the first and second harmonic of the seasonality.*

Now we are really pretty close. Look at the residual—in particular, for values of *x* greater than about 150. The data starts to look quite "random," although there is some systematic behavior for *x* in the range [0:70] that we don't really capture. Let's add some constant ranges to the plot for comparison (see Figure 6-11):

```
plot "data" u 0:($2-f($0)) w l, "" u 0:($2-f($0)):(0.001) s acs w l, 0, 1, -1
```

It looks as if the residual is skewed toward positive values, so let's adjust the vertical offset by 0.1 (see Figure 6-12):

```
f(x) = 315 + 35*(x/350)**1.35 + 3*sin(2*pi*x/12) - 0.75*sin(2*pi*$0/6) + 0.1
plot "data" u 0:($2-f($0)) w l, "" u 0:($2-f($0)):(0.001) s acs w l, 0, 1, -1
```

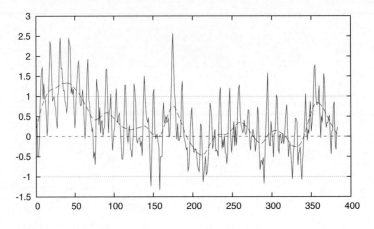

FIGURE 6-11. Adding some grid lines for comparison.

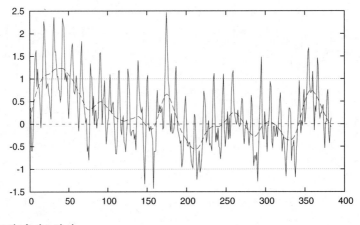

FIGURE 6-12. The final residual.

That's now really close. You should notice how small the last adjustment was—we started out with data ranging from 300 to 350, and now we are making adjustments to the parameters on the order of 0.1. Also note how small the residual has become: mostly in the range from −0.7 to 0.7. That's only about 3 percent of the total variation in the data.

Finally, let's look at the original data again, this time together with our analytical model (see Figure 6-13):

```
f(x) = 315 + 35*(x/350)**1.35 + 3*sin(2*pi*x/12) - 0.75*sin(2*pi*$0/6) + 0.1
plot "data" u 0:2 w l, f(x)
```

All in all, pretty good.

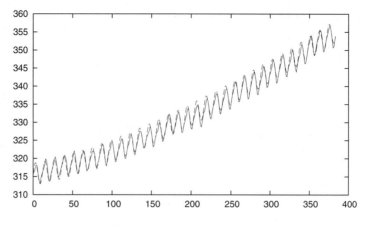

F I G U R E 6-13. The raw data with the final fit.

So what is the point here? The point is that we started out with nothing—no idea at all of what the data looked like. And then, layer by layer, we peeled off components of the data, until only random noise remained. We ended up with an explicit, analytical formula that describes the data remarkably well.

But there is something more. We did so entirely "manually": by plotting the data, trying out some approximations, and wiggling the numbers until they agreed reasonably well with the data. At no point did we resort to a black-box fitting routine—because we didn't have to! We did just fine. (In fact, after everything was finished, I tried to perform a nonlinear fit using the functional form of the analytical model as we have worked it out—only to have it explode terribly! The model depends on seven parameters, which means that convergence of a nonlinear fit can be a bit precarious. In fact, it took me *longer* to try to make the fit work than it took me to work the parameters out manually as just demonstrated.)

I'd go even further. We learned *more* by doing this work manually than if we had used a fitting routine. Some of the observations (such as the idea to include higher harmonics) arose only through direct interaction with the data. And it's not even true that the parameters would be more accurate if they had been calculated by a fitting routine. Sure, they would contain 16 digits but not more information. Our manual wiggling of the parameters enabled us to see quickly and directly the point at which changes to the parameters are so small that they no longer influence the agreement between the data and the model. That's when we have extracted all the information from the data—any further "precision" in the parameters is just insignificant noise.

You might want to try your hand at this yourself and also experiment with some variations of your own. For example, you may question the choice of the power-law behavior for the long-term trend. Does an exponential function (like exp(*x*)) give a better

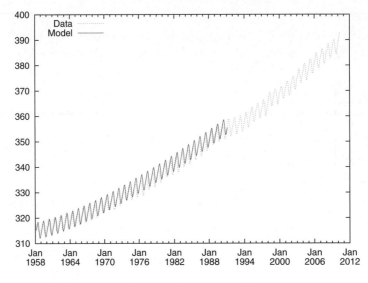

FIGURE 6-14. The extended data set up to early 2010 together with the model (up to 1990).

fit? It is not easy to tell from the data, but it makes a huge difference if we want to project our findings significantly (10 years or more) into the future. You might also take a closer look at the seasonality. Because it is so regular—and especially since its period is known exactly—you should be able to isolate just the periodic part of the data in a separate model by averaging corresponding months for all years. Finally, there is 20 years' worth of additional data available beyond the "classic" data set used in my original exploration.[*] Figure 6-14 shows all the available data together with the model that we have developed. Does the fit continue to work well for the years past 1990?

Workshop: gnuplot

The example commands in this chapter should have given you a good idea what working with gnuplot is like, but let's take a quick look at some of the basics.

Gnuplot (*http://www.gnuplot.info*) is command-line oriented: when you start gnuplot, it presents you with a text prompt at which to enter commands; the resulting graphs are shown in a separate window. Creating plots is simple—the command:

```
plot sin(x) with lines, cos(x) with linespoints
```

will generate a plot of (you guessed it) a sine and a cosine. The sine will be drawn with plain lines, and the cosine will be drawn with symbols ("points") connected by lines.

---

[*] You can obtain the data from the observatory's official website at *http://www.esrl.noaa.gov/gmd/ccgg/ trends/*. Also check out the narrative (with photos of the apparatus!) at *http://celebrating200years.noaa. gov/datasets/mauna/welcome.html*.

(Many gnuplot keywords can be abbreviated: instead of `with lines` I usually type: `w l`, or `w lp` instead of `with linespoints`. These short forms are a major convenience although rather cryptic in the beginning. In this short introductory section, I will make sure to only use the full forms of all commands.)

To plot data from a file, you also use the `plot` command; for instance:

```
plot "data" using 1:2 with lines
```

When plotting data from a file, we use the `using` keyword to specify which columns from the file we want to plot—in the command just given, we use entries from the first column as *x* values and use entries from the second column for *y* values.

One of the nice features of gnuplot is that you can apply arbitrary transformations to the data as it is being plotted. To do so, you put parentheses around each entry in the column specification that you want to apply a transform to. Within these parentheses you can use any mathematical expression. The data from each column is available by prefixing the column index by the dollar sign. An example will make this more clear:

```
plot "data" using (1/$1):($2+$3) with lines
```

This command plots the sum of the second and third columns (that is: `$2+$3`) as a function of one over the value in the first column (`1/$1`).

It is also possible to mix data and functions in a single plot command (as we have seen in the examples in this chapter):

```
plot "data" using 1:2 with lines, cos(x) with lines
```

This is different from the Matlab-style of plotting, where a function must be explicitly *evaluated* for a set of points before the resulting set of values can be plotted.

We can now proceed to add decorations (such as labels and arrows) to the plot. All kinds of options are available to customize virtually every aspect of the plot's appearance: tick marks, the legend, aspect ratio—you name it. When we are done with a plot, we can save all the commands used to create it (including all decorations) via the `save` command:

```
save "plot.gp"
```

Now we can use `load "plot.gp"` to re-create the graph.

As you can see, gnuplot is extremely straightforward to use. The one area that is often regarded as somewhat clumsy is the creation of graphs in common graphics file formats. The reason for this is historical: the first version of gnuplot was written in 1985, a time when one could not expect every computer to be connected to a graphics-capable terminal and when many of our current file formats did not even exist! The gnuplot designers dealt with this situation by creating the so-called "terminal" abstraction. All hardware-specific capabilities were encapsulated by this abstraction so that the rest of gnuplot could be as portable as possible. Over time, this "terminal" came to include different graphics *file formats* as well (not just graphics hardware terminals), and this usage continues to this day.

Exporting a graph to a common file format (such as GIF, PNG, PostScript, or PDF) requires a five-step process:

```
set terminal png
set output "plot.png"
replot
set terminal wxt
set output
```

In the first step, we choose the output device or "terminal": here, a PNG file. In the second step, we choose the file name. In the third step, we explicitly request that the graph be regenerated for this newly chosen device. The remaining commands restore the interactive session by selecting the interactive wxt terminal (built on top of the wxWidgets widget set) and redirecting output back to the interactive terminal. If you find this process clumsy and error-prone, then you are not alone, but rest assured: gnuplot allows you to write macros, which can reduce these five steps to one!

I should mention one further aspect of gnuplot: because it has been around for 25 years, it is extremely mature and robust when it comes to dealing with typical day-to-day problems. For example, gnuplot is refreshingly unpicky when it comes to parsing input files. Many other data analysis or plotting programs that I have seen are pretty rigid in this regard and will bail when encountering unexpected data in an input file. This is the right thing to do in theory, but in practice, data files are often not clean—with ad hoc formats and missing or corrupted data points. Having your plotting program balk over whitespace instead of tabs is a *major* nuisance when doing real work. In contrast, gnuplot usually does an amazingly good job at making sense of almost any input file you might throw at it, and that is indeed a great help. Similarly, gnuplot recognizes undefined mathematical expressions (such as $1/0$, $\log(0)$, and so on) and discards them. This is also very helpful, because it means that you don't have to worry about the domains over which functions are properly defined while you are in the thick of things. Because the output is graphical, there is usually very little risk that this silent discarding of undefined values will lead you to miss essential behavior. (Things are different in a computer program, where silently ignoring error conditions usually only compounds the problem.)

Further Reading

- *Gnuplot in Action: Understanding Data with Graphs.* Philipp K. Janert. Manning Publications. 2010.
  If you want to know more about gnuplot, then you may find this book interesting. It includes not only explanations of all sorts of advanced options, but also helpful hints for working with gnuplot.

## PART II

Analytics: Modeling Data

CHAPTER SEVEN

Guesstimation and the Back
of the Envelope

LOOK AROUND THE ROOM YOU ARE SITTING IN AS YOU READ THIS. NOW ANSWER THE FOLLOWING QUESTION: how many Ping-Pong balls would it take to fill this room?

Yes, I know it's lame to make the reader do jot'em-dot'em exercises, and the question is old anyway, but please make the effort to come up with a number. I am trying to make a point here.

Done? Good—then, tell me, what is the margin of error in your result? How many balls, plus or minus, do you think the room might accommodate as well? Again, numbers, please! Look at the margin of error: can you justify it, or did you just pull some numbers out of thin air to get me off your back? And if you found an argument to base your estimate on: does the result seem right to you? Too large, too small?

Finally, can you state the assumptions you made when answering the first two questions? What did or did you not take into account? Did you take the furniture out or not? Did you look up the size of a Ping-Pong ball, or did you guess it? Did you take into account different ways to pack spheres? Which of these assumptions has the largest effect on the result? Continue on a second sheet of paper if you need more space for your answer.

The game we just played is sometimes called *guesstimation* and is a close relative to the *back-of-the-envelope calculation*. The difference is minor: the way I see it, in guesstimation we worry primarily about finding suitable input values, whereas in a typical back-of-the-envelope calculation, the inputs are reasonably well known and the challenge is to simplify the actual calculation to the point that it can be done on the back of the proverbial envelope. (Some people seem to prefer napkins to envelopes—that's the more sociable crowd.)

Let me be clear about this: I consider proficiency at guesstimation and similar techniques the absolute hallmark of the practical data analyst—the person who goes out and solves *real* problems in the *real* world. It is so powerful because it connects a conceptual understanding (no matter how rough) with the concrete reality of the problem domain; it leaves no place to hide. Guesstimation also generates *numbers* (not theories or models) with their wonderful ability to cut through vague generalities and opinion-based discussions.

For all these reasons, guesstimation is a crucial skill. It is where the rubber meets the road.

The whole point of guesstimation is to come up with an approximate answer—quickly and easily. The flip side of this is that it forces us to think about the accuracy of the result: first how to estimate the accuracy and then how to communicate it. That will be the program for this chapter.

Principles of Guesstimation

Let's step through our introductory Ping-Pong ball example together. This will give me an opportunity to point out a few techniques that are generally useful.

First consider the room. It is basically rectangular in shape. I have bookshelves along several walls; this helps me estimate the length of each wall, since I know that shelves are 90 cm (3 ft) wide—that's a pretty universal standard. I also know that I am 1.80 m (6 ft) tall, which helps me estimate the height of the room. All told, this comes to 5 m by 3.5 m by 2.5 m or about 50 m^3.

Now, the Ping-Pong ball. I haven't had one in my hands for a long time, but I seem to remember that they are about 2.5 cm (1 in) in diameter. That means I can line up 40 of them in a meter, which means I have 40^3 in a cubic meter. The way I calculate this is: $40^3 = 4^3 \cdot 10^3 = 2^6 \cdot 1,000 = 64,000$. That's the number of Ping-Pong balls that fit into a cubic meter.

Taking things together, I can fit $50 \cdot 64,000$ or approximately 3,000,000 Ping-Pong balls into this room. That's a large number. If each ball costs me a dollar at a sporting goods store, then the value of all the balls required to fill this room would be many times greater than the value of the entire house!

Next, the margins of error. The uncertainty in each dimension is at least 10 percent. Relative errors are added to each other in a multiplication (we will discuss error propagation later in this chapter), so the total error turns out to be $3 \cdot 10$ percent = 30 percent! That's pretty large—the number of balls required might be as low as two million or as high as four million. It is uncomfortable to see how the rather harmless-looking 10 percent error in each individual dimension has compounded to lead to a 30 percent uncertainty.

The same problem applies to the diameter of the Ping-Pong balls. Maybe 2.5 cm is a bit low—perhaps 3 cm is more like it. Now, that's a 20 percent increase, which means that the number of balls fitting into one cubic meter is reduced by 60 percent (3 times the relative error, again): now we can fit only about 30,000 of them into a cubic meter. The same goes for the overall estimate: a decrease by half if balls are 5 mm larger than initially assumed. Now the range is something between one and two million.

Finally, the assumptions. Yes, I took the furniture out. Given the uncertainty in the total volume of the room, the space taken up by the furniture does not matter much. I also assumed that balls would stack like cubes, when in reality they pack tighter if we arrange them in the way oranges (or cannonballs) are stacked. It's a slightly nontrivial exercise in geometry to work out the factor, but it comes to about 15 percent more balls in the same space.

So, what can we now say with certainty? We will need a few million Ping-Pong balls—probably not less than one million and certainly not more than five million. The biggest uncertainty is the size of the balls themselves; if we need a more accurate estimate than the one we've obtained so far, then we can look up their exact dimensions and adjust the result accordingly.

(After I wrote this paragraph, I finally looked up the size of a regulation Ping-Pong ball: 38–40 mm. Oops. This means that only about 15,000 balls fit into a cubic meter, and so I must adjust all my estimates down by a factor of 4.)

This example demonstrates all important aspects of guesstimation:

- Estimate sizes of things by comparing them to something you know.
- Establish functional relationships by using simplifying assumptions.
- Originally innocuous errors can compound dramatically, so tracking the accuracy of an estimate is crucial.
- And finally, a few bad guesses on things that are not very familiar can have a devastating effect (I really haven't played Ping-Pong in a long time), but they can be corrected easily when better input is available.

Still, we did find the order of magnitude, one way or the other: a few million.

Estimating Sizes

The best way to estimate the size of an object is to compare it to something you know. The shelves played this role in the previous example, although sometimes you have to work a little harder to find a familiar object to use as reference in any given situation.

Obviously, this is easier to do the more you know, and it can be very frustrating to find yourself in a situation where you don't know anything you could use as a reference. That being said, it is usually possible to go quite far with just a few data points to use as reference values.

(There are stories from the Middle Ages of how soldiers would count how many rows of stone blocks were used in the walls of a fortress before mounting an attack, the better to estimate the height of the walls. Obtaining an accurate value was necessary to prepare scaling ladders of the appropriate length: if the ladders were too short, then the top of the wall could not be reached; if they were too long, the defenders could grab the overhanging tops and topple the ladders back over. Bottom line: you've got to find your reference objects where you can.)

Knowing the sizes of things is therefore the first order of business. The more you know, the easier it is to form an estimate; but also the more you know, the more you develop a feeling for the correct answer. That is an important step when operating with guesstimates: to perform an independent "sanity check" at the end to ensure we did not make some horrible mistake along the way. (In fact, the general advice is that "two (independent) estimates are better than one"; this is certainly true but not always possible—at least I can't think of an independent way to work out the Ping-Pong ball example we started with.)

Knowing the sizes of things can be *learned*. All it takes is a healthy interest in the world around you—please don't go through the dictionary, memorizing data points in alphabetical order. This is not about beating your buddies at a game of Trivial Pursuit! Instead, this is about becoming familiar (I'd almost say intimate) with the world you live in. Feynman once wrote about Hans A. Bethe that "every number was near something he knew." That is the ideal.

The next step is to *look things up*. In situations where one frequently needs relatively good approximations to problems coming from a comparably small problem domain, special-purpose lookup tables can be a great help. I vividly remember a situation in a senior physics lab where we were working on an experiment (I believe, to measure the muon lifetime), when the instructor came by and asked us some guesstimation problem—I forget what it was, but it was nontrivial. None of us had a clue, so he whipped out from his back pocket a small booklet the size of a playing card that listed the physical properties of all kinds of subnuclear particles. For almost any situation that could arise in the lab, he had an approximate answer right there.

Specialized lookup tables exist in all kinds of disciplines, and you might want to make your own as necessary for whatever it is you are working on. The funniest I have seen gave typical sizes (and costs) for all elements of a manufacturing plant or warehouse: so many square feet for the office of the general manager, so many square feet for his assistant (half the size of the boss's), down to the number of square feet per toilet stall, and—not to forget—how many toilets to budget for every 20 workers per 8-hour shift.

Finally, if we don't know anything close and we can't look anything up, then we can try to estimate "from the ground up": starting just with what we know and then piling up arguments to arrive at an estimate. The problem with this approach is that the result may be *way* off. We have seen earlier how errors compound, and the more steps we have in our line of arguments the larger the final error is likely to be—possibly becoming so large that the result will be useless. If that's the case, we can still try and find a cleverer argument that makes do with fewer argument steps. But I have to acknowledge that occasionally we will find ourselves simply stuck: unable to make an adequate estimate with the information we have.

The trick is to make sure this happens only rarely.

Establishing Relationships

Establishing relationships that get us from what we know to what we want to find is usually not that hard. This is true in particular under common business scenarios, where the questions often revolve around rather simple relationships (how something fits into something else, how many items of a kind there are, and the like). In scientific applications, this type of argument can be harder. But for most situations that we are likely to encounter outside the science lab, simple geometric and counting arguments will suffice.

In the next chapter, we will discuss in more detail the kinds of arguments you can use to establish relationships. For now, just one recommendation: *make* it simple! Not: *keep* it simple because, more likely than not, initially the problem is *not* simple; hence you have to make it so in order to make it tractable.

Simplifying assumptions let you cut through the fog and get to the essentials of a situation. You may incur an error as you simplify the problem, and you will want to estimate its effect, but at least you are moving toward a result.

An anecdote illustrates what I mean. When working for Amazon.com, I had a discussion with a rather sophisticated mathematician about how many packages Amazon can typically fit onto a tractor-trailer truck, and he started to work out the different ways you can *stack* rectangular boxes into the back of the truck! This is entirely missing the point because, for a rough calculation, we can make the simplifying assumption that the packages can take any shape at all (*i.e.*, they behave like a liquid) and simply divide the total volume of the truck by the typical volume of a package. Since the individual package is tiny compared to the size of the truck, the specific shapes and arrangements of individual packages are irrelevant: their effect is much smaller than the errors in our estimates for the size of the truck, for instance. (We'll discuss this in more detail in Chapter 8, where we discuss the mean-field approximation.)

The point of back-of-the-envelope estimates is to retain only the core of the problem, stripping away as much nonessential detail as possible. Be careful that your sophistication does not get in the way of finding simple answers.

Working with Numbers

When working with numbers, don't automatically reach for a calculator! I know that I am now running the risk of sounding ridiculous—praising the virtues of old-fashioned reading, 'riting, and 'rithmetic. But that's not my point. My point is that it is *all right* to work with numbers. There is no reason to avoid them.

I have seen the following scenario occur countless times: a discussion is under way, everyone is involved, ideas are flying, concentration is intense—when all of a sudden we need a few numbers to proceed. Immediately, *everything* comes to a screeching halt while several people grope for their calculators and others fire up their computers, followed by hasty attempts to get the required answer, which invariably (given the haste) leads to numerous keying errors and false starts, followed by arguments about the best calculator software to use. In any case, the whole creative process just died. It's a shame.

Besides forcing you to switch context, calculators remove you one step further from the nature of the problem. When working out a problem in your head, you get a feeling for the significant digits in the result: for which digits does the result change as the inputs take on any value from their permissible range? The surest sign that somebody has no clue is when they quote the results from a calculation based on order-of-magnitude inputs to 16 digits!

The whole point here is not to be religious about it—either way. If it actually becomes more complicated to work out a numerical approximation in your head, then by all means use a calculator. But the compulsive habit to avoid working with numbers at all cost should be restrained.

There are a few good techniques that help with the kinds of calculations required for back-of-the-envelope estimates and that are simple enough that they still (even today) hold their own against uncritical calculator use. Only the first is a must-have; the other two are optional.

Powers of ten

The most important technique for deriving order-of-magnitude estimates is to work with orders of magnitudes directly—that is, with powers of ten.

It quickly gets confusing to multiply 9,000 by 17 and then to divide by 400, and so on. Instead of trying to work with the numbers directly, split each number into the most significant digit (or digits) and the respective power of ten. The multiplications now take place among the digits only while the powers of ten are summed up separately. In the example I just gave, we split $9,000 = 9 \cdot 1,000$, $17 = 1.7 \cdot 10 \approx 2 \cdot 10$, and $400 = 4 \cdot 100$. From the leading digits we have 9 times 2 divided by 4 equals 4.5, and from the powers of ten we have 3 plus 1 minus 2 equals 2; so then $4.5 \cdot 10^2 = 450$. That wasn't so hard, was it? (I have replaced 17 with $2 \cdot 10$ in this approximation, so the result is a bit on the high side, by about 15 percent. I might want to correct for that in the end—a better approximation would be closer to 390. The exact value is 382.5.)

More systematically, any number can be split into a decimal fraction and a power of ten. It will be most convenient to require the fraction to have exactly one digit before the decimal point, like so:

$$123.45 = 1.2345 \cdot 10^2$$
$$1,000,000 = 1.0 \cdot 10^6$$
$$0.00321 = 3.21 \cdot 10^{-3}$$

The fraction is commonly known as the *mantissa* (or the *significand* in most recent usage), whereas the power of ten is always referred to as the *exponent*.

This notation significantly simplifies multiplication and division between numbers of very different magnitude: the mantissas multiply (involving only single-digit multiplications, if we restrict ourselves to the most significant digit), and the exponents add. The biggest challenge is to keep the two different tallies simultaneously in one's head.

Small perturbations

The techniques in this section are part of a much larger family of methods known as *perturbation theory*, methods that play a huge role in applied mathematics and related fields. The idea is always the same—we split the original problem into two parts: one that is easy to solve and one that is somehow "small" compared to the first. If we do it right, the effect of the latter part is only a "small perturbation" to the first, easy part of the problem. (You may want to review Appendix B if some of this material is unfamiliar to you.)

The easiest application of this idea is in the calculation of simple powers, such as 12^3. Here is how we would proceed:

$$12^3 = (10 + 2)^3 = 10^3 + 3 \cdot 10^2 \cdot 2 + 3 \cdot 10 \cdot 2^2 + 2^3$$
$$= 1,000 + 600 + \cdots$$
$$= 1,600 + \cdots$$

In the first step, we split 12 into $10 + 2$: here 10 is the easy part (because we know how to raise 10 to an integer power) and 2 is the perturbation (because $2 \ll 10$). In the next step, we make use of the binomial formula (see Appendix B), ignoring everything except the linear term in the "perturbation." The final result is pretty close to the exact value.

The same principle can be applied to many other situations. In the context of this chapter, I am interested in this concept because it gives us a way to estimate and correct for the error introduced by ignoring all but the first digit in powers-of-ten calculations. Let's look at another example:

$$32 \cdot 430$$

Using only the most significant digits, this is $(3 \cdot 10^1) \cdot (4 \cdot 10^2) = (3 \cdot 4) \cdot 10^{1+2} = 12{,}000$. But this is clearly not correct, because we dropped some digits from the factors.

We can consider the nonleading digits as *small perturbations* to the result and treat them separately. In other words, the calculation becomes:

$$(3 + 0.2) \cdot (4 + 0.3) \cdot 10^3 \approx 3(1 + 0.1\ldots) \cdot 4(1 + 0.1\ldots) \cdot 10^3$$

where I have *factored out* the largest factor in each term. On the righthand side I did not write out the correction terms in full—for our purposes, it's enough to know that they are about 0.1.

Now we can make use of the binomial formula:

$$(1 + \epsilon)^2 = 1 + 2\epsilon + \epsilon^2$$

We drop the last term (since it will be very small compared to the other two), but the second term gives us the size of the correction: $+2\epsilon$. In our case, this amounts to about 20 percent, since ϵ is one tenth.

I will admit that this technique seems somewhat out of place today, although I do use it for real calculations when I don't have a calculator on me. But the true value of this method is that it enables me to estimate and reason about the effect that changes to my input variables will have on the overall outcome. In other words, this method is a first step toward *sensitivity analysis*.

Logarithms

This is the method by which generations before us performed numerical calculations. The crucial insight is that we can use logarithms for products (and exponentiation) by making use of the functional equation for logarithms:

$$\log(xy) = \log(x) + \log(y)$$

In other words, instead of *multiplying* two numbers, we can *add* their logarithms. The slide rule was a mechanical calculator based on this idea.

Amazingly, using logarithms for multiplication is *still* relevant—but in a slightly different context. For many statistical applications (in particular when using Bayesian methods), we need to multiply the probabilities of individual events in order to arrive at the probability for the combination of these events. Since probabilities are by construction less than 1, the product of any two probabilities is always smaller than the individual factors. It does not take many probability factors to underflow the floating-point precision of almost any standard computer. Logarithms to the rescue! Instead of multiplying the probabilities, take logarithms of the individual probabilities and then add the logarithms. (The logarithm of a number that is less than 1 is negative, so one usually works with $-\log(p)$.) The resulting numbers, although mathematically equivalent, have much better numerical properties. Finally, since in many applications we mostly care which of a selection of different events has the maximum probability, we don't even need to convert back to probabilities: the event with maximum probability will also be the one with the maximum (negative) logarithm.

More Examples

We have all seen this scene in many a Hollywood movie: the gangster comes in to pay off the hitman (or pay for the drug deal, or whatever it is). Invariably, he hands over an elegant briefcase with the money—cash, obviously. Question: how much is in the case?

Well, a briefcase is usually sized to hold two letter-size papers next to each other; hence it is about 17 by 11 inches wide, and maybe 3 inches tall (or 40 by 30 by 7 centimeters). A bank note is about 6 inches wide and 3 inches tall, which means that we can fit about six per sheet of paper. Finally, a 500-page ream of printer paper is about 2 inches thick. All told, we end up with $2 \cdot 6 \cdot 750 = 9,000$ banknotes. The highest dollar denomination in general circulation is the \$100 bill,[*] so the maximum value of that payoff was about \$1 million, and certainly not more than \$5 million.

Conclusion: for the really big jobs, you need to pay by check. Or use direct transfer.

For a completely different example, consider the following question. What's the typical takeoff weight of a large, intercontinental jet airplane? It turns out that you can come up with an approximate answer even if you don't know *anything* about planes.

A plane is basically an aluminum tube with wings. Ignore the wings for now; let's concentrate on the tube. How big is it? One way to find out is to check your boarding pass: it will display your row number. Unless you are much classier than your author, chances are that it shows a row number in the range of 40–50. You can estimate that the distance between seats is a bit over 50 cm—although it feels closer. (When you stand in the aisle, facing sideways, you can place both hands comfortably on the tops of two consecutive seats; your shoulders are about 30 cm apart, so the distance between seats must be a tad greater than that.) Thus we have the length: $50 \cdot 0.5$ m. We double this to make up for first and business class, and to account for cockpit and tail. Therefore, the length of the tube is about 50 m. How about its diameter? Back in economy, rows are about 9 seats abreast, plus two aisles. Each seat being just a bit wider than your shoulders (hopefully), we end up with a diameter of about 5 m. Hence we are dealing with a tube that is 50 m long and 5 m in diameter.

As you walked through the door, you might have noticed the strength or thickness of the tube: it's about 5 mm. Let's make that 10 mm (1 cm) to account for "stuff": wiring, seats, and all kinds of other hardware that's in the plane. Imagining now that you unroll the entire plane (the way you unroll aluminum foil), the result is a sheet that is

---

[*] Larger denominations exist but—although legal tender—are not officially in circulation and apparently fetch far more than their face value among collectors.

	Length	Width	Diameter	Weight (empty)	Weight (full)	Passengers
B767	50 m	50 m	5 m	90 t	150 t	200
B747	70 m	60 m	6.5 m	175 t	350 t	400
A380	75 m	80 m	7 m	275 t	550 t	500

$50 \cdot \pi \cdot 5 \cdot 0.01 \mathrm{m}^3$. The density of aluminum is a little higher than water (if you have ever been to a country that uses aluminum coins, you know that you can barely make them float), so let's say it's 3 g/cm^3.

It is at this point that we need to employ the proverbial back of the envelope (or the cocktail napkin they gave you with the peanuts) to work out the numbers. It will help to realize that there are $100^3 = 10^6$ cubic centimeters in a cubic meter and that the density of aluminum can therefore be written as 3 tons per cubic meter. The final mass of the "tube" comes out to about 25 ton. Let's double this to take into account the wings (wings are about as long as the fuselage is wide—if you look at the silhouette of a plane in the sky, it forms an approximate square); this yields 50 ton just for the "shell" of the airplane. It does not take into account the engines and most of the other equipment inside the plane.

Now let's compare this number with the load. We have 50 rows, half of them with 9 passengers and the other half with 5; this gives us an average of 7 passengers per row or a total of 350 passengers per plane. Assuming that each passenger contributes 100 kg (body weight and baggage), the load amounts to 35 ton: comparable to the weight of the plane itself. (This weight-to-load ratio is actually not that different than for a car, fully occupied by four people. Of course, if you are driving alone, then the ratio for the car is *much* worse.)

How well are we doing? Actually, not bad at all: Table 7-1 lists typical values for three planes that are common on transatlantic routes: the mid size Boeing 767, the large Boeing 747 (the "Jumbo"), and the extra-large Airbus 380. That's enough to check our calculations. We are not far off.

(What we totally missed is that planes don't fly on air and in-flight peanuts alone: in fact, the greatest single contribution to the weight of a fully loaded and fuelled airplane is the weight of the *fuel*. You can estimate its weight as well, but to do so, you will need one additional bit of information: the fuel consumption of a modern jet airplane per passenger and mile traveled is less than that of a typical compact car with only a single passenger.)

That was a long and involved estimation, and I won't blame you if you skipped some of the intermediate steps. In case you are just joining us again, I'd like to emphasize one point: we came up with a reasonable estimate without having to resort to any "seat of the pants" estimates—even though we had no prior knowledge! Everything that we used, we could either observe directly (such as the number of rows in the plane or the thickness of the fuselage walls) or could relate to something that was familiar to us (such as the distance between seats). That's an important takeaway!

But not all calculations have to be complicated. Sometimes, all you have to do is "put two and two together." A friend told me recently that his company had to cut their budget by a million dollars. We knew that the overall budget for this company was about five million dollars annually. I also knew that, since it was mostly a service company, almost all of its budget went to payroll (there was no inventory or rent to speak of). I could therefore tell my friend that layoffs were around the corner—even with a salary reduction program, the company would have to cut at least 15 percent of their staff. The response was: "Oh, no, our management would *never* do that." Two weeks later, the company eliminated one third of all positions.

Things I Know

Table 7-2 is a collection of things that I know and frequently use to make estimates. Of course, this list may seem a bit whimsical, but it is actually pretty serious. For instance, note the *range* of areas from which these items are drawn! What domains can you reason about, given the information in this table?

Also notice the absence of systematic "scales." That is no accident. I don't need to memorize the weights of a mouse, a cat, and a horse—because I know (or can guess) that a mouse is 1,000 times smaller than a human, a cat 10 times smaller, and a horse 10 times larger. The items in this table are *not* intended to be comprehensive; in fact, they are the bare minimum. Knowing how things relate to each other lets me take it from there.

Of course, this table reflects my personal history and interests. Yours will be different.

How Good Are Those Numbers?

Remember the Ping-Pong ball question that started out this chapter? I once posted that question as a homework problem in a class, and one student's answer was something like 1,020,408.16327. (Did you catch *both* mistakes? Not only does the result of this rough estimate pretend to be accurate to within a single ball; but the answer also includes a fractional part—which is meaningless, given the context.) This type of confusion is incredibly common: we focus so much on the calculation (any calculation) that we forget to interpret the result!

This story serves as a reminder that there are two questions that we should ask *before* any calculation as well as one *afterward*. The two questions to ask before we begin are:

- What level of correctness do I *need*?
- What level of correctness can I *afford*?

TABLE 7-2. *Reference points for guesstimations*

Size of an atomic data type	10 bytes
A page of text	55 lines of 80 characters, or about 4,500 characters total
A record (of anything)	100–1,000 bytes
A car	4 m long, 1 ton weight
A person	2 m tall, 100 kg weight
A shelf	1 m wide, 2 m tall
Swimming pool (not Olympic)	25 × 12.5 meters
A story in a commercial building	4 m high
Passengers on a large airplane	350
Speed of a jetliner	1,000 km/hr
Flight time from NY	6 hr (to the West Coast or Europe)
Human, walking	1 m/s (5 km/hr)
Human, maximum power output	200 W (not sustainable)
Power consumption of a water kettle	2 kW
Electricity grid	100 V (U.S.), 220 V (Europe)
Household fuse	16 A
$3 \cdot 3$	10 (minus 10%)
π	3
Large city	1 million
Population, Germany or Japan	100 million
Population, USA	300 million
Population, China or India	1 billion
Population, Earth	7 billion
U.S. median annual income	$60,000
U.S. federal income tax rate	25% (but also as low as 0% and as high as 40%)
Minimum hourly wage	$10 per hour
Billable hours in a year	2,000 (50 weeks at 40 hours per week)
Low annual inflation	2%
High annual inflation	8%
Price of a B-2 bomber	$2 billion
American Civil War; Franco-Prussian War	1860s; 1870s
French Revolution	1789
Reformation	1517
Charlemagne	800
Great Pyramids	3000 B.C.E.
Hot day	35 Celsius
Very hot kitchen oven	250 Celsius
Steel melts	1200 Celsius
Density of water	1 g/cm^3
Density of aluminum	3 g/cm^3
Density of lead	13 g/cm^3
Density of gold	20 g/cm^3
Ionization energy of hydrogen	13.6 eV
Atomic diameter (Bohr radius)	10^{-10} m
Energy of X-ray radiation	keV
Nuclear binding energy per particle	MeV
Wavelength of the sodium doublet	590 nm

The question to ask afterward is:

- What level of correctness did I *achieve*?

I use the term "correctness" here a bit loosely to refer to the quality of the result. There are actually two different concepts involved: *accuracy* and *precision*.

Accuracy
Accuracy expresses how close the result of a calculation or measurement comes to the "true" value. Low accuracy is due to systematic error.

Precision
Precision refers to the "margin of error" in the calculation or the experiment. In experimental situations, precision tells us how far the results will stray when the experiment is repeated several times. Low precision is due to random noise.

Said another way: accuracy is a measure for the correctness of the result, and precision is a measure of the result's uncertainty.

Before You Get Started: Feasibility and Cost

The first question (what level of correctness is needed) will define the overall approach—if I only need an order-of-magnitude approximation, then the proverbial back of the envelope will do; if I need better results, I might need to work harder. The second question is the necessary corollary: it asks whether I will be able to achieve my goal given the available resources. In other words, these two questions pose a classic engineering trade-off (*i.e.*, they require a regular cost–benefit analysis).

This obviously does not matter much for a throwaway calculation, but it matters a lot for bigger projects. I once witnessed a huge project (involving a dozen developers for over a year) to build a computation engine that had failed to come clear on both counts until it was too late. The project was eventually canceled when it turned out that it would cost *more* to achieve the accuracy required than the project was supposed to gain the company in increased revenue! (Don't laugh—it could happen to you. Or at least in your company.)

This story points to an important fact: correctness is usually expensive, and high correctness is often *disproportionally* more expensive. In other words, a 20 percent approximation can be done on the back of an envelope, a 5 percent solution can be done in a couple of months, but the cost for a 1 percent solution may be astronomical. It is also not uncommon that there is no middle ground (*e.g.*, an affordable 10 percent solution).

I have also seen the opposite problem: projects chasing correctness that is not really necessary—or not achievable because the required input data is not available or of poor quality. This is a particular risk if the project involves the opportunity to play with some attractive new technology.

Finding out the true cost or benefit of higher-quality results can often be tricky. I was working on a project to forecast the daily number of visitors viewing the company's website, when I was told that "we must have absolute forecast accuracy; nothing else matters." I suggested that if this were so, then we should take the entire site *down*, since doing so would guarantee a perfect forecast (zero page views). Yet because this would also imply zero revenue from display advertising, my suggestion focused the client's mind wonderfully to define more clearly what "else" mattered.

After You Finish: Quoting and Displaying Numbers

It is obviously pointless to report or quote results to more digits than is warranted. In fact, it is misleading or at the very least unhelpful, because it fails to communicate to the reader another important aspect of the result—namely its reliability!

A good rule (sometimes known as *Ehrenberg's rule*) is to quote all digits up to and including the *first two variable digits*. Starting from the left, you keep all digits that do not change over the entire range of numbers from one data point to the next; then you also keep the first two digits that vary over the *entire range* from 0 to 9 as you scan over all data points. An example will make this clear. Consider the following data set:

```
121.733
122.129
121.492
119.782
120.890
123.129
```

Here, the first digit (from the left) is always 1 and the second digit takes on only two values (1 and 2), so we retain them both. All further digits can take on any value between 0 and 9, and we retain the first two of them—meaning that we retain a total of *four* digits from the left. The two right-most digits therefore carry no significance, and we can drop them when quoting results. The mean (for instance) should be reported as:

```
121.5
```

Displaying further digits is of no value.

This rule—to retain the first two digits that vary over the entire range of values and all digits to the left of them—works well with the methods described in this chapter. If you are working with numbers as I suggested earlier, then you also develop a sense for the digits that are largely unaffected by reasonable variations in the input parameters as well as for the position in the result after which uncertainties in the input parameters corrupt the outcome.

Finally, a word of warning. The accuracy level of a numerical result should be established from the outset, since doing so later will trigger resistance. I have encountered a system that reported projected sales numbers (which were typically in the hundreds of thousands) to six "significant" digits (*e.g.*, as 324,592 or so). But because these were forecasts that were *at best* accurate to within 30 percent, *all* digits beyond the first were absolute junk! (Note that 30 percent of 300,000 is 100,000, which means that the confidence band for this result was 200,000–400,000.) However, a later release of the same software, which now reported only the actually significant digits, was met by violent opposition from the user community because it was "so much less precise"!

Optional: A Closer Look at Perturbation Theory and Error Propagation

I already mentioned the notion of "small perturbations." It is one of the great ideas of applied mathematics, so it is worth a closer look.

Whenever we can split a problem into an "easy" part and a part that is "small," the problem lends itself to a perturbative solution. The "easy" part we can solve directly (that's what we mean by "easy"), and the part that is "small" we solve in an approximative fashion. By far the most common source of approximations in this area is based on the observation that every function (every curve) is linear (a straight line) in a sufficiently small neighborhood: we can therefore replace the full problem by its linear approximation when dealing with the "small" part—and linear problems are always solvable.

As a simple example, let's calculate $\sqrt{17}$. Can we split this into a "simple" and a "small" problem? Well, we know that $16 = 4^2$ and so $\sqrt{16} = 4$. That's the simple part, and we therefore now write $\sqrt{17} = \sqrt{16 + 1}$. Obviously $1 \ll 16$, so there's the "small" part of the problem. We can now rewrite our problem as follows:

$$\sqrt{17} = \sqrt{16 + 1}$$
$$= \sqrt{16(1 + \epsilon)}$$
$$= \sqrt{16}\sqrt{1 + \epsilon}$$
$$= 4\sqrt{1 + \epsilon}$$

It is often convenient to factor out everything so that we are left with $1 + $ *small stuff* as in the second line here. At this point, we also replaced the small part with ϵ (we will put the numeric value back in at the end).

So far everything has been exact, but to make progress we need to make an approximation. In this case, we replace the square root by a local approximation around 1. (Remember: ϵ is small, and $\sqrt{1}$ is easy.) Every smooth function can be replaced by a straight line locally, and if we don't go too far, then that approximation turns out to be quite good (see Figure 7-1). These approximations can be derived in a systematic fashion by a process known as *Taylor expansion*. The figure shows both the simplest approximation, which is just a straight line, and also the next-higher (second-order) approximation, which is even better.

Taylor expansions are so fundamental that they are almost considered a *fifth* basic operation (after addition, subtraction, multiplication, and division). See Appendix B for a little more information on them.

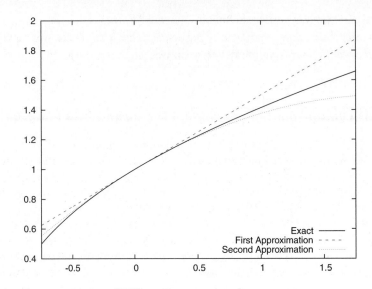

FIGURE 7-1. The square-root function $\sqrt{1+x}$ and the first two approximations around $x = 0$.

With the linear approximation in place, our problem has now become quite tractable:

$$\sqrt{17} \approx 4 \left(1 + \frac{\epsilon}{2} + \cdots \right)$$
$$= 4 + 2\epsilon$$

We can now plug the numeric value $\epsilon = 1/16$ back in: $\sqrt{17} \approx 4 + 2/16 = 4.125$. The exact value is $\sqrt{17} = 4.12310\ldots$. Our approximation is pretty good.

Error Propagation

Error propagation considers situations where we have some quantity x and an associated uncertainty δx. We write $x \pm \delta x$ to indicate that we expect the true value to lie anywhere in the range from $x - \delta x$ to $x + \delta x$. In other words, we have not just a single value for the quantity x, but instead a whole range of possible values.

Now suppose we have several quantities—each with its own error term—and we need to combine them in some fashion. We probably know how to work with the quantities themselves, but what about the uncertainties? For example, we know both the height and width of a rectangle to within some range: $h + \delta h$ and $w + \delta w$. We also know that the area is $A = hw$ (from basic geometry). But what can we say about the uncertainty in the area?

This kind of scenario is ideal for the perturbative methods discussed earlier: the uncertainties are "small," so we can use simplifying approximations to deduce their behavior.

Let's work through the area example:

$$A = (h \pm \delta h)(w \pm \delta w)$$

$$= hw \left(1 \pm \frac{\delta h}{h}\right)\left(1 \pm \frac{\delta w}{w}\right)$$

$$= hw \left(1 \pm \frac{\delta h}{h} \pm \frac{\delta w}{w} + \frac{\delta h}{h}\frac{\delta w}{w}\right)$$

Here again we have factored the primary terms out, to end up with terms of the form $1 + small\ stuff$, because that makes life easier. This also means that, instead of expressing the uncertainty through the *absolute* error δh or δw, we express them through the *relative* error $\delta h / h$ or $\delta w / w$. (Observe that if $\delta h \ll h$, then $\delta h / h \ll 1$.)

So far, everything has been exact. Now comes the approximation: the error terms are small (in fact, smaller than 1); hence their product is extra-small, and we can therefore drop it. Our final result is thus $A = hw \left(1 \pm (\frac{\delta h}{h} + \frac{\delta w}{w})\right)$ or, in words: "When multiplying two quantities, their relative errors add." So if I know both the width and the height to within 10 percent each, then my uncertainty in the area will be 20 percent.

Here are a few more results of this form, which are useful whenever you work with quantities that have associated uncertainties (you might want to try deriving some of these yourself):

$$(x \pm \delta x) + (y \pm \delta y) = x + y \pm (\delta x + \delta y) \qquad \text{Sum}$$

$$(x \pm \delta x) \cdot (y \pm \delta y) = xy \left(1 \pm \left(\frac{\delta x}{x} + \frac{\delta y}{y}\right)\right) \qquad \text{Product}$$

$$\frac{x \pm \delta x}{y \pm \delta y} = \frac{x}{y}\left(1 \pm \left(\frac{\delta x}{x} + \frac{\delta y}{y}\right)\right) \qquad \text{Fraction}$$

$$\sqrt{x + \delta x} = \sqrt{x}\sqrt{1 + \frac{\delta x}{x}} \approx \sqrt{x}\left(1 + \frac{1}{2}\frac{\delta x}{x}\right) \qquad \text{Square root}$$

$$\log(x + \delta x) = \log\left(x\left(1 + \frac{\delta x}{x}\right)\right) \approx \log x + \frac{\delta x}{x} \qquad \text{Logarithm}$$

The most important ones are the first two: when adding (or subtracting) two quantities, their absolute errors add; and when multiplying (or dividing) two quantities, their relative errors add. This implies that, if one of two quantities has a significantly larger error than the other, then the larger error dominates the final uncertainty.

Finally, you may have seen a different way to calculate errors that gives slightly tighter bounds, but it is only appropriate if the errors have been determined by calculating the variances in *repeated measurements* of the same quantity. Only in that case are the statistical assumptions valid upon which this alternative calculation is based. For guesstimation, the simple (albeit more pessimistic) approach described here is more appropriate.

Workshop: The Gnu Scientific Library (GSL)

What do you do when a calculation becomes too involved to do it in your head or even on the back of an envelope? In particular, what can you do if you *need* the extra precision that a simple order-of-magnitude estimation (as practiced in this chapter) will not provide? Obviously, you reach for a numerical library!

The Gnu Scientific Library, or GSL, (*http://www.gnu.org/software/gsl/*) is the best currently available open source library for numerical and scientific calculations that I am aware of. The list of included features is comprehensive, and the implementations are of high quality. Thanks to some unifying conventions, the API, though forbidding at first, is actually quite easy to learn and comfortable to use. Most importantly, the library is mature, well documented, and reliable.

Let's use it to solve two rather different problems; this will give us an opportunity to highlight some of the design choices incorporated into the GSL. The first example involves matrix and vector handling: we will calculate the singular value decomposition (SVD) of a matrix. The second example will demonstrate how the GSL handles non-linear, iterative problems in numerical analysis as we find the minimum of a nonlinear function.

The listing that follows should give you a flavor of what vector and matrix operations look like when using the GSL. First, we allocate a couple of (two-dimensional) vectors and assign values to their elements. We then perform some basic vector operations: adding one vector to another and performing a dot product. (The result of a dot product is a scalar, not another vector.) Finally, we allocate and initialize a matrix and calculate its SVD. (See Chapter 14 for more information on vector and matrix operations.)

```
/* Basic Linear Algebra using the GSL */

#include <stdio.h>
#include <gsl/gsl_vector.h>
#include <gsl/gsl_matrix.h>
#include <gsl/gsl_blas.h>
#include <gsl/gsl_linalg.h>

int main() {
  double r;

  gsl_vector *a, *b, *s, *t;
  gsl_matrix *m, *v;


  /* --- Vectors --- */
  a = gsl_vector_alloc( 2 );    /* two dimensions */
  b = gsl_vector_alloc( 2 );

  /* a = [ 1.0, 2.0 ] */
  gsl_vector_set( a, 0, 1.0 );
  gsl_vector_set( a, 1, 2.0 );
```

```
/* a = [ 3.0, 6.0 ] */
gsl_vector_set( b, 0, 3.0 );
gsl_vector_set( b, 1, 6.0 );

/* a += b (so that now a = [ 4.0, 8.0 ]) */
gsl_vector_add( a, b );
gsl_vector_fprintf( stdout, a, "%f" );

/* r = a . b (dot product) */
gsl_blas_ddot( a, b, &r );
fprintf( stdout, "%f\n", r );

/* --- Matrices --- */
s = gsl_vector_alloc( 2 );
t = gsl_vector_alloc( 2 );

m = gsl_matrix_alloc( 2, 2 );
v = gsl_matrix_alloc( 2, 2 );

/* m = [ [1, 2],
         [0, 3] ] */
gsl_matrix_set( m, 0, 0, 1.0 );
gsl_matrix_set( m, 0, 1, 2.0 );
gsl_matrix_set( m, 1, 0, 0.0 );
gsl_matrix_set( m, 1, 1, 3.0 );

/* m = U s V^T (SVD : singular values are in vector s) */
gsl_linalg_SV_decomp( m, v, s, t );
gsl_vector_fprintf( stdout, s, "%f" );


/* --- Cleanup --- */
gsl_vector_free( a );
gsl_vector_free( b );
gsl_vector_free( s );
gsl_vector_free( t );

gsl_matrix_free( m );
gsl_matrix_free( v );

return 0;
}
```

It is becoming immediately (and a little painfully) clear that we are dealing with plain C, not C++ or any other more modern, object-oriented language! There is no operator overloading; we must use regular functions to access individual vector and matrix elements. There are no namespaces, so function names tend to be lengthy. And of course there is no garbage collection!

What is *not* so obvious is that element access is actually boundary checked: if you try to access a vector element that does not exist (*e.g.*, gsl_vector_set(a, 4, 1.0);), then the GSL internal error handler will be invoked. By default, it will halt the program and print a message to the screen. This is quite generally true: if the library detects an error—including bad inputs, failure to converge numerically, or an out-of-memory situation—it will invoke its error handler to notify you. You can provide your own error handler to respond to errors in a more flexible fashion. For a fully tested program, you can also turn range checking on vector and matrix elements *off* completely, to achieve the best possible runtime performance.

Two more implementation details before leaving the linear algebra example: although the matrix and vector elements are of type `double` in this example, versions of all routines exist for integer and complex data types as well. Furthermore, the GSL will use an optimized implementation of the BLAS (Basic Linear Algebra Subprograms) API if one is available; if not, the GSL comes with its own, basic implementation.

Now let's take a look at the second example. Here we use the GSL to find the minimum of a one-dimensional function. The function to minimize is defined at the top of the listing: $x^2 \log(x)$. In general, nonlinear problems such as this must be solved iteratively: we start with a guess, then calculate a new trial solution based on that guess, and so on until the result meets whatever stopping criteria we care to define.

At least that's what the introductory textbooks tell you.

In the main part of the program, we instantiate a "minimizer," which is an encapsulation of a specific minimization algorithm (in this case, Golden Section Search—others are available, too) and initialize it with the function to minimize as well as our initial guess for the interval containing the minimum.

Now comes the surprising part: an explicit loop! In this loop, the "minimizer" takes a single step in the iteration (*i.e.,* calculates a new, tighter interval bounding the minimum) but then essentially hands control back to us. Why so complicated? Why can't we just specify the desired accuracy of the interval and let the library handle the entire iteration for us? The reason is that real problems more often than not don't converge as obediently as the textbooks suggest! Instead they can (and do) fail in a variety of ways: they converge to the wrong solution, they attempt to access values for which the function is not defined, they attempt to make steps that (for reasons of the larger system of which the routine is only a small part) are either too large or too small, or they diverge entirely. Based on my experience, I have come to the conclusion that *every nonlinear problem is different* (whereas every linear problem is the same), and therefore generic black-box routines don't work!

This brings us back to the way this minimization routine is implemented: the required iteration is not a black box and instead is open and accessible to us. We can simply monitor its progress (as we do in this example, by printing every iteration step to the screen), but we could also interfere with it—for instance to enforce some invariant that is specific to our problem. The "minimizer" does as much as it can by calculating and proposing a new interval; ultimately, however, we are in control over how the iteration progresses. (For the textbook example used here, this doesn't matter, but it makes all the difference when you are doing serious numerical analysis on real problems!)

```
/* Minimizing a function with the GSL */

#include <stdio.h>
#include <gsl/gsl_min.h>

double fct( double x, void *params ) {
  return x*x*log(x);
}

int main() {
  double a = 0.1, b = 1; /* interval which bounds the minimum */

  gsl_function f;          /* pointer to the function to minimize */
  gsl_min_fminimizer *s;   /* pointer to the minimizer instance */


  f.function = &fct;      /* the function to minimize */
  f.params = NULL;        /* no additional parameters needed */

  /* allocate the minimizer, choosing a particular algorithm */
  s = gsl_min_fminimizer_alloc( gsl_min_fminimizer_goldensection );

  /* initialize the minimizer with a function an an initial interval */
  gsl_min_fminimizer_set( s, &f, (a+b)/2.0, a, b );

  while ( b-a > 1.e-6 ) {
    /* perform one minimization step */
    gsl_min_fminimizer_iterate( s );

    /* obtain the new bounding interval */
    a = gsl_min_fminimizer_x_lower( s );
    b = gsl_min_fminimizer_x_upper( s );

    printf( "%f\t%f\n", a, b );
  }

  printf( "Minimum Position: %f\tValue: %f\n",
          gsl_min_fminimizer_x_minimum(s), gsl_min_fminimizer_f_minimum(s) );

  gsl_min_fminimizer_free( s );

  return 0;
}
```

Obviously, we have only touched on the GSL. My primary intention in this section was to give you a sense for the way the GSL is designed and for what kinds of considerations it incorporates. The list of features is extensive—consult the documentation for more information.

Further Reading

- *Guesstimation: Solving the World's Problems on the Back of a Cocktail Napkin.* Lawrence Weinstein and John A. Adam. Princeton University Press. 2008.

This little book contains about a hundred guesstimation problems (with solutions!) from all walks of life. If you are looking for ideas to get you started, look no further.

- *Programming Pearls*. Jon Bentley. 2nd ed., Addison-Wesley. 1999; also, *More Programming Pearls: Confessions of a Coder*. Jon Bentley. Addison-Wesley. 1989.
  These two volumes of reprinted magazine columns are delightful to read, although (or because) they breathe the somewhat dated atmosphere of the old Bell Labs. Both volumes contain chapters on guesstimation problems in a programming context.

- *Back-of-the-Envelope Physics*. Clifford E. Swartz. Johns Hopkins University Press. 2003.
  Physicists regard themselves as the inventors of back-of-the-envelope calculations. This book contains a set of examples from introductory physics (with solutions).

- *The Flying Circus of Physics*. Jearl Walker. 2nd ed., Wiley. 2006.
  If you'd like some hints on how to take an interest in the world around you, try this book. It contains hundreds of everyday observations and challenges you to provide an explanation for each. Why are dried coffee stains always darker around the rim? Why are shower curtains pulled inward? Remarkably, many of these observations are still not fully understood! (You might also want to check out the rather different and more challenging first edition.)

- *Pocket Ref*. Thomas J. Glover. 3rd ed., Sequoia Publishing. 2009.
  This small book is an extreme example of the "lookup" model. It seems to contain almost everything: strength of wood beams, electrical wiring charts, properties of materials, planetary data, first aid, military insignia, and sizing charts for clothing. It also shows the limitations of an overcomplete collection of trivia: I simply don't find it all that useful, but it is interesting for the breadth of topics covered.

## CHAPTER EIGHT

Models from Scaling Arguments

AFTER FAMILIARIZING YOURSELF WITH THE DATA THROUGH PLOTS AND GRAPHS, THE NEXT STEP IS TO START building a model for the data. The meaning of the word "model" is quite hazy, and I don't want to spend much time and effort attempting to define this concept in an abstract way. For our purposes, a *model* is a mathematical description of the data that ideally is guided by our understanding of the system under consideration and that relates the various variables of the system to each other: a "formula."

Models

Models like this are incredibly important. It is at this point that we go from the merely *descriptive* (plots and graphs) to the *prescriptive*: having a model allows us to predict what the system will do under a certain set of conditions. Furthermore, a good or truly useful model—because it helps us to *understand* how the system works—allows us to do so without resorting to the model itself or having to evaluate any particular formula explicitly. A good model ties the different variables that control the system together in such a way that we can see how varying any one of them will influence the outcome. It is this use of models—as an aide to or expression of our understanding—that is the most important one. (Of course, we must still evaluate the model formulas explicitly in order to obtain actual numbers for a specific prediction.)

I should point out that this view of models and what they can do is not universal, and you will find the term used quite differently elsewhere. For instance, statistical models (and this includes machine-learning models) are much more descriptive: they do not purport to *explain* the observed behavior in the way just described. Instead, their purpose is to predict expected outcomes with the greatest level of accuracy possible (numbers in, numbers out). In contrast, my training is in theoretical physics, where the development of *conceptual understanding* of the observed behavior is the ultimate goal. I will use all available information about the system and how it works (or how I *suspect* it works!) wherever I can; I don't restrict myself to using only the information contained in the data itself. (This is a practice that statisticians traditionally frown upon, because it constitutes a form of "pollution" of the data. They may very well be right, but my purpose is different: I don't want to understand the *data*, I want to understand the *system*!) At the same time, I don't consider the absolute accuracy of a model paramount: a model that yields only order-of-magnitude accuracy but helps me understand the system's behavior (so that I can, for instance, make informed trade-off decisions) is much more valuable to me than a model that yields results with 1 percent accuracy but that is a black box otherwise.

To be clear: there are situations when achieving the best possible accuracy is all that matters and conceptual understanding is of little interest. (Often these cases involve repeatable processes in well-understood systems.) If this describes your situation, then you need to use different methods that are appropriate to your problem scenario.

Modeling

As should be clear from the preceding description, building models is basically a creative process. As such, it is difficult (if not impossible) to teach: there are no established techniques or processes for arriving at a useful model in any given scenario. One common approach to teaching this material is to present a large number of case studies, describing the problem situations and attempts at modeling them. I have not found this style to be very effective. First of all, every (nontrivial) problem is different, and tricks and fortuitous insights that work well for one example rarely carry over to a different problem. Second, building effective models often requires fairly deep insight into the particulars of the problem space, so you may end up describing lots of tedious details of the *problem* when actually you wanted to talk about the *model* (or the modeling).

In this chapter, we will take a different approach. Effective modeling is often an exercise in determining "what to leave out": good models should be simple (so that they are workable) yet retain the essential features of the system—certainly those that we are interested in.

As it turns out, there are a few essential arguments and approximations that prove helpful again and again to make a complex problem tractable and to identify the dominant behavior. That's what I want to talk about.

Using and Misusing Models

Just a reminder: models are not reality. They are descriptions or approximations of reality—often quite coarse ones! We need to ensure that we only place as much confidence in a model as is warranted.

How much confidence is warranted? That depends on how well-tested the model is. If a model is based on a good theory, agrees well with a wide range of data sets, and has shown it can predict observations correctly, then our confidence may be quite strong.

At the other extreme are what one might call "pie in the sky" models: ad hoc models, involving half a dozen (or so) parameters—all of which have been estimated independently and not verified against real data. The reliability of such a model is highly dubious: each of the parameters introduces a certain degree of uncertainty, which in combination can make the results of the model meaningless. Recall the discussion in Chapter 7: three parameters known to within 10 percent produce an uncertainty in the final result of 30 percent—and that assumes that the parameters are actually known to within 10 percent! With four to six parameters that possibly are known, only much less precisely than 10 percent, the situation is correspondingly worse. (Many business models fall into this category.)

Also keep in mind that virtually all models have only a limited region of validity. If you try to apply an existing model to a drastically different situation or use input values that are very different from those that you used to build the model, then you may well find that the model makes poor predictions. Be sure to check that the assumptions on which the model is based are actually fulfilled for each application that you have in mind!

Arguments from Scale

Next to the local stadium there is a large, open parking lot. During game days, the parking lot is filled with cars, and—for obvious reasons—a line of portable toilets is set up all along one of the edges of the parking lot. This poses an interesting balancing problem: will this particular arrangement work for all situations, no matter how large the parking lot in question?

The answer is no. The number of people in the parking lot grows with the area of the parking lot, which grows with the square of the edge length (*i.e.*, it "scales as" L^2); but the number of toilets is proportional to the edge length itself (so it scales as L). Therefore, as we make the parking lot bigger and bigger, there comes a point where the number of people overwhelms the number of available facilities. Guaranteed.

Scaling Arguments

This kind of reasoning is an example of a *scaling argument*. Scaling arguments try to capture how some quantity of interest depends on a control parameter. In particular, a scaling argument describes how the output quantity will change as the control parameter changes. Scaling arguments are a particularly fruitful way to arrive at symbolic expressions for phenomena ("formulas") that can be manipulated analytically.

You should have observed that the expressions I gave in the introductory example were not "dimensionally consistent." We had people expressed as the square of a length and toilets expressed as length—what is going on here? Nothing, I merely omitted some detail that was not relevant for the argument I tried to make. A car takes up some amount of space on a parking lot; hence given the size of the parking lot (its area), we can figure out how many cars it can accommodate. Each car seats on average two people (on a game day), so we can figure out the number of people as well. Each person has a certain probability of using a bathroom during the duration of the game and will spend a certain number of minutes there. Given all these parameters, we can figure out the required "toilet availability minutes." We can make a similar argument to find the "availability minutes" provided by the installed facilities. Observe that none of these parameters depend on the size of the parking lot: they are constants. Therefore, we don't need to worry about them if all we want to determine is whether this particular arrangement (with toilets all along one edge, but nowhere else) will work for parking lots of any size. (It is a widely followed convention to use the *tilde*, as in $A \sim B$, to express that A "scales as" B, where A and B do not necessarily have the same dimensions.)

On the other hand, if we actually want to know the exact number of toilets required for a specific parking lot size, then we do need to worry about these factors and try to obtain the best possible estimates for them.

Because scaling arguments free us from having to think about pesky numerical factors, they provide such a convenient and powerful way to begin the modeling process. At the beginning, when things are most uncertain and our understanding of the system is least developed, they free us from having to worry about low-level details (*e.g.*, how long does the average person spend in the bathroom?) and instead help us concentrate on the system's overall behavior. Once the big picture has become clearer (and if the model still seems worth pursuing), we may want to derive some actual numbers from it as well. Only at this point do we need to concern ourselves with numerical constants, which we must either estimate or derive from available data.

A recurring challenge with scaling models is to find the correct scales. For example, we implicitly assumed that the parking lot was square (or at least nearly so) and would remain that shape as it grew. But if the parking lot were growing in one direction only (*i.e.*, becoming longer and longer, while staying the same width), then its area would no longer scale as L^2 but instead scale as L, where L is now the "long" side of the lot. This changes the argument, for if the portable toilets were located along the long side of the lot then the balance between people and available facilities would be the same no matter how large the lot became! On the other hand, if the facilities were set up along the short side, then their number would remain constant while the long side grew, resulting again in an imbalanced situation.

Finding the correct scales is a bit of an experience issue—the important point here is that it is not as simple as saying: "It's an area, therefore it must scale as length squared." It depends on the shape of the area and on which of its lengths controls the size.

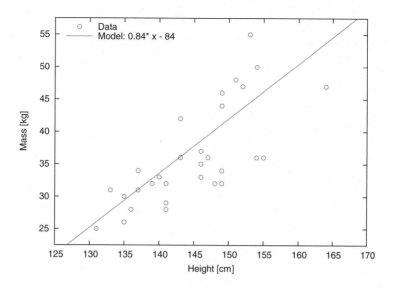

FIGURE 8-1. Heights and weights of a group of middle-school students.

The parking lot example demonstrates one typical application of high-level scaling arguments: what I call a "no-go argument." Even without any specific numbers, the scaling behavior alone was enough to determine that this particular arrangement of toilets to visitors will break down at some point.

Example: A Dimensional Argument

Figure 8-1 shows the heights and weights of a class of female middle-school students.[*] Also displayed is the function $m = 0.84h - 84.0$, where m stands for the mass (or weight) and h for the height. The fit seems to be quite close—is this a good model?

The answer is no, because the model makes unreasonable predictions. Look at it: the model suggests that students have no weight unless they are at least 84 centimeters (almost 3 feet) tall; if they were shorter, their weight would be *negative*. Clearly, this model is no good (although it does *describe* the data over the range shown quite well). We expect that people who have no height also have no weight, and our model should reflect that.

Rather than a model of the form $ax + b$, we might instead try ax^b, because this is the simplest function that gives the expected result for $x = 0$.

[*] A description of this data set can be found in *A Handbook of Small Data Sets*. David J. Hand, Fergus Daly, K. McConway, D. Lunn, and E. Ostrowski. Chapman & Hall/CRC. 1993.

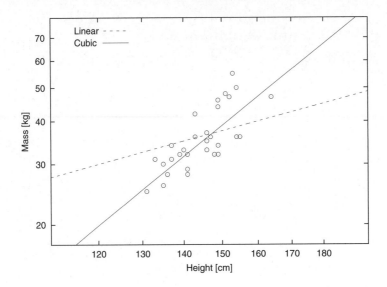

FIGURE 8-2. A double logarithmic plot of the data from Figure 8-1. The cubic function $m = ah^3$ seems to describe the data much better than the linear function $m = ah$.

Figure 8-2 shows the same data but on a double logarithmic plot. Also indicated are functions of the form $y = ax$ and $y = ax^3$. The cubic function ax^3 seems to represent the data quite well—certainly better than the linear function.

But this makes utmost sense! The weight of a body is proportional to its *volume*—that is, to height times width times depth or $h \cdot w \cdot d$. Since body proportions are pretty much the same for all humans (*i.e.*, a person who is twice as tall as another will have shoulders that are twice as wide, too), it follows that the volume of a person's body (and hence its mass) scales as the third power of the height: mass $\sim$ height^3.

Figure 8-3 shows the data one more time and together with the model $m = 1.25 \cdot 10^{-5} h^3$. Notice that the model makes reasonable predictions even for values outside the range of available data points, as you can see by comparing the model predictions with the average body measurements for some different age groups. (The figure also shows the possible limitations of a model that is built using less than perfectly representative data: the model underestimates adult weights because middle-school students are relatively light for their size. In contrast, two-year-olds are notoriously "chubby.")

Nevertheless, this is a very successful model. On the one hand, although based on very little data, the model successfully predicts the weight to within 20 percent accuracy over a range of almost two orders of magnitude in height. On the other hand, and arguably more importantly, it captures the general relationship between body height and weight—a relationship that makes sense but that we might not necessarily have guessed without looking at the data.

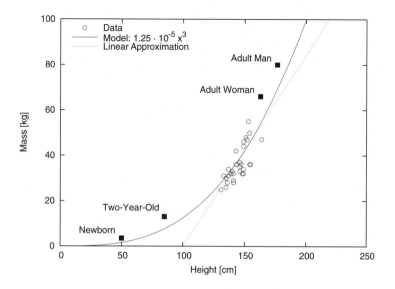

FIGURE 8-3. The data from Figure 8-1, together with the cubic model and the linear approximation to this model around $h = 150\,cm$. Note that the approximation is good over the range of the actual data set but is wildly off farther away from it.

The last question you may ask is why the initial description, $m = 0.84x - 84$ in Figure 8-1 seemed so good. The answer is that this is exactly the linear approximation to the correct model, $m = 1.25 \cdot 10^{-5}h^3$, near $h = 150$ cm. (See Appendix B.) As with all linear approximations, it works well in a small region but fails for values farther away.

Example: An Optimization Problem

Another application of scaling arguments is to cast a question as an optimization problem. Consider a group of people scheduled to perform some task (say, a programming team). The amount of work that this group can perform in a fixed amount of time (its "throughput") is obviously proportional to the number n of people on the team: $\sim n$. However, the members of the team will have to coordinate with each other. Let's assume that each member of the team needs to talk to every other member of the team at least once a day. This implies a communication overhead that scales the *square* of the number of people: $\sim -n^2$. (The minus sign indicates that the communication overhead results in a loss in throughput.) This argument alone is enough to show that for this task, there is an optimal number of people for which the realized productivity will be highest. (Also see Figure 8-4.)

To find the optimal staffing level, we want to maximize the productivity P with respect to the number of workers on the team n:

$$P(n) = cn - dn^2$$

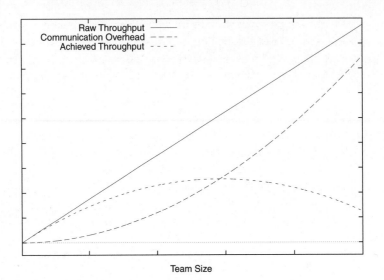

FIGURE 8-4. The work achievable by a team as a function of its size: the raw amount of work that can be accomplished grows with the team size, but the communication overhead grows even faster, which leads to an optimal team size.

where c is the number of minutes each person can contribute during a regular workday, and d is the *effective* number of minutes consumed by each communication event. (I'll return to the cautious "effective" modifier shortly.)

To find the maximum, we take the derivative of $P(n)$ with respect to n, set it equal to 0, and solve for n (see Appendix B). The result is:

$$n_{\text{optimal}} = \frac{c}{2d}$$

Clearly, as the time consumed by each communication event d grows larger, the optimal team size shrinks.

If we now wish to find an actual number for the optimal staffing level, then we need to worry about the numerical factors, and this is where the "effective" comes in. The total number of hours each person can put in during a regular workday is easy to estimate (8 hours at 60 minutes, less time for diversions), but the amount of time spent in a single communication event is more difficult to determine. There are also additional effects that I would lump into the "effective" parameter: for example, not everybody on the team needs to talk to everybody else. Adjustments like this can be lumped into the parameter d which increasingly turns it into a synthetic parameter and less one that can be measured directly.

Example: A Cost Model

Models don't have to be particularly complicated to provide important insights. I remember a situation where we were trying to improve the operation of a manufacturing environment. One particular job was performed on a special machine that had to be retooled for each different type of item to be produced. First the machine would be set up (which took about 5 to 10 minutes), and then a worker would operate the machine to produce a batch of 150 to 200 identical items. The whole cycle lasted a bit longer than an hour and a half to complete the batch, and then the machine was retooled for the next batch.

The retooling part of the cycle was a constant source of management frustration: for 10 minutes (while the machine was being set up), nothing seemed to be happening. Wasted time! (In manufacturing, productivity—defined as "units per hour"—is the most closely watched metric.) Consequently, there had been a long string of process improvement projects dedicated to making the retooling part more efficient and thereby faster. By the time I arrived, it had been streamlined very well. Nevertheless, there were constant efforts underway to reduce the time it took—after all, the sight of the machine sitting idle for 10 minutes seemed to be all the proof that was needed.

It is interesting to set up a minimal cost model for this process. The relevant quantity to study is "minutes per unit." This is essentially the inverse of the productivity, but I find it easier to think in terms of the time it takes to produce a single unit than the other way around. Also note that "time per unit" equates to "cost per unit" after we take the hourly wage into account. Thus, the time per unit is the time T it takes to produce an entire batch, divided by the number of items n in the batch. The total processing time itself consists of the setup time T_1 and n times the amount of time t required to produce a single item:

$$\frac{T}{n} = \frac{T_1 + nt}{n}$$
$$= \frac{T_1}{n} + t$$

The first term on the righthand side is the amount of the setup time that can be attributed to a single item; the second term, of course, is the time it takes to actually produce the item. The larger the batch size, the smaller the contribution of the setup time to the cost of each item as the setup time is "amortized" over more units.

This is one of those situations where the numerical factors actually matter. We know that T_1 is in the range of 300–600 seconds, and that n is between 150 and 200, so that the setup time per item, T_1/n, is between 1–4 seconds. We can also find the time t required to actually produce a single item if we recall that the cycle time for the entire batch was about 90 minutes; therefore $t = 90 \cdot 60/n$, which is about 30 seconds per item. In other words, the setup time that caused management so much grief actually accounted for less than 10 percent of the total time to produce an item!

But we aren't finished yet. Let's assume that, through some strenuous effort, we are able to reduce the setup time by 10 percent. (Not very likely, given that this part of the process had already received a lot of attention, but let's assume—best case!) This would mean that we can reduce the setup time *per item* to 1–3.5 seconds. However, this means that the *total* time per item is reduced by only 1 or 2 percent! This is the kind of efficiency gain that

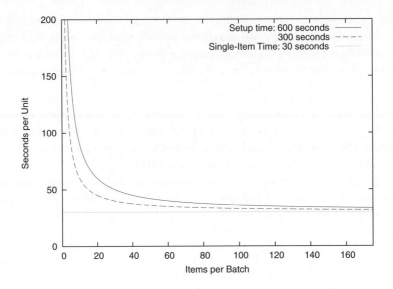

F I G U R E 8-5. Total time required to process a unit, as a function of the batch size.

makes sense only in very, very controlled situations where *everything* else is completely optimized. In contrast, a 10 percent reduction in *t*, the actual work time per item, would result in (almost) a 10 percent improvement in overall productivity (because the amount of time that it takes to produce an item is so much greater than the fraction of the setup time attributable to a single item).

We can see this in Figure 8-5 which shows the "loaded" time per unit (including the setup time) for two typical values of the setup time as a function of the number of items produced in a single batch. Although the setup time contributes significantly to the per-item time when there are fewer than about 50 items per batch, its effect is very small for batch sizes of 150 or more. For batches of this size, the time it takes to actually *make* an item dominates the time to retool the machine.

The story is still not finished. We eventually launched a project to look at ways to reduce *t* for a change, but it was never strongly supported and shut down at the earliest possible moment by plant management in favor of a project to look at, you guessed it, the setup time! The sight of the machine sitting idle for 10 minutes was more than any self-respecting plant manager could bear.

Optional: Scaling Arguments Versus Dimensional Analysis

Scaling arguments may seem similar to another concept you may have heard of: *dimensional analysis*. Although they are related, they are really quite different. Scaling concepts, as introduced here, are based on our intuition of how the system behaves and are a way to capture this intuition in a mathematical expression.

Dimensional analysis, in contrast, applies to physical systems, which are described by a number of quantities that have different physical *dimensions*, such as length, mass, time, or temperature. Because equations describing a physical system must be dimensionally consistent, we can try to deduce the form of these equations by forming dimensionally consistent combinations of the relevant variables.

Let's look at an example. Everybody is familiar with the phenomenon of air resistance, or drag: there is a force F that acts to slow a moving body down. It seems reasonable to assume that this force depends on the cross-sectional area of the body A and the speed (or velocity) v. But it must also depend on some property of the medium (air, in this case) through which the body moves. The most basic property is the density ρ, which is the mass (in grams or kilograms) per volume (in cubic centimeters or meters):

$$F = f(A, v, \rho)$$

Here, $f(x, y, z)$ is an as-yet-unknown function.

Force has units of mass $\cdot$ length^2/time^2, area has units of length^2, velocity of length/time, and density has units of mass/length^3. We can now try to combine A, v, and ρ to form a combination that has the same dimensions as force. A little experimentation leads us to:

$$F = c\rho A v^2$$

where c is a pure (dimensionless) number. This equation expresses the well-known result that air resistance increases with the square of the speed. Note that we arrived at it using purely dimensional arguments without any insight into the physical mechanisms at work.

This form of reasoning has a certain kind of magic to it: why did we choose these specific quantities? Why did we not include the viscosity of air, the ambient air pressure, the temperature, or the length of the body? The answer is (mostly) physical intuition. The viscosity of air is small (viscosity measures the resistance to shear stress, which is the force transmitted by a fluid captured between parallel plates moving parallel to each other but in opposite directions—clearly, not a large effect for air at macroscopic length scales). The pressure enters indirectly through the density (at constant temperature, according to the ideal gas law). And the length of the body is hidden in the numerical factor c, which depends on the shape of the body and therefore on the ratio of the cross-sectional radius $\sqrt{A}$ to the length. In summary: it is impressive how far we came using only very simple arguments, but it is hard to overcome a certain level of discomfort entirely.

Methods of dimensional analysis appear less arbitrary when the governing equations are known. If this is the case, then we can use dimensional arguments to reduce the number of independently variable quantities. For example: *assume* that we already know the drag force is described by $F = c\rho A v^2$. Suppose further that we want to perform experiments to determine c for various bodies by measuring the drag force on them under various conditions. Naively, it might appear as if we had to map out the full three-dimensional parameter space by making measurements for all combinations of (ρ, A, v). But these three parameters only occur in the combination $\gamma = \rho A v^2$, therefore it is sufficient to run a single series of tests that varies γ over the range of values that we are interested in. This constitutes a significant simplification!

Dimensional analysis relies on dimensional consistency and therefore works best for physical and engineering systems, which are described by independently measurable, dimensional quantities. It is particularly prevalent in areas such as fluid dynamics, where the number of variables is especially high, and the physical laws are complicated and often not well understood. It is much less applicable in economic or social settings, where there are fewer (if any) rigorously established, dimensionally consistent relationships.

Other Arguments

There are other arguments that can be useful when attempting to formulate models. They come from the physical sciences, and (like dimensional analysis) they may not work as well in social and economic settings, which are not governed by strict physical laws.

Conservation laws

Conservation laws tell us that some quantity does not change over time. The best-known example is the law of conservation of energy. Conservation laws can be very powerful (in particular when they are exact, as opposed to only approximate) but may not be available: after all, the entire idea of economic growth and (up to a point) manufacturing itself rest on the assumption that more comes out than is being put in!

Symmetries

Symmetries, too, can be helpful in reducing complexity. For example, if an apparently two-dimensional system exhibits the symmetry of a circle, then I know that I'm dealing with a one-dimensional problem: any variation can occur only in the *radial* direction, since a circle looks the same in all directions. When looking for symmetries, don't restrict yourself to geometric considerations—for instance, items entering and leaving a buffer at the same rate exhibit a form of symmetry. In this case, you might only need to solve one of the two processes explicitly while treating the other as a mirror image of the first.

Extreme-value considerations

How does the system behave at the extremes? If there are no customers, messages, orders, or items? If there are infinitely many? What if the items are extremely large or vanishingly small, or if we wait an infinite amount of time? Such considerations can help to "sanity check" an existing model, but they can also provide inspiration when first establishing a model. Limiting cases are often easier to treat because only one effect dominates, which eliminates the complexities arising out of the interplay of different factors.

Mean-Field Approximations

The term *mean-field approximation* comes from statistical physics, but I use it only as a convenient and intuitive expression for a much more general approximation scheme.

Statistical physics deals with large systems of interacting particles, such as gas molecules in a piston or atoms on a crystal lattice. These systems are extraordinarily complicated because every particle interacts with every other particle. If you move one of the particles, then this will affect all the other particles, and so they will move, too; but their movement will, in turn, influence the first particle that we started with! Finding exact solutions for such large, coupled systems is often impossible. To make progress, we ignore the individual interactions between explicit pairs of particles. Instead, we assume that the test particle experiences a field, the "mean-field," that captures the "average" effect of all the other particles.

For example, consider N gas atoms in a bottle of volume V. We may be interested to understand how often two gas atoms collide with each other. To calculate that number exactly, we would have to follow every single atom over time to see whether it bumps into any of the other atoms. This is obviously very difficult, and it certainly seems as if we would need to keep track of a whole lot of detail that should be unnecessary if we are only interested in macroscopic properties.

Realizing this, we can consider this gas in a mean-field approximation: the probability that our test particle collides with another particle should be proportional to the average density of particles in that bottle $\rho = N/V$. Since there are N particles in the bottle, we expect that the number of collisions (over some time frame) will be proportional to $N\rho$. This is good enough to start making some predictions—for example, note that this expression is proportional to N^2. Doubling the number of particles in the bottle therefore means that the number of collisions will grow by a factor of 4. In contrast, reducing the volume of the container by half will increase the number of collisions only by a factor of 2.

You will have noticed that in the previous argument, I omitted lots of detail—for example, any reference to the time frame over which I intend to count collisions. There is also a constant of proportionality missing: $N\rho$ is not really the number of collisions but is merely proportional to it. But if all I care about is understanding how the number of collisions depends on the two variables I consider explicitly (*i.e.*, on N and V), then I don't need to worry about any of these details. The argument so far is sufficient to work out how the number of collisions scales with both N and V.

You can see how mean-field approximations and scaling arguments enhance and support each other. Let's step back and look at the concept behind mean-field approximations more closely.

TABLE 8-1. Mean-field approximations replace an average over functions with functions of averages.

Exact	Mean-Field
$E[x] = \sum\limits_{\text{all outcomes } x} F(x)p(x)$	$E_{\text{MF}}[x] = F\left(\sum\limits_{\text{all outcomes } x} x\, p(x)\right)$

Background and Further Examples

If mean-field approximations were limited to systems of interacting particles, they would not be of much interest in this book. However, the concept behind them is much more general and is very widely applicable.

Whenever we want to calculate with a quantity whose values are distributed according to some probability distribution, we face the challenge that this quantity does not have a single, fixed value. Instead, it has a whole spectrum of possible values, each more or less likely according to the probability distribution. Operating with such a quantity is difficult because at least in principle we have to perform all calculations for each possible outcome and then weight the result of our calculation by the appropriate probability. At the very end of the calculation, we eventually form the average (properly weighted according to the probability factors) to arrive at a unique numerical value.

Given the combinatorial explosion of possible outcomes, attempting to perform such a calculation exactly invariably starts to feel like wading in a quagmire—and that assumes that the calculation can be carried out exactly at all!

The mean-field approach cuts through this difficulty by performing the average *before* embarking on the actual calculation. Rather than working with all possible outcomes (and averaging them at the end), we determine the average outcome first and then only work with that value alone. Table 8-1 summarizes the differences.

This may sound formidable, but it is actually something we do all the time. Do you ever try to estimate how high the bill is going to be when you are waiting in line at the supermarket? You can do this explicitly—by going through all the items individually and adding up their prices (approximately) in your head—or you can apply a mean-field approximation by realizing that the items in your cart represent a sample, drawn "at random," from the selection of goods available. In the mean-field approximation, you would estimate the average single-item price for goods from that store (probably about $5–$7) and then multiply that value by the number of items in your cart. Note that it should be much easier to count the items in your cart than to add up their individual prices explicitly.

This example also highlights the potential pitfalls with mean-field arguments: it will only be reliable if the average item price is a good estimator. If your cart contains two bottles of champagne and a rib roast for a party of eight, then an estimate based on a typical item price of $7 is going to be *way* off.

To get a grip on the expected accuracy of a mean-field approximation, we can try to find a measure for the width of the original distribution (*e.g.*, its standard deviation or inter-quartile range) and then repeat our calculations after adding (and subtracting) the width from the mean value. (We may also treat the width as a small perturbation to the average value and use the perturbation methods discussed in Chapter 7.)

Another example: how many packages does UPS (or any comparable freight carrier) fit onto a truck (to be clear: I don't mean a delivery truck, but one of these 53 feet tractor-trailer long-hauls)? Well, we can estimate the "typical" size of a package as about a cubic foot (0.3^3 m^3), but it might also be as small as half that or as large as twice that size. To find an estimate for the number of packages that will fit, we divide the volume of the truck (17 m long, 2 m wide, 2.5 m high—we can estimate height and width if we realize that a person can stand upright in these things) by the typical size of a package: $(17 \cdot 2 \cdot 2.5/0.3^3) \approx 3,000$ packages. Because the volume (not the length!) of each package might vary by as much as a factor of 2, we end up with lower and upper bounds of (respectively) 1,500 to 6,000 packages.

This calculation makes use of the mean-field idea twice. First, we work with the "average" package size. Second, we don't worry about the actual spatial packing of boxes inside the truck; instead, we pretend that we can reshape them like putty. (This also is a form of "mean-field" approximation.)

I hope you appreciate how the mean-field idea has turned this problem from almost impossibly difficult to trivial—and I don't just mean with regard to the actual computation and the eventual numerical result; but more importantly in the way we thought about it. Rather than getting stuck in the enormous technical difficulties of working out different stacking orders for packages of different sizes, the mean-field notion reduced the problem description to the most fundamental question: into how many small pieces can we divide a large volume? (And if you think that all of this is rather trivial, I fully agree with you—but the "trivial" can easily be overlooked when one is presented with a complex problem in all of its ugly detail. Trying to find mean-field descriptions helps strip away nonessential detail and helps reveal the fundamental questions at stake.)

One common feature of mean-field solutions is that they frequently violate some of the system's properties. For example, at Amazon, we would often consider the typical order to contain 1.7 items, of which 0.9 were books, 0.3 were CDs, and the remaining 0.5 items were other stuff (or whatever the numbers were). This is obviously nonsense, but don't let this disturb you! Just carry on as if nothing happened, and work out the correct breakdown of things at the end. This approach doesn't always work: you'll still have to assign a whole person to a job, even it requires only one tenth of a full-time worker. However, this kind of argument is often sufficient to work out the general behavior of things.

There is a story involving Richard Feynman working on the Connection Machine, one of the earliest massively parallel supercomputers. All the other people on the team were computer scientists, and when a certain problem came up, they tried to solve it using discrete methods and exact enumerations—and got stuck with it. In contrast, Feynman worked with quantities such as "the average number of 1 bits in a message address" (clearly a mean-field approach). This allowed him to cast the problem in terms of partial differential equations, which were easier to solve.[*]

Common Time-Evolution Scenarios

Sometimes we can propose a model based on the way the system under consideration evolves. The "proper" way to do this is to write down a differential equation that describes the system (in fact, this is exactly what the term "modeling" often means) and then proceed to solve it, but that would take us too far afield. (Differential equations relate the change in some quantity, expressed through its derivative, to the quantity itself. These equations can be solved to yield the quantity for all times.)

However, there are a few scenarios so fundamental and so common that we can go ahead and simply write down the solution in its final form. (I'll give a few notes on the derivation as well, but it's the solutions to these differential equations that should be committed to memory.)

Unconstrained Growth and Decay Phenomena

The simplest case concerns pure growth (or death) processes. If the *rate* of change of some quantity is constant in time, then the quantity will follow an *exponential* growth (or decay). Consider a cell culture. At every time step, a certain fraction of all cells in existence at that time step will split (*i.e.*, generate offspring). Here the *fraction* of cells that participate in the population growth at every time step is constant in time; however, because the population itself grows, the total number of new cells at each time step is larger than at the previous time step. Many pure growth processes exhibit this behavior—compound interest on a monetary amount is another example (see Chapter 17).

Pure death processes work similarly, only in this case a constant fraction of the population dies or disappears at each time step. Radioactive decay is probably the best-known example; but another one is the attenuation of light in a transparent medium (such as water). For every unit of length that light penetrates into the medium, its intensity is reduced by a constant fraction, which gives rise to the same exponential behavior. In this case, the independent variable is space, not time, but the argument is exactly the same.

Mathematically, we can express the behavior of a cell culture as follows: if $N(t)$ is the number of cells alive at time t and if a fraction f of these cells split into new cells, then the

[*]This story is reported in "Richard Feynman and the Connection Machine." Daniel Hillis. *Physics Today* 42 (February 1989), p. 78. The paper can also be found on the Web.

number of cells at the next time step $t + 1$ will be:

$$N(t + 1) = N(t) + fN(t)$$

The first term on the righthand side comes from the cells which were already alive at time t, whereas the second term on the right comes from the "new" cells created at t. We can now rewrite this equation as follows:

$$N(t + 1) - N(t) = fN(t)$$

This is a *difference equation*. If we can assume that the time "step" is very small, we can replace the lefthand side with the derivative of N (this process is not always quite as simple as in this example—you may want to check Appendix B for more details on difference and differential quotients):

$$\frac{d}{dt}N = \frac{1}{T}N(t)$$

This equation is true for growth processes; for pure death processes instead we have an additional minus sign on the righthand side.

These equations can be solved or integrated explicitly, and their solutions are:

$$N(t) = N_0 \, e^{t/T} \qquad\qquad \text{Pure birth process}$$
$$N(t) = N_0 \, e^{-t/T} \qquad\qquad \text{Pure death process}$$

Instead of using the "fraction" f of new or dying cells that we used in the difference equation, here we employ a characteristic *time scale T*, which is the time over which the number of cells changes by a factor e or $1/e$, where $e = 2.71828\ldots$. The value for this time scale will depend on the actual system: for cells that multiply rapidly, T will be smaller than for another species that grows more slowly. Notice that such a scale factor *must* be there to make the argument of the exponential function dimensionally consistent! Furthermore, the parameter N_0 is the number of cells in existence at the beginning $t = 0$.

Exponential processes (either birth or death) are very important, but they never last very long. In a pure death process, the population very quickly dwindles to practically nothing. At $t = 3T$, only 5 percent of the original population are left; at $t = 10T$, less than 1 in 10,000 of the original cells has survived; at $t = 20T$, we are down to one in a billion. In other words, after a time that is a small multiple of T, the population will have all but disappeared.

Pure birth processes face the opposite problem: the population grows so quickly that, after a very short while, it will exceed the capacity of its environment. This is so generally true that it is worth emphasizing: exponential growth is not sustainable over extended time periods. A process may start out as exponential, but before long, it must and will saturate. That brings us to the next scenario.

Constrained Growth: The Logistic Equation

Pure birth processes never continue for very long: the population quickly grows to a size that is unsustainable, and then the growth slows. A common model that takes this behavior into account assumes that the members of the population start to "crowd" each other, possibly competing for some shared resource such as food or territory. Mathematically, this can be expressed as follows:

$$\frac{d}{dt}N = \lambda N(K - N) \quad \lambda, K > 0 \text{ fixed}$$

The first term on the righthand side (which equals $\lambda K N$) is the same as in the exponential growth equation. By itself, it would lead to an exponentially growing population $N(t) = C \exp(\lambda K t)$. But the second term $(-\lambda N^2)$ counteracts this: it is negative, so its effect is to *reduce* the population; and it is proportional to N^2, so it grows more strongly as N becomes large. (You can motivate the form of this term by observing that it measures the number of collisions between members of the population and therefore expresses the "crowding" effect.)

This equation is known as the *logistic differential equation*, and its solution is the *logistic function*:

$$N(t) = \frac{K}{1 + \left(\frac{K}{N_0} - 1\right) e^{-\lambda K t}}$$

This is a complicated function that depends on three parameters:

λ The characteristic growth rate

K The carrying capacity $K = N(t \to \infty)$

N_0 The initial number $N_0 = N(t = 0)$ of cells

Compared to a pure (exponential) growth process, the appearance of the parameter K is new. It stands for the system's "carrying capacity"—that is the maximum number of cells that the environment can support. You should convince yourself that the logistic function indeed tends to K as t becomes large. (You will find different forms of this function elsewhere and with different parameters, but the form given here is the most useful one.) Figure 8-6 shows the logistic function for a selection of parameter values.

I should point out that determining values for the three parameters from data can be extraordinarily difficult especially when the only data points available are those to the left of the inflection point (the point with maximum slope, about halfway between N_0 and K). Many different combinations of λ, K, and N_0 may seem to fit the data about equally well. In particular, it is difficult to assess K from early-stage data alone. You may want to try to obtain an independent estimate (even a very rough one) for the carrying capacity and use it when determining the remaining parameters from the data.

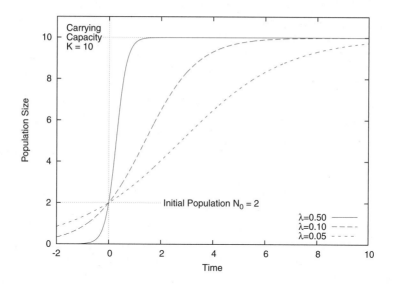

FIGURE 8-6. Logistic growth for different values of the growth rate λ. The initial population N_0 and the overall carrying capacity K are the same in all cases.

The logistic function is the most common model for all growth processes that exhibit some form of saturation. For example, infection rates for contagious diseases can be modeled using the logistic equation, as can the approach to equilibrium for cache hit rates.

Oscillations

The last of the common dynamical behaviors occurs in systems in which some quantity has an equilibrium value and that respond to excursions from that equilibrium position with a restoring effect, which drives the system back to the equilibrium position. If the system does not come to rest in the equilibrium position but instead overshoots, then the process will continue, going back and forth across the neutral position—in other words, the system undergoes *oscillation*. Oscillations occur in many physical systems (from tides to grandfather clocks to molecular bonds), but the "restore and overshoot" phenomenon is much more general. In fact, oscillations can be found almost everywhere: the pendulum that has "swung the other way" is proverbial, from the political scene to personal relationships.

Oscillations are periodic: the system undergoes the same motion again and again. The simplest functions that exhibit this kind of behavior are the trigonometric functions $\sin(x)$ and $\cos(x)$ (also see Appendix B), therefore we can express any periodic behavior, at least approximately, in terms of sines or cosines. Sine and cosine are periodic with period 2π. To express an oscillation with period D, we therefore need to rescale x by $2\pi/D$. It may also be necessary to shift x by a phase factor ϕ: an expression like $\sin(2\pi(x - \phi)/D)$ will at least approximately describe any periodic data set.

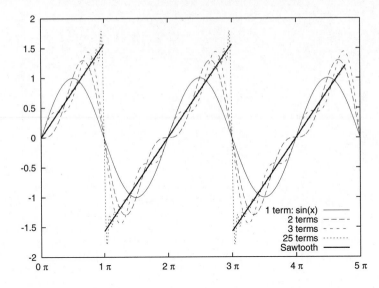

FIGURE 8-7. *The sawtooth function can be composed out of sine functions and their higher harmonics.*

But it gets better: a powerful theorem states that *every* periodic function, no matter how crazy, can be written as a (possibly infinite) combination of trigonometric functions called a *Fourier series*. A Fourier series looks like this:

$$f(x) = \sum_{n=1}^{\infty} a_n \sin\left(2\pi n \frac{x}{D}\right)$$

where I have assumed that $\phi = 0$. The important point is that only integer multiples of $2\pi/D$ are being used in the argument of the sine—the so-called "higher harmonics" of $\sin(2\pi x/D)$. We need to adjust the coefficients a_n to describe a data set. Although the series is in principle infinite, we can usually get reasonably good results by truncating it after only a few terms. (We saw an example for this in Chapter 6, where we used the first two terms to describe the variation in CO_2 concentration over Mauna Loa on Hawaii.)

If the function is known exactly, then the coefficients a_n can be worked out. For the sawtooth function (see Figure 8-7), the coefficients are simply $1, 1/2, 1/3, 1/4, \ldots$ with alternating signs:

$$f(x) = \frac{\sin x}{1} - \frac{\sin 2x}{2} + \frac{\sin 3x}{3} \mp \cdots$$

You can see that the series converges quite rapidly—even for such a crazy, discontinuous function as the sawtooth.

Case Study: How Many Servers Are Best?

To close out this chapter, let's discuss an additional simple case study in model building.

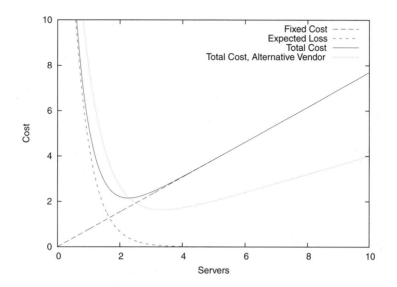

FIGURE 8-8. Costs associated with provisioning a data center, as a function of the number of servers.

Imagine you are deciding how many servers to purchase to power your ecommerce site. Each server costs you a fixed amount E per day—this includes both the operational cost for power and colocation as well as the amortized acquisition cost (*i.e.*, the purchase price divided by the number of days until the server is obsolete and will be replaced). The total cost for n servers is therefore nE.

Given the expected traffic, one server should be sufficient to handle the load. However, each server has a finite probability p of failing on any given day. If your site goes down, you expect to lose B in profit before a new server can be provisioned and brought back online. Therefore, the expected loss when using a single server is pB.

Of course, you can improve the reliability of your site by using multiple servers. If you have n servers, then your site will be down only if all of them fail simultaneously. The probability for this event is p^n. (Note that $p^n < p$, since p is a probability and therefore $p < 1$.)

The total daily cost C that you incur can now be written as the combination of the fixed cost nE and the expected loss due to server downtime $p^n B$ (also see Figure 8-8):

$$C = p^n B + nE$$

Given p, B, and E, you would like to minimize this cost with respect to the number of servers n. We can do this either analytically (by taking the derivative of C with respect to n) or numerically.

But wait, there's more! Suppose we also have an alternative proposal to provision our data center with servers from a different vendor. We know that their reliability q is worse (so that $q > p$), but their price F is significantly lower ($F \ll E$). How does this variant compare to the previous one?

The answer depends on the values for p, B, and E. To make a decision, we must evaluate not only the *location* of the minimum in the total cost (*i.e.*, the number of servers required) but also the actual *value* of the total cost at the minimum position. Figure 8-8 includes the total cost for the alternative proposal that uses less reliable but much cheaper servers. Although we need more servers under this proposal, the total cost is nevertheless lower than in the first one.

(We can go even further: how about a mix of different servers? This scenario, too, we can model in a similar fashion and evaluate it against its alternatives.)

Why Modeling?

Why worry about modeling in a book on data *analysis*? It seems we rarely have touched any actual data in the examples of this chapter.

It all depends on your goals when working with data. If all you want to do is to describe it, extract some features, or even decompose it fully into its constituent parts, then the "analytic" methods of graphical and data analysis will suffice. However, if you intend to use the data to develop an understanding of the *system* that produced the data, then looking at the data itself will be only the first (although important) step.

I consider conceptual modeling to be extremely important, because it is here that we go from the descriptive to the prescriptive. A conceptual model by itself may well be the most valuable outcome of an analysis. But even if not, it will at the very least enhance the purely analytical part of our work, because a conceptual model will lead us to additional hypothesis and thereby suggest additional ways to look at and study the data in an iterative process—in other words, even a purely conceptual model will point us back to the data but with added insight.

The methods described in this chapter and the next are the techniques that I have found to be the most practically useful when thinking about data and the processes that generated it. Whenever looking at data, I always try to understand the system behind it, and I always use some (if not all) of the methods from these two chapters.

Workshop: Sage

Most of the tools introduced in this book work with *numbers*, which makes sense given that we are mostly interested in understanding data. However, there is a different kind of tool that works with formulas instead: *computer algebra systems*. The big (commercial) brand names for such systems have been Maple and Mathematica; in the open source world, the Sage project (*http://www.sagemath.org*) has become somewhat of a front runner.

Sage is an "umbrella" project that attempts to combine several existing open source projects (SymPy, Maxima, and others) together with some added functionality into a single, coherent, Python-like environment. Sage places heavy emphasis on features for number theory and abstract algebra (not exactly everyone's cup of tea) and also includes support for numerical calculations and graphics, but in this section we will limit ourselves to basic calculus and a little linear algebra. (A word of warning: if you are not really comfortable with calculus, then you probably want to skip the rest of this section. Don't worry—it won't be needed in the rest of the book.)

Once you start Sage, it drops you into a text-based command interpreter (a REPL, or read-eval-print loop). Sage makes it easy to perform some simple calculations. For example, let's define a function and take its derivative:

```
sage: a, x = var( 'a x' )
sage: f(x) = cos(a*x)
sage: diff( f, x )
x |--> -a*sin(a*x)
```

In the first line we declare a and x as symbolic variables—so that we can refer to them later and Sage knows how to handle them. We then define a function using the "mathematical" notation f(x) = ... Only functions defined in this way can be used in symbolic calculations. (It is also possible to define Python functions using regular Python syntax, as in def f(x, a): return cos(a*x), but such functions can only be evaluated numerically.) Finally, we calculate the first derivative of the function just defined.

All the standard calculus operations are available. We can combine functions to obtain more complex ones, we can find integrals (both definite and indefinite), and we can even evaluate limits:

```
sage: # Indefinite integral:
sage: integrate( f(x,a) + a*x^2, x )
1/3*a*x^3 + sin(a*x)/a
sage:
sage: # Definite integral on [0,1]:
sage: integrate( f(x,a) + a*x^2, x, 0, 1 )
1/3*(a^2 + 3*sin(a))/a
sage:
sage: # Definite integral on [0,pi], assigned to function:
sage: g(x,a) = integrate( f(x,a) + a*x^2, x, 0, pi )
sage:
sage: # Evaluate g(x,a) for different a:
sage: g(x,1)
1/3*pi^3
sage: g(x,1/2)
1/6*pi^3 + 2
sage: g(x,0)
------------------------------------------------------------
RuntimeError

(some output omitted...)
```

```
RuntimeError: power::eval(): division by zero
sage: limit( g(x,a), a=0 )
pi
```

In the next-to-last command, we tried to evaluate an expression that is mathematically not well defined: the function g(x,a) includes a term of the form $\sin(\pi a)/a$, which we can't evaluate for $a = 0$ because we can't divide by zero. However, the limit $\lim_{a \to 0} \frac{\sin(\pi a)}{a} = \pi$ exists and is found by the limit() function.

As a final example from calculus, let's evaluate some Taylor series (the arguments are: the function to expand, the variable to expand in, the point around which to expand, and the degree of the desired expansion):

```
sage: taylor( f(x,a), x, 0, 5 )
1/24*a^4*x^4 - 1/2*a^2*x^2 + 1
sage: taylor( sqrt(1+x), x, 0, 3 )
1/16*x^3 - 1/8*x^2 + 1/2*x + 1
```

So much for basic calculus. Let's also visit an example from linear algebra. Suppose we have the linear system of equations:

$$
\begin{aligned}
ax + by &= 1 \\
2x + ay + 3z &= 2 \\
b^2x - z &= a
\end{aligned}
$$

and that we would like to find those values of (x, y, z) that solve this system. If all the coefficients were numbers, then we could use a numeric routine to obtain the solution; but in this case, some coefficients are known only symbolically (as a and b), and we would like to express the solution in terms of these variables.

Sage can do this for us quite easily:

```
sage: a, b, x, y, z = var( 'a b x y z' )
sage:
sage: eq1 = a*x + b*y == 1
sage: eq2 = 2*x + a*y + 3*z == 2
sage: eq3 = b^2 - z == a
sage:
sage: solve( [eq1,eq2,eq3], x,y,z )
[[x == (3*b^3 - (3*a + 2)*b + a)/(a^2 - 2*b),
  y == -(3*a*b^2 - 3*a^2 - 2*a + 2)/(a^2 - 2*b),
  z == b^2 - a]]
```

As a last example, let's demonstrate how to calculate the eigenvalues of the following matrix:

$$
M = \begin{pmatrix} a & b & a \\ b & c & b \\ a & b & 0 \end{pmatrix}
$$

Again, if the matrix were given numerically, then we could use a numeric algorithm, but here we would like to obtain a symbolic solution.

Again, Sage can do this easily:

```
sage: m = matrix( [[a,b,a],[b,c,b],[a,b,0]] )
sage: m.eigenvalues()
[-1/18*(-I*sqrt(3) + 1)*(4*a^2 - a*c + 6*b^2 + c^2)/(11/54*a^3 - 7/18*a^2*c + 1/3
*b^2*c + 1/27*c^3 + 1/18*(15*b^2 - c^2)*a + 1/18*sqrt(-5*a^6 - 6*a^4*b^2 + 11*a^2
*b^4 - 5*a^2*c^4 - 32*b^6 + 2*(5*a^3 + 4*a*b^2)*c^3 + (5*a^4 - 62*a^2*b^2 - 4*b^4
)*c^2 - 2*(5*a^5 + 17*a^3*b^2 - 38*a*b^4)*c)*sqrt(3))^(1/3) - 1/2*(I*sqrt(3) + 1)
*(11/54*a^3 - 7/18*a^2*c + 1/3*b^2*c + 1/27*c^3 + 1/18*(15*b^2 - c^2)*a + 1/18*sq
rt(-5*a^6 - 6*a^4*b^2 + 11*a^2*b^4 - 5*a^2*c^4 - 32*b^6 + 2*(5*a^3 + 4*a*b^2)*c^3
 + (5*a^4 - 62*a^2*b^2 - 4*b^4)*c^2 - 2*(5*a^5 + 17*a^3*b^2 - 38*a*b^4)*c)*sqrt(3
))^(1/3) + 1/3*a + 1/3*c, -1/18*(I*sqrt(3) + 1)*(4*a^2 - a*c + 6*b^2 + c^2)/(11/5
4*a^3 - 7/18*a^2*c + 1/3*b^2*c + 1/27*c^3 + 1/18*(15*b^2 - c^2)*a + 1/18*sqrt(-5*
a^6 - 6*a^4*b^2 + 11*a^2*b^4 - 5*a^2*c^4 - 32*b^6 + 2*(5*a^3 + 4*a*b^2)*c^3 + (5*
a^4 - 62*a^2*b^2 - 4*b^4)*c^2 - 2*(5*a^5 + 17*a^3*b^2 - 38*a*b^4)*c)*sqrt(3))^(1/
3) - 1/2*(-I*sqrt(3) + 1)*(11/54*a^3 - 7/18*a^2*c + 1/3*b^2*c + 1/27*c^3 + 1/18*(
15*b^2 - c^2)*a + 1/18*sqrt(-5*a^6 - 6*a^4*b^2 + 11*a^2*b^4 - 5*a^2*c^4 - 32*b^6
+ 2*(5*a^3 + 4*a*b^2)*c^3 + (5*a^4 - 62*a^2*b^2 - 4*b^4)*c^2 - 2*(5*a^5 + 17*a^3*
b^2 - 38*a*b^4)*c)*sqrt(3))^(1/3) + 1/3*a + 1/3*c, 1/3*a + 1/3*c + 1/9*(4*a^2 - a
*c + 6*b^2 + c^2)/(11/54*a^3 - 7/18*a^2*c + 1/3*b^2*c + 1/27*c^3 + 1/18*(15*b^2 -
 c^2)*a + 1/18*sqrt(-5*a^6 - 6*a^4*b^2 + 11*a^2*b^4 - 5*a^2*c^4 - 32*b^6 + 2*(5*a
^3 + 4*a*b^2)*c^3 + (5*a^4 - 62*a^2*b^2 - 4*b^4)*c^2 - 2*(5*a^5 + 17*a^3*b^2 - 38
*a*b^4)*c)*sqrt(3))^(1/3) + (11/54*a^3 - 7/18*a^2*c + 1/3*b^2*c + 1/27*c^3 + 1/18
*(15*b^2 - c^2)*a + 1/18*sqrt(-5*a^6 - 6*a^4*b^2 + 11*a^2*b^4 - 5*a^2*c^4 - 32*b^
6 + 2*(5*a^3 + 4*a*b^2)*c^3 + (5*a^4 - 62*a^2*b^2 - 4*b^4)*c^2 - 2*(5*a^5 + 17*a^
3*b^2 - 38*a*b^4)*c)*sqrt(3))^(1/3)]
```

Whether these results are useful to us is a different question!

This last example demonstrates something I have found to be quite generally true when working with computer algebra systems: it can be difficult to find the right kind of problem for them. Initially, computer algebra systems seem like pure magic, so effortlessly do they perform tasks that took us *years* to learn (and that we still get wrong). But as we move from trivial to more realistic problems, it is often difficult to obtain results that are actually useful. All too often we end up with a result like the one in the eigenvalue example, which—although "correct"—simply does not shed much light on the problem we tried to solve! And before we try manually to simplify an expression like the one for the eigenvalues, we might be better off solving the entire problem with paper and pencil, because using paper and pencil, we can can introduce new variables for frequently occurring terms or even make useful approximations as we go along.

I think computer algebra systems are most useful in scenarios that require the generation of a *very* large number of terms (*e.g.*, combinatorial problems), which in the end are evaluated (numerically or otherwise) entirely by the computer to yield the final result without providing a "symbolic" solution in the classical sense at all. When these conditions are fulfilled, computer algebra systems enable you to tackle problems that would simply not be feasible with paper and pencil. At the same time, you can maintain a greater level of accuracy because numerical (finite-precision) methods, although still required to obtain a useful result, are employed only in the final stages of the calculation (rather than from the outset). Neither of these conditions is fulfilled for relatively straightforward ad hoc symbolic manipulations. Despite their immediate "magic" appeal, computer algebra systems are most useful as specialized tools for specialized tasks!

One final word about the Sage project. As an open source project, it leaves a strange impression. You first become aware of this when you attempt to download the binary distribution: it consists of a 500 MB bundle, which unpacks to 2 GB on your disk! When you investigate what is contained in this huge package, the answer turns out to be *everything*. Sage ships with *all* of its dependencies. It ships with its own copy of all libraries it requires. It ships with its own copy of R. It ships with its own copy of Python! In short, it ships with its own copy of *everything*.

This bundling is partially due to the well-known difficulties with making deeply numerical software portable, but is also an expression of the fact that Sage is an umbrella project that tries to combine a wide range of otherwise independent projects. Although I sincerely appreciate the straightforward pragmatism of this solution, it also feels heavy-handed and ultimately unsustainable. Personally, it makes me doubt the wisdom of the entire "all under one roof" approach that is the whole purpose of Sage: if this is what it takes, then we are probably on the wrong track. In other words, if it is not feasible to integrate different projects in a more organic way, then perhaps those projects should remain independent, with the user free to choose which to use.

Further Reading

There are two or three dozen books out there specifically on the topic of modeling, but I have been disappointed by most of them. Some of the more useful (from the elementary to the quite advanced) include the following.

- *How to Model It: Problem Solving for the Computer Age.* A. M. Starfield, K. A. Smith, and A. L. Bleloch. Interaction Book Company. 1994.
  Probably the best elementary introduction to modeling that I am aware of. Ten (ficticious) case studies are presented and discussed, each demonstrating a different modeling method. (Out of print, but available used.)

- *An Introduction to Mathematical Modeling.* Edward A. Bender. Dover Publications. 2000. Short and idiosyncratic. A bit dated but still insightful.

- *Concepts of Mathematical Modeling.* Walter J. Meyer. Dover Publications. 2004.
  This book is a general introduction to many of the topics required for mathematical modeling at an advanced beginner level. It feels more dated than it is, and the presentation is a bit pedestrian; nevertheless, it contains a lot of accessible, and most of all practical, material.

- *Introduction to the Foundations of Applied Mathematics.* Mark H. Holmes. Springer. 2009.
  This is one of the few books on modeling that places recurring mathematical techniques, rather than case studies, at the center of its discussion. Much of the material is advanced, but the first few chapters contain a careful discussion of

dimensional analysis and nice introductions to perturbation expansions and time-evolution scenarios.

- *Modeling Complex Systems.* Nino Boccara. 2nd ed., Springer. 2010.
  This is a book by a physicist (not a mathematician, applied or otherwise), and it demonstrates how a physicist thinks about building models. The examples are rich, but mostly of theoretical interest. Conceptually advanced, mathematically not too difficult.

- *Practical Applied Mathematics.* Sam Howison. Cambridge University Press. 2005.
  This is a very advanced book on applied mathematics with a heavy emphasis on partial differential equations. However, the introductory chapters, though short, provide one of the most insightful (and witty) discussions of models, modeling, scaling arguments, and related topics that I have seen.

The following two books are not about the process of modeling. Instead, they provide examples of modeling in action (with a particular emphasis on scaling arguments):

- *The Simple Science of Flight.* Henk Tennekes. 2nd ed., MIT Press. 2009.
  This is a short yet fascinating book about the physics and engineering of flying, written at the "popular science" level. The author makes heavy use of scaling laws throughout. If you are interested in aviation, then you will be interested in this book.

- *Scaling Concepts in Polymer Physics.* Pierre-Gilles de Gennes. Cornell University Press. 1979.
  This is a research monograph on polymer physics and probably not suitable for a general audience. But the treatment, which relies almost exclusively on a variety of scaling arguments, is almost elementary. Written by the master of the scaling models.

## CHAPTER NINE

Arguments from Probability Models

WHEN MODELING SYSTEMS THAT EXHIBIT SOME FORM OF RANDOMNESS, THE CHALLENGE IN THE MODELING process is to find a way to handle the resulting uncertainty. We don't know for sure what the system will do—there is a range of outcomes, each of which is more or less likely, according to some probability distribution. Occasionally, it is possible to work out the exact probabilities for all possible events; however, this quickly becomes very difficult, if not impossible, as we go from simple (and possibly idealized systems) to real applications. We need to find ways to simplify life!

In this chapter, I want to take a look at some of the "standard" probability models that occur frequently in practical problems. I shall also describe some of their properties that make it possible to reason about them without having to perform explicit calculations for all possible outcomes. We will see that we can reduce the behavior of many random systems to their "typical" outcome and a narrow range around that.

This is true for many situations but not for all! Systems characterized by power-law distribution functions can *not* be summarized by a narrow regime around a single value, and you will obtain highly misleading (if not outright wrong) results if you try to handle such scenarios with standard methods. It is therefore important to recognize this kind of behavior and to choose appropriate techniques.

The Binomial Distribution and Bernoulli Trials

Bernoulli trials are random trials that can have only two outcomes, commonly called Success and Failure. Success occurs with probability p, and Failure occurs with probability

$1 - p$. We further assume that successive trials are independent and that the probability parameter p stays constant throughout.

Although this description may sound unreasonably limiting, in fact many different processes can be expressed in terms of Bernoulli trials. We just have to be sufficiently creative when defining the class of events that we consider "Successes." A few examples:

- Define Heads as Success in n successive tosses of a fair coin. In this case, $p = 1/2$.

- Using fair dice, we can define getting an "ace" as Success and all other outcomes as Failure. In this case, $p = 1/6$.

- We could just as well define *not* getting an "ace" as Success. In this case, $p = 5/6$.

- Consider an urn that contains b black tokens and r red tokens. If we define drawing a red token as Success, then repeated drawings (with replacement!) from the urn constitute Bernoulli trials with $p = r/(r + b)$.

- Toss two identical coins and define obtaining two Heads as Success. Each toss of the two coins *together* constitutes a Bernoulli trial with $p = 1/4$.

As you can see, the restriction to a binary outcome is not really limiting: even a process that naturally has more than two possible outcomes (such as throwing dice) can be cast in terms of Bernoulli trials if we restrict the definition of Success appropriately. Furthermore, as the last example shows, even combinations of events (such as tossing two coins or, equivalently, two successive tosses of a single coin) can be expressed in terms of Bernoulli trials.

The restricted nature of Bernoulli trials makes it possible to derive some exact results (we'll see some in a moment). More importantly, though, the abstraction forced on us by the limitations of Bernoulli trials can help to develop simplified conceptual models of a random process.

Exact Results

The central formula for Bernoulli trials gives the *probability of observing k Successes in N trials with Success probability p*, and it is also known as the *Binomial distribution* (see Figure 9-1):

$$P(k, N; p) = \binom{N}{k} p^k (1 - p)^{N-k}$$

This should make good sense: we need to obtain k Successes, each occurring with probability p, and $N - k$ Failures, each occurring with probability $1 - p$. The term:

$$\binom{N}{k} = \frac{N!}{k!(N - k)!}$$

consisting of a *binomial coefficient* is combinatorial in nature: it gives the number of distinct arrangements for k successes and $N - k$ failures. (This is easy to see. There are $N!$ ways to

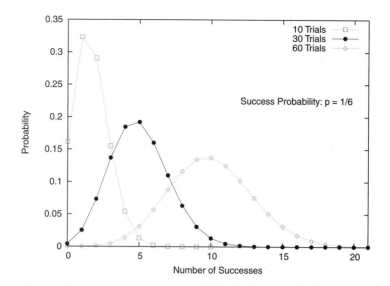

FIGURE 9-1. The Binomial distribution: the probability of obtaining k Successes in N trials with Success probability p.

arrange N *distinguishable* items: you have N choices for the first item, N − 1 choices for the second, and so on. However, the k Successes are indistinguishable from each other, and the same is true for the N − k Failures. Hence the total number of arrangements is reduced by the number of ways in which the Successes can be rearranged, since all these rearrangements are identical to each other. With k Successes, this means that k! rearrangements are indistinguishable, and similarly for the N − k failures.) Notice that the combinatorial factor does not depend on p.

This formula gives the probability of obtaining a specific number k of Successes. To find the expected number of Successes μ in N Bernoulli trials, we need to average over all possible outcomes:

$$\mu = \sum_{k}^{N} k\, P(k, N; p)$$
$$= Np$$

This result should come as no surprise. We use it intuitively whenever we say that we expect "about five Heads in ten tosses of fair coin" ($N = 10$, $p = 1/2$) or that we expect to obtain "about ten aces in sixty tosses of a fair die" ($N = 60$, $p = 1/6$).

Another result that can be worked out exactly is the standard deviation:

$$\sigma = \sqrt{Np(1 - p)}$$

The standard deviation gives us the range over which we expect the outcomes to vary. (For example, assume that we perform m experiments, each consisting of N tosses of a fair coin. The expected number of Successes in each experiment is Np, but of course we won't obtain exactly this number in each experiment. However, over the course of the m experiments, we expect to find the number of Successes in the majority of them to lie between $Np - \sqrt{Np(1-p)}$ and $Np + \sqrt{Np(1-p)}$.)

Notice that σ grows more slowly with the number of trials than does μ ($\sigma \sim \sqrt{N}$ versus $\mu \sim N$). The relative width of the outcome distribution therefore shrinks as we conduct more trials.

Using Bernoulli Trials to Develop Mean-Field Models

The primary reason why I place so much emphasis on the concept of Bernoulli trials is that it lends itself naturally to the development of mean-field models (see Chapter 8). Suppose we try to develop a model to predict the staffing level required for a call center to deal with customer complaints. We know from experience that about one in every thousand orders will lead to a complaint (hence $p = 1/1000$). If we shipped a million orders a day, we could use the Binomial distribution to work out the probability to receive $1, 2, 3, \ldots, 999{,}999, 1{,}000{,}000$ complaints a day and then work out the required staffing levels accordingly—a daunting task! But in the spirit of mean-field theories, we can cut through the complexity by realizing that we will receive "about $Np = 1{,}000$" complaints a day. So rather than working with each possible outcome (and its associated probability), we limit our attention to a single *expected* outcome. (And we can now proceed to determine how many calls a single person can handle per day to find the required number of customer service people.) We can even go a step further and incorporate the uncertainty in the number of complaints by considering the standard deviation, which in this example comes out to $\sqrt{Np(1-p)} \approx \sqrt{1000} \approx 30$. (Here I made use of the fact that $1 - p$ is very close to 1 for the current value of p.) The spread is small compared to the expected number of calls, lending credibility to our initial approximation of replacing the full distribution with only its expected outcome. (This is a demonstration for the observation we made earlier that the width of the resulting distribution grows much more slowly with N than does the expected value itself. As N gets larger, this effect becomes more drastic, which means that mean-field theory gets *better* and more reliable the more urgently we need it! The tough cases can be situations where N is of moderate size—say, in the range of $10, \ldots, 100$. This size is too large to work out all outcomes exactly but not large enough to be safe working only with the expected values.)

Having seen this, we can apply similar reasoning to more general situations. For example, notice that the number of orders shipped each day will probably not equal exactly one million—instead, it will be a random quantity itself. So, by using $N = 1{,}000{,}000$ we have employed the mean-field idea already. It should be easy to generalize to other situations from here.

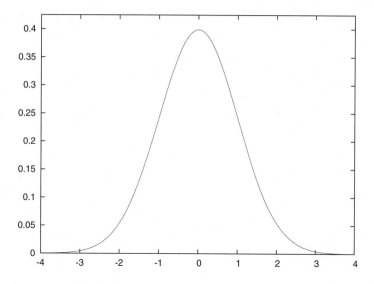

F I G U R E 9-2. The Gaussian probability density.

The Gaussian Distribution and the Central Limit Theorem

Probably the most ubiquitous formula in all of probability theory and statistics is:

$$p(x; \mu, \sigma) = \frac{1}{\sqrt{2\pi}\sigma}\, e^{-\frac{1}{2}\left(\frac{x-\mu}{\sigma}\right)^2}$$

This is the formula for the Gaussian (or *Normal*) probability density. This is the proverbial "Bell Curve." (See Figure 9-2 and Appendix B for additional details.)

Two factors contribute to the elevated importance of the Gaussian distribution: on the foundational side, the Central Limit Theorem guarantees that the Gaussian distribution will arise naturally whenever we take averages (of almost anything). On the sheerly practical side, the fact that we can actually explicitly work out most integrals involving the Gaussian means that such expressions make good building blocks for more complicated theories.

The Central Limit Theorem

Imagine you have a source of data points that are distributed according to some common distribution. The data could be numbers drawn from a uniform random-number generator, prices of items in a store, or the body heights of a large group of people.

Now assume that you repeatedly take a sample of *n* elements from the source (*n* random numbers, *n* items from the store, or measurements for *n* people) and form the total sum of the values. You can also divide by n to get the average. Notice that these sums (or averages) are random quantities themselves: since the points are drawn from a random distribution, their sums will also be random numbers.

Note that we don't necessarily know the distributions from which the original points come, so it may seem it would be impossible to say anything about the distribution of their sums. Surprisingly, the opposite is true: we can make very precise statements about the form of the distribution according to which the sums are distributed. This is the content of the Central Limit Theorem.

The *Central Limit Theorem* states that the sums of a bunch of random quantities will be distributed according to a Gaussian distribution. This statement is not strictly true; it is only an approximation, with the quality of the approximation improving as more points are included in each sample (as n gets larger, the approximation gets better). In practice, though, the approximation is excellent even for quite moderate values of n.

This is an amazing statement, given that we made no assumptions whatsoever about the original distributions (I will qualify this in a moment): it seems as if we got something for nothing! After a moment's thought, however, this result should not be so surprising: if we take a single point from the original distribution, it may be large or it may be small—we don't know. But if we take many such points, then the highs and the lows will balance each other out "on average." Hence we should not be too surprised that the distribution of the sums is a *smooth* distribution with a *central peak*. It is, however, not obvious that this distribution should turn out to be the Gaussian specifically.

We can now state the Central Limit Theorem formally. *Let $\{x_i\}$ be a sample of size n, having the following properties:*

1. *All x_n are mutually independent.*

2. *All x_n are drawn from a common distribution.*

3. *The mean μ and the standard deviation σ for the distribution of the individual data points x_i are finite.*

Then the sample average $\frac{1}{n}\sum_i^n x_i$ is distributed according to a Gaussian with mean μ and standard deviation $\sigma/\sqrt{n}$. The approximation improves as the sample size n increases. In other words, the probability of finding the value x for the sample mean $\frac{1}{n}\sum_i x_i$ becomes Gaussian as n gets large:

$$P\left(\frac{1}{n}\sum_i^n x_i = x\right) \rightarrow \frac{1}{\sqrt{2\pi}}\frac{\sqrt{n}}{\sigma}\exp\left(-\frac{1}{2}\left(\frac{x-\mu}{\sigma/\sqrt{n}}\right)^2\right)$$

Notice that, as for the binomial distribution, the width of the resulting distribution of the average is smaller than the width of the original distribution of the individual data points. This aspect of the Central Limit Theorem is the formal justification for the common practice to "average out the noise": no matter how widely the individual data points scatter, their averages will scatter less.

On the other hand, the reduction in width is not as fast as one might want: it is not reduced linearly with the number n of points in the sample but only by $\sqrt{n}$. This means that if we take 10 times as many points, the scatter is reduced to only $1/\sqrt{10} \approx 30$ percent of its original value. To reduce it to 10 percent, we would need to increase the sample size by a factor of 100. That's a lot!

Finally, let's take a look at the Central Limit Theorem in action. Suppose we draw samples from a uniform distribution that takes on the values $1, 2, \ldots, 6$ with equal probability—in other words, throws of a fair die. This distribution has mean $\mu = 3.5$ (that's pretty obvious) and standard deviation $\sigma = \sqrt{(6^2 - 1)/12} \approx 1.71$ (not as obvious but not terribly hard to work it out, or you can look it up).

We now throw the die a certain number of times and evaluate the average of the values that we observe. According to the Central Limit Theorem, these averages should be distributed according to a Gaussian distribution that becomes narrower as we increase the number of throws used to obtain an average. To see the distribution of values, we generate a histogram (see Chapter 2). I use 1,000 "repeats" to have enough data for a histogram. (Make sure you understand what is going on here: we throw the die a certain number of times and calculate an average based on those throws; and this entire process is repeated 1,000 times.)

The results are shown in Figure 9-3. In the upper-left corner we have thrown the die only once and thus form the "average" over only a single throw. You can see that all of the possible values are about equally likely: the distribution is uniform. In the upper-right corner, we throw the dice *twice* every time and form the average over both throws. Already a central tendency in the distribution of the *average* of values can be observed! We then continue to make longer and longer averaging runs. (Also shown is the Gaussian distribution with the appropriately adjusted width: $\sigma/\sqrt{n}$, where n is the number of throws over which we form the average.)

I'd like to emphasize two observations in particular. First, note how quickly the central tendency becomes apparent—it only takes averaging over two or three throws for a central peak to becomes established. Second, note how well the properly scaled Gaussian distribution fits the observed histograms. This is the Central Limit Theorem in action.

The Central Term and the Tails

The most predominant feature of the Gaussian density function is the speed with which it falls to zero as $|x|$ (the absolute value of x—see Appendix B) becomes large. It is worth looking at some numbers to understand just how quickly it does decay. For $x = 2$, the standard Gaussian with zero mean and unit variance is approximately $p(2, 0, 1) = 0.05 \ldots$. For $x = 5$, it is already on the order of 10^{-6}; for $x = 10$ it's about 10^{-22}; and not much further out, at $x = 15$, we find $p(15, 0, 1) \approx 10^{-50}$. One needs to

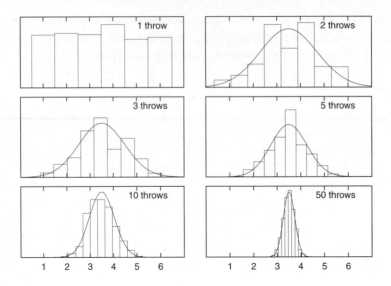

F I G U R E 9-3. The Central Limit Theorem in action. Distribution of the average number of points when throwing a fair die several times. The boxes show the histogram of the value obtained; the line shows the distribution according to the Central Limit Theorem.

keep this in perspective: the age of the universe is currently estimated to be about 15 billion years, which is about $4 \cdot 10^{17}$ seconds. So, even if we had made *a thousand trials per second since the beginning of time*, we would still not have found a value as large or larger than $x = 10$!

Although the Gaussian is defined for all x, its weight is so strongly concentrated within a finite, and actually quite small, interval (about $[-5, 5]$) that values outside this range will not occur. It is not just that only one in a million events will deviate from the mean by more than 5 standard deviations: the decline continues, so that fewer than one in 10^{22} events will deviate by more than 10 standard deviations. Large outliers are not just rare—they don't happen!

This is both the strength and the limitation of the Gaussian model: *if* the Gaussian model applies, then we know that all variation in the data will be relatively small and therefore "benign." At the same time, we know that for some systems, large outliers do occur in practice. This means that, for such systems, the Gaussian model *and theories based on it* will not apply, resulting in bad guidance or outright wrong results. (We will return to this problem shortly.)

Why Is the Gaussian so Useful?

It is the combination of two properties that makes the Gaussian probability distribution so common and useful: because of the Central Limit Theorem, the Gaussian distribution will occur whenever we we dealing with averages; and because so much of the Gaussian's weight is concentrated in the central region, almost any expression can be approximated by concentrating only on the central region, while largely disregarding the tails.

As we will discuss in Chapter 10 in more detail, the first of these two arguments has been put to good use by the creators of classical statistics: although we may not know anything about the distribution of the actual data points, the Central Limit Theorem enables us to make statements about their averages. Hence, if we concentrate on estimating the sample *average* of any quantity, then we are on much firmer ground, theoretically. And it is impressive to see how classical statistics is able to make rigorous statements about the extent of confidence intervals for parameter estimates while using almost no information beyond the data points themselves! I'd like to emphasize these two points again: through clever application of the Central Limit Theorem, classical statistics is able to give *rigorous* (not just intuitive) bounds on estimates—and it can do so without requiring detailed knowledge of (or making additional assumptions about) the system under investigation. This is a remarkable achievement!

The price we pay for this rigor is that we lose much of the richness of the original data set: the distribution of points has been boiled down to a single number—the average.

The second argument is not so relevant from a conceptual point, but it is, of course, of primary practical importance: we can actually do many integrals involving Gaussians, either exactly or in very good approximation. In fact, the Gaussian is so convenient in this regard that it is often the first choice when an integration kernel is needed (we have already seen examples of this in Chapter 2, in the context of kernel density estimates, and in Chapter 4, when we discussed the smoothing of a time series).

Optional: Gaussian Integrals

The basic idea goes like this: we want to evaluate an integral of the form:

$$\int f(x)e^{-x^2/2}\,dx$$

We know that the Gaussian is peaked around $x = 0$, so that only nearby points will contribute significantly to the value of the integral. We can therefore expand $f(x)$ in a power series for small x. Even if this expansion is no good for large x, the result will not be affected significantly because those points are suppressed by the Gaussian. We end up with a series of integrals of the form

$$a_n \int x^n e^{-x^2/2}\,dx$$

which can be performed exactly. (Here, a_n is the expansion coefficient from the expansion of $f(x)$.)

We can push this idea even further. Assume that the kernel is not exactly Gaussian but is still strongly peaked:

$$\int f(x)e^{-g(x)}\,\mathrm{d}x$$

where the function $g(x)$ has a minimum at some location (otherwise, the kernel would not have a peak at all). We can now expand $g(x)$ into a Taylor series around its minimum (let's assume it is at $x = 0$), retaining only the first two terms:
$g(x) \approx g(0) + g''(0)x^2/2 + \cdots$. The linear term vanishes because the first derivative g' must be zero at a minimum. Keeping in mind that the first term in this expansion is a constant not depending on x, we have transformed the original integral to one of Gaussian type:

$$e^{-g(0)}\int f(x)e^{-g''(0)\,x^2/2}\,\mathrm{d}x$$

which we already know how to solve.

This technique goes by the name of *Laplace's method* (not to be confused with "Gaussian integration," which is something else entirely).

Beware: The World Is Not Normal!

Given that the Central Limit Theorem is a rigorously proven theorem, what could possibly go wrong? After all, the Gaussian distribution guarantees the absence of outliers, doesn't it? Yet we all know that unexpected events *do* occur.

There are two things that can go wrong with the discussion so far:

- The Central Limit Theorem only applies to sums or averages of random quantities but not necessarily to the random quantities themselves. The distribution of individual data points may be quite different from a Gaussian, so if we want to reason about individual events (rather than about an aggregate such as their average), then we may need different methods. For example, although the *average* number of items in a shipment may be Gaussian distributed around a typical value of three items per shipment, there is no guarantee that the actual distribution of items per shipment will follow the same distribution. In fact, the distribution will probably be geometrical, with shipments containing only a single item being much more common than any other shipment size.

- More importantly, the Central Limit Theorem *may not apply*. Remember the three conditions listed as requirements for the Central Limit Theorem to hold? Individual events must be independent, follow the same distribution, and must have a finite mean and standard deviation. As it turns out, the first and second of these conditions can be weakened (meaning that individual events can be somewhat correlated and drawn from slightly different distributions), but the third condition *cannot* be weakened: individual events *must* be drawn from a distribution of finite width.

Now this may seem like a minor matter: surely, all distributions occurring in practice are of finite width, aren't they? As it turns out, the answer is *no*! Apparently "pathological" distributions of this kind are much more common in real life than one might expect. Such distributions follow *power-law* behavior, and they are the topic of the next section.

Power-Law Distributions and Non-Normal Statistics

Let's start with an example. Figure 9-4 shows a histogram for the number of visits per person that a sample of visitors made to a certain website over one month. Two things stand out: the huge number of people who made a handful of visits (fewer than 5 or 6) and, at the other extreme, the huge number of visits that a few people made. (The heaviest user made 41,661 visits: that's about one per minute over the course of the month—probably a bot or monitor of some sort.)

This distribution looks nothing like the "benign" case in Figure 9-2. The distribution in Figure 9-4 is not merely skewed—it would be no exaggeration to say that it consists *entirely* of outliers! Ironically, the "average" number of visits per person—calculated naively, by summing the visits and dividing by the number of unique visitors—equals 26 visits per person. This number is clearly not representative of anything: it describes neither the huge majority of light users on the lefthand side of the graph (who made one or two visits), nor the small group of heavy users on the right. (The standard deviation is ±437, which clearly suggests that something is not right, given that the mean is 26 and the number of visits must be positive.)

This kind of behavior is typical for distributions with so-called *fat* or *heavy tails*. In contrast to systems ruled by a Gaussian distribution or another distribution with short tails, data values are not effectively limited to a narrow domain. Instead, we can find a nonnegligible fraction of data points that are very far away from the majority of points.

Mathematically speaking, a distribution is heavy-tailed if it falls to zero much slower than an exponential function. Power laws (*i.e.*, functions that behave as $\sim 1/x^{\beta}$ for some exponent $\beta > 0$) are usually used to describe such behavior.

In Chapter 3, we discussed how to recognize power laws: data points falling onto a straight line on a double logarithmic plot. A double logarithmic plot of the data from Figure 9-4 is shown in Figure 9-5, and we see that eventually (*i.e.*, for more than five visits per person), the data indeed follows a power law (approximately $\sim x^{-1.9}$). On the lefthand side of Figure 9-5 (*i.e.*, for few visits per person), the behavior is different. (We will come back to this point later.)

Power-law distributions like the one describing the data set in in Figures 9-4 and 9-5 are surprisingly common. They have been observed in a number of different (and often colorful) areas: the frequency with which words are used in texts, the magnitude of

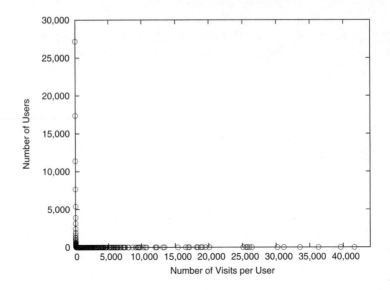

FIGURE 9-4. A histogram of the number of visitors who made x number of visits to a certain website. Note the extreme skewness of the distribution: most visitors made one or two visits, but a few made tens of thousands of visits.

earthquakes, the size of files, the copies of books sold, the intensity of wars, the sizes of sand particles and solar flares, the population of cities, and the distribution of wealth. Power-law distributions go by different names in different contexts—you will find them referred to as "Zipf" of "Pareto" distributions, but the mathematical structure is always the same. The term "power-law distribution" is probably the most widely accepted, general term for this kind of heavy-tailed distribution.

Whenever they were found, power-law distributions were met with surprise and (usually) consternation. The reason is that they possess some unexpected and counterintuitive properties:

- Observations span a wide range of values, often many orders of magnitude.

- There is no typical scale or value that could be used to summarize the distribution of points.

- The distribution is extremely skewed, with many data points at the low end and few (but not negligibly few) data points at *very* high values.

- Expectation values often depend on the sample size. Taking the average over a sample of *n* points may yield a significantly smaller value than taking the average over 2*n* or 10*n* data points. (This is in marked contrast to most other distributions, where the quality of the average improves when it is based on more points. Not so for power-law distributions!)

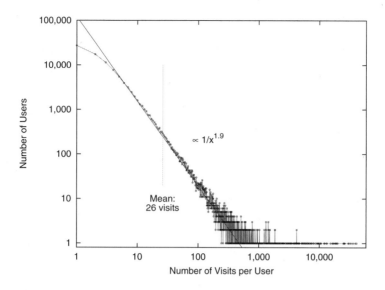

FIGURE 9-5. *The data from Figure 9-4 but on double logarithmic scales. The righthand side of this curve is well described by the power law* $1/x^{1.9}$.

It is the last item that is the most disturbing. After all, didn't the Central Limit Theorem tell us that the scatter of the average was always reduced by a factor of $1/\sqrt{n}$ as the sample size increases? Yes, but remember the caveat at the end of the last section: the Central Limit Theorem applies only to those distributions that have a finite mean and standard deviation. For power-law distributions, this condition is not necessarily fulfilled, and hence the Central Limit Theorem does *not* apply.

The importance of this fact cannot be overstated. Not only does much of our intuition go out the window but most of statistical theory, too! For the most part, distributions without expectations are simply not treated by standard probability theory and statistics.[*]

Working with Power-Law Distributions

So what should you do when you encounter a situation described by a power-law distribution? The most important thing is to *stop using classical methods*. In particular, the mean-field approach (replacing the distribution by its mean) is no longer applicable and will give misleading or incorrect results.

From a practical point of view, you can try segmenting the data (and, by implication, the system) into different groups: the majority of data points at small values (on the lefthand side in Figure 9-5), the set of data points in the tail of the distribution (for relatively large

---

[*]The comment on page 48 (out of 440) of Larry Wasserman's excellent *All of Statistics* is typical: "From now on, whenever we discuss expectations, we implicitly assume that they exist."

values), and possibly even a group of data points making up the intermediate regime. Each such group is now more homogeneous, so that standard methods may apply. You will need insight into the business domain of the data, and you should exercise discretion when determining where to make those cuts, because the data itself will not yield a natural "scale" or other quantity that could be used for this purpose.

There is one more practical point that you should be aware of when working with power-law distributions: the form $\sim 1/x^\beta$ is only valid "asymptotically" for large values of x. For small x, this rule must be supplemented, since it obviously cannot hold for $x \to 0$ (we can't divide by zero). There are several ways to augment the original form near $x = 0$. We can either impose a minimum value x_{min} of x and consider the distribution only for values larger than this. That is often a reasonable approach because such a minimum value may exist naturally. For example there is an obvious "minimum" number of pages (*i.e.*, one page) that a website visitor can view and still be considered a "visitor." Similar considerations hold for the population of a city and the copies of books sold—all are limited on the left by $x_{min} = 1$. Alternatively, the behavior of the observed distribution may be different for small values. Look again at Figure 9-5: for values less than about 5, the curve deviates from the power-law behavior that we find elsewhere.

Depending on the shape that we require near zero, we can modify the original rule in different ways. Two examples stand out: if we want a flat peak for $x = 0$, then we can try a form like $\sim 1/(a + x^\beta)$ for some $a > 0$, and if we require a peak at a nonzero location, we can use a distribution like $\sim \exp(-C/x)/x^\beta$ (see Figure 9-6). For specific values of β, two distributions of this kind have special names:

$$\frac{1}{\pi} \frac{1}{1 + x^2} \quad \text{Cauchy distribution}$$

$$\sqrt{\frac{c}{2\pi}} \frac{e^{-c/2x}}{x^{3/2}} \quad \text{Lévy distribution}$$

Optional: Distributions with Infinite Expectation Values

The *expectation value* $E(f)$ of a function $f(x)$, which in turn depends on some random quantity x, is nothing but the weighted average of that function in which we use the probability density $p(x)$ of x as the weight function:

$$E(f) = \int f(x)p(x)\ dx$$

Of particular importance are the expectation values for simple powers of the variable x, the so called *moments* of the distribution:

$$E(1) = \int p(x)\ dx \qquad \text{(must always equal 1)}$$

$$E(x) = \int x\ p(x)\ dx \qquad \text{Mean or first moment}$$

$$E(x^2) = \int x^2 p(x)\ dx \qquad \text{Second moment}$$

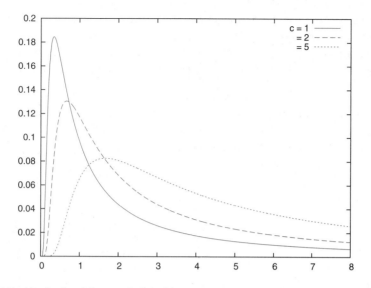

FIGURE 9-6. *The Lévy distribution for several values of the parameter* c.

The first expression must always equal 1, because we expect $p(x)$ to be properly normalized. The second is the familiar mean, as the weighted average of x. The last expression is used in the definition of the standard deviation:

$$\sigma = \sqrt{E(x^2) - E(x)^2}$$

For power-law distributions, which behave as $\sim 1/x^\beta$ with $\beta > 1$ for large x, some of these integrals may not converge—in this case, the corresponding moment "does not exist." Consider the kth moment (C is the normalization constant $C = E(1) = \int p(x)\,\mathrm{d}x$):

$$E(x^k) = C \int^\infty x^k \frac{1}{x^\beta} \,\mathrm{d}x$$
$$= C \int^\infty \frac{1}{x^{\beta-k}} \,\mathrm{d}x$$

Unless $\beta - k > 1$, this integral does not converge at the upper limit of integration. (I assume that the integral is proper at the lower limit of integration, through a lower cutoff $x_{\min}$ or another one of the methods discussed previously.) In particular, if $\beta < 2$, then the mean and all higher moments do not exist; if $\beta < 3$, then the standard deviation does not exist.

We need to understand that this is an analytical result—it tells us that the distribution is ill behaved and that, for instance, the Central Limit Theorem does not apply in this case. Of course, for any *finite* sample of n data points drawn from such a distribution, the mean (or other moment) will be perfectly finite. But these analytical results warn us that, if we continue to draw additional data points from the distribution, then their average (or other moment) will not settle down: it will grow as the number of data points in the sample grows. Any summary statistic calculated from a finite sample of points will therefore not be a good estimator for the true (in this case: infinite) value of that statistic. This poses an obvious problem because, of course, all practical samples contain only a finite number of points.

Power-law distributions have no parameters that could (or need be) estimated—except for the exponent, which we know how to obtain from a double logarithmic plot. There is also a maximum likelihood estimator for the exponent:

$$\beta = 1 + \frac{n}{\sum_{i=0}^{n} \log \frac{x_i}{x_0}}$$

where x_0 is the smallest value of x for which the asymptotic power-law behavior holds.

Where to Go from Here

If you want to dig deeper into the theory of heavy-tail phenomena, you will find that it is a mess. There are two reasons for that: on the one hand, the material is technically hard (since one must make do without two standard tools: expectation values and the Central Limit Theorem), so few simple, substantial, powerful results have been obtained—a fact that is often covered up by excessive formalism. On the other hand, the "colorful" and multi disciplinary context in which power-law distributions are found has led to much confusion. Similar results are being discovered and re-discovered in various fields, with each field imposing its own terminology and methodology, thereby obscuring the mathematical commonalities.

The unexpected and often almost paradoxical consequences of power-law behavior also seem to demand an explanation for *why* such distributions occur in practice and whether they might all be expressions of some common mechanisms. Quite a few theories have been proposed toward this end, but none has found widespread acceptance or proved particularly useful in predicting new phenomena—occasionally grandiose claims to the contrary notwithstanding.

At this point, I think it is fair to say that we don't understand heavy-tail phenomena: not when and why they occur, nor how to handle them if they do.

Other Distributions

There are some other distributions that describe common scenarios you should be aware of. Some of the most important (or most frequently used) ones are described in this section.

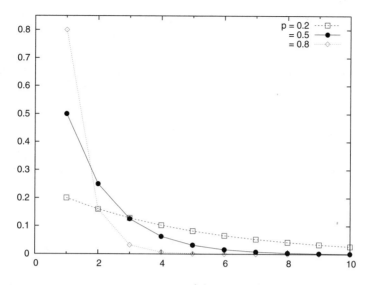

FIGURE 9-7. The geometric distribution: $p(k, p) = p(1 - p)^{k-1}$.

Geometric Distribution

The geometric distribution (see Figure 9-7):

$$p(k, p) = p(1 - p)^{k-1} \quad \text{with } k = 1, 2, 3, \ldots$$

is a special case of the binomial distribution. It can be viewed as the probability of obtaining the first Success at the kth trial (*i.e.*, after observing $k - 1$ failures). Note that there is only a single arrangement of events for this outcome, hence the combinatorial factor is equal to one. The geometric distribution has mean $\mu = 1/p$ and standard deviation $\sigma = \sqrt{1 - p}/p$.

Poisson Distribution

The binomial distribution gives us the probability of observing exactly k events in n distinct trials. In contrast, the Poisson distribution describes the probability of finding k events during some continuous observation *interval* of known length. Rather than being characterized by a probability parameter and a number of trials (as for the binomial distribution), the Poisson distribution is characterized by a *rate* λ and an *interval length* t.

The Poisson distribution $p(k, t, \lambda)$ gives the probability of observing exactly k events during an interval of length t when the rate at which events occur is λ (see Figure 9-8):

$$p(k, t, \lambda) = \frac{(\lambda t)^k}{k!} e^{-\lambda t}$$

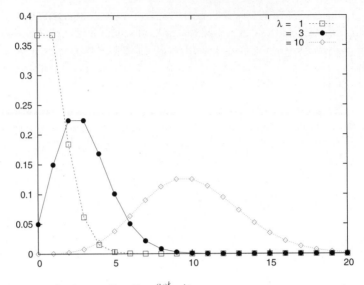

FIGURE 9-8. The Poisson distribution: $p(k, t, \lambda) = \frac{(\lambda t)^k}{k!} e^{-\lambda t}$.

Because t and λ only occur together, this expression is often written in a two-parameter form as $p(k, \nu) = e^{-\nu} \nu^k / k!$. Also note that the term $e^{-\lambda t}$ does not depend on k at all—it is merely there as a normalization factor. All the action is in the fractional part of the equation.

Let's look at an example. Assume that phone calls arrive at a call center at a rate of 15 calls per hour (so that $\lambda = 0.25$ calls/minute). Then the Poisson distribution $p(k, 1, 0.25)$ will give us the probability that $k = 0, 1, 2, \ldots$ calls will arrive in any given minute. But we can also use it to calculate the probability that k calls will arrive during any 5-minute time period: $p(k, 5, 0.25)$. Note that in this context, it makes no sense to speak of independent trials: time passes continuously, and the expected number of events depends on the length of the observation interval.

We can collect a few results. Mean μ and standard deviation σ for the Poisson distribution are given by:

$$\mu = \lambda t$$
$$\sigma = \sqrt{\lambda t}$$

Notice that only a single parameter (λt) controls both the location and the width of the distribution. For large λ, the Poisson distribution approaches a Gaussian distribution with $\mu = \lambda$ and $\sigma = \sqrt{\lambda}$. Only for small values of λ (say, $\lambda < 20$) are the differences notable.

Conversely, to estimate the parameter λ from observations, we divide the number k of events observed by the length t of the observation period: $\lambda = k/t$. Keep in mind that when evaluating the formula for the Poisson distribution, the rate λ and the length t of the interval of interest must be of compatible units. To find the probability of k calls over 6 minutes in our call center example above, we can either use $t = 6$ minutes and $\lambda = 0.25$ calls per minute or $t = 0.1$ hours and $\lambda = 15$ calls per hour, but we cannot mix them. (Also note that $6 \cdot 0.25 = 0.1 \cdot 15 = 1.5$, as it should.)

The Poisson distribution is appropriate for processes in which discrete events occur independently and at a constant rate: calls to a call center, misprints in a manuscript, traffic accidents, and so on. However, you have to be careful: it applies only if you can identify a rate at which events occur *and* if you are interested specifically in the number of events that occur during intervals of varying length. (You cannot expect every histogram to follow a Poisson distribution just because "we are counting events.")

Log-Normal Distribution

Some quantities are inherently asymmetrical. Consider, for example, the time it takes people to complete a certain task: because everyone is different, we expect a distribution of values. However, all values are necessarily positive (since times cannot be negative). Moreover, we can expect a particular shape of the distribution: there will be some minimum time that nobody can beat, then a small group of very fast champions, a peak at the most typical completion time, and finally a long tail of stragglers. Clearly, such a distribution will not be well described by a Gaussian, which is defined for both positive and negative values of x, is symmetric, and has short tails!

The log-normal distribution is an example of an asymmetric distribution that is suitable for such cases. It is related to the Gaussian: a quantity follows the log-normal distribution if its logarithm is distributed according to a Gaussian.

The probability density for the log-normal distribution looks like this:

$$p(x; \mu, \sigma) = \frac{1}{\sqrt{2\pi}\sigma x} \exp\left(-\frac{1}{2}\left(\frac{\log(x/\mu)}{\sigma}\right)^2\right)$$

(The additional factor of x in the denominator stems from the Jacobian in the change of variables from x to $\log x$.) You may often find the log-normal distribution written slightly differently:

$$p(x; \tilde{\mu}, \sigma) = \frac{1}{\sqrt{2\pi}\sigma x} \exp\left(-\frac{1}{2}\left(\frac{\log(x) - \tilde{\mu}}{\sigma}\right)^2\right)$$

This is the same once you realize that $\log(x/\mu) = \log(x) - \log(\mu)$ and make the identification $\tilde{\mu} = \log(\mu)$. The first form is much better because it expresses clearly that μ is the *typical scale* of the problem. It also ensures that the argument of the logarithm is dimensionless (as it must be).

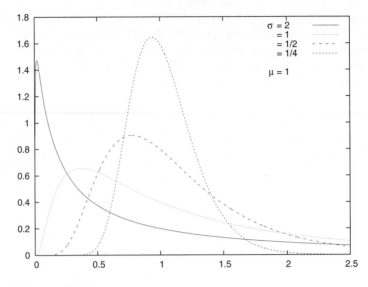

FIGURE 9-9. The log-normal distribution.

Figure 9-9 shows the log-normal distribution for a few different values of σ. The parameter σ controls the overall "shape" of the curve, whereas the parameter μ controls its "scale." In general, it can be difficult to predict what the curve will look like for different values of the parameters, but here are some results (the *mode* is the position of the peak).

$$\text{Mode:} \quad \mu e^{-\sigma^2}$$

$$\text{Mean:} \quad \mu e^{\frac{\sigma^2}{2}}$$

$$\text{Standard deviation:} \quad \mu \sqrt{e^{\sigma^2}\left(e^{\sigma^2}-1\right)}$$

Values for the parameters can be estimated from a data set as follows:

$$\mu = \exp\left(\frac{1}{n}\sum_{i=1}^{n}\log x_i\right)$$

$$\sigma = \sqrt{\frac{1}{n}\sum_{i=1}^{n}\left(\log\frac{x_i}{\mu}\right)^2}$$

The log-normal distribution is important as an example of a standard statistical distribution that provides an alternative to the Gaussian model for situations that require an asymmetrical distribution. That being said, the log-normal distribution can be fickle to use in practice. Not all asymmetric point distributions are described well by a log-normal distribution, and you may not be able to obtain a good fit for your data using a log-normal distribution. For truly heavy-tail phenomena in particular, you will need a power-law distribution after all. Also keep in mind that the log-normal distribution approaches the Gaussian as σ becomes small compared to μ (*i.e.*, $\sigma/\mu \ll 1$), at which point it becomes easier to work with the familiar Gaussian directly.

Special-Purpose Distributions

Many additional distributions have been defined and studied. Some, such as the gamma distribution, are mostly of theoretical importance, whereas others—such as the chi-square, t, and F distributions—are are at the core of classical, frequentist statistics (we will encounter them again in Chapter 10). Still others have been developed to model specific scenarios occurring in practical applications—especially in reliability engineering, where the objective is to make predictions about likely failure rates and survival times.

I just want to mention in passing a few terms that you may encounter. The *Weibull* distribution is used to express the probability that a device will fail after a certain time. Like the log-normal distribution, it depends on both a shape and a scale parameter. Depending on the value of the shape parameter, the Weibull distribution can be used to model different failure modes. These include "infant mortality" scenarios, where devices are more likely to fail early but the failure rate declines over time as defective items disappear from the population, and "fatigue death" scenarios, where the failure rate rises over time as items age.

Yet another set of distributions goes by the name of *extreme-value* or *Gumbel* distributions. They can be used to obtain the probability that the smallest (or largest) value of some random quantity will be of a certain size. In other words, they answer the question: what is the probability that the largest element in a set of random numbers is precisely x?

Quite intentionally, I don't give formulas for these distributions here. They are rather advanced and specialized tools, and if you want to use them, you will need to consult the appropriate references. However, the important point to take away here is that, for many typical scenarios involving random quantities, people have developed explicit models and studied their properties; hence a little research may well turn up a solution to whatever your current problem is.

Optional: Case Study—Unique Visitors over Time

To put some of the ideas introduced in the last two chapters into practice, let's look at an example that is a bit more involved. We begin with a probabilistic argument and use it to develop a mean-field model, which in turn will lead to a differential equation that we proceed to solve for our final answer. This example demonstrates how all the different ideas we have been introducing in the last few chapter can fit together to tackle more complicated problems.

Imagine you are running a website. Users visit this website every day of the month at a rate that is roughly constant. We can also assume that we are able to track the identity of these users (through a cookie or something like that). By studying those cookies, we can see that some users visit the site only once in any given month while others visit it several times. We are interested in the number of *unique users* for the month and, in particular, how this number develops over the course of the month. (The number of unique visitors is a key metric in Internet advertising, for instance.)

The essential difficulty is that some users visit several times during the month, and so the number of unique visitors is smaller than the total number of visitors. Furthermore, we will observe a "saturation effect": on the first day, almost every user is new; but on the last day of the month, we can expect to have seen many of the visitors earlier in the month already.

We would like to develop some understanding for the number of unique visitors that can be expected for each day of the month (*e.g.*, to monitor whether we are on track to meet some monthly goal for the number of unique visitors). To make progress, we need to develop a model.

To see more clearly, we use the following idealization, which is equivalent to the original problem. Consider an urn that contains N identical tokens (total number of potential visitors). At each turn (every day), we draw k tokens randomly from the urn (average number of visitors per day). We mark all of the drawn tokens to indicate that we have "seen" them and then place them back into the urn. This cycle is repeated for every day of the month.

Because at each turn we mark all unmarked tokens from the random sample drawn at this turn, the number of marked tokens in the urn will increase over time. Because each token is marked at most once, the number of marked tokens in the urn at the end of the month is the number of unique visitors that have visited during that time period.

Phrased this way, the process can be modeled as a sequence of Bernoulli trials. We define drawing an already marked token as Success. Because the number of marked tokens in the urn is increasing, the success probability p will change over time. The relevant variables are:

N Total number of tokens in urn

k Number of tokens drawn at each turn

$m(t)$ Number of already-marked tokens drawn at turn t

$n(t)$ Total number of marked tokens in urn at time t

$p(t) = \dfrac{n(t)}{N}$ Probability of drawing an already-marked token at turn t

Each day consists of a new Bernoulli trial in which k tokens are drawn from the urn. However, because the number of marked tokens in the urn increases every day, the probability $p(t)$ is different every day.

On day t, we have $n(t)$ marked tokens in the urn. We now draw k tokens, of which we expect $m(t) = kp(t)$ to be marked (Successes). This is simply an application of the basic result for the expectation value of Bernoulli trials, using the current value for the probability. (Working with the expectation value in this way constitutes a mean-field approximation.)

The number of unmarked tokens in the current drawing is:

$$k - m(t) = k - kp(t) = k(1 - p(t))$$

We now mark these tokens and place them back into the urn, which means that the number of marked tokens in the urn grows by $k(1 - p(t))$:

$$n(t + 1) = n(t) + k(1 - p(t))$$

This equation simply expresses the fact that the new number of marked tokens $n(t + 1)$ consists of the previous number of marked tokens $n(t)$ *plus* the newly marked tokens $k(1 - p(t))$.

We can now divide both sides by N (the total number of tokens). Recalling that $p(t) = n(t)/N$, we write:

$$p(t + 1) = p(t) + f(1 - p(t)) \quad \text{with } f = \frac{k}{N}$$

This is a recurrence relation for $p(t)$, which can be rewritten as:

$$p(t + 1) - p(t) = f(1 - p(t))$$

In the continuum limit, we replace the difference between the "new" and the "old" values by the *derivative* at time t, which turns the recurrence relation into a more convenient differential equation:

$$\frac{dp(t)}{dt} = f(1 - p(t))$$

with initial condition $p(t = 0) = 0$ (because initially there are no marked tokens in the urn). This differential equation has the solution:

$$p(t) = 1 - e^{-ft}$$

Figure 9-10 shows $p(t)$ for various values of the parameter f. (The parameter f has an obvious interpretation as size of each drawing expressed as a fraction of the total number of tokens in the urn.)

This is the result that we have been looking for. Remember that $p(t) = n(t)/N$; hence the probability is directly proportional to the number of unique visitors so far. We can rewrite it more explicitly as:

$$n(t) = N\left(1 - e^{-\frac{k}{N}t}\right)$$

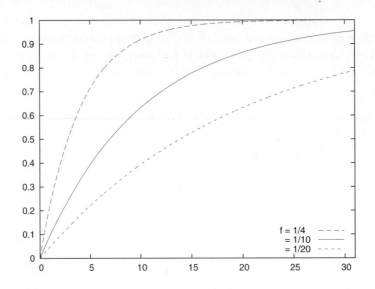

FIGURE 9-10. Fraction of unique visitors seen on day t. The parameter f is the number of daily users expressed as a fraction of all potential users.

In this form, the equation gives us, for each day of the month, the number of unique visitors for the month up to that date. There is only one unknown parameter: N, the total number of *potential* visitors. (We know k, the average number of total visitors per day, because this number is immediately available from the web-server logs.) We can now try to fit one or two months' worth of data to this formula to obtain a value for N. Once we have determined N, the formula predicts the expected number of unique visitors for each day of the month. We can use this information to track whether the actual number of unique visitors for the current month is above or below expectations.

The steps we took in this little example are typical of a lot of modeling. We start with a real problem in a specific situation. To make headway, we recast it in an idealized format that tries to retain only the most relevant information. (In this example: mapping the original problem to an idealized urn model.) Expressing things in terms of an idealized model helps us recognize the problem as one we know how to solve. (Urn models have been studied extensively; in this example, we could identify it with Bernoulli trials, which we know how to handle.) Finding a solution often requires that we make actual approximations in addition to the abstraction from the problem domain to an idealized model. (Working with the expectation value was one such approximation to make the problem tractable; replacing the recurrence relation with a differential equation was another.) Finally, we end up with a "model" that involves some unknown parameters. If we are mostly interested in developing conceptual understanding, then we don't need to go any further, since we can read off the model's behavior directly from the formula.

However, if we actually want to make numerical predictions, then we'll need to find numerical values for those parameters, which is usually done by fitting the model to some already available data. (We should also try to validate the model to see whether it gives a good "fit"; refer to the discussion in Chapter 3 on examining residuals, for instance.)

Finally, I should point out that the model in this example is simplified—as models usually are. The most critical simplification (which would most likely *not* be correct in a real application) is that every token in the urn has the same probability of being drawn at each turn. In contrast, if look at the behavior of actual visitors, we will find that some are much more likely to visit more frequently while others are less likely to visit. Another simplification is that we assumed the total number of potential visitors to be constant. But if we have a website that sees significant growth from one month to the next, this assumption may not be correct, either. You may want to try and build an improved model that takes these (and perhaps other) considerations into account. (The first one in particular is not easy—in fact, if you succeed, then let me know how you did it!)

Workshop: Power-Law Distributions

The crazy effects of power-law distributions have to be seen to be believed. In this workshop, we shall generate (random) data points distributed according to a power-law distribution and begin to study their properties.

First question: how does one actually generate nonuniformly distributed random numbers on a computer? A random generator that produces uniformly distributed numbers is available in almost all programming environments, but generating random numbers distributed according to some other distribution requires a little bit more work. There are different ways of going about it; some are specific to certain distributions only, whereas others are designed for speed in particular applications. We'll discuss a simple method that works for distributions that are analytically known.

The starting point is the cumulative distribution function for the distribution in question. By construction, the distribution function is strictly monotonic and takes on values in the interval [0, 1]. If we now generate uniformly distributed numbers between 0 and 1, then we can find the locations at which the cumulative distribution function assumes these values. These points will be distributed according to the desired distribution (see Figure 9-11).

(A good way to think about this is as follows. Imagine you distribute *n* points *uniformly* on the interval [0, 1] and find the corresponding locations at which the cumulative distribution function assumes these values. These locations are spaced according to the distribution in question—after all, by construction, the probability grows by the same amount between successive locations. Now use points that are randomly distributed, rather than uniformly, and you end up with random points distributed according to the desired distribution.)

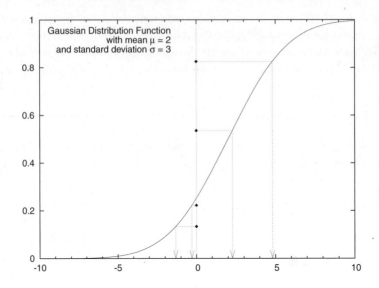

FIGURE 9-11. Generating random numbers from the Gaussian distribution: generate uniformly distributed numbers between 0 and 1, then find the locations values at which the Gaussian distribution function assumes these values. The locations follow a Gaussian distribution.

For power-law distributions, we can easily work out the cumulative distribution function and its inverse. Let the probability density $p(x)$ be:

$$p(x) = \frac{\alpha}{x^{\alpha+1}} \quad x \geq 1, \alpha > 0$$

This is known as the the "standard" form of the Pareto distribution. It is valid for values of x greater than 1. (Values of $x < 1$ have zero probability of occurring.) The parameter α is the "shape parameter" and must be greater than zero, because otherwise the probability is not normalizable. (This is a different convention than the one we used earlier: $\beta = 1 + \alpha$.)

We can work out the cumulative distribution function $P(x)$:

$$P(x) = y = \int_1^x p(t)\,dt$$
$$= 1 - \frac{1}{x^\alpha}$$

This expression can be inverted to give:

$$x = \frac{1}{(1-y)^{1/\alpha}}$$

If we now use uniformly distributed random values for y, then the values for x will be distributed according to the Pareto distribution that we started with. (For other distributions, such as the Gaussian, inverting the expression for the cumulative distribution function is often harder, and you may have to find a numerical library that includes the inverse of the distribution function explicitly.)

Now remember what we said earlier. If the exponent in the denominator is less than 2 (*i.e.*, if $\beta \leq 2$ or $\alpha \leq 1$), then the "mean does not exist." In practice, we can evaluate the mean for any sample of points, and for any *finite* sample the mean will, of course, also be finite. But as we take more and more points, the mean does not settle down—instead it keeps on growing. On the other hand, if the exponent in the denominator is strictly greater than 2 (*i.e.*, if $\beta > 2$ or $\alpha > 1$), then the mean does exist, and its value does not depend on the sample size.

I would like to emphasize again how counterintuitive the behavior for $\alpha \leq 1$ is. We usually expect that larger samples will give us better results with less noise. But in this particular scenario, the opposite is true!

We can explore behavior of this type using the simple program shown below. All it does is generate 10 million random numbers distributed according to a Pareto distribution. I generate those numbers using the method described at the beginning of this section; alternatively, I could have used the `paretovariate()` function in the standard `random` module. We maintain a running total of all values (so that we can form the mean) and also keep track of the largest value seen so far. The results for two runs with $\alpha = 0.5$ and $\alpha = 1.2$ are shown in Figures 9-12 and 9-13, respectively.

```
import sys, random

def pareto( alpha ):
    y = random.random()
    return 1.0/pow( 1-y, 1.0/alpha )


alpha = float( sys.argv[1] )

n, ttl, mx = 0, 0, 0

while n<1e7:
    n += 1

    v = pareto( alpha )

    ttl += v
    mx = max( mx, v )

    if( n%50000 == 0 ):
        print n, ttl/n, mx
```

The typical behavior for situations with $\alpha \leq 1$ versus $\alpha > 1$ is immediately apparent: whereas in Figure 9-13, the mean settles down pretty quickly to a finite value, the mean in Figure 9-12 continues to grow.

We can also recognize clearly what drives this behavior. For $\alpha \leq 1$, very large values occur relatively frequently. Each such occurrence leads to an upward jump in the total sum of values seen, which is reflected in a concomitant jump in the mean. Over time, as more trials are conducted, the denominator in the mean grows, and hence the value of the

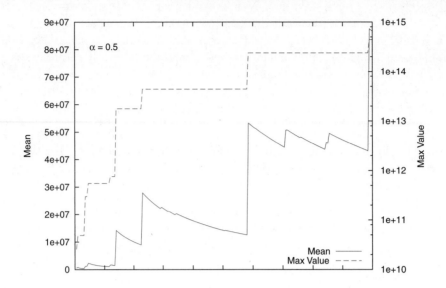

FIGURE 9-12. Sampling from the Pareto distribution $P(x) = \frac{1}{2x^{3/2}}$. *Both the mean and the maximum value grow without bound.*

mean begins to fall. However (and this is what is different for $\alpha \leq 1$ versus $\alpha > 1$), before the mean has fallen back to its previous value, a *further* extraordinarily large value occurs, driving the sum (and hence the mean) up again, with the consequence that the numerator of the expression `ttl/n` in the example program grows faster than the denominator.

You may want to experiment yourself with this kind of system. The behavior at the borderline value of $\alpha = 1$ is particularly interesting. You may also want to investigate how quickly `ttl/n` grows with different values of α. Finally, don't restrict yourself only to the mean. Similar considerations hold for the standard deviation (see our discussion regarding this point earlier in the chapter).

Further Reading

- *An Introduction to Probability Theory and Its Applications, vol. 1.* William Feller. 3rd ed., Wiley. 1968.
  Every introductory book on probability theory covers most of the material in this chapter. This classic is my personal favorite for its deep, yet accessible treatment and for its large selection of interesting or amusing examples.

- *An Introduction to Mathematical Statistics and Its Applications.* Richard J. Larsen and Morris L. Marx. 4th ed., Prentice Hall. 2005.
  This is my favorite book on theoretical statistics. The first third contains a good, practical introduction to many of this chapter's topics.

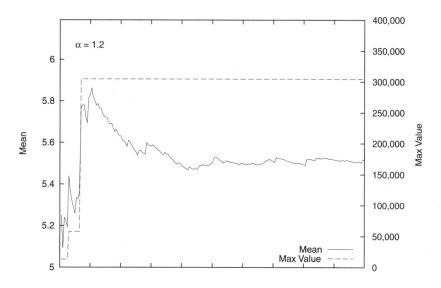

FIGURE 9-13. Sampling from the Pareto distribution $P(x) = \frac{1.2}{x^{2.2}}$. Both the mean and the maximum reach a finite value and retain it as we continue to make further drawings.

- *NIST/SEMATECH e-Handbook of Statistical Methods.* NIST. *http://www.itl.nist.gov/div898/handbook/.* 2010.
  This free ebook is made available by the National Institute for Standards and Technology (NIST). There is a wealth of reliable, high-quality information here.

- *Statistical Distributions.* Merran Evans, Nicholas Hastings, and Brian Peacock. 3rd ed., Wiley. 2000.
  This short and accessible reference includes basic information on 40 of the most useful or important probability distributions. If you want to know what distributions exist and what their properties are, this is a good place to start.

- "Power Laws, Pareto Distributions and Zipf's Law." M. E. J. Newman. *Contemporary Physics* 46 (2005), p. 323.
  This review paper provides a knowledgeable yet very readable introduction to the field of power laws and heavy-tail phenomena. Highly recommended. (Versions of the document can be found on the Web.)

- *Modeling Complex Systems.* Nino Boccara. 2nd ed., Springer. 2010.
  Chapter 8 of this book provides a succinct and level-headed overview of the current state of research into power-law phenomena.

## CHAPTER TEN

What You Really Need to Know About Classical Statistics

BASIC CLASSICAL STATISTICS HAS ALWAYS BEEN SOMEWHAT OF A MYSTERY TO ME: A TOPIC FULL OF OBSCURE notions, such as t-tests and p-values, and confusing statements like "we fail to reject the null hypothesis"—which I can read several times and still not know if it is saying yes, no, or maybe.[*] To top it all off, all this formidable machinery is then used to draw conclusions that don't seem to be all that interesting—it's usually something about whether the means of two data sets are the same or different. Why would I care?

Eventually I figured it out, and I also figured out why the field seemed so obscure initially. In this chapter, I want to explain what classical statistics does, why it is the way it is, and what it is good for. This chapter does not attempt to teach you how to perform any of the typical statistical methods: this would require a separate book. (I will make some recommendations for further reading on this topic at the end of this chapter.) Instead, in this chapter I will tell you what all these other books *omit*.

Let me take you on a trip. I hope you know where your towel is.

Genesis

To understand classical statistics, it is necessary to realize how it came about. The basic statistical methods that we know today were developed in the late 19th and early 20th centuries, mostly in Great Britain, by a very small group of people. Of those, one worked

---

[*] I am not alone—even professional statisticians have the same experience. See, for example, the preface of *Bayesian Statistics*. Peter M. Lee. Hodder & Arnold. 2004.

for the Guinness brewing company and another—the most influential one of them—worked at an agricultural research lab (trying to increase crop yields and the like). This bit of historical context tells us something about their working conditions and primary challenges.

No computational capabilities
> All computations had to be performed with paper and pencil.

No graphing capabilities, either
> All graphs had to be generated with pencil, paper, and a ruler. (And complicated graphs—such as those requiring prior transformations or calculations using the data—were especially cumbersome.)

Very small and very expensive data sets
> Data sets were small (often not more than four to five points) and could be obtained only with great difficulty. (When it always takes a full growing season to generate a new data set, you try *very* hard to make do with the data you already have!)

In other words, their situation was almost entirely the opposite of our situation today:

- Computational power that is essentially free (within reason)

- Interactive graphing and visualization capabilities on every desktop

- Often huge amounts of data

It should therefore come as no surprise that the methods developed by those early researchers seem so out of place to us: they spent a great amount of effort and ingenuity solving problems we simply no longer have! This realization goes a long way toward explaining why classical statistics is the way it is and why it often seems so strange to us today.

By contrast, *modern* statistics is very different. It places greater emphasis on nonparametric methods and Bayesian reasoning, and it leverages current computational capabilities through simulation and resampling methods. The book by Larry Wasserman (see the recommended reading at the end of this chapter) provides an overview of a more contemporary point of view.

However, almost all *introductory* statistics books—that is, those books one is likely to pick up as a beginner—continue to limit themselves to the same selection of slightly stale topics. Why is that? I believe it is a combination of institutional inertia together with the expectations of the "end-user" community. Statistics has always been a support science for other fields: originally agriculture but also medicine, psychology, sociology, and others. And these fields, which merely apply statistics but are not engaged in actively developing it themselves, continue to operate largely using classical methods. However, the machine-learning community—with its roots in computer science but great demand for statistical methods—provides a welcome push for the widespread adoption of more modern methods.

Keep this historical perspective in mind as we take a closer look at statistics in the rest of this chapter.

Statistics Defined

All of statistics deals with the following scenario: we have a *population*—that is the set of all possible outcomes. Typically, this set is large: all male U.S. citizens, for example, or all possible web-server response times. Rather than dealing with the total population (which might be impossible, infeasible, or merely inconvenient), we instead work with a *sample*. A sample is a subset of the total population that is chosen so as to be representative of the overall population. Now we may ask: what conclusions about the overall *population* can we draw given one specific *sample*? It is this particular question that classical statistics answers via a process known as *statistical inference*: properties of the population are inferred from properties of a sample.

Intuitively, we do this kind of thing all the time. For example, given the heights of five men (let's say 178 cm, 180 cm, 179 cm, 178 cm, and 180 cm), we are immediately comfortable calculating the average (which is 179 cm) and concluding that the "typical" body size for all men in the population (not just the five in the sample!) is 179 cm, "more or less." This is where formal classical statistics comes in: it provides us with a way of making the vague "more or less" statement precise and *quantitative*. Given the sample, statistical reasoning allows us to make specific statements about the population, such as, "We expect *x* percent of men to be between *y* and *z* cm tall," or, "We expect fewer than *x* percent of all men to be taller than *y* cm," and so on.

Classical statistics is mostly concerned with two procedures: *parameter estimation* (or "estimation" for short) and *hypothesis testing*. Parameter estimation works as follows. We assume that the population is described by some distribution—for example, the Gaussian:

$$N(x; \mu, \sigma) = \frac{1}{\sqrt{2\pi}\sigma} \exp\left(-\frac{1}{2}\left(\frac{x - \mu}{\sigma}\right)^2\right)$$

and we seek to estimate values for the parameters (μ and σ this case) from a sample. Note that once we have estimates for the parameters, the distribution describing the population is fully determined, and we can (at least in principle) calculate any desired property of the population directly from that distribution. Parameter estimation comes in two flavors: *point estimation* and *interval estimation*. The first just gives us a specific value for the parameter, whereas the second gives us a range of values that is supposed to contain the true value.

Compared with parameter estimation, hypothesis testing is the weirder of the two procedures. It does not attempt to quantify the size of an effect; it merely tries to determine whether there is any effect at all. Note well that this is a largely theoretical argument; from a practical point of view, the existence of an effect cannot be separated entirely from its size. We will come back to this point later, but first let's understand how hypothesis testing works.

Suppose we have developed a new fertilizer but don't know yet whether it actually works. Now we run an experiment: we divide a plot of land in two and treat the crops on half of the plot with the new fertilizer. Finally, we compare the yields: are they different? The specific amounts of the yield will almost surely differ, but is this difference due to the treatment or is it merely a chance fluctuation? Hypothesis testing helps us decide how large the difference needs to be in order to be *statistically significant*.

Formal hypothesis testing now proceeds as follows. First we set up the two hypotheses between which we want to decide: the *null hypothesis* (no effect; that is there is no difference between the two experiments) and the *alternate hypothesis* (there is an effect so that the two experiments have significantly different outcomes). If the difference between the outcomes of the two experiments is statistically significant, then we have sufficient evidence to "reject the null hypothesis," otherwise we "fail to reject the null hypothesis." In other words: if the outcomes are not sufficiently different, then we retain the null hypothesis that there is no effect.

This convoluted, indirect line of reasoning is required because, strictly speaking, no hypothesis can ever be proved correct by empirical means. If we find evidence *against* a hypothesis, then we can surely reject it. But if we *don't* find evidence against the hypothesis, then we retain the hypothesis—at least until we do find evidence against it (which may possibly never happen, in which case we retain the hypothesis indefinitely).

This, then, is the process by which hypothesis testing proceeds: because we can never prove that a treatment was successful, we instead invent a contradicting statement that we can prove to be *false*. The price we pay for this double negative ("it's *not* true that there is *no* effect") is that the test results mean exactly the opposite from what they seem to be saying: "retaining the null hypothesis," which sounds like a success, means that the treatment had no effect; whereas "rejecting the null hypothesis" means that the treatment did work. This is the first problem with hypothesis testing: it involves a convoluted, indirect line of reasoning and a terminology that seems to be saying the exact opposite from what it means.

But there is another problem with hypothesis testing: it makes a statement that has almost no practical meaning! In reducing the outcome of an experiment to the Boolean choice between "significant" and "not significant," it creates an artificial dichotomy that is not an appropriate view of reality. Experimental outcomes are not either strictly significant or strictly nonsignificant: they form a continuum. In order to judge the results of an experiment, we need to know where along the continuum the experimental outcome falls *and* how robust the estimate is. If we have this information, we can decide how to interpret the experimental result and what importance to attach to it.

Classical hypothesis testing exhibits two well-known traps. The first is that an experimental outcome that is *marginally* outside the statistical significance level abruptly changes the interpretation of the experiment from "significant" to "not significant"—a discontinuity in interpretation that is not borne out by the minimal change in the actual outcome of the experiment. The other problem is that almost any effect, no matter how small, can be made "significant" by increasing the sample size. This can lead to "statistically significant" results that nevertheless are too small to be of any practical importance. All of this is compounded by the arbitrariness of the chosen "significance level" (typically 5 percent). Why not 4.99 percent? Or 1 percent, or 0.1 percent? This seems to render the whole hypothesis testing machinery (at least as generally practiced) fundamentally inconsistent: on the one hand, we introduce an absolutely sharp cutoff into our interpretation of reality; and on the other hand, we choose the position of this cutoff in an arbitrary manner. This does not seem right.

(There is a third trap: at the 5 percent significance level, you can expect 1 out of 20 tests to give the wrong result. This means that if you run enough tests, you will always find one that supports whatever conclusion you want to draw. This practice is known as *data dredging* and is strongly frowned upon.)

Moreover, in any practical situation, the actual size of the effect is so much more important than its sheer existence. For this reason, hypothesis testing often simply misses the point. A project I recently worked on provides an example of this. The question arose as to whether two events were statistically independent (this is a form of hypothesis testing). But, for the decision that was ultimately made, it did not matter whether the events truly were independent (they were not) but that treating them as independent made no measurable difference to the company's balance sheet.

Hypothesis testing has its place but typically in rather abstract or theoretical situations where the mere existence of an effect constitutes an important discovery ("Is this coin loaded?" "Are people more likely to die a few days after their birthdays than before?"). If this describes your situation, then you will quite naturally employ hypothesis tests. However, if the *size* of an effect is of interest to you, then you should feel free to ignore tests altogether and instead work out an estimate of the effect—including its confidence interval. This will give you the information that you need. You are not "doing it wrong" just because you haven't performed a significance test somewhere along the way.

Finally, I'd like to point out that the statistics community itself has become uneasy with the emphasis that is placed on tests in some fields (notably medicine but also social sciences). Historically, hypothesis testing was invented to deal with sample sizes so small (possibly containing only four or five events) that drawing any conclusion at all was a challenge. In such cases, the broad distinction between "effect" and "no effect" was about the best one could do. If interval estimates are available, there is no reason to use statistical tests. The Wikipedia entry on *p*-values (explained below) provides some starting points to the controversy.

I have devoted quite a bit of space to a topic that may not seem especially relevant. However, hypothesis tests feature so large in introductory statistics books and courses and, at the same time, are so obscure and counterintuitive, that I found it important to provide some background. In the next section, we will take a more detailed look at some of the concepts and terminology that you are likely to find in introductory (or not-so-introductory) statistics books and courses.

Statistics Explained

In Chapter 9, we already encountered several well-known probability distributions, including the binomial (used for trials resulting in Success or Failure), the Poisson (applicable in situations where events are evenly distributed according to some density), and the ubiquitous Normal, or Gaussian, distribution. All of these distributions describe real-world, observable phenomena.

In addition, classical statistics uses several distributions that describe the distribution of certain quantities that are not observed but calculated. These distributions are not (or not usually) used to describe events in the real world. Instead, they describe how the outcomes of specific typical calculations involving random quantities will be distributed. There are four of these distributions, and they are known as *sampling distributions*.

The first of these (and the only one having much use outside of theoretical statistics) is the Gaussian distribution. As a sampling distribution, it is of interest because we already know that it describes the distribution of a sum of independent, identically distributed random variables. In other words, if $X_1, X_2, \ldots, X_n$ are random variables, then $Z = X_1 + X_2 + \cdots + X_n$ will be normally distributed and (because we can divide by a constant) the average $m = (X_1 + X_2 + \cdots + X_n)/n$ will also follow a Gaussian. It is this last property that makes the Gaussian important as a sampling distribution: it describes *the distribution of averages*. One caveat: to arrive at a closed formula for the Gaussian, we need to know the variance (*i.e.*, the width) of the distribution from which the individual X_i are drawn. For most practical situations this is not a realistic requirement, and in a moment we will discuss what to do if the variance is not known.

The second sampling distribution is the *chi-square (χ^2) distribution*. It describes the distribution of the sum of *squares* of independent, identically distributed Gaussian random variables. Thus, if $X_1, X_2, \ldots, X_n$ are Gaussian random variables with unit variance, then $U = X_1^2 + X_2^2 + \cdots + X_n^2$ will follow a chi-square distribution. Why should we care? Because we form this kind of sum every time we calculate the variance. (Recall that the variance is defined as $\frac{1}{n}\sum(x_i - m)^2$.) Hence, the chi-square distribution is used to describe *the distribution of variances*. The number n of elements in the sum is referred to as *the number of degrees of freedom* of the chi-square distribution, and it is an additional parameter we need to know to evaluate the distribution numerically.

The third sampling distribution describes the behavior of the ratio T of a normally (Gaussian) distributed random variable Z and a chi-square-distributed random variable U. This distribution is the famous *Student t distribution*. Specifically, let Z be distributed according to the standard Gaussian distribution and U according to the chi-square distribution with n degrees of freedom. Then $T = Z/\sqrt{U/n}$ is distributed according to the t distribution with n degrees of freedom. As it turns out, this is the correct formula to use for the *distribution of the average if the variance is not known* but has to be determined from the sample together with the average.

The t distribution is a symmetric, bell-shaped curve like the Gaussian but with fatter tails. How fat the tails are depends on the number of degrees of freedom (*i.e.*, on the number of data points in the sample). As the number of degrees of freedom increases, the t distribution becomes more and more like the Gaussian. In fact, for n larger than about 30, the differences between them are negligible. This is an important point to keep in mind: the distinction between the t distribution and the Gaussian matters only for small samples—that is, samples containing less than approximately 30 data points. For larger samples, it is all right to use the Gaussian instead of the t distribution.

The last of the four sampling distributions is *Fisher's F distribution*, which describes the behavior of the ratio of two chi-square random variables. We care about this when we want to compare two variances against each other (*e.g.*, to test whether they are equal or not).

These are the four sampling distributions of classical statistics. I will neither trouble you with the formulas for these distributions, nor show you their graphs—you can find them in every statistics book. What is important here is to understand what they are describing and why they are important. In short, if you have n independent but identically distributed measurements, then the sampling distributions describe how the average, the variance, and their ratios will be distributed. The sampling distributions therefore allow us to reason about averages and variances. That's why they are important and why statistics books spend so much time on them.

One way to use the sampling distribution is to construct confidence intervals for an estimate. Here is how it works. Suppose we have n observations. We can find the average and variance of these measurements as well as the ratio of the two. Finally, we know that the ratio is distributed according to the t distribution. Hence we can find the interval that has a 95 percent probability of containing the true value (see Figure 10-1). The boundaries of this range are the 95 percent confidence interval; that is, we expect the true value to fall outside this confidence range in only 1 out 20 cases.

A similar concept can be applied to hypothesis testing, where sampling distributions are often used to calculate so-called *p-values*. A *p*-value is an attempt to express the strength of the evidence in a hypothesis test and, in so doing, to soften the sharp binary distinction

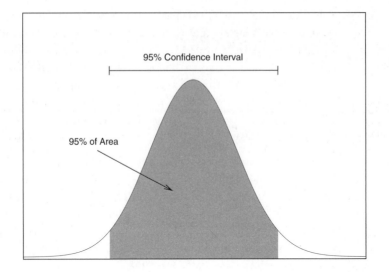

95% Confidence Interval

95% of Area

FIGURE 10-1. The shaded area contains 95 percent of the area under the curve; the boundaries of the shaded region are the bounds on the 95 percent confidence interval.

between significant and not significant outcomes mentioned earlier. A *p*-value is *the probability of obtaining a value as (or more) extreme than the one actually observed* under the assumption that the null hypothesis is true (see Figure 10-2). In other words, if the null hypothesis is that there is no effect, and if the observed effect size is *x*, then the *p*-value is the probability of observing an effect at least as large as *x*. Obviously, a large effect is improbable (small *p*-value) if the null hypothesis (zero effect) is true; hence a small *p*-value is considered strong evidence against the null hypothesis. However, a *p*-value is not "the probability that the null hypothesis is true"—such an interpretation (although appealing!) is incorrect. The *p*-value is the probability of obtaining an effect as large or larger than the observed one *if* the null hypothesis is true. (Classical statistics does not make probability statements about the truth of hypotheses. Doing so would put us into the realm of Bayesian statistics, a topic we will discuss toward the end of this chapter.)

By the way, if you are thinking that this approach to hypothesis testing—with its sliding *p*-values—is quite different from the cut-and-dried significant–not significant approach discussed earlier, then you are right. Historically, two competing theories of significance tests have been developed and have generated quite a bit of controversy; even today they sit a little awkwardly next to each other. (The approach based on sliding *p*-values that need to be interpreted by the researcher is due to Fisher; the decision-rule approach was developed by Pearson and Neyman.) But enough, already. You can consult any statistics book if you want to know more details.

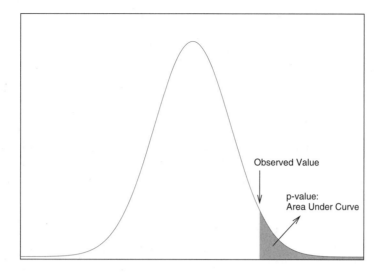

FIGURE 10-2. The p-value is the probability of observing a value as large or larger than the one actually observed if the null hypothesis is true.

Example: Formal Tests Versus Graphical Methods

Historically, classical statistics evolved as it did because working with actual *data* was hard. The early statisticians therefore made a number of simplifying assumptions (mostly that data would be normally distributed) and then proceeded to develop mathematical tools (such as the sampling distributions introduced earlier in the chapter) that allowed them to reason about data sets in a general way and required only the knowledge of a few, easily calculated summary statistics (such as the mean). The ingenuity of it all is amazing, but it has led to an emphasis on formal technicalities as opposed to the direct insight into the data. Today our situation is different, and we should take full advantage of that.

An example will demonstrate what I mean. The listing below shows two data sets. Are they the same, or are they different (in the sense that their means are the same or different)?[*]

0.209	0.225
0.205	0.262
0.196	0.217
0.210	0.240
0.202	0.230
0.207	0.229
0.224	0.235
0.223	0.217
0.220	
0.201	

---

[*]This is a famous data set with history that is colorful but not really relevant here. A Web search for "Quintus Curtius Snodgrass" will turn up plenty of references.

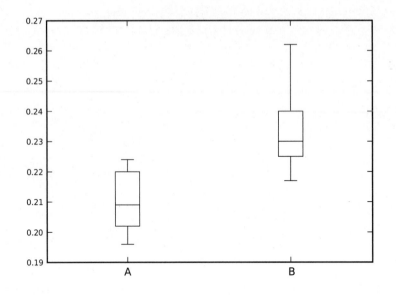

F I G U R E 10-3. Box-and-whisker plots of the two Quintus Curtius Snodgrass data sets. There is almost no overlap between the two.

In case study 9.2.1 of their book, Larsen and Marx (see the recommended reading at the end of this chapter) labor for several pages and finally conclude that the data sets are different at the 99 percent level of significance.

Figure 10-3 shows a box plot for each of the data sets. Case closed.

(In fairness, the formal test does something that a graphical method cannot do: it gives us a quantitative criterion by which to make a decision. I hope that the discussion in this chapter has convinced you that this is not always an advantage, because it can lead to blind faith in "the number." Graphical methods require you to interpret the results and take responsibility for the conclusions. Which is why I like them: they keep you honest!)

Controlled Experiments Versus Observational Studies

Besides the machinery of formal statistical inference (using the sampling distributions just discussed), the early statistics pioneers also developed a general theory of how best to undertake statistical studies. This conceptual framework is sometimes known as *Design of Experiment* and is worth knowing about—not least because so much of typical data mining activity does *not* make use of it.

The most important distinction formalized by the Design of Experiment theory is the one between an *observational study* and a *controlled experiment*. As the name implies, a controlled experiment allows us to control many aspects of the experimental setup and procedure; in particular, we control which treatment is applied to which experimental unit (we will define these terms shortly). For example, in an agricultural experiment, we would treat some (but not all) of the plots with a new fertilizer and then later compare the yields from the two treatment groups. In contrast, with an observational study, we merely collect data as it becomes (or already is) available. In particular, retrospective studies are always observational (not controlled).

In a controlled experiment, we are able to control the "input" of an experiment (namely, the application of a treatment) and therefore can draw much more powerful conclusions from the output. In contrast to observational studies, a properly conducted controlled experiment can provide strong support for cause-and-effect relationships between two observations and can be used to rule out hidden (or confounding) causes. Observational studies can merely *suggest* the existence of a relationship between two observations; however, they can neither prove that one observation is caused by the other nor rule out that additional (unobserved) factors have played a role.

The following (intentionally whimsical) example will serve to make the point. Let's say we have data that suggests that cities with many lawyers also have many espresso stands and that cities with few lawyers have few espresso stands. In other words, there is strong correlation between the two quantities. But what conclusions can we draw about the causal relationship between the two? Are lawyers particularly high consumers of expensive coffee? Or does caffeine make people more litigious? In short, there is no way for us to determine what is cause and what is effect in this example. In contrast, if the fertilized yields in the controlled agricultural experiment are higher than the yields from the untreated control plots, we have strong reason to conclude that this effect is due to the fertilizer treatment.

In addition to the desire to establish that the treatment indeed causes the effect, we also want to rule out the possibility of additional, unobserved factors that might account for the observed effect. Such factors, which influence the outcome of a study but are not themselves part of it, are known as *confounding* (or "hidden" or "lurking") variables. In our agricultural example, differences in soil quality might have a significant influence on the yield—perhaps a greater influence than the fertilizer. The spurious correlation between the number of lawyers and espresso stands is almost certainly due to confounding: larger cities have more of everything! (Even if we account for this effect and consider the per capita *density* of lawyers and espresso stands, there is still a plausible confounding factor: the income generated per head in the city.) In the next section, we will discuss how *randomization* can help to remove the effect of confounding variables.

The distinction between controlled experiments and observational studies is most critical. Many of the most controversial scientific or statistical issues involve observational studies. In particular, reports in the mass media often concern studies that (inappropriately) draw causal inferences from observational studies (about topics such as the relationship between gun laws and homicide rates, for example). Sometimes controlled experiments are not possible, with the result that it becomes almost impossible to settle certain questions once and for all. (The controversy around the connection between smoking and lung cancer is a good example.)

In any case, make sure you understand clearly the difference between controlled and observational studies, as well as the fundamental limitations of the latter!

Design of Experiments

In a controlled experiment, we divide the *experimental units* that constitute our sample into two or more groups and then apply different *treatments* or *treatment levels* to the units in each group. In our agricultural example, the plots correspond to the experimental units, fertilization is the treatment, and the options "fertilizer" and "no fertilizer" are the treatment levels.

Experimental design involves several techniques to improve the quality and reliability of any conclusions drawn from a controlled experiment.

Randomization
> Randomization means that treatments (or treatment levels) are assigned to experimental units in a random fashion. Proper randomization suppresses systematic errors. (If we assign fertilizer treatment randomly to plots, then we remove the systematic influence of soil quality, which might otherwise be a confounding factor, because high-quality and low-quality plots are now equally likely to receive the fertilizer treatment.) Achieving true randomization is not as easy as it looks—I'll come back to this point shortly.

Replication
> Replication means that the same treatment is applied to more than one experimental unit. Replication serves to reduce the variability of the results by averaging over a larger sample. Replicates should be independent of each other, since nothing is gained by repeating the same experiment on the same unit multiple times.

Blocking
> We sometimes know (or at least strongly suspect) that not all experimental units are equal. In this case, it may make sense to group equivalent experimental units into "blocks" and then to treat each such block as a separate sample. For example, if we know that plots A and C have poor soil quality and that B and D have better soil, then we would form two blocks—consisting of (A, C) and (B, D), respectively—before proceeding to make a randomized assignment of treatments *for each block separately*. Similarly, if we know that web traffic is drastically different in the morning and the afternoon, we should collect and analyze data for both time periods separately. This also is a form of blocking.

Factorization
> The last of these techniques applies only to experiments involving several treatments (*e.g.*, irrigation and fertilization, to stay within our agricultural framework). The

simplest experimental design would make only a single change at any given time, so that we would observe yields with and without irrigation as well as with and without fertilizer. But this approach misses the possibility that there are *interactions* between the two treatments—for example, the effect of the fertilizer may be significantly higher when coupled with improved irrigation. Therefore, in a factorial experiment all possible combinations of treatment levels are tried. Even if a fully factorial experiment is not possible (the number of combinations goes up quickly as the number of different treatments grows), there are rules for how best to select combinations of treatment levels for drawing optimal conclusions from the study.

Another term you may come across in this context is ANOVA (analysis of variance), which is a standard way of summarizing results from controlled experiments. It emphasizes the variations within each treatment group for easy comparison with the variances between the treatments, so that we can determine whether the differences between different treatments are significant compared to the variation within each treatment group. ANOVA is a clever bookkeeping technique, but it does not introduce particularly noteworthy new statistical concepts.

A word of warning: when conducting a controlled experiment, make sure that you apply the techniques properly; in particular, beware of *pseudo-randomization* and *pseudo-replication*.

Pseudo-randomization occurs if the assignment of treatments to experimental units is not truly random. This can occur relatively easily, even if the assignment *seems* to be random. For example, if you would like to try out two different drugs on lab rats, it is not sufficient to "pick a rat at random" from the cage to administer the treatment. What does "at random" mean? It might very well mean picking the most active rat first because it comes to the cage door. Or maybe the least aggressive-looking one. In either case, there is a systematic bias!

Here is another example, perhaps closer to home: the web-lab. Two different site designs are to be presented to viewers, and the objective is to measure conversion rate or click-throughs or some other metric. There are multiple servers, so we dedicate one of them (chosen "at random") to serve the pages with the new design. What's wrong with that?

Everything! Do you have any indication that web requests are assigned to servers in a random fashion? Or might servers have, for example, a strong geographic bias? Let's assume the servers are behind some "big-IP" box that routes requests to the servers. How is the routing conducted—randomly, or round-robin, or based on traffic intensity? Is the routing smart, so that servers with slower response times get fewer hits? What about sticky sessions, and what about the relationship between sticky sessions and slower response times? Is the router reordering the incoming requests in some way? That's a lot of questions—questions that randomization is intended to *avoid*. In fact, you are not running a controlled experiment at all: you are conducting an observational study!

The only way that I know to run a controlled experiment is by deciding ahead of time which experimental unit will receive which treatment. In the lab rat example, rats should have been labeled and then treatments assigned to the labels using a (reliable) random number generator or random table. In the web-server example it is harder to achieve true randomization, because the experimental units are not known ahead of time. A simple rule (*e.g.*, show the new design to every nth request) won't work, because there may be significant correlation between subsequent requests. It's not so easy.

Pseudo-replication occurs when experimental units are not truly independent. Injecting the same rat five times with the same drug does not reduce variability! Similarly, running the same query against a database could be misleading because of changing cache utilization. And so on. In my experience, pseudo-replication is easier to spot and hence tends to be less of a problem than pseudo-randomization.

Finally, I should mention one other term that often comes up in the context of proper experimental process: *blind* and *double-blind* experiments. In a blind experiment, the experimental unit should not know which treatment it receives; in a double-blind experiment, the investigator—at the time of the experiment—does not know either. The purpose of blind and double-blind experiments is to prevent the knowledge of the treatment level from becoming a confounding factor. If people know that they have been given a new drug, then this knowledge itself may contribute to their well-being. An investigator who knows which field is receiving the fertilizer might weed that particular field more vigorously and thereby introduce some invisible and unwanted bias. Blind experiments play a huge role in the medical field but can also be important in other contexts. However, I would like to emphasize that the question of "blindness" (which concerns the experimental procedure) is a different issue than the Design of Experiment prescriptions (which are intended to reduce statistical uncertainty).

Perspective

It is important to maintain an appropriate perspective on these matters.

In practice, many studies are observational, not controlled. Occasionally, this is a painful loss and only due to the inability to conduct a proper controlled experiment (smoking and lung cancer, again!). Nevertheless, observational studies can be of great value: one reason is that they may be exploratory and discover new and previously unknown behavior. In contrast, controlled experiments are always confirmatory in deciding between the effectiveness or ineffectiveness of a specific "treatment."

Observational studies can be used to derive predictive models even while setting aside the question of causation. The machine-learning community, for instance, attempts to develop *classification* algorithms that use descriptive attributes or *features* of the unit to predict whether the unit belongs to a given class. They work entirely without controlled experiments and have developed methods for quantifying the accuracy of their results. (We will describe some in Chapter 18.)

That being said, it is important to understand the limitations of observational studies—in particular, their inability to support strong conclusions regarding cause-and-effect relationships and their inability to rule out confounding factors. In the end, the power of controlled experiments can be their limitation, because such experiments require a level of control that limits their application.

Optional: Bayesian Statistics—The Other Point of View

There is an alternative approach to statistics that is based on a different interpretation of the concept of *probability* itself. This may come as a surprise, since probability seems to be such a basic concept. The problem is that, although we have a very strong intuitive sense of what we mean by the word "probability," it is not so easy to give it a rigorous meaning that can be used to develop a mathematical theory.

The interpretation of probability used by classical statistics (and, to some degree, by abstract probability theory) treats probability as a *limiting frequency*: if you toss a fair coin "a large number of times," then you will obtain Heads about half of the time; hence the probability for Heads is 1/2. Arguments and theories starting from this interpretation are often referred to as "frequentist."

An alternative interpretation of probability views it as the degree of our ignorance about an outcome: since we don't know which side will be on top in the next toss of a fair coin, we assign each possible outcome the same probability—namely 1/2. We can therefore make statements about the probabilities associated with individual events without having to invoke the notion of a large number of repeated trials. Because this approach to probability and statistics makes use of *Bayes' theorem* at a central step in its reasoning, it is usually called *Bayesian statistics* and has become increasingly popular in recent years. Let's compare the two interpretations in a bit more detail.

The Frequentist Interpretation of Probability

In the frequentist interpretation, probability is viewed as the limiting frequency of each outcome of an experiment that is repeated a large number of times. This "frequentist" interpretation is the reason for some of the peculiarities of classical statistics. For example, in classical statistics it is incorrect to say that a 95 percent confidence interval for some parameter has a 95 percent chance of containing the true value—after all, the true value is either contained in the interval or not; period. The only statement that we can make that, if we perform an experiment to measure this parameter many times, then in a 95 percent of all cases the experiment will yield a value for this parameter that li the 95 percent confidence interval.

This type of reasoning has a number of drawbacks.

- It is awkward and clumsy, and liable to (possibly even unconscious)

- The constant appeal to a "large number of trials" is artificial even in situations where such a sequence of trials would—at least in principle—be possible (such as tossing a coin). But it becomes wholly ficticious in situations where the trial cannot possibly be repeated. The weather report may state: "There is an 80 percent chance of rain tomorrow." What is that supposed to mean? It is either going to rain tomorrow or not! Hence we must again invoke the unlimited sequence of trials and say that in 8 out of 10 cases where we observe the current meteorological conditions, we expect rain on the following day. But even this argument is illusionary, because we will never observe these *precise* conditions ever again: that's what we have been learning from chaos theory and related fields.

- We would frequently like to make statements such as the one about the chance of rain, or similar ones—for example, "The patient has a 60 percent survival probability," and "I am 25 percent certain that the contract will be approved." In all such cases the actual outcome is not of a probabilistic nature: it will rain or it will not; the patient will survive or not; the contract will be approved or not. Even so, we'd like to express a degree of certainty about the expected outcome even if appealing to an unlimited sequence of trials is neither practical nor even meaningful.

From a strictly frequentist point of view, a statement like "There is an 80 percent chance of rain tomorrow" is nonsensical. Nevertheless, it seems to make so much intuitive sense. In what way can this intuition be made more rigorous? This question leads us to *Bayesian statistics* or *Bayesian reasoning*.

The Bayesian Interpretation of Probability

To understand the Bayesian point of view, we first need to review the concept of *conditional probability*. The conditional probability $P(A|B)$ gives us the probability for the event A, *given* (or assuming) that event B has occurred. You can easily convince yourself that the following is true:

$$P(A|B) = \frac{P(A \cap B)}{P(B)}$$

where $P(A \cap B)$ is the *joint probability* of finding both event A and event B. For example, it is well known that men are much more likely than women to be color-blind: about 10 percent of men are color-blind but fewer than 1 percent of women are color-blind. These are *conditional* probabilities—that is, the probability of being color-blind *given* the gender:

$$P(\text{color-blind}|\text{male}) = 0.1$$
$$P(\text{color-blind}|\text{female}) = 0.01$$

In contrast, if we "randomly" pick a person off the street, then we are dealing with the *joint* probability that this person is color-blind *and* male. The person has a 50 percent chance of being male and a 10 percent conditional probability of being color-blind, given that the person is male. Hence, the joint probability for a random person to be color-blind *and* male is 5 percent, in agreement with the definition of conditional probability given previously.

One can now rigorously prove the following equality, which is known as *Bayes' theorem*:

$$P(A|B) = \frac{P(B|A)P(A)}{P(B)}$$

In words: the probability of finding *A* given *B* is equal to the probability of finding *B* given *A* multiplied by the probability of finding *A* and divided by the probability of finding *B*.

Now, let's return to statistics and data analysis. Assume there is some parameter that we attempt to determine through an experiment (say, the mass of the proton or the survival rate after surgery). We are now dealing with two "events": event *B* is the occurrence of the specific set of measurements that we have observed, and the parameter taking some specific value constitutes event *A*. We can now rewrite Bayes' theorem as follows:

$$P(parameter|data) \propto P(data|parameter)\,P(parameter)$$

(I have dropped the denominator, which I can do because the denominator is simply a constant that does not depend on the parameter we wish to determine. The left- and righthand sides are now no longer equal, so I have replaced the equality sign with $\propto$ to indicate that the two sides of the expression are merely proportional: equal to within a numerical constant.)

Let's look at this equation term by term.

On the lefthand side, we have *the probability of finding a certain value for the parameter, given the data*. That's pretty exciting, because this is an expression that makes an explicit statement about the *probability* of an event (in this case, that the parameter has a certain value), given the data. This probability is called the *posterior probability*, or simply *the posterior*, and is defined solely through Bayes' theorem without reference to any unlimited sequence of trials. Instead, it is a measure of our "belief" or "certainty" about the outcome (*i.e.*, the value of the parameter) given the data.

The first term on the righthand side, $P(data|parameter)$, is known as the *likelihood function*. This is a mathematical expression that links the parameter to the probability of obtaining specific data points in an actual experiment. The likelihood function constitutes our "model" for the system under consideration: it tells us what data we can expect to observe, given a particular value of the parameter. (The example in the next section will help to clarify the meaning of this term.)

Finally, the term $P(parameter)$ is known as the *prior probability*, or simply *the prior*, and captures our "prior" (prior to the experiment) belief of finding a certain outcome—specifically our prior belief that the parameter has a certain value. It is the existence of this prior that makes the Bayesian approach so controversial, because it seems to introduce an inappropriately subjective element into the analysis. In reality, however, the influence of the prior on the final result of the analysis is typically small, in particular when there is plenty of data. One can also find so-called "noninformative" priors that express our complete ignorance about the possible outcomes. But the prior is there, and it forces us to think about our assumptions regarding the experiment and to state some of these assumptions explicitly (in form of the prior distribution function).

Bayesian Data Analysis: A Worked Example

All of this will become much clearer once we demonstrate these concepts in an actual example. The example is very simple, so as not to distract from the concepts.

Assume we have a coin that has been tossed 10 times, producing the following set of outcomes (H for Heads, T for Tails):

T H H H H T T H H H

If you count the outcomes, you will find that we obtained 7 Heads and 3 Tails in 10 tosses of the coin.

Given this data, we would like to determine whether the coin is fair or not. Specifically, we would like to determine the probability p that a toss of this coin will turn out Heads. (This is the "parameter" we would like to estimate.) If the coin is fair, then p should be close to 1/2.

Let's write down Bayes' equation, adapted to this system:

$$P(p | \{\text{T H H H H T T H H H}\}) \propto P(\{\text{T H H H H T T H H H}\} | p) P(p)$$

Notice that at this point, the problem has become *parametric*. All that is left to do is to determine the value of the parameter p or, more precisely, the posterior probability distribution for all values of p.

To make progress, we need to supply the likelihood function and the prior. Given this system, the likelihood function is particularly simple: $P(\text{H}|p) = p$ and $P(\text{T}|p) = 1 - p$. You should convince yourself that this choice of likelihood function gives us exactly what we want: the probability to obtain Heads or Tails, given p.

We also assume that the tosses are independent, which implies that only the total number of Heads or Tails matters but not the order in which they occurred. Hence we don't need to find the combined likelihood for the specific sequence of 10 tosses; instead, the likelihood of the set of events is simply the product of the 10 individual tosses. (The likelihood "factors" for independent events—this argument occurs frequently in Bayesian analysis.)

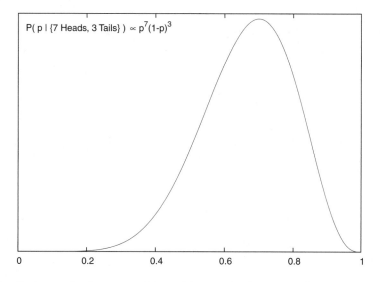

$P(p \mid \{7 \text{ Heads}, 3 \text{ Tails}\}) \propto p^7(1\text{-}p)^3$

| 0 | 0.2 | 0.4 | 0.6 | 0.8 | 1 |

FIGURE 10-4. The (unnormalized) posterior probability of obtaining 7 Heads in 10 tosses of a coin as a function of p.

Finally, we know nothing about this coin. In particular, we have no reason to believe that any value of p is more likely than any other, so we choose as prior probability distribution the "flat" distribution $P(p) = 1$ for all p.

Collecting everything, we end up with the following expression (where I have dropped some combinatorial factors that do not depend on p):

$$P(p \mid \{7 \text{ Heads}, 3 \text{ Tails}\}) \propto p^7(1 - p)^3$$

This is the posterior probability distribution for the parameter p based on the experimental data (see Figure 10-4). We can see that it has a peak near $p = 0.7$, which is the most probable value for p. Note that the absence of tick marks on the y axis in Figure 10-4: the denominator, which we dropped earlier, is still undetermined, and therefore the overall scale of the function is not yet fixed. If we are interested only in the *location* of the maximum, this does not matter.

But we are not restricted to a single (point) estimate for p—the entire distribution function is available to us! We can now use it to construct confidence intervals for p. And because we are now talking about Bayesian probabilities, it would be legitimate to state that "the confidence interval has a 95 percent chance of containing the true value of p."

We can also evaluate any function that depends on p by integrating it against the posterior distribution for p. As a particularly simple example, we could calculate the

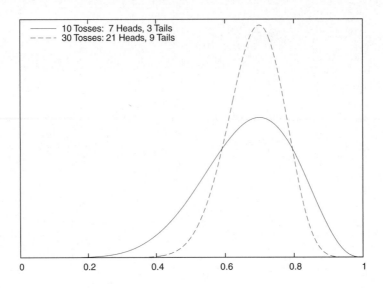

FIGURE 10-5. *The (unnormalized) posterior probability of obtaining 70 percent Heads in 10 and in 30 tosses of a coin. The more data there is, the more strongly peaked the posterior distribution becomes.*

expectation value of p to obtain the single "best" estimate of p (rather than use the most probable value as we did before):

$$E[p] = \frac{\int p\, P(p\,|\,\{7 \text{ Heads, 3 Tails}\})\, dp}{\int P(p\,|\,\{7 \text{ Heads, 3 Tails}\})\, dp}$$

Here we finally need to worry about all the factors that we dropped along the way, and the denominator in the formula is our way of fixing the normalization "after the fact." To ensure that the probability distribution is properly normalized, we divide explicitly by the integral over the whole range of values, thereby guaranteeing that the total probability equals 1 (as it must).

It is interesting to look at the roles played by the likelihood and the prior in the result. In Bayesian analysis, the posterior "interpolates" between the prior and the data-based likelihood function. If there is only very little data, then the likelihood function will be relatively flat, and therefore the posterior will be more influenced by the prior. But as we collect more data (*i.e.*, as the empirical evidence becomes stronger), the likelihood function becomes more and more narrowly peaked at the most likely value of p, regardless of the choice of prior. Figure 10-5 demonstrates this effect. It shows the posterior for a total of 10 trials and a total of 30 trials (while keeping the same ratio of Heads to Tails): as we gather more data, the uncertainty in the resulting posterior shrinks.

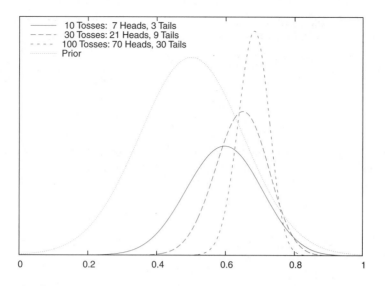

FIGURE 10-6. The effect of a nonflat prior: posterior probabilities for data sets of different sizes, calculated using a Gaussian prior.

Finally, Figure 10-6 demonstrates the effect of the prior. Whereas the posterior distributions shown in Figure 10-5 were calculated using a flat prior, those in Figure 10-6 were calculated using a Gaussian prior—which expresses a rather strong belief that the value of p will be between 0.35 and 0.65. The influence of this prior belief is rather significant for the smaller data set, but as we take more and more data points, its influence is increasingly diminished.

Bayesian Inference: Summary and Discussion

Let's summarize what we have learned about Bayesian data analysis or *Bayesian inference* and discuss what it can do for us—and what it can't.

First of all, the Bayesian (as opposed to the frequentist) approach to inference allows us to compute a true probability distribution for any parameter in question. This has great intuitive appeal, because it allows us to make statements such as "There is a 90 percent chance of rain tomorrow" without having to appeal to the notion of extended trials of identical experiments.

The posterior probability distribution arises as the product of the likelihood function and the prior. The likelihood links experimental results to values of the parameter, and the prior expresses our previous knowledge or belief about the parameter.

The Bayesian approach has a number of appealing features. Of course, there is the intuitive nature of the results obtained using Bayesian arguments: real probabilities and

95 percent confidence intervals that have exactly the kind of interpretation one would expect! Moreover, we obtain the posterior probability distribution in full generality and without having to make limiting assumptions (*e.g.*, having to assume that the data is normally distributed).

Additionally, the likelihood function enters the calculation in a way that allows for great flexibility in how we build "models." Under the Bayesian approach, it is very easy to deal with missing data, with data that is becoming available over time, or with heterogeneous data sets (*i.e.*, data sets in which different attributes are known about each data point). Because the result of Bayesian inference is a probability distribution itself, it can be used as input for a new model that builds on the previous one (hierarchical models). Moreover, we can use the prior to incorporate previous (domain) knowledge that we may have about the problem under consideration.

On the other hand, Bayesian inference has some problems, too—even when we concentrate on practical applications only, leaving the entire philosophical debate about priors and subjectivity aside.

First of all, Bayesian inference is always *parametric*; it is never just exploratory or descriptive. Because Bayesian methods force us to supply a likelihood function explicitly, they force us to be specific about our choice of model assumptions: we must already have a likelihood function in mind, for otherwise we can't even get started (hence such analysis can never be exploratory). Furthermore, the result of a Bayesian analysis is always a posterior distribution—that is, a conditional probability of *something*, given the data. Here, that "something" is some form of hypothesis that we have, and the posterior gives us the probability that this hypothesis is true. To make this prescription operational (and, in particular, expressible through a likelihood function), we pretty much have to parameterize the hypothesis. The inference then consists of finding the best value for this parameter, given the data—which is a parametric problem, given a specific choice for the model (*i.e.*, the likelihood function). (There are so-called "nonparametric" Bayesian methods, but in reality they boil down to parametric models with very large numbers of parameters.)

Additionally, actual Bayesian calculations are often difficult. Recall that Bayesian inference gives us the full explicit posterior distribution function. If we want to summarize this function, we either need to find its maximum or integrate it to obtain an expectation value. Both of these problems are hard, especially when the likelihood function is complicated and there is more than one parameter that we try to estimate. Instead of explicitly integrating the posterior, one can *sample* it—that is, draw random points that are distributed according to the posterior distribution, in order to evaluate expectation values. This is clearly an expensive process that requires computer time and specialized software (and the associated know-how). There can also be additional problems. For example, if the parameter space is very high-dimensional, then evaluating the likelihood function (and hence the posterior) may be difficult.

In contrast, frequentist methods tend to make more assumptions up front and rely more strongly on general analytic results and approximations. With frequentist methods, the hard work has typically already been done (analytically), leading to an asymptotic or approximate formula that you only need to plug in. Bayesian methods give you the full, nonapproximate result but leave it up to you to evaluate it. The disadvantage of the plug-in approach, of course, is that you might be plugging into an inappropriate formula—because some of the assumptions or approximations that were used to derive it do not apply to your system or data set.

To bring this discussion to a close, I'd like to end with a cautionary note. Bayesian methods are very appealing and even exciting—something that is rarely said about classical frequentist statistics. On the other hand, they are probably not very suitable for casual uses.

• Bayesian methods are parametric and specific; they are never exploratory or descriptive. If we already know what specific question to ask, then Bayesian methods may be the best way of obtaining an answer. But if we don't yet know the proper questions to ask, then Bayesian methods are not applicable.

• Bayesian methods are difficult and require a fair deal of sophistication, both in setting up the actual model (likelihood function and prior) and in performing the required calculations.

As far as results are concerned, there is not much difference between frequentist and Bayesian analysis. When there is sufficient data (so that the influence of the prior is small), then the end results are typically very similar, whether they were obtained using frequentist methods or Bayesian methods.

Finally, you may encounter some other terms and concepts in the literature that also bear the "Bayesian" moniker: Bayesian classifier, Bayesian network, Bayesian risk, and more. Often, these have nothing to do with Bayesian (as opposed to frequentist) inference as explained in this chapter. Typically, these methods involve conditional probabilities and therefore appeal at some point to Bayes' theorem. A Bayesian classifier, for instance, is the conditional probability that an object belongs to a certain class, given what we know about it. A Bayesian network is a particular way of organizing the causal relationships that exist among events that depend on many interrelated conditions. And so on.

Workshop: R

R is an environment for data manipulation and numerical calculations, specifically statistical applications. Although it can be used in a more general fashion for programming or computation, its real strength is the large number of built-in (or user-contributed) statistical functions.

R is an open source clone of the S programming language, which was originally developed at Bell Labs in the 1970s. It was one of the first environments to combine the capabilities that today we expect from a scripting language (*e.g.*, memory management, proper strings, dynamic typing, easy file handling) with integrated graphics and intended for an interactive usage pattern.

I tend to stress the word *environment* when referring to R, because the way it integrates its various components is essential to R. It is misleading to think of R as a programming language that also has an interactive shell (like Python or Groovy). Instead, you might consider it as a shell but for handling data instead of files. Alternatively, you might want to view R as a text-based spreadsheet on steroids. The "shell" metaphor in particular is helpful in motivating some of the design choices made by R.

The essential data structure offered by R is the so-called *data frame*. A data frame encapsulates a data set and is the central abstraction that R is built on. Practically all operations involve the handling and manipulation of frames in one way or the other.

Possibly the best way to think of a data frame is as being comparable to a *relational database table*. Each data frame is a rectangular data structure consisting of rows and columns. Each *column* has a designated data type, and all entries in that column must be of that type. Consequently, each *row* will in general contain entries of different types (as defined by the types of the columns), but all rows must be of the same form. All this should be familiar from relational databases. The similarities continue: operations on frames can either project out a subset of columns, or filter out a subset of rows; either operation results in a new data frame. There is even a command (merge) that can perform a join of two data frames on a common column. In addition (and in contrast to databases), we will frequently *add* columns to an existing frame—for example, to hold the results of an intermediate calculation.

We can refer to columns by name. The names are either read from the first line of the input file, or (if not provided) R will substitute synthetic names of the form V1, V2, ... In contrast, we filter out a set of rows through various forms of "indexing magic." Let's look at some examples.

Consider the following input file:

```
Name    Height  Weight  Gender
Joe     6.2     192.2   0
Jane    5.5     155.4   1
Mary    5.7     164.3   1
Jill    5.6     166.4   1
Bill    5.8     185.8   0
Pete    6.1     201.7   0
Jack    6.0     195.2   0
```

Let's investigate this data set using R, placing particular emphasis on how to handle and manipulate data with R—the full session transcript is included below. The commands entered at the command prompt are prefixed by the prompt >, while R output is shown without the prompt:

```
> d <- read.csv( "data", header = TRUE, sep = "\t" )
> str(d)
'data.frame':	7 obs. of  4 variables:
 $ Name  : Factor w/ 7 levels "Bill","Jack",..: 5 3 6 4 1 7 2
 $ Height: num  6.2 5.5 5.7 5.6 5.8 6.1 6
 $ Weight: num  192 155 164 166 186 ...
 $ Gender: int  0 1 1 1 0 0 0
>
> mean( d$Weight )
[1] 180.1429
> mean( d[,3] )
[1] 180.1429
>
> mean( d$Weight[ d$Gender == 1 ] )
[1] 162.0333
> mean( d$Weight[ 2:4 ] )
[1] 162.0333
>
> d$Diff <- d$Height - mean( d$Height )
> print(d)
  Name Height Weight Gender        Diff
1  Joe    6.2  192.2      0  0.35714286
2 Jane    5.5  155.4      1 -0.34285714
3 Mary    5.7  164.3      1 -0.14285714
4 Jill    5.6  166.4      1 -0.24285714
5 Bill    5.8  185.8      0 -0.04285714
6 Pete    6.1  201.7      0  0.25714286
7 Jack    6.0  195.2      0  0.15714286
> summary(d)
     Name        Height          Weight          Gender          Diff
 Bill:1   Min.   :5.500   Min.   :155.4   Min.   :0.0000   Min.   :-3.429e-01
 Jack:1   1st Qu.:5.650   1st Qu.:165.3   1st Qu.:0.0000   1st Qu.:-1.929e-01
 Jane:1   Median :5.800   Median :185.8   Median :0.0000   Median :-4.286e-02
 Jill:1   Mean   :5.843   Mean   :180.1   Mean   :0.4286   Mean   : 2.538e-16
 Joe :1   3rd Qu.:6.050   3rd Qu.:193.7   3rd Qu.:1.0000   3rd Qu.: 2.071e-01
 Mary:1   Max.   :6.200   Max.   :201.7   Max.   :1.0000   Max.   : 3.571e-01
 Pete:1
>
> d$Gender <- factor( d$Gender, labels = c("M", "F") )
> summary(d)
     Name        Height          Weight       Gender        Diff
 Bill:1   Min.   :5.500   Min.   :155.4   M:4     Min.   :-3.429e-01
 Jack:1   1st Qu.:5.650   1st Qu.:165.3   F:3     1st Qu.:-1.929e-01
 Jane:1   Median :5.800   Median :185.8           Median :-4.286e-02
 Jill:1   Mean   :5.843   Mean   :180.1           Mean   : 2.538e-16
 Joe :1   3rd Qu.:6.050   3rd Qu.:193.7           3rd Qu.: 2.071e-01
 Mary:1   Max.   :6.200   Max.   :201.7           Max.   : 3.571e-01
 Pete:1
>
> plot( d$Height ~ d$Gender )
> plot( d$Height ~ d$Weight, xlab="Weight", ylab="Height" )
```

```
> m <- lm( d$Height ~ d$Weight )
> print(m)

Call:
lm(formula = d$Height ~ d$Weight)

Coefficients:
(Intercept)      d$Weight
    3.39918       0.01357

> abline(m)
> abline( mean(d$Height), 0, lty=2 )
```

Let's step through this session in some detail and explain what is going on.

First, we read the file in and assign it to the variable d, which is a data frame as discussed previously. The function str(d) shows us a string representation of the data frame. We can see that the frame consists of five named columns, and we can also see some typical values for each column. Notice that R has assigned a data type to each column: height and weight have been recognized as floating-point values; the names are considered a "factor," which is R's way of indicating a categorical variable; and finally the gender flag is interpreted as an integer. This is not ideal—we will come back to that.

```
> d <- read.csv( "data", header = TRUE, sep = "\t" )
> str(d)
'data.frame':   7 obs. of  4 variables:
 $ Name  : Factor w/ 7 levels "Bill","Jack",..: 5 3 6 4 1 7 2
 $ Height: num  6.2 5.5 5.7 5.6 5.8 6.1 6
 $ Weight: num  192 155 164 166 186 ...
 $ Gender: int  0 1 1 1 0 0 0
```

Let's calculate the mean of the weight column to demonstrate some typical ways in which we can select rows and columns. The most convenient way to specify a column is by name: d$Weight. The use of the dollar-sign ($) to access members of a data structure is one of R's quirks that one learns to live with. Think of a column as a shell variable! (By contrast, the dot (.) is not an operator and can be part of a variable or function name—in the same way that an underscore (_) is used in other languages. Here again the shell metaphor is useful: recall that shells allow the dot as part of filenames!)

```
> mean( d$Weight )
[1] 180.1429
> mean( d[,3] )
[1] 180.1429
```

Although its name is often the most convenient method to specify a column, we can also use its numeric index. Each element in a data frame can be accessed using its row and column index via the familiar bracket notation: d[row,col]. Keep in mind that the vertical (row) index comes first, followed by the horizontal (column) index. Omitting one of them selects all possible values, as we do in the listing above: d[,3] selects *all* rows from the third column. Also note that indices in R start at 1 (mathematical convention), not at 0 (programming convention).

Now that we know how to select a column, let's see how to select rows. In R, this is usually done through various forms of "indexing magic," two examples of which are shown next in the listing. We want to find the mean weight of only the women in the sample. To do so, we take the weight column but now index it with a logical expression. This kind of operation takes some getting used to: inside the brackets, we seem to compare a column (d$Gender) with a scalar—and then use the result to index another column. What is going on here? Several things: first, the scalar on the righthand side of the comparison is expanded into a vector of the same length as the operator on the lefthand side. The result of the equality operator is then a *Boolean* vector of the same length as d$Gender or d$Weight. A Boolean vector of the appropriate length can be used as an index and selects only those rows for which it evaluates as True—which it does in this case only for the women in the sample. The second line of code is much more conventional: the colon operator (:) creates a range of numbers, which are used to index into the d$Weight column. (Remember that indices start at 1, not at 0!)

```
> mean( d$Weight[ d$Gender == 1 ] )
[1] 162.0333
> mean( d$Weight[ 2:4 ] )
[1] 162.0333
```

These kinds of operation are very common in R: using some form of creative indexing to filter out a subset of rows (there are more ways to do this, which I don't show) and mixing vectors and scalars in expressions. Here is another example:

```
> d$Diff <- d$Height - mean( d$Height )
```

Here we create an additional column, called d$Diff, as the residual that remains when the mean height is subtracted from each individual's height. Observe how we mix a column with a scalar expression to obtain another vector.

```
summary(d)
```

Next, we calculate the summary of the entire data frame with the new column added. Take a look at the gender column: because R interpreted the gender flag as an integer, it went ahead and calculated its "mean" and other quantities. This is meaningless, of course; the values in this column should be treated as categorical. This can be achieved using the factor() function, which also allows us to replace the uninformative numeric labels with more convenient string labels.

```
> d$Gender <- factor( d$Gender, labels = c("M", "F") )
```

As you can see when we run summary(d) again, R treats categorical variables differently: it counts how often each value occurs in the data set.

Finally, let's take a look at R's plotting capabilities. First, we plot the height "as a function of" the gender. (R uses the tilde (~) to separate control and response variables; the response variable is always on the left.)

```
> plot( d$Height ~ d$Gender )
```

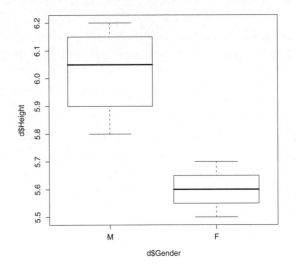

FIGURE 10-7. A box plot, showing the distribution of heights by gender.

This gives us a box plot, which is shown in Figure 10-7. On the other hand, if we plot the height as a function of the weight, then we obtain a scatter plot (see Figure 10-8—without the lines; we will add them in a moment).

```
> plot( d$Height ~ d$Weight, xlab="Weight", ylab="Height" )
```

Given the shape of the data, we might want to fit a linear model to it. This is trivially easy to do in R—it's a single line of code:

```
> m <- lm( d$Height ~ d$Weight )
```

Notice once again the tilde notation used to indicate control and response variable.

We may also want to add the linear model to the scatter plot with the data. This can be done using the abline() function, which plots a line given its offset ("a") and slope ("b"). We can either specify both parameters explicitly, or simply supply the result m of the fitting procedure; the abline function can use either. (The parameter lty selects the line type.)

```
> abline(m)
> abline( mean(d$Height), 0, lty=2 )
```

This short example should have given you an idea of what working with R is like.

R can be difficult to learn: it uses some unfamiliar idioms (such as creative indexing) as well as some obscure function and parameter names. But the greatest challenge to the newcomer (in my opinion) is its indiscriminate use of function overloading. The same function can behave quite differently depending on the (usually opaque) type of inputs it is given. If the default choices made by R are good, then this can be very convenient, but it can be hellish if you want to exercise greater, manual control.

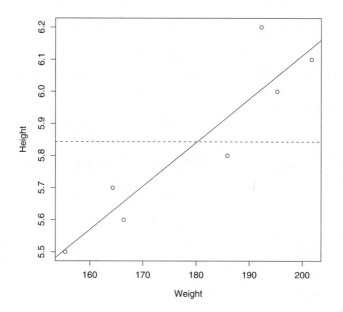

F I G U R E 10-8. A scatter plot with a linear fit.

Look at our example again: the same `plot()` command generates entirely different plot *types* depending on whether the control variable is categorical or numeric (box plot in the first case, scatter plot in the latter). For the experienced user, this kind of implicit behavior is of course convenient, but for the beginner, the apparent unpredictability can be very confusing. (In Chapter 14, we will see another example, where the same `plot()` command generates yet a different type of plot.)

These kinds of issues do not matter much if you use R interactively because you see the results immediately or, in the worst case, get an error message so that you can try something else. However, they can be unnerving if you approach R with the mindset of a contemporary programmer who prefers for operations to be explicit. It can also be difficult to find out which operations are available in a given situation. For instance, it is not at all obvious that the (opaque) return type of the `lm()` function is admissible input to the `abline()` function—it certainly doesn't look like the explicit set of parameters used in the second call to `abline()`. Issues of this sort make it hard to predict what R will do at any point, to develop a comprehensive understanding of its capabilities, or how to achieve a desired effect in a specific situation.

Further Reading

The number of introductory statistics texts seems almost infinite—which makes it that much harder to find good ones. Below are some texts that I have found useful:

- *An Introduction to Mathematical Statistics and Its Applications*. Richard J. Larsen and Morris L. Marx. 4th ed., Prentice Hall. 2005.

  This is my preferred introductory text for the mathematical background of classical statistics: how it all works. This is a math book; you won't learn how to *do* practical statistical fieldwork from it. (It contains a large number of uncommonly interesting examples; however, on close inspection many of them exhibit serious flaws in their experimental design—at least as described in this book.) But as a mathematical treatment, it very neatly blends accessibility with sufficient depth.

- *Statistics for Technology: A Course in Applied Statistics*. Chris Chatfield. 3rd ed., Chapman & Hall/CRC. 1983.

  This book is good companion to the book by Larsen and Marx. It eschews most mathematical development and instead concentrates on the pragmatics of it, with an emphasis on engineering applications.

- *The Statistical Sleuth: A Course in Methods of Data Analysis*. Fred Ramsey and Daniel Schafer. 2nd ed., Duxbury Press. 2001.

  This advanced undergraduate textbook emphasizes the distinction between observational studies and controlled experiments more strongly than any other book I am aware of. After working through some of their examples, you will not be able to look at the description of a statistical study without immediately classifying it as observational or controlled (and questioning the conclusions if it was merely observational). Unfortunately, the development of the general theory gets a little lost in the detailed description of application concerns.

- *The Practice of Business Statistics*. David S. Moore, George P. McCabe, William M. Duckworth, and Layth Alwan. 2nd ed., Freeman. 2008.

  This is a "for business" version of a popular beginning undergraduate textbook. The coverage of topics is comprehensive, and the presentation is particularly easy to follow. This book can serve as a first course, but will probably not provide sufficient depth to develop proper understanding.

- *Problem Solving: A Statistician's Guide*. Chris Chatfield. 2nd ed., Chapman & Hall/CRC. 1995; and *Statistical Rules of Thumb*. Gerald van Belle. 2nd ed., Wiley. 2008.

  Two nice books with lots of practical advice on statistical fieldwork. Chatfield's book is more general; van Belle's contains much material specific to epidemiology and related applications.

- *All of Statistics: A Concise Course in Statistical Inference*. Larry Wasserman. Springer. 2004.

  A thoroughly modern treatment of mathematical statistics, this book presents all kinds of fascinating and powerful topics that are sorely missing from the standard introductory curriculum. The treatment is advanced and very condensed, requiring general previous knowledge in basic statistics and a solid grounding in mathematical methods.

- *Bayesian Methods for Data Analysis.* Bradley P. Carlin, and Thomas A. Louis. 3rd ed., Chapman & Hall. 2008.
  This is a book on Bayesian methods applied to data analysis problems (as opposed to Bayesian theory only). It is a thick book, and some of the topics are fairly advanced. However, the early chapters provide the best introduction to Bayesian methods that I am aware of.

- "Sifting the Evidence—What's Wrong with Significance Tests?" Jonathan A. C. Sterne and George Davey Smith. *British Medical Journal* 322 (2001), p. 226.
  This paper provides a penetrating and nonpartisan overview of the problems associated with classical hypothesis tests, with an emphasis on applications in medicine (although the conclusions are much more generally valid). The full text is freely available on the Web; a search will turn up multiple locations.

## CHAPTER ELEVEN

Intermezzo: Mythbusting—Bigfoot, Least Squares, and All That

EVERYBODY HAS HEARD OF BIGFOOT, THE MYSTICAL FIGURE THAT LIVES IN THE WOODS, BUT NOBODY HAS EVER actually seen him. Similarly, there are some concepts from basic statistics that everybody has heard of but that—like Bigfoot—always remain a little shrouded in mystery. Here, we take a look at three of them: the average of averages, the mystical standard deviation, and the ever-popular least squares.

How to Average Averages

Recently, someone approached me with the following question: given the numbers in Table 11-1, what number should be entered in the lower-right corner? Just adding up the individual defect rates per item and dividing by 3 (in effect, averaging them) did not seem right—if only because it would come out to about 0.75, which is pretty high when one considers that *most* of the units produced (100 out of 103) are not actually defective. The specific question asked was: "Should I weight the individual rates somehow?"

This situation comes up frequently but is not always recognized: we have a set of rates (or averages) and would like to summarize them into an overall rate (or overall average). The

TABLE 11-1. Defect rates: what value should go into the lower-right corner?

Item type	Units produced	Defective units	Defect rate
A	2	1	0.5
B	1	1	1.0
C	100	1	0.01
Total defect rate			**???**

problem is that the naive way of doing so (namely, to add up the individual rates and then to divide by the number of rates) will give an *incorrect* result. However, this is rarely noticed unless the numbers involved are as extreme as in the present example.

The correct way to approach this task is to start from scratch. What is the "defect rate," anyway? It is the number of defective items divided by the number of items produced. Hence, the *total* defect rate is the total number of defective items divided by the total number of items produced: $3/103 \approx 0.03$. There should be no question about that.

Can we arrive at this result in a different way by starting with the individual defect *rates*? Absolutely—provided we weight them appropriately. Each individual defect rate should contribute to the overall defect rate in the same way that the corresponding item type contributes to the total item count. In other words, the weight for item type A is $2/103$, for B is $1/103$, and for C it is $100/103$. Pulling all this together, we have:
$0.5 \cdot 2/103 + 1.0 \cdot 1/103 + 0.01 \cdot 100/103 = (1 + 1 + 1)/103 = 3/103$ as before.

To show that this agreement is not accidental, let's write things out in greater generality:

$$n_k \quad \text{Number of items of type } k$$

$$d_k \quad \text{Number of defective items of type } k$$

$$\epsilon_k = \frac{d_k}{n_k} \quad \text{Defect rate for type } k$$

$$f_k = \frac{n_k}{\sum_i n_i} \quad \text{Contribution of type } k \text{ to total production}$$

Now look at what it means to weight each individual defect rate:

$$f_k \epsilon_k = \frac{n_k}{\sum_i n_i} \frac{d_k}{n_k}$$
$$= \frac{d_k}{\sum_i n_i}$$

In other words, weighting the individual defect rate ϵ_k by the appropriate weight factor f_k has the effect of turning the defect *rate* back to the the defect *count* d_k (normalized by total number of items).

In this example, each item could get only one of two "grades," namely 1 (for defective) or 0 (for not defective), and so the "defect rate" was a measure of the "average defectiveness" of a single item. The same logic as just demonstrated applies if you have a greater (or different) range of values. (You can make up your own example: give items grades from 1 to 5, and then calculate the overall "average grade" to see how it works.)

Simpson's Paradox

Since we are talking about mystical figures that can sometimes be found in tables, we should also mention *Simpson's paradox*. Look at Table 11-2 which shows applications and admissions to a fictional college in terms the applicants' gender and department.

TABLE 11-2. Simpson's paradox: applications and admissions by gender of applicant.

	Male	Female	Overall
Department A	$80/100 = 0.8$	$9/10 = 0.9$	$89/110 = 0.81$
Department B	$5/10 = 0.5$	$60/100 = 0.6$	$65/110 = 0.59$
Total	**$85/110 = 0.77$**	**$69/110 = 0.63$**	

If you look only at the bottom line with the totals, then it might appear that the college is discriminating against women, since the acceptance rate for male applicants is higher than that for female applicants (0.77 versus 0.63).[*] But when you look at the rates for each individual department within the college, it turns out that women have *higher* acceptance rates than men for *every* department. How can that be?

The short and intuitive answer is that many more women apply to department B, which has a lower overall admission rate than department A (0.59 versus 0.81), and this drags down their (gender-specific) acceptance rate.

The more general explanation speaks of a "reversal of association due to a confounding factor." When considering only the totals, it may seem as if there is an association between gender and admission rates, with male applicants being accepted more frequently. However, this view ignores the presence of a hidden but important factor: the choice of department. In fact, the choice of department has a *greater* influence on the acceptance rate than the original explanatory variable (the gender). By lumping the observations for the different departments into a single number, we have in fact masked the influence of this factor—with the consequence that the association between acceptance rate (which favors women for each department) and gender was reversed.

The important insight here is that such "reversal of association" due to a confounding factor is always possible. However, both conditions must occur: the confounding factor must be sufficiently strong (in our case, the acceptance rates for departments A and B were sufficiently different), and the assignment of experimental units to the levels of this factor must be sufficiently imbalanced (in our case, many more women applied to department B than to department A).

As opposed to Bigfoot, Simpson's paradox is known to occur in the real world. The example in this section, for instance, was based on a well-publicized case involving the University of California (Berkeley) in the early 1970s. A quick Internet search will turn up additional examples.

---

[*] You should check that the entries in the bottom row have been calculated properly, per the discussion in the previous section!

The Standard Deviation

The fabled standard deviation is another close relative of Bigfoot. Everybody (it seems) has heard of it, everybody knows how to calculate it, and—most importantly—everybody knows that 68 percent of all data points fall within 1 standard deviation, 95 percent within 2, and virtually all (that is: 99.7 percent) within 3.

Problem is: this is utter nonsense.

It is true that the standard deviation is a measure for the spread (or width) of a distribution. It is also true that, for a given set of points, the standard deviation can always be calculated. But that does not mean that the standard deviation is always a *good* or appropriate measure for the width of a distribution; in fact, it can be quite misleading if applied indiscriminately to an unsuitable data set. Furthermore, we must be careful how to interpret it: the whole 68 percent business applies only if the data set satisfies some very specific requirements.

In my experience, the standard deviation is probably the most misunderstood and misapplied quantity in all of statistics.

Let me tell you a true story (some identifying details have been changed to protect the guilty). The story is a bit involved, but this is no accident: in the same way that Bigfoot sightings never occur in a suburban front yard on a sunny Sunday morning, severe misunderstandings in mathematical or statistical methods usually don't reveal themselves as long as the applications are as clean and simple as the homework problems in a textbook. But once people try to apply these same methods in situations that are a bit less standard, *anything* can happen. This is what happened in this particular company.

I was looking over a bit of code used to identify outliers in the response times from a certain database server. The purpose of this program was to detect and report on uncommonly slow responses. The piece of code in question processed log files containing the response times and reported a threshold value: responses that took longer than this threshold were considered "outliers."

An existing service-level agreement defined an outlier as any value "outside of 3 standard deviations." So what did this piece of code do? It sorted the response times to identify the top 0.3 percent of data points and used those to determine the threshold. (In other words, if there were 1,000 data points in the log file, it reported the response time of the third slowest as threshold.) After all, 99.7 percent of data points fall within 3 standard deviations. Right?

After reading Chapter 2, I hope you can immediately tell where the original programmer went wrong: the threshold that the program reported had *nothing at all* to do with standard deviations—instead, it reported the top 0.3 percentile. In other words, the program completely failed to do what it was supposed to do. Also, keep in mind that it is incorrect to blindly consider the top x percent of any distribution as outliers (review the discussion of box plots in Chapter 2 if you need a reminder).

But the story continues. This was a database server whose typical response time was less than a few seconds. It was clear that anything that took longer than one or two minutes had to be considered "slow"—that is, an outlier. But when the program was run, the threshold value it reported (the 0.3 percentile) was on the order of *hours*. Clearly, this threshold value made no sense.

In what must have been a growing sense of desperation, the original programmer now made a number of changes: from selecting the top 0.3 percent, to the top 1 percent, then the top 5 percent and finally the top 10 percent. (I could tell, because each such change had dutifully been checked into source control!) Finally, the programmer had simply hard-coded some seemingly "reasonable" value (such as 47 seconds or something) into the program, and that's what was reported as "3 standard deviations" regardless of the input.

It was the only case of outright technical fraud that I have ever witnessed: a technical work product that—with the original author's full knowledge—in no way did what it claimed to do.

What went wrong here? Several things. First, there was a fundamental misunderstanding about the definition of the standard deviation, how it is calculated, and some of the properties that in practice it often (but not always) has. The second mistake was applying the standard deviation to a situation where it is not a suitable measure.

Let's recap some basics: we often want to characterize a point distribution by a typical value (its location) and its spread around this location. A convenient measure for the location is the mean: $\mu = \frac{1}{n} \sum_i^n x_i$. Why is the mean so convenient? Because it is easy to calculate: just sum all the values and divide by n.

To find the width of the distribution, we would like see how far points "typically" stray from the mean. In other words, we would like to find the *mean* of the *deviations* $x_i - \mu$. But since the deviations can be positive and negative, they would simply cancel, so instead we calculate the mean of the *squared* deviations: $\sigma^2 = \frac{1}{n} \sum_i^n (x_i - \mu)^2$. This quantity is called the *variance*, and its square root is the *standard deviation*. Why do we bother with the square root? Because it has the same units as the mean, whereas in the variance the units are raised to the second power.

Now, *if and only if* the point distribution is well behaved (which in practice means: it is Gaussian), *then* it is true that about 68 percent of points will fall within the interval $[\mu - \sigma, \mu + \sigma]$ and that 95 percent fall within the interval $[\mu - 2\sigma, \mu + 2\sigma]$ and so on. The inverse is *not* true: you cannot conclude that 68 percent of points define a "standard deviation" (this is where the programmer in our story made the first mistake). If the point distribution is not Gaussian, then there are no particular patterns by which fractions of points will fall within 1, 2, or any number of standard deviations from the mean. However, keep in mind that the definitions of the mean and the standard deviation (as given by the previous equations) both retain their meaning: you can calculate them for any distribution and any data set.

However (and this is the second mistake that was made), if the distribution is strongly asymmetrical, then mean and standard deviation are no longer good measures of location and spread, respectively. You can still *calculate* them, but their values will just not be very informative. In particular, if the distribution has a fat tail then both mean and standard deviation will be influenced heavily by extreme values in the tail.

In this case, the situation was even worse: the distribution of response times was a *power-law* distribution, which is extremely poorly summarized by quantities such as mean and standard deviation. This explains why the top 0.3 percent of response times were on the order of hours: with power-law distributions, all values—even extreme ones—can (and do!) occur; whereas for Gaussian or exponential distributions, the range of values that do occur in practice is pretty well limited. (See Chapter 9 for more information on power-law distributions.)

To summarize, the standard deviation, defined as $\sqrt{\frac{1}{n}\sum_i^n (x_i - \mu)^2}$, is a measure of the width of a distribution (or a sample). It is a good measure for the width only if the distribution of points is well behaved (*i.e.*, symmetric and without fat tails). Points that are far away from the center (compared to the width of the distribution) can be considered outliers. For distributions that are less well behaved, you will have to use other measures for the width (*e.g.*, the inter-quartile range); however, you can usually still identify outliers as points that fall outside the typical range of values. (For power-law distributions, which do not have a "typical" scale, it doesn't make sense to define outliers by statistical means; you will have to justify them differently—for instance by appealing to requirements from the business domain.)

How to Calculate

Here is a good trick for calculating the standard deviation efficiently. At first, it seems you need to make two passes over the data in order to calculate both mean and standard deviation. In the first pass you calculate the mean, but then you need to make a second pass to calculate the deviations from that mean:

$$\sigma^2 = \frac{1}{n}\sum (x_i - \mu)^2$$

It appears as if you can't find the deviations until the mean μ is known.

However, it turns out that you can calculate both quantities in a single pass through the data. All you need to do is to maintain both the sum of the values ($\sum x_i$) and the sum of the squares of the values ($\sum x_i^2$), because you can write the preceding equation for σ^2 in a form that depends only on those two sums:

$$\sigma^2 = \frac{1}{n} \sum (x_i - \mu)^2$$
$$= \frac{1}{n} \sum (x_i^2 - 2x_i\mu + \mu^2)$$
$$= \frac{1}{n} \left(\sum x_i^2 - 2\mu \sum x_i + \mu^2 \sum 1 \right)$$
$$= \frac{1}{n} \sum x_i^2 - 2\mu \frac{1}{n} \sum x_i + \mu^2 \frac{1}{n} n$$
$$= \frac{1}{n} \sum x_i^2 - 2\mu \cdot \mu + \mu^2$$
$$= \frac{1}{n} \sum x_i^2 - \mu^2$$
$$= \frac{1}{n} \sum x_i^2 - \left(\frac{1}{n} \sum x_i \right)^2$$

This is a good trick that is apparently too little known. Keep it in mind; similar situations crop up in different contexts from time to time. (To be sure, the floating-point properties of both methods are different, but if you care enough to worry about the difference, then you should be using a library anyway.)

Optional: One over What?

You may occasionally see the standard deviation defined with an n in the denominator and sometimes with a factor of $n - 1$ instead.

$$\sqrt{\frac{1}{n} \sum_i^n (x_i - \mu)^2} \quad \text{or} \quad \sqrt{\frac{1}{n-1} \sum_i^n (x_i - \mu)^2}$$

What *really* is the difference, and which expression should you use?

The factor $1/n$ applies only if you know the exact value of the mean μ ahead of time. This is usually not the case; instead, you will usually have to calculate the mean from the data. This adds a bit of uncertainty, which leads to the widening of the proper estimate for the standard deviation. A theoretical argument then leads to the use of the factor $1/(n - 1)$ instead of $1/n$.

In short, if you calculated the mean from the data (as is usually the case), then you should really be using the $1/(n - 1)$ factor. The difference is going to be small, unless you are dealing with very small data sets.

Optional: The Standard Error

While we are on the topic of obscure sources of confusion, let's talk about the *standard error*.

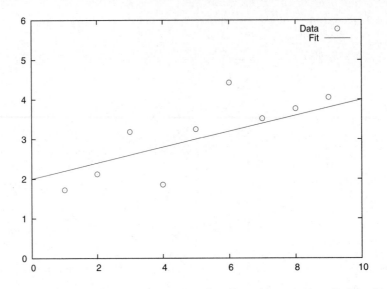

FIGURE 11-1. Fitting for statistical parameter estimation: data affected by random noise. What is the slope of the straight line?

The standard error is the standard deviation of an estimated quantity. Let's say we estimate some quantity (*e.g.*, the mean). If we repeatedly take samples, then the means calculated from those samples will scatter around a little, according to some distribution. The standard deviation of this distribution is the "standard error" of the estimated quantity (the mean, in this example).

The following observation will make this clearer. Take a sample of size n from a normally distributed population with standard deviation σ. Then 68 percent of the members of the *sample* will be within $\pm\sigma$ from the estimated mean (*i.e.*, the sample mean).

However, the mean itself is normally distributed (because of the Central Limit Theorem, since the mean is a sum of random variables) with standard deviation $\sigma/\sqrt{n}$ (again because of the Central Limit Theorem). So if we take several samples, each of size n, then we can expect 68 percent of the estimated means to lie within $\pm\sigma/\sqrt{n}$ of the *true* mean (*i.e.*, the mean of the overall population).

In this situation, the quantity $\sigma/\sqrt{n}$ is therefore the *standard error of the mean*.

Least Squares

Everyone loves least squares. In the confusing and uncertain world of data and statistics, they provide a sense of security—something to rely on! They give you, after all, the "best" fit. Doesn't that say it all?

Problem is, I have *never* (not once!) seen least squares applied appropriately, and I have come to doubt that it should ever be considered a suitable technique. In fact, when today I

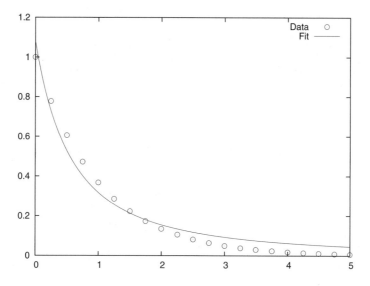

FIGURE 11-2. Fitting a function to approximate a curve known only at discrete locations. Is the fit a good representation of the data?

see someone doing anything involving "least-squares fitting," I am pretty certain this person is at wit's end—and probably does not even know it!

There are two problems with least squares. The first is that it is used for two very different purposes that are commonly confused. The second problem is that least-squares fitting is usually not the best (or even a suitable) method for either purpose. Alternative techniques should be used, depending on the overall purpose (see first problem) and on what, in the end, we want to do with the result.

Let's try to unravel these issues.

Why do we ever want to "fit" a function to data to begin with? There are two different reasons.

Statistical Parameter Estimation
 Data is corrupted by random noise, and we want to extract parameters from it.

Smooth Interpolation or Approximation
 Data is given as individual points, and we would like either to find a smooth interpolation to arbitrary positions between those points or to determine an analytical "formula" describing the data.

These two scenarios are conceptually depicted in Figures 11-1 and 11-2.

Statistical Parameter Estimation

Statistical parameter estimation is the more legitimate of the two purposes. In this case, we have a control variable x and an outcome y. We set the former and measure the latter, resulting in a data set of pairs: $\{(x_1, y_1), (x_2, y_2), \ldots\}$. Furthermore, we assume that the outcome is related to the control variable through some function $f(x; \{a, b, c, \ldots\})$ of known form that depends on the control variable x and also on a set of (initially unknown) parameters $\{a, b, c, \ldots\}$. However, in practice, the actual measurements are affected by some random noise ϵ, so that the measured values y_i are a combination of the "true" value and the noise term:

$$y_i = f(x_i, \{a, b, c, \ldots\}) + \epsilon_i$$

We now ask: how should we choose values for the parameters $\{a, b, c, \ldots\}$, such that the function $f(x, \{a, b, c, \ldots\})$ reproduces the measured values of y most faithfully? The usual answer is that we want to choose the parameters such that the *total mean-square error* E^2 (sometimes called the *residual sum of squares*):

$$E^2 = \sum_i (f(x_i, \{a, b, c, \ldots\}) - y_i)^2$$

is minimized. As long as the distribution of errors is reasonably well behaved (not too asymmetric and without heavy tails), the results are adequate. If, in addition, the noise is Gaussian, then we can even invoke other parts of statistics and show that the estimates for the parameters obtained by the least-squares procedure agree with the "maximum likelihood estimate." Thus the least-squares results are consistent with alternative ways of calculation.

But there is another important aspect to least-squares estimation that is frequently lost: we can obtain not only *point estimates* for the parameters $\{a, b, c, \ldots\}$ but also *confidence intervals*, through a self-consistent argument that links the distribution of the parameters to the distribution of the measured values.

I cannot stress this enough: a point estimate by itself is of limited use. After all, what good is knowing that the point estimate for a is 5.17 if I have no idea whether this means $a = 5.17 \pm 0.01$ or $a = 5.17 \pm 250$? We *must* have some way of judging the range over which we expect our estimate to vary, which is the same as finding a confidence interval for it. Least squares works, when applied in a probabilistic context like this, because it gives us not only an estimate for the parameters but also for their confidence intervals.

One last point: in statistical applications, it is rarely necessary to perform the minimization of E^2 by numerical means. For most of the functions $f(x, \{a, b, c, \ldots\})$ that are commonly used in statistics, the conditions that will minimize E^2 can be worked out explicitly. (See Chapter 3 for the results when the function is linear.) In general, you should be reluctant to resort to numerical minimization procedures—there might be better ways of obtaining the result.

Function Approximation

In practice, however, least-squares fitting is often used for a different purpose. Consider the situation in Figure 11-2, where we have a set of individual data points. These points clearly seem to fall on a smooth curve. It would be convenient to have an explicit formula to summarize these data points rather than having to work with the collection of points directly. So, can we "fit" a formula to them?

Observe that, in this second application of least-squares fitting, there is *no random noise*. In fact, there is no random component at all! This is an important insight, because it implies that statistical methods and arguments don't apply.

This becomes relevant when we want to determine the degree of confidence in the results of a fit. Let's say we have performed a least-squares routine and obtained some values for the parameters. What confidence intervals should we associate with the parameters, and how good is the overall fit? Whatever errors we may incur in the fitting process, they will not be of a random nature, and we therefore cannot make probabilistic arguments about them.

The scenario in Figure 11-2 is typical: the plot shows the data together with the best fit for a function of the form $f(x; a, b) = a/(1 + x)^b$, with $a = 1.08$ and $b = 1.77$. Is this a good fit? And what uncertainty do we have in the parameters? The answer depends on what you want to do with the results—but be aware that the deviations between the fit and the data are not at all "random" and hence that statistical "goodness of fit" measures are inappropriate. We have to find other ways to answer our questions. (For instance, we may find the largest of the residuals between the data points and our fitted function and report that the fit "represents the data with a maximum deviation of . . . .")

This situation is typical in yet another way: given how smooth the curve is that the data points seem to fall on, our "best fit" seems really *bad*. In particular, the fit exhibits a systematic error: for $0 < x < 1.5$, the curve is always smaller than the data, and for $x > 1.5$, it is always greater. Is this really the best we can do? The answer is yes, for functions of the form $a/(1 + x)^b$. However, a different choice of function might give much better results. The problem here is that the least-squares approach forces us to specify the functional form of the function we are attempting to fit, and if we get it wrong, then the results won't be any good. For this reason, we should use less constraining approaches (such as nonparametric or local approximations) unless we have good reasons to favor a particular functional form.

In other words, what we really have here is a problem of function interpolation or approximation: we know the function on a discrete set of points, and we would like to extend it smoothly to all values. How we should do this depends on what we want to do with the results. Here is some advice for common scenarios:

- To find a "smooth curve" for plotting purposes, you should use one of the smoothing routines discussed in Chapter 3, such as splines or LOESS. These nonparametric methods have the advantage that they do not impose a particular functional form on the data (in contrast to the situation in Figure 11-2).

- If you want to be able to evaluate the function easily at an arbitrary location, then you should use a local interpolation method. Such methods build a local approximation by using the three or four data points closest to the desired location. It is not necessary to find a global expression in this case: the local approximation will suffice.

- Sometimes you may want to summarize the behavior of the data set in just a few "representative" values (*e.g.*, so you can more easily compare one data set against another). This is tricky—it is probably a better idea to compare data sets *directly* against each other using similarity metrics such as those discussed in Chapter 13. If you still need to do this, consider a *basis function expansion* using Fourier, Hermite, or wavelet functions. (These are special sets of functions that enable you to extract greater and greater amounts of detail from a data set. Expansion in basis functions also allows you to evaluate and improve the quality of the approximation in a systematic fashion.)

- At times you might be interested in some particular feature of the data: for example, you suspect that the data follows a power law x^b and you would like to extract the exponent; or the data is periodic and you need to know the length of one period. In such cases, it is usually a better idea to transform the data in such a way that you can obtain that particular feature directly, rather than fitting a global function. (To extract exponents, you should consider a logarithmic transform. To obtain the length of an oscillatory period, measure the peak-to-peak (or, better still, the zero-to-zero) distance.)

- Use specialized methods if available and applicable. Time series, for instance, should be treated with the techniques discussed in Chapter 4.

You may have noticed that none of these suggestions involve least squares!

Further Reading

Every introductory statistics book covers the standard deviation and least squares (see the book recommendations in Chapter 10). For the alternatives to least squares, consult a book on numerical analysis, such as the one listed here.

- *Numerical Methods That (Usually) Work.* Forman S. Acton. 2nd ed., Mathematical Association of America. 1997.
  Although originally published in 1970, this book does not feel the least bit dated—it is still one of the best introductions to the art of numerical analysis. Neither a cookbook nor a theoretical treatise, it stresses practicality and understanding first and foremost. It includes an inimitable chapter on "What *Not* to Compute."

## PART III

Computation: Mining Data

## CHAPTER TWELVE

Simulations

IN THIS CHAPTER, WE LOOK AT SIMULATIONS AS A WAY TO UNDERSTAND DATA. IT MAY SEEM STRANGE TO FIND simulations included in a book on data analysis: don't simulations just generate even *more* data that needs to be analyzed? Not necessarily—as we will see, simulations in the form of *resampling methods* provide a family of techniques for extracting information from data. In addition, simulations can be useful when developing and validating models, and in this way, they facilitate our understanding of data. Finally, in the context of this chapter we can take a brief look at a few other relevant topics, such as discrete event simulations and queueing theory.

A technical comment: I assume that your programming environment includes a random-number generator—not only for uniformly distributed random numbers but also for other distributions (this is a pretty safe bet). I also assume that this random-number generator produces random numbers of sufficiently high quality. This is probably a reasonable assumption, but there's no guarantee: although the theory of random-number generators is well understood, broken implementations apparently continue to ship. Most books on simulation methods will contain information on random-number generators—look there if you feel that you need more detail.

A Warm-Up Question

As a warm-up to demonstrate how simulations can help us analyze data, consider the following example. We are given a data set with the results of eight tosses of a coin: six Heads and two Tails. Given this data, would we say the coin is biased?

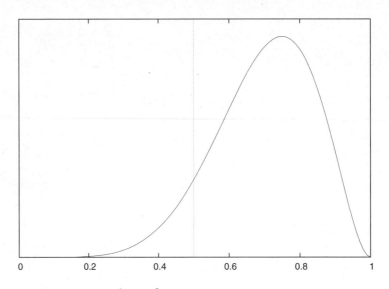

FIGURE 12-1. The likelihood function $p^6(1 - p)^2$ of observing six Heads and two Tails in eight tosses of a coin, as a function of the coin's "balance parameter" p.

The problem is that the data set is small—if there had been 80,000 tosses of which 60,000 came out Heads, then we would have no doubt that the coin was biased. But with just eight tosses, it seems plausible that the imbalance in the results might be due to chance alone—even with a fair coin.

It was for precisely this kind of question that formal statistical methods were developed. We could now either invoke a classical frequentist point of view and calculate the probability of obtaining six or more Heads in eight tosses of a fair coin (*i.e.*, six or more successes in eight Bernoulli trials with $p = 0.5$). The probability comes out to $37/256 \approx 0.14$, which is not enough to "reject the null hypothesis (that the coin is fair) at the 5 percent level." Alternatively, we could adopt a Bayesian viewpoint and evaluate the appropriate likelihood function for the given data set with a noninformative prior (see Figure 12-1). The graph suggests that the coin is not balanced.

But what if we have forgotten how to evaluate either quantity, or (more likely!) if we are dealing with a problem more intricate than the one in this example, so that we neither know the appropriate model to choose nor the form of the likelihood function? Can we find a quick way to make progress on the question we started with?

Given the topic of this chapter, the answer is easy. We can *simulate* tosses of a coin, for various degrees of imbalance, and then compare the simulation results to our data set.

```
import random

repeats, tosses = 60, 8
```

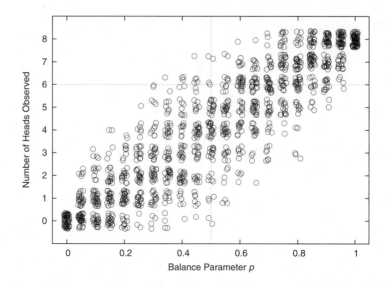

FIGURE 12-2. *Results of 60 simulation runs, each consisting of eight tosses of a coin, for different values of the coin's "balance parameter" p. Shown are the number of Heads observed in each run. Although a slight balance toward Heads ($p \approx 0.7$) seems most probable, note that as many as six Heads can occasionally be observed even with a coin that is balanced toward Tails.*

```
def heads( tosses, p ):
    h = 0
    for x in range( 0, tosses ):
        if random.random() < p: h += 1
    return h

p = 0
while p < 1.01:
    for t in range( 0, repeats ):
        print p, "\t", heads( tosses, p )
    p += 0.05
```

The program is trivial to write, and the results, in the form of a jitter plot, are shown in Figure 12-2. (For each value of the parameter p, which controls the imbalance of the coin, we have performed 60 repeats of 8 tosses each and counted the number of Heads in each repeat.)

The figure is quite clear: for $p = 0.5$ (*i.e.*, a balanced coin), it is pretty unlikely to obtain six or more Heads, although not at all impossible. On the other hand, given that we have observed six Heads, we would expect the parameter to fall into the range $p = 0.6, \ldots, 0.7$. We have thus not only answered the question we started with but also given it some context. The simulation therefore not only helped us understand the actual data set but also allowed us to explore the system that produced it. Not bad for 15 lines of code.

Monte Carlo Simulations

The term *Monte Carlo simulation* is frequently used to describe any method that involves the generation of random points as input for subsequent operations.

Monte Carlo techniques are a major topic all by themselves. Here, I only want to sketch two applications that are particularly relevant in the context of data analysis and modeling. First, simulations allow us to verify analytical work and to experiment with it further; second, simulations are a way of obtaining results from models for which analytical solutions are not available.

Combinatorial Problems

Many basic combinatorial problems can be solved exactly—but obtaining a solution is often difficult. Even when one is able to find a solution, it is surprisingly easy to arrive at incorrect conclusions, missing factors like $1/2$ or $1/n!$ and so on. And lastly, it takes only innocuous looking changes to a problem formulation to render the problem intractable.

In contrast, simulations for typical combinatorial problems are often trivially easy to write. Hence they are a great way to validate theoretical results, and they can be extended to explore problems that are not tractable otherwise.

Here are some examples of questions that can be answered easily in this way:

- If we place n balls into n boxes, what is the probability that no more than two boxes contain two or more balls? What if I told you that *exactly m* boxes are empty? What if *at most m* boxes are empty?

- If we try keys from a key chain containing n different keys, how many keys will we have to try before finding the one that fits the lock? How is the answer different if we try keys randomly (with replacement) as opposed to in order (without replacement)?

- Suppose an urn contains $2n$ tokens consisting of n pairs of items. (Each item is marked in such a way that we can tell to which pair it belongs.) Repeatedly select a single token from the urn and put it aside. Whenever the most recently selected token is the *second* item from a pair, take both items (*i.e.*, the entire pair) and return them to the urn. How many "broken pairs" will you have set aside on average? How does the answer change if we care about triples instead of pairs? What fluctuations can we expect around the average value?

The last problem is a good example of the kind of problem for which the simple case (average number of broken pairs) is fairly easy to solve but that becomes rapidly more complicated as we make seemingly small modifications to the original problem (*e.g.*, going from pairs to triples). However, in a simulation such changes do not pose any special difficulties.

Another way that simulations can be helpful concerns situations that appear unfamiliar or even paradoxical. Simulations allow us to *see* how the system behaves and thereby to develop intuition for it. We already encountered an example in the Workshop section of Chapter 9, where we studied probability distributions without expectation values. Let's look at another example.

Suppose, we are presented with a choice of three closed envelopes. One envelope contains a prize, the other two are empty. After we have selected an envelope, it is revealed that one of the envelopes that we had *not* selected is empty. We are now permitted to choose again. What should we do? Stick with our initial selection? Randomly choose between the two remaining envelopes? Or pick the remaining envelope—that is, not the one that we selected initially and not the one that has been opened?

This is a famous problem, which is sometimes known as the "Monty Hall Problem" (after the host of a game show that featured a similar game).

As it turns out, the last strategy (always switch to the remaining envelope) is the most beneficial. The problem appears to be paradoxical because the additional information that is revealed (that an envelope we did not select is empty) does not seem to be useful in any way. How can this information affect the probability that our initial guess was correct?

The argument goes as follows. Our initial selection is correct with probability $p = 1/3$ (because one envelope among the original three contains the prize). If we stick with our original choice, then we should therefore have a 33 percent chance of winning. On the other hand, if in our second choice, we choose randomly from the remaining options (meaning that we are as likely to pick the initially chosen envelope or the remaining one), then we will select the correct envelope with probability $p = 1/2$ (because now one out of two envelopes contains the prize). A random choice is therefore better than staying put!

But this is still not the best strategy. Remember that our initial choice only had a $p = 1/3$ probability of being correct—in other words, it has probability $q = 2/3$ of being *wrong*. The additional information (the opening of an empty envelope) does not change this probability, but *it removes all alternatives*. Since our original choice is wrong with probability $q = 2/3$ and since now there is only one other envelope remaining, switching to this remaining envelope should lead to a win with 66 percent probability!

I don't know about you, but this is one of those cases where I had to "see it to believe it." Although the argument above seems compelling, I still find it hard to accept. The program in the following listing helped me do exactly that.

```
import sys
import random as rnd

strategy = sys.argv[1]    # must be 'stick', 'choose', or 'switch'

wins = 0
for trial in range( 1000 ):
```

```
            # The prize is always in envelope 0 ... but we don't know that!
            envelopes = [0, 1, 2]

            first_choice = rnd.choice( envelopes )

            if first_choice == 0:
                envelopes = [0, rnd.choice( [1,2] ) ] # Randomly retain 1 or 2
            else:
                envelopes = [0, first_choice] # Retain winner and first choice

            if strategy == 'stick':
                second_choice = first_choice
            elif strategy == 'choose':
                second_choice = rnd.choice( envelopes )
            elif strategy == 'switch':
                envelopes.remove( first_choice )
                second_choice = envelopes[0]

            # Remember that the prize is in envelope 0
            if second_choice == 0:
                wins += 1

        print wins
```

The program reads our strategy from the command line: the possible choices are stick, choose, and switch. It then performs a thousand trials of the game. The "prize" is always in envelope 0, but we don't know that. Only if our second choice equals envelope 0 we count the game as a win.

The results from running this program are consistent with the argument given previously: stick wins in one third of all trials, choose wins half the time, but switch amazingly wins in two thirds of all cases.

Obtaining Outcome Distributions

Simulations can be helpful to verify with combinatorial problems, but the primary reason for using simulations is that they allow us to obtain results that are not available analytically. To arrive at an analytical solution for a model, we usually have to make simplifying assumptions. One particularly common one is to replace all random quantities with their most probable value (the mean-field approximation; see Chapter 8). This allows us to solve the model, but we lose information about the distribution of outcomes. Simulations are a way of retaining the effects of randomness when determining the consequences of a model.

Let's return to the case study discussed at the end of Chapter 9. We had a visitor population making visits to a certain website. Because individual visitors can make repeat visits, the number of *unique* visitors grows more slowly than the number of *total* visitors. We found an expression for the number of unique visitors over time but had to make some approximations in order to make progress. In particular, we assumed that the number of total visitors per day would be the same every day, and be equal to the average number of visitors per day. (We also assumed that the fraction of actual repeat visitors on any given day would equal the fraction of repeat visitors in the total population.)

Both of these assumptions are of precisely the nature discussed earlier: we replaced what in reality is a random quantity with its most probable value. These approximations made the problem tractable, but we lost all sense of the accuracy of the result. Let's see how simulations can help provide additional insight to this situation.

The solution which in Chapter 9 was a *model*: an analytical (mean-field) model. The short program that follows is another model of the same system, but this time it is a *simulation model*. It is a model in the sense that again everything that is not absolutely essential has been stripped away: there is no website, no actual visits, no browsing behavior. But the model retains two aspects that are important and that were missing from the mean-field model. First, the number of visitors per day is no longer fixed, instead it is distributed according to a Gaussian distribution. Second, we have a notion of individual visitors (as elements of the list has_visited), and on every "day" we make a random selection from this set of visitors to determine who does visit on this day and who does not.

```python
import random as rnd

n = 1000    # total visitors
k = 100     # avg visitors per day
s = 50      # daily variation

def trial():
    visitors_for_day = [0]  # No visitors on day 0

    has_visited = [0]*n     # A flag for each visitor
    for day in range( 31 ):
        visitors_today = max( 0, int(rnd.gauss( k, s )) )

        # Pick the individuals who visited today and mark them
        for i in rnd.sample( range( n ), visitors_today ):
            has_visited[i] = 1

        # Find the total number of unique visitors so far
        visitors_for_day.append( sum(has_visited) )

    return visitors_for_day


for t in range( 25 ):
    r = trial()
    for i in range( len(r) ):
        print i, r[i]

    print
    print
```

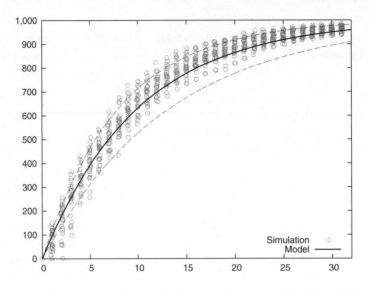

FIGURE 12-3. Unique visitors as a function of time: results from the simulation run, together with predictions from the analytical model. All data points are jittered horizontally to minimize overplotting. The solid line is the most probable number of visitors according to the model; the dashed lines indicate a confidence band.

The program performs 25 trials, where each trial consists of a full, 31-day month of visits. For each day, we find the number of visitors for that day (which must be a positive integer) and then randomly select the same number of "visitors" from our list of visitors, setting a flag to indicate that they have visited. Finally, we count the number of visitors that have the flag set and print this number (which is the number of unique visitors so far) for each day. The results are shown in Figure 12-3.

Figure 12-3 also includes results from the analytical model. In Chapter 9, we found that the number of unique visitors on day t was given by:

$$n(t) = N\left(1 - e^{-\frac{k}{N}t}\right)$$

where N is the total number of visitors ($N = 1{,}000$ in the simulation) and k is the average number of visitors per day ($k = 100$ in the simulation). Accordingly, the solid line in Figure 12-3 is given by $n(t) = 1{,}000\left(1 - \exp\left(-\frac{100}{1000}t\right)\right)$.

The simulation includes a parameter that was not part of the analytical model—namely the width s of the daily fluctuations in visitors. I have chosen the value $s = 50$ for the simulation runs. The dashed lines in Figure 12-3 show the analytical model, with values of $k \pm s/2$ (*i.e.*, $k = 75$ and $k = 125$) to provide a sense for the predicted spread, according to the mean-field model.

First of all, we should note that the analytical model agrees very well with the data from the simulation run: that's a nice confirmation of our previous result! But we should also note the differences; in particular, the simulation results are consistently *higher* than the theoretical predictions. If we think about this for a moment, this makes sense. If on any day there are unusually many visitors, then this irrevocably bumps the number of unique visitors *up*: the number of unique visitors can never shrink, so any outlier above the average can never be neutralized (in contrast to an outlier below the average, which can be compensated by any subsequent high-traffic day).

We can further analyze the data from the simulation run, depending on our needs. For instance, we can calculate the most probable value for each day, and we can estimate proper confidence intervals around it. (We will need more than 25 trials to obtain a good estimate of the latter.)

What is more interesting about the simulation model developed here is that we can use it to obtain *additional* information that would be difficult or impossible to calculate from the analytical formula. For example, we may ask for the *distribution of visits per user* (i.e., how many users have visited once, twice, three times, and so on). The answer to this question is just a snap of the fingers away! We can also extend the model and ask for the number of unique visitors who have paid *two or more* visits (not just one). (For two visits per person, this question can be answered within the framework of the original analytical model, but the calculations rapidly become more tedious as we are asking for higher visit counts per person.)

Finally, we can extend the simulation to include features not included in the analytical model at all. For instance, for a real website, not all possible visitors are equally likely to visit: some individuals will have a higher probability of visiting the website than do others. It would be very difficult to incorporate this kind of generalization into the approach taken in Chapter 9, because it contradicts the basic assumption that the fraction of actual repeat visitors equals the fraction of repeat visitors in the total population. But it is not at all difficult to model this behavior in a simulation model!

Pro and Con

Basic simulations of the kind discussed in this section are often easy to program—certainly as compared with the effort required to develop nontrivial combinatorial arguments! Moreover, when we start writing a simulation project, we can be fairly certain of being successful in the end; whereas there is no guarantee that an attempt to find an exact answer to a combinatorial problem will lead anywhere.

On the other hand, we should not forget that a simulation produces numbers, not insight! A simulation is always only one step in a larger process, which must include a proper analysis of the results from the simulation run and, ideally, also involves an attempt to incorporate the simulation data into a larger conceptual model. I always get a little uncomfortable when presented with a bunch of simulation results that have not been fit into a larger context. Simulations cannot replace analytical modeling.

In particular, simulations do not yield the kind of insight into the mechanisms driving certain developments that a good analytical model affords. For instance, recall the case study near the end of Chapter 8, in which we tried to determine the optimal number of servers. One important insight from that model was that the probability p^n for a total failure dropped extremely rapidly as the number n of servers increased: the exponential decay (with n) is much more important than the reliability p of each individual server. (In other words, redundant commodity hardware beats expensive supercomputers—at least for situations in which this simplified cost model holds!) This is the kind of insight that would be difficult to gain simply by looking at results from simulation runs.

Simulations can be valuable for verifying analytical work and for extending it by incorporating details that would be difficult or impossible to treat in an analytical model. At the same time, the benefit that we can derive from simulations is enhanced by the insight gained from the analytical, conceptual modeling of the the mechanisms driving a system.

The two methods are complementary—although I will give primacy to analytical work. Analytical models without simulation may be crude but will still yield insight, whereas simulations without analysis produce only numbers, not insight.

Resampling Methods

Imagine you have taken a sample of n points from some population. It is now a trivial exercise to calculate the mean from this sample. But how reliable is this mean? If we repeatedly took new samples (of the same size) from the population and calculated *their* means, how much would the various values for the mean jump around?

This question is important. A point estimate (such as the mean by itself) is not very powerful: what we really want is an interval estimate which also gives us a sense of the reliability of the answer.

If we could go back and draw additional samples, then we could obtain the distribution of the mean directly as a histogram of the observed means. But that is not an option: all we have are the n data points of the original sample.

Much of classical statistics deals with precisely this question: how can we make statements about the reliability of an estimate based only on a set of observations? To make progress, we need to make some assumptions about the way values are distributed. This is where the *sampling distributions* of classical statistics come in: all those Normal, t, and chi-square distributions (see Chapter 10). Once we have a theoretical model for the way points are distributed, we can use this model to establish confidence intervals.

Being able to make such statements is one of the outstanding achievements of classical statistics, but at the same time, the difficulties in getting there are a major factor in making classical statistics seem so obscure. Two problems stand out:

- Our assumptions about the shape of those distributions may not be correct, or we may not be able to formulate those distributions at all—in particular, if we are interested in more complicated quantities than just the sample mean or if we are dealing with populations that are ill behaved (*i.e.*, not even remotely Gaussian).

- Even if we know the sampling distribution, determining confidence limits from it may be tedious, opaque, and error-prone.

The Bootstrap

The *bootstrap* is an alternative approach for finding confidence intervals and similar quantities directly from the data. Instead of making assumptions about the distribution of values and then employing theoretical arguments, the bootstrap goes back to the original idea: what if we could draw *additional samples* from the population?

We can't go back to the original population, but the sample that we already have should be a fairly good approximation to the overall population. We can therefore create additional samples (also of size n) by *sampling with replacement* from the original sample. For each of these "synthetic" samples, we can calculate the mean (or any other quantity, of course) and then use this set of values for the mean to determine a measure of the spread of its distribution via any standard method (*e.g.*, we might calculate its inter-quartile range; see Chapter 2).

Let's look at an example—one that is simple enough that we can work out the analytical answer and compare it directly to the bootstrap results. We draw $n = 25$ points from a standard Gaussian distribution (with mean $\mu = 0$ and standard deviation $\sigma = 1$). We then ask about the (observed) sample mean and more importantly, about its standard error. In this case, the answer is simple: we know that the error of the mean is $\sigma/\sqrt{n}$ (see Chapter 11), which amounts to $1/5$ here. This is the analytical result.

To find the bootstrap estimate for the standard error, we draw 100 samples, each containing $n = 25$ points, from our original sample of 25 points. Points are drawn randomly with replacement (so that each point can be selected multiple times). For each of these bootstrap samples, we calculate the mean. Now we ask: what is the spread of the distribution of these 100 bootstrap means?

The data is plotted in Figure 12-4. At the bottom, we see the 25 points of the original data sample; above that, we see the means calculated from the 100 bootstrap samples. (All points are jittered vertically to minimize overplotting.) In addition, the figure shows kernel density estimates (see Chapter 2) of the original sample and also of the bootstrap means. The latter is the answer to our original question: if we repeatedly took samples from the *original* distribution, the sample means would be distributed similarly to the bootstrap means.

(Because in this case we happen to know the original distribution, we can also plot both it and the theoretical distribution of the mean, which happens to be Gaussian as well but

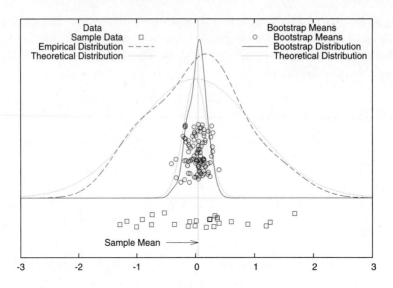

FIGURE 12-4. The bootstrap. The points in the original sample are shown at the bottom; the means calculated from the bootstrap samples are shown above. Also displayed are the original distribution and the distribution of the sample means, both using the theoretical result and a kernel density estimate from the corresponding samples.

with a reduced standard deviation of $\sigma/\sqrt{n}$. As we would expect, the theoretical distributions agree reasonably well with the kernel density estimated calculated from the data.)

Of course, in this example the bootstrap procedure was not necessary. It should be clear, however, that the bootstrap provides a simple method for obtaining confidence intervals even in situations where theoretical results are not available. For instance, if the original distribution had been highly skewed, then the Gaussian assumption would have been violated. Similarly, if we had wanted to calculate a more complicated quantity than the mean, analytical results might have been hard to obtain.

Let me repeat this, because it's important: bootstrapping is a method to estimate the *spread* of some quantity. It is not a method to obtain "better" estimates of the original quantity itself—for that, it is necessary to obtain a larger sample by making additional drawings from the original population. The bootstrap is not a way to give the appearance of a larger sample size by reusing points!

When Does Bootstrapping Work?

As we have seen, the bootstrap is a simple, practical, and relatively transparent method to obtain confidence intervals for estimated quantities. This begs the question: when does it work? The following two conditions must be fulfilled.

1. The original sample must provide a good representation of the entire population.

2. The estimated quantity must depend "smoothly" on the data points.

The first condition requires the original sample to be sufficiently large and relatively clean. If the sample size is too small, then the original estimate for the actual quantity in question (the mean, in our example) won't be very good. (Bootstrapping in a way exacerbates this problem because data points have a greater chance of being reused repeatedly in the bootstrap samples.) In other words, the original sample has to be large enough to allow meaningful estimation of the primary quantity. Use common sense and insight into your specific application area to establish the required sample size for your situation.

Additionally, the sample has to be relatively clean: crazy outliers, for instance, can be a problem. Unless the sample size is very large, outliers have a significant chance of being reused in a bootstrap sample, distorting the results.

Another problem exists in situations involving power-law distributions. As we saw in Chapter 9, estimated values for such distributions may not be unique but depend on the sample *size*. Of course, the same considerations apply to bootstrap samples drawn from such distributions.

The second condition suggests that bootstrapping does not work well for quantities that depend critically on only a few data points. For example, we may want to estimate the maximum value of some distribution. Such an estimate depends critically on the largest observed value—that is, on a single data point. For such applications, the bootstrap is not suitable. (In contrast, the mean depends on *all* data points and with equal weight.)

Another questions concerns the number of bootstrap samples to take. The short answer is: as many as you need to obtain a sufficiently good estimate for the spread you are calculating. If the number of points in the original sample is very small, then creating too many bootstrap samples is counterproductive because you will be regenerating the same bootstrap samples over and over again. However, for reasonably sized samples, this is not much of a problem, since the number of possible bootstrap samples grows very quickly with the number of data points n in the original sample. Therefore, it is highly unlikely that the same bootstrap example is generated more than once—even if we generate thousands of bootstrap samples.

The following argument will help to develop a sense for the order of magnitudes involved. The problem of choosing n data points with replacement from the original n-point sample is equivalent to assigning n elements to n cells. It is a classical problem in occupancy theory to show that there are:

$$\binom{2n-1}{n} = \frac{(2n-1)!}{n!(n-1)!}$$

ways of doing this. This number grows extremely quickly: for $n = 5$ it is 126, for $n = 10$ we have 92,378, but for $n = 20$ it already exceeds 10^{10}.

(The usual proof proceeds by observing that assigning r indistinguishable objects to n bins is equivalent to aligning r objects and $n - 1$ bin dividers. There are $r + n - 1$ spots in total, which can be occupied by either an object or a divider, and the assignment amounts to choosing r of these spots for the r objects. The number of ways one can choose r elements out of $n + r - 1$ is given by the binomial coefficient $\binom{r+n-1}{r}$. Since in our case $r = n$, we find that the number of different bootstrap samples is given by the expression above.)

Bootstrap Variants

There are a few variants of the basic bootstrap idea. The method so far—in which points are drawn directly from the original sample—is known as the *nonparametric bootstrap*. An alternative is the *parametric bootstrap*: in this case, we assume that the original population follows some particular probability distribution (such as the Gaussian), and we estimate its parameters (mean and standard deviation, in this case) from the original sample. The bootstrap samples are then drawn from this distribution rather than from the original sample. The advantage of the parametric bootstrap is that the bootstrap values do not have to coincide exactly with the known data points. In a similar spirit, we may use the original sample to compute a kernel density estimate (as an approximation to the population distribution) and then draw bootstrap samples from it. This method combines aspects of both parametric and nonparametric approaches: it is nonparametric (because it make no assumption about the form of the underlying population distribution), yet the bootstrap samples are not restricted to the values occurring in the original sample. In practice, neither of these variants seems to provide much of an advantage over the original idea (in part because the number of possible bootstrap samples grows so quickly with the number of points in the sample that choosing the bootstrap samples from only those points is not much of a restriction).

Another idea (which historically predates the bootstrap) is the so-called *jackknife*. In the jackknife, we don't draw random samples. Instead, given an original sample consisting of n data points, we calculate the n estimates of the quantity of interest by successively omitting one of the data points from the sample. We can now use these n values in a similar way that we used values calculated from bootstrap samples. Since the jackknife does not contain any random element, it is an entirely deterministic procedure.

Workshop: Discrete Event Simulations with SimPy

All the simulation examples that we considered so far were either static (coin tosses, Monty Hall problem) or extremely stripped down and conceptual (unique visitors). But if we are dealing with the behavior and time development of more complex systems—consisting of many different particles or actors that interact with each other in complicated ways—then we want a simulation that expresses all these entities in a manner that closely resembles the problem domain. In fact, this is probably exactly what most of us think of when we hear the term "simulation."

There are basically two different ways that we can set up such a simulation. In a *continuous time simulation*, time progresses in "infinitesimally" small increments. At each time step, all simulation objects are advanced while taking possible interactions or status changes into account. We would typically choose such an approach to simulate the behavior of particles moving in a fluid or a similar system.

But in other cases, this model seems wasteful. For instance, consider customers arriving at a bank: in such a situation, we only care about the *events* that change the state of the system (*e.g.*, customer arrives, customer leaves)—we don't actually care what the customers do while waiting in line! For such system we can use a different simulation method, known as *discrete event simulation*. In this type of simulation, time does not pass continuously; instead, we determine when the next event is scheduled to occur and then jump ahead to exactly that moment in time.

Discrete event simulations are applicable to a wide variety of problems involving multiple users competing for access to a shared server. It will often be convenient to phrase the description in terms of the proverbial "customers arriving at a bank," but exactly the same considerations apply, for instance, to messages on a computer network.

Introducing SimPy

The SimPy package (*http://simpy.sourceforge.net/*) is a Python project to build discrete event simulation models. The framework handles all the event scheduling and messaging "under the covers" so that the programmer can concentrate on describing the behavior of the actors in the simulation.

All actors in a SimPy simulation must be subclasses of the class `Process`. Congestion points where queues form are modeled by instances of the `Resource` class or its subclasses. Here is a short example, which describes a customer visiting a bank:

```
from SimPy.Simulation import *

class Customer( Process ):
    def doit( self ):
        print "Arriving"
        yield request, self, bank

        print "Being served"
        yield hold, self, 100.0

        print "Leaving"
        yield release, self, bank


# Beginning of main simulation program
initialize()

bank = Resource()

cust = Customer()
cust.start( cust.doit() )

simulate( until=1000 )
```

Let's skip the class definition of the `Customer` object for now and concentrate on the rest of the program. The first function to call in any SimPy program is the `initialize()` method, which sets up the simulation run and sets the "simulation clock" to zero. We then proceed to create a `Resource` object (which models the bank) and a single `Customer` object. After creating the `Customer`, we need to activate it via the `start()` member function. The `start()` function takes as argument the function that will be called to advance the `Customer` through its life cycle (we'll come back to that). Finally, we kick off the actual simulation, requiring it to stop after 1,000 time steps on the simulation clock have passed.

The `Customer` subclasses `Process`, therefore its instances are active agents, which will be scheduled by the framework to receive events. Each agent must define a *process execution method* (PEM), which defines its behavior and which will be invoked by the framework whenever an event occurs.

For the `Customer` class, the PEM is the `doit()` function. (There are no restrictions on its name—it can be called anything.) The PEM describes the customer's behavior: after the customer arrives, the customer *requests* a resource instance (the bank in this case). If the resource is not available (because it is busy, serving other customers), then the framework will add the customer to the waiting list (the *queue*) for the requested resource. Once the resource becomes available, the customer is being serviced. In this simple example, the service time is a fixed value of 100 time units, during which the customer instance is *holding*—just waiting until the time has passed. When service is complete, the customer *releases* the resource instance. Since no additional actions are listed in the PEM, the customer is not scheduled for future events and will disappear from the simulation.

Notice that the `Customer` interacts with the simulation environment through Python `yield` statements, using special yield expressions of the form shown in the example. Yielding control back to the framework in this way ensures that the `Customer` retains its state and its current spot in the life cycle between invocations. Although there are no restrictions on the name and argument list permissible for a PEM, each PEM *must* contain at least one of these special `yield` statements. (But of course not necessarily all three, as in this case; we are free to define the behavior of the agents in our simulations at will.)

The Simplest Queueing Process

Of course the previous example which involved only a *single* customer entering and leaving the bank, is not very exciting—we hardly needed a simulation for that! Things change when we have more than one customer in the system at the same time.

The listing that follows is very similar to the previous example, except that now there is an infinite stream of customers arriving at the bank and requesting service. To generate this infinite sequence of customers, the listing makes use of an idiom that's often used in SimPy programs: a "source" (the `CustomerGenerator` instance).

```
from SimPy.Simulation import *
import random as rnd

interarrival_time = 10.0
service_time = 8.0


class CustomerGenerator( Process ):
    def produce( self, b ):
        while True:
            c = Customer( b )
            c.start( c.doit() )
            yield hold, self, rnd.expovariate(1.0/interarrival_time)


class Customer( Process ):
    def __init__( self, resource ):
        Process.__init__( self )
        self.bank = resource

    def doit( self ):
        yield request, self, self.bank
        yield hold, self, self.bank.servicetime()
        yield release, self, self.bank

class Bank( Resource ):
    def servicetime( self ):
        return rnd.expovariate(1.0/service_time)


initialize()

bank = Bank( capacity=1, monitored=True, monitorType=Monitor )

src = CustomerGenerator()
activate( src, src.produce( bank ) )

simulate( until=500 )


print bank.waitMon.mean()
print

for evt in bank.waitMon:
    print evt[0], evt[1]
```

The CustomerGenerator is itself a subclass of Process and defines a PEM (produce()).
Whenever it is triggered, it generates a new Customer and then goes back to sleep for a
random amount of time. (The time is distributed according to an exponential
distribution—we will discuss this particular choice in a moment.) Notice that we don't
need to keep track of the Customer instances explicitly: once they have been activated
using the start() member function, the framework ensures that they will receive
scheduled events.

There are two changes to the Customer class. First of all, we explicitly inject the resource to request (the bank) as an additional argument to the constructor. By contrast, the Customer in the previous example found the bank reference via lookup in the global namespace. That's fine for small programs but becomes problematic for larger ones—especially if there is more than one resource that may be requested. The second change is that the Customer now asks the *bank* for the service time. This is in the spirit of problem domain modeling—it's usually the server (in this case, the bank) that controls the time it takes to complete a transaction. Accordingly, we have introduced Bank as subclass of Resource in order to accommodate this additional functionality. (The service time is also exponentially distributed but with a different wait time than that used for the CustomerGenerator.)

Subtypes of the Process class are used to model actors in a SimPy simulation. Besides these active simulation objects, the next most important abstraction describes congestion points, modeled by the Resource class and its subclasses. Each Resource instance models a shared resource that actors may request, but its more important function is to manage the *queue* of actors currently waiting for access.

Each Resource instance consists of a single queue and one or more actual "server units" that can fulfill client requests. Think of the typical queueing discipline followed in banks and post offices (in the U.S.—other countries have different conventions!): a single line but multiple teller windows, with the person at the head of the line moving to the next available window. That is the model represented by each Resource instance. The number of server units is controlled through the keyword argument capacity to the Resource constructor. Note that all server units in a single Resource instance are identical. Server units are also "passive": they have no behavior themselves. They only exist so that a Process object can acquire them, hold them for a period of time, and then release them (like a mutex).

Although a Resource instance may have multiple server units, it can contain only a single queue. If you want to model a supermarket checkout situation, where each server unit has its own queue, you therefore need to set up multiple Resource instances, each with capacity=1: one for each checkout stand and each managing its own queue of customers.

For each Resource instance, we can monitor the length of the queue and the events that change it (arrivals and departures) by registering an observer object with the Resource. There are two types of such observers in SimPy: a Monitor records the time stamp and new queue length for every event that affects the queue, whereas a Tally only keeps enough information to calculate summary information (such as the average queue length). Here we have registered a Monitor object with the Bank. (We'll later see an example of a Tally.)

As before, we run the simulation until the internal simulation clock reaches 1,000. The CustomerGenerator produces an infinite stream of Customer objects, each requesting service from the Bank, while the Monitor records all changes to the queue.

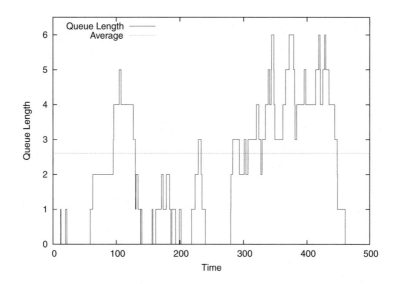

FIGURE 12-5. Number of customers in queue over time.

After the simulation has run to completion, we retrieve the `Monitor` object from the `Bank`: if an observer had been registered with a `Resource`, then it is available in the `waitMon` member variable. We print out the average queue length over the course of the simulation as well as the full time series of events. (The `Monitor` class is a `List` subclass, so we can iterate over it directly.) The time evolution of the queue is shown in Figure 12-5.

One last implementation detail: if you look closely, you will notice that the `CustomerGenerator` is activated using the standalone function `activate()`. This function is an alternative to the `start()` member function of all `Process` objects and is entirely equivalent to it.

Optional: Queueing Theory

Now that we have seen some of these concepts in action already, it is a good time to step back and fill in some theory.

A queue is a specific example of a *stochastic process*. In general, the term "stochastic process" refers to a sequence of random events occurring in time. In the queueing example, customers are joining or leaving the queue at random times, which makes the queue grow and shrink accordingly. Other examples of stochastic processes include random walks, the movement of stock prices, and the inventory levels in a store. (In the latter case, purchases by customers and possibly even deliveries by suppliers constitute the random events.)

In a queueing problem, we are concerned only about arrivals and departures. A particularly important special case assumes that the rate at which customers arrive is constant over time and that arrivals at different times are independent of each other. (Notice that these are reasonable assumptions in many cases.) These two conditions imply that the number of arrivals during a certain time period t follows a Poisson distribution, since the Poisson distribution:

$$p(k, t, \lambda) = \frac{(\lambda t)^k}{k!} e^{-\lambda t}$$

gives the probability of observing k Successes (arrivals, in our case) during an interval of length t if the "rate" of Successes is λ (see Chapter 9).

Another consequence is that the times between arrivals are distributed according to an exponential distribution:

$$p(t, \lambda) = \lambda e^{-\lambda t}$$

The mean of the exponential distribution can be calculated without difficulty and equals $1/\lambda$. It will often be useful to work with its inverse $t_a = 1/\lambda$, the *average interarrival time*.

(It's not hard to show that interarrival times are distributed according to the exponential distribution when the number of arrivals per time interval follows a Poisson distribution. Assume that an arrival occurred at $t = 0$. Now we ask for the probability that *no* arrival has occurred by $t = T$; in other words, $p(0, T, \lambda) = e^{-\lambda T}$ because $x^0 = 1$ and $0! = 1$. Conversely, the probability that the next arrival will have occurred sometime between $t = 0$ and $t = T$ is $1 - p(0, T, \lambda)$. This is the cumulative distribution function for the interarrival time, and from it, we find the probability density for an arrival to occur at t as $\frac{d}{dt}(1 - p(0, t, \lambda)) = \lambda e^{-\lambda t}$.)

The appearance of the exponential distribution as the distribution of interarrival times deserves some comment. At first glance, it may seem surprising because this distribution is greatest for small interarrival times, seemingly favoring very short intervals. However, this observation has to be balanced against the infinity of possible interarrival times, all of which may occur! What is more important is that the exponential distribution is in a sense the most "random" way that interarrival times can be distributed: no matter how long we have waited since the last arrival, the probability that the next visitor will arrive after t more minutes is always *the same*: $p(t, \lambda) = \lambda e^{-\lambda t}$. This property is often referred to as the *lack of memory* of the exponential distribution. Contrast this with a distribution of interarrival times that has a peak for some nonzero time: such a distribution describes a situation of *scheduled* arrivals, as we would expect to occur at a bus stop. In this scenario, the probability for an arrival to occur within the next t minutes will change with time.

Because the exponential distribution arises naturally from the assumption of a constant arrival rate (and from the independence of different arrivals), we have used it as the distribution of interarrival times in the `CustomerGenerator` in the previous example. It is less of a natural choice for the distribution of service times (but it makes some theoretical arguments simpler).

The central question in all queueing problems concerns the expected length of the queue—not only how large it is but also whether it will settle down to a finite value at all, or whether it will "explode," growing beyond all bounds.

In the simple memoryless, single-server–single-queue scenario that we have been investigating, the only two control parameters are the arrival rate λ_a and the service or exit rate λ_e; or rather their ratio:

$$u = \frac{\lambda_a}{\lambda_e}$$

which is the fraction of time the server is busy. The quantity u is the server's *utilization*. It is intuitively clear that if the arrival rate is greater than the exit rate (*i.e.*, if customers are arriving at a faster rate then the server can process them), then the queue length will explode. However, it turns out that even if the arrival rate *equals* the service rate (so that $u = 1$), the queue length still grows beyond all bounds. Only if the arrival rate is strictly lower than the service rate will we end up with a finite queue.

Let's see how this surprising result can be derived. Let p_n be the probability of finding exactly n customers waiting in the queue. The rate at which the queue grows is λ_a, but the rate at which the queue grows from exactly n to exactly $n + 1$ is $\lambda_a p_n$, since we must take into account the probability of the queue having exactly n members. Similarly, the probability of the queue shrinking from $n + 1$ to n members is $\lambda_e p_{n+1}$.

In the steady state (which is the requirement for a finite queue length), these two rates must be equal:

$$\lambda_a p_n = \lambda_e p_{n+1}$$

which we can rewrite as:

$$p_{n+1} = \frac{\lambda_a}{\lambda_e} p_n = u p_n$$

This relationship must hold for all n, and therefore we can repeat this argument and write $p_n = u p_{n-1}$ and so on. This leads to an expression for p_n in terms of p_0:

$$p_n = u^n p_0$$

The probability p_0 is the probability of finding *no* customer in the queue—in other words, it is the probability that the server is idle. Since the utilization is the probability for the server to be busy, the probability p_0 for the server to be idle must be $p_0 = 1 - u$.

We can now ask about the expected length L of the queue. We already know that the queue has length n with probability $p_n = u^n p_0$. Finding the expected queue length L

requires that we sum over all possible queue lengths, each one weighted by the appropriate probability:

$$L = \sum_{n=0}^{\infty} n p_n$$

$$= p_0 \sum_{n=0}^{\infty} n u^n$$

Now we employ a trick that is often useful for sums of this form: observe that $\frac{d}{du} u^n = n u^{n-1}$ and hence that $n u^n = u \frac{d}{du} u^n$. Using this expression in the sum for L leads to:

$$L = p_0 \sum_{n=0}^{\infty} u \frac{d}{du} u^n$$

$$= p_0 u \frac{d}{du} \sum_{n=0}^{\infty} u^n$$

$$= p_0 u \frac{d}{du} \frac{1}{1-u} \qquad \text{(geometric series)}$$

$$= p_0 \frac{u}{(1-u)^2}$$

$$= \frac{u}{1-u}$$

where we have used the sum of the geometric series (see Appendix B) and the expression for $p_0 = 1 - u$. We can rewrite this expression directly in terms of the arrival and exit rates as:

$$L = \frac{u}{1-u} = \frac{\lambda_a}{\lambda_e - \lambda_a}$$

This is a central result. It gives us the expected length of the queue in terms of the utilization (or in terms of the arrival and exit rates). For low utilization (*i.e.*, an arrival rate that is much lower than the service rate or, equivalently, an interarrival time that is much larger than the service time), the queue is very short on average. (In fact, whenever the server is idle, then the queue length equals 0, which drags down the average queue length.) But as the arrival rate approaches the service rate, the queue grows in length and becomes infinite when the arrival rate equals the service rate. (An intuitive argument for why the queue length will explode when the arrival rate equals the service time is that, in this case, the server never has the opportunity to "catch up." If the queue becomes longer due to a chance fluctuation in arrivals, then this backlog will persist forever, since overall the server is only capable of keeping up with arrivals. The cumulative effect of such chance fluctuations will eventually make the queue length diverge.)

Running SimPy Simulations

In this section, we will try to confirm the previous result regarding the expected queue length by simulation. In the process, we will discuss a few practical points of using SimPy to understand queueing systems.

First of all, we must realize that each simulation run is only a particular realization of the sequence of events. To draw conclusions about the system in general, we therefore always need to perform several simulation runs and average their results.

In the previous listing, the simulation framework maintained its state in the global environment. Hence, in order to rerun the simulation, you had to restart the entire program! The program in the next listing uses an alternative interface that encapsulates the entire environment for each simulation run in an instance of class Simulation. The global functions initialize(), activate(), and simulate() are now member functions of this Simulation object. Each instance of the Simulation class provides a separate, isolated simulation environment. A completely new simulation run now requires only that we create a new instance of this class.

The Simulation class is provided by SimPy. Using it does not require any changes to the previous program, except that the current instance of the Simulation class must be passed explicitly to all simulation objects (*i.e.*, instances of Process and Resource and their subclasses):

```
from SimPy.Simulation import *
import random as rnd

interarrival_time = 10.0

class CustomerGenerator( Process ):
    def produce( self, bank ):
        while True:
            c = Customer( bank, sim=self.sim )
            c.start( c.doit() )
            yield hold, self, rnd.expovariate(1.0/interarrival_time)


class Customer( Process ):
    def __init__( self, resource, sim=None ):
        Process.__init__( self, sim=sim )
        self.bank = resource

    def doit( self ):
        yield request, self, self.bank
        yield hold, self, self.bank.servicetime()
        yield release, self, self.bank

class Bank( Resource ):
    def setServicetime( self, s ):
        self.service_time = s

    def servicetime( self ):
        return rnd.expovariate(1.0/self.service_time )


def run_simulation( t, steps, runs ):
    for r in range( runs ):
```

```
        sim = Simulation()
        sim.initialize()

        bank = Bank( monitored=True, monitorType=Tally, sim=sim )
        bank.setServicetime( t )

        src = CustomerGenerator( sim=sim )
        sim.activate( src, src.produce( bank ) )

        sim.startCollection( when=steps//2 )
        sim.simulate( until=steps )

        print t, bank.waitMon.mean()


    t = 0
    while t <= 11.0:
        t += 0.5
        run_simulation( t, 100000, 10 )
```

Another important change is that we don't start recording until half of the simulation time steps have passed (that's what the startCollection() method is for). Remember that we are interested in the queue length in the *steady state*—for that reason, we don't want to start recording until the system has settled down and any transient behavior has disappeared.

To record the queue length, we now use a Tally object instead of a Monitor. The Tally will not allow us to replay the entire sequence of events, but since we are only interested in the average queue length, it is sufficient for our current purposes.

Finally, remember that as the utilization approaches $u = 1$ (*i.e.*, as the service time approaches the interarrival time), we expect the queue length to become infinite. Of course, in any finite simulation it is impossible for the queue to grow to infinite length: the length of the queue is limited by the finite duration of the simulation run. The consequence of this observation is that, for utilizations near or above 1, the queue length that we will observe depends on the number of steps that we allow in the simulation. If we terminate the simulation too quickly, then the system will not have had time to truly reach its fully developed steady state and so our results will be misleading.

Figure 12-6 shows the results obtained when running the example program with 1,000 and 100,000 simulation steps. For low utilization (*i.e.*, short queue lengths), the results from both data sets agree with each other (and with the theoretical prediction). However, as the service time approaches the interarrival time, the short simulation run does not last long enough for the steady state to form, and so the observed queue lengths are too short.

Summary

This concludes our tour of discrete event simulation with SimPy. Of course, there is more to SimPy than mentioned here—in particular, there are two additional forms of resources:

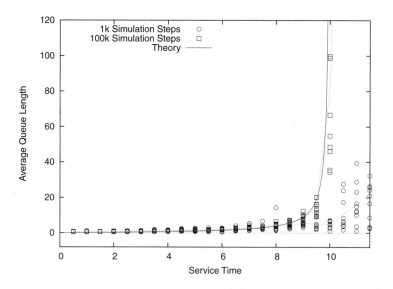

F I G U R E 12-6. Average queue length as a function of the service time for a fixed interarrival time of $t_a = 10$.

the `Store` and `Level` abstractions. Both of them not only encapsulate a queue but also maintain an inventory (of individual items for `Store` and of an undifferentiated amount for `Level`). This inventory can be consumed or replenished by simulation objects, allowing us to model inventory systems of various forms. Other SimPy facilities to explore include asynchronous events, which can be received by simulation objects as they are waiting in queue and additional recording and tracing functionality. The project documentation will provide further details.

Further Reading

- *A First Course in Monte Carlo*. George S. Fishman. Duxbury Press. 2005.
  This book is a nice introduction to Monte Carlo simulations and includes many topics that we did not cover. Requires familiarity with calculus.

- *Bootstrap Methods and Their Application*. A. C. Davison and D. V. Hinkley. Cambridge University Press. 1997.
  The bootstrap is actually a fairly simple and practical concept, but most books on it are very theoretical and difficult, including this one. But it is comprehensive and relatively recent.

- *Applied Probability Models*. Do Le Paul Minh. Duxbury Press. 2000.
  The theory of random processes is difficult, and the results often don't seem commensurate with the amount of effort required to obtain them. This book (although possibly hard to find) is one of the more accessible ones.

- *Introduction to Stochastic Processes.* Gregory F. Lawler. Chapman & Hall/CRC. 2006.
  This short book is much more advanced and theoretical than the previous one. The treatment is concise and to the point.

- *Introduction to Operations Research.* Frederick S. Hillier and Gerald J. Lieberman. 9th ed., McGraw-Hill. 2009.
  The field of operations research encompasses a set of mathematical methods that are relevant for many problems arising in a business or industrial setting, including queueing theory. This text is a standard introduction.

- *Fundamentals of Queueing Theory.* Donald Gross, John F. Shortle, James M. Thompson, and Carl M. Harris. 4th ed., Wiley. 2008.
  The standard textbook on queueing theory. Not for the faint of heart.

## CHAPTER THIRTEEN

Finding Clusters

THE TERM *CLUSTERING* REFERS TO THE PROCESS OF FINDING GROUPS OF POINTS WITHIN A DATA SET THAT ARE IN some way "lumped together." It is also called *unsupervised learning*—unsupervised because we don't know ahead of time where the clusters are located or what they look like. (This is in contrast to *supervised learning* or *classification*, where we attempt to assign data points to preexisting classes; see Chapter 18.)

I regard clustering as an *exploratory* method: a computer-assisted (or even computationally driven) approach to discovering structure in a data set. As an exploratory technique, it usually needs to be followed by a confirmatory analysis that validates the findings and makes them more precise.

Clustering is a lot of fun. It is a rich topic with a wide variety of different problems, as we will see in the next section, where we discuss the different *kinds* of cluster one may encounter. The topic also has a lot of intuitive appeal, and most clustering methods are rather straightforward. This allows for all sorts of ad hoc modifications and enhancements to accommodate the specific problem one is working on.

What Constitutes a Cluster?

Clustering is not a very rigorous field: there are precious few established results, rigorous theorems, or algorithmic guarantees. In fact, the whole notion of a "cluster" is not particularly well defined. Descriptions such as "groups of points that are similar" or "close to each other" are insufficient, because clusters must also be *well separated* from each other. Look at Figure 13-1: some points are certainly closer to each other than to other points, yet there are no discernible clusters. (In fact, it is an interesting exercise to define

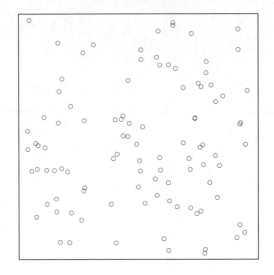

FIGURE 13-1. A uniform point distribution. Any "clusters" that we may recognize are entirely spurious.

what constitutes the *absence* of clusters.) This leads to one possible definition of clusters: *contiguous regions of high data point density separated by regions of lower point density*. Although not particularly rigorous either, this description does seem to capture the essential elements of typical clusters. (For a different point of view, see the next section.)

The definition just proposed allows for very different kinds of clusters. Figures 13-2 and 13-3 show two very different types. Of course, Figure 13-2 is the "happy" case, showing a data set consisting of well-defined and clearly separated regions of high data point density. The clusters in Figure 13-3 are of a different type, one that is more easily thought of by means of nearest-neighbor (graph) relationships than by point density. Yet in this case as well, there are higher density regions separated by lower density regions—although we might want to exploit the nearest-neighbor relationship instead of the higher density when developing with a practical algorithm for this case.

Clustering is not limited to points in space. Figures 13-4 and 13-5 show two rather different cases for which it nevertheless makes sense to speak of clusters. Figure 13-4 shows a bunch of street addresses. No two of them are exactly the same, but if we look closely, we will easily recognize that all of them can be grouped into just a few neighborhoods. Figure 13-5 shows a bunch of different time series: again, some of them are more alike than others. The challenge in both of these examples is finding a way to express the "similarity" among these nonnumeric, nongeometric objects!

Finally, we should keep in mind that clusters may have complicated *shapes*. Figure 13-6 shows two very well-behaved clusters as distinct regions of high point density. However, complicated and intertwined shapes of the regions will challenge many commonly used clustering algorithms.

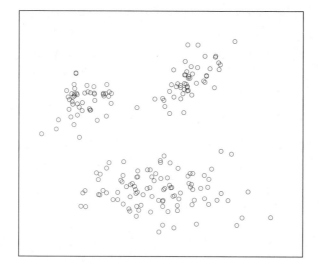

FIGURE 13-2. The "happy" case: three well-separated, globular clusters.

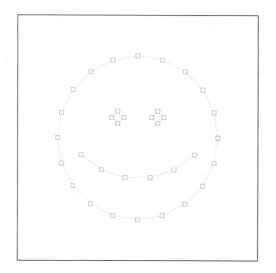

FIGURE 13-3. Examples of non-globular clusters in a smiley face. Some of the clusters are nested, meaning that they are entirely contained within other clusters.

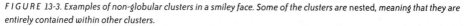

A bit of terminology can help to distinguish different cluster shapes. If the line connecting any two points lies entirely within the cluster itself (as in Figure 13-2), then the cluster is *convex*. This is the easiest shape to handle. A cluster is convex only if the connecting line between two points lies entirely within the cluster for *all* pairs of points. Sometimes this is not the case, but we can still find at least one point (the *center*) such that the connecting line from the center to any other point lies entirely within the cluster: such a cluster is

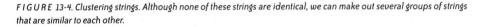

First Avenue 35	48 Second Street	Main Boulevard 9
First Avenue 53	Main Blvd 19	Mn Boulevard 11
45 Second Street E	45 Second St	First Ave 35
Furst Avenue 33	44 second street	Main Boulevrd 1
1st Avenue 53	Second Street, 48	Main Bulevard 19

FIGURE 13-4. Clustering strings. Although none of these strings are identical, we can make out several groups of strings that are similar to each other.

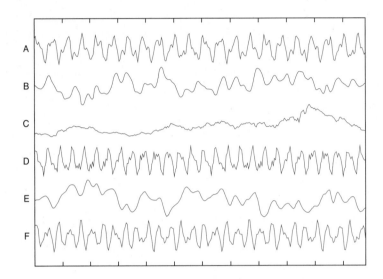

FIGURE 13-5. Six time series. We can recognize groups of time series that seem more similar to each other than to others.

called *star convex*. Notice that the clusters in Figure 13-6 are neither convex nor star convex. Sometimes one cluster is entirely surrounded by another cluster without actually being part of it: in this case we speak of a *nested* cluster. Nested clusters can be particularly challenging (see Figure 13-3).

A Different Point of View

In the absence of a precise (mathematical) definition, a cluster can be whatever we consider as one. That is important because our minds have a different, alternative way of grouping ("clustering") objects: not by proximity or density but rather by the way objects fit into a larger structure. Figures 13-7 and 13-8 show two examples.

Intuitively, we have no problem grouping the points in Figure 13-7 into two overlapping clusters. Yet, the density-based definition of a cluster we proposed earlier will not support such a conclusion. Similar considerations apply to the set of points in Figure 13-8. The distance between any two adjacent points is the same, but we perceive the larger

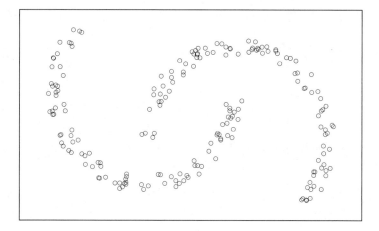

FIGURE 13-6. Two clusters that are well separated but not globular. Some algorithms (e.g., the k-means algorithm) will not be able to handle such clusters.

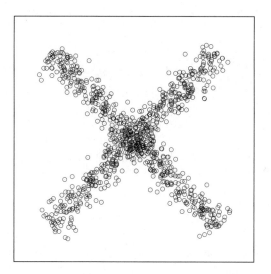

FIGURE 13-7. An impossible situation for most clustering algorithms: although we believe to recognize two crossed clusters, no strictly local algorithm will be able to separate them.

structures of the vertical and horizontal arrangements and assign points to clusters based on them.

This notion of a cluster does not hinge on the similarity or proximity of any pair of points to each other but instead on the similarity between a point and a property of the *entire cluster*. For any algorithm that considers a single point (or a single pair of points) at a time, this leads to a problem: to determine cluster membership, we need the property of the whole cluster; but to determine the properties of the cluster, we must first assign points to clusters.

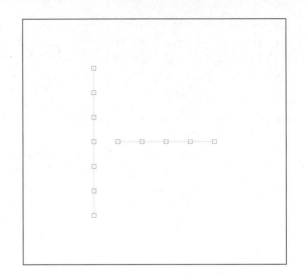

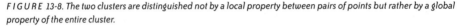

FIGURE 13-8. The two clusters are distinguished not by a local property between pairs of points but rather by a global property of the entire cluster.

To handle such situations, we would need to perform some kind of global structure analysis—a task our minds are incredibly good at (which is why we tend to think of clusters this way) but that we have a hard time teaching computers to do. For problems in two dimensions, *digital image processing* has developed methods to recognize and extract certain features (such as edge detection). But general clustering methods, such as those described in the rest of this chapter, deal only with local properties and therefore can't handle problems such as those in Figures 13-7 and 13-8.

Distance and Similarity Measures

Given how strongly our intuition about clustering is shaped by geometric problems such as those in Figures 13-2 and 13-3, it is an interesting and perhaps surprising observation that clustering does not actually require data points to be embedded into a geometric space: all that is required is a *distance* or (equivalently) a *similarity measure* for any *pair of points*. This makes it possible to perform clustering on a set of strings, such as those in Figure 13-4 that do not map to points in space. However, if the data points have properties of a vector space (see Appendix C), then we can develop more efficient algorithms that exploit these properties.

A *distance* is any function $d(x, y)$ that takes two points and returns a scalar value that is a measure for how different these points are: the more different, the larger the distance. Depending on the problem domain, it may make more sense to express the same information in terms of a *similarity* function $s(x, y)$, which returns a scalar that tells us how similar two points are: the more different they are, the smaller the similarity. Any distance can be transformed into a similarity and vice versa. For example if we know that our similarity measure s can take on values only in the range [0, 1], then we can form an equivalent distance by setting $d = 1 - s$. In other situations, we might decide to use $d = 1/s$, or $s = e^{-d}$, and so on; the choice will depend on the problem we are working on. In what follows, I will express problems in terms of either distances or similarities, whichever seems more natural. Just keep in mind that you can always transform between the two.

How we define a distance function is largely up to us, and we can express different semantics about the data set through the appropriate choice of distance. For some problems, a particular distance measure will present itself naturally (if the data points are points in space, then we will most likely employ the Euclidean distance or a measure similar to it), but for other problems, we have more freedom to define our own metric. We will see several examples shortly.

There are certain properties that a distance (or similarity) function should have. Mathematicians have developed a set of properties that a function must possess to be considered a metric (or distance) in a mathematical sense. These properties can provide valuable guidance, but don't take them too seriously: for our purposes, different properties might be more important. The four axioms of a mathematical metric are:

$$d(x, y) \geq 0$$
$$d(x, y) = 0 \quad \text{if and only if } x = y$$
$$d(x, y) = d(y, x)$$
$$d(x, y) + d(y, z) \geq d(x, z)$$

The first two axioms state that a distance is always positive and that it is null only if the two points are equal. The third property ("symmetry") states that the distance between x and y is the same as the distance between y and x—no matter which way we consider the pair. The final property is the so-called triangle inequality, which states that to get from x to z, it is never shorter to take a detour through a third point y instead of going directly (see Figure 13-9).

This all seems rather uncontroversial, but these conditions are not necessarily fulfilled in practice. A funny example for an asymmetric distance occurs if you ask everyone in a group of people how much they like every other member of the group and then use the responses to construct a distance measure: it is not at all guaranteed that the feelings of person A for person B are requited by B. (Using the same example, it is also possible to construct scenarios that violate the triangle inequality.) For technical reasons, the symmetry property is usually highly desirable. You can always construct a symmetric distance function from an asymmetric one:

$$d_S(x, y) = \frac{d(x, y) + d(y, x)}{2}$$

is always symmetric.

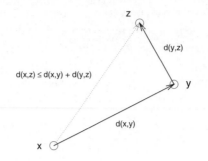

F I G U R E 13-9. The triangle inequality: the direct path from x to z is always shorter than any path that goes through an intermediate point y.

One property of great practical importance but not included among the distance axioms is *smoothness*. For example, we could define a rather simple-minded distance function that is 0 if and only if both points are equal to each other and that is 1 if the two points are not equal:

$$d(x, y) = \begin{cases} 0 & \text{if } x = y \\ 1 & \text{otherwise} \end{cases}$$

You can convince yourself that this distance fulfills all four of the distance axioms. However, this is not a very informative distance measure, because it gives us no information about *how* different two nonidentical points are! Most clustering algorithms require this information. A certain kind of tree-based algorithm, for example, works by successively considering the pairs of points with the smallest distance between them. When using this binary distance, the algorithm will make only limited progress before having exhausted all information available to it.

The practical upshot of this discussion is that a good distance function for clustering should change smoothly as its inputs become more or less similar. (For classification tasks, a binary one as in the example just discussed might be fine.)

Common Distance and Similarity Measures

Depending on the data set and the purpose of our analysis, there are different distance and similarity measures available.

First, let's clarify some terminology. We are looking for ways to measure the distance between any two data points. Very often, we will find that a point has a number of *dimensions* or *features*. (The first usage is more common for numerical data, the latter for categorical data.) In other words, each point is a collection of individual values: $x = \{x_1, x_2, \ldots, x_d\}$, where d is the number of dimensions (or features). For example, the data point {0, 1} has two dimensions and describes a point in space; whereas the tuple ['male', 'retired', 'Florida'], which describes a person, has three features.

TABLE 13-1. Commonly used distance and similarity measures for numeric data

Name	Definition
Manhattan	$d(x, y) = \sum_i^d |x_i - y_i|$
Euclidean	$d(x, y) = \sqrt{\sum_i^d (x_i - y_i)^2}$
Maximum	$d(x, y) = \max_i |x_i - y_i|$
Minkowski	$d(x, y) = \left(\sum_i^d |x_i - y_i|^p\right)^{1/p}$
Dot product	$x \cdot y = \dfrac{\sum_i^d x_i y_i}{\sqrt{\sum_i^d x_i^2}\sqrt{\sum_i^d y_i^2}}$
Correlation coefficient	$\mathrm{corr}(x, y) = \dfrac{\sum_i^d (x_i - \bar{x})(y_i - \bar{y})}{\sqrt{\sum_i^d (x_i - \bar{x})^2}\sqrt{\sum_i^d (y_i - \bar{y})^2}}$
	$\bar{x} = \frac{1}{d}\sum_i^d x_i \qquad \bar{y} = \frac{1}{d}\sum_i^d y_i$

For any given data set containing n elements, we can form n^2 pairs of points. The set of all distances for all possible pairs of points can be arranged in a quadratic table known as the *distance matrix*. The distance matrix embodies all information about the mutual relationships between all points in the data set. If the distance function is symmetric, as is usually the case, then the matrix is also symmetric. Furthermore, the entries along the main diagonal typically are all 0, since $d(x, x) = 0$ for most well-behaved distance functions.

Numerical data

If the data is numerical and also "mixable" or vector-like (in the sense of Appendix C), then the data points bear a strong resemblance to points in space; hence we can use a metric such as the familiar *Euclidean distance*. The Euclidean distance is the most commonly used from a large family of related distance measures, which also contains the so-called *Manhattan* (or *taxicab*) *distance* and the *maximum* (or *supremum*) *distance*. All of these are in fact special cases of a more general *Minkowski* or *p-distance*.* Table 13-1 shows some examples. (The Manhattan distance is so named because it measures distances the way a New York taxicab moves: at right angles, along the city blocks. The Euclidean distance measures distances "as the crow flies." Finally, it is an amusing exercise to show that the maximum distance corresponds to the Minkowski *p*-distance as $p \to \infty$.)

All these distance measures have very similar properties, and the differences between them usually do not matter much. The Euclidean distance is by far the most commonly used. I list the others here mostly to give you a sense of the kind of leeway that exists in defining a suitable distance measure—without significantly affecting the results!

---

*The Minkowski *distance* defined here should not be confused with the Minkowski *metric*, which defines the metric of the four-dimensional space-time in special relativity.

If the data is numeric but *not* mixable (so that it does not make sense to add a random fraction of one data set to a random fraction of a different data set), then these distance measures are not appropriate. Instead, you may want to consider a metric based on the *correlation* between two data points.

Correlation-based measures are measures of *similarity*: they are large when objects are similar and small when the objects are dissimilar. There are two related measures: the *dot product* and the *correlation coefficient*, which are also defined in Table 13-1. The only difference is that when calculating the correlation coefficient, we first center both data points by subtracting their respective means.

In both measures, we multiply entries for the same "dimension" and sum the results; then we divide by the correlation of each data point with itself. Doing so provides a *normalization* and ensures that the correlation of any point with itself is always 1. This normalization step makes correlation-based distance measures suitable for data sets containing data points with widely different numeric values.

By construction, the value of a dot product always falls in the interval $[0, 1]$, and the correlation coefficient always falls in the interval $[-1, 1]$. You can therefore transform either one into a distance measure if need be (*e.g.*, if d is the dot product, then $1 - d$ is a proper distance).

I should point out that the dot product has a geometric meaning. If we regard the data points as vectors in some suitable space, then the dot product of two points is the cosine of the angle that the two vectors make with each other. If they are perfectly aligned (*i.e.*, they fall onto each other), then the angle is 0 and the cosine (and the correlation) is 1. If they are at right angles to each other, the cosine is 0.

Correlation-based distance measures are suitable whenever numeric data is not readily mixable—for instance, when evaluating the similarity of the time series in Figure 13-5.

Categorical data

If the data is categorical, then we can count the number of features that do *not* agree in both data points (*i.e.*, the number of mismatched features); this is the *Hamming distance*. (We might want to divide by the total number of features to obtain a number between 0 and 1, which is the *fraction of mismatched features*.)

In certain data mining problems, the number of features is large, but only relatively few of them will be present for each data point. Moreover, the features may be binary: we care only whether or not they are present, but their values don't matter. (As an example, imagine a patient's health record: each possible medical condition constitutes a feature, and we want to know whether the patient has ever suffered from it.) In such situations, where features are not merely categorical but binary and sparse (meaning that just a few of the features are On), we may be more interested in matches between features that are On than in matches between features that are Off. This leads us to the *Jaccard coefficient* s_J, which is the number of matches between features that are On for both points, divided by the number of features that are On in at least one of the data points. The Jaccard coefficient is a *similarity* measure; the corresponding distance function is the *Jaccard distance* $d_J = 1 - s_J$.

n_{00} features that are Off in both points

n_{10} features that are On in the first point, and Off in the second point

n_{01} features that are Off in the first point, and On in the second point

n_{11} features that are On in both points

$$s_J = \frac{n_{11}}{n_{10} + n_{01} + n_{11}}$$

$$d_J = \frac{n_{10} + n_{01}}{n_{10} + n_{01} + n_{11}}$$

There are many other measures of similarity or dissimilarity for categorical data, but the principles are always the same. You calculate some fraction of matches, possibly emphasizing one aspect (*e.g.,* the presence or absence of certain values) more than others. Feel free to invent your own—as far as I can see, none of these measures has achieved universal acceptance or is fundamentally better than any other.

String data

If the data consists of strings, then we can use a form of Hamming distance and count the number of mismatches. If the strings in the data set are not all of equal length, we can pad the shorter string and count the number of characters added as mismatches.

If we are dealing with many strings that are rather similar to each other (distorted through typos, for instance), then we can use a more detailed measure of the difference between them—namely the *edit* or *Levenshtein distance*. The Levenshtein distance is the minimum number of single-character operations (insertions, deletions, and substitutions) required to transform one string into the other. (A quick Internet search will give many references to the actual algorithm and available implementations.)

Another approach is to find the length of the *longest common subsequence*. This metric is often used for gene sequence analysis in computational biology.

This may be a good place to make a more general point: the best distance measure to use does not follow automatically from data type; rather, it depends on the semantics of the data—or, more precisely, on the semantics that you care about for your current analysis! In some cases, a simple metric that only calculates the difference in string length may be perfectly sufficient. In another case, you might want to use the Hamming distance. If you really care about the details of otherwise similar strings, the Levenshtein distance is most appropriate. You might even want to calculate how often each letter appears in a string and then base your comparison on that. It all depends on what the data means and on what aspect of it you are interested at the moment (which may also change as the analysis progresses). Similar considerations apply everywhere—there are no "cookbook" rules.

Special-purpose metrics

A more abstract measure for the similarity of two points is based on the number of neighbors that the two points have in common; this metric is known as the *shared nearest neighbor* (SNN) similarity. To calculate the SNN for two points x and y, you find the k nearest neighbors (using any suitable distance function) for both x and y. The number of neighbors shared by both points is their mutual SNN.

The same concept can be extended to cases in which there is some property that the two points may have in common. For example, in a social network we could define the "closeness" of two people by the number of friends they share, by the number of movies they have both seen, and so on. (This application is equivalent to the Hamming distance.) Nearest-neighbor-based metrics are particularly suitable for high-dimensional data, where other distance measures can give spuriously small results.

Finally, let me remind you that sometimes the solution does not consist of inventing a new metric. Instead, the trick is to map the problem to a different space that already has a predefined, suitable metric.

As an example, consider the problem of measuring the degree of similarity between different text documents (we here assume that these documents are long—hundreds or thousands of words). The standard approach to this problem is to count how often each word appears in each document. The resulting data structure is referred to as the *document vector*. You can now form a dot product between two document vectors as a measure of their correspondence.

Technically speaking, we have mapped each document to a point in a (high-dimensional) vector space. Each distinct word that occurs in any of the documents spans a new dimension, and the frequency with which each word appears in a document provides the position of that document along this axis. This is very interesting, because we have transformed highly structured data (text) into numerical, even vector-like data and can therefore now manipulate it much more easily. (Of course, the benefit comes at a price: in doing so we have lost all information about the sequence in which words appeared in the text. It is a separate consideration whether this is relevant for our purpose.)

One last comment: one can overdo it when defining distance and similarity measures. Complicated or sophisticated definitions are usually not necessary as long as you capture the fundamental semantics. The Hamming distance and the document vector correlation are two good examples of simplified metrics that intentionally discard a lot of information yet still turn out to be highly successful in practice.

Clustering Methods

In this section, we will discuss several very different clustering algorithms. As you will see, the basic ideas behind all three algorithms are rather simple, and it is straightforward to come up with perfectly adequate implementations of them yourself. These algorithms are also important as starting points for more sophisticated clustering routines, which usually augment them with various heuristics or combine ideas from different algorithms.

Different algorithms are suitable for different kinds of problems—depending, for example, on the shape and structure of the clusters. Some require vector-like data, whereas others require only a distance function. Different algorithms tend to be misled by different kinds of pitfalls, and they all have different performance (*i.e.*, computational complexity) characteristics. It is therefore important to have a variety of different algorithms at your disposal so that you can choose the one most appropriate for your problem *and* for the kind of solution you seek! (Remember: it is pretty much the choice of algorithm that defines what constitutes a "cluster" in the end.)

Center Seekers

One of the most popular clustering methods is the *k-means algorithm*. The *k*-means algorithm requires the number of expected clusters *k* as input. (We will later discuss how to determine this number.) The *k*-means algorithm is an iterative scheme. The main idea is to calculate the position of each cluster's center (or *centroid*) from the positions of the points belonging to the cluster and then to assign points to their nearest centroid. This process is repeated until sufficient convergence is achieved. The basic algorithm can be summarized as follows:

```
choose initial positions for the cluster centroids

repeat:
  for each point:
    calculate its distance from each cluster centroid
    assign the point to the nearest cluster

  recalculate the positions of the cluster centroids
```

The *k*-means algorithm is nondeterministic: a different choice of starting values may result in a different assignment of points to clusters. For this reason, it is customary to run the *k*-means algorithm several times and then compare the results. If you have previous knowledge of likely positions for the cluster centers, you can use it to precondition the algorithm. Otherwise, choose random data points as initial values.

What makes this algorithm efficient is that you don't have to search the existing data points to find one that would make a good centroid—instead you are free to *construct* a new centroid position. This is usually done by calculating the cluster's center of mass. In two dimensions, we would have:

$$x_c = \frac{1}{n} \sum_{i}^{n} x_i$$

$$y_c = \frac{1}{n} \sum_{i}^{n} y_i$$

where each sum is over all points in the cluster. (Generalizations to higher dimensions are straightforward.) You can only do this for vector-like data, however, because only such data allows us to form arbitrary "mixtures" in this way.

For strictly categorical data (such as the strings in Figure 13-4), the k-means algorithm cannot be used (because it is not possible to "mix" different points to construct a new centroid). Instead, we have to use the *k-medoids* algorithm. The k-medoids algorithm works in the same way as the k-means algorithm except that, instead of calculating the new centroid, we search through all points in the cluster to find the data point (the *medoid*) that has the smallest average distance to all other points in the cluster.

The k-means algorithm is surprisingly modest in its resource consumption. On each iteration, the algorithm evaluates the distance function once for each cluster and each point; hence the computational complexity per iteration is $\mathcal{O}(k \cdot n)$, where k is the number of clusters and n is the number of points in the data set. This is remarkable because it means that the algorithm is *linear* in the number of points. The number of iterations is usually pretty small: 10–50 iterations are typical. The k-medoids algorithm is more costly because the search to find the medoid of each cluster is an $\mathcal{O}(n^2)$ process. For very large data sets this might be prohibitive, but you can try running the k-medoids algorithm on random *samples* of all data points. The results from these runs can then be used as starting points for a run using the full data set.

Despite its cheap-and-cheerful appearance, the k-means algorithm works surprisingly well. It is pretty fast and relatively robust. Convergence is usually quick. Because the algorithm is simple and highly intuitive, it is easy to augment or extend it—for example, to incorporate points with different weights. You might also want to experiment with different ways to calculate the centroid, possibly using the median position rather than the mean, and so on.

That being said, the k-means algorithm can fail—annoyingly in situations that exhibit especially strong clustering! Because of its iterative nature, the algorithm works best in situations that involve gradual density changes. If your data sets consists of very dense and widely separated clusters, then the k-means algorithm can get "stuck" if initially two centroids are assigned to the same cluster: moving one centroid to a different cluster would require a large move, which is not likely to be found by the mostly local steps taken by the k-means algorithm.

Among variants, a particularly important one is *fuzzy clustering*. In fuzzy clustering, we don't assign each point to a single cluster; instead, for each point and each cluster, we determine the probability that the point belongs to that cluster. Each point therefore acquires a set of k probabilities or weights (one for each cluster; the probabilities must sum to 1 for each point). We then use these probabilities as weights when calculating the centroid positions. The probabilities also make it possible to declare certain points as "noise" (having low probability of belonging to *any* cluster) and thus can help with data sets that contain unclustered "noise" points and with ambiguous situations such as the one shown in Figure 13-7.

To summarize:

- The k-means algorithms and its variants work best for globular (at least star-convex) clusters. The results will be meaningless for clusters with complicated shapes and for nested clusters (Figures 13-6 and 13-3, respectively).

- The expected number of clusters is required as an input. If this number is not known, it will be necessary to repeat the algorithm with different values and compare the results.

- The algorithm is iterative and nondeterministic; the specific outcome may depend on the choice of starting values.

- The k-means algorithm requires vector data; use the k-medoids algorithm for categorical data.

- The algorithm can be misled if there are clusters of highly different size or different density.

- The k-means algorithm is linear in the number of data points; the k-medoids algorithm is quadratic in the number of points.

Tree Builders

Another way to find clusters is by successively combining clusters that are "close" to each other into a larger cluster until only a single cluster remains. This approach is known as *agglomerative hierarchical clustering*, and it leads to a treelike hierarchy of clusters. Clusters that are close to each other are joined early (near the leaves of the tree) and more distant clusters are joined late (near the root of the tree). (One can also go in the opposite direction, continually splitting the set of points into smaller and smaller clusters. When applied to classification problems, this leads to a *decision tree*—see Chapter 18.)

The basic algorithm proceeds exactly as just outlined:

1. Examine all pairs of clusters.
2. Combine the two clusters that are closest to each other into a single cluster.
3. Repeat.

What do we mean by the distance between *clusters*? The distance measures that we have defined are valid only between points! To apply them, we need to select (or construct) a single "representative" point from each cluster. Depending on this choice, hierarchical clustering will lead to different results. The most important alternatives are as follows.

Minimum or single link
   We define the distance between two clusters as the distance between the two points (one from each cluster) that are *closest* to each other. This choice leads to extended,

thinly connected clusters. Because of this, this approach can handle clusters of complicated shapes, such as those in Figure 13-6, but it can be sensitive to noise points.

Maximum or complete link

The distance between two clusters is defined as the distance between the two points (one from each cluster) that are *farthest away* from each other. With this choice, two clusters are not joined until all points within each cluster are connected to each other—favoring compact, globular clusters.

Average

In this case, we form the average over the distances between all pairs of points (one from each cluster). This choice has characteristics of both the single- and complete-link approaches.

Centroid

For each cluster, we calculate the position of a centroid (as in k-means clustering) and define the distance between clusters as the distance between centroids.

Ward's method

Ward's method measures the distance between two clusters in terms of the decrease in coherence that occurs when the two clusters are combined: if we combine clusters that are closer together, the resulting cluster should be more coherent than if we combine clusters that are farther apart. We can measure coherence as the average distance of all points in the cluster from a centroid, or as their average distance from each other. (We'll come back to cohesion and other cluster properties later.)

The result of hierarchical clustering is not actually a set of clusters. Instead, we obtain a treelike structure that contains the individual data points at the leaf nodes. This structure can be represented graphically in a *dendrogram* (see Figure 13-10). To extract actual clusters from it, we need to walk the tree, evaluate the cluster properties for each subtree, and then cut the tree to obtain clusters.

Tree builders are expensive: we need at least the full distance matrix for all pairs of points (requiring $\mathcal{O}(n^2)$ operations to evaluate). Building the complete tree takes $\mathcal{O}(n)$ iterations: there are n clusters (initially, points) to start with, and at each iteration, the number of clusters is reduced by one because two clusters are combined. For each iteration, we need to search the distance matrix for the closest pair of clusters—naively implemented, this is an $\mathcal{O}(n^2)$ operation that leads to a total complexity of $\mathcal{O}(n^3)$ operations. However, this can be reduced to $\mathcal{O}(n^2 \log n)$ by using indexed lookup.

One outstanding feature of hierarchical clustering is that it does more than produce a flat list of clusters; it also shows their relationships in an explicit way. You need to decide whether this information is relevant for your needs, but keep in mind that the choice of measure for the cluster distance (single- or complete-link, and so on) can have a significant influence on the appearance of the resulting tree structure.

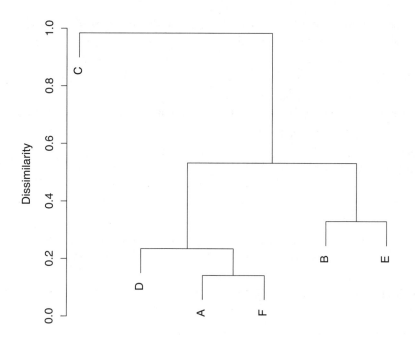

FIGURE 13-10. A typical dendrogram for data like the data in Figure 13-5. Individual data points are at the leaf nodes. The vertical distance between the tree nodes represents the dissimilarity between the nodes.

Neighborhood Growers

A third kind of clustering algorithm could be dubbed "neighborhood growers." They work by connecting points that are "sufficiently close" to each other to form a cluster and then keep doing so until all points have been classified. This approach makes the most direct use of the definition of a cluster as a region of high density, and it makes no assumptions about the overall *shape* of the cluster. Therefore, such methods can handle clusters of complicated shapes (as in Figure 13-6), interwoven clusters, or even nested clusters (as in Figure 13-3). In general, neighborhood-based clustering algorithms are more of a special-purpose tool: either for cases that other algorithms don't handle well (such as the ones just mentioned) or for polishing, in a second pass, the features of a cluster found by a general-purpose clustering algorithm such as *k*-means.

The DBSCAN algorithm which we will introduce in this section is one such algorithm, and it demonstrates some typical concepts. It requires two parameters. One is the *minimum density* that we expect to prevail inside of a cluster—points that are less densely packed will not be considered part of any cluster. The other parameter is the *size of the region* over which we expect this density to be maintained: it should be larger than the average distance between neighboring points but smaller than the entire cluster. The choice of parameters is rather subtle and clearly requires an appropriate balance.

In a practical implementation, it is easier to work with two slightly different parameters: the neighborhood radius r and the minimum number of points n that we expect to find within the neighborhood of each point in a cluster. The DBSCAN algorithm distinguishes between three types of points: noise, edge, and core points. A *noise point* is a point which has fewer than n points in its neighborhood of radius r, such a point does not belong to any cluster. A *core point* of a cluster has more than n neighbors. An *edge point* is a point that has fewer neighbors than required for a core point but that is itself the neighbor of a core point. The algorithm discards noise points and concentrates on core points. Whenever it finds a core point, the algorithm assigns a cluster label to that point and then continues to add all its neighbors, and *their* neighbors recursively to the cluster, until all points have been classified.

This description is simple enough, but actually deriving a concrete implementation that is both correct and efficient is less than straightforward. The pseudo-code in the original paper[*] appears needlessly clumsy; on the other hand, I am not convinced that the streamlined version that can be found (for example) on Wikipedia is necessarily correct. Finally, the basic algorithm lends itself to elegant recursive implementations, but keep in mind that the recursion will not unwind until the current cluster is complete. This means that, in the worst case (of a single connected cluster), you will end up putting the entire data set onto the stack!

As pointed out earlier, the main advantage of the DBSCAN algorithm is that it handles clusters of complicated shapes and nested clusters gracefully. However, it does depend sensitively on the appropriate choice of values for its two control parameters, and it provides little help in finding them. If a data set contains several clusters with widely varying densities, then a single set of parameters may not be sufficient to classify all of the clusters. These problems can be ameliorated by coupling the DBSCAN algorithm with the k-means algorithm: in a first pass, the k-means algorithm is used to identify candidates for clusters. Moreover, statistics on these subsets of points (such as range and density) can be used as input to the DBSCAN algorithm.

The DBSCAN algorithm is dominated by the calculations required to find the neighboring points. For each point in the data set, all other points have to be checked; this leads to a complexity of $\mathcal{O}(n^2)$. In principle, algorithms and data structures exist to find candidates for neighboring points more efficiently (*e.g.*, kd-trees and global grids), but their implementations are subtle and carry their own costs (grids can be very memory intensive). Coupling the DBSCAN algorithm with a more efficient first-pass algorithm (such as k-means) may therefore be a better strategy.

---

[*] "A Density-Based Algorithm for Discovering Clusters in Large Spatial Databases with Noise." Martin Ester, Hans-Peter Kriegel, Jörg Sander, and Xiaowei Xu. Proceedings of 2nd International Conference on Knowledge Discovery and Data Mining (KDD-96). 1996.

Pre- and Postprocessing

The core algorithm for grouping data points into clusters is usually only part (though the most important one) of the whole strategy. Some data sets may require some cleanup or normalization before they are suitable for clustering: that's the first topic in this section.

Furthermore, we need to inspect the results of every clustering algorithm in order to validate and characterize the clusters that have been found. We will discuss some concepts and quantities used to describe clusters and to measure the clustering quality.

Finally, several cluster algorithms require certain input parameters (such as the number of clusters to find), and we need to confirm that the values we provided are consistent with the outcome of the clustering process. That will be our last topic in this section.

Scale Normalization

Look at Figures 13-11 and 13-12. Wouldn't you agree that the data set in Figure 13-11 exhibits two reasonably clearly defined and well-separated clusters while the data set in Figure 13-12 does not? Yet both figures show the *same* data set—only drawn to different scales! In Figure 13-12, I used identical units for both the x axis and the y axis; whereas Figure 13-11 was drawn to maintain a suitable aspect ratio for this data set.

This example demonstrates that clustering is not independent of the units in which the data is measured. In fact, for the data set shown in Figures 13-11 and 13-12, points in two different clusters may be closer to each other than to other points in the same cluster! This is clearly a problem.

If, as in this example, your data spans very different ranges along different dimensions, you need to normalize the data before starting a clustering algorithm. An easy way to achieve this is to divide the data, dimension for dimension, by the range of the data along that dimension. Alternatively, you might want to divide by the standard deviation along that dimension. This process is sometimes called *whitening* or *prewhitening,* particularly in signal-theoretic literature.

You only need to worry about this problem if you are working with vector-like data and are using a distance measure like the Euclidean distance. It does not affect correlation-based similarity measures. In fact, there is a special variant of the Euclidean distance that performs the appropriate rescaling for each dimension on the fly: the *Mahalanobis distance*.

Cluster Properties and Evaluation

It is easiest to think about cluster properties in the context of vector-like data and a straightforward clustering algorithm such as k-means. The algorithm already gives us the

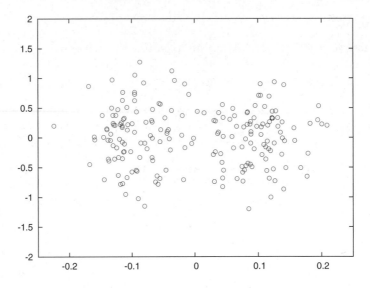

FIGURE 13-11. It is easy to argue that there are two clusters in this graph. (Compare Figure 13-12.)

coordinates of the cluster centroids directly, hence we have the cluster *location*. Two additional quantities are the *mass* of the cluster (*i.e.,* the number of points in the cluster) and its radius. The *radius* is simply the average deviation of all points from the cluster center—basically the standard deviation, when using the Euclidean distance:

$$r^2 = \sum_i (x_c - x_i)^2 + (y_c - y_i)^2$$

in two dimensions (equivalently in higher dimensions). Here x_c and y_c are the coordinates of the center of the cluster, and the sum runs over all points i in the cluster. Dividing the mass by the radius gives us the *density* of the cluster. (These values can be used to construct input values for the DBSCAN algorithm.)

We can apply the same principles to develop a measure for the overall quality of the clustering. The key concepts are *cohesion* within a cluster and *separation* between clusters. The average distance for all points within one cluster is a measure of the cohesion, and the average distance between all points in one cluster from all points in another cluster is a measure of the separation between the two clusters. (If we know the centroids of the clusters, we can use the distance between the centroids as a measure for the separation.) We can go further and form the average (weighted by the cluster mass) of the cohesion for all clusters as a measure for the overall quality.

If a data set can be cleanly grouped into clusters, then we expect the distance between the clusters to be large compared to the radii of the clusters. In other words, we expect the ratio:

$$\frac{\text{separation}}{\text{cohesion}}$$

to be large.

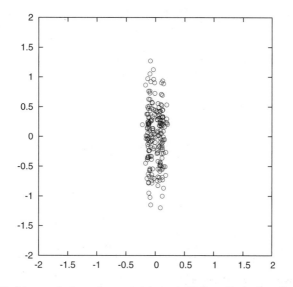

FIGURE 13-12. It is difficult to recognize two well-separated clusters in this figure. Yet the data is the same as in Figure 13-11 but drawn to a different scale! (Compare the horizontal and vertical scales in both graphs.)

A particular measure based on this concept is the *silhouette coefficient S*. The silhouette coefficient is defined for individual points as follows. Let a_i be the average distance (the cohesion) that point i has from all other points in the cluster to which it belongs. Evaluate the average distance that point i has from all points in any cluster to which it does *not* belong, and let b_i be the smallest such value (*i.e.*, b_i is the separation from the "closest" other cluster). Then the silhouette coefficient of point i is defined as:

$$S_i = \frac{b_i - a_i}{\max(a_i, b_i)}$$

The numerator is a measure for the "empty space" between clusters (*i.e.*, it measures the amount of distance between clusters that is not occupied by the original cluster). The denominator is the greater of the two length scales in the problem—namely the cluster radius and the distance between clusters.

By construction, the silhouette coefficient ranges from -1 to 1. Negative values indicate that the cluster radius is *greater* than the distance between clusters, so that clusters overlap; this suggests poor clustering. Large values of S suggest good clustering. We can form the average of the silhouette coefficients for all points belonging to a single cluster and thereby develop a measure for the quality of the entire cluster. We can further define the average over the silhouette coefficients for all individual points as the overall silhouette coefficient for the entire data set; this would be a measure for the quality of the clustering result.

The overall silhouette coefficient can be useful to determine the number of clusters present in the data set. If we run the k-means algorithm several times for different values

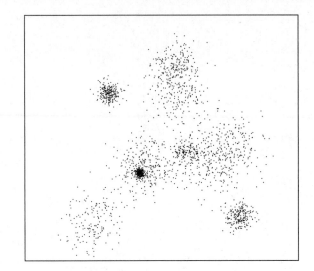

FIGURE 13-13. How many clusters are in this data set?

of the expected number of clusters and calculate the overall silhouette coefficient each time, then it should exhibit a peak near the optimal number of clusters.

Let's work through an example to see how the the silhouette coefficient performs in practice. Figure 13-13 shows the points of a two-dimensional data set. This is an interesting data set because, even though it exhibits clear clustering, it is not at all obvious how many *distinct* clusters there really are—any number between six and eight seems plausible. The total silhouette coefficient (averaged over all points in the data set) for this data set (see Figure 13-14) confirms this expectation, clearly leaning toward the lower end of this range. (It is interesting to note that the data set was generated, using a random-number generator, to include *10* distinct clusters, but some of those clusters are overlapping so strongly that it is not possible to distinguish them.) This example also serves as a cautionary reminder that it may not always be so easy to determine what actually constitutes a cluster!

Another interesting question concerns distinguishing legitimate clusters from a random (unclustered) background. Of the algorithms that we have seen, only the DBSCAN algorithm explicitly labels some points as background; the k-means and the tree-building algorithm perform what is known as *complete clustering* by assigning every point to a cluster. We may want to relax this behavior by trimming those points from each cluster that exceed the average cohesion within the cluster by some amount. This is easiest for fuzzy clustering algorithms, but it can be done for other algorithms as well.

Other Thoughts

The three types of clustering algorithms introduced in this chapter are probably the most popular and widely used, but they certainly don't exhaust the range of possibilities.

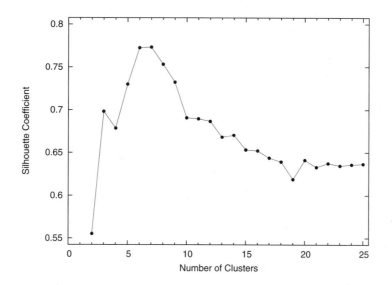

FIGURE 13-14. The silhouette coefficient for the data in Figure 13-13. According to this measure, six or seven clusters give optimal results for this data set.

Here is a brief list of other ideas that can (and have) been used to develop clustering algorithms.

- We can impose a specific *topology*, such as a grid on the data points. Each data point will fall into a single grid cell, and we can use this information to find cells containing unusually many points and so guide clustering. Cell-based methods will perform poorly in many dimensions, because most cells will be empty and have few occupied neighbors (the "curse of dimensionality").

- Among grid-based approaches, Kohonen maps (which we will discuss in Chapter 14) have a lot of intuitive appeal.

- Some special methods have been suggested to address the challenges posed by high-dimensional feature spaces. In *subspace clustering*, for example, clustering is performed on only a subset of all available features. These results are then successively extended by including features ignored in previous iterations.

- Remember kernel density estimates (KDEs) from Chapter 2? If the dimensionality is not too high, then we can generate a KDE for the data set. The KDE provides a smooth approximation to the local point density. We can then identify clusters by finding the maxima of this density directly, using standard methods from numerical analysis.

- The QT ("quality threshold") algorithm is a center-seeking algorithm that does not require the number of clusters as input; instead, we have to fix a maximum *radius*. The QT algorithm treats *every* point in the cluster as a potential centroid and adds neighboring points (in the order of increasing distance from the centroid) until the maximum radius is exceeded. Once all candidate clusters have been completed in this way, the cluster with the greatest number of points is removed from the data set, and then the process starts again with the remaining points.

- There is a well-known correspondence between graphs and distance matrices. Given a set of points, a graph tells us which points are directly connected to each other—but so does a distance matrix! We can exploit this equivalence by treating a distance matrix as the adjacency matrix of a graph. The distance matrix is pruned (by removing connections that are too long) to obtain a sparse graph, which can be interpreted as the backbone of a cluster.

- Finally, *spectral clustering* uses powerful but abstract methods from linear algebra (similar to those used for principal component analysis; see Chapter 14) to structure and simplify the distance matrix.

Obviously, much depends on our prior knowledge about the data set: if we expect clusters to be simple and convex, then the k-means algorithm suggests itself. On the other hand, if we have a sense for the typical radius of the clusters that we expect to find, then QT clustering would be a more natural approach. If we expect clusters of complicated shapes or nested clusters, then an algorithm like DBSCAN will be required. Of course, it might be difficult to develop this kind of intuition—especially for problems that have significantly more than two or three dimensions!

Besides thinking of different ways to combine points into clusters, we can also think of different ways to define clusters to begin with. All methods discussed so far have relied (directly or indirectly) on the information contained in the distance between any two points. We can extend this concept and begin to think about *three-point* (or higher) *distance functions*. For example, it is possible to determine the *angle* between any three consecutive points and use this information as the measure of the similarity between points. Such an approach might help with cases like the one shown in Figure 13-8. Yet another idea is to measure not the similarity between *points* but instead the similarity between a point and a *property of the cluster*. For example, there is a straightforward generalization of the k-means algorithm in which the centroids are no longer pointlike but are straight lines, representing the "axis" of an elongated cluster. Rather than measuring the distance for each point from the centroid, this algorithm calculates the distance from this axis when assigning points to clusters. This algorithm would be suitable for cases like that shown in Figure 13-7. I don't think any of these ideas that try to generalize beyond pairwise distances have been explored in detail yet.

A Special Case: Market Basket Analysis

Which items are frequently bought together? This and similar questions arise in *market basket analysis* or—more generally—in *association analysis*. Because association analysis is looking for items that occur together, it is in some ways related to clustering. However, the specific nature of the problem is different enough to require a separate toolset.

The starting point for association analysis is usually a data set consisting of *transactions*—that is, items that have been purchased together (we will often stay with the market basket metaphor when illustrating these concepts). Each transaction corresponds to a single "data point" in regular clustering.

For each transaction, we keep track of all items that have occurred together but typically ignore whether or not any particular item was purchased multiple times: all attributes are Boolean and indicate only the presence or absence of a certain item. Each item spans a new dimension: if the store sells N different items, then each transaction can have up to N different (Boolean) attributes, although each transaction typically contains only a tiny subset of the entire selection. (Note that we do not necessarily need to know the dimensionality N ahead of time: if we don't know it, we can infer an approximation from the number of different items that actually occur in the data set.)

From this description, you can already see how association analysis differs from regular clustering: data points in association analysis are typically very high-dimensional but also very sparse. It also differs from clustering (as we have discussed it so far) in that we are not necessarily interested in grouping entire "points" (*i.e.*, transactions) but would like to identify those dimensions that frequently occur together.

A group of zero or more items occurring together is known as an *item set* (or *itemset*). Each transaction consists of an item set, but every one of its subsets is also an item set. We can construct arbitrary item sets from the selection of available items. For each such item set, its *support count* is the number of actual transactions that contain the candidate item set as a subset.

Besides simply identifying frequent item sets, we can also try to derive *association rules*—that is, rules of the form "if items A and B are bought, then item C is also likely to be bought." Two measures are important when evaluating the strength of an association rule: its support s and its confidence c. The *support* of a rule is the fraction of transactions in the entire data set that contain the combined item set (*i.e.*, the fraction of transactions that contain all three items A, B, and C). A rule with low support is not very useful because it is rarely applicable.

The *confidence* is a measure for the reliability of an association rule. It is defined as the number of transactions in which the rule is *correct*, divided by the number of transactions in which it is *applicable*. In our example, it would be the number of times A, B, and C occur together divided by the number of times A and B occur together.

How do we go about finding frequent item sets (and association rules)? Rather than performing an open-ended search for the "best" association rule, it is customary to set thresholds for the minimum support (such as 10 percent) and confidence (such as 80 percent) required of a rule and then to generate all rules that meet these conditions.

To identify rules, we generate candidate item sets and then evaluate them against the set of transactions to determine whether they exceed the required thresholds. However, the naive approach—to create and evaluate *all* possible item sets of k elements—is not feasible because of the huge number (2^k) of candidate item sets that could be generated, most of which will *not* be frequent! We must find a way to generate candidate item sets more efficiently.

The crucial observation is that *an item set can occur frequently only if all of its subsets occur frequently*. This insight is the basis for the so-called *apriori algorithm*, which is the most fundamental algorithm for association analysis.

The apriori algorithm is a two-step algorithm: in the first step, we identify frequent item sets; in the second step, we extract association rules. The first part of the algorithm is the more computationally expensive one. It can be summarized as follows.

```
Find all 1-item item sets that meet the minimum support threshold.

repeat:
    from the current list of k-item item sets, construct (k+1)-item item sets
    eliminate those item sets that do not meet the minimum support threshold
    stop when no (k+1)-item item set meets the minimum support threshold
```

The list of frequent item sets may be all that we require, or we may postprocess the list to extract explicit association rules. To find association rules, we split each frequent item set into two sets, and evaluate the confidence associated with this pair. From a practical point of view, rules that have a 1-item item set on the "righthand side" are the easiest to generate and the most important. (In other words, rules of the form "people who bought A and B also bought C," rather than rules of the form "people who bought A and B also bought C and D.")

This basic description leaves out many technical details, which are important in actual implementations. For example: how exactly do we create a $(k + 1)$-item item set from the list of k-item item sets? We might take every single item that occurs among the k-item item sets and add it, in turn, to every one of the k-item item sets; however, this would generate a large number of duplicate item sets that need to be pruned again. Alternatively, we might combine two k-item item sets only if they agree on all but one of their items. Clearly, appropriate data structures are essential for obtaining an efficient implementation. (Similar considerations apply when determining the support count of a candidate item set, and so on.)[*]

Although the apriori algorithm is probably the most popular algorithm for association analysis, there are also very different approaches. For example, the *FP-Growth Algorithm* (where FP stands for "Frequent Pattern") identifies frequent item sets using something

---

[*] An open source implementation of the apriori algorithm (and many other algorithms for frequent pattern identification), together with notes on efficient implementation, can be found at *http://borgelt.net/apriori.html*. The arules package for R is an alternative. It can be found on CRAN.

like a string-matching algorithm. Items in transactions are sorted by their support count, and a treelike data structure is built up by exploiting data sets that agree in the first k items. This tree structure is then searched for frequently occurring item sets.

Association analysis is a relatively complicated problem that involves many technical (as opposed to conceptual) challenges as well. The discussion in this section could only introduce the topic and attempt to give a sense of the kinds of approaches that are available. We will see some additional problems of a similar nature in Chapter 18.

A Word of Warning

Clustering can lead you astray, and when done carelessly it can become a huge waste of time. There are at least two reasons for this: although the algorithms are deceptively simple, it can be surprisingly difficult to obtain useful results from them. Many of them depend quite sensitively on several heuristic parameters, and you can spend hours fiddling with the various knobs. Moreover, because the algorithms are simple and the field has so much intuitive appeal, it can be a lot of fun to play with implementations and to develop all kinds of modifications and variations.

And that assumes there actually are any clusters present! (This is the second reason.) In the absence of rigorous, independent results, you will actually spend *more* time on data sets that are totally worthless—perpetually hunting for those clusters that "the stupid algorithm just won't find." Perversely, additional domain knowledge does not necessarily make the task any easier: knowing that there should be exactly 10 clusters present in Figure 13-13 is of no help in finding the clusters that actually can be identified!

Another important question concerns the value that you ultimately derive from clustering (assuming now that at least one of the algorithms has returned something apparently meaningful). It can be difficult to distinguish spurious results from real ones: like clustering algorithms, cluster evaluation methods are not particularly rigorous or unequivocal either (Figure 13-14 does not exactly inspire confidence). And we still have not answered the question of what you will actually *do* with the results—assuming that they turn out to be significant.

I have found that understanding the actual question that needs to be answered, developing some pertinent hypotheses and models around it, and then verifying them on the data through specific, focused analysis is usually a far better use of time than to go off on a wild-goose clustering search.

Finally, I should emphasize that, in keeping with the spirit of this book, the algorithms in this chapter are suitable for moderately sized data sets (a few thousand data points and a dozen dimensions, or so) and for problems that are not too pathological. Highly developed algorithms (*e.g.*, CURE and BIRCH) exist for very large or very high-dimensional problems; these algorithms usually combine several different cluster-finding approaches together with a set of heuristics. You need to evaluate whether such specialized algorithms make sense for your situation.

Workshop: Pycluster and the C Clustering Library

The C Clustering Library (*http://bonsai.hgc.jp/~mdehoon/software/cluster/software.htm*) is a mature and relatively efficient clustering library originally developed to find clusters among gene expressions in microarray experiments. It contains implementations of the *k*-means and *k*-medoids algorithms, tree clustering, and even self-organized (Kohonen) maps. It comes with its own GUI frontend as well as excellent Perl and Python bindings. It is easy to use and very well documented. In this Workshop, we use Python to demonstrate the library's center-seeker algorithms.

```
import Pycluster as pc
import numpy as np
import sys

# Read data filename and desired number of clusters from command line
filename, n = sys.argv[1], int( sys.argv[2] )

# x and y coordinates, whitespace-separated
data = np.loadtxt( filename, usecols=(0,1) )

# Perform clustering and find centroids
clustermap = pc.kcluster( data, nclusters=n, npass=50 )[0]
centroids = pc.clustercentroids( data, clusterid=clustermap )[0]

# Obtain distance matrix
m = pc.distancematrix( data )

# Find the masses of all clusters
mass = np.zeros( n )
for c in clustermap:
    mass[c] += 1

# Create a matrix for individual silhouette coefficients
sil = np.zeros( n*len(data) )
sil.shape = ( len(data), n )

# Evaluate the distance for all pairs of points
for i in range( 0, len(data) ):
    for j in range( i+1, len(data) ):
        d = m[j][i]

        sil[i, clustermap[j] ] += d
        sil[j, clustermap[i] ] += d

# Normalize by cluster size (that is: form average over cluster)
for i in range( 0, len(data) ):
    sil[i,:] /= mass
```

```
# Evaluate the silhouette coefficient
s = 0
for i in range( 0, len(data) ):
    c = clustermap[i]
    a = sil[i,c]
    b = min( sil[i, range(0,c)+range(c+1,n) ] )
    si = (b-a)/max(b,a) # This is the silhouette coeff of point i
    s += si

# Print overall silhouette coefficient
print n, s/len(data)
```

The listing shows the code used to generate Figure 13-14, showing how the silhouette coefficient depends on the number of clusters. Let's step through it.

We import both the Pycluster library itself as well as the NumPy package. We will use some of the vector manipulation abilities of the latter. The point coordinates are read from the file specified on the command line. (The file is assumed to contain the x and y coordinates of each point, separated by whitespace; one point per line.) The point coordinates are then passed to the kcluster() function, which performs the actual k-means algorithm. This function takes a number of optional arguments: nclusters is the desired number of clusters, and npass holds the number of trials that should be performed with *different* starting values. (Remember that k-means clustering is nondeterministic with regard to the initial guesses for the positions of the cluster centroids.) The kcluster() function will make npass different trials and report on the best one.

The function returns three values. The first return value is an array that, for each point in the original data set, holds the index of the cluster to which it has been assigned. The second and third return values provide information about the quality of the clustering (which we ignore in this example). This function signature is a reflection of the underlying C API, where you pass in an array of the same length as the data array and then the cluster assignments of each point are communicated via this additional array. This frees the kcluster() function from having to do its own resource management, which makes sense in C (and possibly also for extremely large data sets).

All information about the result of the clustering procedure are contained in the clustermap data structure. The Pycluster library provides several functions to extract this information; here we demonstrate just one: we can pass the clustermap to the clustercentroids() function to obtain the coordinates of the cluster centroids. (However, we won't actually use these coordinates in the rest of the program.)

You may have noticed that we did not specify the distance function to use in the listing. The C Clustering Library does *not* give us the option of a user-defined distance function with k-means. It does include several standard distance measures (Euclidean, Manhattan, correlation, and several others), which can be selected through a keyword argument to kcluster() (the default is to use the Euclidean distance). Distance calculations can be a rather expensive part of the algorithm, and having them implemented in C makes the

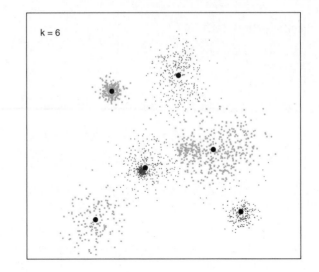

FIGURE 13-15. The result of running the k-means algorithm on the data from Figure 13-13, finding six clusters. Different clusters are shown in black and gray, and the cluster centroids are indicated by filled dots.

overall program faster. (If we want to define our own distance function, then we have to use the `kmedoids()` function, which we will discuss in a moment.)

To evaluate the silhouette coefficient we need the point-to-point distances, and so we obtain the distance matrix from the `Pycluster` library. We will also need the number of points in each cluster (the cluster's "mass") later.

Next, we calculate the individual silhouette coefficients for all data points. Recall that the silhouette coefficient involves both the average distance to the all points in the *same* cluster as well as the average distance to all points in the *nearest* cluster. Since we don't know ahead of time which one will be the nearest cluster to each point, we simply go ahead and calculate the average distance to *all* clusters. The results are stored in the matrix `sil`.

(In the implementation, we make use of some of the vector manipulation features of NumPy: in the expression `sil[i,:] /= mass`, each entry in row i is divided componentwise by the corresponding entry in `mass`. Further down, we make use of "advanced indexing" when looking for the minimum distance between the point i and a cluster to which it does not belong: in the expression `b = min( sil[i, range(0,c)+range(c+1,n) ] )`, we construct an indexing vector that includes indices for all clusters except the one that the point i belongs to. See the Workshop in Chapter 2 for more details.)

Finally, we form the average over all single-point silhouette coefficients and print the results. Figure 13-14 shows them as a graph.

Figures 13-15 and 13-16 show how the program assigned points to clusters in two runs, finding 6 and 10 clusters, respectively. These results agree with Figure 13-14: $k = 6$ is

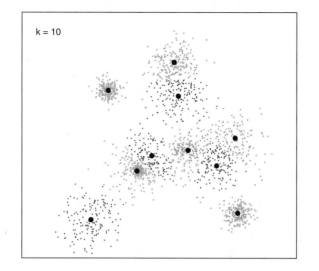

$FIGURE$ *13-16. Similar to Figure 13-15 but for* $k = 10$. *Ten seems too high a number of clusters for this data set, which agrees with the results from calculating the silhouette coefficient in Figure 13-14.*

close to the optimal number of clusters, whereas $k = 10$ seems to split some clusters artificially.

The next listing demonstrates the `kmedoids()` function, which we have to use if we want to provide our own distance function. As implemented by the `Pycluster` library, the k-medoids algorithm does *not* require the data at all—all it needs is the distance matrix!

```
import Pycluster as pc
import numpy as np
import sys

# Our own distance function: maximum norm
def dist( a, b ):
    return max( abs( a - b ) )

# Read data filename and desired number of clusters from command line
filename, n = sys.argv[1], int( sys.argv[2] )

# x and y coordinates, whitespace-separated
data = np.loadtxt( filename, usecols=(0,1) )
k = len(data)

# Calculate the distance matrix
m = np.zeros( k*k )
m.shape = ( k, k )

for i in range( 0, k ):
    for j in range( i, k ):
        d = dist( data[i], data[j] )
```

```
        m[i][j] = d
        m[j][i] = d

    # Perform the actual clustering
    clustermap = pc.kmedoids( m, n, npass=20 )[0]

    # Find the indices of the points used as medoids, and the cluster masses
    medoids = {}
    for i in clustermap:
        medoids[i] = medoids.get(i,0) + 1


    # Print points, grouped by cluster
    for i in medoids.keys():
        print "Cluster=", i, " Mass=", medoids[i], " Centroid: ", data[i]

        for j in range( 0, len(data) ):
            if clustermap[j] == i:
                print "\t", data[j]
```

In the listing, we calculate the distance matrix using the maximum norm (which is not supplied by Pycluster) as distance function. Obviously, we could use any other function here—such as the Levenshtein distance if we wanted to cluster the strings in Figure 13-4.

We then call the kmedoids() function, which returns a clustermap data structure similar to the one returned by kcluster(). For the kmedoids() function, the data structure contains—for each data point—the index of the data point that is the centroid of the assigned cluster.

Finally, we calculate the masses of the clusters and print the coordinates of the cluster medoids as well as the coordinates of all points assigned to that cluster.

The C Clustering Library is small and relatively easy to use. You might also want to explore its tree-clustering implementation. The library also includes routines for Kohonen maps and principal component analysis, which we will discuss in Chapter 14.

Further Reading

- *Introduction to Data Mining.* Pang-Ning Tan, Michael Steinbach, and Vipin Kumar. Addison-Wesley. 2005.
  This is my favorite book on data mining. The presentation is compact and more technical than in most other books on this topic. The section on clustering is particularly strong.

- *Data Clustering: Theory, Algorithms, and Applications.* Guojun Gan, Chaoqun Ma, and Jianhong Wu. SIAM. 2007.
  This book is a recent survey of results from clustering research. The presentation is too terse to be useful, but it provides a good source of concepts and keywords for further investigation.

- *Algorithms for Clustering Data.* Anil K. Jain and Richard C. Dubes. Prentice Hall. 1988. An older book on clustering as freely available at *http://www.cse.msu.edu/~jain/Clustering_Jain_Dubes.pdf*.

- *Metric Spaces: Iteration and Application.* Victor Bryant. Cambridge University Press. 1985. If you are interested in thinking about distance measures in arbitrary spaces in a more abstract way, then this short (100-page) book is a wonderful introduction. It requires no more than some passing familiarity with real analysis, but it does a remarkable job of demonstrating the power of purely abstract reasoning—both from a conceptual point of view but also with an eye to real applications.

## CHAPTER FOURTEEN

Seeing the Forest for the Trees: Finding Important Attributes

WHAT DO YOU DO WHEN YOU DON'T KNOW WHERE TO START? WHEN YOU ARE DEALING WITH A DATA SET THAT offers no structure that would suggest an angle of attack?

For example, I remember looking through a company's contracts with its suppliers for a certain consumable. These contracts all differed in regards to the supplier, the number of units ordered, the duration of the contract and the lead time, the destination location that the items were supposed to be shipped to, the actual shipping date, and the procurement agent that had authorized the contract—and, of course, the unit price. What I tried to figure out was which of these quantities had the greatest influence on the unit price.

This kind of problem can be very difficult: there are so many different variables, none of which seems, at first glance, to be predominant. Furthermore, I have no assurance that the variables are all independent; many of them may be expressing related information. (In this case, the supplier and the shipping destination may be related, since suppliers are chosen to be near the place where the items are required.)

Because all variables arise on more or less equal footing, we can't identify a few as the obvious "control" or independent variables and then track the behavior of all the other variables in response to these independent variables. We can try to look at all possible pairings—for example, using graphical techniques such as scatter-plot matrices (Chapter 5)—but that may not really reveal much either, particularly if the number of variables is truly large. We need some form of computational guidance.

In this chapter, we will introduce a number of different techniques for exactly this purpose. All of them help us select the most important variables or *features* from a multivariate data set in which all variables appear to arise on equal footing. In doing so, we reduce the dimension of the data set from the original number of variables (or features) to a smaller set, which (hopefully) captures most of the "interesting" behavior of the data. These methods are therefore also known as *feature selection* or *dimensionality reduction* techniques.

A word of warning: the material in this chapter is probably the most advanced and least obvious in the whole book, both conceptually and also with respect to actual implementations. In particular, the following section (on principal component analysis) is very abstract, and it may not make much sense if you haven't had some previous exposure to matrices and linear algebra (including eigentheory). Other sections are more accessible.

I include these techniques here nevertheless, because they are of considerable practical importance but also to give you a sense of the kinds of (more advanced) techniques that are available, and also as a possible pointer for further study.

Principal Component Analysis

Principal component analysis (PCA) is the primary tool for dimensionality reduction in multivariate problems. It is a foundational technique that finds applications as part of many other, more advanced procedures.

Motivation

To understand what PCA can do for us, let's consider a simple example. Let's go back to the contract example given earlier and now assume that there are only two variables for each contract: its lead time and the number of units to be delivered. What can we say about them? Well, we can draw histograms for each to understand the distribution of values and to see whether there are "typical" values for either of these quantities. The histograms (in the form of kernel density estimates—see Chapter 2) are shown in Figure 14-1 and don't reveal anything of interest.

Because there are only two variables in this case, we can also plot one variable against the other in a scatter plot. The resulting graph is shown in Figure 14-2 and is very revealing: the lead time of the contract grows with its size. So far, so good.

But we can also look at Figure 14-2 in a different way. Recall that the contract data depends on two variables (lead time and number of items), so that we would expect the points to fill the two-dimensional space spanned by the two axes (lead time and number of items). But in reality, all the points fall very close to a straight line. A straight line, however, is only one-dimensional, and this means that we need only a *single* variable to describe the position of each point: the distance along the straight line. In other words, although it appears to depend on two variables, the contract data *mostly* depends on a single variable that lies halfway between the original ones. In this sense, the data is of lower dimensionality than it originally appeared.

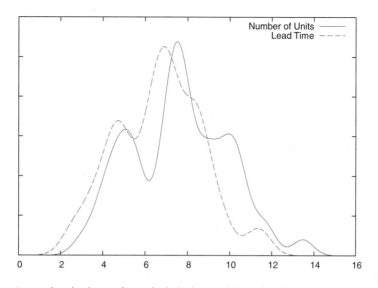

FIGURE 14-1. Contract data: distribution of points for the lead time and the number of units per order. The distributions do not reveal anything in particular about the data.

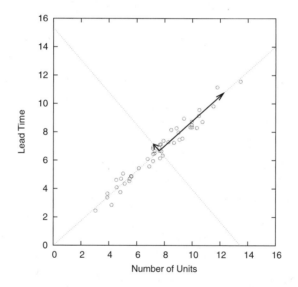

FIGURE 14-2. Contract data: individual contracts in a scatter plot spanned by the two original variables. All the points fall close to a straight line that is not parallel to either of the original coordinate axes.

Of course, the data still depends on two variables—as it did originally. But most of the *variation* in the data occurs along only one direction. If we were to measure the data only along this direction, we would still capture most of what is "interesting" about the data. In Figure 14-3, we see another kernel density estimate of the same data, but this time not taken along the original variables but instead showing the distribution of data points along

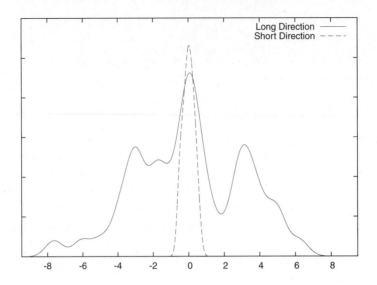

FIGURE 14-3. Contract data: distribution of points along the principal directions. Most of the variation is along the "long" direction, whereas there is almost no variation perpendicular to it. (The vertical scales have been adjusted to make the curves comparable.)

the two "new" directions indicated by the arrows in the scatter plot of Figure 14-2. In contrast to the variation occurring along the "long" component, the "short" component is basically irrelevant.

For this simple example, which had only two variables to begin with, it was easy enough to find the lower-dimensional representation just by looking at it. But that won't work when there are significantly more than two variables involved. If there aren't too many variables, then we can generate a scatter-plot matrix (see Chapter 5) containing all possible pairs of variables, but even this becomes impractical once there are more than seven or eight variables. Moreover, scatter-plot matrices can never show us more than the combination of any two of the original variables. What if the data in a three-dimensional problem falls onto a straight line that runs along the *space* diagonal of the original three-dimensional data cube? We will not find this by plotting the data against any (two-dimensional!) pair of the original variables.

Fortunately, there is a calculational scheme that—given a set of points—will give us the principal directions (in essence, the arrows in Figure 14-2) as a combination of the original variables. That is the topic of the next section.

Optional: Theory

We can make progress by using a technique that works for many multi-dimensional problems. If we can summarize the available information regarding the multi-dimensional system in *matrix form*, then we can invoke a large and powerful body of results from linear algebra to transform this matrix into a form that reveals any underlying structure (such as the structure visible in Figure 14-2).

In what follows, I will often appeal to the two-dimensional example of Figure 14-2, but the real purpose here is to develop a procedure that will be applicable to any number of dimensions. These techniques become necessary when the number of dimensions exceeds two or three so that simple visualizations like the ones discussed so far will no longer work.

To express what we know about the system, we first need to ask ourselves how best to summarize the way any two variables relate to each other. Looking at Figure 14-2, the *correlation coefficient* suggests itself. In Chapter 13, we introduced the correlation coefficient as a measure for the similarity between two multi-dimensional *data points x* and *y*. Here, we use the same concept to express the similarity between two *dimensions* in a multivariate data set. Let x and y be two different dimensions ("variables") in such a data set, then the correlation coefficient is defined by:

$$\text{corr}(x, y) = \frac{1}{N} \frac{\sum_i (x_i - \bar{x})(y_i - \bar{y})}{\sigma(x)\sigma(y)}$$

where the sum is over all data points, $\bar{x}$ and $\bar{y}$ are the means of the x_i and the y_i, respectively, and $\sigma(x) = \sqrt{\frac{1}{N}\sum_i (x_i - \bar{x})^2}$ is the standard deviation of x (and equivalently for y). The denominator in the expression of the correlation coefficient amounts to a rescaling of the values of both variables to a standard interval. If that is not what we want, then we can instead use the *covariance* between the x_i and the y_i:

$$\text{cov}(x, y) = \frac{1}{N} \sum_i^N (x_i - \bar{x})(y_i - \bar{y})$$

All of these quantities can be defined for *any* two variables (just supply values for, say x_i and z_i). For a p-dimensional problem, we can find all the $p(p-1)/2$ different combinations (remember that these coefficients are symmetric: $\text{cov}(x, y) = \text{cov}(y, x)$).

It is now convenient to group the values in a matrix, which is typically called Σ (not to be confused with the summation sign!)

$$\Sigma = \begin{pmatrix} \text{cov}(x, x) & \text{cov}(x, y) & \cdots \\ \text{cov}(y, x) & \text{cov}(y, y) & \\ \vdots & & \ddots \end{pmatrix}$$

and similarly for the correlation matrix. Because the covariance (or correlation) itself is symmetric under an interchange of its arguments, the matrix Σ is also symmetric (so that it equals its transpose).

We can now invoke an extremely important result from linear algebra, known as the *spectral decomposition theorem*, as follows. *For any real, symmetric N × N matrix A, there exists an orthogonal matrix U such that:*

$$B = \begin{pmatrix} \lambda_1 & & & \\ & \lambda_2 & & \\ & & \ddots & \\ & & & \lambda_N \end{pmatrix} = U^{-1}AU$$

is a diagonal matrix.

Let's explain some of the terminology. A matrix is *diagonal* if its only nonzero entries are along the main diagonal from the top left to the bottom right. A matrix is *orthogonal* if its transpose equals its inverse: $U^T = U^{-1}$ or $U^T U = U U^T = 1$.

The entries λ_i in the diagonal matrix are called the *eigenvalues* of matrix A, and the column vectors of U are the *eigenvectors*. The spectral theorem also implies that all eigenvectors are mutually orthogonal. Finally, the ith column vector in U is the eigenvector "associated" with the eigenvalue λ_i; each eigenvalue has an associated eigenvector.

What does all of this mean? In a nutshell, it means that we can perform a change of variables that turns any symmetric matrix A into a diagonal matrix B. Although it may not be obvious, the matrix B contains the same information as A—it's just packaged differently.

The change of variables required for this transformation consists of a *rotation* of the original coordinate system into a new coordinate system in which the correlation matrix has a particularly convenient (diagonal) shape. (Notice how in Figure 14-2, the new directions are rotated with respect to the original horizontal and vertical axes.)

When expressed in the original coordinate system (*i.e.*, the original variables that the problem was initially expressed in), the matrix Σ is a complicated object with off-diagonal entries that are nonzero. However, the eigenvectors span a new coordinate system that is rotated with respect to the old one. In this new coordinate system, the matrix takes on a simple, diagonal form in which all entries that are not on the diagonal vanish. The arrows in Figure 14-2 show the directions of the new coordinate axes, and the histogram in Figure 14-3 measures the distribution of points along these new directions.

The purpose of performing a matrix diagonalization is to find the directions of this new coordinate system, which is more suitable for describing the data than was the original coordinate system.

Because the new coordinate system is merely rotated relative to the original one, we can express its coordinate axes as linear combinations of the original ones. In Figure 14-2, for instance, to make a step in the new direction (along the diagonal), you take a step along the (old) x axis, followed by a step along the (old) y axis. We can therefore express the new direction (call it $\hat{x}$) in terms of the old ones: $\hat{x} = (x + y)/\sqrt{2}$ (the factor $\sqrt{2}$ is just a normalization factor).

Interpretation

The spectral decomposition theorem applies to *any* symmetric matrix. For any such matrix, we can find a new coordinate system, in which the matrix is diagonal. But the *interpretation* of the results (what do the eigenvalues and eigenvectors mean?) depends on the specific application. In our case, we apply the spectral theorem to the covariance or correlation matrix of a set of points, and the results of the decomposition will give us the *principal axes of the distribution of points* (hence the name of the technique).

Look again at Figure 14-2. Points are distributed in a region shaped like an extremely stretched ellipse. If we calculate the eigenvalues and eigenvectors of the correlation matrix of this point distribution, we find that the eigen*vectors* lie in the directions of the principal axes of the ellipse while the eigen*values* give the relative length of the corresponding principal axes.

Put another way, the eigenvalues point along the directions of greatest variance: the data is most stretched out if we measure it along the principal directions. Moreover, the eigenvalue corresponding to each eigenvector is a measure of the width of the distribution along this direction.

(In fact, the eigenvalue is the square of the standard deviation along that direction; remember that the diagonal entries of the covariance matrix Σ are $\sigma^2(x) = \sum_i (x_i - \bar{x})^2$. Once we diagonalize Σ, the entries along the diagonal—that is, the eigenvalues—are the variances along the "new" directions.)

You should also observe that the variables measured along the principal directions are uncorrelated with each other. (By construction, their correlation matrix is diagonal, which means that the correlation between any two different variables is zero.)

This, then, is what the principal component analysis does for us: if the data points are distributed as a globular cloud in the space spanned by all the original variables (which may be more than two!), then the eigenvectors will give us the *directions* of the principal axes of the ellipsoidal cloud of data points and the eigenvalues will give us the *length* of the cloud along each of these directions. The eigenvectors and eigenvalues therefore describe the shape of the point distribution. This becomes especially useful if the data set has more than just two dimensions, so that a simple plot (as in Figure 14-2) is no longer feasible. (There are special varieties of PCA, such as "Kernel PCA" or "ISOMAP," that work even with point distributions that do not form globular ellipsoids but have more complicated, contorted shapes.)

The description of the shape of the point distribution provided by the PCA is already helpful. But it gets even better, because we may suspect that not all of the original variables are really needed. Some of them may be redundant (expressing more or less the same thing), and others may be irrelevant (carrying little information).

An indication that variables may be redundant (*i.e.*, express the "same thing") is that they are correlated. (That's pretty much the definition of correlation: knowing that if we change one variable, then there will be a corresponding change in the other.) The PCA uses the information contained in the mutual correlations between variables to identify those that are redundant. By construction, the principal coordinates are *uncorrelated* (*i.e.*, not redundant), which means that the information contained in the original (redundant) set of variables has been concentrated in only a few of the new variables while the remaining variables have become irrelevant. The irrelevant variables are those corresponding to small eigenvalues: the point distribution will have only little spread in the corresponding directions (which means that these variables are almost constants and can therefore be ignored).

The price we have to pay for the reduction in dimensions is that the new directions will not, in general, map neatly to the original variables. Instead, the new directions will correspond to *combinations* of the original variables.

There is an important consequence of the preceding discussion: the principal component analysis works with the correlation between variables. If the original variables are uncorrelated, then there is no point in carrying out a PCA! For instance, if the data points in Figure 14-2 had shown no structure but had filled the entire two-dimensional parameter space randomly, then we would not have been able to simplify the problem by reducing it to a one-dimensional one consisting of the new direction along the main diagonal.

Computation

The theory just described would be of only limited interest if there weren't practical algorithms for calculating both eigenvalues and eigenvectors. These calculations are always numerical. You may have encountered algebraic methods matrix diagonalization methods in school, but they are impractical for matrices larger than 2×2 and infeasible for matrices larger than about 4×4.

However, there are several elegant *numerical* algorithms to invert and diagonalize matrices, and they tend to form the foundational part of any numerical library. They are not trivial to understand, and developing high-quality implementations (that avoid, say round-off error) is a specialized skill. There are no good reasons to write your own, so you should always use an established library. (Every numerical library or package will include the required functionality.)

Matrix operations are relatively expensive, and run time performance can be a serious concern for large matrices. Matrix operations tend to be of $\mathcal{O}(N^3)$ complexity, which means that doubling the size of the matrix will increase the time to perform an operation by a factor of $2^3 = 8$. In other words, doubling the problem size will result in nearly a *tenfold* increase in runtime! This is not an issue for small matrices (up to 100×100 or so), but you will hit a brick wall at a certain size (somewhere between $5{,}000 \times 5{,}000$ and $50{,}000 \times 50{,}000$). Such large matrices do occur in practice but usually not in the context of the topic of this chapter. For even larger matrices there are alternative algorithms—which, however, calculate only the most important of the eigenvalues and eigenvectors.

I will not go into details about different algorithms, but I want to mention one explicitly because it is of particular importance in this context. If you read about principal component analysis (PCA), then you will likely encounter the term *singular value decomposition* (SVD); in fact, many books treat PCA and SVD as equivalent expressions for the same thing. That is not correct; they are really quite different. PCA is the application of spectral methods to covariance or correlation matrices; it is a conceptual technique, not an algorithm. In contrast, the SVD is a specific algorithm that can be applied to many different problems one of which is the PCA.

The reason that the SVD features so prominently in discussions of the PCA is that the SVD combines two required steps into one. In our discussion of the PCA, we assumed that you first calculate the covariance or correlation matrix explicitly from the set of data points and then diagonalize it. The SVD performs these two steps in one fell swoop: you pass the set of data points directly to the SVD, and it calculates the eigenvalues and eigenvectors of the correlation matrix directly from those data points.

The SVD is a very interesting and versatile algorithm, which is unfortunately rarely included in introductory classes on linear algebra.

Practical Points

As you can see, principal component analysis is an involved technique—although with the appropriate tools it becomes almost ridiculously easy to perform (see the Workshop in this chapter). But convenient implementations don't make the conceptual difficulties go away or ensure that the method is applied appropriately.

First, I'd like to emphasize that the mathematical operations underlying principal component analysis (namely, the diagonalization of a matrix) are very general: they consist of a set of formal transformations that apply to *any* symmetric matrix. (Transformations of this sort are used for many different purposes in literally all fields of science and engineering.)

In particular, there is nothing specific to data analysis about these techniques. The PCA thus does not involve any of the concepts that we usually deal with in statistics or analysis: there is no mention of populations, samples, distributions, or models. Instead, principal component analysis is a set of formal transformations, which are applied to the covariance matrix of a data set. As such, it can be either *exploratory* or *preparatory*.

As an exploratory technique, we may inspect its results (the eigenvalues and eigenvectors) for anything that helps us develop an understanding of the data set. For example, we may look at the contributions to the first few principal components to see whether we can find an intuitive interpretation of them (we will see an example of this in the Workshop section). Biplots (discussed in the following section) are a graphical technique that can be useful in this context.

But we should keep in mind that this kind of investigation is exploratory in nature: there is no guarantee that the results of a principal component analysis will turn up anything useful. In particular, we should not expect the principal components to have an intuitive interpretation in general.

On the other hand, PCA may also be used as a preparatory technique. Keep in mind that, by construction, the principal components are uncorrelated. We can therefore transform any multivariate data set into an equivalent form, in which all variables are mutually independent, before performing any subsequent analysis. Identifying a subset of principal components that captures most of the variability in the data set—for the purpose of reducing the dimensionality of the problem, as we discussed earlier—is another preparatory use of principal component analysis.

As a preparatory technique, principal component analysis is always applicable but may not always be useful. For instance, if the original variables are already uncorrelated, then the PCA cannot do anything for us. Similarly, if none of the eigenvalues are significantly smaller (so that their corresponding principal components can be dropped), then again we gain nothing from the PCA.

Finally, let me reiterate that PCA is just a mathematical transformation that can be applied to any symmetric matrix. This means that its results are not uniquely determined by the data set but instead are sensitive to the way the inputs are prepared. In particular, the results of a PCA depend on the actual *numerical values* of the data points and therefore on the *units* in which the measurements have been recorded. If the numerical values for one of the original variables are consistently larger than the values of the other variables, then the variable with the large values will unduly dominate the spectrum of eigenvalues. (We will see an example of this problem in the Workshop.) To avoid this kind of problem, all variables should be of comparable scale. A systematic way to achieve this is to work with the correlation matrix (in which all entries are normalized by their autocorrelation) instead of the covariance matrix.

Biplots

Biplots are an interesting way to visualize the results of a principal component analysis. In a biplot, we plot the data points in a coordinate system spanned by the first two principal components (*i.e.*, those two of the *new* variables corresponding to the largest eigenvalues). In addition, we also plot a representation of the *original* variables but now projected into the space of the new variables. The data points are represented by symbols, whereas the directions of the original variables are represented by arrows. (See Figure 14-5 in the Workshop section.)

In a biplot, we can immediately see the distribution of points when represented through the new variables (and can also look for clusters, outliers, or other interesting features). Moreover, we can see how the original variables relate to the first two principal components and to each other: if any of the original variables are approximately aligned with the horizontal (or vertical) axis, then they are approximately aligned with the first (or second) principal component (because in a biplot, the horizonal and vertical axes coincide with the first and second principal components). We can thus see which of the original variables contribute strongly to the first principal components, which might help us develop an intuitive interpretation for those components. Furthermore, any of the original variables that are roughly redundant will show up as more or less parallel to each other in a biplot—which can likewise help us identify such combinations of variables in the original problem.

Biplots may or may not be helpful. There is a whole complicated set of techniques for interpreting biplots and reading off various quantities from them, but these techniques seem rarely used, and I have not found them to be very practical. If I do a PCA, I will routinely also draw a biplot: if it tells me something worthwhile, that's great; but if not, then I'm not going to spend much time on it.

Visual Techniques

Principal component analysis is a rigorous prescription, and example of a "data-centric" technique: it transforms the original data in a precisely prescribed way, without ambiguity and without making further assumptions. The results are an expression of properties of the data set. It is up to us to interpret them, but the results are true regardless of whether we find them useful or not.

In contrast, the methods described in this section are convenience methods that attempt to make multi-dimensional data sets more "palatable" for human consumption. These methods do not calculate any rigorous properties inherent in the data set; instead, they try to transform the data in such a way that it can be plotted while at the same time trying to be as faithful to the data as possible.

We will not discuss any of these methods in depth, since personally, I do not find them worth the effort: on the one hand, they are (merely) exploratory in nature; on the other hand, they require rather heavy numerical computations and some nontrivial theory. Their primary results are projections (*i.e.*, graphs) of data sets, which can be difficult to interpret if the number of data points or their dimensionality becomes large—which is exactly when I expect a computationally intensive method to be helpful! Nevertheless, there are situations where you might find these methods useful, and they do provide some interesting concepts for how to *think* about data. This last reason is the most important to me, which is why this section emphasizes concepts while skipping most of the technical details.

The methods described in this section try to calculate specific "views" or projections of the data into a lower number of dimensions. Instead of selecting a specific projection, we can also try to display many of them in sequence, leaving it to the human observer to choose those that are "interesting." That is the method we introduced in Chapter 5, when we discussed Grand Tours and Projection Pursuits—they provide yet another approach to the problem of dimensionality reduction for multivariate data sets.

Multidimensional Scaling

Given a set of data points (*i.e.*, the *coordinates* of each data point), we can easily find the distance between any pair of points (see Chapter 13 for a discussion of distance measures). Multidimensional scaling (MDS) attempts to answer the opposite question: given a distance matrix, can we recover the explicit coordinates of the points?

This question has a certain intellectual appeal in its own right, but of course, it is relevant in situations where our information about a certain system is limited to the differences between data points. For example, in usability studies or surveys we may ask respondents to list which of a set of cars (or whiskeys, or pop singers) they find the most or the least alike; in fact, the entire method was first developed for use in psychological studies. The question is: given such a matrix of relative preferences or distances, can we come up with a set of absolute positions for each entry?

First, we must choose the desired number of dimensions of our points. The dimension $D = 2$ is used often, so that the results can be plotted easily, but other values for D are also possible.

If the distance measure is Euclidean—that is, if the distance between two points is given by:

$$d(x, y) = \sqrt{\sum_i^D (x_i - y_i)^2}$$

where the sum is running over all dimensions—then it turns out that we can invert this relationship explicitly and find expressions for the coordinates in terms of the distances. (The only additional assumption we need to make is that the center of mass of the entire data set lies at the origin, but this amounts to no more than an arbitrary translation of all points.) This technique is known as *classical* or *metric scaling*.

The situation is more complicated if we cannot assume that the distance measure is Euclidean. Now we can no longer invert the relationship exactly and must resort instead to iterative approximation schemes. Because the resulting coordinates may not replicate the original distances exactly, we include an additional constraint: the distance matrix calculated from the new positions must obey the same rank order as the original distance matrix: if the original distances between any three points obeyed the relationship $d(x, y) < d(x, z)$, then the calculated coordinates of the three points must satisfy this also. For this reason, this version of multidimensional scaling is known as *ordinal scaling*.

The basic algorithm makes an initial guess for the coordinates and calculates a distance matrix based on the guessed coordinates. The coordinates are then changed iteratively to minimize the discrepancy (known as the "stress") between the new distance matrix and the original one.

Both versions of multidimensional scaling lead to a set of coordinates in the desired number of dimensions (usually two), which we can use to plot the data points in a form of scatter plot. We can then inspect this plot for clusters, outliers, or other features.

Network Graphs

In passing, I'd like to mention *force-based algorithms* for drawing network graphs because they are similar in spirit to multidimensional scaling.

Imagine we have a network consisting of nodes, some of which are connected by vertices (or edges), and we would like to find a way to plot this network in a way that is "attractive" or "pleasing." One approach is to treat the edges as springs, in such a way that each spring has a preferred extension and exerts an opposing force—in the direction of the spring—if compressed or extended beyond its preferred length. We can now try to find a configuration (*i.e.*, a set of coordinates for all nodes) that will minimize the overall tension of the springs.

There are basically two ways we can go about this. We can write down the the total energy due to the distorted springs and then minimize it with respect to the node coordinates using a numerical minimization algorithm. Alternatively, we can "simulate" the system by initializing all nodes with random coordinates and then iteratively moving each node in response to the spring forces acting on it. For smaller networks, we can update all nodes at the same time; for very large networks, we may randomly choose a single node at each iteration step for update and continue until the configuration no longer changes. It is easy to see how this basic algorithm can be extended to include richer situations—for instance, edges carrying different weights.

Note that this algorithm makes no guarantees regarding the distances that are maintained between the nodes in the final configuration. It is purely a visualization technique.

Kohonen Maps

Self-organizing maps (SOMs), often called Kohonen maps after their inventor, are different from the techniques discussed so far. In both principal component analysis and multidimensional scaling, we attempted to find a new, more favorable arrangement of points by moving them about in a continuous fashion. When constructing a Kohonen map, however, we map the original data points to cells in a *lattice*. The presence of a lattice forces a fixed topology on the system; in particular, each point in a lattice has a fixed set of neighbors. (This property is typically and confusingly called "ordering" in most of the literature on Kohonen maps.)

The basic process of constructing a Kohonen map works as follows. We start with a set of k data points in p dimensions, so that each data point consists of a tuple of p numeric values. (I intentionally avoid the word "vector" here because there is no requirement that the data points must satisfy the "mixable" property characteristic of vectors—see Appendix C and Chapter 13.)

Next we prepare a lattice. For simplicity, we consider a two-dimensional square lattice consisting of $n \times m$ cells. Each cell contains a p-dimensional tuple, similar to a data point, which is called the *reference tuple*. We initialize this tuple with random values. In other words, our lattice consists of a collection of random data points, arranged on a regular grid.

Now we perform the following iteration. For each data point, we find that cell in the lattice with the smallest distance between its contained p-tuple and the data point; then we assign the data point to this cell. Note that multiple data points can be assigned to the same cell if necessary.

Once all the data points have been assigned to cells in the lattice, we update the p-tuples of all cells based on the values of the data points assigned to the cell itself and to its neighboring cells. In other words, we use the data points assigned to each cell, as well as those assigned to the cell's neighbors, to compute a new tuple for the cell.

When all lattice points have been updated, we restart the iteration and begin assigning data points to cells again (after erasing the previous assignments). We stop the iteration if the assignments no longer change or if the differences between the original cell values and their updates are sufficiently small.

This is the basic algorithm for the construction of a Kohonen map. It has certain similarities with the k-means algorithm discussed in Chapter 13. Both are iterative procedures in which data points are assigned to cells or clusters, and the cell or cluster is updated based on the points assigned to it. However, two features are specific to Kohonen maps:

- Each data point is mapped to a cell in the lattice, and this implies that each data point is placed in a specific neighborhood of other data points (which have been mapped to neighboring cells).

- Because the updating step for each cell relies not only on the current cell but also on neighboring cells, the resulting map will show a "smooth" change of values: changes are averaged or "smeared out" over all cells in the neighborhood. Viewed the other way around, this implies that points that are similar to each other will map to lattice cells that are in close proximity to each other.

Although the basic algorithm seems fairly simple, we still need to decide on a number of technical details if we want to develop a concrete implementation. Most importantly, we still need to give a specific prescription for how the reference tuples will be updated by the data points assigned to the current cell and its neighborhood.

In principle, it would be possible to recalculate the values for the reference tuple from scratch every time by forming a componentwise average of all data points assigned to the cell. In practice, this may lead to instability during iteration, and therefore it is usually recommended to perform an incremental update of the reference value instead, based on the difference between the current value of the reference tuple and the assigned data points. If $y_i(t)$ is the value of the reference tuple at position i and at iteration t, then we can write its value at the next iteration step $t + 1$ as:

$$y_i(t + 1) = y_i(t) + \sum_k h(i, j; t) (x_k(j; t) - y_i(t))$$

where $x_k(j; t)$ is the data point k which has been assigned to lattice point j at iteration step t and where the sum runs over all data points. The weight function $h(i, j; t)$ is now chosen to be a decreasing function of the distance between the lattice cells i and j, and it is also made to shrink in value as the iteration progresses. A typical choice is a Gaussian:

$$h(i, j; t) = \alpha(t) \exp \left(-\frac{d_{ij}}{2\sigma(t)} \right)^2$$

where d_{ij} is the Euclidean distance between lattice points i and j and where $\alpha(t)$ and $\sigma(t)$ are decreasing functions of t. Choices other than the Gaussian are also possible—for instance, we may choose a step function to delimit the effective neighborhood.

Even with these definitions, we still need to decide on further details:

- What is the topology of the lattice? Square lattices (like quad-ruled paper) are convenient but strongly single out two specific directions. Hexagonal lattices (like a honeycomb) are more isotropic. We also need to fix the boundary conditions. Do cells at the edge of the lattice have fewer neighbors than cells in the middle of the lattice, or do we wrap the lattice around and connect the opposite edges to form periodic boundary conditions?

- What is the size of the lattice? Obviously, the number of cells in the lattice should be smaller than the number of data points (otherwise, we end up with unoccupied cells). But how much smaller? Is there a preferred ratio between data points and lattice cells? Also, should the overall lattice be square ($n \times n$) or rectangular ($n \times m$)? In principle, we can even consider lattices of different shape—triangular, for example, or circular. However, if we choose a lattice of higher symmetry (square or circular), then the *orientation* of the final result within the lattice is not fixed; for this reason, it has been suggested that the lattice should always be oblongated (*e.g.*, rectangular rather than square).

- We need to choose a distance or similarity measure for measuring the distance between data points and reference tuples.

- We still need to fix the numerical range of $\alpha(t)$ and $\sigma(t)$ and define their behavior as functions of t.

In addition, there are many opportunities for low-level tuning, in particular with regard to performance and convergence. For example, we may find it beneficial to initialize the lattice points with values other than random numbers.

Finally, we may ask what we can actually do with the resulting lattice of converged reference tuples. Here are some ideas.

- We can use the lattice to form a smooth, "heat map" visualization of the original data set. Because cells in the lattice are closely packed, a Kohonen map interpolates smoothly between different points. This is in contrast to the result from either PCA or MDS, which yield only individual, scattered points.

- One problem when plotting a Kohonen map is deciding which feature to show. If the original data set was p-dimensional, you may have to plot p different graphs to see the distribution of all features.

- The situation is more favorable if one of the features of interest is categorical and has only a few possible values. In this case, you can plot the labels on the graph and study their relationships (which labels are close to each other, and so on). In this situation, it is also possible to use a "trained" Kohonen map to classify new data points or data points with missing data.

- If the number of cells in the lattice was chosen much smaller than the number of original data points, then you can try mapping the reference tuples *back* into the original data space—for example, to use them as *prototypes* for clustering purposes.

Kohonen maps are an interesting technique that occupy a space between clustering and dimensionality reduction. Kohonen maps group similar points together like a clustering algorithm, but they also generate a low-dimensional representation of all data points by mapping all points to a low-dimensional lattice. The entire concept is very ad hoc and heuristic; there is little rigorous theory, and thus there is little guidance on the choice of specific details. Nonetheless, the hands-on, intuitive nature of Kohonen maps lends itself to exploration and experimentation in a way that a more rigorous (but also more abstract) technique like PCA does not.

Workshop: PCA with R

Principal component analysis is a complicated technique, so it makes sense to use specialized tools that hide most of the complexity. Here we shall use R, which is the best-known open source package for statistical calculations. (We covered some of the basics of R in the Workshop section of Chapter 10; here I want to demonstrate some of the advanced functionality built into R.)

Let's consider a nontrivial example. For a collection of nearly 5,000 wines, almost a dozen physico-chemical properties were measured, and the results of a subjective "quality" or taste test were recorded as well.[*] The properties are:

```
 1 - fixed acidity
 2 - volatile acidity
 3 - citric acid
 4 - residual sugar
 5 - chlorides
 6 - free sulfur dioxide
 7 - total sulfur dioxide
 8 - density
 9 - pH
10 - sulphates
11 - alcohol
12 - quality (score between 0 and 10)
```

This is a complicated data set, and having to handle 11 input variables is not comfortable. Can we find a way to make sense of them and possibly even find out which are most important in determining the overall quality of the wine?

This is a problem that is perfect for an application of the PCA. And as we will see, R makes this really easy for us.

For this example, I'll take you on a slightly roundabout route. Be prepared that our initial attempt will lead to an incorrect conclusion! I am including this detour here for a number of reasons. I want to remind you that real data analysis, with real and interesting data sets, usually does not progress linearly. Instead, it is very important that, as we work with a data set, we constantly keep checking and questioning our results as we go along. Do they make sense? Might we be missing something? I also want to demonstrate how R's interactive programming model facilitates the required exploratory work style: try something and look at the results; if they look wrong, go back and make sure you are on the right track, and so on.

Although it can be scripted for batch operations, R is primarily intended for interactive use, and that is how we will use it here. We first load the data set into a heterogeneous "data frame" and then invoke the desired functions on it. Functions in turn may return data structures themselves that can be used as input to other functions, that can be printed in a human readable format to the screen, or that can be plotted.

R includes many statistical functions as built-in functions. In our specific case, we can perform an entire principal component analysis in a single command:

```
wine <- read.csv( "winequality-white.csv", sep=';', header=TRUE )
pc <- prcomp( wine )
plot( pc )
```

[*] This example is taken from the "Wine Quality" data set, available at the UCI Machine Learning repository at *http://archive.ics.uci.edu/ml/*.

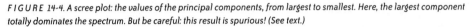

FIGURE 14-4. A scree plot: the values of the principal components, from largest to smallest. Here, the largest component totally dominates the spectrum. But be careful: this result is spurious! (See text.)

This snippet of code reads the data from a file and assigns the resulting data frame to the variable wine. The prcomp() function performs the actual principal component analysis and returns a data structure containing the results, which we assign to the variable pc. We can now examine this returned data structure in various ways.

R makes heavy use of function overloading—a function such as plot() will accept different forms of input and try to find the most useful action to perform, given the input. For the data structure returned by prcomp(), the plot() function constructs a so-called *scree plot*[*] (see Figure 14-4), showing the magnitudes of the variances for the various principal components, from the greatest to the smallest.

We see that the first eigenvalue entirely dominates the spectrum, suggesting that the corresponding new variable is all that matters (which of course would be great). To understand in more detail what is going on, we look at the corresponding eigenvector. The print() function is another overloaded function, which for this particular data structure prints out the eigenvalues and eigenvectors:

```
print( pc )

(some output omitted...)
```

	PC1	PC2	PC3
fixed.acidity	-1.544402e-03	-9.163498e-03	-1.290026e-02
volatile.acidity	-1.690037e-04	-1.545470e-03	-9.288874e-04
citric.acid	-3.386506e-04	1.403069e-04	-1.258444e-03
residual.sugar	-4.732753e-02	1.494318e-02	-9.951917e-01
chlorides	-9.757405e-05	-7.182998e-05	-7.849881e-05
free.sulfur.dioxide	-2.618770e-01	9.646854e-01	2.639318e-02
total.sulfur.dioxide	-9.638576e-01	-2.627369e-01	4.278881e-02
density	-3.596983e-05	-1.836319e-05	-4.468979e-04
pH	-3.384655e-06	-4.169856e-05	7.017342e-03
sulphates	-3.409028e-04	-3.611112e-04	2.142053e-03
alcohol	1.250375e-02	6.455196e-03	8.272268e-02

```
(some output omitted...)
```

[*] *Scree* is the rubble that collects at the base of mountain cliffs.

This is disturbing: if you look closely, you will notice that both the first and the second eigenvector are dominated by the sulfur dioxide concentration—and by a wide margin! That does not seem right. I don't understand much about wine, but I would not think that the sulfur dioxide content is all that matters in the end.

Perhaps we were moving a little too fast. What do we actually know about the data in the data set? Right: absolutely nothing! Time to find out. One quick way to do so is to use the summary() function on the *original* data:

```
summary(wine)
 fixed.acidity    volatile.acidity  citric.acid     residual.sugar
 Min.   : 3.800   Min.   :0.0800   Min.   :0.0000   Min.   : 0.600
 1st Qu.: 6.300   1st Qu.:0.2100   1st Qu.:0.2700   1st Qu.: 1.700
 Median : 6.800   Median :0.2600   Median :0.3200   Median : 5.200
 Mean   : 6.855   Mean   :0.2782   Mean   :0.3342   Mean   : 6.391
 3rd Qu.: 7.300   3rd Qu.:0.3200   3rd Qu.:0.3900   3rd Qu.: 9.900
 Max.   :14.200   Max.   :1.1000   Max.   :1.6600   Max.   :65.800
   chlorides       free.sulfur.dioxide total.sulfur.dioxide   density
 Min.   :0.00900   Min.   :  2.00     Min.   :  9.0       Min.   :0.9871
 1st Qu.:0.03600   1st Qu.: 23.00     1st Qu.:108.0       1st Qu.:0.9917
 Median :0.04300   Median : 34.00     Median :134.0       Median :0.9937
 Mean   :0.04577   Mean   : 35.31     Mean   :138.4       Mean   :0.9940
 3rd Qu.:0.05000   3rd Qu.: 46.00     3rd Qu.:167.0       3rd Qu.:0.9961
 Max.   :0.34600   Max.   :289.00     Max.   :440.0       Max.   :1.0390
      pH           sulphates         alcohol         quality
 Min.   :2.720   Min.   :0.2200   Min.   : 8.00   Min.   :3.000
 1st Qu.:3.090   1st Qu.:0.4100   1st Qu.: 9.50   1st Qu.:5.000
 Median :3.180   Median :0.4700   Median :10.40   Median :6.000
 Mean   :3.188   Mean   :0.4898   Mean   :10.51   Mean   :5.878
 3rd Qu.:3.280   3rd Qu.:0.5500   3rd Qu.:11.40   3rd Qu.:6.000
 Max.   :3.820   Max.   :1.0800   Max.   :14.20   Max.   :9.000
```

I am showing the output in its entire length to give you a sense of the kind of output generated by R. If you look through this carefully, you will notice that the two sulfur dioxide columns have values in the tens to hundreds, whereas all other columns have values between 0.01 and about 10.0. This explains a lot: the two sulfur dioxide columns dominate the eigenvalue spectrum simply because they were measured in units that make the numerical values much larger than the other quantities. As explained before, if this is the case, then we need to *scale* the input variables before performing the PCA. We can achieve this by passing the scale option to the prcomp() command, like so:

```
pcx <- prcomp( wine, scale=TRUE )
```

Before we examine the result of this operation, I'd like to point out something else. If you look really closely, you will notice that the quality column is not what it claims to be. The description of the original data set stated that quality was graded on a scale from 1 to 10. But as we can see from the data summary, only grades between 3 and 9 have actually been assigned. Worse, the first quartile is 5 and the third quartile is 6, which means that at least half of all entries in the data set have a quality ranking of either 5 or 6. In other words, the actual range of qualities is much narrower than we might have expected (given the original description of the data) and is strongly dominated by the center. This makes sense (there are more mediocre wines than outstanding or terrible ones), but it also makes this data set much less interesting because whether a wine will be ranked 5 versus 6 during the sensory testing is likely a toss-up.

We can use the `table()` function to see how often each quality ranking occurs in the data set (remember that the dollar sign is used to select a single column from the data frame):

```
table( wine$quality )
```

```
   3    4    5    6    7    8    9
  20  163 1457 2198  880  175    5
```

As we suspected, the middling ranks totally dominate the distribution. We might therefore want to change our goal and instead try to predict the outliers, either good or bad, rather than spending too much effort on the undifferentiated middle.

Returning to the results of the scaled PCA, we can look at the spectrum of eigenvalues for the scaled version by using the `summary()` function (again, overloaded!) on the return value of `prcomp()`:

```
summary( pcx )
Importance of components:
                         PC1    PC2    PC3    PC4     PC5     PC6
Standard deviation     1.829  1.259  1.171 1.0416  0.9876  0.9689
Proportion of Variance 0.279  0.132  0.114 0.0904  0.0813  0.0782
Cumulative Proportion  0.279  0.411  0.525 0.6157  0.6970  0.7752
                         PC7    PC8    PC9   PC10    PC11    PC12
Standard deviation    0.8771 0.8508 0.7460 0.5856  0.5330 0.14307
Proportion of Variance 0.0641 0.0603 0.0464 0.0286 0.0237 0.00171
Cumulative Proportion  0.8393 0.8997 0.9460 0.9746  0.9983 1.00000
```

No single eigenvalue dominates now, and the first 5 (out of 12) eigenvalues account for only 70 percent of the total variance. That's not encouraging—it doesn't seem that we can significantly reduce the number of variables this way.

As a last attempt, we can create a biplot. This, too, is very simple; all we need to do is execute (see Figure 14-5)

```
biplot( pcx )
```

This is actually a fascinating graph! We see that three of the original variables—alcohol content, sugar content, and density— are parallel to the first principal component (the horizontal axis). Moreover, alcohol content is aligned in the direction opposite to the other two quantities.

But this makes utmost sense. If you recall from chemistry class, alcohol has a lower density than water, and sugar syrup has a higher density. So the result of the PCA reminds us that density, sugar concentration, and alcohol content are not independent: if you

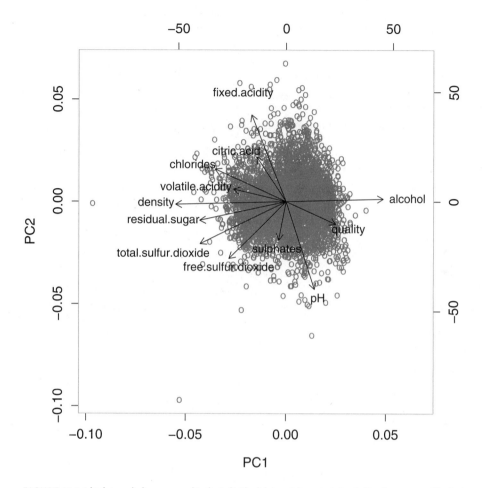

FIGURE 14-5. A biplot: symbols correspond to the individual data points projected onto the plane spanned by the two largest principal components. Also shown are the original variables projected onto the same plane.

change one, the others will change accordingly. And because these variables are parallel to the first principal component, we can conclude that the overall density of the wine is an important quantity.

The next set of variables that we can read off are the fixed acidity, the citric acid concentration, and the pH value. Again, this makes sense: the pH is a measure of the acidity of a solution (with higher pH values indicating less acidity). In other words, these three variables are also at least partially redundant.

The odd one out, then, is the overall sulfur content, which is a combination of sulfur dioxide and sulphate concentration.

And finally, it is interesting to see that the quality seems to be determined primarily by the alcohol content and the acidity. This suggests that the more alcoholic and the less sour the wine, the more highly it is ranked—quite a reasonable conclusion!

We could have inferred all of this from the original description of the data set, but I must say that I, for one, failed to see these connections when initially scanning the list of columns. In this sense, the PCA has been a tremendous help in interpreting and understanding the content of the data set.

Finally, I'd like to reflect one more time on our use of R in this example. This little application demonstrates both the power and the shortcomings of R. On the one hand, R comes with many high-level, powerful functions built in, often for quite advanced statistical techniques (even an unusual and specialized graph like a biplot can be created with a single command). On the other hand, the heavy reliance on high-level functions with implicit behavior leads to opaque programs that make it hard to understand exactly what is going on. For example, such a critical question as deciding whether or not to rescale the input data is handled as a rather obscure option to the `prcomp()` command. In particular, the frequent use of overloaded functions—which can exhibit widely differing functionality depending on their input—makes it hard to predict the precise outcome of an operation and makes discovering ways to perform a specific action uncommonly difficult.

Further Reading

- *Introduction to Multivariate Analysis.* Chris Chatfield and Alexander Collins. Chapman & Hall/CRC. 1981.
  A bit dated but still one of the most practical, hands-on introductions to the mathematical theory of multivariate analysis. The section on PCA is particularly clear and practical but entirely skips computational issues and makes no mention of the SVD.

- *Principal Component Analysis.* I. T. Jolliffe. 2nd ed., Springer. 2002.
  The definitive reference on principal component analysis. Not an easy read.

- *Multidimensional Scaling.* Trevor F. Cox and Michael A. A. Cox. Chapman & Hall/CRC. 2001.
  The description of multidimensional scaling given in this chapter is merely a sketch—mostly, because I find it hard to imagine scenarios where this technique is truly useful. However, it has a lot of appeal and is fun to tinker with. Much more information, including some extensions, can be found in this book.

- *Introduction to Data Mining.* Pang-Ning Tan, Michael Steinbach, and Vipin Kumar. Addison-Wesley. 2005.
  This is my favorite reference on data mining. The presentation is compact and more technical than in most other books on this topic.

Linear Algebra

Linear algebra is a foundational topic. It is here that one encounters for the first time abstract concepts such as spaces and mappings treated as objects of interest in their own right. It takes time and some real mental effort to get used to these notions, but one gains a whole different perspective on things.

The material is also of immense practical value—particularly its central result, which is the spectral decomposition theorem. The importance of this result cannot be overstated: it is used in *every* multi-dimensional problem in mathematics, science, and engineering.

However, the material is abstract and unfamiliar, which makes it hard for the beginner. Most introductory books on linear algebra try to make the topic more palatable by emphasizing applications, but that only serves to confuse matters even more, because it never becomes clear why all that abstract machinery is needed when looking at elementary examples. The abstract notions at the heart of linear algebra are best appreciated, and most easily understood, when treated in their own right.

The resources listed here are those I have found most helpful in this regard.

- *Linear Algebra Done Right.* Sheldon Axler. 2nd ed., Springer. 2004.
  The book lives up to its grandiose title. It treats linear algebra as an abstract theory of mappings but on a very accessible, advanced undergraduate level. Highly recommended but probably not as the first book on the topic.

- *Matrix Methods in Data Mining and Pattern Recognition.* Lars Eldén. SIAM. 2007.
  This short book is an introduction to linear algebra with a particular eye to applications in data mining. The pace is fast and probably requires at least some previous familiarity with the subject.

- *Understanding Complex Datasets: Data Mining with Matrix Decompositions.* David Skillicorn. Chapman & Hall/CRC. 2007.
  An advanced book, concentrating mostly on applications of the SVD and its variants.

- "A Singularly Valuable Decomposition: The SVD of a Matrix." Dan Kalman. *The College Mathematics Journal* 27 (1996), p. 2. This article, which can be found on the Web, is a nice introduction to the SVD. It's not for beginners, however.

## CHAPTER FIFTEEN

Intermezzo: When More Is Different

WHEN DEALING WITH SOME OF THE MORE COMPUTATIONALLY INTENSIVE DATA ANALYSIS OR MINING algorithms, you may encounter an unexpected obstacle: *the brick wall*. Programs or algorithms that seemed to work just fine turn out not to work once in production. And I don't mean that they work slower than expected. I mean they do not work at all!

Of course, performance and scalability problems are familiar to most enterprise developers. However, the kinds of problems that arise in data-centric or computationally intensive applications are different, and most enterprise programmers (and, in fact, most computer science graduates) are badly prepared for them.

Let's try an example: Table 15-1 shows the time required to perform 10 matrix multiplications for square matrices of various size. (The details of matrix multiplication don't concern us here; suffice it to say that it's the basic operation in almost all problems involving matrices and is at the heart of operator decomposition problems, including the principal component analysis introduced in Chapter 14.)

TABLE 15-1. Time required to perform 10 matrix multiplications for square matrices of different sizes

Size n	Time [seconds]
100	0.00
200	0.06
500	2.12
1,000	22.44
2,000	176.22

Would you agree that the data in Table 15-1 does not look too threatening? For a 2,000 × 2,000 matrix, the time required is a shade under three minutes. How long might it take to perform the same operation for a 10,000 × 10,000 matrix? Five, maybe ten minutes? Yeah, right. It takes *five hours*! And if you need to go a little bit bigger still—say, 30,000 × 30,000, the computation will take five *days*.

What we observe here is typical of many computationally intensive algorithms: they consume disproportionately more time as the problem size becomes larger. Of course, we have all heard about this in school, but our intuition for the reality of this phenomenon is usually not very good. Even if we run a few tests on small data sets, we fail to spot the trouble: sure, the program takes longer as the data sets get larger, but it all seems quite reasonable. Nevertheless, we tend to be unprepared for what appears to be a huge *jump* in the required time as we increase the data set by a seemingly not very large factor. (Remember: what took us from three minutes to five hours was an increase in the problem size by a factor of 5—not even an order of magnitude!)

The problem is that, unless you have explicitly worked on either a numerical or a combinatorial problem in the past, you probably have never encountered the kind of scaling behavior exhibited by computational or combinatorial problems. This skews our perception.

Where are you most likely to encounter perceptible performance problems in an enterprise environment? Answer: slow database queries! We all have encountered the frustration resulting from queries that perform a full table scan instead of using an indexed lookup (regardless whether no index is available or the query optimizer fails to use it). Yet a query that performs a full table scan rather than using an index exhibits one of the most benign forms of scaling: from $\mathcal{O}(\log n)$ (meaning that the response time is largely insensitive to the size of the table) to $\mathcal{O}(n)$ (meaning that doubling the table size will double the response time).

In contrast, matrix operations—such as the matrix multiplication encountered in the earlier example—scale as $\mathcal{O}(n^3)$; this means that if the problem doubles in size, then the time required grows by a factor of *8* (because $2^3 = 8$). In other words, as you go from a 2,000 × 2,000 matrix to a 4,000 × 4,000 matrix, the problem will take almost 10 times as long; and if you go to a 10,000 × 10,000 matrix, it will take $5^3 = 125$ times as long. Oops.

And this is the good news. Many combinatorial problems (such as the Traveling Salesman problem and similar problems) don't scale according to a power law (such as $\mathcal{O}(n^3)$) but instead scale exponentially ($\mathcal{O}(e^n)$). In these cases, you will hit the brick wall *much* faster and much more brutally. For such problems, an incremental increase in the size of the problem (*i.e.*, from n to $n + 1$) will typically at least *double* the runtime. In other words, the last element to calculate takes as much time as all the previous elements *taken together*. System sizes of around $n = 50$ are frequently the end of the line. With extreme effort you might be able to push it to $n = 55$, but $n = 100$ will be entirely out of reach.

The reason I stress this kind of problem so much is that in my experience, not only are most enterprise developers unprepared for the reality of it but also that the standard set of software engineering practices and attitudes is entirely inadequate to deal with them. I once heard a programmer say, "It's all just engineering" in response to challenges about the likely performance problems of a computational system he was working on. Nothing could be further from the truth: no amount of low-level performance tuning will save a program of this nature that is algorithmically hosed—and no amount of faster hardware, either. Moreover, "standard software engineering practices" are either of no help or are even entirely inapplicable (we'll see an example in a moment).

Most disturbing to me was his casual, almost blissful ignorance—this coming from a guy who definitely *should* have known better.

A Horror Story

I was once called into a project in its thirteenth hour—they had far exceeded both their budget and their schedule and were about to be shut down for good because they could not make their system work. They had been trying to build an internal tool that was intended to solve what was, essentially, a combinatorial problem. The tool was supposed to be used interactively: the user supplies some inputs and receives an answer within, at most, a few minutes. By the time I got involved, the team had labored for over a year, but the minimum response time achieved by their system exceeded *12 hours*—even though it ran on a very expensive (and very expensive to operate) supercomputer.

After a couple of weeks, I came up with an improved algorithm that calculated answers in real time and could run on a laptop.

No amount of "engineering" will be able to deliver that kind of speed-up.

How was this possible? By attacking the problem on many different levels. First of all, we made sure we fully *understood the problem domain*. The original project team had always been a little vague about what exactly the program was trying to calculate, as a result their "domain model" was not truly logically consistent. Hence the first thing to do was to put the whole problem on sound mathematical footing. Second, we *redefined the problem*: the original program had attempted to calculate a certain quantity by explicit enumeration of all possible combinations, whereas the new solution calculated an approximation instead. This was warranted because the input data was not known very precisely, anyway, and because we were able to show that the uncertainty introduced by the approximation was less than the uncertainty already present in the data. Third, we *treated hot spots differently than the happy case*: the new algorithm could calculate the result to higher accuracy, but it did so only when the added accuracy was needed. Fourth, we used efficient data structures and implemented some core pieces ourselves instead of relying on general-purpose libraries; we also judiciously precalculated and cached some frequently used intermediate results.

After putting the whole effort on a conceptually consistent footing, the most important contribution was changing the problem definition: dropping the exact approach, which was unnecessary and infeasible, and adopting an approximate solution that was cheap and all that was required.

Some Suggestions

Computational and combinatorial programming is really different. It runs into different limits and requires different techniques. Most important is the appropriate choice of algorithm at the outset, since no amount of low-level tuning or "engineering" will save a program that is algorithmically flawed.

Here is a list of recommendations in case you find yourself setting out on a project that involves heavy computation or deals with combinatorial complexity issues:

Do your homework.   Understand computational complexity, know the complexity of the algorithm you intend to use, and research the different algorithms (and their trade-offs) available for your kind of problem. Read broadly—although the exact problem as specified may turn out to be intractable, you may find that a small change in the requirements may lead to a much simpler problem. It is definitely worth it to renegotiate the problem with the customer or end users than setting out on a project that is infeasible from the outset. (Skiena's *Algorithm Design Manual* is a particularly good resource for algorithms grouped by problems.)

Run a few numbers.   Do a few tests with small programs and evaluate their scaling performance. Don't just look at the actual numbers themselves—also consider the scaling behavior as you vary the problem size. If the program does not exhibit the scaling behavior you expect theoretically, it has a bug. If so, fix the bug before proceeding! (In general, algorithms follow the theoretical scaling prediction quite closely for all but the smallest of problem sizes.) Extrapolate to real-sized problems: can you live with the expected runtime predictions?

Forget standard software engineering practices.   It is a standard assumption in current software engineering that developer time is the scarcest resource and that programs should be designed and implemented accordingly. Computationally intensive programs are one case where this is not true: if you are likely to max out the machine, then it's worth having the developer—rather than the computer—go the extra mile. Additional developer time may very well make the difference between an "infeasible" problem and a solved one.

For instance, in situations where you are pressed for space, it might very well make sense to write your own container implementations instead of relying on the system-provided hash map. Beware of the trap of conditioned thinking, though: in one project I worked on, we knew that we would have a memory size problem and that we therefore had to keep the size of individual elements small. On the other hand, it was not clear at first whether the 4-byte Java `int` data type would be sufficient to represent all required values or whether we would have to use the 8-bye Java `long` type. In response, someone suggested that we *wrap* the atomic data type in an object so we could swap out the implementation, in case the 4-byte `int` turned out to be insufficient. That's a fine approach in a standard software engineering scenario ("encapsulation" and all that), but in this situation—where space was at a premium—it missed the point entirely: the space that the Java wrapper would have consumed (in addition to its data members) would have been larger than the payload!

Remember: standard software engineering practices are typically intended to trade machine resources for developer resources. However, for computationally intensive problems, machine resources (not developer time) are the limiting factor.

Don't assume that parallelization will be possible.   Don't assume that you'll be able to partition the problem in such a way that simultaneous execution on multiple machines (*i.e.*, parallelization) will be possible, until you have developed an actual, concrete, implementable algorithm—many computational problems don't parallelize well. Even if you can come up with a parallel algorithm, performance may be disappointing: hidden costs (such as communication overhead) often lead to performance that is much poorer than predicted; a cluster consisting of twice as many nodes often exhibits a behavior *much* less than double the original one! Running realistic tests (on realistically sized data sets and on realistically sized clusters) is harder for parallel programs than for single processor implementations—but even more important.

Leave yourself some margin.   Assume that the problem size will be larger by a factor of 3 and that hardware will deliver only 50 percent of theoretically predicted performance.

If the results are not wholly reassuring, explore alternatives.   Take the results for the expected runtime and memory requirements that you obtained from theoretical predictions and the tests that you have performed seriously. Unless you seem able to meet your required benchmarks *comfortably*, explore alternatives. Consider better algorithms, research whether the problem can be simplified or whether the problem can be approached in an entirely different manner, and look into approximate or heuristic solutions. If you feel yourself stuck, get help!

If you can't make it work on paper, STOP.   It won't work in practice, either. It is a surprisingly common anti-pattern to see the warning signs early but to press on regardless with the hopeful optimism that "things will work themselves out during implementation." This is entirely misguided: nothing will work out better as you proceed with an implementation; everything is always a bit worse than expected.

Unless you can make it work on paper and make it work *comfortably*, there is no point in proceeding!

The recurring recommendation here is that nobody is helped by a project that ultimately fails, because it was impossible (or at least infeasible) from the get-go. Unless you can demonstrate at least the feasibility of a solution (at an acceptable price point!), there is no use to proceed. And everybody is much better off knowing this ahead of time.

What About Map/Reduce?

Won't the map/reduce family of techniques make most of these considerations obsolete? The answer, in general, is *no*.

It is important to understand that map/reduce is not actually a clever algorithm or even an algorithm at all. It is a piece of *infrastructure* that makes naive algorithms convenient.

That's a whole different ball game. The map/reduce approach does not speed up any particular algorithm at all. Instead, it makes the parallel execution of many subproblems convenient. For map/reduce to be applicable, therefore, it must be possible to *partition* the problem in such a way that individual partitions don't need to talk to each other. Search is such an application that is trivially parallelizable, and many (if not all) successful current applications of map/reduce that I am aware of seem to be related to generalized forms of search.

This is not to say that map/reduce is not a very important advance. (Any device that makes an existing technique orders of magnitudes more convenient is an important innovation!) At the moment, however, we are still in the process of figuring how which problems are most amenable to the map/reduce approach and how best to adapt them. I suspect that the algorithms that will work best on map/reduce will *not* be straightforward generalizations of serial algorithms but instead will be algorithms that would be entirely unattractive on a serial computer.

It is also worth remembering that parallel computation is not new. What has killed it in the past was the need for different partitions of the problem to communicate with each other: very quickly, the associated communication overhead annihilated the benefit from parallelization. This problem has not gone away, it is merely masked by the current emphasis on search and searchlike problems, which allow trivial parallelization without any need for communication among partitions. I worry that more strictly computational applications (such as the matrix multiplication problem discussed earlier or the simulation of large physical systems) will require so much sharing of information among nodes that the map/reduce approach will appear unattractive.

Finally, amid the excitement currently generated by map/reduce, it should not be forgotten that its total cost of ownership (including the long-term *operational* cost of maintaining the required clusters as well as the associated network and storage infrastructure) is not yet known. Although map/reduce installations make distributed computing "freely" available to the individual programmer, the required hardware installations and their operations are anything but "free."

In the end, I expect map/reduce to have an effect similar to the one that compilers had when they came out. The code that they produced was less efficient than handcoded assembler code, but the overall efficiency gain far outweighed this local disadvantage.

But keep in mind that even the best compilers have rendered neither Quicksort nor indexed lookup obsolete.

Workshop: Generating Permutations

Sometimes, you have to see it to believe it. In this spirit, let's write a program that calculates all permutations (*i.e.,* all possible rearrangements) of a set. (That is, if the set is [1,2,3], then the program will generate [1,2,3], [1,3,2], [2,1,3], [2,3,1], [3,1,2], [3,2,1].) You can imagine this routine to be part of a larger program: in order to solve the Traveling Salesman problem exactly, for example, one needs to generate all possible trips (*i.e.,* all permutations of the cities to visit) and evaluate the associated distances.

Of course, we all "know" that the number of permutations grows as $n! = 1 \cdot 2 \cdot 3 \cdots n$, where n is the number of elements in the set and that the factorial function grows "quickly." Nevertheless, you have to see it to believe it. (Even I was shocked by what I found when developing and running the program below!)

The program that follows reads a positive integer n from the command line and then generates all permutations of a list of n elements, using a recursive algorithm. (It successively removes one element of the list, generates all permutations of the remainder, and then tacks the removed element back on to the results.) The time required is measured and printed.

```python
import sys, time

def permutations( v ):
    if len(v) == 1: return [ [v[0]] ]

    res = []
    for i in range( 0, len(v) ):
        w = permutations( v[:i] + v[i+1:] )
        for k in w:
            k.append( v[i] )
        res += w

    return res


n = int(sys.argv[1])
v = range(n)
```

```
t0 = time.clock()
z = permutations( v )
t1 = time.clock();

print n, t1-t0
```

(You may object to the use of recursion here, pointing out that Python does not allow infinite depth of recursion. This is true but is not a factor: we will run into trouble long before that constraint comes into play.)

I highly recommend that you try it. Because we know (or suspect) that this program might take a while to run when the number of elements is large, we probably want to start out with three elements. Or with four. Then maybe we try five, six, or seven. In all cases, the program finishes almost *instantaneously*. Then go ahead and run it with n=10. Just 10 elements. Go ahead, do it. (But I suggest you save all files and clean up your login session first, so you can reboot without losing too much work if you have to.)

Go ahead. You have to *see* it to believe it![*]

Further Reading

- *The Algorithm Design Manual.* Steven S. Skiena. 2nd ed., Springer. 2008.
  This is an amazing book, because it presents algorithms not as abstract entities to be studied for their own beauty but as potential solutions to real problems. Its second half consists of a "hitchhiker's guide to algorithms": a catalog of different algorithms for common problems. It helps you find an appropriate algorithm by asking detailed questions about your specific problem and provides pointers to existing implementations. In addition, the author's "war stories" of past successes and failures in the real world provide a vivid reminder that algorithms are *real*.

---

[*]Anybody who scoffs that this example is silly, because "you should not store all the intermediate results; use a generator" or because "everyone knows you can't find all permutations exhaustively; use heuristics" is absolutely correct—and entirely missing the point. I know that this implementation is naive, but—cross your heart—would you really have assumed that the naive implementation would be in trouble for $n = 10$? Especially, when it didn't even blink for $n = 7$?

## PART IV

Applications: Using Data

## CHAPTER SIXTEEN

Reporting, Business Intelligence, and Dashboards

DATA ANALYSIS DOES NOT JUST CONSIST OF CRUNCHING NUMBERS. IT ALSO INCLUDES NAVIGATING THE CONTEXT and environment in which the need for data analysis arises. In this chapter and the next, we will look at two areas that often have a demand for data analysis and analytical modeling but that tend to be unfamiliar if you come from a technical background: in this chapter, we discuss business intelligence and corporate metrics; in the next chapter, financial calculations and business plans.

This material may seem a little out of place because it is largely not technical. But that is precisely why it is important to include this topic here: to a person with a technical background, this material is often totally new. Yet it is precisely in these areas that sound technical and analytical advice is often required: the primary consumers of these services are "business people," who may not have the necessary background and skills to make appropriate decisions without help. This places additional responsibility on the person working with the data to understand the problem domain thoroughly, in order to make suitable recommendations.

This is no joke. I have seen otherwise very smart people at high-quality companies completely botch business metrics programs simply because they lacked basic software engineering and math skills. As the person who (supposedly!) "understands data," I see it as part of my responsibility to understand what my clients actually want to *do* with the data—and advise them accordingly on the things they *should* be doing. But to do so effectively, it is not enough to understand the data—I also need to understand my clients.

That's the spirit in which these chapters are intended. The aim is to describe some of the ways that demand for data arises in a business environment, to highlight some of the traps for the unwary, and to give some advice on using data more successfully.

Business Intelligence

Businesses have been trying to make use of the data that they collect for years and, in the process, have accumulated a fair share of disappointments. I think we need to accept that the problem is hard: you need to find a way to represent, store, and make accessible a comprehensive view of all available data in such a way that is useful to anybody and for any purpose. That's just hard. In addition, to be comprehensive, such an initiative has to span the entire company (or at least a very large part of it), which brings with it a whole set of administrative and political problems.

This frustrating state of affairs has brought forth a number of attempts to solve what is essentially a conceptual and political problem using *technical* means. In particular, the large enterprise tool vendors saw (and see) this problem space as an opportunity!

The most recent iteration on this theme was data warehouses—that is, long-term, comprehensive data stores in which data is represented in a denormalized schema that is intended to be more general than the schema of the transactional databases and also easier to use for nontechnical users. Data is imported into the data warehouse from the transactional databases using so-called ETL (extraction, transformation, and load) processes.

Overall, there seems to be a feeling that data warehouses fell short of expectations for three reasons. First of all, since data warehouses are enterprise-wide, they respond slowly to changes in any one business unit. In particular, changes to the transactional data schema tend to propagate into the data warehouse at a glacial pace, if at all. The second reason is that accessing the data in the data warehouse never seems to be as convenient as it should be. The third and final reason is that doing something useful with the data (once obtained) turns out to be difficult—in part because the typical query interface is often clumsy and not designed for analytic work.

While data warehouses were the most recent iteration in the quest for making company data available and useful, the current trend goes by the name of *business intelligence*, or BI. The term is not new (Wikipedia tells me that it was first used in the 1950s), but only in the last one or two years have I seen the term used regularly.

The way I see it, business intelligence is an accessibility layer sitting on top of a data warehouse or similar data store, trying to make the underlying data more useful through better reporting, improved support for ad hoc data analysis, and even some attempts at canned predictive analytics.

Because it sits atop a database, all business intelligence stays squarely within the database camp; and what it aspires to do is constrained by what a database (or a database developer!) can do. The "analytics" capabilities consist mostly of various aggregate operations (sums, averages, and so on) that are typically supported by *OLAP* (Online

Analytical Processing) *cubes*. OLAP cubes are multi-dimensional contingency tables (*i.e.*, with more than two dimensions) that are precomputed and stored in the database and that allow for (relatively) quick summaries or projections along any of the axes. These "cubes" behave much like spreadsheets on steroids, which makes them familiar and accessible to the large number of people comfortable with spreadsheets and pivot tables.

In my experience, the database heritage (in contrast to a software engineering heritage) of BI has another consequence: the way people involved with business intelligence relate to it. While almost all software development has an element of *product* development to it, business intelligence often feels like *infrastructure* maintenance. And while the purpose of the former typically involves innovation and the development of new ways to please the customer, the latter tends to be more reactive and largely concerned with "keeping the trains on time." This is not necessarily a bad thing, as long as one pays attention to the difference in cultures.

What is the take away here? First of all, I think it is important to have realistic expectations: when it comes right down to it, business intelligence initiatives are mostly about better reporting. That is fine as far as it goes, but it does not require (or provide) much data analysis per se. The business users who are the typical customers of such projects usually don't need much help in defining the numbers they would like to see. There may be a need for help with visualization and overall user interface design, but the possibilities here tend to be mostly defined (and that means limited) by the set of tools being used.

More care needs to be taken when any of the "canned" analysis routines are being used that come bundled with many BI packages. Most (if not all) of these tools are freebies, thrown in by the vendor to pad the list of supported features, but they are likely to lack production strength and instead emphasize "ease of use." These tools will produce results, all right—but it will be our job to decide how *significant* and how *relevant* these results are.

We should first ask what these routines are actually doing "under the hood." For example, a clustering package may employ any one of a whole range of clustering algorithms (as we saw in Chapter 13) or even use a combination of algorithms together with various heuristics. Once we understand what the package does, we can then begin asking questions about the quality and, in particular, the significance of the results. Given that the routine is largely a black box to us, we will not have an intuitive sense regarding the extent of the region of validity of its results, for example. And because it is intended as an easy-to-use give away, it is not likely to have support for (or report at length about) nasty details such as confidence limits on the results. Finally, we should ask how relevant and useful these results are. Was there an original question that is being addressed—or was the answer mostly motivated by the ease with which it could be obtained?

One final observation: when there are no commercial tool vendors around, there is not much momentum for developing business intelligence implementations. Neither of the two major open source databases (MySQL and Postgres) has developed BI functionality or the kinds of ad hoc analytics interfaces that are typical of BI tools. (There are, however, a few open source projects that provide reporting and OLAP functionality.)

Reporting

The primary means by which data is used for "analysis" purposes in an enterprise environment is via reports. Whether we like it or not, much of "business intelligence" revolves around reporting, and "reporting" is usually a big part of what companies do with their data.

It is also one of the greatest sources of frustration. Given the ubiquity of reporting and the resources spent on it, one would think that the whole area would be pretty well figured out by now. But this is not so: in my experience, nobody seems to like what the reporting team is putting out—including the reporting team itself.

I have come to the conclusion that reporting, as currently understood and practiced, has it all wrong. Reporting is the one region of the software universe that has so far been barely touched by the notions of "agility" and "agile development." Reporting solutions are invariably big, bulky, and bureaucratic, slow to change, and awkward to use. Moreover, I think with regards to two specific issues they get it *exactly* wrong:

1. In an attempt to conserve resources, reporting solutions are often built generically: a single reporting system that supports all the needs of all the users. The reality, of course, is that the system does not serve the needs of *any* user (certainly not well), even as the overhead of the general-purpose architecture drives the cost through the roof.

2. Most reporting that I have seen confuses "up to date" with "real time." Data for reports is typically pulled in immediate response to a user's query, which ensures that the data is up to date but also (for many reports) that it will take a while before the report is available—often quite a while! I believe that this delay is the single greatest source of frustration with all reports, anywhere. For a user, it typically matters much more to get the data *right this minute* than to get it *up to this minute*!

Can we conceive of an alternative to the current style of reporting, one that actually delivers on its promise and is easy and fun to use? I think so (in fact, I have seen it in action), but first we need to slaughter a sacred cow: namely, that *one* reporting system should be able to handle all kinds of *different* requirements. In particular, I think it will be helpful to distinguish very clearly between *operational* and *representative* reports.

Representative reports are those intended for external users. Quarterly filings certainly fall into this category, as do reports the company may provide to its customers on various metrics. In short, anything that gets published.

Operational reports, in contrast, are those used by managers within the company to actually run the business. Such reports include information on the the number of orders shipped today, the size of the backlog, or the CPU loads of various servers.

These two report types have almost nothing in common! Operational reports need to be fast and convenient—little else matters. Representative reports need to be definitive and optically impressive. It is not realistic to expect a single reporting system to support both requirements simultaneously! I'd go further and say that the preparation of representative reports is always somewhat of a special operation and should be treated as such: "making it look good." If you have to do this a lot (*e.g.*, because you regularly send invoices to a large number of customers), then by all means automate the process—but don't kid yourself into thinking that this is still merely "reporting." (Billing is a *core* business activity for all service businesses!)

When it comes to operational reports, there are several ideas to consider:

Think "simple, fast, convenient."   Reports should be simple to understand, quick (instantaneous) to run, and convenient to use. Convenience dictates that the users *must not* be required to fill in an input mask with various parameters. The most the user can be expected to do is to select one specific report from a fixed list of available ones.

Don't waste real estate.   The whole point of having a report is the *data*. Don't waste space on other things, especially if they never change. I have seen reports in which fully one third of the screen was taken up by a header showing the company logo! In another case, a similar amount of space was taken up by an input mask. Column headers and explanations are another common culprit: once people have seen the report twice, they will know what the columns are. (You will still need headers, but they can be short.) Move explanatory material to a different location and provide a link to it. Remember: the reason people ran the report is to see the *data*.

Make reports easy to read.   In particular, this means putting lots of data onto a single page that can be read by scrolling (instead of dividing the data across several pages that require reloading those pages). Use a large enough font and consider (gently!) highlighting every second line. Less is more.

Consider expert help for the visual design.   Reports don't have to be ugly. It may be worth enlisting an expert to design and implement a report that *looks* pleasant and is easy to use. Good design will emphasize the content and avoid distracting embellishments. Developing good graphic designs is a specialized skill, and some people are simply better at this task than others. Remember: a report's ease of use is not an unnecessary detail but an essential quality!

Provide raw data, and let the user handle filtering and aggregation. This is a potentially radical idea: instead of providing a complicated input mask whereby the user has to specify a bunch of selection criteria and the columns to return, a report can simply return *everything* (within reason, of course) and leave it to the user to perform any desired filtering and aggregation. This idea is based on the realization that most people who use reports are going to be comfortable working with Excel (or an equivalent spreadsheet program). Hence, we can regard a report not as an end product but rather as a data feed for spreadsheets.

This approach has a number of advantages: it is simple, cheap, and flexible (because users are free to design their own reports). It also implies that the report needs to include additional columns, which are required for user-level filtering and aggregation.

Consider cached reports instead of real-time queries. Once the input mask has been removed, the content of a report is basically fixed. But once it is fixed, it can be run ahead of time and cached—which means that we can return the data to the user instantaneously. It also means that the database is hit only once no matter how often the report is viewed.

Find out what your users are doing with reports—and then try to provide it for them. I cannot tell how often I've witnessed the following scenario. The reporting team spends significant time and effort worrying about the details and layout of its reports. But a few doors down the hall, the first thing that the report's actual users do is cut-and-paste the results from the reporting system and import them into, yes, Excel. And then they often spend a lot of time manually editing and formatting the results so that they reflect the information that the users actually need. This occurs *every day* (or every week, or every hour—each time the report is accessed).

These edits are often painfully simple: the users need the report sorted on some numerical column, but this is impossible because the entry in that column is text: "Quantity 17." Or they need the difference between two columns rather than the raw values. In any case, it's usually something that could be implemented in half an hour, solving the problem once and for all. (These informal needs tend not to be recognized in formal "requirements" meetings, but they become immediately apparent if you spend a couple of hours tracking the the users' daily routines.)

Reports are for consumers, not producers. A common response to the previous item is that every user seems to have his own unique set of needs, and trying to meet all of them would lead to a proliferation of different reports.

There is of course some truth to that. But in my experience, certain reports are used by work groups in a fairly standard fashion. It is in these situations that the time spent on repetitive, routine editing tasks (such as those just described) is especially painful—and avoidable. In such cases it might also be worthwhile to work with the group (or its management) to standardize their processes, so that in the end, a single report can meet everybody's needs.

But there is a bigger question here, too. Whose convenience is more important—the producers' or the users'? More broadly: for *whom* are the reports intended—for the reporting team or for the people looking at them?

Think about the proper metrics to show.   For reports that show some form of summary statistics (as opposed to raw counts), think about which quantities to show. Will a mean (*e.g.*, "average time spent in queue") be sufficient, or is the distribution of values skewed, so that the median would be more appropriate? Do you need to include a measure for the width of the distribution (standard deviation or inter-quartile range)? (Answer: probably!) Also, don't neglect cumulative information (see Chapter 2).

Don't mix drill-down functionality with standard reporting.   This may be a controversial item. In my opinion, reports are exactly that: standard overviews of the status of the system. Every time I run a report, I expect to find the same picture. (The numbers will change, of course, but not the overall view.) Drill-downs, on the other hand, are always different. After all, they are usually conducted in response to something out of the ordinary. Hence I don't think it makes sense devising a general-purpose framework for them; ad hoc work is best done using ad hoc tools.

Consider this: general-purpose frameworks are always clumsy and expensive yet they rarely deliver the functionality required. Would it be more cost-effective to forget about maintaining drill-down functionality in the reporting system itself and instead deploy the resources (*i.e.*, the developers) liberated thereby to address drill-down tasks on an ad hoc basis?

Don't let your toolset strangle you.   Don't let your toolset limit the amount of value you can deliver. Many reporting solutions that I have seen can be awfully limiting in terms of the kind of information you can display and the formatting options that are available. As with any tool: if it gets in the way, evaluate again whether it is a net gain!

This is the list. I think the picture I'm trying to paint is pretty clear: fast, *simple*, and convenient reports that show lots of data but little else. Minimal overhead and a preference for cheap one-offs as opposed to expensive, general-purpose solutions. It's not all roses—in particular, the objection that a large number of cheap one-off reports might incur a significant total cost of ownership in the long run is well taken. On the other hand, every general-purpose reporting solution that I have seen incurred a similar cost of ownership—but did not deliver the same level of flexibility and convenience.

I think it is time to rethink reporting. The agile movement (whether right or wrong in all detail) has brought fresh life to software development processes. We should start applying its lessons to reporting.

Finally, a word about reporting tools. The promise of the reporting tools that I have seen is to consume data from "many sources" and to deliver reports to "many formats" (such as HTML, PDF, and Excel).

I have already suggested why I consider this largely an imaginary problem: I cannot conceive of a situation where you really need to deliver the same report in both HTML and PDF versions. If there is a requirement to support both formats, on close examination we will probably find that the HTML report is an operational report, whereas the PDF report is to be representational. There are probably additional differences between the two versions (besides the output format), in terms of layout, content, life cycle, and audience—just about everything.

Similar considerations apply regarding the need to pull data from many sources. Although this *does* occur, does it occur often enough that it should form the basis for the entire reporting architecture? Or does, in reality, most of the data come from relational databases and the odd case where some information comes from a different source (*e.g.*, an XML document, an LDAP server, or a proprietary data store) is best handled as a special case? (If you do in fact need to pull data from very different sources, then you should consider implementing a proper intermediate layer, one that extracts and *stores* data from all sources in a robust, common format. Reporting requires a solid and reliable data model. In other words, you want to isolate your reporting solution from the vagaries of the data sources—especially if these sources are "weird.")

The kinds of problems that reporting tools promise to solve strike me as classic examples of cases where a framework *seems* like a much better idea than it actually is. Sure, a lot of the tasks involved in reporting are lame and repetitive. However, designing a framework that truly has the flexibility required to function as a general-purpose tool is difficult, which leads to frameworks that are hard to use for everyone—and you still have to work around their limitations. The alternative is to write some boring but straightforward and most of all *simple* boilerplate code that solves *your* specific problems simply and well. I tend to think that some simple, problem-specific boilerplate code is in every way preferable to a big, complicated, all-purpose framework.

As for the actual delivery technology, I am all for simple tables and static, precomputed graphics—provided they are useful and well thought-out (which is not always as easy as it may seem). Specifically, I don't think that animated or interactive graphics—for example, using Adobe Flash, Microsoft Silverlight, or some other "Thick Client" technology—work well for reporting. Test yourself: how often do you want to wait for 5–10 seconds while some bar chart is slowly rendering itself (with all the animated bars growing individually from the base line)? Once you have seen this a few times, the "cute" effect has worn off, and the waiting becomes a drag. Remember that reports should be convenient, and that mostly means *quick*.

Thick clients do make sense as technologies for building "control consoles": complex user interfaces designed to operate a complex system that needs to be controlled in real time. But that's a very different job than reporting and should be (and usually is) treated as a core product with a dedicated software team.

Corporate Metrics and Dashboards

It is always surprising when a company doesn't have good, real-time, and consistent visibility into some of its own fundamental processes. It can be amazingly difficult to obtain insight into data such as: orders fulfilled today, orders still pending, revenue by item type, and so on.

But this lack of visibility should not come as surprise because up close, the problem is harder than it appears. Any business of sufficient size will have complex business rules, which furthermore may be inconsistent across divisions or include special exceptions for major customers. The IT infrastructure that provides the data will have undergone several iterations over the years and be a mixture of "legacy" and more current systems—none of which were primarily designed for our current purposes! The difficulties in presenting the desired data are nothing more than a reflection of the complexity of the business.

You may encounter two concepts that try to address the visibility problem just described: special *dashboards* and more general *metrics programs*. The goals of a metrics program are to *define* those quantities that are most relevant and should be tracked and to design and develop the infrastructure required to collect the appropriate data and make it accessible.

A dashboard might be the visible outcome of a metrics program. The purpose of a dashboard is to provide a high-level view of all relevant metrics in a single report (rather than a collection of individual, more detailed reports). Dashboards often include information on whether any given metric is within its desired range.

Dashboard implementations can be arbitrarily fancy, with various forms of graphical displays for individual quantities. An unfortunate misunderstanding results from taking the word "dashboard" too seriously and populating the report with graphical images of dials, as one might find in a car. Of course, this is beside the point and actually detracts from a legitimate, useful idea: to have a comprehensive, unified view of the whole set of relevant metrics.

I think it is important to keep dashboards simple. Stick to the original idea of all the relevant data on a single page—together with clear indications of whether each value is within the desired range or not.

As already explained when discussing reports, I do not believe that drill-down functionality should be part of the overall infrastructure. The purpose of the dashboard is to highlight areas that need further attention, but the actual work on these areas is better done using individual, detailed research.

Recommendations for a Metrics Program

In case you find yourself on a project team to implement a metrics program, tasked to define the metrics to track and to design the required infrastructure, here are some concrete recommendations that you might want to consider.

Understand the cost of metrics programs. Metrics aren't free. They require development effort and deployment infrastructure of production-level strength, both of which have costs and overhead. Once in production, these systems will also require regular maintenance. None of this is free.

I think the single biggest mistake is to assume that a successful metrics program can be run as an add-on project without additional resources. It can't.

Have realistic expectations for the achievable benefit. The short-term effect of any sort of metrics program is likely to be small and possibly nondetectable. Metrics provide visibility and *only* visibility, but they don't improve performance. Only the decisions based on these metrics will (perhaps!) improve performance. But here the *marginal* gain can be quite small, since many of the same decisions might have been made anyway, based on routine and gut feeling.

The more important effect of a metrics program stems from the long-term effect it has on the organizational culture. A greater sense of accountability, or even the realization that there *are* different levels of performance, can change the way the business runs. But these effects take time to materialize.

Start with the actions that the metrics should drive. When setting out to define a set of metrics to collect, make sure to ask yourself: what decision would I make differently in response to the value of this metric? If none comes to mind, you don't need to collect it!

Don't define what you can't measure. This is a good one. I remember a metrics program where the set of metrics to track had been decided at the executive management level, based on what would be "useful" to see. Problem was, for a significant fraction of those quantities, no data was being collected and none could be collected because of limitations in the physical processes.

Build appropriate infrastructure. For a metrics program to be successful, it must be technically reliable, and the data must be credible. In other words, the systems that support it must be of *production-level quality* in regard to robustness, uptime, and reliability. For a company of any size, this requires databases, network infrastructure, monitoring—the whole nine yards. Plan on them! It will be difficult to be successful with only flat files and a CGI script (or with Excel sheets on a SharePoint, for that matter).

There is an important difference here between a more comprehensive *program* that purports to be normative and widely available, and an ad hoc report. Ad hoc reports can be extremely effective precisely because they do not require any infrastructure beyond a CGI script (or an Excel sheet), but they *do not scale*. They won't scale to more metrics, larger groups of users, more facilities, longer historical time frames, or whatever it is.

That being said, if all you need is an ad hoc report, by all means go for it.

Steer clear of manually collected metrics.   First of all, manually collected metrics are neither reliable nor credible (people will forget to enter numbers and, if pressed, will make them up). Second, most people will resist having to enter numbers (especially in detail—think timesheets!), which will destroy the acceptance and credibility of the program. Avoid manually collected metrics at all cost.

Beware of aggregates.   It can be very appealing to aggregate values as much as possible: "Just give me *one number* so that I see how my business is doing." The problem is that every aggregation step loses information that is impossible to regain: you can't unscramble an egg. And *actionable* information is typically *detailed* information. Knowing that my aggregated performance score has tanked is not actionable but knowing which *specific* system has failed is!

This leads us to questions about user interface design, roll-ups, and drill-downs. I think most of this is unnecessary. All that's required is a simple, high-level report. If details are required, one can always dig deeper in an ad hoc fashion.

Think about the math involved.   The math required for corporate metrics is rarely advanced, but it still offers opportunities for mistakes. A common example occurs whenever we are forming a ratio—for example, to calculate the defect rate as the number of defects divided by the number of items produced. The problem is that the denominator can become zero (no items produced during the observation time frame), which makes it impossible to calculate a defect rate. There are different ways you can handle this (report as "not available," treat zero items produced as a special case, especially slick: add a small number to the denominator in your definition of the defect rate, so that it can never become zero), but you need to handle this possibility somehow (also see Appendix B).

There are other problems for which careful thinking about the best mathematical representation can be helpful. For example, to compare metrics they need to be normalized through rescaling by an appropriate scaling factor. For quantities that vary over many orders of magnitude, it might be more useful to track the logarithm instead of the raw quantity. Consider getting expert help: a specialist with sufficient analytical background can recognize trouble spots *and* make recommendations for how best to deal with them that may not be obvious.

Be careful with statistical methods that might not apply.   Mean and standard deviation are good representations for the typical value and the typical spread only if the distribution of data points is roughly symmetrical. In many practical situations, this is *not* the case—waiting times, for instance, can never be negative and, although the "typical" waiting time may be quite short, there is likely to be a tail of events that take a very long time to complete. This tail will corrupt both mean and standard deviation. In such cases, median-based statistics are a better bet (see Chapter 2 and Chapter 9).

In general, it is necessary to study the nature of the data *before* settling on an appropriate way to summarize it. Again, consider expert help if you don't have the competency in-house.

Don't buy what you don't need.   It is tempting to ask for a lot of detail that is not really required. Generally, it is not necessary to track sales numbers on a millisecond basis because we cannot respond to changes at that speed—and even if we could, the numbers would not be very meaningful because sales normally fluctuate over the course of a day.

Establish a meaningful time scale or the frequency with which to track changes. This time scale should be similar to the time scale in which we can make decisions and also similar to the time scale after which we see the results of those decisions. Note that this time scale might vary drastically: daily is probably good enough for sales, but for, say, the reactor temperature, a much shorter time scale is certainly appropriate!

Don't oversteer.   This recommendation is the logical consequence of the previous one. Every "system" has a certain response time within which it reacts to changes. Applying changes more frequently than this response time is useless and possibly harmful (because it prevents the system from reaching a steady state).

Learn to distinguish trend and variation.   Most metrics will be tracked over time, so what we have learned about time-series analysis (see Chapter 4) applies. The most important skill is to develop an understanding for the duration and magnitude of typical "noise" fluctuations and to distinguish them from significant changes (trends) in the data. Suppose sales dipped today by 20 percent: this is no cause for alarm if we know that sales fluctuate by ± 25 percent from day to day. But if sales fall by 5 percent for five days in a row, that could possibly be a warning sign.

Don't forget the power of perverted incentives.   When metrics are used to manage staff performance, this often means changing from a vague yet broad sense of "performance" to a much narrower focus on specifically those quantities that are being measured. This development can result in creating perverted incentives.

Take, for instance, the primary performance metric in a customer service call center: the number of calls a worker handles per hour, or "calls per hour." The best way for a call center worker who is evaluated solely in terms of calls per hour to improve her standing is by picking up the phone when it rings and hanging up immediately! By making calls per hour the dominant metric, we have implicitly deemphasized other important aspects, such as customer satisfaction (*i.e.*, quality).

Beware of availability bias.   Some quantities are easier to measure than others and therefore tend to receive greater attention. In my experience, productivity is generally easier to measure than quality, with all the unfortunate consequences this entails.

Just because it can't be measured does not mean it does not exist.   Some quantities cannot be measured. This includes "soft" factors such as culture, commitment, and fun; but also some very "hard" factors like customer satisfaction. You can't measure that—all you can measure directly are proxies (*e.g.*, the return rate). An alternative are surveys, but because participants decide themselves whether they reply, the results may be misleading. (This is known as *self-selection bias*.)

Above all, don't forget that a metrics program is intended to help the business by providing visibility—it should never become an end in itself. Also keep in mind that it is an effort to support others, not the other way around.

Data Quality Issues

All reporting and metrics efforts depend on the availability and quality of the underlying data. If the required data is improperly captured (or not captured at all), there is nothing to work with!

The truth of the matter is that if a company wants to have a successful business intelligence or metrics program, then its data model and storage solution *must be designed with reporting needs in mind*. By the time the demand for data analysis services rolls around, it is too late to worry about data modeling!

Two problems in particular occur frequently when one is trying to prepare reports or metrics: data may not be *available* or it may not be *consistent*.

Data Availability

Data may not be collected at all, often with the innocent argument that "nobody wanted to use it." That's silly: data that's directly related to a company's business is always relevant—whether or not anybody is looking at it right now.

If data is not available, this does not necessarily mean that it is not being collected. Data may be collected but not at the required level of granularity. Or it is collected but immediately aggregated in a way that loses the details required for later analysis. (For instance, if server logs are aggregated daily into hits per page, then we lose the ability to associate a specific user to a page, and we also lose information about the order in which pages were visited.)

Obviously, there is a trade-off between the amount of data that can be stored and the level of detail that we can achieve in an analysis. My recommendation: try to keep as much detail as you can, even if you have to spool it out to tape (or whatever offline storage mechanism is available). Keep in mind that operational data, once lost, can *never* be restored. Furthermore, gathering new data takes *time* and cannot be accelerated. If you know that data will be needed for some planned analysis project, start collecting it *today*. Don't wait for the "proper" extraction and storage solution to be in place—that could easily take weeks or even months. If necessary, I do not hesitate to pull daily snapshots of relevant data to my local desktop, to preserve it temporarily, while a long-term storage solution is being worked out. Remember: every day that data is not collected is another day by which your results will be delayed.

Even when data is in principle collected at the appropriate level of detail, it may still not be available in a practical sense, if the storage schema was not designed with reporting needs in mind. (I assume here that the data in question comes from a corporate database—certainly the most likely case by far.) Three problems stand out to me in this context: lack of revision history, business logic commingled with data, and awkward encodings.

Some entities have a nontrivial life cycle: orders will go through several status updates, contracts have revisions, and so on. In such cases, it is usually important to preserve the full revision history—that is, all life-cycle events. The best way to do this is to model the time-varying state as a *separate entity*. For instance, you might have the `Order` entity (which contains, for example, the order ID and the customer ID) and the `OrderStatus`, which represents the actual status of the order (placed, accepted, shipped, paid, completed, ...), as well as a timestamp for the time that the status change took place. The current status is the one with the most recent status change. (A good way to handle this is with two timestamps: `ValidFrom` and `ValidTo`, where the latter is `NULL` for the current status.) Such a model preserves all the information necessary to study quantities like the typical time that orders remain in any one state. (In contrast, the presence of history tables with `OldValue` and `NewValue` columns suggests improper relational modeling.)

The important principle is that data is never *updated*—we only append to the revision history. Keep in mind that every time a database field is updated, the previous value is destroyed. Try to avoid this whenever you can! (I'd go so far as to say that CRUD—create, read, update, delete—is indeed a four-letter word. The only two operations that should ever be used are create and read. There may be valid operational reasons to move very old data to offline storage, but the data model should be designed in such a way that we never clobber existing data. In my experience, this point is far too little understood and even less heeded.)

The second common problem is business logic that is commingled with data in such a way that the data alone does not present an accurate picture of the business. A sure sign of this situation is a statement like the following: "Don't try to read from the database directly—you have to go through the access layer API to get all the business rules." What this is saying is that the DB schema was not designed so that the data can stand by itself: the business rules in the access layer are required to interpret the data correctly. (Another indicator is the presence of long, complicated stored procedures. This is worse, in fact, because it suggests that the situation developed inadvertently, whereas the presence of an access layer is proof of at least some degree of foreplanning.)

From a reporting point of view, the difficulty with a mandatory access layer like this is that a reporting system typically has to consume the data in bulk, whereas application-oriented access layers tend to access individual records or small collections of items. The problem is not the access layer as such—in fact, an abstraction layer between the database and the application (or applications) often makes sense. But it should be exactly that: an abstraction and access layer without embedded business logic, so that it can be bypassed if necessary.

Finally, the third problem that sometimes arises is the use of weird data representations, which (although complete) make bulk reporting excessively difficult. As an example, think of a database that stores only updates (to inventory levels, for example) but not the grand total. To get a view of the current state, it is now necessary to replay the entire transaction history since the beginning of time. (This is why your bank statement lists both a transaction history *and* an account balance!) In such situations it may actually make sense to invest in the required infrastructure to pull out the data and store it in a more manageable fashion. Chances are good that plenty of uses for the sanitized data will appear over time (build it, and they will come).

Data Consistency

Problems of data consistency (as opposed to data availability) occur in every company of sufficient size, and they are simply an expression of the complexity of the underlying business. Here are some typical examples that I have encountered.

- Different parts of the company use different definitions for the same metric. Operations, for example, may consider an order to be completed when it has left the warehouse, whereas the finance department does consider an order to be complete once the payment for it has been received.

- Reporting time frames may not be aligned with operational process flows. A seemingly simple question such as, "How many orders did we complete yesterday?" can quickly become complicated, depending on whose definition of "yesterday" we use. For example, in a warehouse, we may only be able to obtain a total for the number of orders completed per shift—but then how do we account for the shift that stretches from 10 at night to 6 the next morning? How do we deal with time zones? Simply stating that "yesterday" refers to the local time at the corporate headquarters sounds simple but is probably not practical, since all the facilities will naturally do their bookkeeping and reporting according to their local time.

- Time flows backward. How does one account for an order that was later returned? If we want to recognize revenue in the quarter in which the order was completed but an item is later returned, then we have a problem. We can still report on the revenue accurately—but not in a timely manner. (In other words, final quarterly revenue reports cannot be produced until the time allowed to return an item has elapsed. Keep in mind that this may be a *long* time in the case of extended warranties or similar arrangements.)

Additional difficulties will arise if information has been lost—for instance, because the revision history of a contract has not been kept (recall our earlier discussion). You can probably think of still other scenarios in which problems of data or metric inconsistency occur.

The answer to this set of problems is not technical but administrative or political. Basically it comes down to agreeing on a common definition of all metrics. An even more drastic recommendation to deal with conflicting metrics is to declare one data source as the "normative" one; this does not make the data any more accurate, but it can help to stop fruitless efforts to reconcile different sources at any cost. At least that's the theory. Unfortunately, if the manager of an off-site facility can expect to have his feet held to the fire by the CEO over why the facility missed its daily goal of two million produced units by a handful of units last Friday, he will look for ways to pass the blame. And pointing to inconsistencies in the reports is an easy way out. (In my experience, one major drawback of all metrics programs is the amount of work generated to reconcile minute inconsistencies between different versions of the same data. The costs—in terms of frustration and wasted developer time—can be stunning.)

As practical advice I recommend striving as much as possible for clear definitions of all metrics, so that at least we know what we're talking about. Furthermore, wherever possible, try to make those metrics normative that are *practical* to gather, rather than those "correct" from a theoretical point of view (*e.g.*, report metrics in local instead of global time coordinates). Apply conversion factors behind the scenes, if necessary, but try to make sure that humans only need to deal with quantities that are meaningful and familiar to them.

Workshop: Berkeley DB and SQLite

For analysis purposes, the most suitable data format is usually the flat file. Most of the time, we will want all (or almost all) of the records in a data set for our analysis. It therefore makes more sense to read the whole file, possibly filter out the unneeded records, and process the rest, rather than to do an indexed lookup of only the records that we want.

Common as this scenario is, it does not always apply. Especially when it comes to reporting, it can be highly desirable to have access to a data storage solution that supports structured data, indexed lookup, and even the ability to merge and aggregate data. In other words, we want a database.

The problem is that most databases are *expensive*—and I don't (just) mean in terms of money. They require their own process (or processes), they require care and feeding, they require network access (so that people and processes can actually get to them). They must be designed, installed, and provisioned; very often, they require architectural approval before anything else. (The latter point can become such an ordeal that it makes anything requiring changes to the database environment virtually impossible; one simply has to invent solutions that do without them.) In short, most databases are expensive: both technically and politically.

Fortunately, other people have recognized this and developed database solutions that are cheap: so-called *embedded databases*. Their distinguishing feature is that they do not run in a separate process. Instead, embedded databases store their data in a regular file, which is accessed through a library linked into the application. This eliminates most of the overhead for provisioning and administration, and we can replicate the entire database simply by copying the data file! (This is occasionally very useful to "deploy" databases.)

Let's take a look at the two most outstanding examples of (open source) embedded databases: the Berkeley DB, which is a key/value hash map stored on disk, and SQLite, which is a complete relational database "in a box." Both have bindings to almost any programming language—here, we demonstrate them from Python. (Both are included in the Python Standard Library and therefore should already be available wherever Python is.)

Berkeley DB

The Berkeley DB is a key/value hash map (a "dictionary") persisted to disk. The notion of a persistent key/value database originated on Unix; the first implementation being the Unix dbm facility. Various reimplementations (ndbm, gdbm, and so on) exist. The original "Berkeley DB" was just one specific implementation that added some additional capabilities—mostly multiuser concurrency support. It was developed and distributed by a commercial company (Sleepycat) that was acquired by Oracle in 2008. However, the name "Berkeley DB" is often used generically for any key/value database.

Through the magic of operator overloading, a Berkeley DB also *looks* like a dictionary to the programmer[*] (with the requirement that keys and values must be *strings*):

```
import dbm

db = dbm.open( "data.db", 'c' )
```

---

[*] In Perl, you use a "tied hash" to the same effect.

```
db[ 'abc' ] = "123"
db[ 'xyz' ] = "Hello, World!"
db[ '42' ] = "42"

print db[ 'abc' ]

del db[ 'xyz' ]

for k in db.keys():
    print db[k]

db.close()
```

That's all there is to it. In particular, notice that the overhead ("boilerplate") required is precisely zero. You can't do much better than that.

I used to be a great fan of the Berkeley DB, but over time I have become more aware of its limitations. Berkeley DBs store single-key/single-value pairs—period. If that's what you want to do, then a Berkeley DB is great. But as soon as that's not *exactly* what you want to do, then the Berkeley DB simply is the wrong solution. Here are a few things you *cannot* do with a Berkeley DB:

- Range searches: 3 < x < 17

- Regular expression searches: x like 'Hello%'

- Aggregation: count(*)

- Duplicate keys

- Result sets consisting of multiple records and iteration over result sets

- Structured data values

- Joins

In fairness, you can achieve some of these features, but you have to build them yourself (*e.g.*, provide your own serialization and deserialization to support structured data values) or be willing to lose almost all of the benefit provided by the Berkeley DB (you can have range or regular expression searches, as long as you are willing to suck in *all* the keys and process them sequentially in a loop).

Another area in which Berkeley DBs are weak is administrative tasks. There are no standard tools for browsing and (possibly) editing entries, with the consequence that you have to write your own tools to do so. (Not hard but annoying.) Furthermore, Berkeley DBs don't maintain administrative information about themselves (such as the number of records, most recent access times, and so on). The obvious solution—which I have seen implemented in just about every project using a Berkeley DB—is to maintain this information explicitly and to store it in the DB under a special, synthetic key. All of this is easy enough, but it does bring back some of the "boilerplate" code that we hoped to avoid by using a Berkeley DB in the first place.

SQLite

In contrast to the Berkeley DB, SQLite (*http://www.sqlite.org/*) is a full-fledged relational database, including tables, keys, joins, and WHERE clauses. You talk to it in the familiar fashion through SQL. (In Python, you can use the DB-API 2.0 or one of the higher-level frameworks built on top of it.)

SQLite supports almost all features found in standard SQL with very few exceptions. The price you pay is that you have to design and define a schema. Hence SQLite has a bit more overhead than a Berkeley DB: it requires some up-front design as well as a certain amount of boilerplate code.

A simple example exercising many features of SQLite is shown in the following listing. It should pose few (if any) surprises, but it does demonstrate some interesting features of SQLite:

```
import sqlite3

# Connect and obtain a cursor
conn = sqlite3.connect( 'data.db1' )
conn.isolation_level = None            # use autocommit!
c = conn.cursor()


# Create tables
c.execute( """CREATE TABLE orders
              ( id INTEGER PRIMARY KEY AUTOINCREMENT,
                customer )""" )
c.execute( """CREATE TABLE lineitems
              ( id INTEGER PRIMARY KEY AUTOINCREMENT,
                orderid, description, quantity )""" )

# Insert values
c.execute( "INSERT INTO orders ( customer ) VALUES ( 'Joe Blo' )" )
id = str( c.lastrowid )
c.execute( """INSERT INTO lineitems ( orderid, description, quantity )
              VALUES ( ?, 'Widget 1', '2' )""", ( id, ) )
c.execute( """INSERT INTO lineitems ( orderid, description, quantity )
              VALUES ( ?, 'Fidget 2', '1' )""", ( id, ) )
c.execute( """INSERT INTO lineitems ( orderid, description, quantity )
              VALUES ( ?, 'Part 17', '5' )""", ( id, ) )

c.execute( "INSERT INTO orders ( customer ) VALUES ( 'Jane Doe' )" )
id = str( c.lastrowid )
```

```
c.execute( """INSERT INTO lineitems ( orderid, description, quantity )
            VALUES ( ?, 'Fidget 2', '3' )""", ( id, ) )
c.execute( """INSERT INTO lineitems ( orderid, description, quantity )
            VALUES ( ?, 'Part 9', '2' )""", ( id, ) )


# Query
c.execute( """SELECT li.description FROM orders o, lineitems li
            WHERE o.id = li.orderid AND o.customer LIKE '%Blo'""" )
for r in c.fetchall():
    print r[0]

c.execute( """SELECT orderid, sum(quantity) FROM lineitems
            GROUP BY orderid ORDER BY orderid desc""" )
for r in c.fetchall():
    print "OrderID: ", r[0], "\t Items: ", r[1]


# Disconnect
conn.close()
```

Initially, we "connect" to the database—if it doesn't exist yet, it will be created. We specify autocommit mode so that each statement is executed immediately. (SQLite also supports concurrency control through explicit transaction.)

Next we create two tables. The first column is specified as a primary key (which implies that it will be indexed automatically) with an autoincrement feature. All other columns do not have a data type associated with them, because basically all values are stored in SQLite as strings. (It is also possible to declare certain type conversions that should be applied to the values, either in the database or in the Python interface.)

We then insert two orders and some associated line items. In doing so, we make use of a convenience feature provided by the sqlite3 module: the last value of an autoincremented primary key is available through the lastrowid attribute (data member) of the current cursor object.

Finally, we run two queries. The first one demonstrates a join as well as the use of SQL wildcards; the second uses an aggregate function and also sorts the result set. As you can see, basically everything you know about relational databases carries over directly to SQLite!

SQLite supports some additional features that I have not mentioned. For example, there is an "in-memory" mode, whereby the entire database is kept entirely in memory: this can be very helpful if you want to use SQLite as a part of a performance-critical application. Also part of SQLite is the command-line utility sqlite3, which allows you to examine a database file and run ad hoc queries against it.

I have found SQLite to be extremely useful—basically everything you expect from a relational database but without most of the pain. I recommend it highly.

Further Reading

- *Information Dashboard Design: The Effective Visual Communication of Data.* Stephen Few. O'Reilly. 2006.
  This book addresses good graphical design of dashboards and reports. Many of the author's points are similar in spirit to the recommendations in this chapter. After reading his book, you might consider hiring a graphic or web designer to design your reports for you!

CHAPTER SEVENTEEN

Financial Calculations and Modeling

I RECENTLY RECEIVED A NOTICE FROM A MAGAZINE REMINDING ME THAT MY SUBSCRIPTION WAS RUNNING OUT. It's a relatively expensive weekly magazine, and they offered me three different plans to renew my subscription: one year (52 issues) for $130, two years for $220, or three years for $275. Table 17-1 summarizes these options and also shows the respective cost per issue.

TABLE 17-1. Pricing plans for a magazine subscription

Subscription	Total price	Price per issue
Single issue	n/a	6.00
1 year	130	2.50
2 years	220	2.12
3 years	275	1.76

Assuming that I want to continue the subscription, which of these three options makes the most sense? From Table 17-1, we can see that each issue of the magazine becomes cheaper as I commit myself to a longer subscription period, but is this a good deal? In fact, what does it mean for a proposal like this to be a "good deal"? Somehow, stumping up nearly three hundred dollars right now seems like a stretch, even if I remind myself that it saves me more than half the price on each issue.

This little story demonstrates the central topic of this chapter: the *time value of money*, which expresses the notion that a hundred dollars today are worth more than a hundred dollars a year from now. In this chapter, I shall introduce some standard concepts and calculational tools that are required whenever we need to make a choice between different investment decisions—whether they involve our own personal finances or the evaluation of business cases for different corporate projects.

I find the material in this chapter fascinating—not because it is rocket science (it isn't) but because it is so fundamental to how the economy works. Yet very few people, in particular, very few tech people, have any understanding of it. (I certainly didn't.) This is a shame, not just because the topic is obviously important but also because it is not really all that mystical. A little familiarity with the basic concepts goes a long way toward removing most of the confusion (and, let's face it, the intimidation) that many of us experience when reading the Wall Street pages.

More important in the context of this book is that a lot of data analysis is done specifically to evaluate different business proposals and to support decisions among them. To be able to give effective, appropriate advice, you want to understand the concepts and terminology of this particular problem domain.

The Time Value of Money

Let's return to the subscription problem. The essential insight is that—instead of paying for the second and third year of the subscription *now*—I could invest that money, reap the investment benefit, and pay for the subsequent years of the subscription later. In other words, the discount offered by the magazine must be *greater* than the investment income I can expect if I were instead to invest the sum.

It is this ability to gain an investment benefit that makes having money *now* more valuable than having the same amount of money *later*. Note well that this has nothing to do with the concept of *inflation*, which is the process by which a certain amount of money tends to buy a lesser amount of goods as time passes. For our purposes, inflation is an external influence over which we have no control. In contrast, investment and purchasing decisions (such as the earlier magazine subscription problem) are under our control, and time value of money calculations can help us make the best possible decisions in this regard.

A Single Payment: Future and Present Value

Things are easiest when there is only a single payment involved. Imagine we are given the following choice: receive $1,000 today, or receive $1,050 a year from now. Which one should we choose?

Well, that depends on what we could do with $1,000 right now. For this kind of analysis, it is customary to assume that we would put the money in a "totally safe form of

investment" and use the returns generated in this way as a benchmark for comparison.[*]
Now we can compare the alternatives against the interest that would be generated by this
"safe" investment. For example, assume that the current interest rate that we could gain
on a "safe" investment is 5 percent annually. If we invest $1,000 for a full year, then at the
year's end, we will receive back our principal ($1,000) and, in addition, the accrued
interest ($0.05 \cdot \$1000 = \$50$), for a total of $1,050.

In this example, both options lead to the same amount of money after one year; we say
that they are *equivalent*. In other words, receiving $1,000 now is *equivalent* to receiving
$1,050 a year from now, *given* that the current interest rate on a safe form of investment is
5 percent annually. Equivalence always refers to a specific time frame and interest rate.

Clearly, any amount of money that we now possess has a *future value* (or *future worth*) at
any point in the future; likewise, a payment that we will receive at some point in the
future has a *present value* (or *present worth*) now. Both values depend on the interest rate
that we could achieve by investing in a safe alternative investment instead. The present or
future values must be equivalent at equal times.

There is a little bit of math behind this that is not complicated but is often a little messy.
The future value V_f of some base amount M (the *principal*), after a single time period
during which the amount earns p percent of interest, is calculated as follows:

$$V_f = M + \frac{p}{100} M$$
$$= \left(1 + \frac{p}{100}\right) M$$

The first term on the righthand side expresses that we get our principal back, and the
second term is the amount of interest we receive in addition. Here and in what follows, I
explicitly show the denominator 100 that is used to translate a statement such as "p
percent" into the equivalent numerical factor $p/100$.

Conversely, if we want to know how much a certain amount of money in the future is
worth today, then we have to *discount* that amount to its present value. To find the present
value, we work the preceding equation backward. The present value V_p is unknown, but
we do know the amount of money M that we will have at some point in the future, hence
the equation becomes:

$$M = \left(1 + \frac{p}{100}\right) V_p$$

This can be solved for V_p:

$$V_p = \frac{M}{1 + \frac{p}{100}}$$

Note how we find the future or present value by multiplying the base amount by an appropriate *equivalencing factor*—namely, the future-worth factor $1 + p/100$ and the present-worth factor $1/(1 + p/100)$. Because most such calculations involve discounting a future payment to the present value, the percentage rate p used in these formulas is usually referred to as the *discount rate*.

This example was the simplest possible because there was only a single payment involved—either at the beginning or at the end of the period under consideration. Next, we look at scenarios where there are multiple payments occurring over time.

Multiple Payments: Compounding

Matters become a bit more complicated when there is not just a single payment involved as in the example above but a series of payments over time. Each of these payments must be discounted by the appropriate time-dependent factor, which leads us to *cash-flow analysis*. In addition, payments made or received may alter the base amount on which we operate, this leads to the concept of *compounding*.

Let's consider compounding first, since it is so fundamental. Again, the idea is simple: if we put a sum of money into an interest-bearing investment and then *reinvest* the generated interest, we will start to receive interest on the interest itself. In other words, we will start receiving *compound interest*.

Here is how it works: we start with principal M and invest it at interest rate p. After one year, we have:

$$V(1) = \left(1 + \frac{p}{100}\right) M$$

In the second year, we receive interest on the combined sum of the principal and the interest from the first year:

$$V(2) = \left(1 + \frac{p}{100}\right) V(1)$$
$$= \left(1 + \frac{p}{100}\right)^2 M$$

and so on. After n years, we will have:

$$V(n) = \left(1 + \frac{p}{100}\right)^n M$$

These equations tell us the future worth of our investment at any point in time. It works the other way around, too: we can determine the present value of a payment that we expect to receive n years from now by working the equations backward (much as we did previously for a single payment) and find:

$$V(\text{present}) = \frac{M}{\left(1 + \frac{p}{100}\right)^n}$$

We can see from these equations that, if we continue to reinvest our earnings, then the total amount of money grows exponentially with time (*i.e.*, as a^t for some constant a)—in other words, *fast*. The growth law that applies to compound interest is the same that describes the growth of bacteria cultures or similar systems, where at each time step new members are added to the population *and* start producing offspring themselves. In such systems, not only does the population grow, but the rate at which it grows is constantly increasing as well.

On the other hand, suppose you take out a loan without making payments and let the lender add the accruing interest back onto your principal. In this case, you not only get deeper into debt every month, but you do so at a faster rate as time goes by.

Calculational Tricks with Compounding

Here is a simple trick that is quite convenient when making approximate calculations of future and present worth. The single-payment formula for future worth, $V = (1 + p/100)M$, is simple and intuitive: the principal *plus* the interest after one period. In contrast, the corresponding formula for present worth $V = \frac{M}{1+p/100}$, seems to make less intuitive sense and is harder to work with (how much is \$1,000 divided by 1.05?). But this is again one of those situations where guesstimation techniques (see Chapter 7; also see Appendix B) can be brought to bear. We can approximate the discounting factor as follows:

$$\frac{1}{1 + \frac{p}{100}} \approx 1 - \frac{p}{100} + \left(\frac{p}{100}\right)^2 \mp \cdots$$

Since p is typically small (single digits), it follows that $p/100$ is very small, and so we can terminate the expansion after the first term. Using this approximation, the discounting equation for the present worth becomes $V = (1 - p/100)M$, which has an intuitive interpretation: the present value is equal to the future value, less the interest that we will have received by then.

We can use similar formulas even in the case of compounding, since:

$$\left(1 + \frac{p}{100}\right)^n \approx 1 + n\frac{p}{100} + \cdots$$
$$\left(1 + \frac{p}{100}\right)^{-n} \approx 1 - n\frac{p}{100} + \cdots$$

However, keep in mind that the overall perturbation must be small for the approximation to be valid. In particular, as the number of years n grows, the perturbation term $np/100$ may no longer be small. Still, even for 5 percent over 5 years, the approximation gives $1 \pm 25/100 = 1.25$ or 0.75, respectively. Compare this with the exact values of 1.28 and 0.79. However, for 10 percent over 10 years, the approximation starts to break down, yielding 2 and 0, respectively, compared to the exact values of 2.59 and 0.39.

Similar logic is behind "Einstein's Rule of 72." This rule of thumb states that if you divide 72 by the applicable interest rate, you obtain the number of years it would take for your investment to double. So if you earn 7 percent interest, your money will double in 10 years, but if you only earn 3.5 percent, it will take 20 years to double.

What's the basis for this rule? By now, you can probably figure it out yourself, but here is the solution in a nutshell: for your investment to double, the compounding factor must equal 2. Therefore, we need to solve $(1 + p/100)^n = 2$ for n. Applying logarithms on both sides we find $n = \log(2)/\log(1 + p/100)$. In a second step, we expand the logarithm in the denominator (remember that $p/100$ is a small perturbation!) and end up with $n = \log(2) \cdot (100/p) = 69/p$, since the value of $\log(2)$ is approximately 0.69. The number 69 is awkward to work with, so it is usually replaced by the number 72—which has the advantage of being evenly divisible by 2, 3, 4, 6, 8, and 9 (you can replace 72 with 70 for interest rates of 5 or 7 percent).

Here is another calculational tool that you may find useful. Strictly speaking, an expression such as x^n is defined only for integer n. For general exponents, the power function is defined as $x^n = \exp(n \log x)$. We can use this when calculating compounding factors as follows:

$$\left(1 + \frac{p}{100}\right)^n = \exp\left(n \log\left(1 + p/100\right)\right)$$
$$\approx e^{np/100}$$

where in the second step we have expanded the logarithm again and truncated the expansion after the first term. This form of the compounding factor is often convenient (*e.g.*, it allows us to use arbitrary values for the time period n, not just full years). It becomes exact in the limit of continuous compounding (discussed shortly).

Interest rates are conventionally quoted "per year," as in "5 percent annually." But payments may occur more frequently than that. Savings accounts, for example, pay out any accrued interest on a monthly basis. That means that (as long as we don't withdraw anything) the amount of money that earns us interest grows every month; we say it is *compounded monthly*. (This is in contrast to other investments, which pay out interest or dividends only on a quarterly or even annual basis.) To take advantage of the additional compounding, it is of course in our interest (pun intended) to receive payments as early as possible.

This monthly compounding is the reason for the difference between the *nominal* interest rate and the annual *yield* that you will find stated on your bank's website: the nominal interest rate is the rate p that is used to determine the amount of interest paid out to you each month. The yield tells you by how much your money will grow over the course of the year when the monthly compounding has been factored in. With our knowledge, we can now calculate the yield from the nominal rate:

$$\left(1 + \frac{p_{\text{yield}}}{100}\right) = \left(1 + \frac{\frac{p_{\text{nominal}}}{12}}{100}\right)^{12}$$

One more bit of terminology: the interest rate $p/12$ that is used to determine the value of the monthly payout is known as the *effective* interest rate.

Of course, other payment periods are possible. Many mutual funds pay out quarterly. In contrast, many credit cards compound daily. In theory, we can imagine payments being made constantly (but at an appropriately reduced effective interest rate); this is the case of *continuous compounding* mentioned earlier. In this case, the compounding factor is given by the exponential function. (Mathematically, you replace the 12 in the last formula by n and then let n go to infinity, using the identity $\lim_{n\to\infty}(1 + x/n)^n = \exp(x)$.)

The Whole Picture: Cash-Flow Analysis and Net Present Value

We now have all the tools at our disposal to evaluate the financial implications of any investment decision, no matter how complicated. Imagine we are running a manufacturing plant (or perhaps an operation like Amazon's, where books and other goods are put into boxes and mailed to customers—that's how *I* learned about all these things). We may consider buying some piece of automated equipment for some part of the process (*e.g.*, a sorting machine that sorts boxes onto different trucks according to their destination). Alternatively, we can have people do the same job manually. Which of these two alternatives is better from an economic point of view?

The manual solution has a simple structure: we just have to pay out the required wages every year. If we decide to buy the machine, then we have to pay the purchase price now (this is also known as the *first cost*) and also pay a small maintenance fee each year. For the sake of the argument, assume also that we expect to use the machine for ten years and then sell it on for scrap value.

In economics texts, you will often find the sequence of payments visualized using *cash-flow diagrams* (see Figure 17-1). Time progresses from left to right; inflows are indicated by upward-pointing arrows and outflows by downward-pointing arrows.

To decide between different alternatives, we now proceed as follows:

1. Determine all individual net cash flows (*net* cash flows, because we offset annual costs against revenues).
2. Discount each cash flow to its present value.
3. Add up all contributions.

The quantity obtained in the last step is known either as the *net present value* (NPV) or the *discounted net cash flow*: it is the total value of all cash flows, each properly discounted to its present value. In other words, our financial situation will be the same, whether we execute the entire series of cash flows *or* receive the net present value today. Because the net present value contains all inflows and outflows (properly discounted to the present value), it is a comprehensive single measure that can be used to compare the financial outcomes of different investment strategies.

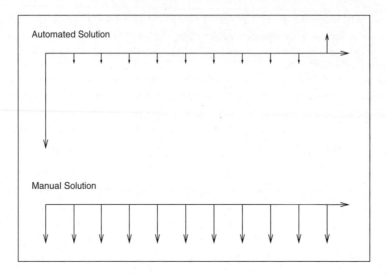

FIGURE 17-1. Examples of cash-flow diagrams. Arrows pointing up correspond to money received; arrows pointing down, to money spent.

We can express the net present value of a series of cash flows in a single formula:

$$\text{NPV} = \sum_i \frac{c(i)}{(1 + p/100)^i}$$

where $c(i)$ is the net cash flow at payment period i and $1/(1 + p/100)^i$ is the associated discounting factor.

There is one more concept that is interesting in this context. What should we use for the discount rate p in the second step above? Instead of supplying a value, we can ask how much interest we would have to receive elsewhere (on a "safe" investment) to obtain the same (or higher) payoff than that expected from the planned project. Let's consider an example. Assume we are evaluating a project that would require us to purchase some piece of equipment at the beginning but that would then result in a series of positive cash flows over the next so many years. Is this a "good" investment? It is if its net present value is positive! (That's pretty much the definition of "net present value": the NPV takes into account the first cost to purchase the equipment as well as the subsequent positive cash flows. If the discounted cash flows are greater than the first cost, we come out ahead.) But the net present value depends on the discount rate p, so we need to find that value of p for which the NPV first becomes zero: if we can earn a higher interest rate elsewhere, then the project does not make financial sense and we should instead take our money to the bank. But if the bank would pay us less than the *rate of return* just calculated, then the project is financially the better option. (To find a numeric value for the rate of return, plug your cash flow structure $c(i)$ into the equation for NPV and then solve for p. Unless the cash flows are particularly simple, you will have to do this numerically.)

The net present value is such an important criterion when making investment decisions because it provides us with a single number that summarizes the financial results of any planned project. It gives us an objective (financial) quantity to decide among different investment alternatives.

Up to a point, that is. The process described here is only as good as its inputs. In particular, we have assumed that we know all inputs perfectly—possibly for many years into the future. Of course we don't have perfect knowledge, and so we better accommodate for that uncertainty somehow. That will be the topic of the next section.

There is another, more subtle problem when evaluating different options solely based on net present value: different investment alternatives may have nonfinancial benefits or drawbacks that are not captured by the net present value. For example, using manual labor may lead to greater flexibility: if business grows more strongly than expected, then the company can hire additional workers, and if business slows down, then it can reduce the number of workers. In contrast, any piece of equipment has a maximum capacity, which may be a limiting factor if business grows more strongly than expected. The distinction arising here is that between fixed and variable cost, and we will come back to it toward the end of the chapter.

Uncertainty in Planning and Opportunity Costs

Now we are ready to revisit the magazine subscription problem from the beginning of this chapter. Let's consider only two alternatives: paying the entire amount for a two-year subscription up front or making two single-year payments. The NPV for the second option is $(1 + 1/(1 + p/100)) C_{1yr}$, where we have left the discount rate p undetermined for the moment. We can now ask: what interest rate would we have to earn elsewhere to make the second option worthwhile? In other words, we want to know the discount rate we'd have to apply to make the NPV of the multiple-payment option equal to the cost of the single-payment plan:

$$\left(1 + \frac{1}{1 + \frac{p}{100}}\right) C_{1yr} = C_{2yr}$$

This equation can be solved for p. The result is $p = 30$ percent! In other words, the two-year subscription is so much cheaper that we would have to find an investment yielding 30 percent annually before it would be worthwhile to pay for the subscription year by year and invest the saved money elsewhere. No investment (and certainly no "safe" investment) yields anywhere near that much. Clearly, something is amiss. (Exercise for the reader: find the net present value for the three-year subscription and verify that it leads to the same value for p.)

Using Expectation Values to Account for Uncertainty

The two- and three-year plans carry a hidden cost for us: once we have signed up, we can no longer freely decide over our money—we're committed ourselves for the long haul. In contrast, if we pay on a yearly basis, then we can reevaluate every year whether we want to continue the subscription. The price for this freedom is a higher subscription fee. However, we will probably not find it easy to determine the exact dollar value that this freedom is worth to us.

From the magazine's perspective, the situation is simpler. They can simply ask how much money they expect to make from an individual subscriber under either option. If I sign up for the two-year subscription, they make C_{2yr} with certainty; if I sign up for the one-year subscription, they make C_{1yr} with certainty now and another C_{1yr} later—*provided* I renew my subscription! In this case, then, the amount of money the magazine expects to make on me is $C_{1yr} + \gamma C_{1yr}$, where γ is the probability that I will renew the subscription. From the magazine's perspective, both options must be equally favorable (otherwise they would adjust the price of the two-year subscription to make them equal), so we can equate the expected revenues and solve for γ. The result comes out to about $\gamma = 0.7$—in other words, the magazine expects (based on past experience, and so on) that about 70 percent of its current subscribers will renew their subscription. For three years, the equation becomes $(1 + \gamma + \gamma^2)C_{1yr} = C_{3yr}$ because, to sign up for three years, a subscriber must decide *twice* to renew the subscription. If you work through the algebra, you will find that γ again comes out to about $\gamma = 0.7$, providing a nice consistency check.

There are two takeaways in this example that are worth emphasizing: the first concerns making economic decisions that are subject to uncertainty. The second is the concept of opportunity cost, which is the topic of the following section.

When making economic decisions that are subject to uncertainty, you may want to take this uncertainty into account by replacing the absolute cash flows with their expected values. A simple probability model for the likely payout is often sufficient. In the magazine example there were just two outcomes: the subscriber renews with probability $\gamma = 0.7$ and value C_{1yr}, or the subscriber does not renew with probability $\gamma = 0.3$ and value 0, hence the expected value is $0.3 \cdot 0 + 0.7 \cdot C_{1yr}$. If your situation warrants it and if you can specify the probability distribution for various payout alternatives in more detail, then you can calculate the expected value accordingly. (See Chapter 8 and Chapter 9 for more information on how to build models to support this kind of conclusion.)

Working with expectation values is convenient, because once you have determined the expected value of the payout, you no longer need to worry about the probabilities for the various outcomes: they have been entirely absorbed into the expectation values. What you lose is insight into the probable spread of outcomes. For a quick order-of-magnitude check, that's acceptable, but for a more serious study, an estimate of the spread should be included. There are two ways to do this: repeat your calculation multiple times using different values (low, medium, high) for the expected payouts at every step to develop a sense for the range of possible outcomes. (If there are many different options, you may want to do this through simulation; see Chapter 12.) Alternatively, you can evaluate both the expectation value and the spread directly from the probability distribution to obtain a range for each estimated value: $\mu \pm \sigma$. Now you can use this sum in your calculations, treating σ as a small perturbation and evaluate the effect of this perturbation on your model (see Chapter 7).

Opportunity Costs

The second point that I would like to emphasize is the concept of *opportunity cost.* Opportunity costs arise when we miss out on some income (the "opportunity") because we were not in a position to take advantage of it. Opportunity costs formalize the notion that resources are finite and that, if we apply them to one purpose, then those resources are not available for other uses. In particular, if we commit resources to a project, then we want that project to generate a benefit greater than the opportunity costs that arise, because those resources are no longer available for other uses.

I find it easiest to think about opportunity cost in the context of certain business situations. For instance, suppose a company takes on a project that pays $15,000. While this contract is under way, someone else offers the company a project that would pay $20,000. Assuming that the company cannot break its initial engagement, it is now incurring an opportunity cost of $5,000.

I find the *concept* of opportunity cost useful as a way to put a price on alternatives, particularly when no money changes hands. In textbooks, this is often demonstrated by the example of the student who takes a trip around the world instead of working at a summer job. Not only does the student have to pay the actual expenses for the trip but also incurs an opportunity cost equal to the amount of forgone wages. The concept of opportunity cost allows us to account for these forgone wages, which would otherwise be difficult because they do not show up on any account statement (since they were never actually paid).

On the other hand, I often find opportunity cost a somewhat shadowy concept because it totally hinges on a competing opportunity actually arising. Imagine you try to decide between two opportunities: an offer for a project that would pay $15,000 and the prospect of a project paying $20,000. If you take the first job and then the second opportunity comes through as well, you are incurring an opportunity cost of $5,000. But if the second project falls through, your opportunity cost just dropped to zero! (The rational way to make this decision would be to calculate the total revenue expected from each prospect but *weighted by the probability* that the contract will actually be signed. This brings us back to calculations involving *expected* payouts, as discussed in the preceding section.)

To be clear: the concept of opportunity cost has nothing to do with uncertainty in planning. It is merely a way to evaluate the relative costs of competing opportunities. However, when evaluating competing deals, we must often decide between plans that have a different likelihood of coming to fruition, and therefore opportunity cost and planning for uncertainty often arise together.

Cost Concepts and Depreciation

The methods described in the previous sections might suggest that the net present value is all there is to financial considerations. This is not so—other factors may influence our decision. Some factors are entirely outside the financial realm (*e.g.*, ethical or strategic considerations); others might have direct business implications but are not sufficiently captured by the quantities we have discussed so far.

For example, let's go back to the situation discussed earlier where we considered the choice between two alternatives: buying a sorting machine or having the same task performed manually. Once we identify all arising costs and discount them properly to their present value, it would seem we have accounted for all financial implications. But that would be wrong: the solution employing manual labor is more flexible, for instance. If the pace of the business varies over the course of the year, then we need to buy a sorting machine that is large enough to handle the busiest season—which means it will be underutilized during the rest of the year. If we rely on manual labor, then we can more flexibly scale capacity up through temporary labor or overtime—and we can likewise respond to unexpectedly strong (or weak) growth of the overall business more flexibly, again by adjusting the number of workers. (This practice may have further consequences—for example, regarding labor relations.) In short, we need to look at the costs, and how they arise, in more detail.

To understand the cost structure of a business or an operation better, it is often useful to discuss it in terms of three pairs of complementary concepts:

1. Direct versus indirect cost

2. Fixed versus variable cost

3. Capital expenditure versus operating cost

For good measure, I'll also throw in the concept of *depreciation*, although it is not a cost in the strict sense of the word.

Direct and Indirect Costs

Labor and materials that are applied in creating the *product* (*i.e.*, in the creation of something the company will *sell*) are considered direct labor or direct materials cost. Indirect costs, on the other hand, arise from activities that the company undertakes to maintain *itself*: management, maintenance, and administrative tasks (payroll and accounting) but also training, for example. Another term for such indirect costs is *overhead*.

I should point out that this is a slightly different definition of direct and indirect costs than the one you will find in the literature. Most textbooks define direct cost as the cost that is "easily attributable" to the production process, whereas indirect cost is "not easily attributable." This definition makes it seem as if the distinction between direct and indirect costs is mostly one of convenience. Furthermore, the textbook definition provides no reason why, for example, maintenance and repair activities are usually considered indirect costs. Surely, we can keep track of which machine needed how much repair and therefore assign the associated cost to the product made on that specific machine. On the other hand, by my definition, it is clear that maintenance should be considered an indirect cost because it is an activity the company undertakes to keep *itself* in good order—not to generate value for the customer.

I have used the term "product" for whatever the company is selling. For manufacturing or retail industries this is a straightforward concept, but for a service industry the "product" may be intangible. Nevertheless, in probably all businesses we can introduce the concept of a single produced unit or *unit of production*. In manufacturing and retail there are actual "units," but in other industries the notion of a produced unit is a bit more artificial: in service industries, for instance, one often uses "billable hours" as a measure of production. Other industries have specialized conventions: the airline industry uses "passenger miles," for example.

The unit is an important concept because it is the basis for the most common measure of productivity—namely the unit cost or *cost per unit* (CPU). The cost per unit is obtained by dividing the total (dollar) amount spent during a time period (per month, for instance) by the total number of units produced during that time. If we include not only the direct cost but also the indirect cost in this calculation, we obtain what is called the *loaded* or *burdened* cost per unit.

We can go further and break out the various contributions to the unit cost. For example, if there are multiple production steps, then we can determine how much each step contributes to the total cost. We can also study how much indirect costs contribute to the overall cost as well as how material costs relate to labor. Understanding the different contributions to the total cost per unit is often a worthwhile exercise because it points directly to where the money is spent. And appearances can be deceiving. I have seen situations where literally hundreds of people were required for a certain processing step whereas, next door, a single person was sufficient to oversee a comparable but highly automated process. Yet once you calculated the cost per unit, it all looked very different: because the number of units going through the automated process was low, its total cost per unit was actually higher than for the manual process. And because so many units where processed manually, their labor cost *per unit* turned out to be very low.

In general, it is desirable to have low overhead relative to the direct cost: a business should spend relatively less time and money on managing itself than on generating value for the customer. In this way, the ratio of direct to indirect cost can be a telling indicator for "top-heavy" organizations that seem mostly occupied with managing themselves. On the other hand, overeager attempts to improve the direct/indirect cost ratio can lead to pretty unsanitary manipulations. For example, imagine a company that considers software engineers *direct* labor, while any form of management (team leads and project managers) is considered *indirect*. The natural consequence is that management responsibilities are pushed onto developers to avoid "indirect" labor. Of course, this does not make these tasks go away; they just become invisible. (It also leads to the inefficient use of a scarce resource: developers are always in short supply—and they are expensive.) In short, beware the danger of perverted incentives!

Fixed and Variable Costs

Compared to the previous distinction (between direct and indirect costs), the distinction between fixed and variable costs is clearer. The *variable* costs are those that change in response to changing demand, while *fixed* costs don't. For a car manufacturer, the cost of steel is a variable cost: if fewer cars are being built, less steel is consumed. Whether labor costs are fixed or variable depends on the type of labor and the employment contracts. But the capital cost for the machines in the production line is a fixed cost, because it has to be paid regardless of whether the machines are busy or idle.

It is important not to confuse direct and variable costs. Although direct costs are more likely to be variable (and overhead, in general, is fixed), these are unrelated concepts; one can easily find examples of fixed, yet direct costs. For example, consider a consultancy with salaried employees: their staff of consultants is a *direct* cost, yet it is also a *fixed* cost because the consultants expect their wages regardless of whether the consultancy has projects for them or not. (We'll see another example in a moment.)

In general, having high fixed costs relative to variable ones makes a business or industry less flexible and more susceptible to downturns. An extreme example is the airline industry: its cost structure is almost exclusively fixed (pretty much the only variable cost is the price of the in-flight meal), but its demand pattern is subject to extreme cyclical swings.

The numbers are interesting. Let's do a calculation in the spirit of Chapter 7. A modern jet airplane costs about $100M new and has a useful service life of about 10 years. The cost attributable to a single 10-hour transatlantic flight (the depreciation—see below) comes to about $30k (*i.e.*, $100M/(10 · 365)—half that, if the plane is turned around immediately, completing a full round-trip within 24 hours). Fuel consumption is about 6 gallons per mile; if we assume a fuel price of $2 per gallon, then the 4,000-mile flight between New York and Frankfurt (Germany) will cost $50k for fuel. Let's say there are 10 members of the cabin crew at $50k yearly salary and two people in the cockpit at $150k each. Double these numbers for miscellaneous benefits, and we end up with about $2M in yearly labor costs, or $10k attributable to this one flight. In contrast, the cost of an in-flight meal (wholesale) is probably less than $10 per person. For a flight with 200 passengers, this amounts to $1,000–2,000 dollars total. It is interesting to see that—all things considered—the influence of the in-flight meal on the overall cost structure of the flight is as high as it is: about 2 percent of the total. In a business with thin margins, improving profitability by 2 percent is usually seen as worthwhile. In other words, we should be grateful that we get *anything* at all! A final cross-check: the cost per passenger for the entire flight from the airline's point of view is $375—and at the time of this writing, the cheapest fare I could find was $600 round-trip, equivalent to $300 for a single leg. As is well known, airlines break even on economy class passengers but don't make any profits.

Capital Expenditure and Operating Cost

Our final distinction is the one between *capital expenditure* (CapEx) and *operating expense* (OpEx—the abbreviation is rarely used). Capital expenses are money spent to purchase long-lived and typically tangible assets: equipment, installations, real estate. Operating expenses are everything else: payments for rents, raw materials, fees, salaries. In most companies, separate budgets exist for both types of expense, and the availability of funds may be quite different for each. For example, in a company that is financially strapped but does have a revenue stream, it might be quite acceptable to hire and "throw people" at a problem (even at great cost), but it might very well be impossible to buy a piece of equipment that would take care of the problem for good. Conversely, in companies that do have money in the bank, it is often *easier* to get a lump sum approved for a specific purchase than to hire more people or to perform maintenance. Decision makers often are more inclined to approve funding for an identifiable and visible purchase than for spending money on "business as usual." Political and vanity considerations may play a role as well.

The distinction between CapEx and operating costs is important because, depending on the availability of funds from either source, different solutions will be seen as feasible. (I refer to such considerations as "color of money" issues—although all dollars are green, some are greener than others!)

In the context of capital expenditure, there is one more concept that I'd like to introduce because it provides an interesting and often useful way of thinking about money: the notion of *depreciation*.[*] The idea is this: any piece of equipment that we purchase will have a useful service life. We can now distribute the total cost of that purchase across the entire life of the asset. For example, if I purchase a car for $24,000 and expect to drive it for 10 years, then I can say that this car costs me $200 per month "in depreciation" alone and before taking into account any operating costs (such as gas and insurance). I may want to compare this number with monthly lease payment options on the same kind of vehicle.

In other words, depreciation is a formalized way of capturing how an asset loses value over time. There are different standard ways to calculate it: "straight-line" distributes the purchase cost (less any *salvage value* that we might expect to obtain for the asset at the end

---

[*] Do not confuse *to depreciate*, which is the process by which an asset loses value over time, with *to deprecate*, which is an expression of disapproval. The latter word is used most often to mark certain parts of a software program or library as *deprecated*, meaning that they should no longer be used in future work.

of its life) evenly over the service life. The "declining balance" method assumes that the asset loses a certain constant fraction of its value every year. And so on. (Interestingly, land is never depreciated—because it does not wear out in the way a machine does and therefore does not have a finite service life.)

I find depreciation a useful concept, because it provides a good way to think about large capital expenses: as an ongoing cost rather than as an occasional lump sum. But depreciation is just that: a way of thinking. It is important to understand that depreciation is *not* a cash flow and therefore does not show up in any sort of financial accounting. What's in the books is the money actually spent, when it is spent.

The only occasion where depreciation is treated as a cash flow is when it comes to taxes. The IRS (the U.S. tax authority) requires that certain long-lived assets purchased for business purposes be depreciated over a number of years, with the annual depreciation counted as a business expense for that year. For this reason, depreciation is usually introduced in conjunction with tax considerations. But I find the concept more generally useful as a way to think about and account for the cost of assets and their declining value over time.

Should You Care?

What does all this talk about money, business plans, and investment decisions have to do with data analysis? Why should you even care?

That depends. If you take a purely technical stance, then all of these questions are outside your area of competence and responsibility. That's a valid position to take, and many practitioners will make exactly that decision.

Personally, I disagree. I don't see it as my job to provide *answers* to *questions*. I see it as my responsibility to provide *solutions* to *problems*, and to do this effectively, I need to understand the context in which questions arise, and I need to understand how answers will be evaluated and used. Furthermore, when it comes to questions having to do with abstract topics like data and mathematical modeling, I have found that few clients are in a good position to ask meaningful questions. *Coaching* the client on what makes a good question (one that is both operational for me and actionable for the client) is therefore a large part of what I do—and to do that, I must understand and speak the client's language.

There are two more reasons why I find it important to understand issues such as those discussed in this (and the previous) chapter: to establish my own *credibility* and to provide advice and counsel on the *mathematical details* involved.

The decision makers—that is, the people who request and use the results of a data analysis study—are "business people." They tend to see decisions as *investment* decisions and thus will evaluate them using the methods and terminology introduced in this chapter. Unless I understand how they will look at my results and unless I can defend my results in those terms, I will be on weak ground—especially since I am supposed to be "the expert." I learned this the hard way: once, while presenting the results of a rather sophisticated and involved analysis, some MBA bully fresh out of business school challenged me with: "OK, now which of these options has the best discounted net cash flow?" I had no idea what he was talking about. I looked like an idiot. That did *not* help my credibility! (No matter how right I was in everything else I was presenting.)

Another reason why I think it is important to understand the concepts in this chapter is that the math can get a little tricky. This is why the standard textbooks resort to large collections of precooked scenarios—which is not only confusing but can become downright misleading if none of them fit exactly and people start combining several of the standard solutions in ad hoc (and probably incorrect) ways. Often the most important skill I bring to the table is basic calculus. In one place I worked for, which was actually staffed by some of the smartest people in the industry, I discovered a problem because people did not fully understand the difference between $1/x$ and $-x$. Of course, if you put it like this, everybody understands the difference. But if you muddy the waters a little bit and present the problem in the business domain setting in which it arose, it's no longer so easy to see the difference. (And I virtually guarantee you that nobody will understand why $1/(1 - x)$ is actually close to $1 - x$ for small x, when $1/x$ is not equal $-x$.)

In my experience, the correct and meaningful application of basic math outside a purely mathematical environment poses a nearly insurmountable challenge even for otherwise very bright people. Understanding exactly what people are trying to do (*e.g.*, in calculating a total rate of return) allows me to help them avoid serious mistakes.

But in the end, I think the most important reason for mastering this material is to be able to understand the *context* in which questions arise and to be able to answer those questions appropriately with a sense for the *purpose* driving the original request.

Is This All That Matters?

In this chapter, we discussed several financial concepts and how to use them when deciding between different business or investment options.

This begs the question: are these the only issues that matter? Should you automatically opt for the choice with the highest net present value and be done with it?

Of course, the short answer is no. Other aspects matter and may even be more important (strategic vision, sustainability, human factors, personal interest, commitment). What makes these factors different is that they are *intangible*. You have to decide on them yourself.

The methods and concepts discussed in this chapter deal specifically and exclusively with the *financial* implications of certain decisions. Those concerns are important—otherwise, you would not even *be* in business. But this focus should not be taken to imply that financial considerations are the *only* ones that matter.

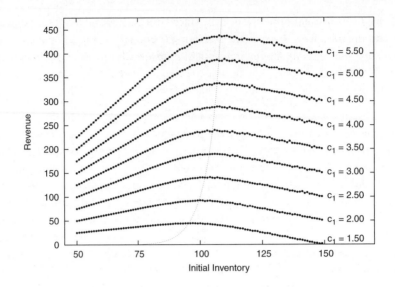

FIGURE 17-2. Simulation results for the newsvendor problem: total revenue as a function of the initial inventory, for several values of the sales price c_1. Also shown is the (theoretical) locus of the initial inventory size that leads to maximum revenue.

However, I am in no better position than you to give advice on ethical questions. It's up to each of us individually—what kind of life do we want to live?

Workshop: The Newsvendor Problem

In this workshop, I'd like to introduce one more idea that is often relevant when dealing with business plans and calculations on how to find the optimal price or, alternatively, the optimal inventory level for some item. The basic problem is often presented in the following terms.

Imagine you run a newsstand. In the morning, you buy a certain number n of newspapers at price c_0. Over the course of the day, you try to sell this inventory at price c_1; anything that isn't sold in the evening is discarded (no salvage value). If you knew how many papers you would actually sell during the course of the day (the *demand m*), then it would be easy: you would buy exactly m papers in the morning. However, the demand is not known exactly, although we know the probability $p(k)$ of selling exactly k copies. The question is: how many papers should you buy in the morning in order to maximize your net earnings (the *revenue*)?

A first guess might be to use the average number of papers that we expect to sell—that is, the mean of $p(k)$. However, this approach may not be good enough: suppose that c_1 is much larger than c_0 (so that your markup is high). In that case, it makes sense to purchase more papers in the hope of selling them, because the gain from selling an additional paper outweighs the loss from having purchased too many. (In other words, the *opportunity cost* that we incur if we have too few papers to satisfy all demand is greater than the cost of purchasing the inventory.) The converse also holds: if the markup is small, then each unsold paper significantly reduces our overall revenue.

This problem lends itself nicely to simulations. The listing that follows shows a minimal program for simulating the newsvendor problem. We fix the purchase price c_0 at $1 and read the projected sales price c_1 from the command line. For the demand, we assume a Gaussian distribution with mean $\mu = 100$ and standard deviation $\sigma = 10$. Now, for each possible initial level of inventory n, we make 1,000 random trials. Each trial corresponds to a single "day"; we randomly generate a level of demand m and calculate the resulting revenue for that day. The revenue consists of the sales price for the number of units that were actually sold *less* the purchase price for the inventory. You should convince yourself that the number of units sold is the lesser of the inventory and the demand: in the first case, we sold out; in the second case, we ended up discarding inventory. Finally, we average all trials for the current level of starting inventory and print the average revenue generated. The results are shown in Figure 17-2 for several different sales prices c_1:

```
from sys import argv
from random import gauss

c0, c1 = 1.0, float( argv[1] )
mu, sigma = 100, 10
maxtrials = 1000

for n in range( mu-5*sigma, mu+5*sigma ):
    avg = 0
    for trial in range( maxtrials ):
        m = int( 0.5 + gauss( mu, sigma ) )
        r = c1*min( n, m ) - c0*n
        avg += r

    print c1, n, avg/maxtrials
```

Of course, the total revenue depends on the actual sales price—the higher the price, the more we take home. But we can also see that, for each value of the sales price, the revenue curve has a maximum at a different horizontal location. The corresponding value of n gives us the optimal initial inventory level for that sales price. Thus we have achieved our objective: we have found the optimal number of newspapers to buy at the beginning of the day to maximize our earnings.

This simple idea can be extended in different ways. More complicated situations may involve *different* types of items, each with its own demand distribution. How much of each item should we hold in inventory now? Alternatively, we can turn the problem around by asking: given a fixed inventory, what would be the optimal *price* to maximize earnings? To answer this question, we need to know how the demand varies as we change the price—that is, we need to know the *demand curve*, which takes the role of the demand distribution in our example.

Optional: Exact Solution

For this particular example, involving only a single type of product at a fixed price, we can actually work out the optimum exactly. (This means that running a simulation wasn't strictly necessary in this case. Nevertheless, this is one of those cases where a simulation may actually be easier to do and less error-prone than an analytical model. For more complicated scenarios, such as those involving different types of items with different demands, simulations are unavoidable.)

To solve this problem analytically, we want to find the optimum of the expected revenue. The revenue—as we already saw in our example simulation program—is given by

$$r(m) = c_1 \min(n, m) - c_0 n$$

The revenue depends on the demand m. However, the demand is a random quantity: all that we know is that it is distributed according to some distribution $p(m)$. The *expected revenue* $E[r(m)]$ is the average of the revenue over all possible values of m, where each value is weighted by the appropriate probability factor:

$$E[r(m)] = \int_0^\infty r(m)\, p(m)\, dm$$

We can now plug in the previous expression for $r(m)$, using the lesser of n and m in the integral:

$$E[r(m)] = c_1 \int_0^n m\, p(m)\, dm + c_1 \int_n^\infty n\, p(m)\, dm - c_0 n \int_0^\infty p(m)\, dm$$

$$= c_1 \int_0^n m\, p(m)\, dm + c_1 n \left(1 - \int_0^n p(m)\, dm\right) - c_0 n$$

where we have made use of the fact that $\int_0^\infty p(m)\, dm = 1$ and that $\int_0^n p(m)\, dm + \int_n^\infty p(m)\, dm = \int_0^\infty p(m)\, dm$.

We now want to find the maximum of the expected revenue with respect to the initial inventory level n. To locate the maximum, we first take the derivative with respect to n:

$$\frac{d}{dn} E[r(m)] = c_1 n\, p(n) + c_1 \left(1 - \int_0^n p(m)\, dm\right) - c_1 n\, p(n) - c_0$$

$$= c_1 - c_0 - c_1 \int_0^n p(m)\, dm$$

where we have used the product rule and the fundamental theorem of calculus: $\frac{d}{dx} \int^x f(s)\, ds = f(x)$.

Next we equate the derivative to zero (that is the condition for the maximum) and rearrange terms to find

$$\int_0^n p(m)\, dm = 1 - \frac{c_0}{c_1}$$

This is the final result. The lefthand side is the *cumulative distribution function* of the demand, and the righthand side is a simple expression involving the ratio of the purchase price and the sales price. Given the cumulative distribution function for the demand, we can now find the value of n for which the cumulative distribution function equals $1 - c_0/c_1$—that value of n is the optimal initial inventory level.

The lighter dotted line in Figure 17-2 shows the location of the optimum revenue obtained by plugging the optimal inventory calculated in this way back into the expression for the revenue. As we would expect, this line goes right through the peaks in all the revenue curves. Notice that the maximum in the revenue curve occurs for $n < 100$ for $c_1 < 2.00$: in other words, our markup has to be at least 100 percent, before it makes sense to hold *more* inventory than the expected average demand. (Remember that we expect to sell 100 papers on average.) If our markup is less than that, then we are better-off selling our inventory out entirely, rather than having to discard some items. (Of course, details such as these depend on the specific choice of the probability distribution $p(m)$ that is used to model the demand.)

Further Reading

If you want to read up on some of the details that I have (quite intentionally) skipped, you should look for material on "engineering economics" or "engineering economic analysis." Some books that I have found useful include the following.

- *Industrial Mathematics: Modeling in Industry, Science and Government.* Charles R. MacCluer. Prentice Hall. 1999.
  In his preface, MacCluer points out that most engineers leaving school "will have no experience with problems incorporating the unit $." This observation was part of the inspiration for this chapter. MacCluer's book contains an overview over many more advanced mathematical techniques that are relevant in practical applications. His choice of topics is excellent, but the presentation often seems a bit aloof and too terse for the uninitiated. (For instance, the material covered in this chapter is compressed into only three pages.)

- *Schaum's Outline of Engineering Economics.* Jose Sepulveda, William Souder, and Byron Gottfried. McGraw-Hill. 1984.
  If you want a quick introduction to the details left out of my presentation, then this inexpensive book is a good choice. Includes many worked examples.

- *Engineering Economy.* William G. Sullivan, Elin M. Wicks, and C. Patrick Koelling. 14th ed., Prentice Hall. 2008.
  Engineering Economic Analysis. Donald Newnan, Jerome Lavelle, and Ted Eschenbach. 10th ed., Oxford University Press. 2009.

Principles of Engineering Economic Analysis. John A. White, Kenneth E. Case, and David B. Pratt. 5th ed., Wiley. 2000.
Three standard, college-level textbooks that treat largely the same material on many more pages.

The Newsvendor Problem

- *Pricing and Revenue Optimization.* Robert Phillips. Stanford Business Books. 2005.
  Finding the optimal price for a given demand is the primary question in the field of "revenue optimization." This book provides an accessible introduction.

- *Introduction to Operations Research.* Frederick S. Hillier and Gerald J. Lieberman. 9th ed., McGraw-Hill. 2009.
  The field of operations research encompasses a set of mathematical methods that are useful for many problems that arise in a business setting, including inventory management. This text is a standard introduction.

## CHAPTER EIGHTEEN

Predictive Analytics

DATA ANALYSIS CAN TAKE MANY DIFFERENT FORMS—NOT ONLY IN THE TECHNIQUES THAT WE APPLY BUT ALSO in the *kind* of results that we ultimately achieve. Looking back over the material that we have covered so far, we see that the results obtained in Part I were mostly *descriptive*: we tried to figure out what the data was telling us and to describe it. In contrast, the results in Part II were primarily *prescriptive*: data was used as a guide for building models which could then be used to infer or prescribe phenomena, including effects that had not actually been observed yet. In this form of analysis, data is not used directly; instead it is used only indirectly to guide (and verify) our intuition when building models. Additionally, as I tried to stress in those chapters, we don't just follow data blindly, but instead we try to develop an understanding of the processes that generate the data and to capture this understanding in the models we develop. The predictive power of such models derives from this *understanding* we develop by studying data and the circumstances in which it is generated.[*]

In this chapter, we consider yet another way to use data—we can call it *predictive*, since the purpose will be to make predictions about future events. What is different is that now we try to make predictions *directly from the data* without necessarily forming the kind of conceptual model (and the associated deeper understanding of the problem domain) as discussed in Part II. This difference is obviously both a strength and a weakness. It's a strength in that it enables us to deal with problems for which we have no hope of developing a conceptual model, given the complexity of the situation. It is also a weakness because we may end up with only a black-box solution and no deeper understanding.

---

[*] The techniques discussed in Part III are different: for the most part they were strictly computational and can be applied to any purpose, depending on the context.

There are technical difficulties also: this form of analysis tends to require huge data sets because we are lacking the consistency and continuity guarantees provided by a conceptual model. (We will come back to this point.)

Topics in Predictive Analytics

The phrase *predictive analytics* is a bit of an umbrella term (others might say: marketing term) for various tasks that share the intent of deriving predictive information directly from data. Three different specific application areas stand out:

Classification or supervised learning
> Assign each record to exactly one of a set of predefined classes. For example, classify credit card transactions as "valid" or "fraudulent." Spam filtering is another example. Classification is considered "supervised," because the classes are known ahead of time and don't need to be inferred from the data. Algorithms are judged on their ability to assign records to the correct class.

Clustering or unsupervised learning
> Group records into clusters, where the size and shape—and often even the number—of clusters is unknown. Clustering is considered "unsupervised," because no information about the clusters is available ahead of the clustering procedure.

Recommendation
> Recommend a suitable item based on past interest or behavior. Recommendation can be seen as a form of clustering, where you start with an anchor and then try to find items that are similar or related to it.

A fourth topic that is sometimes included is time-series forecasting. However, I find that it does not share many characteristics with the other three, so I usually don't consider it part of predictive analytics itself. (We discussed time-series analysis and forecasting in Chapter 4.)

Of the three application areas, classification is arguably the most important and the best developed; the rest of this chapter will try to give an overview over the most important classification algorithms and techniques. We discussed unsupervised learning in Chapter 13 on clustering techniques—and I'll repeat my impression that clustering is more an exploratory than a predictive technique. Recommendations are the youngest branch of predictive analytics and quite different from the other two. (There are at least two major differences. First, on the technical side, many recommendation techniques boil down to network or graph algorithms, which have little in common with the statistical techniques used for classification and clustering. Second, recommendations tend to be *explicitly* about predicting human behavior; this poses additional difficulties not shared by systems that follow strictly deterministic laws.) For these reasons, I won't have much to say about recommendation techniques here.

TABLE 18-1. The confusion matrix for a binary classification problem

	Predicted: A	Predicted: B
Actual: A	Correct	Incorrect
Actual: B	Incorrect	Correct

Let me emphasize that this chapter can serve only as an overview of classification. Entire books could (and have!) been written about it. But we can outline the problem, introduce some terminology, and give the flavor of different solution approaches.

Some Classification Terminology

We begin with a data set containing multiple elements, records, or *instances*. Each instance consists of several *attributes* or *features*. One of the features is special: it denotes the record's *class* and is known as the *class label*. Each record belongs to exactly one class.

A large number of classification problems are binary, consisting only of two classes (valid or fraudulent, spam or not spam); however, multiclass scenarios do also occur. Many classification algorithms can deal only with binary problems, but this is not a real limitation because any multiclass problem can be treated as a *set* of binary problems (belongs to the target class or does belong to any other class).

A *classifier* takes a record (*i.e.*, a set of attribute values) and produces a class label for this record. Building and using a classifier generally follows a three-step process of training, testing, and actual application.

We first split the existing data set into a *training set* and a *test set*. In the training phase, we present each record from the training set to the classification algorithm. Next we compare the class label produced by the algorithm to the true class label of the record in question; then we adjust the algorithm's "parameters" to achieve the greatest possible accuracy or, equivalently, the lowest possible error rate. (Of course, the details of this "fitting" process vary greatly from one algorithm to the next; we will look at different ways of how this is done in the next section.)

The results can be summarized in a so-called *confusion matrix* whose entries are the number of records in each category. (Table 18-1 shows the layout of a generic confusion matrix.)

Unfortunately, the error rate derived from the training set (the *training error*) is typically way too optimistic as an indicator of the error rate the classifier would achieve on new data—that is, on data that was not used during the learning phase. This is the purpose of the test set: after we have optimized the algorithm using *only* the training data, we let the classifier operate on the elements of the test set to see how well it classifies them. The error rate obtained in this way is the *generalization error* and is a much more reliable indicator of the accuracy of the classifier.

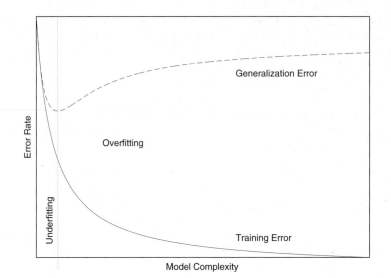

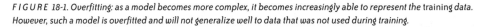

FIGURE 18-1. Overfitting: as a model becomes more complex, it becomes increasingly able to represent the training data. However, such a model is overfitted and will not generalize well to data that was not used during training.

To understand the need for a separate testing phase (using a separate data set!), keep in mind that as long as we use enough parameters (*i.e.*, making the classifier more and more complex) we can always tweak a classifier until it works very well on the training set. But in doing so, we train the classifier to memorize every aspect of the training set, including those that are atypical for the system in general. We therefore need to find the right level of complexity for the classifier. On the one hand, if it is too simple, then it cannot represent the desired behavior very well, and both its training and generalization error will be poor; this is known as *underfitting*. On the other hand, if we make the classifier too complex, then it will perform very well on the training set (low training error) but will not generalize well to unknown data points (high generalization error); this is known as *overfitting*. Figure 18-1 summarizes these concepts.

Once a classifier has been developed and tested, it can be used to classify truly new and unknown data points—that is, data points for which the correct class label is not known. (This is in contrast to the test set, where the class labels were known but not used by the classifier when making a prediction.)

Algorithms for Classification

At least half a dozen different families of classification algorithms have been developed. In this section, we briefly characterize the basic idea underlying each algorithm, emphasizing how it differs from competing methods. The first two algorithms (nearest-neighbor and Bayesian classifiers) are simpler, both technically and conceptually, than the other; I discuss them in more detail since you may want to implement them yourself. For the other algorithms, you probably want to use existing libraries instead!

Instance-Based Classifiers and Nearest-Neighbor Methods

The idea behind instance-based classifiers is dead simple: to classify an unknown instance, find an existing instance that is "most similar" to the new instance and assign the class label of the known instance to the new one!

This basic idea can be generalized in a variety of ways. First of all, the notion of "most similar" brings us back to the notion of distance and similarity measures introduced in Chapter 13; obviously we have considerable flexibility in the choice of which distance measure to use. Furthermore, we don't have to stop at a single "most similar" existing instance. We might instead take the nearest k neighbors and use them to classify the new instance, typically by using a majority rule (*i.e.*, we assign the new instance to the class that occurs most often among the k neighbors). We could even employ a weighted-majority rule whereby "more similar" neighbors contribute more strongly than those farther away.

Instance-based classifiers are atypical in that they don't have a separate "training" phase; for this reason, they are also known as "lazy learners." (The only adjustable parameter is the extent k of the neighborhood used for classification.) However, a (possibly large) set of known instances must be kept available during the final application phase. For the same reason, classification can be relatively expensive because the set of existing instances must be searched for appropriate neighbors.

Instance-based classifiers are *local*: they do not take the overall distribution of points into account. Additionally, they impose no particular shape or geometry on the decision boundaries that they generate. In this sense they are especially flexible. On the other hand, the are also susceptible to noise.

Finally, instance-based classifiers depend on the proper choice of distance measure, much as clustering algorithms do. We encountered this situation before, when we discussed the need for scale normalization in Chapters 13 and 14; the same considerations apply here as well.

Bayesian Classifiers

A Bayesian classifier takes a probabilistic (*i.e.*, nondeterministic) view of classification. Given a set of attributes, it calculates the *probability* of the instance to belong to this or that class. An instance is then assigned the class label with the highest probability.

A Bayesian classifier calculates a *conditional* probability. This is the probability of the instance to belong to a specific class C, *given* the set of attribute values:

$$P(\text{class } C \,|\, \{x_1, x_2, x_3, \dots, x_n\})$$

Here C is the class label, and the set of attribute values is $\{x_1, x_2, x_3, \ldots, x_n\}$. Note that we don't yet know the value of the probability—if we did, we'd be finished.

To make progress, we invoke Bayes' theorem (hence the name of the classifier—see also Chapter 10 for a discussion of Bayes' theorem) to invert this probability expression as follows:

$$P(\text{class } C \mid \{x_i\}) = \frac{P(\{x_i\} \mid \text{class } C) \cdot P(\text{class } C)}{P(\{x_i\})}$$

where I have collapsed the set of n features into $\{x_i\}$ for brevity.

The first term in the numerator (the likelihood) is the probability of observing a set of features $\{x_i\}$ *if* the instance belongs to class C (in the language of conditional probability: *given* the class label C). We can find an empirical value for this probability from the set of training instances: it is simply the frequency with which we observe the set of specific attribute values $\{x_i\}$ among instances belonging to class C. Empirically, we can approximate this distribution by a set of *histograms* of the $\{x_i\}$, one for each class label. The second term in the numerator, $P(\text{class } C)$, is the prior probability of any instance belonging to class C. We can estimate this probability from the fraction of instances in the training set that belong to class C. The denominator does not depend on the class label and—as usual with Bayesian computations—is ignored until the end, when the probabilities are normalized.

Through the use of Bayes' theorem, we have been able to express the probability for an instance to belong to class C, given a set of features, entirely through expressions that can be determined from the training set.

At least in theory. In practice, it will be almost impossible to evaluate this probability directly. Look closely at the expression (now written again in its long form), $P(\{x_1, x_2, x_3, \ldots, x_n\} \mid \text{class } C)$. For each possible combination of attribute values, we must have enough examples in our training set to be able to evaluate their frequency with some degree of reliability. This is a combinatorial nightmare! Assume that each feature is binary (*i.e.*, it can take on one of only two values). The number of possible combinations is then 2^n, so for $n = 5$ we already have 32 different combinations. Let's say we need about 20 example instances for each possible combination in order to evaluate the frequency, then we'll need a training set of at least 600 instances. In practice, the problem tends to be worse because features frequently can take more than two values, the number of features can easily be larger than five, and—most importantly—some combinations of features occur much less frequently than others. We therefore need a training set large enough to guarantee that even the least-frequent attribute combination occurs sufficiently often.

In short, the "brute force" approach of evaluating the likelihood function for all possible feature combinations is not feasible for problems of realistic size. Instead, one uses one of two simplifications.

The *naive Bayesian classifier* assumes that all features are independent of each other, so that we can write:

$$P(\{x_1, x_2, x_3, \ldots, x_n\} \,|\, C) = P(x_1|C)P(x_2|C)P(x_3|C) \cdots P(x_n|C)$$

This simplifies the problem greatly, because now we need only determine the frequencies for each attribute value for a *single* attribute at a time. In other words, each probability distribution $P(x_i|C)$ is given as the histogram of a single feature x_i, separately for each class label. Despite their simplicity, naive Bayesian classifiers are often surprisingly effective. (Many spam filters work this way.)

Another idea is to use a *Bayesian network*. Here we prune the set of all possible feature combinations by retaining only those that have a causal relationship with each other.

Bayesian networks are best discussed through an example. Suppose we want to build a classifier that predicts whether we will be late to work in the morning, based on three binary features:

- Alarm clock went off: Yes or No
- Left the house on time: Yes or No
- Traffic was bad: Yes or No

Although we don't assume that *all* features are independent (as we did for the naive Bayesian classifier), we do observe that the traffic situation is independent of the other two features. Furthermore, whether we leave the house on time does depend on the proper working of the alarm clock. In other words, we can split the full probability:

P(Arrive on time | Alarm clock, Leave on time, Traffic)

into the following combination of events:

P(Arrive on time | Leave on time)
P(Leave on time | Alarm clock)
P(Arrive on time | Traffic)

Notice that only two of the terms give the probability for the class label ("Arrive on time") and that one gives the probability of an intermediate event (see Figure 18-2).

For such a small example (containing only three features), the savings compared with maintaining all feature combinations are not impressive. But since the number of combinations grows exponentially with the number of features, restricting our attention to only those factors that have a causal relationship with each other can significantly reduce the number of combinations we need to retain for larger problems.

The structure (or *topology*) of a Bayesian network is usually not inferred from the data; instead, we use domain knowledge to determine which pathways to keep. This is exactly

All Combinations

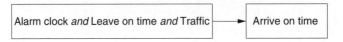

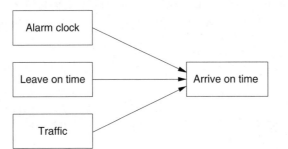

Naive Bayesian

Bayesian Network

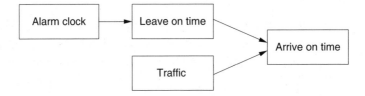

F I G U R E 18-2. The structure of different Bayesian classifiers.

what we did in the example: we "knew" that traffic conditions were independent of the situation at home and used this knowledge to prune the network accordingly.

There are some practical issues that need to be addressed when building Bayesian classifiers. The description given here silently assumes that all attributes are categorical (*i.e.*, take on only a discrete set of values). Attributes that take on continuous numerical values either need to be discretized, or we need to find the probability $P(\{x_i\} | C)$ through a kernel density estimate (see Chapter 2) for all the points in class C in the training set. If the training set is large, the latter process may be expensive.

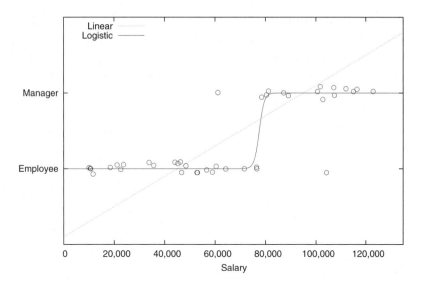

F I G U R E 18-3. Using regression for classification: the data points show the they employee type (employee or manager) as a function of the salary; managers tend to have higher salaries. (Data points are jittered in the vertical direction to avoid overplotting.)

Another tricky detail concerns attribute values that do not occur in the training set: the corresponding probability is 0. But a naive Bayesian classifier consists of a product of probabilities and therefore becomes 0 as soon as a single term is 0! In particular with small training sets, this is a problem to watch out for. On the other hand, naive Bayesian classifiers are robust with regard to *missing* features: when information about an attribute value is unknown for some of the instances, the corresponding probability simply evaluates to 1 and does not affect the final result.

Regression

Sometimes we have reason to believe that there is a functional relationship between the class label and the set of features. For example, we might assume that there is some relationship between an employee's salary and his status (employee or manager). See Figure 18-3.

If it is reasonable to assume a functional relationship, then we can try to build a classifier based on this relationship by "fitting" an appropriate function to the data. This turns the classification problem into a *regression* problem.

However, as we can see in Figure 18-3, a linear function is usually not very appropriate because it takes on all values, whereas class labels are discrete. Instead of fitting a straight line, we need something like a step function: a function that is 0 for points belonging to the one class, and 1 for points belonging to the other class. Because of its discontinuity, the step function is hard to work with; hence one typically uses the logistic function (see Appendix B) as a smooth approximation to the step function. The logistic function gives this technique its name: *logistic regression*. Like all regression methods, it is a global technique that tries to optimize a fit over all points and not just over a particularly relevant subset.

Logistic regression is not only important in practical applications but has deep roots in theoretical statistics as well. Until the arrival of support vector machines, it was the method of choice for many classification problems.

Support Vector Machines

Support vector machines are a relative newcomer among classification methods. The name is a bit unfortunate: there is nothing particularly "machine-y" about them. They are, in fact, based on a simple geometrical construction.

Consider training instances in a two-dimensional feature space like the one in Figure 18-4. Now we are looking for the "best" dividing line (or *decision boundary*) that separates instances belonging to one class from instances belonging to the other.

We need to decide what we mean by "best." The answer given by support vector machines is that the "best" dividing line is one that has the largest *margin*. The margin is the space, parallel to the decision boundary, that is free of any training instances. Figure 18-4 shows two possible decision boundaries and their respective margins. Although this example is only two-dimensional, the reasoning generalizes directly to higher dimensions. In such cases, the decision boundary becomes a hyperplane, and support vector machines therefore find the *maximum margin hyperplanes* (a term you might find in the literature).

I will not go through the geometry and algebra required to construct a decision boundary from a data set, since you probably don't want to implement it yourself, anyway. (The construction is not difficult, and if you have some background in analytic geometry, you will be able to do it yourself or look it up elsewhere.) The important insight is that support vector machines turn the task of finding a decision boundary first into the geometric task of constructing a line (or hyperplane) from a set of points (this is an elementary task in analytic geometry). The next step—find the decision boundary with the largest margin—is then just a multi-dimensional optimization problem, with a particularly simple and well-behaved objective function (namely, the square of the distance of each point from the decision boundary), for which good numerical algorithms exist.

One important property of support vector machines is that they perform a strict global optimization without having to rely on heuristics. Because of the nature of the objective function, the algorithm is guaranteed to find the global optimum, not merely a local one. On the other hand, the final solution does not depend on all points; instead it depends only on those closest to the decision boundary, points that lie right on the edge of the margin. (These are the *support vectors*, see Figure 18-4.) This means that the decision

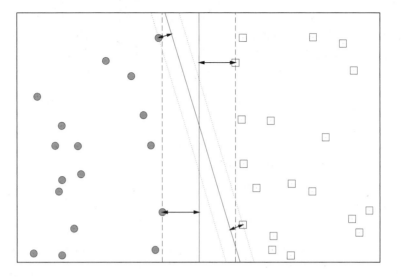

FIGURE 18-4. Two decision boundaries and their margins. Note that the vertical decision boundary has a wider margin than the other one. The arrows indicate the distance between the respective support vectors and the decision boundary.

boundary depends only on instances close to it and is not influenced by system behavior far from the decision boundary. However, the global nature of the algorithm implies that, for those support vectors, the optimal hyperplane will be found!

Two generalizations of this basic concept are of great practical importance. First, consider Figure 18-4 again. We were lucky that we could find a straight line (in fact, more than one) to separate the data points exactly into two classes, so that both decision boundaries shown have zero training error. In practice, it is not guaranteed that we will always find such a decision boundary, and there may be some stray instances that cannot be classified correctly by any straight-line decision boundary. More generally, it may be advantageous to have a few misclassified training instances—in return for a much wider margin— because it is reasonable to assume that a larger margin will lead to a lower generalization error later on. In other words, we want to find a balance between low training error and large margin size. This can be done by introducing *slack variables*. Basically, they associate a cost with each misclassified instance, and we then try to solve the extended optimization problem, in which we try to minimize the cost of misclassified instances while at the same time trying to maximize the margins.

The other important generalization allows us to use curves other than straight lines as decision boundaries. This is usually achieved through *kernelization* or the "kernel trick." The basic idea is that we can replace the dot product between two vectors (which is central to the geometric construction required to find the maximum margin hyperplane) with a more general function of the two vectors. As long as this function meets certain requirements (you may find references to "Mercer's theorem" in the literature), it can be shown that all the previous arguments continue to hold.

One disadvantage of support vector machines is that they lead to especially opaque results: they truly are black boxes. The final classifier may work well in practice, but it does not shed much light on the nature of the problem. This is in contrast to techniques such as regression or decision trees (see the next section), which often lead to results that can be interpreted in some form. (In regression problems, for instance, one can often see which attributes are the most influential ones, and which are less relevant.)

Decision Trees and Rule-Based Classifiers

Decision trees and rule-based classifiers are different from the classifiers discussed so far in that they do not require a distance measure. For this reason, they are sometimes referred to as *nonmetric classifiers*.

Decision trees consist of a hierarchy of decision points (the nodes of the tree). When using a decision tree to classify an unknown instance, a single feature is examined at each node of the tree. Based on the value of that feature, the next node is selected. Leaf nodes on the tree correspond to classes; once we have reached a leaf node, the instance in question is assigned the corresponding class label. Figure 18-5 shows an example of a simple decision tree.

The primary algorithm (*Hunt's algorithm*) for deriving a decision tree from a training set employs a greedy approach. The algorithm is easiest to describe when all features are categorical and can take only one of two values (binary attributes). If this is the case, then the algorithm proceeds as follows:

1. For each instance in the training set, examine each feature in turn.

2. Split the training instances into two subsets based on the value of the current feature.

3. Select the feature that results in the "purest" subsets; the value of this attribute will be the decision condition employed by the current node.

4. Repeat this algorithm recursively on the two subsets until the resulting subsets are sufficiently pure.

To make this concrete, we must be able to measure the *purity* of a set. Let f_C be the fraction of instances in the set belonging to class C. Obviously, if $f_C = 1$ for any class label C, then the set is totally pure because all of its elements belong to the same class. We can therefore define the a purity of a set as the frequency of its most common constituent. (For example, if a set consists of 60 percent of items from class A, 30 percent from class B, and 10 percent from class C, then its purity is 60 percent.) This is not the only way to define purity. Other ways of measuring it are acceptable provided they reach a maximum when all elements of a set belong to the same class and reach a minimum when the elements of the set are distributed uniformly across classes.

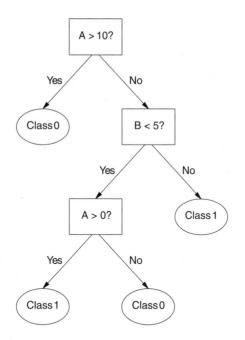

FIGURE 18-5. A very simple decision tree.

Another important quantity related to decision trees is the *gain ratio* Δ from a parent node to its children. This quantity measures the gain in purity from parent to children, weighted by the relative size of the subsets:

$$\Delta = I(\text{parent}) - \sum_{\text{children } j} \frac{N_j}{N} I(\text{child } j)$$

where I is the purity (or impurity) of a node, N_j is the number of elements assigned to child node j, and N is the total number of elements at the parent node. We want to find a splitting that maximizes this gain ratio.

What I have described so far is the outline of the basic algorithm. As with all greedy algorithms, there is no guarantee that it will find the optimal solution, and therefore various heuristics play a large role to ensure that the solution is as good as possible. Hence the various published (and proprietary) algorithms for decision trees (you may find references to CART, C4.5, and ID3) differ in such details such as the following:

- What choice of purity/impurity measure is used?

- At what level of purity does the splitting procedure stop? (Continuing to split a training set until all leaf nodes are entirely pure usually results in overfitting.)

- Is the tree binary, or can a node have more than two children?

- How should noncategorical attributes be treated? (For attributes that take on a continuum of values, we need to define the optimal splitting point.)

- Is the tree postprocessed? (To reduce overfitting, some algorithms employ a pruning step that attempts to eliminate leaf nodes having too few elements.)

Decision trees are popular and combine several attractive features: with good algorithms, decision trees are relatively cheap to build and are always very fast to evaluate. They are also rather robust in the presence of noise. It can even be instructive to examine the decision points of a decision tree, because they frequently reveal interesting information about the distribution of class labels (such as when 80 percent of the class information is contained in the topmost node). However, algorithms for building decision trees are almost entirely black-box and do not lend themselves to ad hoc modifications or extensions.

There is an equivalence between decision trees and *rule-based classifiers*. The latter consist of a set of rules (*i.e.*, logical conditions on attribute values) that, when taken in aggregate, determine the class label of a test instance. There are two ways to build a rule-based classifier. We can build a decision tree first and then transform each complete path through the decision tree into a single rule. Alternatively, we can build rule-based classifiers directly from a training set by finding a subset of instances that can be described by a simple rule. These instances are then removed from the training set, and the process is repeated. (This amounts to a bottom-up approach, whereas using a variant of Hunt's algorithm to build a decision-tree follows a top-down approach.)

Other Classifiers

In addition to the classifiers discussed so far, you will find others mentioned in the literature. I'll name just two—mostly because of their historical importance.

Fisher's linear discriminant analysis (LDA) was one of the first classifiers developed. It is similar to principal component analysis (see Chapter 14). Whereas in PCA, we introduce a new coordinate system to maximize the spread along the new coordinates axes, in LDA we introduce new coordinates to maximize the separation between two classes that we try to distinguish. The position of the means, calculated separately for each class, are taken as the location of each class.

Artificial neural networks were conceived as extremely simplified models for biological brains. The idea was to have a network of nodes; each node receives input from several other nodes, forms a weighted average of its input, and then sends it out to the next layer of nodes. During the learning stage, the weights used in the weighted average are adjusted to minimize training error. Neural networks were very popular for a while but have recently fallen out of favor somewhat. One reason is that the calculations required are more complicated than for other classifiers; another is that the whole concept is very ad hoc and lacks a solid theoretical grounding.

The Process

In addition to the primary algorithms for classification, various techniques are important for dealing with practical problems. In this section, we look at some standard methods commonly used to enhance accuracy—especially for the important case when the most "interesting" type of class occurs much less frequently than the other types.

Ensemble Methods: Bagging and Boosting

The term *ensemble methods* refers to a set of techniques for improving accuracy by combining the results of individual or "base" classifiers. The rationale is the same as when performing some experiment or measurement multiple times and then averaging the results: as long as the experimental runs are independent, we can expect that errors will cancel and that the average will be more accurate than any individual trial. The same logic applies to classification techniques: as long as the individual base classifiers are independent, combining their results will lead to cancellation of errors and the end result will have greater accuracy than the individual contributions.

To generate a set of independent classifiers, we have to introduce some randomness into the process by which they are built. We can manipulate virtually any aspect of the overall system: we can play with the selection of training instances (as in bagging and boosting), with the selection of features (often in conjunction with random forests), or with parameters that are specific to the type of classifier used.

Bagging is an application of the bootstrap idea (see Chapter 12) to classification. We generate additional training sets by sampling with replacement from the original training set. Each of these training sets is then used to train a separate classifier instance. During production, we let each of these instances provide a separate assessment for each item we want to classify. The final class label is then assigned based on a majority vote or similar technique.

Boosting is another technique to generate additional training sets using a bootstrap approach. In contrast to bagging, boosting is an iterative process that assigns higher weights to instances misclassified in previous rounds. As the iteration progresses, higher emphasis is placed on training instances that have proven hard to classify correctly. The final result consists of the aggregate result of all base classifiers generated during the iteration. A popular variant of this technique is known as "AdaBoost."

Random forests apply specifically to decision trees. In this technique, randomness is introduced not by sampling from the training set but by randomly choosing what features to use when building the decision tree. Instead of examining all features at every node to find the feature that gives the greatest gain ratio, only a subset of features is evaluated for each tree.

Estimating Prediction Error

Earlier, we already talked about the difference between the training and the generalization error: the training error is the final error rate that the classifier achieves on the training set. It is usually not a good measure for the accuracy of the classifier on *new* data (*i.e.*, on data that was not used to train the classifier). For this reason, we hold some of the data back during training, and use it later as a test set. The error that the classifier achieves on this test set is a much better measure for the generalization error that we can expect when using the classifier on entirely new data.

If the original data set is very large, there is no problem in splitting it into a training and a test set. In reality, however, available data sets are always "too small," so that we need to make sure we use the available data most efficiently, using a process known as *cross-validation*.

The basic idea is that we randomly divide the original data set into k equally sized chunks. We then perform k training and test runs. In each run, we omit one of the chunks from the training set and instead use it as the test set. Finally, we average the generalization errors from all k runs to obtain the overall expected generalization error.

A value of $k = 10$ is typical, but you can also use a value like $k = 3$. Setting $k = n$, where n is the number of available data points, is special: in this so-called "leave-one-out" cross-validation, we train the classifier on all data points except one and then try to predict the omitted data point—this procedure is then repeated for all data points. (This prescription is similar to the jackknife process that was mentioned briefly in Chapter 12.)

Yet another method uses the idea of random sampling *with replacement*, which is characteristic of bootstrap techniques (see Chapter 12). Instead of dividing the available data into k nonoverlapping chunks, we generate a bootstrap sample by drawing n data points with replacement from the original n data points. This bootstrap sample will contain some of the data points more than once, and some not at all: overall, the fraction of the unique data points included in the bootstrap sample will be about $1 - e^{-1} \approx 0.632$ of the available data points—for this reason, the method is often known as the *0.632 bootstrap*. The bootstrap sample is used for training, and the data points not included in the bootstrap sample become the test set. This process can be repeated several times, and the results averaged as for cross-validation, to obtain the final estimate for the generalization error.

(By the way, this is basically the "unique visitor" problem that we discussed in Chapters 9 and 12—after n days (draws) with one random visitor each day (one data point selected per draw), we will have seen $1 - e^{-\frac{1}{n}n} = 1 - e^{-1}$ unique visitors (unique data points).)

	Predicted: *Bad*	Predicted: *Good*
Actually: *Bad*	True positive: "Hit"	False negative: "Miss"
Actually: *Good*	False positive: "False alarm"	True negative: "Correct rejection"

Class Imbalance Problems

A special case of particular importance concerns situations where one of the classes occurs much less frequently than any of the other classes in the data set—and, as luck would have it, that's usually the class we are interested in! Consider credit card fraud detection, for instance: only one of every hundred credit card transactions may be fraudulent, but those are exactly the ones we are interested in. Screening lab results for patients with elevated heart attack risk or inspecting manufactured items for defects falls into the same camp: the "interesting" cases are rare, perhaps extremely rare, but those are precisely the cases that we want to identify.

For cases like this, there is some additional terminology as well as some special techniques for overcoming the technical difficulties. Because there is one particular class that is of greater interest, we refer to an instance belonging to this class as a *positive event* and the class itself as the *positive class*. With this terminology, entries in the confusion matrix (see Table 18-1) are often referred to as true (or false) positives (or negatives).

I have always found this terminology very confusing, in part because what is called "positive" is usually something *bad*: a fraudulent transaction, a defective item, a bad heart. Table 18-2 shows a confusion matrix employing the special terminology for problems with a class imbalance—and also an alternative terminology that may be more intuitive.

The two different types of errors may have very different costs associated with them. From the point of view of a merchant accepting credit cards as payment, a false negative (*i.e.*, a fraudulent transaction incorrectly classified as "not fraudulent"—a "miss") results in the total loss of the item purchased, whereas a false positive (a valid transaction incorrectly classified as "not valid"—a "false alarm") results only in the loss of the profit margin on that item.

The usual metrics by which we evaluate a classifier (such as accuracy and error rate), may not be very meaningful in situations with pronounced class imbalances: keep in mind that the trivial classifier that labels *every* credit card transaction as "valid" is 99 percent accurate—and entirely useless! Two metrics that provide better insight into the ability of a classifier to detect instances belonging to the positive class are *recall* and *precision*. The precision is the fraction of correct classifications among all instances labeled positive; the

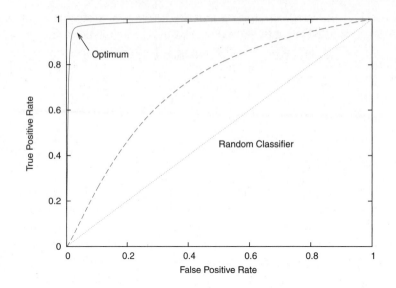

FIGURE 18-6. A ROC (receiver operating characteristic) curve: the trade-off between true positives ("hits") and false positives ("false alarms"), for three different classifier implementations.

recall is the fraction of correct classifications among all instances labeled negative:

$$\text{precision} = \frac{\text{true positives}}{\text{true positives} + \text{false positives}}$$

$$\text{recall} = \frac{\text{true positives}}{\text{true positives} + \text{false negatives}}$$

You can see that we will need to strike a balance. On the one hand, we can build a classifier that is very aggressive, labeling many transactions as "bad," but it will have a high false-positive rate, and therefore low precision. On the other hand, we can build a classifier that is highly selective, marking only those instances that are blatantly fraudulent as "bad," but it will have a high rate of false negatives and therefore low recall. These two competing goals (to have few false positives and few false negatives) can be summarized in a graph known as a *receiver operating characteristic* (ROC) curve. (The concept originated in signal processing, where it was used to describe the ability of a receiver to distinguish a true signal from a spurious one in the presence of noise, hence the name.)

Figure 18-6 shows an example of a ROC curve. Along the horizontal axis, we plot the false positive rate (good events that were labeled as bad—"false alarms") and along the vertical axis we plot the true positive rate (bad events labeled as bad—"hits"). The lower-left corner corresponds to a maximally conservative classifier, which labels every instance as good; the upper-right corner corresponds to a maximally aggressive classifier, which labels everything as bad. We can now imagine tuning the parameters and thresholds of our classifier to shift the balance between "misses" and "false alarms" and thereby mapping out the characteristic curve for our classifier. The curve for a random classifier (which assigns a positive class label with fixed probability p, irrespective of attribute values) will be close to the diagonal: it is equally likely to classify a good instance as good as it is to classify a bad one as good, hence its false positive rate equals its true positive rate. In contrast, the ideal classifier would have a true positive rate equal to 1 throughout. We want to tune our classifier so that it approximates the ideal classifier as nearly as possible.

Class imbalances pose some technical issues during the training phase: if positive instances are extremely rare, then we want to make sure to retain as much of their information as possible in the training set. One way to achieve this is by oversampling (*i.e.*, resampling) from the positive class instances—and undersampling from the negative class instances—when generating a training set.

The Secret Sauce

All this detail about different algorithms and processes can easily leave the impression that that's all there is to classification. That would be unfortunate, because it leaves out what can be the most important but also the most difficult part of the puzzle: finding the right attributes!

The choice of attributes matters for successful classification—arguably more so than the choice of classification algorithm. Here is an interesting case story. Paul Graham has written two essays on using Bayesian classifiers for spam filtering.[*] In the second one, he describes how using the information contained in the email *headers* is critical to obtaining good classification results, whereas using only information in the *body* is not enough. The punch line here is clear: in practice, it matters a lot which features or attributes you choose to include.

Unfortunately, when compared with the extremely detailed information available on different classifier algorithms and their theoretical properties, it is much more difficult to find good guidance regarding how best to choose, prepare, and encode features for classification. (None of the current books on classification discuss this topic at all.)

I think there are several reasons for this relative lack of easily available information—despite the importance of the topic. One of them is lack of rigor: whereas one can prove rigorous theorems on classification algorithms, most recommendations for feature preparation and encoding would necessarily be empirical and heuristic. Furthermore, every problem domain is different, which makes it difficult to come up with recommendations that would be applicable more generally. The implication is that factors such as experience, familiarity with the problem domain, and lots of time-consuming trial and error are essential when choosing attributes for classification. (A last reason for the

---

[*] "A Plan for Spam" (*http://www.paulgraham.com/spam.html*) and "Better Bayesian Filtering" (*http://www.paulgraham.com/better.html*).

relative lack of available information on this topic may be that some prefer to keep their cards a little closer to their chest: they may tell you how it works "in theory," but they won't reveal all the tricks of the trade necessary to fully replicate the results.)

The difficulty of developing some recommendations that work in general and for a broad range of application domains may also explain one particular observation regarding classification: the apparent scarcity of spectacular, well-publicized successes. Spam filtering seems to be about the only application that clearly works and affects many people directly. Credit card fraud detection and credit scoring are two other widely used (if less directly visible) applications. But beyond those two, I see only a host of smaller, specialized applications. This suggests again that every successful classifier implementation depends strongly on the details of the particular problem—probably more so than on the choice of algorithm.

The Nature of Statistical Learning

Now that we have seen some of the most commonly used algorithms for classification as well as some of the related practical techniques, it's easy to feel a bit overwhelmed—there seem to be so many different approaches (each nontrivial in its own way) that it can be hard to see the commonalities among them: the "big picture" is easily lost. So let's step back for a moment and reflect on the specific challenges posed by classification problems and on the overall strategy by which the various algorithms overcome these challenges.

The crucial problem is that from the outset, we don't have good insight into which features are the most relevant in predicting the class—in fact, we may have no idea at all about the processes (if any!) that link observable features to the resulting class. Because we don't know ahead of time which features are likely to be most important, we need to retain them all and perhaps even expand the feature set in an attempt to include any possible clue we can get. In this way, the problem quickly becomes very multi-dimensional. That's the first challenge.

But now we run into a problem: multi-dimensional data sets are invariably *sparse* data sets. Think of a histogram with (say) 5 bins per dimension. In one dimension, we have 5 bins total. If we want on average at least 5 items per bin, we can make do with 25 items total. Now consider the same data set in two dimensions. If we still require 5 bins per dimension, we have a total of 25 bins, so that each bin contains on average only a single element. But it is in three dimensions that the situation becomes truly dramatic: now there are 125 bins, so we can be sure that the majority of bins will contain *no* element at all! It gets even worse in higher dimensions. (Mathematically speaking, the problem is that the number of bins grows exponentially with the number of dimensions: N^d, where d is the number of dimensions and N is the number of bins per dimension. No matter what you do, the number of cells is going to grow faster than you can obtain data. This problem is known as the *curse of dimensionality*.) That's the second challenge.

It is this combinatorial explosion that drives the need for larger and larger data sets. We have just seen that the the number of possible attribute value combinations grows exponentially; therefore, if we want to have a reasonable chance of finding at least one instance of each possible combination in our training data, we need to have very large data sets indeed. Yet despite our best efforts, we will frequently end up with a sparse data set (as discussed above). Nevertheless, we will often deal with inconveniently large data sets. That's the third challenge.

Basically all classification algorithms deal with these challenges by using some form of *interpolation* between points in the sparse data set. In other words, they attempt to smoothly fill the gaps left in the high-dimensional feature space, supported only by a (necessarily sparse) set of points (*i.e.*, the training instances).

Different algorithms do this in different ways: nearest-neighbor methods and naive Bayesian classifiers explicitly "smear out" the training instances to fill the gaps locally, whereas regression and support vector classifiers construct global structures to form a smooth decision boundary from the sparse set of supporting points. Decision trees are similar to nearest-neighbor methods in this regard but provide a particularly fast and efficient lookup of the most relevant neighbors. Their differences aside, all algorithms aim to fill the gaps between the existing data points in some smooth, consistent way.

This brings us to the question of what can actually be predicted in this fashion. Obviously, class labels must depend on attribute values, and they should do so in some smooth, predictable fashion. If the relationship between attribute values and class labels is too crazy, no classifier will be very useful.

Furthermore, the distribution of attribute values for different classes must *differ*, for otherwise no classifier will be able to distinguish classes by examining the attribute values.

Unfortunately, there is—to my knowledge—no independent, rigorous way of determining whether the information contained in a data set is sufficient to allow the data to be classified. To find out, we must build an actual classifier. If it works, then obviously there *is* enough information in the data set for classification. But if it does *not* work, we have learned nothing, because it is always possible that a different or more sophisticated classifier *would* work. But without an independent test, we can spend an infinite amount of time building and refining classifiers on data sets that contain no useful information. We encountered this kind of difficulty already in Chapter 13 in the context of clustering algorithms, but it strikes me as even more of a problem here. The reason is that classification is by nature predictive (or at least should be), whereas uncertainty of this sort seems more acceptable in an exploratory technique such as clustering.

To make this more clear, suppose we have a large, rich data set: many records with many features. We then arbitrarily assign class labels A and B to the records in the data set. Now, by construction, it is clear that there is no way to predict the labels from the "data"—they are, after all, purely random! However, there is no unambiguous test that will clearly say so. We can calculate the correlation coefficients between each feature (or combination of features) and the class label, we can look at the distribution of feature values and see whether they differ from class to class, and so eventually convince ourselves that we won't be able to build a good classifier given this data set. But there is no clear test or diagnostic that would give us, for instance, an upper bound on the quality of any classifier that could be built based on this data set. If we are not careful, we may spend a lot of time vainly attempting to build a classifier capable of extracting useful information from this data set. This kind of problem is a trap to be aware of!

Workshop: Two Do-It-Yourself Classifiers

With classification especially, it is really easy to end up with a black-box solution: a tool or library that provides an implementation of a classification algorithm—but one that we would not be able to write ourselves if we had to. This kind of situation always makes me a bit uncomfortable, especially if the algorithms require any parameter tuning to work properly. In order to adjust such parameters intelligently, I need to understand the algorithm well enough that I could at least provide a rough-cut version myself (much as I am happy to rely on the library designer for the high-performance version).

In this spirit, instead of discussing an existing classification library, I want to show you how to write straightforward (you might say "toy version") implementations for two simple classifiers: a nearest-neighbor lazy learner and a naive Bayesian classifier. (I'll give some pointers to other libraries near end of the section.)

We will test our implementations on *the* classic data set in all of classification: Fisher's Iris data set.[*] The data set contains measurements of four different parts of an iris flower (sepal length and width, petal length and width). There are 150 records in the data set, distributed equally among three species of Iris (*Iris setosa*, *versicolor*, and *virginica*). The task is to predict the species based on a given a set of measurements.

First of all, let's take a quick look at the distributions of the four quantities, to see whether it seems feasible to distinguish the three classes this way. Figure 18-7 shows histograms (actually, kernel density estimates) for all four quantities, separately for the three classes. One of the features (sepal width) does not seem very promising, but the distributions of the other three features seem sufficiently separated that it should be possible to obtain good classification results.

---

[*] First published in 1936. The data set is available from many sources, for example in the "Iris" data set on the UCI Machine Learning repository at *http://archive.ics.uci.edu/ml/*.

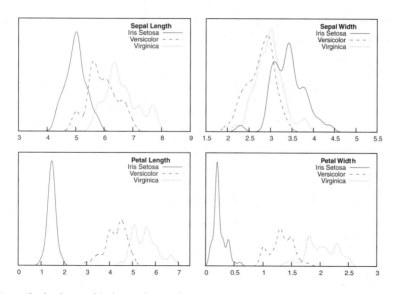

FIGURE 18-7. The distribution of the four attributes in the Iris data set, displayed separately for the three classes.

As preparation, I split the original data set into two parts: a training set (in the file iris.trn) and a test set (in file iris.tst). I randomly selected five records from each class for the test set; the remaining records were used for training. The test set is shown in full below: the columns are (in order) sepal length, sepal width, petal length, petal width, and the class label. (All measurements are in centimeters and to millimeter precision.)

```
5.0,3.6,1.4,0.2,Iris-setosa
4.8,3.0,1.4,0.1,Iris-setosa
5.2,3.5,1.5,0.2,Iris-setosa
5.1,3.8,1.6,0.2,Iris-setosa
5.3,3.7,1.5,0.2,Iris-setosa
5.7,2.8,4.5,1.3,Iris-versicolor
5.2,2.7,3.9,1.4,Iris-versicolor
6.1,2.9,4.7,1.4,Iris-versicolor
6.1,2.8,4.7,1.2,Iris-versicolor
6.0,3.4,4.5,1.6,Iris-versicolor
6.3,2.9,5.6,1.8,Iris-virginica
6.2,2.8,4.8,1.8,Iris-virginica
7.9,3.8,6.4,2.0,Iris-virginica
5.8,2.7,5.1,1.9,Iris-virginica
6.5,3.0,5.2,2.0,Iris-virginica
```

Our implementation of the nearest-neighbor classifier is shown in the next listing. The implementation is exceedingly simple—especially once you realize that about two thirds of the listing deal with file input and output. The actual "classification" is a matter of three lines in the middle:

```
# A Nearest-Neighbor Classifier

from numpy import *

train = loadtxt( "iris.trn", delimiter=',', usecols=(0,1,2,3) )
trainlabel = loadtxt( "iris.trn", delimiter=',', usecols=(4,), dtype=str )

test = loadtxt( "iris.tst", delimiter=',', usecols=(0,1,2,3) )
testlabel = loadtxt( "iris.tst", delimiter=',', usecols=(4,), dtype=str )

hit, miss = 0, 0
for i in range( test.shape[0] ):
    dist = sqrt( sum( (test[i] - train)**2, axis=1 ) )
    k = argmin( dist )

    if trainlabel[k] == testlabel[i]:
        flag = '+'
        hit += 1
    else:
        flag = '-'
        miss += 1

    print flag, "\t Predicted: ", trainlabel[k], "\t True: ", testlabel[i]

print
print hit, "out of", hit+miss, "correct - Accuracy: ", hit/(hit+miss+0.0)
```

The algorithm loads both the training and the test data set into two-dimensional NumPy arrays. Because all elements in a NumPy array must be of the same type, we store the class labels (which are strings, not numbers) in separate vectors.

Now follows the actual classification step: for each element of the test set, we calculate the Euclidean distance to each element in the training set. We make use of NumPy "broadcasting" (see the Workshop in Chapter 2) to calculate the distance of the test instance test[i] from *all* training instances in one fell swoop. (The argument axis=1 is necessary to tell NumPy that the sum in the Euclidean distance should be taken over the *inner* (horizontal) dimension of the two-dimensional array.) Next, we use the argmin() function to obtain the index of the training record that has the smallest distance to the current test record: this is our predicted class label. (Notice that we base our result only on a single record—namely the closest training instance.)

Simple as it is, the classifier works very well (on this data set). For the test set shown, all records in the test set are classified correctly!

The naive Bayesian classifier implementation is next. A naive Bayesian classifier needs an estimate of the probability distribution P(class C | feature x), which we find from a histogram of attribute values, separately for each class. In this case, we need a total of 12 histograms (3 classes × 4 features). I maintain this data in a triply nested data structure: histo[label][feature][value]. The first index is the class label, the second index specifies the feature, and the third contains the values of the feature that occur in the histogram. The value stored in the histogram is the number of times that each value has been observed:

```
# A Naive Bayesian Classifier

total = {}  # Training instances per class label
histo = {}  # Histogram

# Read the training set and build up a histogram
train = open( "iris.trn" )
for line in train:
    # seplen, sepwid, petlen, petwid, label
    f = line.rstrip().split( ',' )
    label = f.pop()

    if not total.has_key( label ):
        total[ label ] = 0
        histo[ label ] = [ {}, {}, {}, {} ]

    # Count training instances for the current label
    total[label] += 1

    # Iterate over features
    for i in range( 4 ):
        histo[label][i][f[i]] = 1 + histo[label][i].get( f[i], 0.0 )

train.close()

# Read the test set and evaluate the probabilities
hit, miss = 0, 0
test = open( "iris.tst" )
for line in test:
    f = line.rstrip().split( ',' )
    true = f.pop()

    p = {} # Probability for class label, given the test features
    for label in total.keys():
        p[label] = 1
        for i in range( 4 ):
            p[label] *= histo[label][i].get(f[i],0.0)/total[label]

    # Find the label with the largest probability
    mx, predicted = 0, -1
    for k in p.keys():
        if p[k] >= mx:
            mx, predicted = p[k], k

    if true == predicted:
        flag = '+'
        hit += 1

    else:
        flag = '-'
        miss += 1
```

```
        print flag, "\t", true, "\t", predicted, "\t",
        for label in p.keys():
            print label, ":", p[label], "\t",
        print

    print
    print hit, "out of", hit+miss, "correct - Accuracy: ", hit/(hit+miss+0.0)

    test.close()
```

I'd like to point out two implementation details. The first is that the second index is an integer, which I use instead of the feature names; this simplifies some of the loops in the program. The second detail is more important: I know that the feature values are given in centimeters, with exactly one digit after the decimal point. In other words, the values are already discretized, and so I don't need to "bin" them any further—in effect, each bin in the histogram is one millimeter wide. Because I never need to operate on the feature values, I don't even convert them to numbers: I read them as strings from file and use them (as strings) as keys in the histogram. Of course, if we wanted to use a different bin width, then we would have to convert them into numerical values so that we can operate on them.

In the evaluation part, the program reads data points from the test set and then evaluates the probability that the record belongs to a certain class for all three class labels. We then pick the class label that has the highest probability. (Notice that we don't need an explicit factor for the prior probability, since we know that each class is equally likely.)

On the test set shown earlier, the Bayesian classifier does a little worse than the nearest neighbor classifier: it correctly classifies 12 of 15 instances for a total accuracy of 80 percent.

If you look at the results of the classifier more closely, you will immediately notice a couple of problems that are common with Bayesian classifiers. First of all, the posterior probabilities are *small*. This should come as no surprise: each Bayes factor is smaller than 1 (because it's a probability), so their product becomes very small very quickly. To avoid underflows, it's usually a good idea to add the logarithms of the probabilities instead of multiplying the probabilities directly. In fact, if you have a greater number of features, this becomes a necessity. The second problem is that many of the posterior probabilities come out as exactly zero: this occurs whenever no entry in the histogram can be found for at least one of the feature values in the test record; in this case the histogram evaluates to zero, which means the entire product of probabilities is also identical to zero. There are different ways of dealing with this problem—in our case, you might want to experiment with replacing the histogram of discrete feature values with a kernel density estimate (similar to those in Figure 18-7), which, by construction, is nonzero everywhere. Keep in mind that you will need to determine a suitable bandwidth for each histogram!

Let me be clear: the implementations of both classifiers are extremely simpleminded. My intention here is to demonstrate the basic ideas behind these algorithms in as few lines of code as possible—and also to show that there is nothing mystical about writing a simple classifier. Because the implementations are so simple, it is easy to continue experimenting with them: can we do better if we use a larger number of neighbors in our nearest-neighbor classifier? How about a different distance function? In the naive Bayesian classifier, we can experiment with different bin widths in the histogram or, better yet, replace the histogram of discrete bins with a kernel density estimate. In either case, we need to start thinking about runtime efficiency: for a data set of only 150 elements this does not matter much, but evaluating a kernel density estimate of a few thousand points can be quite expensive!

If you want to use an established tool or library, there are several choices in the open source world. Three projects have put together entire data analysis and mining "toolboxes," complete with graphical user interface, plotting capabilities, and various plug-ins: RapidMiner (*http://rapid-i.com/*) and WEKA (*http://www.cs.waikato.ac.nz/ml/weka/*), which are both in Java as well as Orange (*http://www.ailab.si/orange/*), which is in Python. WEKA has been around for a long time and is very well established; RapidMiner is part of a more comprehensive tool suite (and includes WEKA as a plug-in). Orange is an alternative using Python.

All three of these projects use a "pipeline" metaphor: you select different processing steps (discretizers, smoothers, principal component analysis, regression, classifiers) from a toolbox and string them together to build up the whole analysis workflow entirely within the tool. Give it a shot—the idea has a lot of appeal, but I must confess that I have *never* succeeded in doing anything nontrivial with any of them!

There are some additional libraries worth checking out that have Python interfaces: libSVM (*http://www.csie.ntu.edu.tw/~cjlin/libsvm/*) and Shogun (*http://www.shogun-toolbox.org/*) provide implementations of support vector machines, while the Modular toolkit for Data Processing (*http://mdp-toolkit.sourceforge.net/*) is more general. (The latter also adheres to the "pipeline" metaphor.)

Finally, all classification algorithms are also available as R packages. I'll mention just three: the class package for nearest-neighbor classifiers and the rpart package for decision trees (both part of the R standard distribution) as well as the e1071 package (which can be found on CRAN) for support vector machines and naive Bayesian classifiers.

Further Reading

- *Introduction to Data Mining.* Pang-Ning Tan, Michael Steinbach, and Vipin Kumar. Addison-Wesley. 2005.
  This is my favorite book on data mining. It contains two accessible chapters on classification.

- *The Elements of Statistical Learning.* Trevor Hastie, Robert Tibshirani, and Jerome Friedman. 2nd ed., Springer. 2009.
  This book exemplifies some of the problems with current machine-learning theory: an entire book of highly nontrivial mathematics—and what feels like not a single real-world example or discussion of "what to use when."

## CHAPTER NINETEEN

Epilogue: Facts Are Not Reality

THE LAST (NOT LEAST) IMPORTANT SKILL WHEN WORKING WITH DATA IS TO KEEP IN MIND THAT DATA IS ONLY part of the picture. In particular, when one is working intensely with data oneself, it is all too easy to forget that just about everyone else will have a different perspective.

When the data contradicts appearances, appearances will win.   Almost always, at least. Abstract "data" will have little or no credibility when compared with direct, immediate observation. This has been one of my most common experiences. A manager observes a pile of defective items—and no amount of "data" will convince him that avoiding those defects will cost more than the defects themselves. A group of workers spends an enormous amount of effort on some task—and no amount of "data" will convince them that their efforts make no measurable difference to the quality of the product.

If something strongly *appears* to be one way, then it will be very, very difficult to challenge that appearance based on some abstract analysis—no matter how "hard" your facts may be.

And it can get ugly. If your case is watertight, so that your analysis cannot be refuted, then you may next find that your *personal* credibility or integrity is being challenged.

Never underestimate the persuasive power of appearance.

Data-driven decision making is a contradiction in terms.   Making a decision means that someone must stick his or her neck out and *decide*. If we wait until the situation is clear or let "the data" dictate what we do, then there is no longer any decision involved. This also means that if things don't turn out well, then nobody will accept the blame (or the responsibility) for the outcome: after all, we did what "the data" told us to do.

It is a fine line. Gut-level decisions can be annoyingly random (this way today, that way tomorrow). They can also lead to a lack of accountability: "It was my decision to do X that led to Y!"—without a confirming look at some data, who can say?

Studying data can help us understand the situation in more detail and therefore make better-informed decisions. On the other hand, data can be misleading in subtle ways. For instance, by focusing on "data" it is easy to overlook aspects that are important but for which no data is available (including but not limited to "soft factors"). Also, keep in mind that data is always *backward* looking: there is no data available to evaluate any truly novel idea!

Looking at data can help illuminate the situation and thereby help us make better decisions. But it should not be used to absolve everyone from taking individual responsibility.

Sometimes the only reason you need is that it is the right thing to do. Some organizations feel as if you would not put out a fire in the mail room, unless you first ran a controlled experiment and developed a business case for the various alternatives. Such an environment can become frustrating and stifling; if the same approach is being applied to human factors such as creature comforts (better chairs, larger monitors) or customer service ("sales don't dip proportionally if we lower the quality of our product"), then it can start to feel toxic pretty quickly.

Don't let "data" get in the way of ethical decisions.

The most important things in life can't be measured. It is a fallacy to believe that, just because something can't be measured, it doesn't matter or doesn't even exist. And a pretty tragic fallacy at that.

Programming Environments for Scientific Computation and Data Analysis

MOST DATA ANALYSIS INVOLVES A GOOD DEAL OF DATA MANIPULATION AND NUMERICAL COMPUTATION. OF course, we use computers for these tasks, hence we also need appropriate software.

This appendix is intended to give a brief survey of several popular software systems suitable for the kind of data analysis discussed in the rest of the book. I am mostly interested in open source software, although I also mention some of the most important commercial players.

The emphasis here is on *programming environments* for scientific applications (*i.e.*, libraries or packages intended for general data manipulation and computation) because being able to operate with data easily and conveniently is a fundamental capability for all data analysis efforts. On the other hand, I do not include programs intended exclusively for graphing data: not because visualization is not important (it is), but because the choice of plotting or visualization software is less fundamental.

Software Tools

In many ways, our choice of a data manipulation environment determines what problems we can solve; it certainly determines which problems we consider to be "easy" problems. For data analysis, the hard problem that we should be grappling with is always the data and what it is trying to tell us—the mechanics of handling it should be sufficiently convenient that we don't even think about them.

Properties I look for in a tool or programming environment include:

- Low overhead or ceremony; it must be easy to get started on a new investigation.
- Facilitates iterative, interactive use.

- No arbitrary limitations (within reasonable limits).

- Scriptable—not strictly required but often nice to have.

- Stable, correct, mature; free of random defects and other annoying distractions.

Most of these items are probably not controversial. Given the investigative nature of most data analysis, the ability to support iterative, interactive use is a requirement. Scriptability and the absence of arbitrary limitations are both huge enablers. I have been in situations where the ability to generate and compare hundreds of graphs revealed obvious similarities and differences that had never been noticed before—not least because everyone else was using tools (mostly Excel) that allowed graphs to be created only one at a time. (Excel is notorious for unnecessarily limiting what can be done, and so is SQL. Putting even minimal programming abilities on top of SQL greatly expands the range of problems that can be tackled.)

In addition to these rather obvious requirements, I want to emphasize two properties that may appear less important, but are, in fact, essential for successful data analysis. First, it is very important that the tool or environment itself does not impose much overhead or "ceremony": we will be hesitant to investigate an ad hoc idea if our programming environment is awkward to use or time-consuming to start. Second, the tool must be stable and correct. Random defects that we could "work around" if we used it as a component in a larger software project are unacceptable when we use the tool by itself.

In short: whatever we use for data manipulation must not get in our way! (I consider this more important than how "sophisticated" the tool or environment might be: a dumb tool that works is better than a cutting-edge solution that does not deliver—a point that is occasionally a little bit forgotten.)

Before leaving this section, let me remind you that it is not only the size of the toolbox that matters but also our mastery of the various elements within it. Only tools we know well enough that using them feels effortless truly leverage our abilities. Balancing these opposing trends (breadth of tool selection and depth of mastery) is a constant challenge. When in doubt, I recommend you opt for depth—superficiality does not pay.

Scientific Software Is Different

It is important to realize that scientific software (for a sufficiently wide definition of "scientific") faces some unusual challenges. First of all, scientific software is *hard*. Writing high-quality scientific programs is difficult and requires rather rare and specialized skills. (We'll come back to this later.) Second, the market for scientific software is *small*, which makes it correspondingly harder for any one program or vendor to gain critical mass.

Both of these issues affect all players equally, but a third problem poses a particular challenge for open source offerings: many users of scientific software are transients. Graduate students graduate, moving on from their projects and often leaving the research environment entirely. As a result, "abandonware" is common among open source scientific software projects. (And not just there—the long-term viability of commercial offerings is also far from assured.)

Before investing significant time and effort into mastering any one tool, it is therefore necessary to evaluate it with regard to two questions:

- Is the project of sufficiently high *quality*?
- Does the project have strong enough *momentum* and *support*?

A Catalog of Scientific Software

There are currently three main contenders for interactive, numeric programming available: Matlab (and its open source clone, Octave), R (and its commercial predecessor, S/S-Plus), and the NumPy/SciPy set of libraries for Python. Fundamentally, all three are vector and matrix packages: they treat vectors and matrices as atomic data types and allow mathematical functions to operate on them directly (addition, multiplication, application of a function to all elements in a vector or matrix). Besides this basic functionality, all three offer various other mathematical operations, such as special functions, support for function minimization, or numerical integration and nonlinear equation solving. It is important to keep in mind that all three are packages for *numerical* computations that operate with floating-point numbers. None of these three packages handles *symbolic* computations, such as the expansion of a function into its Taylor series. For this you need a symbolic math package, such as Mathematica or Maple (both commercial) or Maxima, Sage, or Axiom (all three open source). (Matlab has recently acquired the ability to perform symbolic operations as well.)

Matlab

Matlab has been around since the mid-1980s; it has a very large user base, mostly in the engineering professions but also in pure mathematics and in the machine-learning community. Rather than do all the heavy lifting itself, Matlab was conceived as a user-friendly frontend to existing high-performance numerical linear algebra libraries (LINPACK and EISPACK, which have been replaced by LAPACK). Matlab was one of the first widely used languages to treat complex data structures (such as vectors and matrices) as atomic data types, allowing the programmer to work with them as if they were scalar variables and without the need for explicit looping. (In this day and age, when object-oriented programming and operator overloading are commonly used and entirely mainstream, it is hard to imagine how revolutionary this concept seemed when it was first developed.[*]) In 2008, The MathWorks (the company that develops Matlab) acquired the

---

[*] I remember how blown away I personally was when I first read about such features in the programming language APL in the mid-1980s!

rights to the symbolic math package MuPAD and incorporated it into subsequent Matlab releases.

Matlab was mainly designed to be used interactively, and its programming model has serious deficiencies for larger programming projects. (There are problems with abstraction and encapsulation as well as memory management issues.) It is a commercial product but quite reasonably priced.

Matlab places particular emphasis on the quality of its numerical and floating-point algorithms and implementations.

There is an open source clone of Matlab called Octave. Octave (*http://www.gnu.org/software/octave/*) strives to be fully compatible; however, there are reports of difficulties when porting programs back and forth.

R

R is the open source clone of the S/S-Plus statistical package originally developed at Bell Labs. R (*http://www.r-project.org*) has a very large user base, mostly in the academic statistics community and a healthy tradition of user-contributed packages. The *Comprehensive R Archive Network* (CRAN) is a large central repository of user-contributed modules.

When first conceived, S was revolutionary in providing an integrated system for data analysis, including capabilities that we today associate with scripting languages (built-in support for strings, hash maps, easy file manipulations, and so on), together with extensive graphics functionality—and all that in an interactive environment! On the other hand, S was not conceived as a general-purpose programming language but is strongly geared toward statistical applications. Its programming model is quite different from current mainstream languages, which can make it surprisingly difficult for someone with a strong programming background to switch to S (or R). Finally, its primarily academic outlook makes for a sometimes awkward fit within a commercial enterprise environment.

The strongest feature of R is the large number of built-in (or user-contributed) functions for primarily *statistical* calculations. In contrast to Matlab, R is not intended as a general numerical workbench (although it can, with some limitations, be used for that purpose). Moreover—and perhaps contrary to expectations—it is not intended as a general-purpose data manipulation language, although it can serve as scripting language for text and file manipulations and similar tasks.

A serious problem when working with R is its dated programming model. It relies strongly on implicit behavior and "reasonable defaults," which leads to particularly opaque programs. Neither the language nor the libraries provide strong support for organizing information into larger structures, making it uncommonly difficult to locate pertinent information. Although it is easy to pick up isolated "tricks," it is notoriously difficult to develop a comprehensive understanding of the whole environment.

Like Matlab, R is here to stay. It has proven its worth (for 30 years!); it is mature; and it has a strong, high-caliber, and vocal user base. Unlike Matlab, it is free and open source, making it easy to get started.

Python

Python has become the scripting language of choice for scientists and scientific applications, especially in the machine-learning field and in the biological and social sciences. (Hard-core, large-scale numerical applications in physics and related fields continue to be done in C/C++ or even—*horresco referens*—in Fortran.)

The barrier to programming in Python is low, which makes it easy to start new projects. This is somewhat of a mixed blessing: on the one hand, there is an abundance of exciting Python projects out there; on the other hand, they seem to be particularly prone to the "abandonware" problem mentioned before. Also, scientists are not programmers, and it often shows (especially with regard to long-term, architectural vision and the cultivation of a strong and committed community).

In addition to a large number of smaller and more specialized projects, there have been five major attempts to provide a *comprehensive* Python library for scientific applications. It can be confusing to understand how they relate to each other, so they are summarized here:[*]

Numeric
> This is the original Python module for the manipulation of numeric arrays, initiated in 1995 at MIT. Superceded by NumPy.

Numarray
> An alternative implementation from the Space Telescope Science Institute (2001). Considered obsolete, replaced by NumPy.

NumPy
> The NumPy project was begun in 2005 to provide a unified framework for numerical matrix calculations. NumPy builds on (and supercedes) Numeric, and it includes the additional functionality developed by numarray.

SciPy
> Started in 2001, the SciPy project evolved out of an effort to combine several previously separate libraries for scientific computing. Builds on and includes NumPy.

ScientificPython
> An earlier (started in 1997) general-purpose library for scientific applications. In contrast to SciPy, this library tries to stay with "pure Python" implementations for better portability.

---

[*]For more information on the history and interrelations of these libraries, check out the first chapter in Travis B. Oliphant's "Guide to NumPy," which can be found on the Web.

Today, the NumPy/SciPy project has established itself as the clear winner among general-purpose libraries for scientific applications in Python, and we will take a closer look at it shortly.

A strong point in favor of Python is the convenient support it has for relatively fancy and animated graphics. The matplotlib library is the most commonly used Python library for generating standard plots, and it has a particularly close relationship with NumPy/SciPy. Besides matplotlib there are Chaco and Mayavi (for two- and three-dimensional graphics, respectively) and libraries such as PyGame and Pyglet (for animated and interactive graphics)—and, of course, many more.

Uncertainties associated with the future and adoption of Python3 affect all Python projects, but they are particularly critical for many of the scientific and graphics libraries just mentioned: to achieve higher performance, these libraries usually rely heavily on C bindings, which do not port easily to Python3. Coupled with the issue of "abandonware" discussed earlier, this poses a particular challenge for all scientific libraries based on Python at this time.

NumPy/SciPy

The NumPy/SciPy project (*http://www.scipy.org*) has become the dominant player in scientific programming for Python. NumPy provides efficient vector and matrix operations; SciPy consists of a set of higher-level functions built on top of NumPy. Together with the matplotlib graphing library and the IPython interactive shell, NumPy/SciPy provides functionality resembling Matlab. NumPy/SciPy is open source (BSD-style license) and has a large user community; it is supported and distributed by a commercial company (Enthought).

NumPy is intended to contain low-level routines for handling vectors and matrices, and SciPy is meant to contain all higher-level functionality. However, some additional functions are included in NumPy for backward compatibility, and all NumPy functions are aliased into the SciPy namespace for convenience. As a result, the distinction between NumPy and SciPy is not very clear in practice.

NumPy/SciPy can be a lot of fun. It contains a wide selection of features and is very easy to get started with. Creating graphical output is simple. Since NumPy/SciPy is built on Python, it is trivial to integrate it into other software projects. Moreover, it does not require you to learn (yet another) restricted, special-purpose language: everything is accessible from a modern, widely used scripting language.

On the other hand, NumPy/SciPy has its own share of problems. The project has a tendency to emphasize quantity over quality: the number of features is very large, but the design appears overly complicated and is often awkward to use. Edge and error cases are not always handled properly. On the scientific level, NumPy/SciPy feels amateurish. The choice of algorithms appears to reflect some well-known textbooks more than deep, practical knowledge arising from real experience.

What worries me most is that the project does not seem to be managed very well: although it has been around for nearly 10 years and has a large and active user base, it has apparently not been able to achieve and maintain a consistent level of reliability and maturity throughout. Features seem to be added haphazardly, without any long-term vision or discernible direction. Despite occasional efforts in this regard, the documentation remains patchy.

NumPy/SciPy is interesting because, among scientific and numeric projects, it probably has the lowest barrier to entry and is flexible and versatile. That makes it a convenient environment for getting started and for casual use. However, because of the overall quality issues, I would not want to rely on it for "serious" production work at this point.

What About Java?

Java is not a strong player when it comes to heavily *numerical* computations—so much so that a Java Numerics Working Group ceased operations years ago (around the year 2002) for lack of interest.

Nevertheless, a lot of production-quality machine-learning programming is done in Java, where its relatively convenient string handling (compared to C) and its widespread use for *enterprise* programming come into play. One will have to see whether these applications will over time lead to the development of high-quality numerical libraries as well.

If you want a comfortable programming environment for large (possibly distributed) systems that's relatively fast, then Java is a reasonable choice. However, Java programming has become very heavy-weight (with tools to manage your frameworks, and so on), which does not encourage ad hoc, exploratory programming. Groovy carries less programming overhead but is slow. A last issue concerns Java's traditionally weak capabilities for interactive graphics and user interfaces, especially on Linux.

Java is very strong in regard to Big Data; in particular, Hadoop—the most popular open source map/reduce implementation—is written in Java. Java is also popular for text processing and searching.

A relatively new project is Incanter (*http://incanter.org/*), which uses Clojure (a Lisp dialect running on top of the Java virtual machine) to develop an "R-like statistical computing and graphics environment." Incanter is an interesting project, but I don't feel that it has stood the test of time yet, and one will have to see how it will position itself with respect to R.

Other Players

The preceding list of programs and packages is, of course, far from complete. Among the other players, I shall briefly mention three.

SAS   SAS is a classical statistics packages with strongly established uses in credit scoring and medical trials. SAS was originally developed for OS/360 mainframes, and it shows. Its command language has a distinct 1960s feel, and the whole development cycle is strongly batch oriented (neither interactive nor exploratory). SAS works best when well-defined procedures need to be repeated often and on large data sets. A unique feature of SAS is that it works well with data sets that are too large to fit into memory and therefore need to be processed on disk.

SAS, like the mainframes it used to run on, is very expensive and requires specially trained operators—it is not for the casual user. (It is not exactly fun, either. The experience has been described as comparable to "scraping down the wallpaper with your fingernails.")

SciLab   SciLab is an open source project similar to Matlab. It was created by the French research institute INRIA.

GSL   The GSL (Gnu Scientific Library) is a C library for classical numerical analysis: special functions, linear algebra, nonlinear equations, differential equations, the lot. The GSL was designed and implemented by a relatively small team of developers, who clearly knew what they were doing—beyond the standard textbook treatment. (This is evident from some design choices that specifically address ugly but important real-world needs.)

The API is wonderfully clear and consistent, the implementations are of high quality, and even the documentation is complete and finished. I find the GSL thoroughly enjoyable to use. (If you learned numerical analysis from *Numerical Recipes*,[*] this is the software that should have shipped with the book—but didn't.)

The only problem with the GSL is that it is written in C. You need to be comfortable with C programming, including memory management and function pointers, if you want to use it. Bindings to scripting languages exist, but they are not part of the core project and may not be as complete or mature as the GSL itself.

Recommendations

So, which to pick? No clear winner emerges, and every single program or environment has significant (not just superficial) drawbacks. However, here are some qualified recommendations:

- Matlab is the 800-pound gorilla of scientific software. As a commercially developed product, it also has a certain amount of "polish" that many open source alternatives

---

[*] *Numerical Recipes 3rd Edition: The Art of Scientific Computing.* William H. Press, Saul A. Teukolsky, William T. Vetterling, and Brian P. Flannery. Cambridge University Press. 2007.

lack. If you don't have a preferred programming environment yet, *and* if you can afford it (or can make your employer pay for it), then Matlab is probably the most comprehensive, most mature, and best supported all-purpose tool. Octave is a cheap way to get started and "try before you buy."

- If you work with statisticians or have otherwise a need for formal statistical methods (tests, models), then R is a serious contender. It can also stand in as a scripting language for data manipulation if you don't already have a favorite one yet. Since it is open source software, its financial cost to you is zero, but be prepared for a significant investment of time and effort before you start feeling comfortable and proficient.

- NumPy/SciPy is particularly easy to get started with and can be a lot of fun for casual use. However, you may want to evaluate carefully whether it will meet your needs in the long run if you are planning to use it for a larger or more demanding project.

- NumPy/SciPy, together with some of its associated graphics packages, is also of interest if you have a need for fancier, possibly interactive, graphics.

- If you have a need for serious numerical analysis *and* you know C well, then the GSL is a mature, high-quality library.

I am well aware that this list of options does not cover all possibilities that may occur in practice!

Writing Your Own

Given the fragmented tool situation, it may be tempting to write your own. There is nothing wrong with that: it can be very effective to write a piece of software specifically for *your* particular problem and application domain. It is much harder to write general-purpose scientific software.

Just how much harder is generally underappreciated. When P. J. Plauger worked on his reference implementation of the standard C library,[*] he found that he "spent about as much time writing and debugging the functions declared in `<math.h>` as [he] did all the rest of this library combined"! Plauger then went on to state his design goals for his implementation of those functions.

This should startle you: *design goals*? Why should a reference implementation need any design goals beyond faithfully and correctly representing the standard?

The reason is that scientific and numerical routines can fail in more ways than most people expect. For such routines, correctness is not so much a binary property, as a floating-point value itself. Numerical routines have more complicated contracts than `strlen(char *)`.

---

[*] *The Standard C Library.* P. J. Plauger. Prentice Hall. 1992.

My prime example for this kind of problem is the sine function. What could possibly go wrong with it? It is analytic everywhere, strictly bounded by $[-1, 1]$, perfectly smooth, and with no weird behavior anywhere. Nonetheless, it is impossible to evaluate the sine accurately for sufficiently large values of x. The reason is that the sine sweeps out its entire range of values when x changes by as little as 2π. Today's floating-point values carry about 16 digits of precision. Once x has become so large that all of these digits are required to represent the value of x to the left of the decimal point, we are no longer able to resolve the location of x within the interval of length 2π with sufficient precision to be meaningful—hence the "value" returned by $\sin(x)$ is basically random. In practice, the quality of the results starts to degrade long before we reach this extreme regime. (More accurately the problem lies not so much in the implementation of the sine but in the inability to express its input values with the precision required for obtaining a meaningful result. This makes no difference for the present argument.)

There are two points to take away here. First, note how "correctness" is a relative quality that can degrade smoothly depending on circumstances (*i.e.*, the inputs). Second, you should register the sense of surprise that a function, which in mathematical theory is perfectly harmless, can turn nasty in the harsh reality of a computer program!

Similar examples can be found all over and are not limited to function evaluations. In particular for iterative algorithms (and almost all numerical algorithms are iterative), one needs to monitor and confirm that all intermediate values are uncorrupted—even in cases where the final result is perfectly reasonable. (This warning applies to many matrix operations, for instance.)

The punch line here is that although it is often not hard to produce an implementation that works well for a limited set of input values and in a narrow application domain, it is much more difficult to write routines that work equally well for all possible arguments. It takes a lot of experience to anticipate all possible applications and provide built-in diagnostics for likely failure modes. If at all possible, leave this work to specialists!

Further Reading

Matlab

- *Numerical Computing with MATLAB.* Cleve B. Moler. Revised reprint, SIAM. 2008.
  The literature on Matlab is vast. I mention this title because its author is Cleve Moler, the guy who started it all.

R

- *A Beginner's Guide to R.* Alain F. Zuur, Elena N. Ieno, and Erik H. W. G. Meesters. Springer. 2009.
  Probably the most elementary introduction into the mechanics of R. A useful book to get started, but it won't carry you very far. Obviously very hastily produced.

- *R in a Nutshell.* Joseph Adler. O'Reilly. 2009.
  This is the first book on R that is organized by the *task* that you want to perform. This makes it an invaluable resource in those situations where you know exactly what you want to do but can't find the appropriate commands that will tell R how to do it. The first two thirds of the book address data manipulation, programming, and graphics in general; the remainder is about statistical methods.

- *Using R for Introductory Statistics.* John Verzani. Chapman & Hall/CRC. 2004.
  This is probably my favorite introductory text on how to perform basic statistical analysis using R.

NumPy/SciPy

There is no comprehensive introduction to NumPy/SciPy currently available that takes a user's perspective. (The "Guide to NumPy" by Travis Oliphant, which can be found on the NumPy website, is too concerned with implementation issues.) Some useful bits, together with an introduction to Python and some other libraries, can be found in either of the following two books.

- *Python Scripting for Computational Science.* Hans Petter Langtangen. 3rd ed., Springer. 2009.

- *Beginning Python Visualization: Crafting Visual Transformation Scripts.* Shai Vaingast. Apress. 2009.

Results from Calculus

IN THIS APPENDIX, WE REVIEW SOME OF THE RESULTS FROM CALCULUS THAT ARE EITHER NEEDED EXPLICITLY IN the main part of the book or are conceptually sufficiently important when doing data analysis and mathematical modeling that you should at least be aware that they *exist*.

Obviously, this appendix cannot replace a class (or two) in beginning and intermediate calculus, and this is also not the intent. Instead, this appendix should serve as a reminder of things that you probably know already. More importantly, the results are presented here in a slightly different context than usual. Calculus is generally taught with an eye toward the theoretical development—it has to be, because the intent is to teach the entire body of knowledge of calculus and therefore the theoretical development is most important. However, for applications you need a different sort of tricks (based on the same fundamental techniques, of course), and it generally takes *years* of experience to make out the tricks from the theory. This appendix assumes that you have seen the theory at least once, so I am just reminding you of it, but I want to emphasize those elementary techniques that are most useful in applications of the kind explained in this book.

This appendix is also intended as somewhat of a teaser: I have included some results that are particularly interesting, noteworthy, or fascinating as an invitation for further study.

The structure of this appendix is as follows:

1. To get a head start, we first look at some common functions and their graphs.
2. Then we discuss the core concepts of calculus proper: derivative, integral, limit.
3. Next I mention a few practical tricks and techniques that are frequently useful.

4. Near the end, there is a section on notation and *very* basic concepts. *If you start feeling truly confused, check here!* (I did not want to start with that section because I'm assuming that most readers know this material already.)

5. I conclude with some pointers for further study.

A note for the mathematically fussy: this appendix quite intentionally eschews much mathematical sophistication. I know that many of the statements can be made either more general or more precise. But the way they are worded here is sufficient for my purpose, and I want to avoid the obscurity that is the by-product of presenting mathematical statements in their most general form.

Common Functions

Functions are mappings, which map a real number into another real number: $f : \mathbb{R} \mapsto \mathbb{R}$. This mapping is always unique: every input value x is mapped to exactly one result value $f(x)$. (The converse is not true: many input values may be mapped to the same result. For example, the mapping $f(x) = 0$, which maps *all* values to zero, is a valid function.)

More complicated functions are often built up as combinations of simpler functions. The most important simple functions are powers, polynomials and rational functions, and trigonometric and exponential functions.

Powers

The simplest nontrivial function is the *linear* function:

$$f(x) = ax$$

The constant factor a is the *slope*: if x increases by 1, then $f(x)$ increases by a. Figure B-1 shows linear functions with different slopes.

The next set of elementary functions are the simple powers:

$$f(x) = x^k$$

The power k can be greater or smaller than 1. The exponent can be positive or negative, and it can be an integer or a fraction. Figure B-2 shows graphs of some functions with positive integer powers, and Figure B-3 shows functions with fractional powers.

Simple powers have some important properties:

- All simple powers go through the two points $(0, 0)$ and $(1, 1)$.

- The linear function $f(x) = x$ is a simple power with $k = 1$.

- The square-root function $f(x) = \sqrt{x}$ is a simple power with $k = 1/2$.

- Integer powers ($k = 1, 2, 3, \ldots$) can be evaluated for negative x, but for fractional powers we have to be more careful.

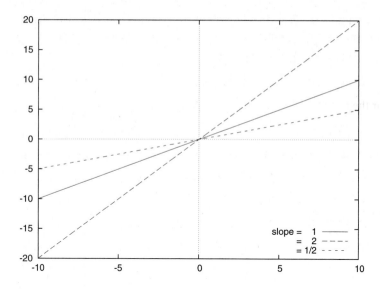

FIGURE B-1. The linear function $y = ax$.

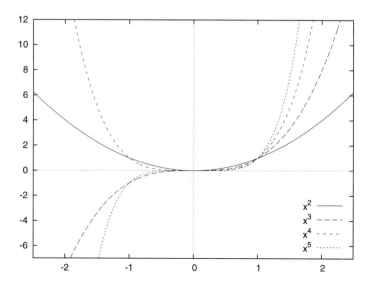

FIGURE B-2. Simple powers: $y = ax^k$.

Powers obey the following laws:

$$x^n x^m = x^{n+m}$$

$$x^n x^{-m} = \frac{x^n}{x^m}$$

$$x^0 = 1$$

$$x^1 = x$$

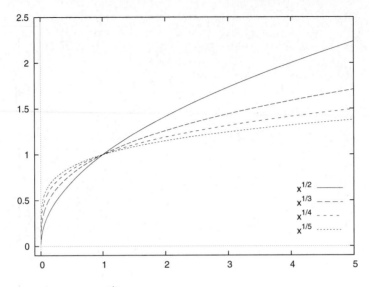

FIGURE B-3. Fractional powers: $y = a^{p/q}$.

If the exponent is negative, it turns the expression into a *fraction*:

$$x^{-n} = \frac{1}{x^n}$$

When dealing with fractions, we must always remember that the denominator must not become zero. As the denominator of a fraction approaches zero, the value of the overall expression goes to infinity. We say: the expression *diverges* and the function has a *singularity* at the position where the denominator vanishes. Figure B-4 shows graphs of functions with negative powers. Note the divergence for $x = 0$.

Polynomials and Rational Functions

Polynomials are sums of integer powers together with constant coefficients:

$$p(x) = a_n x^n + a_{n-1} x^{n-1} + \cdots + a_2 x^2 + a_1 x + a_0$$

Polynomials are nice because they are extremely easy to handle mathematically (after all, they are just sums of simple integer powers). Yet, more complicated functions can be approximated very well using polynomials. Polynomials therefore play an important role as approximations of more complicated functions.

All polynomials exhibit some "wiggles" and eventually diverge as x goes to plus or minus infinity (see Figure B-5). The highest power occurring in a polynomial is known as that *degree* of the polynomial.

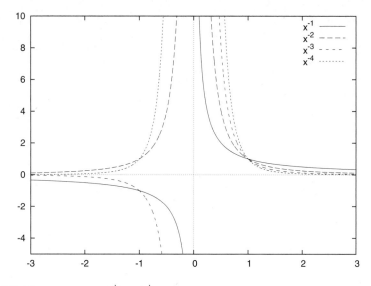

FIGURE B-4. *Negative powers:* $y = ax^{-k} = a/x^k$.

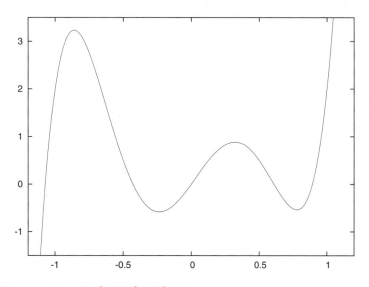

FIGURE B-5. *A polynomial:* $y = 16x^5 - 20x^3 + 2x^2 + 4x$.

Rational functions are fractions that have polynomials in both the numerator and the denominator:

$$r(x) = \frac{p(x)}{q(x)} = \frac{a_n x^n + a_{n-1} x^{n-1} + \cdots + a_2 x^2 + a_1 x + a_0}{b_m x^m + b_{m-1} x^{m-1} + \cdots + b_2 x^2 + b_1 x + b_0}$$

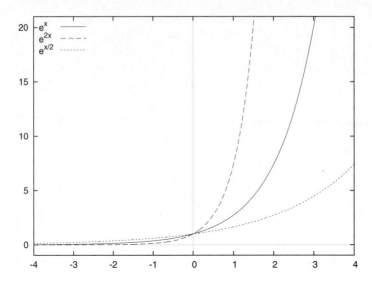

FIGURE B-6. The exponential function $y = e^x$.

Although they may appear equally harmless, rational functions are entirely more complicated beasts than polynomials. Whenever the denominator becomes zero, they blow up. The behavior as x approaches infinity depends on the relative size of the largest powers in numerator and denominator, respectively. Rational functions are *not* simple functions.

Exponential Function and Logarithm

Some functions cannot be expressed as polynomials (or as fraction of polynomials) of finite degree. Such functions are known as *transcendental functions*. For our purposes, the most important ones are the exponential function $f(x) = e^x$ (where $e = 2.718281\ldots$ is Euler's number) and its inverse, the logarithm.

A graph of the exponential function is shown in Figure B-6. For positive argument the exponential function grows *very* quickly, and for negative argument it decays equally quickly. The exponential function plays a central role in growth and decay processes.

Some properties of the exponential function follow from the rules for powers:

$$e^x e^y = e^{x+y}$$

$$e^{-x} = \frac{1}{e^x}$$

The logarithm is the inverse of the exponential function; in other words:

$$y = e^x \iff \log y = x$$

$$e^{\log(x)} = x \quad \text{and} \quad \log(e^x) = x$$

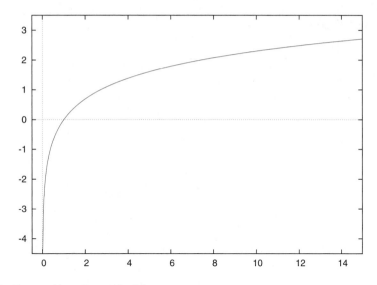

FIGURE B-7. The natural logarithm: $y = \log(x)$.

A plot of the logarithm is shown in Figure B-7. The logarithm is defined only for strictly positive values of x, and it tends to negative infinity as x approaches zero. In the opposite direction, as x becomes large the logarithm grows without bounds, but it grows almost unbelievably slowly. For $x = 2$, we have $\log 2 = 0.69\ldots$ and for $x = 10$ we find $\log 10 = 2.30\ldots$, but for $x = 1{,}000$ and $x = 10^6$ we have only $\log 1000 = 6.91\ldots$ and $\log 10^6 = 13.81\ldots$, respectively. Yet the logarithm does not have an upper bound: it keeps on growing but at an ever-decreasing rate of growth.

The logarithm has a number of basic properties:

$$\log(1) = 0$$
$$\log(x\, y) = \log x + \log y$$
$$\log(x^k) = k\, \log x$$

As you can see, logarithms turn products into sums and powers into products. In other words, logarithms "simplify" expressions. This property was (and is!) used in numerical calculations: instead of multiplying two numbers (which is complicated), you add their logarithms (which is easy—provided you have a logarithm table or a slide rule) and then exponentiate the result. This calculational scheme is still relevant today, but not for the kinds of simple products that previous generations performed using slide rules. Instead, logarithmic multiplication can be necessary when dealing with products that would generate intermediate over- or underflows even though the final result may be of reasonable size. In particular, certain kinds of combinatorial and probabilistic problems require finding the maximum of expressions such as $p^n(1 - p)^k$, where $p < 1$ is a probability and n and k may be large numbers. Brute-force evaluation will underflow

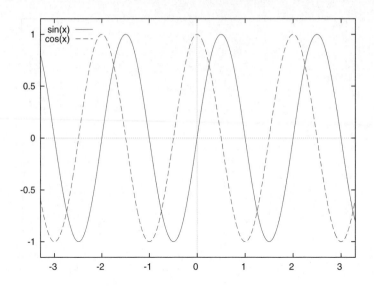

FIGURE B-8. The trigonometric functions $\sin(x)$ *and* $\cos(x)$.

even for modest values of the exponents, but taking logarithms first will result in a numerically harmless expression.

Trigonometric Functions

The trigonometric functions describe oscillations of all kinds and thus play a central role in sciences and engineering. Like the exponential function, they are transcendental functions, meaning they cannot be written down as a polynomial of finite degree.

Figure B-8 shows graphs of the two most important trigonometric functions: $\sin(x)$ and $\cos(x)$. The cosine is equal to the sine but is shifted by $\pi/2$ (90 degrees) to the left. We can see that both functions are *periodic*: they repeat themselves *exactly* after a period of length 2π. In other words, $\sin(x + 2\pi) = \sin(x)$ and $\cos(x + 2\pi) = \cos(x)$.

The length of the period is 2π, which you may recall is the *circumference of a circle with radius equal to* 1. This should make sense, because $\sin(x)$ and $\cos(x)$ repeat themselves after advancing by 2π and so does the circle: if you go around the circle once, you are back to where you started. This similarity between the trigonometric functions and the geometry of the circle is no accident, but this is not the place to explore it.

Besides their periodicity, the trigonometric functions obey a number of rules and properties ("trig identities"), only one of which is important enough to mention here:

$$\sin^2 x + \cos^2 x = 1 \quad \text{for all } x$$

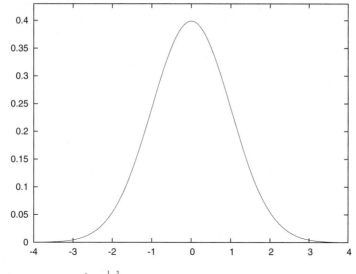

FIGURE B-9. The Gaussian: $y = \frac{1}{\sqrt{2\pi}}e^{-\frac{1}{2}x^2}$.

Finally, I should mention the tangent function, which is occasionally useful:

$$\tan x = \frac{\sin(x)}{\cos(x)}$$

Gaussian Function and the Normal Distribution

The Gaussian function arises frequently and in many different contexts. It is given by the formula:

$$\phi(x) = \frac{1}{\sqrt{2\pi}}e^{-\frac{1}{2}x^2}$$

and its plot is shown in Figure B-9. (This is the form in which the Gaussian should be memorized, with the factor $1/2$ in the exponent and the factor $1/\sqrt{2\pi}$ up front: they ensure that the integral of the Gaussian over all x will be equal to 1.)

Two applications of the Gaussian stand out. First of all, a strong result from probability theory, the *Central Limit Theorem* states that (under rather weak assumptions) if we add many random quantities, then their sum will be distributed according to a Gaussian distribution. In particular, if we take several samples from a population and calculate the mean for each sample, then the sample means will be distributed according to a Gaussian. Because of this, the Gaussian arises *all the time* in probability theory and statistics.

It is because of this connection that the Gaussian is often identified as "the" bell curve—quite incorrectly so, since there are many bell-shaped curves, many of which have drastically different properties. In fact, there are important cases where the Central Limit

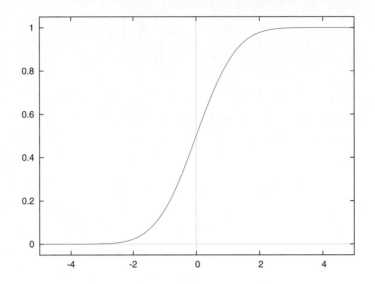

FIGURE B-10. The Gaussian distribution function.

Theorem fails, and the Gaussian is *not* a good way to describe the behavior of a random system (see the discussion of power-law distributions in Chapter 9).

The other context in which the Gaussian arises frequently is as a *kernel*—that is, as a strongly peaked and localized yet very smooth function. Although the Gaussian is greater than zero everywhere, it falls off to zero so quickly that almost the entire area underneath it is concentrated on the interval $-3 \leq x \leq 3$. It is this last property that makes the Gaussian so convenient to use as a kernel. Although the Gaussian is defined and nonzero everywhere (so that we don't need to worry about limits of integration), it can be multiplied against almost any function and integrated. The integral will retain only those values of the function near zero; values at positions far from the origin will be suppressed (smoothly) by the Gaussian.

In statistical applications, we are often interested in the area under certain parts of the curve because that will provide the answer to questions such as: "What is the probability that the point lies between -1 and 1?" The antiderivative of the Gaussian cannot be expressed in terms of elementary functions; instead it is defined through the integral directly:

$$\Phi(x) = \frac{1}{\sqrt{2\pi}} \int_{-\infty}^{x} e^{-\frac{1}{2}t^2}\, dt$$

This function is known as the *Normal distribution function* (see Figure B-10). As previously mentioned, the factor $1/\sqrt{2\pi}$ is a normalization constant that ensures the area under the entire curve is 1.

Given the function $\Phi(x)$, a question like the one just given can be answered easily: the area over the interval $[-1, 1]$ is simply $\Phi(1) - \Phi(-1)$.

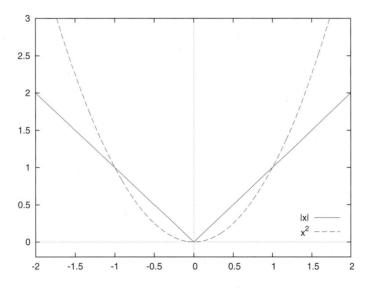

FIGURE B-11. *The absolute value function $y = |x|$ and the square $y = x^2$.*

Other Functions

There are some other functions that appear in applications often enough that we should be familiar with them but are a bit more exotic than the families of functions considered so far.

The *absolute value* function is defined as:

$$|a| = \begin{cases} a & \text{if } a \geq 0 \\ -a & \text{otherwise} \end{cases}$$

In other words, it is the positive ("absolute") value of its argument. From a mathematical perspective, the absolute value is hard to work with because of the need to treat the two possible cases separately and because of the kink at $x = 0$, which poses difficulties when doing analytical work. For this reason, one instead often uses the square x^2 to guarantee a positive value. The square relieves us of the need to worry about special cases explicitly, and it is smooth throughout. However, the square is relatively smaller than the absolute value for small values of x but relatively larger for large values of x. Weight functions based on the square (as in least-squares methods, for instance) therefore tend to overemphasize outliers (see Figure B-11).

Both the *hyperbolic tangent* $\tanh(x)$ (pronounced: tan-sh) and the *logistic function* are S-shaped or sigmoidal functions. The latter function is the solution to the *logistic differential equation*, hence the name. The logistic differential equation is used to model constrained

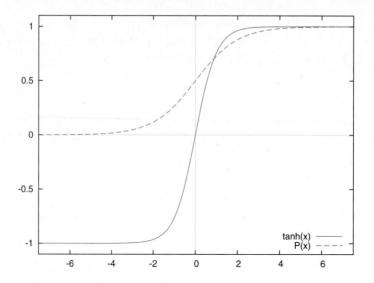

FIGURE B-12. *Two sigmoid (step) functions: the hyperbolic tangent* $y = \tanh(x)$ *and the logistic function* $y = 1/(1 + e^{-x})$.

growth processes such as bacteria competing for food and infection rates for contagious diseases. Both these functions are defined in terms of the exponential functions as follows:

$$\tanh(x) = \frac{e^x - e^{-x}}{e^x + e^{-x}}$$

$$P(x) = \frac{1}{1 + e^{-x}}$$

Both functions are smooth approximations to a step function, and they differ mostly in the range of values they assume: the $\tanh(x)$ takes on values in the interval $[-1, 1]$, whereas the logistic function takes on only positive values between 0 and 1 (see Figure B-12). It is not hard to show that the two functions can be transformed into each other; in fact, we have $P(x) = (\tanh(x/2) + 1)/2$.

These two functions are each occasionally referred to as *the* sigmoid function. That is incorrect: there are infinitely many functions that smoothly interpolate a step function. But among those functions, the two discussed here have the advantage that—although everywhere smooth—they basically consist of three straight lines: very flat as x goes to plus or minus infinity and almost linear in the transition regime. The position and steepness of the transition can be changed through a standard variable transformation; for example, $\tanh((x - m)/a)$ will have a transition at m with local slope $1/a$.

The last function to consider here is the *factorial*: $n!$. The factorial is defined only for nonnegative integers, as follows:

$$0! = 1$$

$$n! = 1 \cdot 2 \cdot \cdots \cdot (n - 1) \cdot n$$

The factorial plays an important role in combinatorial problems, since it is the number of ways that n distinguishable objects can be arranged. (To see this, imagine that you have to fill n boxes with n items. To fill the first box, you have n choices. To fill the second box, you have $n - 1$ choices. And so on. The total number of arrangements or *permutations* is therefore $n \cdot (n - 1) \cdots 1 = n!$.)

The factorial grows *very* quickly; it grows faster even than the exponential. Because the factorial grows so quickly, it is often convenient to work with its logarithm. An important and widely used approximation for the logarithm of the factorial is *Stirling's approximation*:

$$\log n! \approx n \log(n) - n \qquad \text{for large } n$$

For the curious: it is possible to define a function that smoothly interpolates the factorial for all positive numbers (not just integers). It is known as the *Gamma function*, and it is another example (besides the Gaussian distribution function) for a function defined through an integral:

$$\Gamma(x) = \int_0^\infty t^{x-1} e^{-t} \, dt$$

The variable t in this expression is just a "dummy" variable of integration—it does not appear in the final result. You can see that the first term in the integral grows as a power while the second falls exponentially, with the effect that the value of the integral is finite. Note that the limits of integration are fixed. The independent variable x enters the expression only as a parameter. Finally, it is easy to show that the Gamma function obeys the rule $n \Gamma(n) = \Gamma(n + 1)$, which is the defining property of the factorial function.

We do not need the Gamma function in this book, but it is interesting as an example of how integrals can be used to define and construct new functions.

The Inverse of a Function

A function maps its argument to a result: given a value for x, we can find the corresponding value of $f(x)$. Occasionally, we want to turn this relation around and ask: given a value of $f(x)$, what is the corresponding value of x?

That's what the *inverse function* does: if $f(x)$ is some function, then its inverse $f^{-1}(x)$ is defined as the function that, when applied to $f(x)$, returns the original argument:

$$f^{-1}(f(x)) = x$$

Sometimes we can invert a function explicitly. For example, if $f(x) = x^2$, then the inverse function is the square root, because $\sqrt{x^2} = x$ (which is the definition of the inverse function). In a similar way, the logarithm is the inverse function of the exponential: $\log(e^x) = x$.

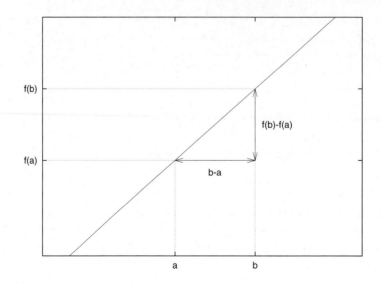

FIGURE B-13. The slope of a linear function is the ratio of the growth in the vertical direction, $f(b) - f(a)$, divided by the corresponding growth in the horizontal direction, $b - a$.

In other cases, it may not be possible to find an explicit form for the inverse function. For example, we sometimes need the inverse of the Gaussian distribution function $\Phi(x)$. However, no simple form for this function exists, so we write it symbolically as $\Phi^{-1}(x)$, which refers to the function for which $\Phi^{-1}(\Phi(x)) = x$ is true.

Calculus

Calculus proper deals with the consideration of limit processes: how does a sequence of values behave if we make infinitely many steps? The slope of a function and the area underneath a function are both defined through such limit processes (the derivative and the integral, respectively).

Calculus allows us to make statements about properties of functions and also to develop approximations.

Derivatives

We already mentioned the slope as the rate of change of a linear function. The same concept can be extended to nonlinear functions, though for such functions, the slope itself will vary from place to place. For this reason, we speak of the *local slope* of a curve at each point.

Let's examine the slope as the *rate of change* of a function in more detail, because this concept is of fundamental importance whenever we want to interpolate or approximate some data by a smooth function. Figure B-13 shows the construction used to calculate the

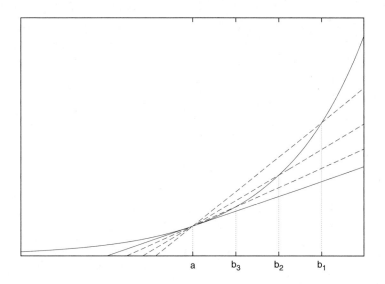

FIGURE B-14. As b_i approaches a, the slope found for these two points becomes closer and closer to the local slope at a.

slope of a linear function. As x goes from a to b, the function changes from $f(a)$ to $f(b)$. The rate of change is the ratio of the change in $f(x)$ to the change in x:

$$\text{slope} = \frac{f(b) - f(a)}{b - a}$$

Make sure that you really understand this formula!

Now, let's apply this concept to a function that is nonlinear. Because the slope of the curve varies from point to point, we cannot find the slope directly using the previous formula; however, we can use the formula to *approximate* the local slope.

Figure B-14 demonstrates the concept. We fix two points on a curve and put a straight line through them. This line has a slope, which is $\frac{f(b)-f(a)}{b-a}$. This is only an approximation to the slope at point a. But we can improve the approximation by moving the second point b closer to a. If we let b go all the way to a, we end up with the (local) slope *at* the point a exactly. This is called the *derivative*. (It is a central result of calculus that, although numerator and denominator in $\frac{f(b)-f(a)}{b-a}$ each go to zero separatcly in this process, the fraction itself goes to a well-defined value.)

The construction just performed was done graphically and for a single point only, but it can be carried out analytically in a fully general way. The process is sufficiently instructive that we shall study a simple example in detail—namely finding a general rule for the derivative of the function $f(x) = x^2$. It will be useful to rewrite the interval $[a, b]$ as

TABLE B-1. *Derivatives and antiderivatives (integrals) for a few elementary functions.*

Function	Derivative	Integral
x^n	nx^{n-1}	$\frac{1}{n+1}x^{n+1}$
e^x	e^x	e^x
$\log x$	$1/x$	$x \log x - x$
$\sin x$	$\cos x$	$-\cos x$
$\cos x$	$-\sin x$	$\sin x$

$[x, x + \epsilon]$. We can now go ahead and form the familiar ratio:

$$
\begin{aligned}
\frac{f(b) - f(a)}{b - a} &= \frac{f(x + \epsilon) - f(x)}{(x + \epsilon) - x} \\
&= \frac{(x + \epsilon)^2 - x^2}{x + \epsilon - x} \\
&= \frac{x^2 + 2x\epsilon + \epsilon^2 - x^2}{\epsilon} \\
&= \frac{2x\epsilon + \epsilon^2}{\epsilon} \\
&= 2x + \epsilon \\
&\rightarrow 2x \quad \text{as } \epsilon \text{ goes to zero}
\end{aligned}
$$

In the second step, the terms not depending on ϵ cancel each other; in the third step, we cancel an ϵ between the numerator and the denominator, which leaves an expression that is perfectly harmless as ϵ goes to zero! The (harmless) result is the sought-for derivative of the function. Notice that the result is true for *any* x, so we have obtained an expression for the derivative of x^2 that holds for all x: the derivative of x^2 is $2x$. Always. Similar rules can be set up for other functions (you may try your hand at finding the rule for x^3 or even x^k for general k). Table B-1 lists a few of the most important ones.

There are two ways to indicate the derivative. A short form uses the prime, like this: $f'(x)$ is the derivative of $f(x)$. Another form uses the *differential operator* $\frac{d}{dx}$, which acts on the expression to its right. Using the latter, we can write:

$$
\frac{d}{dx}x^2 = 2x
$$

Finding Minima and Maxima

When a smooth function reaches a local minimum or maximum, its slope at that point is zero. This is easy to see: as you approach a peak, you go uphill (positive slope); once over the top, you go downhill (negative slope). Hence, you must have passed a point where you were going neither uphill nor downhill—in other words, where the slope was zero. (From a mathematically rigorous point of view, this is not quite as obvious as it may seem; you may want to check for "Rolle's theorem" in a calculus text.)

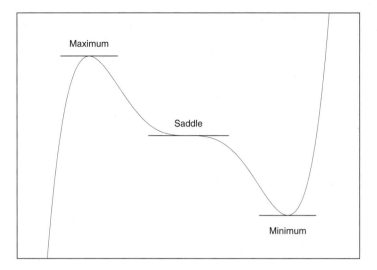

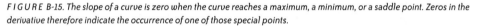

F I G U R E B-15. The slope of a curve is zero when the curve reaches a maximum, a minimum, or a saddle point. Zeros in the derivative therefore indicate the occurrence of one of those special points.

The opposite is also true: if the slope (*i.e.*, the derivative) is zero somewhere, then the function has either a minimum or a maximum at that position. (There is also a third possibility: the function has a so-called saddle point there. In practice, this occurs less frequently.) Figure B-15 demonstrates all these cases.

We can therefore use derivatives to locate minima or maxima of a function. First we determine the derivative of the function, and then we find the locations where the derivative is zero (the derivative's *roots*). The roots are the locations of the extrema of the original function.

Extrema are important because they are the solution to *optimization* problems. Whenever we want to find the "best" solution in some context, we are looking for an extremum: the lowest price, the longest duration, the greatest utilization, the highest efficiency. Hence, if we have a mathematical expression for the price, duration, utilization, or efficiency, we can take its derivative with respect to its parameters, set the derivative to zero, and solve for those values of the parameters that maximize (or minimize) our objective function.

Integrals

Derivatives find the local rate of change of a curve as the limit of a sequence of better and better approximations. Integrals calculate the area underneath a curve by a similar method.

Figure B-16 demonstrates the process. We approximate the area underneath a curve by using rectangular boxes. As we make the boxes narrower, the approximation becomes more accurate. In the limit of infinitely many boxes of infinitely narrow width, we obtain the exact area under the curve.

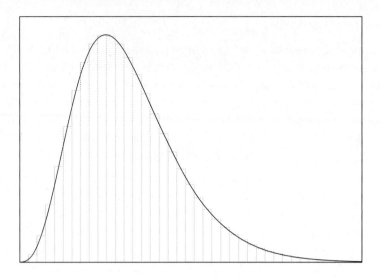

F I G U R E B-16. *The integral is the area under a curve. It can be approximated by filling the area under the curve with narrow rectangles and adding up their areas. The approximation improves as the width of the rectangles becomes smaller.*

Integrals are conceptually very simple but analytically much more difficult than derivatives. It is always possible to find a closed-form expression for the derivative of a function. This is not so for integrals in general, but for some simple functions an expression for the integral can be found. Some examples are included in Table B-1.

Integrals are often denoted using uppercase letters, and there is a special symbol to indicate the "summing" of the area underneath a curve:

$$F(y) = \int f(x)\,dx$$

We can include the limits of the domain over which we want to integrate, like this:

$$A = \int_a^b f(x)\,dx$$

Notice that A is a *number*, namely the area underneath the curve between $x = a$ and $x = b$, whereas the indefinite integral (without the limits) is a *function*, which can be evaluated at any point.

Limits, Sequences, and Series

The central concept in all of calculus is the notion of a *limit*. The basic idea is as follows. We construct some process that continues indefinitely and approximates some value ever more closely as the process goes on—but without reaching the limit in any finite number of steps, no matter how many. The important insight is that, even though the limit is never reached, we can nevertheless make statements about the limiting value. The derivative (as the limit of the difference ratio) and the integral (as the limit of the sum of approximating "boxes") are examples that we have already encountered.

As simpler example, consider the numbers $1/1$, $1/2$, $1/3$, $1/4$, ... or $1/n$ in general as n goes to infinity. Clearly, the numbers approach zero ever more closely; nonetheless, for any finite n, the value of $1/n$ is always greater than zero. We call such an infinite, ordered set of numbers a *sequence*, and zero is the limit of this particular sequence.

A *series* is a sum:

$$s_n = \sum_{i=0}^{n} a_n$$

$$= a_0 + a_1 + a_2 + a_3 + \cdots + a_n$$

As long as the number of terms in the series is finite, there is no problem. But once we let the number of terms go to infinity, we need to ask whether the sum still converges to a finite value. We have already seen a case where it does: we defined the integral as the value of the infinite sum of infinitely small boxes.

It may be surprising that an *infinite* sum can still add up to a *finite* value. Yet this can happen provided the terms in the sum become smaller rapidly enough. Here's an example: if you sum up 1, 0.1, 0.01, 0.001, 0.0001, ... , you can see that the sum approaches 1.1111... but will never be larger than 1.2. Here is a more dramatic example: I have a piece of chocolate. I break it into two equal parts and give you one. Now I repeat the process with what I have left, and so on. Obviously, we can continue like this forever because I always retain half of what I had before. However, you will never accumulate more chocolate than what I started out with!

An infinite series converges to a finite value only if the magnitude of the terms decreases sufficiently quickly. If the terms do not become smaller fast enough, the series diverges (*i.e.*, its value is infinite). An important series that does *not* converge is the *harmonic series*:

$$\sum_{k=1}^{\infty} \frac{1}{k} = 1 + \frac{1}{2} + \frac{1}{3} + \cdots = \infty$$

One can work out rigorous tests to determine whether or not a given series converges. For example, we can compare the terms of the series to those from a series that is known to converge: if the terms in the new series become smaller more quickly than in the converging series, then the new series will also converge.

Finding the value of an infinite sum is often tricky, but there is one example that is rather straightforward. The solution involves a trick well worth knowing. Consider the infinite *geometric series*:

$$s = \sum_{i=0}^{\infty} = 1 + q + q^2 + q^3 + \cdots \qquad \text{for } |q| < 1$$

Now, let's multiply by q and add 1:

$$qs + 1 = q(1 + q + q^2 + q^3 + \cdots) + 1$$
$$= q + q^2 + q^3 + q^4 + \cdots + 1$$
$$= s$$

To understand the last step, realize that the righthand side equals our earlier definition of s. We can now solve the resulting equation for s and obtain:

$$s = \frac{1}{1 - q}$$

This is a good trick that can be applied in similar cases: if you can express an infinite series in terms of itself, the result may be an equation that you can solve explicitly for the unknown value of the infinite series.

Power Series and Taylor Expansion

An especially important kind of series contains consecutive powers of the variable x multiplied by the constant coefficients a_i. Such series are called *power series*. The variable x can take on any value (it is a "dummy variable"), and the sum of the series is therefore a function of x:

$$s(x) = \sum_{i=0}^{n} a_i x^i$$

If n is finite, then there is only a finite number of terms in the series: in fact, the series is simply a polynomial (and, conversely, every polynomial is a finite power series). But the number of terms can also be infinite, in which case we have to ask for what values of x does the series converge. Infinite power series are of great theoretical interest because they are a (conceptually straightforward) generalization of polynomials and hence represent the "simplest" nonelementary functions.

But power series are also of the utmost *practical* importance. The reason is a remarkable result known as *Taylor's theorem*. Taylor's theorem states that any reasonably smooth function can be *expanded into a power series*. This process (and the resulting series) is known as the *Taylor expansion* of the function.

Taylor's theorem gives an explicit construction for the coefficients in the series expansion:

$$f(x) = f(0) + f'(0)x + \frac{f''(0)}{2!}x^2 + \frac{f'''(0)}{3!}x^3 + \cdots$$

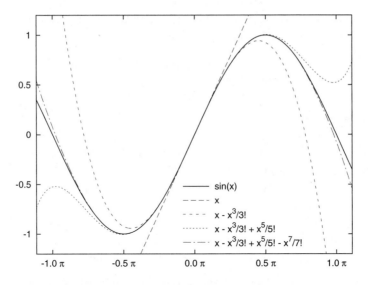

FIGURE B-17. The sine function $\sin(x)$ and its Taylor expansions around zero, truncated after retaining different numbers of terms. If more terms are kept, the approximation is acceptable over a greater range of values.

In other words, the coefficient of the nth term is the nth derivative (evaluated at zero) divided by $n!$. The Taylor series converges for *all* x—the factorial in the denominator grows so quickly that convergence is guaranteed no matter how large x is.

The Taylor series is an exact representation of the function on the lefthand side if we retain all (infinitely many) terms. But we can also *truncate* the series after just a few terms and so obtain a good *local approximation* of the function in question. The more terms we keep, the larger will be the range over which the approximation is good. For the sine function, Figure B-17 shows how the Taylor expansion improves as a greater number of terms is kept. Table B-2 shows the Taylor expansions for some functions we have encountered so far.

It is this last step that makes Taylor's theorem so useful from a practical point of view: it tells us that *we can approximate any smooth function locally by a polynomial.* And polynomials are always easy to work with—often much easier than the complicated functions that we started with.

One important practical point: the approximation provided by a truncated Taylor series is good only *locally*—that is, near the point around which we expand. This is because in that case x is small (*i.e.*, $x \ll 1$) and so higher powers become negligible fast. Taylor series are usually represented in a form that assumes that the expansion takes place around zero. If this is not the case, we need to remove or factor out some large quantity so that we are left with a "small parameter" in which to expand. As an example, suppose we want to obtain an approximation to e^x for values of x near 10. If we expanded in the usual fashion around zero, then we would have to sum *many* terms before the approximation becomes

TABLE B-2. The first few terms of the Taylor expansion of some important functions

Function	Taylor expansion	Comment
e^x	$1 + x + \frac{x^2}{2!} + \frac{x^3}{3!} + \cdots$	all x
$\sin x$	$x - \frac{x^3}{3!} + \frac{x^5}{5!} \mp \cdots$	all x
$\cos x$	$1 - \frac{x^2}{2!} + \frac{x^4}{4!} \mp \cdots$	all x
$\log(1 + x)$	$x - \frac{x^2}{2} + \frac{x^3}{3} \mp \cdots$	$-1 < x \leq 1$
$\sqrt{1 + x}$	$1 + \frac{x}{2} + \frac{x^2}{8} + \frac{x^3}{16} + \cdots$	$\|x\| \leq 1$
$1/(1 + x)$	$1 - x + x^2 - x^3 \pm \cdots$	$\|x\| < 1$

good (the terms grow until $10^n < n!$, which means we need to keep more than 20 terms). Instead, we proceed as follows: we write $e^x = e^{10+\delta} = e^{10} e^{\delta} = e^{10} (1 + \delta + \frac{\delta^2}{2} + \cdots)$. In other words, we set it up so that δ is small allowing us to expand e^{δ} around zero as before.

Another important point to keep in mind is that the function must be smooth at the point around which we expand: it must not have a kink or other singularity there. This is why the logarithm is usually expanded around one (not zero): recall that the logarithm diverges as x goes to zero.

Useful Tricks

The Binomial Theorem

Probably everyone has encountered the binomial formulas at some point:

$$(a + b)^2 = a^2 + 2ab + b^2$$
$$(a - b)^2 = a^2 - 2ab + b^2$$

The binomial theorem provides an extension of this result to higher powers. The theorem states that, for an arbitrary integer power n, the expansion of the lefthand side can be written as:

$$(a + b)^n = \sum_{k=0}^{n} \binom{n}{k} a^{n-k} b^k$$
$$= \binom{n}{0} a^n b^0 + \binom{n}{1} a^{n-1} b^1 + \binom{n}{2} a^{n-2} b^2 + \cdots + \binom{n}{n} a^0 b^n$$

This complicated-looking expression involves the *binomial coefficients*:

$$\binom{n}{k} = \frac{n!}{k! \, (n - k)!} \qquad 0 \leq k \leq n$$

The binomial coefficients are combinatorial factors that count the number of different ways one can choose k items from a set of n items, and in fact there is a close relationship between the binomial theorem and the binomial probability distribution.

As is the case for many exact results, the greatest practical use of the binomial theorem comes from an approximate expression. Assume that $b < a$, so that $b/a < 1$. Now we can write:

$$(a + b)^n = a^n \left(1 + \frac{b}{a}\right)^n$$

$$\approx a^n \left(1 + n\frac{b}{a} + \frac{n(n-1)}{2}\left(\frac{b}{a}\right)^2 + \cdots\right)$$

Here we have neglected terms involving higher powers of b/a, which are small compared to the retained terms, since $b/a < 1$ by construction (so that higher powers of b/a, which involve multiplying a small number repeatedly by itself, quickly become negligible).

In this form, the binomial theorem is frequently useful as a way to generate approximate expansions. In particular, the first-order approximation:

$$(1 + x)^n \approx 1 + nx \qquad \text{for } |x| < 1$$

should be memorized.

The Linear Transformation

Here is a quick, almost trivial, trick that is useful enough to be committed to memory. Any variable can be transformed to a similar variable that takes on only values from the interval $[0, 1]$, via the following linear transformation, where x_{min} and x_{max} are the minimum and maximum values that x can take on:

$$y = \frac{x - x_{min}}{x_{max} - x_{min}}$$

This transformation is frequently useful—for instance, if we have two quantities and would like to compare how they develop over time. If the two quantities have very different magnitudes, then we need to reduce both of them to a common range of values. The transformation just given does exactly that.

If we want the transformed quantity to *fall* whenever the original quantity goes up, we can do this by writing:

$$\bar{y} = 1 - y = 1 - \frac{x - x_{min}}{x_{max} - x_{min}}$$

We don't have to shift by x_{min} and rescale by the original range $x_{max} - x_{min}$. Instead, we can subtract any "typical" value and divide by any "typical" measure of the range. In statistical applications, for example, it is frequently useful to subtract the mean μ and to divide by the standard deviation σ. The resulting quantity is referred to as the *z-score*:

$$z = \frac{x - \mu}{\sigma}$$

Alternatively, you might also subtract the median and divide by the inter-quartile range. The exact choice of parameters is not crucial and will depend on the specific application context. The important takeaway here is that we can normalize any variable by:

- Subtracting a typical value (shifting) and
- Dividing by the typical range (rescaling)

Dividing by Zero

Please remember that *you cannot divide by zero!* I am sure you know this—but it's surprisingly easy to forget (until the computer reminds us with a fatal "divide by zero" error).

It is instructive to understand what happens if you try to divide by zero. Take some fixed number (say, 1), and divide it by a sequence of numbers that approach zero:

$$\frac{1}{10} = 0.1$$

$$\frac{1}{5} = 0.2$$

$$\frac{1}{1} = 1.0$$

$$\frac{1}{1/5} = 5$$

$$\frac{1}{1/10} = 10$$

$$\frac{1}{0} = ?$$

In other words, as you divide a constant by numbers that *approach* zero, the result becomes larger and larger. Finally, if you let the divisor go to zero, the result grows beyond all bounds: it diverges. Figure B-18 shows this graphically.

What you should take away from this exercise and Figure B-18 is that you cannot replace 1/0 by something else—for instance, it is *not* a smart move to replace 1/0 by 0 "because both don't really mean anything, anyway." If you need to find a numeric value for 1/0, then it should be something like "infinity," but this is not a useful value to operate with in practical applications.

Therefore, *whenever you encounter a fraction $\frac{a}{b}$ of any kind, you* must *check whether the denominator can become zero and exclude these points from consideration.*

Failing to do so is one of the most common sources of error. What is worse, these errors are difficult to recover from—not just in implementations but also conceptually. A typical

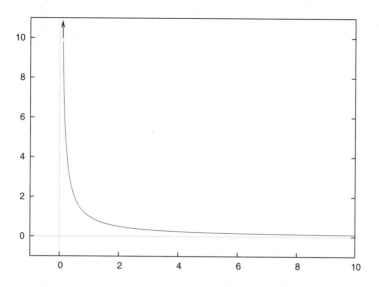

FIGURE B-18. As you divide a constant value by smaller and smaller numbers, the result is getting larger and larger. If you divide by zero, it blows up!

example involves "relative errors," where we divide the difference between the observed and the expected value by the expected value:

$$\text{relative error} = \frac{\text{observed} - \text{expected}}{\text{expected}}$$

What happens if for one day the expected value drops to zero? You are toast. There is no way to assign a meaningful value to the error in this case. (If the observed value is also zero, then you can treat this as a special case and *define* the relative error to be zero in this case, but if the observed value is not zero, then this definition is obviously inappropriate.)

These kinds of problems have an unpleasant ability to sneak up on you. A quantity such as the relative error or the defect rate (which is also a ratio: the number of defects found divided by the number of units produced) is a quantity commonly found in reports and dashboards. You don't want your entire report to crash because no units were produced for some product on this day rendering the denominator zero in one of your formulas!

There are a couple of workarounds, neither of which is perfect. In the case of the defect rate, where you can be sure that the numerator will be zero if the denominator is (because no defects can be found if no items were produced), you can add a small positive number to the denominator and thereby prevent it from ever becoming exactly zero. As long as this number is small compared to the number of items typically produced in a day, it will not significantly affect the reported defect rate, but will relieve you from having to check for the $\frac{0}{0}$ special case explicitly. In the case of calculating a relative error, you might want to replace the numerator with the average of the expected and the observed values. The advantage is that now the denominator can be zero only if the numerator is zero, which brings us back to the suggestion for dealing with defect rates just discussed. The problem with this method is that when no events are observed but some number was expected, the relative error is reported as -2 (negative 200 percent instead of negative 100 percent); this is due to the factor $1/2$ in the denominator, which comes from calculating the average there.

So, let me say it again: whenever you are dealing with fractions, you *must* consider the case of denominators becoming zero. Either rule them out or handle them explicitly.

Notation and Basic Math

This section is not intended as a comprehensive overview of mathematical notation or as your first introduction to mathematical formulas. Rather, it should serve as a general reminder of some basic facts and to clarify some conventions used in this book. (All my conventions are pretty standard—I have been careful not to use any symbols or conventions that are not generally used and understood.)

On Reading Formulas

A mathematical formula combines different components, called *terms*, by use of operators. The most basic operators are *plus* and *minus* (+ and −) and *multiplied by* and *divided by* (· and /). Plus and minus are always written explicitly, but the multiplication operator is usually silent—in other words, if you see two terms next to each other, with nothing between them, they should be multiplied. The division operator can be written in two forms: $1/n$ or $\frac{1}{n}$, which mean exactly the same thing. The former is more convenient in text such as this; the latter is more clear for long, "display" equations. An expression such as $1/n + 1$ is ambiguous and should not be used, but if you encounter it, you should assume that it means $\frac{1}{n} + 1$ and not $1/(n + 1)$ (which is equivalent to $\frac{1}{n+1}$).

Multiplication and division have higher precedence than addition and subtraction, therefore $ab + c$ means that first you multiply a and b and then add c to the result. To change the priority, you need to use parentheses: $a(b + c)$ means that first you add b and c and then multiply the result by a. Parentheses can either be round $(\ldots)$ or square $[\ldots]$, but their meaning is the same.

Functions take one (or several) arguments and return a result. A function always has a *name* followed by the *arguments*. Usually the arguments are enclosed in parentheses: $f(x)$. Strictly speaking, this notation is ambiguous because an expression such as $f(a + b)$ could mean either "add a and b and then multiply by f" or "add a and b and then pass the result to the function f." However, the meaning is usually clear from the context.

(There is a slightly more advanced way to look at this. You can think of f as an operator, similar to a differential operator like $\frac{d}{dx}$ or an integral operator like $\int dt$. This operator is now applied to the expression to the right of it. If f is a function, this means applying the function to the argument; if the operator is a differential operator, this means taking the derivative; and if f is merely a number, then applying it simply means multiplying the term on its right by it.)

A function may take more than one argument; for example, the function $f(x, y, z)$ takes three arguments. Sometimes you may want to emphasize that not all of these arguments are equivalent: some are actual variables, whereas others are "parameters," which are kept constant while the variables change. Consider $f(x) = ax + b$. In this function, x is the variable (the quantity usually plotted along the horizontal axis) while a and b would be considered parameters. If we want to express that the function f does depend on the parameters as well as on the actual variable, we can do this by including the parameters in the list of arguments: $f(x, a, b)$. To visually separate the parameters from the actual variable (or variables), a semicolon is sometimes used: $f(x; a, b)$. There are no hard-and-fast rules for when to use a semicolon instead of a comma—it's simply a convenience that is sometimes used and other times not.

One more word on functions: several functions are regarded as "well known" in mathematics (such as sine and cosine, the exponential function, and the logarithm). The names of such well-known functions are always written in upright letters, whereas functions in general are denoted by an italic letter. (Variables are always written in italics.) For well-known functions, the parentheses around the arguments can be omitted if the argument is sufficiently simple. (This is another example of the "operator" point of view mentioned earlier.) Thus we may write $\sin(x + 1) + \log x - f(x)$ (note the upright letters for sine and logarithm, and the parentheses around the argument for the logarithm have been omitted, because it consists of only a single term). This has a different meaning than: $\sin(x + 1) + \log(x - f(x))$.

Elementary Algebra

For numbers, the following is generally true:

$$a(b + c) = ab + ac$$

This is often applied in situations like the following, where we *factor out* the a:

$$a + b = a(1 + b/a)$$

If a is much greater than b, then we have now converted the original expression $a + b$ into another expression of the form:

$$something\ large \cdot (1 + something\ small)$$

which makes it easy to see which terms matter and which can be neglected in an approximation scheme. (The small term in the parentheses is "small" compared to the 1 in the parentheses and can therefore be treated as a perturbation.)

Quantities can be multiplied together, which gives rise to *powers*:

$$a \cdot a = a^2$$
$$a \cdot a \cdot a = a^3$$
$$\ldots$$

The raised quantity (the superscript) is also referred to as the *exponent*. In this book, superscripts always denote powers.

The three binomial formulas should be committed to memory:

$$(a + b)^2 = a^2 + 2ab + b^2$$
$$(a - b)^2 = a^2 - 2ab + b^2$$
$$(a + b)(a - b) = a^2 - b^2$$

Because the easiest things are often the most readily forgotten, let me just work out the first of these identities explicitly:

$$(a + b)^2 = (a + b)(a + b)$$
$$= a(a + b) + b(a + b)$$
$$= a^2 + ab + ba + b^2$$
$$= a^2 + 2ab + b^2$$

where I have made use of the fact that $ab = ba$.

Working with Fractions

Let's review the basic rules for working with fractions. The expression on top is called the *numerator*, the one at the bottom is the *denominator*:

$$\frac{\text{numerator}}{\text{denominator}}$$

If you can factor out a common factor in both numerator and denominator, then this common factor can be canceled:

$$\frac{2 + 4x}{2 + 2\sin(y)} = \frac{2(1 + 2x)}{2(1 + \sin(y))} = \frac{1 + 2x}{1 + \sin y}$$

To add two fractions, you have to bring them onto a common denominator in an operation that is the opposite of canceling a common factor:

$$\frac{1}{a} + \frac{1}{b} = \frac{a}{ab} + \frac{b}{ab} = \frac{a + b}{ab}$$

Here is a numeric example:

$$\frac{1}{2} + \frac{1}{3} = \frac{3}{6} + \frac{2}{6} = \frac{5}{6}$$

Sets, Sequences, and Series

A *set* is a grouping of elements in no particular order. In a *sequence*, the elements occur in a fixed order, one after the other.

The individual elements of sets and sequences are usually shown with subscripts that denote the index of the element in the set or its position in the sequence (similar to indexing into an array). In this book, subscripts are used only for the purpose of indexing elements of sets or sequences in this way.

Sets are usually indicated by curly braces. The following expressions are equivalent:

$$\{x_1, x_2, x_3, \ldots, x_n\}$$
$$\{x_i \mid i = 1, \ldots, n\}$$

For brevity, it is customary to suppress the range of the index if it can be understood from context. For example, if it is clear that there are n elements in the set, I might simply write $\{x_i\}$.

One often wants to sum a finite or infinite sequence of numbers; the result is known as a *series*:

$$x_1 + x_2 + x_3 + \cdots + x_n$$

Instead of writing out the terms explicitly, it is often useful to use the sum notation:

$$\sum_{i=1}^{n} x_i = x_1 + x_2 + x_3 + \cdots + x_n$$

The meaning of the summation symbol should be clear from this example. The variable used as index (here, i) is written underneath the summation sign followed by the lower limit (here, 1). The upper limit (here, n) is written above the summation sign. As a shorthand, any one of these specifications can be omitted. For instance, if it is clear from the context that the lower limit is 1 and the upper limit is n, then I might simply write $\sum_i x_i$ or even $\sum x_i$. In the latter form, it is understood that the sum runs over the index of the summands.

It is often convenient to describe the terms to be summed over in words, rather than giving specific limits:

$$\sum_{\text{all data points}} x_i$$

Some standard transformations involving the summation notation are used fairly often. For example, one frequently needs to shift indices. The following three expressions are equal, as you can easily see by writing out explicitly the terms of the sum in each case:

$$\sum_{i=0}^{n} x_i = \sum_{i=1}^{n+1} x_{i-1} = x_0 + \sum_{i=1}^{n} x_i$$

Keep in mind that the summation notation is just a shorthand for the explicit form given at the start of this section. If you become confused, you can always write out the terms explicitly to understand what is going on.

Finally, we may take the upper limit of the sum to be infinity, in which case the sum runs over infinitely many terms. Infinite series play a fundamental role in the theoretical development of mathematics, but all series that you will encounter in applications are, of course, finite.

Special Symbols

A few mathematical symbols are either indispensable or so useful that I wouldn't do without them.

Binary relationships

There are several special symbols to describe the relationship between two expressions. Some of the most useful ones are listed in Table B-3.

TABLE B-3. Commonly used relational operators

Operator	Meaning
$=\neq$	equal to, not equal to
$< >$	less than, greater than
$\leq \geq$	less than or equal to, greater than or equal to
$\ll \gg$	much less than, much greater than
$\propto$	proportional to
$\approx$	approximately equal to
$\sim$	scales as

The last three might require a word of explanation. We say two quantities are *approximately equal* when they are equal up to a "small" error. Put differently, the difference between the two quantities must be small compared to the quantities themselves: x and $1.1x$ are approximately equal, $x \approx 1.1x$, because the difference (which is $0.1x$) is small compared to x.

One quantity is *proportional* to another if they are equal up to a constant factor that has been omitted from the expression. Often, this factor will have units associated with it. For example, when we say "time is money," what we really mean is:

$$\text{money} \propto \text{time}$$

Here the omitted constant of proportionality is the hourly rate (which is also required to fix the units: hours on the left, dollars on the right; hence hourly rate must have units of "dollars per hour" to make the equation dimensionally consistent).

We say that a quantity *scales as* some other quantity if we want to express how one quantity depends on another one in a very general way. For example, recall that the area of a circle is πr^2 (where r is the length of the radius) but that the area of a square is a^2 (where a is the length of the side of the square). We can now say that "the area *scales as* the square of the length." This is a more general statement than saying that the area is proportional to the square of the length: the latter implies that they are equal up to a constant factor, whereas the scaling behavior allows for more complicated dependencies. (In this example, the constant of proportionality depends on the *shape* of the figure, but the scaling behavior area $\sim$ length^2 is true for all symmetrical figures.)

In particular when evaluating the complexity of algorithms, there is another notation to express a very similar notion: the so-called *big O* notation. For example, the expression $\mathcal{O}(n^2)$ states that the complexity of an algorithm grows ("scales") with the square of the number of elements in the input.

Parentheses and other delimiters

Round parentheses (...) are used for two purposes: to group terms together (establishing precedence) and to indicate the arguments to a function:

$$ab + c \neq a(b + c)$$ Parentheses to establish precedence

$$f(x, y) = x + y$$ Parentheses to indicate function arguments

Square brackets [...] are mostly used to indicate an interval:

$$[a, b]$$ all x such that $a \leq x \leq b$

For the purpose of this book, we don't need to worry about the distinction between closed and open intervals (*i.e.*, intervals that do or don't contain their endpoints, respectively).

Very rarely I use brackets for other purposes—for example as an alternative to round parentheses to establish precedence, or indicate that a function takes another *function* as its argument, as in the expectation value: $E[f(x)]$.

Curly braces {...} always denote a set.

Miscellaneous symbols

Two particular constants are indispensable. Everybody has heard of $\pi = 3.141592\ldots$, which is the ratio of the circumference of a circle to its diameter:

$$\pi = \frac{\text{circumference}}{\text{diameter}} = 3.141592\ldots$$

Equally important is the "base of the natural logarithm" $e = 2.718281\ldots$, sometimes called Euler's number. It is defined as the value of the infinite series:

$$e = \sum_{n=0}^{\infty} \frac{1}{n!} = 2.718281\ldots$$

The function e^x obtained by raising e to the xth power has the property that its derivative also equals e^x, and it is the only function that equals its derivative (up to a multiplicative constant, to be precise).

The number e also shows up in the definition of the Gaussian function:

$$e^{-x^2}$$

(Any function that contains e raised to $-x^2$ power is called a "Gaussian"; what's crucial is that the x in the exponent is squared and enters with a negative sign. Other constants may appear also, but the $-x^2$ in the exponent is the defining property.)

Because the exponents are often complicated expressions themselves, there is an alternative notation for the exponential function that avoids superscripts and instead uses the function name exp(...). The expression $\exp(x)$ means exactly the same as e^x, and the following two expressions are equivalent, also—but the one on the right is easier to write:

$$e^{-\left(\frac{x-\mu}{\sigma}\right)^2} = \exp\left(-\left(\frac{x-\mu}{\sigma}\right)^2\right)$$

A value of infinite magnitude is indicated by a special symbol:

$$\infty \qquad \text{a value of infinite magnitude}$$

The square root sign $\sqrt{x}$ states that:

$$\text{if} \quad y = \sqrt{x} \quad \text{then} \quad y^2 = x$$

Finally, the integral sign $\int$, which always occurs together with an expression of the form dx (or dt, or so), is used to denote a generalized form of summation: the expression to the right of the integral sign is to be "summed" for all values of x (or t). If explicit limits of the integration are given, they are attached to the integral sign:

$$\int_0^1 f(x)\, dx$$

This means: "sum all values of $f(x)$ for x ranging from 0 to 1."

The Greek Alphabet

Greek letters are used all the time in mathematics and other sciences and should be committed to memory. (See Table B-4.)

TABLE B-4. The Greek alphabet

Lowercase	Uppercase	Name
α	A	Alpha
β	B	Beta
γ	Γ	Gamma
δ	Δ	Delta
ϵ	E	Epsilon
ζ	Z	Zeta
η	H	Eta
θ	Θ	Theta
ι	I	Iota
κ	K	Kappa
λ	Λ	Lambda
μ	M	Mu
ν	N	Nu
ξ	Ξ	Xi
o	O	Omicron
π	Π	Pi
ρ	R	Rho
σ	Σ	Sigma
τ	T	Tau
υ	Υ	Upsilon
ϕ	Φ	Phi
χ	X	Chi
ψ	Ψ	Psi
ω	Ω	Omega

Where to Go from Here

This appendix can of course only give a cartoon version of the topics mentioned, or—if you have seen this material before—at best serve as a reminder. But most of all, I hope it serves as a *teaser*: mathematics is a wonderfully rich and stimulating topic, and I would hope that in this appendix (and in the rest of this book) I have been able to convey some of its fascination—and perhaps even convinced you to dig a little deeper.

If you want to learn more, here are a couple of hints.

The first topic to explore is calculus (or real analysis). All modern mathematics starts here, and it is here that some of the most frequently used concepts (derivative, integral, Taylor expansion) are properly introduced. It is a must-have.

But if you limit your attention to calculus, you will never get over the idea that mathematics is about "calculating something." To get a sense of what math is *really* all about, you have to go beyond analysis. The next topic in a typical college syllabus is linear algebra. In linear algebra, we go beyond relatively tangible things like curves and numbers and for the first time start to consider concepts in a fully abstract way: spaces, transformations, mappings. What can we say about them *in general* without having to appeal to any particular realization? Understanding this material requires real mental effort—you have to change the way you think. (Similarly to how you have to change the way you think if you try to learn Lisp or Haskell.) Linear algebra also provides the theoretical underpinnings of all matrix operations and hence for most frequently used numerical routines. (You can't do paper-and-pencil mathematics without calculus, and you can't do numerical mathematics without linear algebra.)

With these two subjects under your belt, you will be able to pick up pretty much any mathematical topic and make sense of it. You might then want to explore complex calculus for the elegance and beauty of its theorems, or functional analysis and Fourier theory (which blend analysis and linear algebra) because of their importance in all application-oriented areas, or take a deeper look at probability theory, with its obvious importance for anything having to do with random data.

On Math

I have observed that there are two misconceptions about mathematics that are particularly prevalent among people coming from a software or computing background. The first misconception holds that mathematics is primarily a prescriptive, calculational (not necessarily numerical) scheme and similar to an Algol-derived programming language: a pseudo-code for expressing algorithms. The other misconception views mathematics as mostly an abstract method for formal reasoning, not dissimilar to certain logic programming environments: a way to manipulate logic statements.

What both of them miss is that mathematics is not a *method* but first and foremost a body of *content* in its own right. You will never understand what mathematics is if you see it only as something you *use* to obtain certain results. Mathematics is, first and foremost, a rich and exciting story in itself.

There is an unfortunate perception among nonmathematicians (and even partially reinforced by this book) that mathematics is about "calculating things." This is not so, and it is probably the most unhelpful misconception about mathematics of all.

In fairness, this point of view is promulgated by many introductory college textbooks. In a thoroughly misguided attempt to make their subject "interesting," they try to motivate mathematical concepts with phony applications to the design of bridges and airplanes, or to calculating the probability of winning at poker. This not only obscures the beauty of the subject but also creates the incorrect impression of mathematics as a utilitarian fingering exercise and almost as a necessary evil.

Finally, I strongly recommend that you stay away from books on popular or recreational math, for two reasons. First, they tend to focus on a small set of topics that can be treated using "elementary" methods (mostly geometry and some basic number theory), and tend to omit most of the conceptually important topics. Furthermore, in their attempt to present amusing or entertaining snippets of information, they fail to display the rich, interconnected structure of mathematical theory: all you end up with is a book of (stale) jokes.

Further Reading

Calculus

- *The Hitchhiker's Guide to Calculus.* Michael Spivak. Mathematical Association of America. 1995.
  If the material in this appendix is really new to you, then this short (120-page) booklet provides a surprisingly complete, approachable, yet mathematically respectable introduction. Highly recommended for the curious and the confused.

- *Precalculus: A Prelude to Calculus.* Sheldon Axler. Wiley. 2008.
  Axler's book covers the basics: numbers, basic algebra, inequalities, coordinate systems, and functions—including exponential, logarithmic, and trigonometric functions—but it stops short of derivatives and integrals. If you want to brush up on foundational material, this is an excellent text.

- *Calculus.* Michael Spivak. 4th ed., Publish or Perish. 2008.
  This is a comprehensive book on calculus. It concentrates exclusively on the clear development of the mathematical theory and thereby avoids the confusion that often results from an oversupply of (more or less) artificial examples. The presentation is written for the reader who is relatively new to formal mathematical reasoning, and the author does a good job motivating the peculiar arguments required by formal mathematical manipulations. Rightly popular.

- *Yet Another Introduction to Analysis.* Victor Bryant. Cambridge University Press. 1990.
  This short book is intended as a quick introduction for those readers who already possess passing familiarity with the topic and are comfortable with abstract operations.

Linear Algebra

- *Linear Algebra Done Right.* Sheldon Axler. 2nd ed., Springer. 2004.
  This is the best introduction to linear algebra that I am aware of, and it fully lives up to its grandiose title. This book treats linear algebra as abstract theory of mappings, but on a very accessible, advanced undergraduate level. Highly recommended.

- *Linear Algebra.* Klaus Jänich. Springer. 1994.
  This book employs a greater amount of abstract mathematical formalism than the previous entry, but the author tries very hard to explain and motivate all concepts. This book might therefore give a better sense of the nature of abstract algebraic arguments than Axler's streamlined presentation. The book is written for a first-year course at German universities; the style of the presentation may appear exotic to the American reader.

Complex Analysis

- *Complex Analysis.* Joseph Bak and Donald J. Newman. 2nd ed., Springer. 1996.
  This is a straightforward, and relatively short, introduction to all the standard topics of classical complex analysis.

- *Complex Variables.* Mark J. Ablowitz and Athanassios S. Fokas. 2nd ed., Cambridge University Press. 2003.
  This is a much more comprehensive and advanced book. It is split into two parts: the first part developing the theory, the second part discussing several nontrivial applications (mostly to the theory of differential equations).

- *Fourier Analysis and Its Applications.* Gerald B. Folland. American Mathematical Society. 2009.
  This is a terrific introduction to Fourier theory. The book places a strong emphasis on the solution of partial differential equations but in the course of it also develops the basics of function spaces, orthogonal polynomials, and eigenfunction expansions. The later chapters give an introduction to distributions and Green's functions. This is a very accessible book, but you will need a strong grounding in real and complex analysis, as well as some linear algebra.

Mindbenders

If you *really* want to know what math is like, pick up any one of these. You don't have to understand everything—just get the flavor of it all. None of them are "useful," all are fascinating.

- *A Primer of Analytic Number Theory.* Jeffrey Stopple. Cambridge University Press. 2003.
  This is an amazing book in every respect. The author takes one of the most advanced, obscure, and "useless" topics—namely analytic number theory—and makes it completely accessible to anyone having even minimal familiarity with calculus concepts (and even those are not strictly required). In the course of the book, the author introduces series expansions, complex numbers, and many results from calculus, finally arriving at one of the great unsolved problems in mathematics: the Riemann hypothesis. If you want to know what math *really* is, read this book!

- *The Computer As Crucible: An Introduction to Experimental Mathematics.* Jonathan Borwein and Keith Devlin. AK Peters. 2008.
  If you are coming from a programming background, you might be comfortable with this book. The idea behind "experimental mathematics" is to see whether we can use a computer to provide us with intuition about mathematical results that can later be verified through rigorous proofs. Some of the observations one encounters in the process are astounding. This book tries to maintain an elementary level of treatment.

- *Mathematics by Experiment.* Jonathan M. Borwein and David H. Bailey. 2nd ed., AK Peters. 2008.

This is a more advanced book coauthored by one of the authors of the previous entry on much the same topic.

- *A Mathematician's Lament: How School Cheats Us Out of Our Most Fascinating and Imaginative Art Form*. Paul Lockhart. Bellevue Literary Press. 2009.

  This is not a math book at all: instead it is a short essay by a mathematician (or math teacher) on *what* mathematics is and *why* and *how* it should be taught. The author's philosophy is similar to the one I've tried to present in the observations toward the end of this appendix. Read it and weep. (Then go change the world.) Versions are also available on the Web (for example, check *http://www.maa.org/devlin/devlin_03_08. html*).

Working with Data

ONE OF THE UNCOMFORTABLE (AND EASILY OVERLOOKED) TRUTHS OF WORKING WITH DATA IS THAT USUALLY only a small fraction of the time is spent on the actual "analysis." Often a far greater amount of time and effort is expended on a variety of tasks that may appear "menial" by comparison but that are absolutely critical nevertheless: obtaining the data; verifying, cleaning and possibly reformatting it; and dealing with updates, storage, and archiving. For someone new to working with data (and even, periodically, for someone not so new), it typically comes as a surprise that these preparatory tasks are not only necessary but also take up as much time as they do.

By their nature, these housekeeping and auxiliary tasks tend to be very specific: specific to the data, specific to the environment, and specific to the particular question being investigated. This implies that there is little that can be said about them in generality—it pretty much all comes down to ad hoc hackery. Of course, this absence of recognizable nontrivial techniques is one of the main reasons these activities receive as little attention as they do.

That being said, we can try to increase our awareness of such issues typically arising in practical situations.

Sources for Data

The two most common sources for data in an enterprise environment are *databases* and *logfiles*. As data sources, the two sources tend to address different needs. Databases will contain data related to the "business," whereas logfiles are a source for "operational" data: databases answer the question "what did we sell to whom?" whereas logfiles answer the question "what did we do, and when?"

Databases can be either "online transaction processing" (OLTP) or "production" databases, or "data warehouses" for long-term storage. Production databases tend to be normalized, fast, and busy. You may or may not be able to get read access to them for ad hoc queries, depending on company policy. Data warehouses tend to be denormalized, slow, and often accessed through a batch processing facility (submit your query tonight and find out tomorrow that you omitted a field you needed). Production databases tend to be owned (at least in spirit) by the application development teams. Data warehouses are invariably owned by the IT department, which implies a different culture (see also the discussion in Chapter 17). In either form, databases tend to provide a stable foundation for data needs—provided you are interested in something the company already considers part of its "business."

In contrast, logfiles are often an important source of data for new initiatives. If you want to evaluate a new business idea, chances are that the data required for your analysis will not be available in the database—not *yet*, since there has never been a reason to store it before. In such situations you may still be able to find the information you need in logfiles that are regularly produced.

One *very* important distinction is that databases and logfiles have different life cycles: making changes to the design of a database is always a slow (often, excruciatingly slow) process, but the data itself lives in the database forever (if the database is properly designed). In contrast, logfiles often contain much more information than the database, but they are usually deleted very quickly. If your organization keeps logfiles for two weeks, consider yourself lucky!

Therefore, if you want to begin a project using data contained in logfiles then you need to move *fast*: start saving all files to your desktop or another safe location immediately, *then* figure out what you want to do with them! Frequently, you will need several weeks' (or months') worth of data for a conclusive analysis, and every day that you wait can never be made up. Also keep in mind that logfiles are usually generated on production servers to which access may be heavily restricted. It is not uncommon to spend *weeks* in negotiations with network administrators if you need to move significant amounts of data off of production systems.

The same consideration applies if information is not available in the logfiles, so that existing code needs to be instrumented to support collection of the required data. In this situation, you will likely find yourself captive to preexisting release schedules and other constraints. Again: start to think about *collecting* data early.

Because databases and logfiles are so common and so directly useful sources of data in an enterprise environment, it's easy to forget that they're not the only available sources.

A separate data source that sometimes can be extremely useful is the company's finance department. Companies are required to report on various financial metrics, which means that such information *must* be available, although possibly only in a highly aggregated form (*e.g.*, quarterly) and possibly quite late. On other hand, this information is normative and therefore reliable: after all, it's what the company is paying taxes on! (I am ignoring the possibility that the data provided by the finance department might be *wrong*, but don't get me wrong: forensic data analysis is also an interesting field of study.)

What works internally may also work with competitors. The quarterly filings that publicly listed companies are required to make can make interesting reading!

So far we have assumed that you had to find and extract the data you need from whatever sources are available; in my experience, this is by far the most common scenario. However, your data may also be handed to you—for example, if it is experimental data or if it comes from an external source. In this case, it may come in a domain-specific file format (we'll return to data formats shortly). The problem with this situation is, of course, that now you have no control over what is in the data!

Cleaning and Conditioning

Raw data, whether it was obtained from a database query or by parsing a logfile, typically needs to be cleaned or conditioned. Here are some areas that often need attention.

Missing values
> If individual attributes or entire data points are missing, we need to decide how to handle them. Should we discard the whole record, mark the information in question as missing, or backfill it in some way? Your choice will depend strongly on your specific situation and goals.

Outliers
> In general, you should be extremely careful when removing outliers—you may be removing the effect that you are looking for. *Never* should data points be removed silently. (There is a (partly apocryphal) story[*] that the discovery of the hole in the ozone layer over Antarctica was delayed by several years because the automated data gathering system discarded readings that it considered to be "impossibly low.")

Junk
> Data that comes over a network may contain nonprintable characters or similar junk. Such data is not only useless but can also seriously confuse downstream applications that are attempting to process the data (*e.g.*, when nonprintable characters are interpreted as control characters—many programming environments will not issue helpful diagnostics if this happens). This kind of problem frequently goes unnoticed, because such junk is typically rare and not easily noticed simply by scanning the beginning of a data set.

Formatting and normalizing
> Individual values may not be formatted in the most useful way for subsequent analysis. Examples of frequently used transformations for this purpose include: forcing upper- or

---

[*] *http://www.nas.nasa.gov/About/Education/Ozone/history.html.*

lowercase; removing blanks within strings, or replacing them with dashes; replacing timestamps with Unix Epoch seconds, the Julian day number, or a similar numerical value; replacing numeric codes with string labels, or vice versa; and so on.

Duplicate records

Data sets often contain duplicate records that need to be recognized and removed ("de-duped"). Depending on what you consider "duplicate," this may require a nontrivial effort. (I once worked on a project that tried to recognize misspelled postal addresses and assign them to the correctly spelled one. This also is a form of de-duping.)

Merging data sets

The need to merge data sets from different sources is arises pretty often—for instance, when the data comes from different database instances. Make sure the data is truly compatible, especially if the database instances are geographically dispersed. Differing time zones are a common trouble spot, but don't overlook things like monetary units. In addition, you may need to be aware of localization issues, such as font encodings and date formatting.[*]

Reading this list, you should realize that the process of *cleaning* data cannot be separated from *analyzing* it. For instance: outlier detection and evaluation require some pretty deep analysis to be reliable. On the other hand, you may need to remove outliers before you can calculate meaningful values for certain summary statistics. This is an important insight, which we will make time and again: data analysis is an *iterative* process, in which each operation is at the same time the result of a previous step and the preparation for a subsequent step.

Data files may also be defective in ways that only become apparent when subsequent analysis fails or produces nonsensical results. Some common problems are:

Clerical errors

These are basically data entry errors: 0.01 instead of 0.001, values entered in the wrong column, all that. Because most data these days is computer generated, the classic occasional typo seems to be mostly a thing of the past. But watch out for its industrial counterpart: entire data sets that are systematically corrupted. (Once, we didn't realize that a certain string field in the database was of fixed width. As we went from entries of the form ID1, ID2, and so on to entries like ID10, the last character was silently truncated by the database. It took a long time before we noticed—after all, the results we got back *looked* all right.)

---

[*] Regarding time zones, I used to be a strong proponent of keeping all date/time information in Coordinated Universal Time (UTC, "Greenwich Time"), always. However, I have since learned that this is not always appropriate: for some information, such as customer behavior, it is the *local* time that matters, not the absolute time. Nevertheless, I would prefer to store such information in two parts: timestamp in UTC *and* in addition, the local time zone of the user. (Whether we can actually determine the user's time zone accurately is a different matter.)

Numerical "special" values

Missing values in a data set may be encoded using special numerical values (such as −1 or 9999). Unless these values are filtered out, they will obviously corrupt any statistical analysis. There is less of a need for special values like this when data is kept in text files (because you can indicate missing values with a marker such as ???), but be aware that it's still an issue when you are dealing with binary files.

Crazy business rules and overloaded database fields

Bad schema design can thoroughly wreck your analysis. A pernicious problem is overloaded database fields: fields that change their meaning depending on the values of *other* fields in the database. I remember a case where the `Quantity` field in a table contained the number of items shipped—unless it was zero—in which case it signaled a discount, a promotion, or an out-of-stock situation depending on whether an entry with the same order ID existed in the `Discounts`, `Promotions`, or `BackOrders` tables—or it contained not the number of items shipped but rather the number of multi-item packages that had been shipped (if the `IsMulti` flag was set), or it contained the ID (!) of the return order associated with this line item (if some other flag was set). What made the situation so treacherous was that running a query such as `select avg(Quantity) from ...` would produce a number that *seemed* sensible even though it was, of course, complete nonsense. What's worse, most people were unaware of this situation because the data was usually accessed only through (massive) stored procedures that took all these crazy business rules into account.

Sampling

When dealing with very large data sets, we can often simplify our lives significantly by working with a *sample* instead of the full data set—provided the sample is *representative* of the whole. And therein lies the problem.

In practice, sampling often means partitioning the data on some property of the data: picking all customers whose names begin with the letter "t," for instance, or whose customer ID ends with "0"; or using the logfile from one server only (out of 10); or all transactions that occurred today. The problem is that it can be very difficult to establish a priori whether these subpopulations are at all representative of the entire population. Determining this would require an in-depth study on the *whole* population—precisely what we wanted to avoid!

Statistical lore is full of (often quite amusing) stories about the subtle biases introduced through improper sampling. Choosing all customers whose first names end in "a" will probably introduce a bias toward female customers. Surveying children for the number of siblings will overestimate the number of children per household because it excludes households without children. A long-term study of mutual funds may report overly optimistic average returns on investment because it ignores funds that have been shut down because of poor performance ("survivorship bias"). A trailing zero may indicate a customer record that was created long ago by the previous version of the software. The server you selected for your logfile may be the "overflow" server that comes online during peak hours only. And we haven't even mentioned the problems involved with collecting data in the first place! (A phone survey is inherently biased against those who don't have a phone or don't answer it.) Furthermore, strange biases may exist that nobody is aware of. (It is not guaranteed that the network administrators will know or understand the algorithm that the load balancer uses to assign transactions to servers, particularly if the load balancer itself is "smart" and changes its logic based on traffic patterns.)

A relatively safe way to create a sample is to take the whole data set (or as large a chunk of it as possible) and randomly pick some of the records. The keyword is *randomly*: don't take every tenth record; instead, evaluate each record and retain it with a probability of 1/10. Also make sure that the data set does not contain duplicates. (For instance, to sample customers given their purchases, you must first extract the customer IDs and de-dupe them, then sample from the de-duped IDs. Sampling from the transactions alone will introduce a bias toward repeat customers.)

Sampling in this way pretty much requires that the data be available as a file. In contrast, sampling from a database is more difficult because, in general, we don't have control (or even full understanding) over how records are sorted internally. We can dump all records to file and then sample from there, but this is rather awkward and may not even be feasible for very large tables.

A good trick to enable random sampling from databases is to include an additional column, which *at the time the record is created* is filled with a random integer between (say) 0 and 99. By selecting on this column, we can extract a sample consisting of 1 percent of all records. This column can even be indexed (although the database engine may ignore the index if the result set is too large). Even when it is not possible to add such a column to the actual table, the same technique can still be used by adding a cross-reference table that contains only the primary key of the table we want to sample from and the random integer. It is critical that the the random number is assigned at the time the record is created and is never changed or updated thereafter.

Whichever approach you take, you should verify that your sampling process does lead to representative samples. (Take two independent samples and compare their properties.)

Sampling can be truly useful—even necessary. Just be very careful.

Data File Formats

When it comes to file formats for data, my recommendation is to keep it simple, even dead-simple. The simpler the file format, the greater flexibility you have in terms of the tools you can use on the data. Avoid formats that require a nontrivial parser!

My personal favorite is that old standby, the delimiter-separated text file, with one record per line and a single data set per file. (Despite the infamous difficulties with the Unix make utility, I nevertheless like tab-delimited files: since numbers don't contain tabs, I never need to quote or escape anything; and the tabs make it easy to visually inspect a file—easier than do commas.) In fairness, delimiter-separated text files do not work well for one-to-many relationships or other situations where each record can have a varying number of attributes. On the other hand, such situations are rare and tend to require special treatment, anyway.

One disadvantage of this format is that it does not allow you to keep information about the data ("metadata") within the file itself, except possibly the column names as first row. One solution is to use two files—one for the data and one for the metadata—and to adopt a convenient naming convention (*e.g.*, using the same basename for both files while distinguishing them by the extensions `.data` and `.names`).[*]

In general, I strongly recommend that you stay with text files and avoid binary files. Text files are portable (despite the annoying newline issue), robust, and self-explanatory. They also compress nicely. If you nevertheless decide to use binary files, I suggest that you use an established format (for which mature libraries exist!) instead of devising an ad hoc format of your own.

I also don't find XML very suitable as a file format for data: the ratio of markup to payload is poor which leads to unnecessarily bloated files. XML is also notoriously expensive to parse, in particular for large files. Finally, the flexibility provided by XML is rarely necessary for data sets, which typically have a very regular structure. (It may seem as if XML might be useful for metadata, but even here I disagree: the value of XML is to make data machine-readable, whereas the primary consumers of metadata are humans!)

Everything I have said so far assumes that the data files are primarily for yourself (you don't want to distribute them) and that you are willing to read in the entire file sequentially (so that you don't need to perform seeks within the file). There are file formats that allow you to bundle multiple data sets into a single file and efficiently extract parts of them (for example, check out the Hierarchical Data Format (HDF) and its variants, such as netCDF), but I have never encountered them in real life. It should not be lost on you that the statistics and machine-learning communities use delimiter-separated text almost exclusively as format for data sets on their public data repositories. (And if you need indexed lookup, you may be better off setting up a minimal standalone database for yourself: see the Workshop in Chapter 16.)

Finally, I should point out that some (scientific) disciplines have their own specialized file formats as well as the tools designed to handle them. Use them when appropriate.

---

[*]This convention is used by many data sets available from the UCI Machine Learning Repository.

The Care and Feeding of Your Data Zoo

If you work in the same environment for a while, you are likely to develop a veritable collection of different data sets. Not infrequently, it is this ready access to relevant data sets that makes you valuable to the organization (quite aside from your more celebrated skills). On the downside, *maintaining* that collection in good order requires a certain amount of effort.

My primary advice is make sure that all data sets are *self-explanatory* and *reproducible*.

To ensure that a data set is self-explanatory, you should not only include the minimal metadata with or in the file itself, but include *all* the information necessary to make sense of it. For instance, to represent a time series (*i.e.*, a data set of measurements taken over time at regular intervals), it is strictly necessary to store only the values, the starting time, and the length of the interval between data points. However, it is safer to store the corresponding timestamp with each measured value—this way, the data set still makes sense even if the metadata has been lost or garbled. Similar considerations apply more generally: I tend to be fairly generous when it comes to including information that might seem "redundant."

To keep data reproducible, you should keep track of its source *and* the cleaning and conditioning transformations. This can be tedious because so much of the latter consists of ad hoc, manual operations. I usually keep logs with my data sets to record the URLs (if the data came from the Web) or the database queries. I also capture the commands and pipelines issued at the shell prompt and keep copies of all transformation scripts. Finally, if I combine data from multiple sources into a single data set, I always retain the original data sets.

This kind of housekeeping is very important: not only to produce an audit trail (should it ever be needed) but also because data sets tend to be reused again and again and for different purposes. Being able to determine *exactly* what is in the data is crucial.

I have not found many opportunities to automate these processes; the tasks just vary too much. The one exception is the automated scheduled collection and archiving of volatile data (*e.g.*, copying logfiles to a safe location). Your needs may be different.

Finally, here are three pieces of advice on the physical handling of data files. They should be obvious but aren't necessarily.

Keep data files readily available
> Being able to run a minimal script on a file residing on a local drive to come up with an answer in seconds (compared to the 12–24 hour turnaround typical of may data warehouse installations) is a huge enabler.

Compress your data files
> I remember a group of statisticians who constantly complained about the lack of disk space and kept requesting more storage. None of them used compression or had even

heard of it. And all their data sets were kept in a textlike format that could be compressed by 90 percent! (Also keep in mind that gzip can read from and write to a pipe, so that the uncompressed file never needs to exist on disk.)

Have a backup strategy

This is important especially if all of your data resides only on your local workstation. At the very least, get a second drive and mirror files to it. Of course, a remote (and, ideally, managed) storage location is much better. Keep in mind that data sets can easily become large, so you might want to sit down with your network administrators early in the process so that your storage needs can be budgeted appropriately.

Skills

I hope that I've convinced you that obtaining, preparing, and transforming data makes up a large part of day-to-day activities when working with data. To be effective in this role, I recommend you acquire and develop some skills that facilitate these aspects of your role.

For the most part, these skills come down to easy, ad hoc programming. If you come from software development, you will hardly find anything new here. But if you come from a scientific (or academic) background, you might want to broaden your expertise a little.

A special consideration is due to those who come to "data analysis" from a database-centric, SQL programming point of view. If this describes your situation, I *strongly* encourage you to pick up a language besides SQL. SQL is simply too restricted in what it can do and therefore limits the kinds of problems you will choose to tackle—whether you realize it or not! It's also a good idea to do the majority of your work "offline" so that there is less of a toll on the database (which is, after all, usually a shared resource).

Learn a scripting language

A scripting language such as Perl, Python, or Ruby is required for easy manipulation of data files. Knowledge of a "large-scale" programming language like C/C++/Java/C# is *not* sufficient. Scripting languages eliminate the overhead ("boilerplate code") typically associated with common tasks such as input/output and file or string handling. This is important because most data transformation tasks are tiny and therefore the typical cost of overhead, relative to the overall programming task, is simply not acceptable.

Note that R (the statistics package) can do double duty as a scripting language for these purposes.

Master regular expressions

If you are dealing with strings (or stringlike objects, such as timestamps), then regular expressions are the solution (and an amazingly powerful solution) to problems you didn't even realize you had! You don't need to develop intimate familiarity with the whole regular expression bestiary, but working knowledge of the basics is required.

Be comfortable browsing a database

Pick a graphical database frontend[*] and become proficient with it. You should be able to figure out the schema of a database and the semantics of the data simply by browsing the tables and their values, requiring only minimal help.

Develop a good relationship with your system administrator and DBA

System administrators and DBAs are in the position to make your life significantly easier (by granting you access, creating accounts, saving files, providing storage, running jobs for you, ...). However, they were not hired to do that—to the contrary, they are paid to "keep the trains on time." A rogue (and possibly clueless or oblivious) data analyst, running huge batch jobs during the busiest time of the day, does *not* help with that task!

I would like to encourage you to take an interest in the situation of your system administrators: try to understand their position and the constraints they have to work under. System administrators tend to be paranoid—that's what they're paid for! Their biggest fear is that *something* will upset the system. If you can convince them that you do not pose a great risk, you will probably find them to be incredibly helpful.

(Finally, I tend to adopt the attitude that any production job by default has higher priority than the research and analysis I am working on, and therefore I better be patient.)

Work on Unix

I mean it. Unix was developed for *precisely* this kind of ad hoc programming with files and data, and it continues to provide the most liberating environment for such work.

Unix (and its variants, including Linux and Mac OS X) has some obvious technical advantages, but its most important property in the present context is that it *encourages you to devise solutions*. It does not try (or pretend) to do the job for you, but it goes out of its way to give you tools that you might find handy—without prescribing how or for what you use them. In contrast, other operating systems tend to encourage you to stay within the boundaries of certain familiar activity patterns—which does *not* encourage the development of your problem-solving abilities (or, more importantly, your problem-solving *attitudes*).

True story: I needed to send a file containing several millions of keys to a coworker. (The company did not work on Unix.) Since the file was too large to fit safely into an email message, I posted it to a web server on my desktop and sent my coworker the link. (I dutifully had provided the file with the extension .txt, so that he would be able to open it.) Five minutes later, he calls me back: "I can't open that"—"What do you mean?"—"Well, I click the link, but ScrapPaper [the default text editor for small text

---

[*]The SQuirreL project (*http://squirrel-sql.sourceforge.net*) is a good choice. Free, open source, and mature, it is also written in Java—which means that it can run anywhere and connect to any database for which JDBC drivers exist.

files on this particular system] dies because the file is too big." This coworker was not inept (in fact, he was quite good at his primary job), but he displayed the particular non-problem-solving attitude that develops in predefined work environments: "link, click." It did not even occur to him to think of something else to try. That's a problem!

If you want to be successful working with data, you want to work in an environment that encourages you to devise your own solutions.

You want to work on Unix.

Terminology

When working with data, there is some terminology that is frequently used.

Types of Data

We can distinguish different types of data. The most important distinction is the one between *numerical* and nonnumerical or *categorical* data.

Numerical data is the most convenient to handle because it allows us to perform arbitrary calculations. (In other words, we can calculate quantities like the mean.) Numerical data can be *continuous* (taking on all values) or *discrete* (taking on only a discrete set of values). It is often necessary to discretize or *bin* continuous data.

You will sometimes find numerical data subdivided further into *interval* and *ratio* data. Interval data is data that does not have a proper origin, whereas ratio data does. Examples of interval data (without proper origin) are calendar dates and temperatures in units of Fahrenheit or Celsius. You can subtract such data to form *intervals* (there are 7 days between 01 April 09 and 07 April 09) but you cannot form ratios: it does not make sense to say that 60 Celsius is "twice as hot" as 30 Celsius. In contrast, quantities like length or weight measurements are ratio data: 0 kilograms truly means "no mass," and 0 centimeters truly means "no length." For ratio data, it makes sense to say that a mass of 2 kilograms is "twice as heavy" as a mass of 1 kilogram.

The distinction between ratio and interval data is not very important in practice, because interval data occurs rarely (I can think of no examples other than the two just mentioned) and can always be avoided through better encoding. The data is numeric by construction, so a zero must exist; hence an encoding can be found that measures magnitudes from this origin (the Kelvin scale for temperatures does exactly that).

All nonnumerical data is categorical—in practice, you will usually find categorical data encoded as strings. Categorical data is less powerful than numerical data because there are fewer things we can do with it. Pretty much the only available operation is counting how often each value occurs.

Categorical data can be subdivided into *nominal* and *ordinal* data. The difference is that for ordinal data, a natural sort order between values exists, whereas for nominal data no such sort order exists. An example for ordinal (sortable) data is a data set consisting of values like Like, Dislike, Don't Care, which have a clear sort order (namely, Like > Don't Care > Dislike). In contrast, the colors Red, Blue, Green when used to describe (say) a sweater are nominal, because there is no natural order in which to arrange these values.

Sortability is an important property because it implies that the data is "almost" numerical. If categorical data is sortable then it can be mapped to a set of numbers, which are more convenient to handle. For example, we can map Like, Dislike, Don't Care to the numbers 1, −1, and 0, which allows us to calculate an average value after all! However, there is no such thing as the "average color" of all sweaters that were sold.

Another property I look for determines whether data is "mixable." Can I combine arbitrary multiples of data points to construct a new data point? For data to be mixable in this way, it is not enough to be able to *combine* data points (*e.g.*, concatenating two strings) I must also be able to combine *arbitrary* multiples of all data points. If I can do this, then I can construct a *new* data point that lies, for example, "halfway" between the original ones, like so: $x/2 + y/2$. Being able to construct new data points in this way can speed up certain algorithms (see Chapter 13 for some applications).

When data is mixable it is similar to points in space, and a lot of geometric intuition can be brought to bear. (Technically, the data forms a vector space over the real numbers.)

The Data Type Depends on the Semantics

It is extremely important to realize that *the type of the data is determined by the semantics of the data*. The data type is *not* inherent in the data—it only arises from its *context*.

Postal codes are a good example: although a postal code like 98101 may *look* like a number, it does not *behave* like a number. It just does not make sense to add two postal codes together or to form the average of a bunch of postal codes! Similarly, the colors Red, Yellow, Green may be either nominal (if they refer to the colors of a sweater) or ordinal (if they are status indicators, in which case they obey a sort order akin to that of a traffic light).

Whether data is numerical or categorical, sortable or not, depends on its meaning. You can't just look at a data set in isolation to determine its type. You need to know what the data *means*.

Data by itself does not provide information. It is only when we take the data *together* with its context that defines its semantics that data becomes meaningful. (This point is occasionally overlooked by people with an overly formalistic disposition.)

Types of Data Sets

Data sets can be classified by the number of variables or columns they contain. Depending on the type of data set, we tend to be interested in different questions.

Univariate

A data set containing values only for a single variable. The weights of all students in a class, for example, form a univariate data set. For univariate data sets, we usually want to know how the individual points are distributed: the shape of the distribution, whether it is symmetric, does it have outliers, and so on.

Bivariate

A data set containing two variables. For such data sets, we are mostly interested in determining whether there is a relationship between the two quantities. If we had the heights in addition to the weights, for instance, we would ask whether there is any discernible relationship between heights and weights (*e.g.*, are taller students heavier?).

Multivariate

If a data set contains more than two variables, then it is considered multivariate. When dealing with multivariate problems, we typically want to find a smaller group of variables that still contains most of the information about the data set.

Of course, any bivariate or multivariate data set can be *treated* as a univariate one if we consider a single variable at a time. Again, the nature of the data set is not inherent in the data but depends on how we look at it.

Further Reading

- *Problem Solving: A Statistician's Guide.* Chris Chatfield. 2nd ed., Chapman & Hall/CRC. 1995.
  This is a highly informative book about all the messy realities that are usually *not* mentioned in class: from botched experimental setups to effective communication with the public. The book is geared toward professional statisticians, and some of the technical discussion may be too advanced, but it is worthwhile for the practicality of its general advice nonetheless.

- *Unix Power Tools.* Shelley Powers, Jerry Peek, Tim O'Reilly, and Mike Loukides. 3rd ed., O'Reilly. 2002.
  The classic book on getting stuff done with Unix.

- *The Art of UNIX Programming.* Eric S. Raymond. Addison-Wesley. 2003.
  The Unix philosophy has been expounded many times before but rarely more eloquently. This is a partisan book, and one need not agree with every argument the author makes, but some of his observations on good design and desirable features in a programming environment are well worth contemplating.

Data Set Repositories

Although I assume that you have your own data sets that you would like to analyze, it's nice to have access to a wider selection of data sets—for instance, when you want to try out and learn a new method.

Several data set repositories exist on the Web. These are the ones that I have found particularly helpful.

- *The Data and Story Library at statlib.* A smaller collection of data sets, together with their motivating "stories," intended for courses in introductory statistics. (*http://lib.stat.cmu.edu/DASL*)

- *Data Archive at the Journal of Statistics Education.* A large collection of often uncommonly interesting data sets. In addition to the data sets, the site provides links to the full text of the articles in which these data sets were analyzed and discussed. (*http://www.amstat.org/publications/jse*—then select "Data Archive" in the navigation bar)

- *UCI Machine Learning Repository.* A large collection of data sets, mostly suitable for classification tasks. (*http://archive.ics.uci.edu/ml/*)

- *Time Series Data Library.* An extensive collection of times series data. Unfortunately, many of the data sets are poorly documented. (*http://robjhyndman.com/TSDL/*)

- *Frequent Itemset Mining Dataset Repository.* A specialized repository with data sets for methods to find frequent item sets. (*http://fimi.cs.helsinki.fi/data/*)

- *UCINET IV Datasets.* Another specialized collection: this one includes data sets with information about social networks. (*http://vlado.fmf.uni-lj.si/pub/networks/data/Ucinet/UciData.htm*)

- *A Handbook of Small Data Sets.* David J. Hand, Fergus Daly, K. McConway, D. Lunn, and E. Ostrowski. Chapman & Hall/CRC. 1993.
  This is a rather curious resource: a book containing over 500 individual data sets (with descriptions) from all walks of life. Most of the data sets are "small," containing from a handful to a few hundred points. The data sets themselves can be found all over the Web, but only the book gives you the descriptions as well.

INDEX

C

C Library: *See GSL*

C Clustering Library, 320–324

calculus, 447–483
  absolute value function, 457
  binomial theorem, 468
  derivatives, 460–462
  dividing by zero, 470
  exponential functions, 452–454
  factorial function, 458
  Gaussian function and the Normal
    distribution, 455
  hyperbolic tangent function, 457
  integrals, 463
  inverse of a function, 459
  limits, sequences and series, 465
  linear transformation, 469
  logarithms, 452–454
  mathematical notation, 472–478
  minima and maxima, 462
  on math, 480
  polynomials, 450
  power series and Taylor
    expansion, 466
  powers, 448
  rational functions, 450
  trigonometric functions, 454

capital expenditures (CapEx), 397

carrying capacity (logistic
  equation), 180

cash-flow analysis, 386, 389–391

categorical data
  about, 495
  clustering, 302

CDF (cumulative distribution
  function), 23–29

Central Limit Theorem
  Gaussian distribution, 195–201, 455
  power-law distributions, 203

centroids, clusters, 305, 308

Chaco library (Python), 124

chi-square (χ^2) distribution, 226

class imbalance problems, 421

classical statistics, *See statistics*

classification, *See also predictive analytics*
  about, 406

terminology, 407

cleaning and conditioning data, 487

clustering, 293–325
  about, 293–298, 406
  distance and similarity measures,
    298–304
  market basket analysis, 316
  methods, 304–310
  pre- and postprocessing, 311–314
  Pycluster and the C Clustering
    Library, 320–324

CO_2 measurements above Mauna Loa
  on Hawaii, 80, 127–136

cohesion, clusters, 312

color, false-color plots, 100–105

combinatorial problems, 270

complete clustering, 314

composition, multivariate analysis,
  110–116

compounding, 386–389

compression, data files, 492

conditional probability, 236

confidence intervals
  bootstrap, 277
  example, 227
  least squares, 262

confidence, association rules, 317

confounding variables, 231

confusion matrix, 407

conservation laws, 174

consistency, data consistency, 375–376

contingency tables, 113

continuous time simulations, 280

contour plots, 101

convex clusters, 295

convolution, 95

coplots, 107–109

correlation coefficient
  clustering, 302
  PCA, 331

correlation function, 91–95

correlations, clustering, 302

costs
  cost concepts and depreciation,
    394–398
  cost model example, 170

About the Author

After previous careers in physics and software development, **Philipp K. Janert** currently provides consulting services for data analysis, algorithm development, and mathematical modeling. He has worked for small start-ups and in large corporate environments, both in the U.S. and overseas. He prefers simple solutions that work to complicated ones that don't, and thinks that purpose is more important than process. Philipp is the author of "Gnuplot in Action: Understanding Data with Graphs" (Manning Publications), and has written for the O'Reilly Network, IBM developerWorks, and IEEE Software. He is named inventor on a handful of patents, and is an occasional contributor to CPAN. He holds a Ph.D. in theoretical physics from the University of Washington. Visit his company website at *www.principal-value.com*.

Colophon

The animal on the cover of *Data Analysis with Open Source Tools* is a common kite, most likely a member of the genus *Milvus*. Kites are medium-size raptors with long wings and forked tails. They are noted for their elegant, soaring flight. They are also called "gledes" (for their gliding motion) and, like the flying toys, they appear to ride effortlessly on air currents.

The genus *Milvus* is a group of Old World kites, including three or four species and numerous subspecies. These kites are opportunistic feeders that hunt small animals, such as birds, fish, rodents, and earthworms, and also eat carrion, including sheep and cow carcasses. They have been observed to steal prey from other birds. They may live 25 to 30 years in the wild.

The genus dates to prehistoric times; an Israeli *Milvus pygmaeus* specimen is thought to be between 1.8 million and 780,000 years old. Biblical references to kites probably refer to birds of this genus. In *Coriolanus*, Shakespeare calls Rome "the city of kites and crows," commenting on the birds' prevalence in urban areas.

The most widespread member of the genus is the black kite (*Milvus migrans*), found in Europe, Asia, Africa, and Australia. These kites are very common in many parts of their habitat and are well adapted to city life. Attracted by smoke, they sometimes hunt by capturing small animals fleeing from fires.

The other notable member of *Milvus* is the red kite (*Milvus milvus*), which is slightly larger than the black kite and is distinguished by a rufous body and tail. Red kites are found only in Europe. They were very common in Britain until 1800, but the population was devastated by poisoning and habitat loss, and by 1930, fewer than 20 birds remained. Since then, kites have made a comeback in Wales and have been reintroduced elsewhere in Britain.

The cover image is from Cassell's *Natural History*, Volume III. The cover font is Adobe ITC Garamond; the text font is Adobe's Meridien-Roman; the heading font is Adobe Myriad Condensed; and the code font is LucasFont's TheSansMonoCondensed.

Related Titles from O'Reilly

Scripting Languages

Enterprise Rails

Essential PHP Security

Exploring Expect

Head First Rails

JRuby Cookbook

Jython Essentials

Learning Python, *3rd Edition*

Learning PHP and MySQL, *2nd Edition*

Learning Rails

Learning Ruby

Learning PHP 5

PHP Cookbook, *2nd Edition*

PHP Hacks

PHP in a Nutshell

PHP Pocket Reference, *2nd Edition*

PHPUnit Pocket Guide

Programming PHP, *2nd Edition*

Programming Python, *3rd Edition*

Python & XML

Python Cookbook, *2nd Edition*

Python for Unix and Linux System Administration

Python in a Nutshell, *2nd Edition*

Python Pocket Reference, *3rd Edition*

Python Standard Library

Rails Pocket Reference

Rails: Up and Running, *2nd Edition*

The Ruby Programming Language

Upgrading to PHP 5